HANDBOOKS
ON THE
HISTORY OF RELIGIONS

48594.

8° H
6262
(2)

HANDBOOKS

ON THE

HISTORY OF RELIGIONS

EDITED BY

MORRIS JASTROW, Jr., Ph.D.

Professor of Semitic Languages in the University of Pennsylvania

VOLUME II

Handbooks on the History of Religions

THE RELIGION

OF

BABYLONIA AND ASSYRIA

BY

MORRIS JASTROW, JR., PH.D.
(LEIPZIG)
PROFESSOR OF SEMITIC LANGUAGES IN THE UNIVERSITY OF PENNSYLVANIA

GINN & COMPANY
BOSTON · NEW YORK · CHICAGO · LONDON

Copyright, 1898
By MORRIS JASTROW, Jr.

ALL RIGHTS RESERVED

35.11

The Athenæum Press
GINN & COMPANY · PRO-
PRIETORS · BOSTON · U.S.A.

In order that the book may serve as a guide to students, the names of those to whose researches our present knowledge of the subject is due have frequently been introduced, and it will be found, I trust, that I have been fair to all.[1] At the same time, I have naturally not hesitated to indicate my dissent from views advanced by this or that scholar, and it will also be found, I trust, that in the course of my studies I have advanced the interpretation of the general theme or of specific facts at various points. While, therefore, the book is only in a secondary degree sent forth as an original contribution, the discussion of mooted points will enhance its value, I hope, for the specialist, as well as for the general reader and student for whom, in the first place, the volumes of this series are intended.

The disposition of the subject requires a word of explanation. After the two introductory chapters (common to all the volumes of the series) I have taken up the pantheon as the natural means to a survey of the field. The pantheon is treated, on the basis of the historical texts, in four sections: (1) the old Babylonian period, (2) the middle period, or the pantheon in the days of Hammurabi, (3) the Assyrian pantheon, and (4) the latest or neo-Babylonian period. The most difficult phase has naturally been the old Babylonian pantheon. Much is uncertain here. Not to speak of the chronology which is still to a large extent guesswork, the identification of many of the gods occurring in the oldest inscriptions, with their later equivalents, must be postponed till future discoveries shall have cleared away the many obstacles which beset the path of the scholar. The discoveries at Telloh and Nippur have occasioned a recasting of our views, but new problems have arisen as rapidly as old ones have been solved. I have been especially careful in this section not to pass beyond the range of

---

[1] In the Index, however, names of scholars have only been introduced where absolutely necessary to the subject.

what is definitely *known*, or, at the most, what may be regarded as tolerably certain. Throughout the chapters on the pantheon, I have endeavored to preserve the attitude of being 'open to conviction' — an attitude on which at present too much stress can hardly be laid.

The second division of the subject is represented by the religious literature. With this literature as a guide, the views held by the Babylonians and Assyrians regarding magic and oracles, regarding the relationship to the gods, the creation of the world, and the views of life after death have been illustrated by copious translations, together with discussions of the specimens chosen. The translations, I may add, have been made direct from the original texts, and aim to be as literal as is consonant with presentation in idiomatic English.

The religious architecture, the history of the temples, and the cult form the subject of the third division. Here again there is much which is still uncertain, and this uncertainty accounts for the unequal subdivisions of the theme which will not escape the reader.

Following the general plan of the series, the last chapter of the book is devoted to a general estimate and to a consideration of the influence exerted by the religion of Babylonia and Assyria.

In the transliteration of proper names, I have followed conventional methods for well-known names (like Nebuchadnezzar), and the general usage of scholars in the case of others. In some cases I have furnished a transliteration of my own; and for the famous Assyrian king, to whom we owe so much of the material for the study of the Babylonian and Assyrian religion, Ashurbanabal, I have retained the older usage of writing it with a *b*, following in this respect Lehman, whose arguments [1] in favor of this pronunciation for the last element in the name I regard as on the whole acceptable.

---

[1] In his work. *Šamassum-ukin König von Babylonien*, pp. 16–21. Hence, I also write Ashurnaṣirbaḷ.

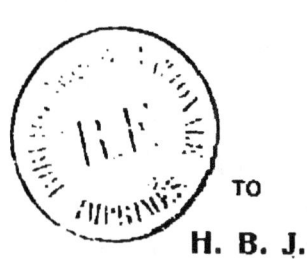 TO
H. B. J.

MY FAITHFUL COLLABORATOR

PREFACE.

IT requires no profound knowledge to reach the conclusion that the time has not yet come for an exhaustive treatise on the religion of Babylonia and Assyria. But even if our knowledge of this religion were more advanced than it is, the utility of an exhaustive treatment might still be questioned. Exhaustive treatises are apt to be exhausting to both reader and author; and however exhaustive (or exhausting) such a treatise may be, it cannot be final except in the fond imagination of the writer. For as long as activity prevails in any branch of science, all results are provisional. Increasing knowledge leads necessarily to a change of perspective and to a readjustment of views. The chief reason for writing a book is to prepare the way for the next one on the same subject.

In accordance with the general plan of this Series[1] of Handbooks, it has been my chief aim to gather together in convenient arrangement and readable form what is at present known about the religion of the Babylonians and Assyrians. The investigations of scholars are scattered through a large variety of periodicals and monographs. The time has come for focusing the results reached, for sifting the certain from the uncertain, and the uncertain from the false. This work of gathering the *disjecta membra* of Assyriological science is essential to future progress. If I have succeeded in my chief aim, I shall feel amply repaid for the labor involved.

[1] Set forth in the announcement of the series at the back of the book and in the Editor's Prefatory Note to Volume I.

I have reasons to regret the proportions to which the work has grown. These proportions were entirely unforeseen when I began the book, and have been occasioned mainly by the large amount of material that has been made available by numerous important publications that appeared after the actual writing of the book had begun. This constant increase of material necessitated constant revision of chapters; and such revision was inseparable from enlargement. I may conscientiously say that I have studied these recent publications thoroughly as they appeared, and have embodied at the proper place the results reached by others and which appeared to me acceptable. The work, therefore, as now given to the public may fairly be said to represent the state of present knowledge.

In a science that grows so rapidly as Assyriology, to which more than to many others the adage of *dies diem docet* is applicable, there is great danger of producing a piece of work that is antiquated before it leaves the press. At times a publication appeared too late to be utilized. So Delitzsch's important contribution to the origin of cuneiform writing [1] was published long after the introductory chapters had been printed. In this book he practically abandons his position on the Sumerian question (as set forth on p. 22 of this volume) and once more joins the opposite camp. As far as my own position is concerned, I do not feel called upon to make any changes from the statements found in chapter i., even after reading Weissbach's *Die Sumerische Frage* (Leipzig, 1898), — the latest contribution to the subject, which is valuable as a history of the controversy, but offers little that is new. Delitzsch's name must now be removed from the list of those who accept Halévy's thesis; but, on the other hand, Halévy has gained a strong ally in F. Thureau-Dangin, whose *special* studies in the old Babylonian inscriptions lend great weight to his utterances on the origin of the cuneiform script. Dr. Alfred Jeremias, of

[1] *Die Entstehung des ältesten Schriftsystems* (Leipzig, 1897).

Leipzig, is likewise to be added to the adherents of Halévy. The Sumero-Akkadian controversy is not yet settled, and meanwhile it is well to bear in mind that not *every* Assyriologist is qualified to pronounce an opinion on the subject. A special study is required, and but few Assyriologists have made such a study. Accepting a view or a tradition from one's teacher does not constitute a person an authority, and one may be a very good Assyriologist without having views on the controversy that are of any particular value.

Lastly, I desire to call attention to the Bibliography, on which much time has been spent, and which will, I trust, be found satisfactory. In a list of addenda at the end of the book, I have noted some errors that slipped into the book, and I have also embodied a few additions. The copious index is the work of my student, Dr. S. Koppe, and it gives me pleasure to express my deep obligations to him for the able and painstaking manner in which he has carried out the work so kindly undertaken by him. The drawing for the map was made by Mr. J. Horace Frank of Philadelphia.

To my wife more thanks are due than I can convey in words for her share in the work. She copied almost all of the manuscript, and in doing so made many valuable suggestions. Without her constant aid and encouragement I would have shrunk from a task which at times seemed too formidable to be carried to a successful issue. As I lay down my pen after several years of devotion to this book, my last thought is one of gratitude to the beloved partner of my joys and sorrows.

MORRIS JASTROW, Jr.

University of Pennsylvania,
June, 1898.

CORRECTIONS AND ADDITIONS.

Page, line.

22. See Preface.

35, 10. Isin or Nisin, see Lehmann's Šamaš-šumukin, I. 77; Meissner's Beiträge zum altbabylonischen Privatrecht, p. 122.

61. Bau also appears as Nin-din-dug, i.e., 'the lady who restores life.' See Hilprecht, Old Babylonian Inscriptions, I. 2, Nos. 95, 106, 111.

74. On Â, see Hommel, Journal of Transactions of Victoria Institute, XXVIII. 35–36.

99, 24. Ur-shul-pa-uddu is a ruler of Kish.

102, 13. For Ku-anna, see IIIR. 67, 32 c–d.

102, 24. For another U-mu as a title of Adad, see Delitzsch, Das Babylonische Weltschöpfungsepos, p. 125, note.

111, 2. Nisaba is mentioned in company with the great gods by Nebopolassar (Hilprecht, Old Babylonian Inscriptions, I. 1. Pl. 32, col. II. 15).

165. Note 2. On these proper names, see Delitzsch's "Assyriologische Miscellen" (Berichte der phil.-hist. Classe der kgl. sächs. Gesell. d. Wiss., 1893, pp. 183 seq.).

488. Note 1. See now Scheil's article "Recueil de Travaux," etc., XX. 55–59.

529. The form Di-ib-ba-ra has now been found. See Scheil's "Recueil de Travaux," etc., XX. 57.

589. Note 3. See now Hommel, Expository Times, VIII. 472, and Baudissin, ib. IX. 40–45.

CONTENTS.

CHAPTER		PAGE
I.	INTRODUCTION	1
II.	THE LAND AND THE PEOPLE	26
III.	GENERAL TRAITS OF THE OLD BABYLONIAN PANTHEON	48
IV.	BABYLONIAN GODS PRIOR TO THE DAYS OF HAMMURABI	51
V.	THE CONSORTS OF THE GODS	104
VI.	GUDEA'S PANTHEON	106
VII.	SUMMARY	112
VIII.	THE PANTHEON IN THE DAYS OF HAMMURABI	116
IX.	THE GODS IN THE TEMPLE LISTS AND IN THE LEGAL AND COMMERCIAL DOCUMENTS	165
X.	THE MINOR GODS IN THE PERIOD OF HAMMURABI	171
XI.	SURVIVALS OF ANIMISM IN THE BABYLONIAN RELIGION	180
XII.	THE ASSYRIAN PANTHEON	188
XIII.	THE TRIAD AND THE COMBINED INVOCATION OF DEITIES	235
XIV.	THE NEO-BABYLONIAN PERIOD	239
XV.	THE RELIGIOUS LITERATURE OF BABYLONIA	245
XVI.	THE MAGICAL TEXTS	253
XVII.	THE PRAYERS AND HYMNS	294
XVIII.	PENITENTIAL PSALMS	312
XIX.	ORACLES AND OMENS	328
XX.	VARIOUS CLASSES OF OMENS	352
XXI.	THE COSMOLOGY OF THE BABYLONIANS	407
XXII.	THE ZODIACAL SYSTEM OF THE BABYLONIANS	454
XXIII.	THE GILGAMESH EPIC	467
XXIV.	MYTHS AND LEGENDS	518
XXV.	THE VIEWS OF LIFE AFTER DEATH	556
XXVI.	THE TEMPLES AND THE CULT	612
XXVII.	CONCLUSION	690

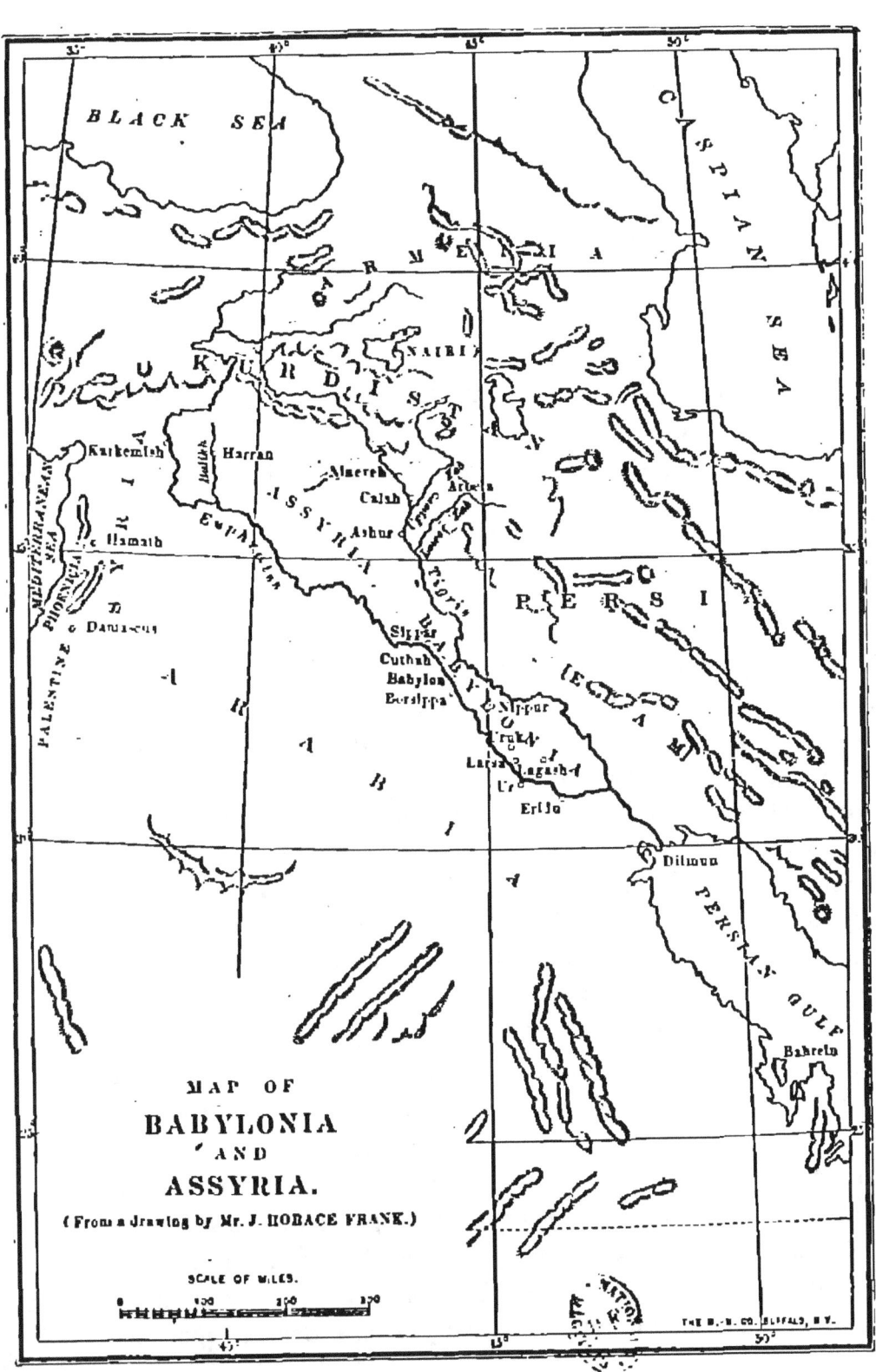

MAP OF BABYLONIA AND ASSYRIA.
(From a drawing by Mr. J. HORACE FRANK.)

THE RELIGION OF BABYLONIA AND ASSYRIA.

CHAPTER I.—INTRODUCTION.

SOURCES AND METHODS OF STUDY.

I.

UNTIL about the middle of the 19th century, our knowledge of the religion of the Babylonians and Assyrians was exceedingly scant. No records existed that were contemporaneous with the period covered by Babylonian-Assyrian history; no monuments of the past were preserved that might, in default of records, throw light upon the religious ideas and customs that once prevailed in Mesopotamia. The only sources at command were the incidental notices — insufficient and fragmentary in character — that occurred in the Old Testament, in Herodotus, in Eusebius, Syncellus, and Diodorus. Of these, again, only the two first-named, the Old Testament and Herodotus, can be termed direct sources; the rest simply reproduce extracts from other works, notably from Ctesias, the contemporary of Xenophon, from Berosus, a priest of the temple of Bel in Babylonia, who lived about the time of Alexander the Great, or shortly after, and from Apollodorus, Abydenus, Alexander Polyhistor, and Nicolas of Damascus, all of whom being subsequent to Berosus, either quote the latter or are dependent upon him.

Of all these sources it may be said, that what information they furnish of Babylonia and Assyria bears largely upon the political history, and only to a very small degree upon the religion. In the Old Testament, the two empires appear only as they enter into relations with the Hebrews, and since Hebrew history is not traced back beyond the appearance of the clans of Terah in Palestine, there is found previous to this period, barring the account of the migrations of the Terahites in Mesopotamia, only the mention of the Tigris and Euphrates among the streams watering the legendary Garden of Eden, the incidental reference to Nimrod and his empire, which is made to include the capitol cities of the Northern and Southern Mesopotamian districts, and the story of the founding of the city of Babylon, followed by the dispersion of mankind from their central habitation in the Euphrates Valley. The followers of Abram, becoming involved in the attempts of Palestinian chieftains to throw off the yoke of Babylonian supremacy, an occasion is found for introducing Mesopotamia again, and so the family history of the Hebrew tribes superinduces at odd times a reference to the old settlements on the Euphrates, but it is not until the political struggles of the two Hebrew kingdoms against the inevitable subjection to the superior force of Assyrian arms, and upon the fall of Assyria, to the Babylonian power, that Assyria and Babylonia engage the frequent attention of the chronicler's pen and of the prophet's word. Here, too, the political situation is always the chief factor, and it is only incidentally that the religion comes into play, — as when it is said that Sennacherib, the king of Assyria, was murdered while worshipping in the temple dedicated to a deity, Nisroch; or when a prophet, to intensify the picture of the degradation to which the proud king of Babylon is to be reduced, introduces Babylonian conceptions of the nether world into his discourse.[1] Little, too, is furnished by the Book of Daniel, despite the fact that Babylon is the center of action, and what little there is

---

[1] Isaiah, xlv. For the Babylonian views contained in this chapter, see Alfred Jeremias, *Die Babylonisch-Assyrischen Vorstellungen vom Leben nach dem Tode*, pp. 112–116.

bearing on the religious status, such as the significance attached to dreams, and the implied contrast between the religion of Daniel and his companions, and that of Nebuchadnezzar and the Babylonians, loses some of its force by the late origin of the book. The same applies, only in a still stronger degree, to the Book of Judith, in which Nineveh is the center of the incidents described.

The rabbinical literature produced in Palestine and Babylonia is far richer in notices bearing on the religious practices of Mesopotamia, than is the Old Testament. The large settlements of Jews in Babylonia, which, beginning in the sixth century B.C., were constantly being increased by fresh accessions from Palestine, brought the professors of Judaism face to face with religious conditions abhorrent to their souls. In the regulations of the Rabbis to guard their followers from the influences surrounding them, there is frequent reference, open or implied, to Babylonish practices, to the festivals of the Babylonians, to the images of their gods, to their forms of incantations, and other things besides; but these notices are rendered obscure by their indirect character, and require a commentary that can only be furnished by that knowledge of the times which they take for granted. To this difficulty, there must be added the comparatively late date of the notices, which demands an exercise of care before applying them to the very early period to which the religion of the Babylonians may be traced.

Coming to Herodotus, it is a matter of great regret that the history of Assyria, which he declares it was his intention to write,[1] was either never produced, or if produced, lost. In accordance with the general usage of his times, Herodotus included under Assyria the whole of Mesopotamia, both Assyria proper in the north and Southern Mesopotamia. His history would therefore have been of extraordinary value, and since nothing escaped his observant eye and well-trained mind,

[1] Book i. sec. 184.

the religious customs of the country would have come in for their full share of attention. As it is, we have only a few notices about Babylonia and Assyria, incidental to his history of Persia.[1] Of these, the majority are purely historical, chief among which is an epitome of the country's past — a curious medley of fact and legend — and the famous account of the capture of Babylon by Cyrus. Fortunately, however, there are four notices that treat of the religion of the inhabitants: the first, a description of an eight-storied tower, surmounted by a temple sacred to the god Bel; a second furnishing a rather detailed account of another temple, also sacred to Bel, and situated in the same precinct of the city of Babylon; a third notice speaks, though with provoking brevity, of the funeral customs of the Babylonians; while in a fourth he describes the rites connected with the worship of the chief goddess of the Babylonians, which impress Herodotus, who failed to appreciate their mystic significance, as shameful. We have no reason to believe that Ctesias' account of the Assyrian monarchy, under which he, like Herodotus, included Babylonia, contained any reference to the religion at all. What he says about Babylonia and Assyria served merely as an introduction to Persian history — the real purpose of his work — and the few fragments known chiefly through Diodorus and Eusebius, deal altogether with the succession of dynasties. As is well known, the lists of Ctesias have fallen into utter discredit by the side of the ever-growing confidence in the native traditions as reported by Berosus.

The loss of the latter's history of Babylon is deplorable indeed; its value would have been greater than the history of Herodotus, because it was based, as we know, on the records and documents preserved in Babylonian temples. How much of the history dealt with the religion of the people, it is difficult to determine, but the extracts of it found in various writers show

[1] Book I. ("Clio"), secs. 95, 102, 178–200.

that starting, like the Old Testament, with the beginning of things, Berosus gave a full account of the cosmogony of the Babylonians. Moreover, the early history of Babylonia being largely legendary, as that of every other nation, tales of the relations existing between the gods and mankind — relations that are always close in the earlier stages of a nation's history — must have abounded in the pages of Berosus, even if he did not include in his work a special section devoted to an account of the religion that still was practiced in his days. The quotations from Berosus in the works of Josephus are all of a historical character; those in Eusebius and Syncellus, on the contrary, deal with the religion and embrace the cosmogony of the Babylonians, the account of a deluge brought on by the gods, and the building of a tower. It is to be noted, moreover, that the quotations we have from Berosus are not direct, for while it is possible, though not at all certain, that Josephus was still able to consult the works of Berosus, Eusebius and Syncellus refer to Apollodorus, Abydenus, and Alexander Polyhistor as their authorities for the statements of Berosus. Passing in this way through several hands, the authoritative value of the comparatively paltry extracts preserved, is diminished, and a certain amount of inaccuracy, especially in details and in the reading of proper names,[1] becomes almost inevitable. Lastly, it is to be noted that the list of Babylonian kings found in the famous astronomical work of Claudius Ptolemaeus, valuable as it is for historical purposes, has no connection with the religion of the Babylonians.

[1] An instructive instance is furnished by the mention of a mystic personage, "Homoroka," which now turns out to be — as Professor J. H. Wright has shown — a corruption of Marduk. (See *Zeitschrift für Assyriologie*, x. 71–74.)

II.

The sum total of the information thus to be gleaned from ancient sources for an elucidation of the Babylonian-Assyrian religion is exceedingly meagre, sufficing scarcely for determining its most general traits. Moreover, what there is, requires for the most part a control through confirmatory evidence which we seek for in vain, in biblical or classical literature.

This control has now been furnished by the remarkable discoveries made beneath the soil of Mesopotamia since the year 1842. In that year the French consul at Mosul, P. E. Botta, aided by a government grant, began a series of excavations in the mounds that line the banks of the Tigris opposite Mosul. The artificial character of these mounds had for some time been recognized. Botta's first finds of a pronounced character were made at a village known as Khorsabad, which stood on one of the mounds in question. Here, at a short distance below the surface, he came across the remains of what proved to be a palace of enormous extent. The sculptures that were found in this palace — enormous bulls and lions resting on backgrounds of limestone, and guarding the approaches to the palace chambers, or long rows of carvings in high relief lining the palace walls, and depicting war scenes, building operations, and religious processions — left no doubt as to their belonging to an ancient period of history. The written characters found on these monuments substantiated the view that Botta had come across an edifice of the Assyrian empire, while subsequent researches furnished the important detail that the excavated edifice lay in a suburb of the ancient capitol of Assyria, Nineveh, the exact site of which was directly opposite Mosul. Botta's labors extended over a period of two years; by the end of which time, having laid bare the greater part of the palace, he had gathered a large mass of material including many smaller objects — pottery, furniture, jewelry, and ornaments — that might serve for the study of Assyrian art and of Assyrian antiquities, while the written records accompanying the monuments placed for the first time an equally considerable quantity of original material at the disposal of scholars for the history of Assyria. All that could be transported was sent to the Louvre, and this material was subsequently published. Botta was followed by Austen Henry Layard, who, acting as the agent of the British Museum, conducted excavations during the years 1845–52, first at a mound Nimrud, some fifteen miles to the south of Khorsabad, and afterwards on the site of Nineveh proper, the mound Koyunjik, opposite Mosul, besides visiting and examining other mounds still further to the south within the district of Babylonia proper.

The scope of Layard's excavations exceeded, therefore, those of Botta; and to the one palace at Khorsabad, he added three at Nimrud and two at Koyunjik, besides finding traces of a temple and other buildings. The construction of these edifices was of the same order as the one unearthed by Botta; and as at the latter, there was a large yield of sculptures, inscriptions, and miscellaneous objects. A new feature, however, of Layard's excavations was the finding of several rooms filled with fragments of small and large clay tablets closely inscribed on both sides in the cuneiform characters. These tablets, about 30,000 of which found their way to the British Museum, proved to be the remains of a royal library. Their contents ranged over all departments of thought, — hymns, incantations, prayers, epics, history, legends, mythology, mathematics, astronomy constituting some of the chief divisions. In the corners of the palaces, the foundation records were also found, containing in each case more or less extended annals of the events that occurred during the reign of the monarch whose official residence was thus brought to light. Through Layard, the foundations were laid for the Assyrian and Babylonian collections of the British

Museum, the parts of which exhibited to the public now fill six large halls. Fresh sources of a direct character were thus added for the study, not only of the historical unfolding of the Assyrian empire, but through the tablets of the royal library, for the religion of ancient Mesopotamia as well.

The stimulus given by Botta and Layard to the recovery of the records and monuments of antiquity that had been hidden from view for more than two thousand years, led to a refreshing rivalry between England and France in continuing a work that gave promise of still richer returns by further efforts. Victor Place, a French architect of note, who succeeded Botta as the French consul at Mosul, devoted his term of service, from 1851 to 1855, towards completing the excavations at Khorsabad. A large aftermath rewarded his efforts. Thanks, too, to his technical knowledge and that of his assistant, Felix Thomas, M. Place was enabled more accurately to determine the architectural construction of the temples and palaces of ancient Assyria. Within this same period (1852–1854) another exploring expedition was sent out to Mesopotamia by the French government, under the leadership of Fulgence Fresnel, in whose party were the above-mentioned Thomas and the distinguished scholar Jules Oppert. The objective point this time was Southern Mesopotamia, the mounds of which had hitherto not been touched, many not even identified as covering the remains of ancient cities. Much valuable work was done by this expedition in its careful study of the site of the ancient Babylon, — in the neighborhood of the modern village Hillah, some forty miles south of Baghdad. Unfortunately, the antiquities recovered at this place, and elsewhere, were lost through the sinking of the rafts as they carried their precious burden down the Tigris. In the south again, the English followed close upon the heels of the French. J. E. Taylor, in 1854, visited many of the huge mounds that were scattered throughout Southern Mesopotamia in much larger numbers than in the north, while his compatriot, William K. Loftus, a few years previous had begun excavations, though on a small scale, at Warka, the site of the ancient city of Erech. He also conducted some investigations at a mound Mugheir, which acquired special interest as the supposed site of the famous Ur, — the home of some of the Terahites before the migration to Palestine. Of still greater significance were the examinations made by Sir Henry Rawlinson, in 1854, of the only considerable ruins of ancient Babylonia that remained above the surface, — the tower of Birs Nimrud, which proved to be the famous seven-staged temple as described by Herodotus. This temple was completed, as the foundation records showed, by Nebuchadnezzar II., in the sixth century before this era; but the beginnings of the structure belong to a much earlier period. Another sanctuary erected by this same king was found near the tower. Subsequent researches by Hormuzd Rassam made it certain that Borsippa, the ancient name of the place where the tower and sanctuaries stood, was a suburb of the great city of Babylon itself, which lay directly opposite on the east side of the Euphrates. The scope of the excavations continued to grow almost from year to year, and while new mounds were being attacked in the south, those in the north, especially Koujunjik, continued to be the subject of attention.

Rassam, who has just been mentioned, was in a favorable position, through his long residence as English consul at Mosul, for extracting new finds from the mounds in this vicinity. Besides adding more than a thousand tablets from the royal library discovered by Layard, his most noteworthy discoveries were the unearthing of a magnificent temple at Nimrud, and the finding of a large bronze gate at Balawat, a few miles to the northeast of Nimrud. Rassam and Rawlinson were afterwards joined by George Smith of the British Museum, who, instituting a further search through the ruins of Koujunjik, Nimrud,

Kalah-Shergat, and elsewhere, made many valuable additions to the English collections, until his unfortunate death in 1876, during his third visit to the mounds, cut him off in the prime of a brilliant and most useful career. The English explorers extended their labors to the mounds in the south. Here it was, principally at Abu-Habba, that they set their forces to work. The finding of another temple dedicated to the sun-god rewarded their efforts. The foundation records showed that the edifice was one of great antiquity, which was permitted to fall into decay and was then restored by a ruler whose date can be fixed at the middle of the ninth century B.C. The ancient name of the place was shown to be Sippar, and the fame of the temple was such, that subsequent monarchs vied with one another in adding to its grandeur. It is estimated that the temple contained no less than three hundred chambers and halls for the archives and for the accommodation of the large body of priests attached to this temple. In the archives many thousands of little clay tablets were again found, not, however, of a literary, but of a legal character, containing records of commercial transactions conducted in ancient Sippar, such as sales of houses, of fields, of produce, of stuffs, money loans, receipts, contracts for work, marriage settlements, and the like. The execution of the laws being in the hands of priests in ancient Mesopotamia, the temples were the natural depositories for the official documents of the law courts. Similar collections to those of Sippar have been found in almost every mound of Southern Mesopotamia that has been opened since the days of Rassam. So at Djumdjuma, situated near the site of the ancient city of Babylon, some three thousand were unearthed that were added to the fast growing collections of the British Museum. At Borsippa, likewise, Rawlinson and Rassam recovered a large number of clay tablets, most of them legal but some of them of a literary character, which proved to be in part duplicates of those in the royal library of Ashurbanabal. In this way, the latter's statement, that he sent his scribes to the large cities of the south for the purpose of collecting and copying the literature that had its rise there, met with a striking confirmation. Still further to the south, at a mound known as Telloh, a representative of the French government, Ernest de Sarzec, began a series of excavations in 1877, which, continued to the present day, have brought to light remains of temples and palaces exceeding in antiquity those hitherto discovered. Colossal statues of diorite, covered with inscriptions, the pottery, tablets and ornaments, showed that at a period as early as 3500 B.C. civilization in this region had already reached a very advanced stage. The systematic and thorough manner in which De Sarzec, with inexhaustible patience, explored the ancient city, has resulted in largely extending our knowledge of the most ancient period of Babylonian history as yet known to us. The Telloh finds were forwarded to the Louvre, which in this way secured a collection from the south that formed a worthy complement to the Khorsabad antiquities.

Lastly, it is gratifying to note the share that our own country has recently taken in the great work that has furnished the material needed for following the history of the Mesopotamian states. In 1887, an expedition was sent out under the auspices of the University of Pennsylvania, to conduct excavations at Niffer, — a mound to the southeast of Babylon, situated on a branch of the Euphrates, and which was known to be the site of one of the most famous cities in this region. The Rev. John P. Peters (now in New York), who was largely instrumental in raising the funds for the purpose, was appointed director of the expedition. Excavations were continued for two years under Dr. Peters' personal supervision, and since then by Mr. John H. Haynes, with most satisfactory success. A great temple dedicated to the god Bel was discovered, and work has hitherto been confined chiefly to laying bare the various parts of the edifice. The foundation of the building goes back to an earlier period than the ruins of Telloh. It survived the varying fortunes of the city in which it stood, and each period of Babylonian history left its traces at Niffer through the records of the many rulers who sought the favor of the god by enlarging or beautifying his place of worship. The temple became a favorite spot to which pilgrims came from all sides on the great festivals, to offer homage at the sacred shrines. Votive offerings, in the shape of inscribed clay cones, and little clay images of Bel and of his female consort, were left in the temple as witnesses to the piety of the visitors. The archives were found to be well stocked with the official legal documents dating chiefly from the period of 1700 to 1200 B.C., when the city appears to have reached the climax of its glory. Other parts of the mound were opened at different depths, and various layers which followed the chronological development of the place were determined.[1] After its destruction, the sanctity of the city was in a measure continued by its becoming a burial-place. The fortunes of the place can thus be followed down to the ninth or the tenth century of our era, a period of more than four thousand years. Already more than 20,000 tablets have been received at the University of Pennsylvania, besides many specimens of pottery, bowls, jars, cones, and images, as well as gold, copper, and alabaster work.

From this survey of the work done in the last decades in exploring the long lost and almost forgotten cities of the Tigris and of the Euphrates Valley, it will be apparent that a large amount of material has been made accessible for tracing the course of civilization in this region. Restricting ourselves to that portion of it that bears on the religion of ancient Mesopotamia, it may be grouped under two heads, (1) literary, and (2) archaeological. The religious texts of Ashurbanabal's

---

[1] The excavations are still being continued, thanks to the generosity of some public-spirited citizens of Philadelphia.

library occupy the first place in the literary group. The incantations, the prayers and hymns, lists of temples, of gods and their attributes, traditions of the creation of the world, legends of the deities and of their relations to men, are sources of the most direct character; and it is fortunate that among the recovered portions of the library, such texts are largely represented. Equally direct are the dedicatory inscriptions set up by the kings in the temples erected to the honor of some god, and of great importance are the references to the various gods, their attributes, their powers, and their deeds, which are found at every turn in the historical records which the kings left behind them. Many of these records open or close with a long prayer to some deity; in others, prayers are found interspersed, according to the occasion on which they were offered up. Attributing the success of their undertakings — whether it be a military campaign, or the construction of some edifice, or a successful hunt — to the protection offered by the gods, the kings do not tire of singing the praises of the deity or deities as whose favorites they regarded themselves. The gods are constantly at the monarch's side. Now we are told of a dream sent to encourage the army on the approach of a battle, and again of some portent which bade the king be of good cheer. To the gods, the appeal is constantly made, and to them all good things are ascribed. From the legal documents, likewise, much may be gathered bearing on the religion. The protection of the gods is invoked or their curses called down; the oath is taken in their name; while the manner in which the temples are involved in the commercial life of ancient Babylonia renders these tablets, which are chiefly valuable as affording us a remarkable insight into the people's daily life, of importance also in illustrating certain phases of the religious organization of the country. Most significant for the position occupied by the priests, is the fact that the latter are invariably the scribes who draw up the documents.

The archaeological material furnished by the excavations consists of the temples of the gods, their interior arrangement, and provisions for the various religious functions; secondly, the statues of the gods, demi-gods, and the demons, the altars and the vessels; and thirdly, the religious scenes, — the worship of some deity, the carrying of the gods in procession, the pouring of libations, the performance of rites, or the representation of some religious symbols sculptured on the palace wall or on the foundation stone of a sacred building, or cut out on the seal cylinders, used as signatures[1] and talismans.

Large as the material is, it is far from being exhausted, and, indeed, far from sufficient for illustrating all the details of the religious life. This will not appear surprising, if it be remembered that of the more than one hundred mounds that have been identified in the region of the Tigris and Euphrates as containing remains of buried cities, only a small proportion have been explored, and of these scarcely more than a half dozen with an approach to completeness. The soil of Mesopotamia unquestionably holds still greater treasures than those which it has already yielded. The links uniting the most ancient period — at present, c. 4000 B.C. — to the final destruction of the Babylonian empire by Cyrus, in the middle of the sixth century B.C., are far from being complete. For entire centuries we are wholly in the dark, and for others only a few skeleton facts are known; and until these gaps shall have been filled, our knowledge of the religion of the Babylonians and Assyrians must necessarily remain incomplete. Not as incomplete, indeed, as their history, for religious rites are not subject to many changes, and the progress of religious ideas does not keep pace with the constant changes in the political kaleidoscope of a country; but, it is evident that no exhaustive treat-

---

[1] The parties concerned rolled their cylinders over the clay tablet recording a legal or commercial transaction.

ment of the religion can be given until the material shall have become adequate to the subject.

III.

Before proceeding to the division of the subject in hand, some explanation is called for of the method by which the literary material found beneath the soil has been made intelligible.

The characters on the clay tablets and cylinders, on the limestone slabs, on statues, on altars, on stone monuments, are generally known as cuneiform, because of their wedge-shaped appearance, though it may be noted at once that in their oldest form the characters are linear rather than wedge-shaped, presenting the more or less clearly defined outlines of objects from which they appear to be derived. At the time when these cuneiform inscriptions began to be found in Mesopotamia, the language which these characters expressed was still totally unknown. Long previous to the beginning of Botta's labors, inscriptions also showing the cuneiform characters had been found at Persepolis on various monuments of the ruins and tombs still existing at that place. The first notice of these inscriptions was brought to Europe by a famous Italian traveler, Pietro della Valle, in the beginning of the seventeenth century. For a long time it was doubted whether the characters represented anything more than mere ornamentation, and it was not until the close of the 18th century, after more accurate copies of the Persepolitan characters had been furnished through Carsten Niebuhr, that scholars began to apply themselves to their decipherment. Through the efforts chiefly of Gerhard Tychsen, professor at Rostock, Frederick Münter, a Danish scholar, and the distinguished Silvestre de Sacy of Paris, the beginnings were made which finally led to the discovery of the key to the mysterious writings, in 1802, by Georg Friedrich Grotefend, a teacher at a public school in Göttingen. The observation was made previous to the days of Grotefend that the inscriptions at Persepolis invariably showed three styles of writing. While in all three the characters were composed of wedges, yet the combination of wedges, as well as their shape, differed sufficiently to make it evident, even to the superficial observer, that there was as much difference between them as, say, between the English and the German script. The conclusion was drawn that the three styles represented three languages, and this conclusion was strikingly confirmed when, upon the arrival of Botta's finds in Europe, it was seen that one of the styles corresponded to the inscriptions found at Khorsabad; and so in all subsequent discoveries in Mesopotamia, this was found to be the case. One of the languages, therefore, on the monuments of Persepolis was presumably identical with the speech of ancient Mesopotamia. Grotefend's key to the reading of that style of cuneiform writing which invariably occupied the first place when the three styles were ranged one under the other, or occupied the most prominent place when a different arrangement was adopted, met with universal acceptance. He determined that the language of the style which, for the sake of convenience, we may designate as No. 1, was Old Persian,—the language spoken by the rulers, who, it was known through tradition and notices in classical writers, had erected the series of edifices at Persepolis, one of the capitols of the Old Persian or, as it is also called, the Achaemenian empire. By the year 1840 the decipherment of these Achaemenian inscriptions was practically complete, the inscriptions had been read, the alphabet was definitely settled, and the grammar, in all but minor points, known. It was possible, therefore, in approaching the Mesopotamian style of cuneiform, which, as occupying the third place, may be designated as No. 3, to use No. 1 as a guide, since it was only legitimate to conclude that Nos. 2 and 3 represented translations of No. 1 into two languages, which, by the side of Old Persian, were spoken by the subjects of the Achaemenian kings. That one of these languages should have been the current speech of Mesopotamia was exactly what was to be expected, since Babylonia and Assyria formed an essential part of the Persian empire.

The beginning was made with proper names, the sound of which would necessarily be the same or very similar in both, or, for that matter, in all the three languages of the Persepolitan inscriptions.[1] In this way, by careful comparisons between the two styles, Nos. 1 and 3, it was possible to pick out the signs in No. 3 that corresponded to those in No. 1, and inasmuch as the same sign occurred in various names, it was, furthermore, possible to assign, at least tentatively, certain values to the signs in question. With the help of the signs thus determined, the attempt was made to read other words in style No. 3, in which these signs occurred, but it was some time before satisfactory results were obtained. An important advance was made when it was once determined, that the writing was a mixture of signs used both as words and as syllables, and that the language on the Assyrian monuments belonged to the group known as Semitic. The cognate languages — chiefly Hebrew and Arabic — formed a help towards determining the meaning of the words read and an explanation of the morphological features they presented. For all that, the task was one of stupendous proportions, and many were the obstacles that had to be overcome, before the principles underlying the cuneiform writing were determined, and the decipherment placed on a firm and scientific basis. This is not the place to enter upon a detailed illustration of the method adopted by ingenious scholars, —

---

[1] Besides those at Persepolis, a large tri-lingual inscription was found at Behistun, near the city of Kirmenshah, in Persia, which, containing some ninety proper names, enabled Sir Henry Rawlinson definitely to establish a basis for the decipherment of the Mesopotamian inscriptions.

notably Edward Hincks, Isidor Löwenstern, Henry Rawlinson, Jules Oppert, — to whose united efforts the solution of the great problems involved is due;[1] and it would also take too much space, since in order to make this method clear, it would be necessary to set forth the key discovered by Grotefend for reading the Old Persian inscriptions. Suffice it to say that the guarantee for the soundness of the conclusions reached by scholars is furnished by the consideration, that it was from small and most modest beginnings that the decipherment began. Step by step, the problem was advanced by dint of a painstaking labor, the degree of which cannot easily be exaggerated, until to-day the grammar of the Babylonian-Assyrian language has been clearly set forth in all its essential particulars: the substantive and verb formation is as definitely known as that of any other Semitic language, the general principles of the syntax, as well as many detailed points, have been carefully investigated, and as for the reading of the cuneiform texts, thanks to the various helps at our disposal, and the further elucidation of the various principles that the Babylonians themselves adopted as a guide, the instance is a rare one when scholars need to confess their ignorance in this particular. At most there may be a halting between two possibilities. The difficulties that still hinder the complete understanding of passages in texts, arise in part from the mutilated condition in which, unfortunately, so many of the tablets and cylinders are found, and in part from a still imperfect knowledge of the lexicography of the language. For many a word occurring

---

[1] The best account is to be found in Hommel's *Geschichte Babyloniens und Assyriens*, pp. 58-134. A briefer statement was furnished by Professor Fr. Delitzsch in his supplements to the German translation of George Smith's *Chaldaean Genesis* (*Chaldäische Genesis*, pp. 257-262). A tolerably satisfactory account in English is furnished by B. T. A. Evetts in his work, *New Light on the Bible and the Holy Land*, pp. 79-129. For a full account of the excavations and the decipherment, together with a summary of results and specimens of the various branches of the Babylonian-Assyrian literature, the reader may be referred to Kaulen's *Assyrien und Babylonien nach den neuesten Entdeckungen* (5th edition).

only once or twice, and for which neither text nor comparison with cognate languages offers a satisfactory clue, ignorance must be confessed, or at best, a conjecture hazarded, until its more frequent occurrence enables us to settle the question at issue. Such settlements of disputed questions are taking place all the time; and with the activity with which the study of the language and antiquities of Mesopotamia is being pushed by scholars in this country, in England, France, Austria, Germany, Italy, Norway, and Holland, and with the constant accession of new material through excavations and publications, there is no reason to despair of clearing up the obscurities, still remaining in the precious texts that a fortunate chance has preserved for us.

IV.

A question that still remains to be considered as to the origin of the cuneiform writing of Mesopotamia, may properly be introduced in connection with this account of the excavations and decipherment, though it is needless to enter into it in detail.

The "Persian" style of wedge-writing is a direct derivative of the Babylonian, introduced in the times of the Achaemenians, and it is nothing but a simplification in form and principle of the more cumbersome and complicated Babylonian. Instead of a combination of as many as ten and fifteen wedges to make one sign, we have in the Persian never more than five, and frequently only three; and instead of writing words by syllables, sounds alone were employed, and the syllabary of several hundred signs reduced to forty-two, while the ideographic style was practically abolished.

The second style of cuneiform, generally known as Median or Susian,[1] is again only a slight modification of the "Persian."

[1] The most recent investigations show it to have been a ' Turanian ' language. See Weissbach, *Achämeniden Inschriften zweiter Art*, Leipzig, 1893.

Besides these three, there is a fourth language (spoken in the northwestern district of Mesopotamia between the Euphrates and the Orontes), known as "Mitanni," the exact status of which has not been clearly ascertained, but which has been adapted to cuneiform characters. A fifth variety, found on tablets from Cappadocia, represents again a modification of the ordinary writing met with in Babylonia. In the inscriptions of Mitanni, the writing is a mixture of ideographs and syllables, just as in Mesopotamia, while the so-called "Cappadocian" tablets are written in a corrrupt Babylonian, corresponding in degree to the "corrupt" forms that the signs take on. In Mesopotamia itself, quite a number of styles exist, some due to local influences, others the result of changes that took place in the course of time. In the oldest period known, that is from 4000 to 3000 B.C., the writing is linear rather than wedge-shaped. The linear writing is the modification that the original pictures underwent in being adapted for engraving on stone; the wedges are the modification natural to the use of clay, though when once the wedges became the standard method, the greater frequency with which clay as against stone came to be used, led to an imitation of the wedges by those who cut out the characters on stone. In consequence, there developed two varieties of wedge-writing : the one that may be termed lapidary, used for the stone inscriptions, the official historical records, and such legal documents as were prepared with especial care; the other cursive, occurring only on legal and commercial clay tablets, and becoming more frequent as we approach the latest period of Babylonian writing, which extends to within a few decades of our era. In Assyria, finally, a special variety of cuneiform developed that is easily distinguished from the Babylonian by its greater neatness and the more vertical position of the wedges.

The origin of all the styles and varieties of cuneiform writing is, therefore, to be sought in Mesopotamia; and within Mesopotamia, in that part of it where culture begins — the extreme south; but beyond saying that the writing is a direct development from picture writing, there is little of any definite character that can be maintained. We do not know when the writing originated, we only know that in the oldest inscriptions it is already fully developed.

We do not know who originated it; nor can the question be as yet definitely answered, whether those who originated it spoke the Babylonian language, or whether they were Semites at all. Until about fifteen years ago, it was generally supposed that the cuneiform writing was without doubt the invention of a non-Semitic race inhabiting Babylonia at an early age, from whom the Semitic Babylonians adopted it, together with the culture that this non-Semitic race had produced. These inventors, called Sumerians by some and Akkadians by others, and Sumero-Akkadians by a third group of scholars, it was supposed, used the "cuneiform" as a picture or 'ideographic' script exclusively; and the language they spoke being agglutinative and largely monosyllabic in character, it was possible for them to stop short at this point of development. The Babylonians however, in order to adapt the writing to their language, did not content themselves with the 'picture' method, but using the non-Semitic equivalent for their own words, employed the former as syllables, while retaining, at the same time, the sign as an ideograph. To make this clearer by an example, the numeral 'I' would represent the word 'one' in their own language, while the non-Semitic word for 'one,' which let us suppose was "*ash*," they used as the phonetic value of the sign, in writing a word in which this sound occurred, as *e.g.*, *ash-es*. Since each sign, in Sumero-Akkadian as well as in Babylonian, represented some general idea, it could stand for an entire series of words, grouped about this idea and associated with it, 'day,' for example, being used for 'light,' 'brilliancy,' 'pure,' and so forth. The variety of syllabic and ideographic values which the cuneiform characters show could thus be accounted for.

This theory, however, tempting as it is by its simplicity, cannot be accepted in this unqualified form. Advancing knowledge has made it certain that the ancient civilization, including the religion, is Semitic in character. The assumption therefore of a purely non-Semitic culture for southern Babylonia is untenable. Secondly, even in the oldest inscriptions found, there occur Semitic words and Semitic constructions which prove that the inscriptions were composed by Semites. As long, therefore, as no traces of purely non-Semitic inscription are found, we cannot go beyond the Semites in seeking for the origin of the culture in this region. In view of this, the theory first advanced by Prof. Joseph Halévy of Paris, and now supported by the most eminent of German Assyriologists, Prof. Friedrich Delitzsch, which claims that the cuneiform writing is Semitic in origin, needs to be most carefully considered. There is much that speaks in favor of this theory, much that may more easily be accounted for by it, than by the opposite one, which was originally proposed by the distinguished Nestor of cuneiform studies, Jules Oppert, and which is with some modifications still held by the majority of scholars.[1] The question is one which cannot be answered by an appeal to philology alone. This is the fundamental error of the advocates of the Sumero-Akkadian theory, who appear to overlook the fact that the testimony of archaeological and anthropological research must be confirmatory of a philological hypothesis before it can be accepted as an indisputable fact.[2] The time however has not yet come for these two sciences to pronounce their verdict definitely, though it may be added that the supposition of a variety of races once

---

[1] Besides Delitzsch, however, there are others, as Pognon, Jäger, Guyard, McCurdy and Brinton, who side with Halévy.

[2] See now Dr. Brinton's paper, "The Protohistoric Ethnography of Western Asia" (*Proceed. Amer. Philos. Soc.*, 1895), especially pp. 18-22.

inhabiting Southern Mesopotamia finds support in what we know from the pre-historic researches of anthropologists. Again, it is not to be denied that the theory of the Semitic origin of the cuneiform writing encounters obstacles that cannot easily be set aside. While it seeks to explain the syllabic values of the signs on the general principle that they represent elements of Babylonian words, truncated in this fashion in order to answer to the growing need for phonetic writing of words for which no ideographs existed, it is difficult to imagine, as Halévy's theory demands, that the "ideographic" style, as found chiefly in religious texts, is the deliberate invention of priests in their desire to produce a method of conveying their ideas that would be regarded as a mystery by the laity, and be successfully concealed from the latter. Here again the theory borders on the domain of archaeology, and philology alone will not help us out of the difficulty. An impartial verdict of the present state of the problem might be summed up as follows:

1. It is generally admitted that all the literature of Babylonia, including the oldest and even that written in the "ideographic" style, whether we term it "Sumero-Akkadian" or "hieratic," is the work of the Semitic settlers of Mesopotamia.

2. The culture, including the religion of Babylonia, is likewise a Semitic production, and since Assyria received its culture from Babylonia, the same remark holds good for entire Mesopotamia.

3. The cuneiform syllabary is largely Semitic in character. The ideas expressed by the ideographic values of the signs give no evidence of having been produced in non-Semitic surroundings; and, whatever the origin of the system may be, it has been so shaped by the Babylonians, so thoroughly adapted to their purposes, that it is to all practical purposes Semitic.

4. Approached from the theoretical side, there remains, after making full allowance for the Semitic elements in the system, a residuum that has not yet found a satisfactory explanation, either by those who favor the non-Semitic theory or by those who hold the opposite view.

5. Pending further light to be thrown upon this question, through the expected additions to our knowledge of the archaeology and of the anthropological conditions of ancient prehistoric Mesopotamia, philological research must content itself with an acknowledgment of its inability to reach a conclusion that will appeal so forcibly to all minds, as to place the solution of the problem beyond dispute.

6. There is a presumption in favor of assuming a mixture of races in Southern Mesopotamia at an early day, and a possibility, therefore, that the earliest form of picture writing in this region, from which the Babylonian cuneiform is derived, may have been *used* by a non-Semitic population, and that traces of this are still apparent in the developed system after the important step had been taken, marked by the advance from picture to phonetic writing.

The important consideration for our purpose is, that the religious conceptions and practices as they are reflected in the literary sources now at our command, are distinctly Babylonian. With this we may rest content, and, leaving theories aside, there will be no necessity in an exposition of the religion of the Babylonians and Assyrians to differentiate or to attempt to differentiate between Semitic and so-called non-Semitic elements. Local conditions and the long period covered by the development and history of the religion in question, are the factors that suffice to account for the mixed and in many respects complicated phenomena which this religion presents.

Having set forth the sources at our command for the study of the Babylonian-Assyrian religion, and having indicated the manner in which these sources have been made available for our purposes, we are prepared to take the next step that will fit us for an understanding of the religious practices that prevailed in Mesopotamia, — a consideration of the land and of its people, together with a general account of the history of the latter.

CHAPTER II.

THE LAND AND THE PEOPLE.

I.

THE Babylonians and Assyrians with whom we are concerned in this volume dwelt in the region embraced by the Euphrates and the Tigris, — the Babylonians in the south, or the Euphrates Valley, the Assyrians to the northeast, in the region extending from the Tigris into the Kurdish Mountain districts; while the northwestern part of Mesopotamia — the northern half of the Euphrates district — was the seat of various empires that were alternately the rivals and the subjects of either Babylonia or Assyria.

The entire length of Babylonia was about 300 miles; the greatest breadth about 125 miles. The entire surface area was some 23,000 square miles, or about the size of West Virginia. The area of Assyria, with a length of 350 miles and a breadth varying from 170 to 300 miles, covered 75,000 square miles, which would make it somewhat smaller than the state of Nebraska. In the strict sense, the term Mesopotamia should be limited to the territory lying between the Euphrates and the Tigris above their junction, in the neighborhood of Baghdad, and extending northwards to the confines of the Taurus range; while the district to the south of Baghdad, and reaching to the Persian Gulf, may more properly be spoken of as the Euphrates Valley; and a third division is represented by the territory to the east of the Tigris, from Baghdad, and up to the Kurdish Mountains; but while this distinction is one that may be justly maintained, in view of the different character that the southern valley presents from the northern plain, it has become so customary, in popular parlance, to think of the entire territory along and between the Euphrates and Tigris as one country, that the term Mesopotamia in this broad sense may be retained, with the division suggested by George Rawlinson, into Upper and Lower Mesopotamia. The two streams, as they form the salient traits of the region, are the factors that condition the character of the inhabitants and the culture that once flourished there. The Euphrates, or, to give the more correct pronunciation, Purat, signifies the 'river' *par excellence*. It is a quiet stream, flowing along in majestic dignity almost from its two sources, in the Armenian mountains, not far from the town of Erzerum, until it is joined by the Tigris in the extreme south. As the Shatt-el Arab, *i.e.*, Arabic River, the two reach the Persian Gulf. Receiving many tributaries as long as it remains in the mountains, it flows first in a westerly direction, as though making direct for the Mediterranean Sea, then, veering suddenly to the southeast, it receives but few tributaries after it once passes through the Taurus range into the plain, — on the right side, only the Sadschur, on the left the Balichus and the Khabur. From this point on for the remaining distance of 800 miles, so far from receiving fresh accessions, it loses in quantity through the marsh beds that form on both sides. When it reaches the alluvial soil of Babylonia proper, its current and also its depth are considerably diminished through the numerous canals that form an outlet for its waters. Of its entire length, 1780 miles, it is navigable only for a small distance, cataracts forming a hindrance in its northern course and sandbanks in the south. In consequence, it never became at any time an important avenue for commerce; and besides rafts, which could be floated down to a certain distance, the only means of communication ever used were wicker baskets coated within and without with bitumen, or some form of a primitive ferry for passing from one shore to another.

An entirely different stream is the Tigris — a corrupted form of 'Idiklat.' It is only 1146 miles in length, and is marked, as the native name indicates, by the 'swiftness' of its flow. Starting, like the Euphrates, in the rugged regions of Armenia, it continues its course through mountain clefts for a longer period, and joined at frequent intervals by tributaries, both before it merges into the plain and after doing so, the volume of its waters is steadily increased. Even when it approaches the alluvial soil of the south, it does not lose its character until well advanced in its course to the gulf. Advancing towards the Euphrates and again receding from it, it at last joins the latter at Korna, and together they pour their waters through the Persian Gulf into the great ocean. It is navigable from Diabekr in the north, for its entire length. Large rafts may be floated down from Mosul to Baghdad and Basra, and even small steamers have ascended as far north as Nimrud. The Tigris, then, in contrast to the Euphrates, is the avenue of commerce for Mesopotamia, forming the connecting bond between it and the rest of the ancient world, — Egypt, India, and the lands of the Mediterranean. Owing, however, to the imperfect character of the means of transportation in ancient and, for that matter, in modern times, the voyage up the stream was impracticable. The rafts, resting on inflated bags of goat or sheep skin, can make no headway against the rapid stream, and so, upon reaching Baghdad or Basra, they are broken up, and the bags sent back by the shore route to the north.

The contrast presented by the two rivers is paralleled by the traits distinguishing Upper from Lower Mesopotamia. Shut off to the north and northeast by the Armenian range, to the northwest by the Taurus, Upper Mesopotamia retains, for a considerable extent, and especially on the eastern side, a rugged aspect. The Kurdish mountains run close to the Tigris' bed for some distance below Mosul, while between the Tigris and the Euphrates proper, small ranges and promontories stretch as far as the end of the Taurus chain, well on towards Mosul.

Below Mosul, the region begins to change its character. The mountains cease, the plain begins, the soil becomes alluvial and through the regular overflow of the two rivers in the rainy season, develops an astounding fertility. This overflow begins, in the case of the Tigris, early in March, reaches its height in May, and ceases about the middle of June. The overflow of the Euphrates extends from the middle of March till the beginning of June, but September is reached before the river resumes its natural state. Not only does the overflow of the Euphrates thus extend over a longer period, but it oversteps its banks with greater violence than does the Tigris, so that as far north as the juncture with the Khabur, and still more so in the south, the country to both sides is flooded, until it assumes the appearance of a great sea. Through the violence of these overflows, changes constantly occur in the course that the river takes, so that places which in ancient times stood on its banks are to-day removed from the main river-bed. Another important change in Southern Babylonia is the constant accretion of soil, due to the deposits from the Persian Gulf.

This increase proceeding on an average of about one mile in fifty years has brought it about that the two rivers to-day, instead of passing separately into the Gulf, unite at Korna — some distance still from the entrance. The contrast of seasons is greater, as may be imagined, in Upper Mesopotamia than in the south. The winters are cold, with snowfalls that may last for several months, but with the beginning of the dry season, in May, a tropical heat sets in which lasts until the beginning of November, when the rain begins. Assyria proper, that is, the eastern side of Mesopotamia, is more affected by the mountain ranges than the west. In the Euphrates Valley, the heat during the dry season, from about May till November, when for weeks, and even months, no cloud is to be seen, beggars description; but strange enough, the Arabs who dwell there at present, while enduring the heat without much discomfort, are severely affected by a winter temperature that for Europeans and Americans is exhilarating in its influence.

From what has been said, it will be clear that the Euphrates is, *par excellence*, the river of Southern Mesopotamia or Babylonia, while the Tigris may be regarded as the river of Assyria. It was the Euphrates that made possible the high degree of culture, that was reached in the south. Through the very intense heat of the dry season, the soil developed a fertility that reduced human labor to a minimum. The return for sowing of all kinds of grain, notably wheat, corn, barley, is calculated, on an average, to be fifty to a hundred-fold, while the date palm flourishes with scarcely any cultivation at all. Sustenance being thus provided for with little effort, it needed only a certain care in protecting oneself from damage through the too abundant overflow, to enable the population to find that ease of existence, which is an indispensable condition of culture. This was accomplished by the erection of dikes, and by directing the waters through channels into the fields.

Assyria, more rugged in character, did not enjoy the same advantages. Its culture, therefore, not only arose at a later period than that of Babylonia, but was a direct importation from the south. It was due to the natural extension of the civilization that continued for the greater part of the existence of the two empires to be central in the south. But when once Assyria was included in the circle of Babylonian culture, the greater effort required in forcing the natural resources of the soil, produced a greater variety in the return. Besides corn, wheat and rice, the olive, banana and fig tree, mulberry and vine were cultivated, while the vicinity of the mountain ranges furnished an abundance of building material — wood and limestone — that was lacking in the south. The fertility of Assyria proper, again, not being dependent on the overflow of the Tigris, proved to be of greater endurance. With the neglect of the irrigation system, Babylonia became a mere waste, and the same river that was the cause of its prosperity became the foe that, more effectually than any human power, contributed to the ruin and the general desolation that marks the greater part of the Euphrates Valley at the present time. Assyria continued to play a part in history long after its ancient glory had departed, and to this day enjoys a far greater activity, and is of considerable more significance than the south.

II.

In so far as natural surroundings affect the character of two peoples belonging to the same race, the Assyrians present that contrast to the Babylonians which one may expect from the differences, just set forth, between the two districts. The former were rugged, more warlike, and when they acquired power, used it in the perfection of their military strength; the latter, while not lacking in the ambition to extend their dominion, yet, on the whole, presented a more peaceful aspect that led to the cultivation of commerce and industrial arts. Both, however, have very many more traits in common than they have marks of distinction. They both belong not only to the Semitic race, but to the same branch of the race. Presenting the same physical features, the languages spoken by them are identical, barring differences that do not always rise to the degree of dialectical variations, and affect chiefly the pronunciation of certain consonants. At what time the Babylonians and Assyrians settled in the district in which we find them, whence they came, and whether the Euphrates Valley or the northern Tigris district was the first to be settled, are questions that cannot, in the present state of knowledge, be answered. As to the time of their settlement, the high degree of culture that the Euphrates Valley shows at the earliest period known to us, — about 4000 B.C., — and the indigenous character of this culture, points to very old settlement, and makes it easier to err on the side of not going back far enough, than on the side of going too far. Again, while, as has been several times intimated, the culture in the south is older than that of the north, it does not necessarily follow that the settlement of Babylonia antedates that of Assyria. The answer to this question would depend upon the answer to the question as to the original home of the Semites.[1] The probabilities, however, are in favor of assuming a movement of population, as of culture, from the south to the north. At all events, the history of Babylonia and Assyria begins with the former, and as a consequence we are justified also in beginning with that phase of the religion for which we have the earliest records, — the Babylonian.

III.

At the very outset of a brief survey of the history of the Babylonians, a problem confronts us of primary importance. Are there any traces of other settlers besides the Semitic Babylonians in the earliest period of the history of the Euphrates Valley? Those who cling to the theory of a non-Semitic origin of the cuneiform syllabary will, of course, be ready to answer in the affirmative. Sumerians and Akkadians are the names given to these non-Semitic settlers who preceded the Babylonians in the control of the Euphrates Valley. The names are derived from the terms Sumer and Akkad, which are frequently found in Babylonian and Assyrian inscriptions, in connection with the titles of the kings. Unfortunately, scholars are not a unit in the exact location of the districts comprised by these names, some declaring Sumer to be in the north and

---

[1] I may be permitted to refer to a publication by Dr. Brinton and myself, *The Cradle of the Semites* (Philadelphia, 1889), in which the various views as to this home are set forth.

Akkad in the south; others favoring the reverse position. The balance of proof rests in favor of the former supposition; but however that may be, Sumer and Akkad represent, from a certain period on, a general designation to include the whole of Babylonia. Professor Hommel goes so far as to declare that in the types found on statues and monuments of the oldest period of Babylonian history — the monuments coming from the mound Telloh — we have actual representations of these Sumerians, who are thus made out to be a smooth-faced race with rather prominent cheek-bones, round faces, and shaven heads.[1] He pronounces in favor of the highlands lying to the east of Babylonia, as the home of the Sumerians, whence they made their way into the Euphrates Valley. Unfortunately, the noses on these old statues are mutilated, and with such an important feature missing, anthropologists, at least, are unwilling to pronounce definitely as to the type represented. Again, together with these supposed non-Semitic types, other figures have been found which, as Professor Hommel also admits, show the ordinary Semitic features. It would seem, therefore, that even accepting the hypothesis of a non-Semitic type existing in Babylonia at this time, the Semitic settlers are just as old as the supposed Sumerians; and since it is admitted that the language found on these statues and figures contains Semitic constructions and Semitic words, it is, to say the least, hazardous to give the Sumerians the preference over the Semites so far as the period of settlement and origin of the Euphratean culture is concerned. As a matter of fact, we are not warranted in going beyond the statement that all evidence points in favor of a population of mixed races in the Euphrates Valley from the earliest period known to us. No positive proof is forthcoming that Sumer and Akkad were ever employed or understood in any other sense than as geographical terms.

[1] It has been suggested that since the statues of Telloh are those of the priest-kings, only the priestly classes shaved their hair off.

This one safe conclusion, however, that the Semitic settlers of Babylonia were not the sole occupants, but by their side dwelt another race, or possibly a variety of races, possessing entirely different traits, is one of considerable importance. At various times the non-Semitic hordes of Elam and the mountain districts to the east of Babylonia swept over the valley, and succeeded, for a longer or shorter period, in securing a firm foothold. The ease with which these conquerors accommodated themselves to their surroundings, continuing the form of government which they found there, making but slight changes in the religious practices, can best be accounted for on the supposition that the mixture of different races in the valley had brought about an interchange and interlacing of traits which resulted in the approach of one type to the other. Again, it has recently been made probable that as early at least as 2000, or even 2500 B.C., Semitic invaders entering Babylonia from the side of Arabia drove the native Babylonian rulers from the throne;[1] and at a still earlier period intercourse between Babylonia and distant nations to the northeast and northwest was established, which left its traces on the political and social conditions. At every point we come across evidence of this composite character of Babylonian culture, and the question as to the origin of the latter may, after all, resolve itself into the proposition that the contact of different races gave the intellectual impetus which is the first condition of a forward movement in civilization; and while it is possible that, at one stage, the greater share in the movement falls to the non-Semitic contingent, the Semites soon obtained the intellectual ascendency, and so absorbed the non-Semitic elements as to give to the culture resulting from the combination, the homogeneous character it presents on the surface.

[1] See an interesting discussion of the question by Professor Hommel, " Arabia according to the Latest Discoveries and Researches." — *Sunday School Times*, 1895, nos. 41 and 43.

IV.

Our present knowledge of Babylonian history reaches back to the period of about 4000 B.C. At that time we find the Euphrates Valley divided into a series of states or principalities, parcelling North and South Babylonia between them. These states group themselves around certain cities. In fact, the Babylonian principalities arise from the extension of the city's jurisdiction, just as the later Babylonian empire is naught but the enlargement, on a greater scale, of the city of Babylon.

Of these old Babylonian cities the most noteworthy, in the south, are Eridu, Lagash,[1] Ur, Larsa, Uruk, Isin; and in the north, Agade, Sippar, Nippur, Kutha, and Babylon. The rulers of these cities call themselves either 'king' (literally 'great man') or 'governor,' according as the position is a purely independent one, or one of subjection to a more powerful chieftain. Thus the earliest rulers of the district of Lagash, of whom we have inscriptions (c. 3200 B.C.) have the title of 'king,' but a few centuries later Lagash lost its independent position and its rulers became 'patesis,' *i.e.*, governors. They are in a position of vassalage, as it would appear, to the contemporaneous kings of Ur, though this does not hinder them from engaging in military expeditions against Elam, and in extensive building operations. The kings of Ur, in addition to their title as kings of Ur, are styled kings of Sumer and Akkad. Whether at this time, Sumer and Akkad included the whole of Babylonia, or, as seems more likely, only the southern part, in either case, Lagash would fall under the jurisdiction of these kings, if their title is to be regarded as more than an empty boast. Again, the rulers of Uruk are known simply as kings of that place, while those of Isin incorporate in their titles, kingship over Ur as well as Sumer and Akkad.

[1] Also known as Shirpurla which Jensen (*Keils Bibl.* 3, 1, 5) thinks was the later name.

For this early period, extending from about 4000 B.C. to 2300, the chronology is as yet uncertain. Beyond the titles of the rulers over Babylonian states, there are but few safe indications for determining the succession of dynasties. So much, however, is now certain,—that simultaneous with the governors of Lagash and the older kings of Ur, there was an independent state in Northern Babylonia with its seat at Agade. Indeed the history of this state can now be traced back six centuries beyond that of Lagash. Two rulers of Agade, Naram-Sin (c. 3800 B.C.) and Sargon (or to give his fuller name, Shargani-shar-ali[1]), are the earliest rulers as yet known. These kings of Agade extended their jurisdiction as far north, at least, as Nippur on the one side and Sippar on the other. The city of Babylon itself, if it existed at this period, was therefore included within the territory of these kings; and it follows that if there existed rulers of Babylon at this time, which is doubtful (since the city is not mentioned), they were in the same position of dependency upon the rulers of Agade as the 'governors' of Lagash were upon some greater power. It is not until about the middle of the third millennium before this era, that Babylon comes into prominence.

In the south, as already intimated, the rulers of Lagash and the dynasty of Ur are the earliest of which we have any record. There is every reason to believe that further excavations at Mugheir will bring to light the names of older kings, and the presumption is in favor of regarding the southern states, or at least some of them, earlier than any in the north. The climax in the power of the kings of Ur, the period when

---

[1] See Hilprecht, *Old Babylonian Inscriptions*, i. 16–18. Naram-Sin signifies 'beloved of the god Sin' (the moon-god); Shargani-shar-ali—'the legitimate king, king of the city.' The excavations of the University of Pennsylvania have cast new light upon this most ancient period of Babylonian history. It is now known that the temple of Bel at Nippur antedates the reign of Naram-Sin, and in the further publications of the University, we may look for material which will enable us to pass beyond the period of Sargon.

they exerted, in fact as well as in name, the sovereignty over all Sumer and Akkad may be fixed approximately at 3000 B.C. How far we shall be able to go beyond that, for the beginnings of this state, must, for the present, remain doubtful, with the chances in favor of a considerably earlier date; and it may be that prior to Ur and Lagash there were dynasties established elsewhere, — at Eridu, perhaps, — the existence of which will be revealed by future discoveries. An independent state with its seat at Uruk follows upon the culminating period of the glory of Ur, and may be regarded, indeed, as an indication that the rulers of Ur had lost their control over the whole of Southern Babylonia. Isin, whose site has not yet been determined, but which lay probably to the north of Uruk, was another political center. Its rulers, so far as we know them, curiously assign the fourth place to the title 'king of Isin,' giving precedence to their control over Nippur, Eridu, and Uruk. We may conclude from this, that at the time when Isin extended its supremacy, the greater luster attaching to the old towns of Nippur and Uruk, was emphasized by the precedence given to these centers over Isin, although the Isin kings are only 'shepherds' and 'merciful lords' over Nippur and Uruk, and not kings.

At a subsequent period, the kings of Ur appear to have regained the supremacy, which was wrested from them by Isin; and the rulers of the latter acknowledge their dependence upon the kings of Ur. This so-called second dynasty of Ur includes Nippur. The kings are proud of calling themselves the guardians of the temple of Bel in Nippur, nominated to the office by the god himself, and reviving an old title of the kings of Agade, style themselves also 'king of the four regions.' Another change in the political horoscope is reflected in the subjection of Ur to a district whose center was Larsa, not far from Ur, and represented by the mound Senkereh. There are two kings, Nur-Ramman (*i.e.*, light of Ramman) and Sin-iddina (*i.e.*, Sin judges), who call themselves guardians of Ur and kings of Larsa, showing that the center of this principality was Larsa, with Ur as a dependent district. That these rulers take up the dominion once held by the kings of Ur is further manifest in the additional title that they give to themselves, as 'kings of Sumer and Akkad,' whereas the omission of the title 'king of the four regions' indicates apparently the exclusion of Agade and Nippur; and with these, probably North Babylonia in general, from their supremacy. The power of Larsa receives a fatal check through the invasion of Babylonia by the Elamites (*c.* 2350 B.C.).

These variations in official titles are a reflection of the natural rivalry existing between the various Babylonian states, which led to frequent shiftings in the political situation. Beyond this, the inscriptions of these old Babylonian rulers, being ordinarily commemorative of the dedication to a deity, of some temple or other construction — notably canals — or of some votive offering, a cone or tablet, unfortunately tell us little of the events of the time. Pending the discovery of more complete annals, we must content ourselves with the general indications of the civilization that prevailed, and of the relations in which the principalities stood to one another, and with more or less doubtful reconstructions of the sequence in the dynasties. In all of this period, however, the division between North and South Babylonia was kept tolerably distinct, even though occasionally, and for a certain period, a North Babylonian city, like that of Agade and Nippur, extended its jurisdiction over a section bordering on the south and *vice versa*. It remained for a great conqueror, Hammurabi, the sixth king of a dynasty having its seat in the city of Babylon itself, who about the year 2300 B.C. succeeded in uniting North and South Babylonia under one rule. With him, therefore, a new epoch in the history of the Euphrates Valley begins. Henceforth the supremacy of the city of Babylon remains undisputed, and the other ancient centers, losing their political importance, retain their significance only by virtue of the sanctuaries existing there, to which pilgrimages continued to be made, and through the commercial activity that, upon the union of the various Babylonian districts, set in with increased vigor.

Attention was directed a few years ago by Pognon and Sayce to the fact that the name of Hammurabi, as well as the names of four kings that preceded him, and of a number that followed, are not Babylonian. Sayce expressed the opinion that they were Arabic, and Professor Hommel has recently reënforced the position of Sayce by showing the close resemblance existing between these names and those found on the monuments of Southern Arabia.[1] While no evidence has as yet been found to warrant us in carrying back the existence of the Minean empire in Southern Arabia beyond 1500 B.C., still since at this period, this empire appears in a high state of culture, with commercial intercourse established between it and Egypt, as well as Palestine, the conclusion drawn by Hommel that Babylonia was invaded about 2500 B.C. by an Arabic-speaking people is to be seriously considered. Elam, as we have seen, was constantly threatening Babylonia from the East, and shortly before Hammurabi's appearance, succeeded in putting an end to the dynasty of Larsa. It now appears that the inhabitants of the Euphrates Valley were also threatened by an enemy lodged somewhere in the southwest. Though Hommel's hypothesis still needs confirmation, and may perhaps be somewhat modified by future researches, still so much seems certain: that the great union of the Babylonian states and the supremacy of the city of Babylon itself was achieved not by Babylonians but by foreigners who entered Babylonia from its western (or southwestern) side. The dynasty of which Hammurabi is the chief representative comes to an end c. 2100, and is followed by an-

---

[1] *Sunday School Times*, 1895, no. 41.

other known as Shish-Kha,[1] whose rulers likewise appear to be foreigners; and when this dynasty finally disappears after a rule of almost four centuries, Babylonia is once more conquered by a people coming from the northern parts of Elam and who are known as the Cassites.[2] These Cassites, of whose origin, character, and language but little is known as yet, ruled over Babylonia for a period of no less than 576 years; but adapting themselves to the customs and religion of the country, their presence did not interfere with the normal progress of culture in the Euphrates Valley. We may therefore embrace the period of Hammurabi and his successors, down through the rule of the Cassite kings, under one head. It is a period marked by the steady growth of culture, manifesting itself in the erection of temples, in the construction of canals, and in the expansion of commerce. Active relationships were maintained between Babylonia and distant Egypt.

This movement did not suffer an interruption through the invasion of the Cassites. Though Nippur, rather than Babylon, appears to have been the favorite city of the dynasty, the course of civilization flows on uninterruptedly, and it is not until the growing complications between Babylonia and Assyria, due to the steady encroachment on the part of the latter, that decided changes begin to take place.

About 1500 B.C. the first traces of relationship between Babylonia and the northern Mesopotamian power, Assyria, appear. These relations were at first of a friendly character, but it is not long before the growing strength of Assyria becomes a serious menace to Babylonia. In the middle of the thirteenth century, Assyrian arms advance upon the city of Babylon. For some decades, Babylon remains in subjection to

---

[1] For various views regarding the name and character of this dynasty see Winckler, *Geschichte*, pp. 67, 68, 328; Hilprecht, *Assyriaca*, pp. 25-28, 102, 103; Winckler, *Altorientalische Forschungen*, I. 275-277, and Rogers, *Outlines*, 32, note.

[2] See Delitzsch, *Die Sprache der Kossaer*.

Assyria, and although she regains her independence once more, and even a fair measure of her former glory, the power of the Cassites is broken. Internal dissensions add to the difficulties of the situation and lead to the overthrow of the Cassites (1151 B.C.). Native Babylonians once more occupy the throne, who, although able to check the danger still threatening from Elam, cannot resist the strong arms of Assyria. At the close of the twelfth century Tiglathpileser I. secures a firm hold upon Babylonia, which now sinks to the position of a dependency upon the Assyrian kings.

V.

In contrast to Babylonia, which is from the start stamped as a civilizing power, Assyria, from its rise till its fall, is essentially a military empire, seeking the fulfillment of its mission in the enlargement of power and in incessant warfare. Its history may be traced back to about 1800 B.C., when its rulers, with their seat in the ancient city of Ashur, first begin to make their presence felt. The extension of their power proceeds, as in Babylonia, from the growing importance of the central city, and soon embraces all of Assyria proper. They pass on into the mountain regions to the east, and advancing to the west, they encounter the vigorous forces of Egypt, whose Asiatic campaigns begin about the same time as the rise of Assyria. The Egyptians, abetted by the Hittites — the possessors of the strongholds on the Orontes — successfully check the growth of Assyria on this side, at least for a period of several centuries. In the meanwhile, the Assyrian king gathers strength enough to make an attack upon Babylonia.

The conflict, once begun, continues, as has been indicated, with varying fortunes. Occasional breathing spells are brought about by a temporary agreement of peace between the two empires, until at the end of the twelfth century, Assyria, under Tiglathpileser I., secures control over the Babylonian empire. Her kings add to their long list of titles that of 'ruler of Babylonia.' They either take the government of the south into their hands or exercise the privilege of appointing a governor of their choice to regulate the affairs of the Euphrates Valley. From this time on, the history of Babylonia and Assyria may be viewed under a single aspect. The third period of Babylonian history — the second of Assyrian history — thus begins about 1100 B.C., and continues till the fall of Assyria in the year 606 B.C. These five centuries represent the most glorious epoch of the united Mesopotamian empire. During this time, Assyria rises to the height of an all-embracing power. With far greater success than Egypt, she securely established her sovereignty over the lands bordering on the Mediterranean. After severe struggles, the Hittites are overcome, the names of their strongholds on the Orontes changed, in order to emphasize their complete possession by the Assyrians, and the principalities of Northern Syria become tributary to Assyria. Phoenicia and the kingdom of Israel are conquered, while the southern kingdom of Judah purchases a mere shadow of independence by complete submission to the conditions imposed by the great and irresistible monarchy. Far to the northeast Assyria extends her sway, while Babylonia, though occasionally aroused to a resistance of the tyrannical bonds laid upon her, only to be still further weakened, retains a distinctive existence chiefly in name. The culture of the south is the heritage bequeathed by old Babylonia to the north. Babylonian temples become the models for Assyrian architecture. The literary treasures in the archives of the sacred cities of the south are copied by the scribes of the Assyrian kings, and placed in the palaces of the latter. Meanwhile, the capital of Assyria moves towards the north. Ashur gives way under the glorious reign of Ashurnasirbal to Calah, which becomes the capitol in the year 880 B.C.;

and Calah, in turn, yields to Nineveh, which becomes, from the time of Tiglathpileser II., in the middle of the eighth century, the center of the great kingdom. Under Ashurbanabal, who rules from 668 to 626 B.C., the climax of Assyrian power is reached. He carries his arms to the banks of the Nile, and succeeds in realizing the dreams of his ancestors of a direct control over the affairs of Egypt. A patron of science and literature, as so many great conquerors, Ashurbanabal succeeds in making Nineveh a literary as well as a military center.

A vast collection of the cuneiform literature of Babylonia is gathered by him for the benefit of his subjects, as he is at constant pains to tell us. The city is further embellished with magnificent structures, and on every side he establishes his sovereignty with such force, that the might of Assyria appears invincible. The fatal blow, dealt with a suddenness that remains a mystery, came from an unexpected quarter. A great movement of wild northern hordes, rather vaguely known as the Cimmerians and Scythians, and advancing towards the south, set in shortly after the death of Ashurbanabal, and created great political disturbances. The vast number of these hordes, their muscular strength, and their unrestrained cruelty, made them a foe which Assyria found as hard to withstand, as Rome the approach of the Vandals and Goths. The sources for our knowledge of the last days of the Assyrian empire are not sufficient to enable us to grasp the details, but it is certain that the successful attempt of the Babylonians to throw off the Assyrian yoke almost immediately after Ashurbanabal's death, was a symptom of the ravages which the hordes made in reducing the vitality of the Assyrian empire. Her foes gained fresh courage from the success that crowned the revolt of Babylonia. The Medes, a formidable nation to the east of Assyria, and which had often crossed arms with the Assyrians, entered into combination with Babylonia, and the two making several united assaults upon Nineveh, under the leadership of Kyaxares, at last succeeded in effecting an entrance. The city was captured and burned to the ground. With the fall of Assyria, a feeling of relief passed over the entire eastern world. A great danger, threatening to extinguish the independence of all of the then known nations of the globe, was averted. The Hebrew prophets living at the time of this downfall, voice the general rejoicing that ensued when they declared, that even the cedars of Lebanon leaped for joy. The province of Assyria proper, fell into the hands of the Medes, but Babylonia, with her independence established on a firm footing, was the real heir of Assyria's spirit. Her most glorious monarch, Nebuchadnezzar II. (604–561 B.C.), seems to have dreamed of gaining for Babylon the position, once held by Nineveh, of mistress of the world. Taking Ashurbanabal as his model, he carried his arms to the west, subdued the kingdom of Judah, and, passing on to Egypt, strove to secure for Babylon, the supremacy exercised there for a short time by Assyrian monarchs. In addition to his military campaigns, however, he also appears in the light of a great builder, enlarging and beautifying the temples of Babylonia, erecting new ones in the various cities of his realm, strengthening the walls of Babylon, adorning the capital with embankment works and other improvements, that gave it a permanent place in the traditions of the ancient world as one of the seven wonders of the universe.

The glory of this second Babylonian empire was of short duration. Its vaulting ambition appears to have overleaped itself. Realizing for a time the Assyrian ideal of a world monarchy, the fall was as sudden as its rise was unexpected. Internal dissensions gave the first indication of the hollowness of the state. Nebuchadnezzar's son was murdered in 560 B.C., within two years after reaching the throne, by his own brother-in-law, Neriglissar; and the latter dying after a reign of only four years, his infant child was put out of the way and Nabonnedos, a high officer of the state, but without royal prerogative, mounted the throne. In the year 550 news reached Babylon that Cyrus, the king of Anzan, had dealt a fatal blow to the Median empire, capturing its king, Astyages, and joining Media to his own district. He founded what was afterwards known as the Persian empire.

The overthrow of the Medes gave Cyrus control over Assyria, and it was to be expected that his gaze should be turned in the direction of Babylonia. Nabonnedos recognized the danger, but all his efforts to strengthen the powers of resistance to the Persian arms were of no avail. Civil disturbances divided the Babylonians. The cohesion between the various districts was loosened, and within the city of Babylon itself, a party arose antagonistic to Nabonnedos, who in their short-sightedness hailed the advance of Cyrus. Under these circumstances, Babylon fell an easy prey to the Persian conqueror. In the autumn of the year 539 Cyrus entered the city in triumph, and was received with such manifestations of joy by the populace, as to make one almost forget that with his entrance, the end of a great empire had come. Politically and religiously, the history of Babylonia and Assyria terminates with the advent of Cyrus; and this despite the fact that it was his policy to leave the state of affairs, including religious observances, as far as possible, undisturbed. A new spirit had, however, come into the land with him. The official religion of the state was that practiced by Cyrus and his predecessors in their native land. The essential doctrines of the religion, commonly known as Mazdeism or Zoroastrianism, presented a sharp contrast to the beliefs that still were current in Babylonia, and it was inevitable that with the influx of new ideas, the further development of Babylonian worship was cut short. The respect paid by Cyrus to the Babylonian gods was a mere matter of policy. Still, the religious rites continued to be practiced as of old in Babylonia and Assyria for a long time, and when the religion finally disappeared, under the subsequent conquests of the Greeks, Romans, and Arabs, it left its traces in the popular superstitions and in the ineradicable traditions that survived. But so far as the *history* of this religion is concerned, it comes to an end with the downfall of the second Babylonian empire.

The period, then, to be covered by a treatment of the religion of the Babylonians and Assyrians extends over the long interval between about 4000 B.C. and the middle of the sixth century. The development of this religion follows closely the course of civilization and of history in the territory under consideration. The twofold division, accordingly, into Babylonia and Assyria, is the one that suggests itself also for the religion. The beginning, as is evident from the historical sketch given, must be made with Babylonia. It will be seen that, while the rites there and in Assyria are much the same, the characters of the gods as they developed in the south were quite different from those of the north; and, again, it was inevitable that the Assyrian influence manifest in the second Babylonian empire should give to the religion of the south at this time, some aspects which were absent during the days of the old Babylonian empire. In Babylonia, again, the political changes form the basis for the transformation to be observed in the position occupied by the deities at different periods; and the same general remark applies to the deities peculiar to Assyria, who must be studied in connection with the course pursued by the Assyrian empire.

The division of the subject which thus forces itself upon us is twofold, (1) geographical, and (2) historical.

It will be necessary to treat first of the beliefs and pantheon developed during the first two periods of Babylonian history, down to the practical conquest of Babylonia by

Assyria. Then, turning to Assyria, the traits of the pantheon peculiar to Upper Mesopotamia will be set forth. In the third place, the history of the religion will be traced in Babylonia during the union of the Babylonian-Assyrian empire; and, lastly, the new phases of that religion which appeared in the days of the second Babylonian empire. Turning after this to other aspects of the religion, it will be found that the religious rites were only to a small degree influenced by political changes, while the literature and religious art are almost exclusively products of Babylonia. In treating of these subjects, accordingly, no geographical divisions are called for, in setting forth their chief features.

The general estimate to be given at the close of the volume will furnish an opportunity of making a comparison between the Babylonian-Assyrian religion and other religions of the ancient world, with a view to determining what foreign influences may be detected in it, as well as ascertaining the influence it exerted upon others.

CHAPTER III.

GENERAL TRAITS OF THE OLD BABYLONIAN PANTHEON.

The Babylonian religion in the oldest form known to us may best be described as a mixture of local and nature cults. Starting with that phase of religious beliefs known as Animism, which has been ascertained to be practically universal in primitive society, the Babylonians, from ascribing life to the phenomena of nature, to trees, stones, and plants, as well as to such natural events, as storm, rain, and wind, and as a matter of course to the great luminaries and to the stars—would, on the one hand, be led to invoke an infinite number of spirits who were supposed to be, in some way the embodiment of the life that manifested itself in such diverse manners; and yet, on the other hand, this tendency would be restricted by the experience which would point to certain spirits, as exercising a more decisive influence upon the affairs of man than others. The result of this would be to give a preponderance to the worship of the sun and moon and the water, and of such natural phenomena as rain, wind, and storms, with their accompaniment of thunder and lightning, as against the countless sprites believed to be lurking everywhere. The latter, however, would not for this reason be ignored altogether. Since everything was endowed with life, there was not only a spirit of the tree which produced the fruit, but there were spirits in every field. To them the ground belonged, and upon their mercy depended the success or failure of the produce. To secure the favor of the rain and the sun was not sufficient to the agriculturist; he was obliged to obtain the protection of the guardian spirits of the soil, in order to be sure of reaping the fruit of his labors. Again, when through association, the group of arable plots grew into a hamlet, and then through continued growth into a town, the latter, regarded as a unit by virtue of its political organization under a chief ruler, would necessarily be supposed to have some special power presiding over its destinies, protecting it from danger, and ready to defend the rights and privileges of those who stood immediately under its jurisdiction. Each Babylonian city, large or small, would in this way obtain a deity devoted to its welfare, and as the city grew in extent, absorbing perhaps others lying about, and advancing in this way to the dignity of a district, the city's god would correspondingly increase his jurisdiction. As it encroached upon the domain of other local deities, it would by conquest annihilate the latter, or reduce them to a subservient position. The new regime would be expressed by making the conquered deity, the servant of the victorious, or the two might be viewed in the relation of father to son; and again, in the event of a peaceful amalgamation of two cities or districts, the protecting deities might join hands in a compact, mirroring the partnership represented by the conjugal tie. In this way, there arose in Babylon a selection, as it were, out of an infinite variety of personified forces, manifest or concealed, that at one time may have been objects of worship. The uniformity of the spirit world, which is the characteristic trait of primitive Animism, gave way to a differentiation regulated by the political development and the social growth of Babylonia. The more important natural forces became gods, and the inferior ones were, as a general thing, relegated to the secondary position of mere sprites, — like the *jinns*, in Arabic beliefs. Only in the case of the guardian spirit of an entire city or district, would there result — and even this not invariably — an elevation to the grade of deity, in the proper sense of the word. In many cases, however, this guardian deity might be a heavenly body, as the moon or sun or stars, all of which were supposed to regulate the fate of mankind or some force of nature, as the rain or the storm; and even if this were not originally the case, the protecting deity might, in the course of time, become identified with one of the forces of nature; and, if for no other reason, simply because of the prominence which the worship of the force in question acquired in the place. As a consequence, the mixture of local and nature cults is so complete that it is often impossible to distinguish the one from the other. It is hard in many cases to determine whether the deity which is identified with a certain city was originally a mere local spirit watching over a certain restricted territory, or a personification of a natural force associated in some way with a certain section of Babylonia.

CHAPTER IV.

BABYLONIAN GODS PRIOR TO THE DAYS OF HAMMURABI.

With these preliminary remarks, we may turn, as the first part of our subject, to a consideration of the oldest of the Babylonian gods. Our main sources are the inscriptions of the old Babylonian rulers, above referred to. These are, in most cases, of a dedicatory character, being inscribed on statues, cylinders, or tablets, placed in the temples or on objects — cones, knobs, stones — presented as votive offerings to some god. Besides the inscriptions of the rulers, we have those of officials and others. Many of these are likewise connected directly or indirectly with religious worship.

The advantage of the historical texts over the purely religious ones consists in their being dated, either accurately or approximately. For this reason, the former must be made the basis for a rational theory of the development of the Babylonian pantheon through the various periods above instanced. The data furnished by the religious texts can be introduced only, as they accord with the facts revealed by the historical inscriptions in each period.

Taking up the group of inscriptions prior to the union of the Babylonian States under Hammurabi, *i.e.*, prior to 2300 B.C., we find these gods mentioned: Bel, Belit, Nin-khar-sag, Nin-gir-su, also appearing as Shul-gur, Bau, Ga-tum-dug, Ea, Nin-a-gal, Nergal, Shamash, under various forms Â, who is the consort of Shamash, Nannar or Sin, Nanâ, Anunit, Ishtar, Innanna or Ninni, Ninâ, Nin-mar, Dun-shagga, Gal-alim, Anu, Nin-gish-zida, Nin-si-a, Nin-shakh, Dumu-zi, Lugal-banda and his consort Nin-gul, Dumuzi-zu-aba, Nisaba, Ku(?)anna, Lugal-erima(?), Dagan, Ishum, Umu, Pa-sag, Nin-e-gal, Nin-gal, Shul(or Dun)-pa-uddu, and Nin-akha-kuddu.

Regarding these names, it may be said at once that the reading, in many cases, is to be looked upon as merely provisional. Written, as they usually are, in the ideographic "style," the phonetic reading can only be determined when the deity in question can be identified with one, whose name is written at some place phonetically, or when the ideographs employed are so grouped as to place the phonetic reading beyond doubt. The plan to be followed in this book will be to give the ideographic reading[1] as provisional wherever the real pronunciation is unknown or uncertain. The ideographic designation of a deity is of great value, inasmuch as the ideographs themselves frequently reveal the character of the god, though of course the additional advantage is obvious when the name appears in both the ideographic and the phonetic writing. It will, therefore, form part of a delineation of the Babylonian pantheon to interpret the picture, as it were, under which each deity is viewed.

En-lil or Bel.

Taking up the gods in the order named, the first one, Bel, is also the one who appears on the oldest monuments as yet unearthed — the inscriptions of Nippur. His name is, at this time, written invariably as En-lil. In the Babylonian theology, he is 'the lord of the lower world.' He represents, as it were, the unification of the various forces whose seat and sphere of action is among the inhabited parts of the globe, both on the surface and beneath, for the term 'lower world' is here used in contrast to the upper or heavenly world. Such a conception manifestly belongs to the domain of abstract thought, and it may be concluded, therefore, that either the deity belongs to an advanced stage of Babylonian culture, or that the original view of the deity was different from the one just mentioned.

[1] Indicated by separating the syllables composing the name.

The latter is the case. Primarily, the ideograph Lil is used to designate a 'demon' in general, and En-lil is therefore the 'chief demon.' Primitive as such a conception is, it points to some system of thought that transcends primitive Animism, which is characterized rather by the equality accorded to all spirits. The antiquity of the association of En-lil with Nippur justifies the conclusion that we have before us a local deity who, originally the protecting spirit merely, of a restricted territory, acquires the position of 'chief demon' as the town of Nippur grows to be the capitol of a large and powerful district. The fame and sanctity of Nippur survives political vicissitudes; and, indeed, in proportion as Nippur loses political prestige, the great deity of the place is released from the limitations due to his local origin and rises to the still higher dignity of a great power whose domain is the entire habitable universe. As the 'lord of the lower world,' En-lil is contrasted to a god Anu, who presides over the heavenly bodies. The age of Sargon (3800 B.C.), in whose inscriptions En-lil already occurs, is one of considerable culture, as is sufficiently evidenced by the flourishing condition of art, and there can therefore be no objection against the assumption that even at this early period, a theological system should have been evolved which gave rise to beliefs in great powers whose dominion embraces the 'upper' and 'lower' worlds. It was because of this wide scope of his power that he became known as Bel, *i.e.*, the lord *par excellence;* and it is equally natural to find his worship spread over the whole of Babylonia. In the south, the patron deity of Lagash is designated by Gudea as "the mighty warrior of Bel," showing the supremacy accorded to the latter. A temple to En-lil at Lagash, and known as E-adda, 'house of the father,' by virtue of the relationship existing between the god of Nippur and Nin-girsu, is mentioned by Uru-kagina. The temple is described as a lofty structure 'rising up to heaven.' In the north, Nippur remains the place where his worship acquired the greatest importance, so that Nippur was known as the "land of Bel." The temple sacred to him at that place was a great edifice, famous throughout Babylonian history as E-Kur, *i.e.*, mountain house, in the construction of which, a long line of Babylonian rulers took part. From Naram-Sin, ruler of Agade, on through the period of Cassite rule, the kings of Nippur proudly include in their titles that of 'builder of the Temple of Bel at Nippur,' measuring their attachment to the deity by the additions and repairs made to his sacred edifice.[1] Besides the kings of Agade, the rulers of other places pay their devotions to Bel of Nippur. So, a king of Kish, whose name is read Alu-usharshid by Professor Hilprecht,[2] brings costly vases of marble and limestone from Elam and offers them to Bel as a token of victory; and this at a period even earlier than Sargon. Even when En-lil is obliged to yield a modicum of his authority to the growing supremacy of the patron deity of the city of Babylon, the highest tribute that can be paid to the latter, is to combine with his real name, Marduk, the title of "Bel," which of right belongs to En-lil. We shall see how this combination of En-lil, or Bel, with Marduk reflects political changes that took place in the Euphrates Valley; and it is a direct consequence of this later association of the old Bel of Nippur with the chief god of Babylon, that the original traits of the former become obscured in the historical and religious texts. Dimmed popular traditions, which will be set forth in their proper place, point to his having been at one time regarded as a powerful chieftain armed with mighty weapons, but engaged in conflicts for the ultimate benefit of mankind. On the whole, he is a beneficent deity, though ready to inflict

---

[1] At the period when the kings of Ur extend their rule over Nippur, they, too, do not omit to refer to the distinction of having been called to the service of the great god at his temple.

[2] The name signifies, 'He has founded the city,' the subject of the verb being some deity whose name is omitted.

severe punishment for disobedience to his commands. We must distinguish, then, in the case of En-lil, at least four phases:

1. His original rôle as a local deity;
2. The extension of his power to the grade of a great 'lord' over a large district;
3. Dissociation from local origins to become the supreme lord of the lower world; and
4. The transfer of his name and powers as god of Nippur to Marduk, the god of Babylon.

The last two phases can best be set forth when we come to the period, marked by the political supremacy of the city of Babylon. It is sufficient, at this point, to have made clear his position as god of Nippur.

Nin-lil or Belit.

The consort of En-lil is Nin-Lil, the 'mistress of the lower world.' She is known also as Belit, the feminine form to Bel, *i.e.*, the lady *par excellence*. She, too, had her temple at Nippur, the age of which goes back, at least, to the first dynasty of Ur. But the glory of the goddess pales by the side of her powerful lord. She is naught but a weak reflection of Bel, as in general the consorts of the gods are. Another title by which this same goddess was known is

Nin-khar-sag,[1]

which means the 'lady of the high or great mountain.' The title may have some reference to the great mountain where the gods were supposed to dwell, and which was known to Baby-

---

[1] Jensen, *Keils Bibl.* 3, 1, p. 23, proposes to read Nin-Ur-sag, but without sufficient reason, it seems to me. The writing being a purely ideographic form, an *epi-theton ornans*, the question of how the ideographs are to be read is not of great moment.

lonians as the 'mountain of the lands.' Bel, as the chief of the gods, is more particularly associated with this mountain. Hence his temple is called the 'mountain house.' From being regarded as the inhabitant of the mountain, he comes to be identified with the mountain itself. Accordingly, he is sometimes addressed as the "great mountain,"[1] and his consort would therefore be appropriately termed 'the lady of the great mountain.' Besides the temple at Nippur, Belit, as Nin-khar-sag, had a sanctuary at Girsu, one of the quarters at Lagash (see under Nin-girsu), the earliest mention of which occurs on an inscription of Ur-Bau. The latter calls the goddess 'the mother of the gods,' which further establishes her identity with the consort of Bel. Entemena, another governor of Lagash, places his domain under the protection of Nin-khar-sag. The worship at Nippur, however, remained most prominent. The continued popularity of her cult is attested by the fortress Dur-zakar, which a later king, Samsuiluna (*c.* 2200), erected in her honor.

NIN-GIR-SU.

In the inscriptions of Gudea and of his time, the god most prominently mentioned is the "Lord of Girsu." Girsu itself, as the inscriptions show, is one of the four sections into which the capitol city of Lagash was divided. It was there that the temple stood which was sacred to the patron deity, and we may conclude from this that Girsu is the oldest part of the city. Afterwards, Lagash became the general name for the capitol through being the quarter where the great palace of the king was erected. That Girsu was once quite distinct from Lagash is also evident from the title of "king of Girsu," with which a certain Uru-kagina, who is to be placed somewhat before Gudea, contents himself. The other three quarters, all of

---

[1] We may compare the poetic application 'rock' to Yahweh in the Old Testament, *e.g.*, Job 1. 12, and frequently in Psalms, — lxii. 3, 7; xcii. 16, 18, etc.

which were originally independent cities, are Uru-azagga, Ninâ, and apparently Gish-galla.[1]

Nin-girsu is frequently termed the warrior of Bel, — the one who in the service of the 'lord of the lower world,' appears in the thick of the fight, to aid the subjects of Bel. In this rôle, he is identical with a solar deity who enjoys especial prominence among the warlike Assyrians, whose name is provisionally read Nin-ib, but whose real name may turn out to be Adar.[2] The rulers of Lagash declare themselves to have been chosen for the high office by Nin-girsu, and as if to compensate themselves for the degradation implied in being merely *patesis*, or governors, serving under some powerful chief, they call themselves the patesis of Nin-girsu, implying that the god was the master to whom they owed allegiance. The temple sacred to him at Girsu was called E-ninnu, and also by a longer name that described the god as the one 'who changes darkness into light,' — the reference being to the solar character of the god Nin-ib with whom Nin-girsu is identified. In this temple, Gudea and other rulers place colossal statues of themselves, but temper the vanity implied, by inscribing on the front and back of these statues, an expression of their devotion to their god. To Nin-girsu, most of the objects found at Tell-loh are dedicated; conspicuous among which are the many clay cones, that became the conventional objects for votive offerings. There was another side, however, to his nature, besides the belligerent one. As the patron of Lagash, he also presided

---

[1] Reading doubtful Jensen suggests Erim. Hommel (*Proc. Soc. Bibl. Arch.* xv. 37 *seq.*) endeavored to identify the place with Babylon, but his views are untenable. If Gish-galla was not a part of Lagash, it could not have been far removed from it. It was Amiaud who first suggested that Shir-pur-la (or Lagash) was the general name for a city that arose from an amalgamation of four originally distinct quarters. ("Sirpurla" in *Revue Archéologique*, 1888.) The suggestion has been generally, though not universally accepted.

[2] That Ninib is only an ideographic form is sufficiently clear from the element NIN-, lord. The proof, however, that Ninib is Adar, is still wanting. See Jensen, *Kosmologie der Babylonier*, pp. 457, 458.

over the agricultural prosperity of the district. In this rôle he is addressed as Shul-gur or Shul-gur-an, *i.e.*, the "god of the corn heaps"; Entemena and his son Enanna-tuma in erecting a kind of storehouse which they place under the protection of Nin-girsu, declare that their god is Shul-gur;[1] and an old hymn[2] identifies him with Tammuz, the personification of agricultural activity. Such a combination of apparently opposing attributes is a natural consequence of the transformation of what may originally have been the personification of natural forces, into local deities. Each field had its protecting spirit, but for the city as a whole, a local deity, whose rule mirrored the control of the human chief over his subjects, alone was available. To him who watched over all things pertaining to the welfare of the territory coming under his jurisdiction, various attributes, as occasion required, were ascribed, and quite apart from his original character, the god could thus be regarded, as the warrior and the peaceful husbandman at the same time.

BAU.

Perhaps the most prominent of the goddesses in the ancient Babylonian period was Bau. One of the rulers of Lagash has embodied the name of the goddess in his name, calling himself Ur-Bau. It is natural, therefore, to find him more especially devoted to the worship of this deity. He does not tire of singing her praises, and of speaking of the temple he erected in her honor. Still, Ur-Bau does not stand alone in his devotion; Uru-kagina, Gudea, and others refer to Bau fre-

---

[1] From the context (De Sarzec, *Découvertes*, pl. 6, no. 4, ll. 13–21, and pl. 31, no. 3, col. iii. ll. 2–6), there can be no doubt that Shul-gur (or Shul-gur-ana) is an epithet of Nin-girsu. The ideographs descriptive of the edifice suggest a corn magazine of some kind. One is reminded of the storehouses for grain in Egypt. See Jensen's Notes, *Keils Bibl.* 3, 1, pp. 15, 18, 73. A comparison of the two texts in question makes it probable that Ab-gi and E-bi-gar are synonymous.

[2] Rawlinson, iv. 27, no. 6; 11, 45–46.

quently, while in the incantation texts, she is invoked as the great mother, who gives birth to mankind and restores the body to health. In the old Babylonian inscriptions she is called the chief daughter of Anu, the god of heaven. Among her titles, the one most frequently given is that of 'good lady.' She is the 'mother' who fixes the destinies of men and provides 'abundance' for the tillers of the soil. Gudea calls her his mistress, and declares that it is she who "fills him with speech," — a phrase whose meaning seems to be that to Bau he owes the power he wields. Locally, she is identified with Uru-azagga (meaning 'brilliant town'), a quarter of Lagash; and it was there that her temple stood. As a consequence, we find her in close association with Nin-girsu, the god of Girsu. We may indeed go further and assume that Girsu and Uru-azagga are the two oldest quarters of the city, the combination of the two representing the first natural steps in the development of the principality, afterwards known as Lagash, through the addition of other quarters.[1] . She is indeed explicitly called the consort of Nin-girsu; and this relation is implied also, in the interesting phrase used by Gudea, who presents gifts to Bau in the name of Nin-girsu, and calls them 'marriage gifts.'[2] It is interesting to find, at this early period, the evidence for the custom that still prevails in the Orient, which makes the gifts of the bridegroom to his chosen one, an indispensable formality.[3] These gifts were offered on the New Year's Day, known as Zag-muk, and the importance of the worship of Bau is evidenced by the designation of this day, as the festival of Bau.

The offerings, themselves, consist of lambs, sheep, birds, fish, cream, besides dates and various other fruits. When

---

[1] It is noticeable that there is no mention made of a special god of Lagash, which points to the later origin of the name.

[2] Inscr. D, col. li. 13; G, col. ii. ll. 1–8; iii. 4 *seq.*

[3] See Gen. xxiv. 53. Burkhardt, *Notes on the Bedouins*, i. 109, gives an example of the custom.

Uru-azagga becomes a part of Lagash, Bau's dignity is heightened to that of 'mother of Lagash.' As the consort of Nin-girsu, she is identified with the goddess Gula, the name more commonly applied to the 'princely mistress' of Nin-ib, whose worship continues down to the days of the neo-Babylonian monarchy.

It is quite certain, however, that Bau is originally an independent goddess, and that the association of Uru-azagga and Girsu[1] lead to her identification with Gula. Regarding her original nature, a certain index is her character as " daughter of Anu." Anu being the god of heaven, Bau must be sought in the upper realm of personified forces, rather than elsewhere; but exactly which one she is, it is difficult to say. Hommel, indeed,[2] is of opinion that she is the personified watery depth, the primitive chaos which has only the heavens above it ; but in giving this explanation, he is influenced by the desire to connect the name of Bau with the famous term for chaos in Genesis, *Tohu-wa-bohu*. There is, however, no proof whatsoever that Bau and Bohu have anything to do with one another. A goddess who can hardly be distinguished from Bau is

GA-TUM-DUG.[3]

Indeed, from the fact that she is also the 'mother of Lagash,' it might seem that this is but another name for Bau. However, elsewhere, in two lists of deities invoked by Gudea (Inscr. B, col. ii. 17), Ga-tum-dug is given a separate place by the side of Bau, once placed before and once after the latter ; and it is clear therefore that she was originally distinct from Bau. For Gudea, Ga-tum-dug is the mother who produced him. He is

---

[1] The two names are used by Gudea (Inscr. G, col. iii. 12) in a way to indicate that they embrace the whole district of Lagash.

[2] *Semit. Völker*, p. 382.

[3] See Jensen, *Keils Bibl.* 3, 1, 28, note 2.

her servant and she is his mistress. Lagash is her beloved city, and there he prepares for her a dwelling-place, which later rulers, like Entena, embellish. She is called the 'brilliant' (*Azag*), but as this title is merely a play upon the element found in the city, Uru-azagga, sacred to Bau, not much stress is to be laid upon this designation. Unfortunately, too, the elements composing her name are not clear,[1] and it must be borne in mind that the reading is purely provisional. So much, at least, seems certain: that Bau and Ga-tum-dug are two forms under which one and the same natural element was personified. Bau is called in the incantation texts, the mother of Ea. The latter being distinctly a water god, we may conclude that in some way, Bau is to be connected with water as a natural element. The conjecture may be hazarded that she personifies originally the waters of the upper realm — the clouds. Since Ea, who is her son, represents the waters of the lower realm, the relation of mother and son reflects perhaps a primitive conception of the origin of the deep, through the descent of the upper waters. When we come to the cosmogony of the Babylonians, it will be seen that this conception of a distinction between the two realms of waters is a fundamental one. This character as a spirit of the watery elements is shared by others of the goddesses appearing in the old Babylonian inscriptions.[2]

EN-KI OR EA.

This god, who, as we shall see, becomes most prominent in the developed form of Babylonian theology, does not occupy the place one should expect in the early Babylonian inscriptions. Ur-Bau erects a sanctuary to Ea, at Girsu. Another of the governors of Lagash calls himself, priest of Ea, describing the

---

[1] The first signifies 'to make,' the third means "good, favorable," but the second, upon which so much depends, is not clear. Amiaud reads *tum* instead of *sig*.

[2] *E.g.*, Nina (see below).

god as the "supreme councillor." From him, the king receives "wisdom."[1] A ruler, Rim-Sin, of the dynasty of Larsa, associates Ea with Bel, declaring that these "great gods" entrusted Uruk into his hands with the injunction to rebuild the city that had fallen in ruins. The ideograms, with which his name is written, En-ki, designate him as god of that 'which is below,'—the earth in the first place; but with a more precise differentiation of the functions of the great gods, Ea becomes the god of the waters of the deep. When this stage of belief is reached, Ea is frequently associated with Bel, who, it will be recalled, is the 'god of the lower region,' but who becomes the god of earth *par excellence*. When, therefore, Bel and Ea are invoked, it is equivalent, in modern parlance, to calling upon earth and water; and just as Bel is used to personify, as it were, the unification of the earthly forces, so Ea becomes, in a comprehensive sense, the watery deep. Ea and Bel assume therefore conspicuous proportions in the developed Babylonian cosmogony and theology. In the cosmogony, Bel is the creator and champion of mankind, and Ea is the subterranean deep which surrounds the earth, the source of wisdom and culture; in the theology, Ea and Bel are pictured in the relation of father and son, who, in concert, are appealed to, when misfortune or disease overtakes the sons of man; Ea, the father, being the personification of knowledge, and Bel, the practical activity that 'emanates from wisdom,' as Professor Sayce,[2] adopting the language of Gnosticism, aptly puts it; only that, as already suggested, Marduk assumes the rôle of the older Bel.

Confining ourselves here to the earlier phases of Ea, it seems probable that he was originally regarded as the god of Eridu, — one of the most ancient of the holy cities of Southern Babylonia, now represented by Abu-Shahrein, and which once stood on the shores of the Persian Gulf. Ur-Bau expressly calls the

---

[1] De Sarzec, pl. 7, col. i. 12.
[2] *Hibbert Lectures*, p. 104.

god the 'king of Eridu.' The sacredness of the place is attested by Gudea, who boasts of having made the temple of Nin-girsu as sacred as Eridu.[1] It is over this city that Ea watches. The importance of the Persian Gulf to the growth of the city, would make it natural to place the seat of the god in the waters themselves. The cult of water-deities arises, naturally, at places which are situated on large sheets of water; and in the attributes of wisdom which an older age ascribed to Ea, there may be seen the embodiment of the tradition that the course of civilization proceeds from the south. The superiority of the Persian Gulf over the other waters of Babylon — over the two great rivers with their tributary streams and canals — would be another factor that would lead to the god of the Persian Gulf being regarded as the personification of the watery element in general. For the Babylonians, the Persian Gulf, stretching out indefinitely, and to all appearances one with the great ocean whose ulterior shores could not be reached, was the great 'Okeanos,' that flowed around the earth and on which the earth rested. Ea, accordingly (somewhat like En-lil), was delocalized, as it were, and his worship was maintained long after the recollection of his connection with Eridu had all but disappeared. At the same time, for the very reason that he was cut loose from local associations, no place could lay claim to being the seat of the deity. Ur-Bau, when erecting a sanctuary to Ea at Girsu, significantly calls the god 'the king of Eridu.' The sanctuary is not, in this case, the dwelling-place of the god.

We are justified, therefore, in going back many centuries, before reaching the period when Ea was, merely, the local god of Eridu. Whether Ea is to be regarded as the real name of the god, or is also an ideograph like En-ki, is again open to doubt. If Ea is the real pronunciation, then the writing of the name is a play upon the character of the deity, for it is com-

[1] Inscr. D, col. iv. ll. 7, 8.

posed of two elements that signify 'house' and 'water,'—the name thus suggesting the character and real seat of the deity. A point in favor of regarding Ea as the real name, albeit not decisive, is the frequent use of the unmistakable ideographic description of the god as En-ki. The consort of Ea who is Dam-kina also occurs in the historical texts of the first period.

The origin of Babylonian civilization at the Persian Gulf, together with the dependence of Babylonia for her fertility upon the streams and canals, account for the numerous water-deities to be found in the ancient Babylonian pantheon, some of which have already been discussed. We will meet with others further on. Every stream, large or small, having its special protecting deity, the number of water-deities naturally increases as the land becomes more and more dissected by the canal system that conditioned the prosperity of the country.

Ea, as we shall see, appears under an unusually large number of names.[1] One of these is

NIN-A-GAL,

which, signifying 'god of great strength,' is given to him as the patron of the smith's art.[2] A god of this name is mentioned by Ur-Bau,[3] who speaks of a sanctuary erected in honor of this deity. But since the king refers to Ea (as En-ki) a few lines previous, it would appear that at this period Nin-agal is still an independent deity. The later identification with Ea appears to be due to the idea of 'strength' involved in the name of Nin-agal. In the same way, many of the names of Ea were originally descriptive of independent gods who, because of the similarity of their functions to those of the great Ea,

---

[1] In Rawlinson, ii. 58, no. 6, there is a list of some seventy names.
[2] Rawlinson, ii. 58, no. 6, 58.
[3] De Sarzec, pl. 8, col. v. ll. 4-6.

were absorbed by the latter. Their names transferred to Ea, are frequently the only trace left of their original independent existence.

NERGAL.

Nergal, the local deity of Cuthah (or Kutu), represented by the mound Tell-Ibrahim, some distance to the east of Babylon, was of an entirely different character from Ea, but his history in the development of the Babylonian religion is hardly less interesting. The first mention of his famous temple at Cuthah is found in an inscription of Dungi (to be read Ba'u-ukin, according to Winckler[1]) who belongs to the second dynasty of Ur (c. 2700 B.C.). Its origin, however, belongs to a still earlier period. Such was the fame of the temple known as E-shid-lam, and the closeness of the connection between the deity and his favorite seat, that Nergal himself became known as shid-lam-ta-ud-du-a, *i.e.*, the god that rises up from E-shid-lam. It is by this epithet that the same Dungi describes him in one of his inscriptions.[2] Down to the latest period of Assyro-Babylonian history, Nergal remains identified with Kutu, being known at all times as the god of Kutu.[3] When Sargon, the king of Assyria, upon his conquest of the kingdom of Israel (c. 722 B.C.), brought people from Babylon, Cuthah, Ava, and so forth, across to the lands of the Jordan to take the place of the deported Israelites, the Hebrew narrator (II Kings, xvii. 24–35) tells us in an interesting manner of the obnoxious foreign worship which these people brought to the land, each division bringing the gods of their place with them. The men of Cuthah, he adds (v. 30), made a

---

[1] *Keils Bibl.* 3, 1, 80, note 3.

[2] Rawlinson, iv. 35, no. 2, 1.

[3] See a syllabary giving lists of gods, Rawlinson, ii. 60, 12. Dungi, indeed, calls Nergal once the king of lawful control over Lagash (Rawlinson, iv. 35, no. 2, ll. 2, 3). The exact force of the title is not clear, but in no case are we permitted to conclude as Amiaud does (*Rec. of the Past*, N. S., i. 59) that Shid-lam-ta-udda is identical with Nin-girsu.

statue of Nergal. Singamil, of the dynasty, having its capital at Uruk (*c.* 2750 B.C.), likewise testifies to his devotion to Nergal by busying himself with improvements and additions to his temple at Cuthah. His worship, therefore, was not confined to those who happened to reside at Cuthah; and closely as he is identified with the place, the character of the god is a general and not a special one. The full form of his name appears to have been Ner-unu-gal, of which Nergal, furnished by the Old Testament passage referred to, would then be a contraction or a somewhat corrupt form. The three elements composing his name signify "the mighty one of the great dwelling-place," but it is, again, an open question whether this is a mere play upon the character of the god, as in the name of Ea (according to one of the interpretations above suggested), or whether it is an ideographic form of the name. The Old Testament shows, conclusively, that the name had some such pronunciation as Nergal. Jensen, from other evidences, inclines to the opinion that the writing Ner-unu-gal is the result of a species of etymology, brought about by the prominence given to Nergal as the god of the region of the dead. It is in this capacity that he already appears in the inscription of Singamil, who calls him 'king of the nether world.' The "great dwelling-place," therefore, is clearly the dominion over which Nergal rules, and when we come to the cosmogony of the Babylonians,[1] it will be found that this epithet for the nether world — the great dwelling-place — accords with their conception of the life after death. But while Nergal, with a host of lesser demons about him, appears as the Babylonian Pluto, particularly in the religious texts, his functions are not limited to the control of the dead. He is the personification of some of the evils that bring death to mankind, particularly pestilence and war. The death that follows in his path is a violent one, and his destructive force is one that acts upon large masses rather than

[1] See Jensen, *Kosmologie der Babylonier*, pp. 476–87.

upon the individual. Hence, one of the most common ideographs used to express his name is that which signifies 'sword.'

War and pestilence are intimately associated in the mind of the Babylonians. Among other nations, the sword is, similarly, the symbol of the deity, as the plague-bringer as well as the warrior.

To this day, a pestilence is the general accompaniment of war in the East, or follows in its wake. Different from Nin-ib, who is also a god of war, Nergal symbolizes more particularly the *destruction* which accompanies war, and not the strong champion who aids his subjects in the fight. Nergal is essentially a destroyer, and the various epithets applied to him in the religious texts, show that he was viewed in this light. He is at times the 'god of fire,' again 'the raging king,' 'the violent one' 'the one who burns'; and finally identified with the glowing heat of flame. Often, he is described by these attributes, instead of being called by his real name.[1] Dr. Jensen has recently shown in a satisfactory manner, that this phase of his character must be the starting-point in tracing the order of his development. As the 'glowing flame,' Nergal is evidently a phase of the sun, and Jensen proves that the functions and aspects of the sun at different periods being differentiated among the Babylonians, Nergal is more especially the hot sun of midsummer or midday, the destructive force of which was the chief feature that distinguished it. The hot sun of Babylonia, that burns with fierce intensity, brings pestilence and death, and carries on a severe contest against man. From being the cause of death, it is but a step, and a natural one, to make Nergal preside over the region, prepared for those whom he has destroyed. The course taken by Babylonian theology is responsible for the prominence given to the latter rôle of Nergal, which finally overshadows his other phases to the extent of suggesting the fanciful interpretation of his name as

[1] See Jensen, *Kosmologie der Babylonier*, pp. 476–87.

the 'ruler of the great dwelling-place for the dead.' In the light of the facts set forth, another explanation for his name must be looked for that would connect the god with solar functions. The name may in fact be divided into two elements, the first having the force of chief or ruler, the second 'great.' The combination would be an appropriate designation for the sun, in the rôle of a destructive power. But Nergal, after all, represents only one phase of the sun-god. The god who was worshipped as the personification of the sun *par excellence* and the sun as a whole, was

SHAMASH.

Written with an ideograph that describes him as the 'god of the day,' there is no deity whose worship enjoys an equally continued popularity in Babylonia and Assyria. Beginning at the earliest period of Babylonian history, and reaching to the latest, his worship suffers no interruption. Shamash, moreover, maintains his original character with scarcely any modification throughout this long period. For all that, he bears a name which signifies 'attendant' or 'servitor,' and which sufficiently shows the subsidiary position that he occupied in the Babylonian pantheon. One of the rulers belonging to the dynasty of Isin calls the sun-god, the offspring of Nannar, — one of the names of the moon-god, — and the last king of Babylonia, Nabonnedos, does the same. In combination with the moon-god, the latter takes precedence of Shamash,[1] and in the enumeration of the complete pantheon, in the inscriptions of both Assyrian and Babylonian kings, the same order is preserved. Other evidence that points to the superior rank accorded to Sin, the moon-god over the sun-deity in Babylonia, is the reckoning of time by the moon phases. The day begins with the evening, and not with sunrise. The moon, as

[1] So in the inscription of Rim-Sin (*Keils Bibl.* 3, 1, p. 97).

the chief of the starry firmament, and controlling the fate of mankind, was the main factor in giving to the orb of night, this peculiar prominence. The 'service,' accordingly implied in the name of Shamash appears to have been such as was demanded by his subsidiary position to the moon-god. Beyond the general recognition, however, of this relationship between the two, it does not appear that the worship paid to Shamash, was at all affected by the secondary place, that he continued to hold in the theoretically constructed pantheon. Less than is the case with the other gods, is he identified with any particular city, and we therefore find in the most ancient period, two centers of Southern Babylonia claiming Shamash as their patron saint,— Larsa, represented by the mound of Senkereh, and Sippar, occupying the site of the modern Abu-Habba. It is difficult to say which of the two was the older; the latter, in the course of time, overshadowed the fame of the former, and its history can be traced back considerably beyond the sun-worship at Larsa, the first mention of which occurs in the inscriptions of rulers of the second dynasty of Ur (*c.* 2900 B.C.). Since Ur, as we shall see, was sacred to the moon-god, it is hardly likely that the Shamash cult was introduced at Larsa by the rulers of Ur. The kings of Ur would not have forfeited the protection of Sin, by any manifestation of preference for Shamash. When Ur-Gur, therefore, tells us that he 'built' a temple to Shamash at Larsa, he must mean, as Sin-iddina of the dynasty of Larsa does, in using the same phrase, that he enlarged or improved the edifice. What makes it all the more likely that Ur-Gur found sun-worship at Larsa in existence is, that in the various places over which this ruler spread his building activity, he is careful in each case to preserve the status of the presiding deity. So at Nippur, he engages in work at the temples of En-lil and of Nin-lil; while at Uruk he devotes himself to the temple of Nanâ. In thus connecting their names with the various sacred edifices of Babylonia, the rulers emphasized, on the one hand, their control of the territory in which the building lay, and on the other, their allegiance to the deity of the place, whose protection and favor they sought to gain.

The mention of a temple to Shamash at Sippar reverts to a still earlier period than that of its rival. Nabonnedos tells us that it was founded by Naram-Sin. Sargon has put his name on some object[1] that he dedicates to the sun-god at Sippar. That there was an historical connection between the two temples may be concluded from the fact that the name of the sacred edifices was the same in both, — E-babbara, signifying the 'house of lustre.' Such a similarity points to a dependence of one upon the other, and the transfer or extension of the worship directly from one place to the other; but, as intimated, we have no certain means of determining which of the two is the older. In view of the general observation to be made in what pertains to the religion of the Babylonians, that fame and age go hand in hand, the balance is in favor of Sippar, which became by far the more famous of the two, received a greater share of popular affection, and retained its prominence to the closing days of the neo-Babylonian monarchy. We shall have occasion in a succeeding chapter to trace the history of the sun-temple at Sippar so far as known. It is interesting to note that Nabonnedos, feeling the end of his power to be near, undertakes, as one of the last resorts, the restoration of this edifice, in the hope that by thus turning once more to the powerful Shamash, he might secure his protection, in addition to that of Marduk, the head of the later Babylonian pantheon.

In Ur itself, Shamash was also worshipped in early days by the side of the moon-god. Eannatum, of the dynasty of Isin (*c*. 2800 B.C.), tells of two temples erected to him at that place; and still a third edifice, sacred to both Nannar (the moon-god) and Shamash at Ur, is referred to by a king of the

---

[1] Perhaps the knob of a sceptre. *Proc. Soc. Bibl. Arch.* viii. 68.

Larsa dynasty, Rim-Sin (*c.* 2300 B.C.). The titles given to Shamash by the early rulers are sufficiently definite to show in what relation he stood to his worshippers, and what the conceptions were that were formed of him. He is, alternately, the king and the shepherd. Since the kings also called themselves shepherds, no especial endearment is conveyed by this designation. In the incantations, Shamash is frequently appealed to, either alone, or when an entire group of spirits and deities are enumerated. He is called upon to give life to the sick man. To him the body of the one who is smitten with disease is confided. As the god of light, he is appropriately called upon to banish 'darkness' from the house, darkness being synonymous with misfortune; and the appeal is made to him more particularly as the 'king of judgment.' From this, it is evident that the beneficent action of the sun, was the phase associated with Shamash. He was hailed as the god that gives light and life to all things, upon whose favor the prosperity of the fields and the well-being of man depend. He creates the light and secures its blessings for mankind. His favor produces order and stability; his wrath brings discomfiture and ruin to the state and the individual. But his power was, perhaps, best expressed by the title of "judge" — the favorite one in the numerous hymns that were composed in his honor. He was represented as seated on a throne in the chamber of judgment, receiving the supplications of men, and according as he manifested his favor or withdrew it, enacting the part of the decider of fates. He loosens the bonds of the imprisoned, grants health to the sick, and even revivifies the dead. On the other hand, he puts an end to wickedness and destroys enemies. He makes the weak strong, and prevents the strong from crushing the weak. From being the judge, and, moreover, the supreme judge of the world, it was but natural that the conception of justice was bound up with him. His light became symbolical of righteousness, and the absence of it, or darkness, was viewed as wickedness. Men and gods look expectantly for his light. He is the guide of the gods, as well as the ruler of men.

While there are no direct indications in the historical texts known at present, that this conception of the sun-god existed in all its details before the days of Hammurabi, there is every reason to believe that this was the case; the more so, in that it does not at all transcend the range of religious ideas that we have met with in the case of the other gods of this period. Nor does this conception in any way betray itself, as being due to the changed political conditions that set in, with the union of the states under Hammurabi. Still, the age of the religious texts not being fixed, it is thus necessary to exercise some caution before using them without the basis of an allusion in the historical texts.

Utu.

It but remains, before passing on, to note that the same deity appears under various names. Among these are Utu[1] and apparently also Babbar[2] in the old Babylonian inscriptions. For the latter, a Semitic etymology is forthcoming, and we may therefore regard it as representing a real pronunciation, and not an ideographic writing. Babbar, a contracted form from Barbar, is the reduplication of the same stem *bar*[3] that we have already met with, in the name of the temple sacred to Shamash. Like E-babbara, therefore, Babbar is the "brilliantly shining one,"—a most appropriate name for the sun, and one frequently applied to him in the religious texts. As to Utu, there is some doubt whether it represents a real pronunciation or not. My own opinion is that it does, and that the underlying stem is

---

[1] *E.g.*, Hammurabi (*Revue d'Assyriologie*, ii. col. 1. 21); but also Gudea and a still earlier king.

[2] So Amiaud; and there seems some reason to believe that the name was used by the side of Utu, though perhaps only as an epithet.

[3] Compare *birbiru*, 'sheen,' and the stem *barû*, 'to see,' etc.

atû, which in Babylonian has almost the same meaning as *bar* or *barû*, viz., 'to see.' 'Utu' would thus again designate the sun as 'that which shines forth.'

It will be recalled, that other instances have been noted of the same god appearing under different names. The most natural explanation for this phenomenon is, that the variation corresponds to the different localities where the god was worshipped. The identification would not be made until the union of the various Babylonian states had been achieved. Such a union would be a potent factor in systematizing the pantheon. When once it was recognized that the various names represented, in reality, one and the same deity, it would not be long before the name, peculiar to the place where the worship was most prominent, would set the others aside or reduce them to mere epithets.

It may well be that Shamash was the name given to the god at Sippar, whereas at Ur he may have been known as Utu. Ur-Bau (of the first Ur dynasty) calls him Utu also, when speaking of the temple at Larsa, but it would be natural for the kings of Ur to call the sun-god of Larsa by the same name that he had in Ur. That Hammurabi, however, calls the sungod of Larsa, Utu, may be taken as an indication that, as such he was known at that place, for since we have no record of a sun-temple at Babylon in these days, there would be no motive that might induce him to transfer a name, otherwise known to him, to another place. The testimony of Hammurabi is therefore as direct as that of Sargon, who calls the sun-god of Sippar, Shamash. It is not always possible to determine, with as much show of probability, as in the case of the sun-god, the distribution of the various names, but the general conclusion, for all that, is warranted in every instance, that a variety of names refers, originally, to an equal variety of places over which the worship was spread, — only that care must be exercised to distinguish between distinctive names and mere epithets.

Â.

A consort of the sun-deity, appearing frequently at his side in the incantation texts, is Â. It is more particularly with the Shamash of Sippar, that Â is associated. She is simply the 'beloved one' of the sun-deity, with no special character of her own. In the historical texts, her rôle is quite insignificant, and for the period with which we are at present concerned she is only mentioned once by a North Babylonian ruler, Ma-an-ish-tu-su,[1] who dedicates an object to her. The reading of the ideogram Â, or Nin-Â (*i.e.*, Lady Â), is doubtful. Malkatu ("mistress" or "queen") is offered as a plausible conjecture.[2] Lehman (*Keils Bibl.* iii. 1, 202) suggests *A-ja*, but on insufficient grounds. In any case Â has the force of mistress, and Nin-Â simply designates the goddess as the lady, mistress, or queen. It is likely that Â was originally an independent deity, and one of the names of the sun-god in a particular locality. It occurs in proper names as a title of Shamash. Instead, however, of becoming identified with Shamash, Â degenerated into a pale reflection of Shamash, pictured under the relationship of consort to him. This may have been due to the union of Shamash with the place where Â was worshipped. If, as seems likely, that near Sippar, there was another city on the other side of the Euphrates, forming a suburb to it (as Borsippa did to Babylon), the conclusion is perhaps warranted that Â was originally the sun-god worshipped at the place which afterwards became incorporated with Sippar.[3] Such an amalgamation of two originally male deities into a combination of

---

[1] See *Keils Bibl.* 3, 1, 100. Reading of name uncertain.
[2] Suggested by Rawlinson, ii. 57, 10. See Schrader, *Zeits. f. Assyr.* iii. 33 *seq.*
[3] On Sippar, see Sayce, *Hibbert Lectures*, etc., 168-169, who finds in the Old Testament form "Sepharvayim" a trace of this double Sippar. Dr. Ward's suggestion, however, in regard to Anbar, as representing this 'second' Sippar, is erroneous.

male and female, strange as it may seem to us, is in keeping with the lack of sharp distinction between male and female in the oldest forms of Semitic religions. In the old cuneiform writing the same sign is used to indicate "lord" or "lady" when attached to deities. Ishtar appears among Semites both as a male[1] and as a female deity. Sex was primarily a question of strength. The stronger god was viewed as masculine; the weaker as feminine.

Nannar and Sin.

Nannar, a reduplicated form like Babbar, with the assimilation of the first r to n (nar-nar = nannar), has very much the same meaning as Babbar. The latter, as we have seen, is the "lustrous one," the former, the "one that furnishes light." The similarity in meaning is in keeping with the similarity of function of the two deities, thus named: Babbar being the sun and Nannar, the moon. It was under the name of Nannar that the moon-god was worshipped at Ur, the most famous and probably the oldest of the cities over which the moon-god presided. The association of Nannar with Ur is parallel to that of Shamash with Sippar, — not that the moon-god's jurisdiction or worship was confined to that place, but that the worship of the deity of that place eclipsed others, and the fame and importance at Ur led to the overshadowing of the moon-worship there, over the obeisance to him paid elsewhere.

What further motives led to the choice of the moon-god as the patron of Ur, lies beyond the scope of our knowledge. Due allowance must be made for that natural selection, which takes place in the realm of thought as much as in the domain of nature. Attention has already been called to the predominance given by the Babylonians to the moon over the sun.

---

[1] *E.g.*, in Southern Arabia. See W. Robertson Smith, *The Religion of the Semites*, I. 59.

The latter is expressly called the "offspring of the lord of brilliant beginning," that is, the moon-god (Delitzsch, *Assyr. Hdw.*, p. 234 *a*). It is needless, therefore, to do more, at this place, than to emphasize the fact anew. The moon serving much more as a guide to man, through the regular character of its constant changes, than the sun, was connected in the religious system with both the heavenly and the terrestrial forces. In view of Nannar's position in the heavens, he was called the "heifer of Anu." Anu, it will be recalled, was the god of heaven (and heaven itself), while the "heifer"[1] is here used metaphorically for offspring, the picture being suggested probably by the "horn" that the moon presents at a certain phase. This 'horn' constitutes his crown, and he is frequently represented on seal cylinders with a crescent over his head, and with a long flowing beard, that is described as having the color of lapislazuli. A frequent title is the 'lord of the crown.' On the other hand, by virtue of its influence on the earth, regulating, as the ancients observed, the tides, the moon was connected by the Babylonians with the reckoning of time. Because of this connection with the 'lower world,' it seems, he was also regarded as the first-born of Bel. His sacred edifice at Ur was one to which all rulers of the place devoted themselves. Ur-Gur, Nur-Ramman, Sin-iddina, and Kudur-mabuk tell of their embellishment of the temple, each one appropriating to himself the title of 'builder,' in which they gloried. So close, again, was the identification of the city with the deity, that the latter was frequently known simply as the god of Ur, and the former, as the city of Nannar.

Another name of the moon-god was Sin, — the meaning of which escapes us. At the side of Ur, Harran is the place most celebrated by reason of its moon-worship, and there is every reason to believe that the name Sin was originally attached to

---

[1] In Rabbinical literature, the moon is compared to a 'heifer' (Talmud Babli Rosh-hashana 22 *b*).

Harran. The migrations of the ancient Hebrews were connected as we now know with political movements in Babylonia. They proceed from Ur — or Ur-Kasdim, *i.e.*, Chaldean Ur — northward to Harran, which, by virtue of its position, became a town of much importance. This association of Ur with Harran furnishes an indication for historical relations of some sort, existing between the two places. It is therefore not accidental, that the patron deity of both places was the same. As yet, no excavations have been made at Harran, and we are, therefore, dependent upon incidental notices for our knowledge of its history. These sufficiently show that the place continued through a long period to preserve its sacred character. The old temple there, was one of the many that stirred up the religious zeal of Nabonnedos; and previous to this, we find several Assyrian kings occupied in embellishing and restoring the structure. An interesting reference to Harran, bearing witness to its ancient dignity, is found in an inscription of Sargon II. of Assyria (722-706 B.C.), who enumerates among his claims to the favor of the gods, that he restored the "laws and customs of Harran," by which he evidently means that he was instrumental in giving the place, the dignity it once enjoyed. A curious feature connected with Sin, is the occurrence of the name in Mount Sinai, in the wilderness of Sin, as well as in an inscription of Southern Arabia. May not this be a further testimony to the association of Harran with Sin, since it is from Harran that the departure of the Hebrews for the west took place? What more natural than that in the migrations which carried the Hebrews to the west, the worship of Sin should have been transferred to Arabia?[1] Important as Ur and Harran are as sacred towns, politically they do not retain their prominence after the days of Hammurabi. The amalgamation of Nannar

---

[1] That the name of Sin should have been introduced into Mesopotamia through the 'Arabic' dynasty (see above, p. 39) is less probable, though not impossible in the light of recent discoveries.

with Sin, and the almost exclusive occurrence of the latter name in later times, does not of necessity point to a preponderating influence of Harran over Ur, but may be due to the greater fame which the former place acquired as the goal of religious pilgrimages. The situation of Harran — the name itself signifies 'road' — as the highway leading to the west, must have been an important factor, in bringing this about. However this may be, Sin and Nannar are as thoroughly identical in the period following Hammurabi, as Babbar and Shamash. The attributes of the one are transferred to the other so completely, that a separation of the two is no longer possible.

The ideographs with which the name of Sin is written show him to have been regarded as the god of wisdom, but while wisdom and light may be connected, it is Nannar's character as the "illuminator" that becomes the chief trait of the god. No doubt the preëminence of Ea in this respect, who is the personification of wisdom, *par excellence*, made it superfluous to have another deity possessing the same trait. It is, accordingly, as the god of light, that Sin continues to be adored in the Babylonian religion; and when he is referred to, in the historical texts and hymns, this side of his nature is the one dwelt upon. Through his light, the traps laid by the evil spirits, who are active at night, are revealed. In later times, apparently through Assyrian influence, the reckoning of time was altered to the extent of making the day begin with sunrise, instead of with the approach of night; and this, together with the accommodation of the lunar cycle to the movements of the sun, brought about a partial change of the former conditions, and gave somewhat greater prominence to Shamash. As a consequence, the rôle of Sin is not as prominent in the hymns that belong to a later period as in those of earlier days.

The oracles of the Assyrian kings are addressed to Shamash, and not to Sin. Moreover, the personal factor in the case of Sin, if one may express oneself thus, is not as strong as in that of some other gods. His traits are of a more general kind. He is supreme; there is none like him, and the spirits are subservient to his will. But terms of endearment are few, while on the mythological side, comparatively little is made of him. He is strong and he is holy. He is called upon to clothe the evil-doer with leprosy, as with a dress. In a robe, befitting his dignity, he stalks about. Without him, no city is founded, no district restored to former glory. Sin is called the father of the gods, but in a metaphorical rather than in a real sense. The only one of his children who takes an important part in the later phases of Babylonian-Assyrian worship is his daughter Ishtar. She seems to have taken to herself some of the traits of right belonging to Sin, and the prominence of her worship may be regarded as an additional factor in accounting for the comparative obscurity to which Sin gradually is assigned. At all events, Sin is a feature of the earlier period of the Babylonian religion rather than of the later periods.

Innanna.

The secondary position held by the female deities in the Babylonian pantheon has been repeatedly referred to. This trait of the religion finds an illustration not only in the 'shadowy' character of the consorts of the gods, but also in the manner in which goddesses, originally distinct from one another and enjoying an existence independent of any male consort, lose their individuality, as it were, and become merely so many forms of one and the same deity. Indeed, as we approach the moment when the gods of the Babylonian pantheon are ranged into a system, the tendency becomes pronounced to recognize only *one* goddess, representative of the principle of generation — one 'great mother,' endowed with a variety of traits according to the political and social conditions prevailing at different times in Babylonia and Assyria.

In the earliest period which we are now considering, we can still distinguish a number of goddesses who afterwards became merged into this one great goddess. These are Ninni (or Innanna), Nanâ, and Anunit.

Ninni and Innanna are names that appear to have a common origin.[1] Both embody the notion of 'ladyship.' The worship of this goddess centers in the district of Lagash. Ur-Bau (c. 3000 B.C.), who addresses her as 'glorious and supreme,' builds a temple in her honor at Gishgalla, and Gudea refers to a temple known as E-anna, i.e., heavenly house in Girsu.[2] For Gudea, Ninni is the "mistress of the world." Another ruler of Lagash whose name is doubtfully read as E-dingir-ra-na-gin,[3] but who is even earlier than Ur-Bau, declares that he has been 'called' by Innanna to the throne. She is mentioned by the side of Nin-khar-sag. We are still in the period where local associations formed a controlling factor in ensuring the popularity of a deity, and while the goddesses attached to the gods of the important centers are still differentiated, the tendency already exists to designate the female consorts simply as the 'goddess,'—to apply to all, the traits that may once have been peculiar to one. As we pass from one age to the other, there is an increasing difficulty in keeping the various local 'goddesses' apart. Even the names become interchangeable; and since these goddesses all represented essentially the same principle of generation and fertility, it was natural that with the union of the Babylonian states they should become merged into one great mother-goddess. A 'local' goddess who retains rather more of her individuality than others, is

---

[1] Innanna may be separated into *In* = lord or lady, and *nanna*; *in* and *nanna* would then be elements added to "lady," conveying perhaps the idea of greatness. See Jensen's remarks, *Keils Bibl.* 3, 1, 20, note 4.

[2] *Rec. of the Past*, N.S., ii. p. 104.

[3] *Keils Bibl.* 3, 1, 16. See Jensen's note on the reading of the name.

Nanâ.

Her name is again playfully interpreted by the Babylonians — through association with Nin — as 'the lady' *par excellence*. She was the chief goddess of the city of Uruk. Her temple at Uruk is first mentioned by Ur-Gur, of the second dynasty of Ur. It is restored and enlarged by Dungi, the successor of Ur-Bau, and so thoroughly is she identified with her edifice known as E-anna (again a play upon her name), that she becomes known as the Lady of E-anna.[1] She appears to have had a temple also at Ur, and it is to this edifice that later rulers of Larsa — Kudur-Mabuk and Rim-Sin, as well as the kings of the Isin dynasty, Gamil-Ninib, Libit-Ishtar, and Ishme-Dagan — refer in their inscriptions.

The members of the Isin dynasty pride themselves upon their control over Uruk, and naturally appear as special devotees to Nanâ, whose chosen "consort" they declare themselves to be, wielding the sceptre, as it were, in union with her. Already at this period, Nanâ is brought into connection with the moon-god, being called by Kudur-Mabuk the daughter of Sin. The relationship in this case indicates, primarily, the supremacy exercised by Ur, and also a similarity in the traits of the two deities. In the fully developed cosmology, Nanâ is the planet Venus, whose various aspects, as morning and evening star, suggested an analogy with the phases of the moon.

Venus, like the moon, served as a guide to man, while her inferiority in size and importance to the former, would naturally come to be expressed under the picture of father and daughter. In a certain sense, all the planets appearing at the same time and in the same region with the moon were the children of the latter. Sin, therefore, is appropriately called

---

[1] The fame of this temple outlasts the political importance of the place, and as late as the days of the Assyrian monarchy is an object of fostering care on the part of the kings.

the father of gods, just as Anu, the personification of the heaven itself, is the supreme father of Sin and Shamash, and of all the heavenly bodies. The metaphorical application of 'father' as 'source,' throughout Oriental parlance, must be kept in mind in interpreting the relationship between the gods. Still another name of the goddess is Anunit, which appears to have been peculiar to the North Babylonian city Agade, and emphasizes her descent from "Anu," the god of heaven. Her temple at Agade, known as E-ul-mash, is the object of Sargon's devotion, which makes her, with Bel and Shamash, the oldest triad of gods mentioned in the Babylonian inscriptions. But the name which finally displaces all others, is

Ishtar.

Where the name originated has not yet been ascertained, as little as its etymology,[1] but it seems to belong to Northern Babylonia rather than to the south.

In time, all the names that we have been considering—Innanna, Nanâ, and Anunit—became merely so many designations of Ishtar. She absorbs the titles and qualities of all, and the tendency which we have pointed out finds its final outcome in the recognition of Ishtar as the one and only goddess endowed with powers and an existence independent of association with any male deity, though even this independence does not hinder her from being named at times as the associate of the chief god of Assyria—the all-powerful Ashur. The attempt has been made by Sayce and others to divide the various names of Ishtar among the aspects of Venus as morning and evening star, but there is no evidence to show that the

---

[1] That the name is Semitic is no longer seriously questioned by any scholar. The underlying stem suggests etymological relationship with the god Ashur. If this be so, Ishtar may mean 'the goddess that brings blessing' to mankind, but all this is tentative, as are the numerous other etymologies suggested.

Babylonians distinguished the one from the other so sharply as to make two goddesses of one and the same planet.

It is more in accord with what, as we have seen, has been the general character of the Babylonian pantheon, to account for the identification of Ninni, Nanâ, and Anunit with Ishtar on the supposition that the different names belonged originally to different localities. Ishtar was appropriately denominated the brilliant goddess. She is addressed as the mother of gods, which signals her supreme position among the female deities. 'The mistress of countries' alternating with 'the mistress of mountains,'[1] is one of her common titles; and as the growing uniqueness of her position is one of the features of the Babylonian-Assyrian religion, it is natural that she should become simply *the* goddess. This was especially the case with the Assyrians, to whom Ishtar became a goddess of war and battle, the consort, at times, of the chief god of the Assyrian pantheon. At the same time it is important to note that the warlike character of the goddess goes back to the time of Hammurabi (*Keils Bibl.* 3, 1, 113), and is dwelt upon by other Babylonian kings (*e.g.*, Nebuchadnezzar I., *c.* 1130 B.C.) prior to the rise of the Assyrian power. How Ishtar came to take on so violent a character is not altogether clear. There are no indications of this rôle in the incantation texts, where she is simply the kind mother who is appealed to, to release the sufferer from the power of the disease-bringing spirits. In the prayers, as will be shown in the proper place, she becomes the vehicle for the expression of the highest religious and ethical thought attained by the Babylonians. On the other hand, in the great Babylonian epic,[2] dealing with the adventures of a famous hero, Gilgamesh, Ishtar, who

---

[1] The ideographs for 'country' and 'mountain' are identical Assyrian. The alternation in the title of Ishtar must not be taken to point to a mountainous origin of the goddess.

[2] A full account of this epic will be given at its proper place.

makes her appearance at the summer solstice, is a raging goddess who smites those who disobey her commands with wasting disease. Starting with this phase of the goddess' character, one can at least understand the process of her further development into a fierce deity presiding over the fortunes of war. The epic just referred to belongs to the old Babylonian period. It embodies ancient traditions of rivalry between the Babylonian principalities, though there are traces of several recastings which the epic received. The violent Ishtar, therefore, is a type going back to the same period as the other side of her character that is emphasized elsewhere. Since, moreover, the Ishtar in the Gilgamesh epic is none other than the chief goddess of Uruk, all further doubt as to the union of such diverging traits in one and the same personage falls to the ground. In this same epic, Ishtar appears as sympathizing with the sufferings of mankind, and bewailing the destruction that was at one time decreed by the gods. It is noteworthy that the violent Ishtar appears in that portion of the epic which, on the assumption of a zodiacal interpretation for the composition, corresponds to the summer solstice, whereas, the destruction which arouses her sympathy takes place in the eleventh month. It is quite possible, therefore, that the two aspects of Venus, as evening and morning stars, corresponding, as they do, to the summer and winter seasons, are reflected in this double character of the goddess. We are not justified, however, in going further and assuming that her double rôle as daughter of Sin and daughter of Anu is to be accounted for in the same manner. In the Gilgamesh epic, she is found in association with Anu, and to the latter she appeals for protection as her father, and yet it is as the daughter of Sin that she enters the world of the dead to seek for the waters that may heal her bridegroom, Tammuz.[1] Evidently, the distinction between

---

[1] Again, in the incantation texts she appears only as the daughter of Anu, coördinate with Sin and Shamash.

Ishtar as the daughter of Anu and as the daughter of Sin is not an important one, the term daughter in both cases being a metaphor to express a relationship both of physical nature and of a political character. Of the various forms under which the goddess appears, that of Anunit — a feminine form indicating descent from and appertaining to Anu — attaches itself most clearly to the god of heaven, and it may be that it was not until the assimilation of Anunit and Nanâ with Ishtar that the goddess is viewed as at once the daughter of Anu and of Sin. If this be so, there is surely nothing strange in the fact that a planet like Venus should be regarded in one place as the daughter of heaven and in another brought into relationship with the moon. She actually belongs to both.

Just as in Babylonia, so in Assyria, there were various Ishtars, or rather various places where the goddess was worshipped as the guardian spirit, but her rôle in the north is so peculiar that all further consideration of it must be postponed until we come to consider, in due time, the Assyrian pantheon. There will be occasion, too, when treating of the Gilgamesh epic, to dwell still further on some of her traits. All that need be said here is to emphasize the fact that the popularity of the Babylonian Ishtar in Assyria, as manifested by Esarhaddon's zeal in restoring her temple at Uruk, and Ashurbanabal's restoration of Nanâ's statue (*c.* 635 B.C.) which had been captured by the Elamites 1635 years before Ashurbanabal's reign, is largely due to the effected identity with the goddess who, for the Assyrians, was regarded chiefly as the goddess of war and strife. In worshipping the southern Ishtars, the Assyrian kings felt themselves to be showing their allegiance to the same deity to whom, next to Ashur, most of their supplications were addressed, and of whom as warriors they stood in dread.

NINÂ.

A goddess who, while sharing the fate of her sister goddesses in being overshadowed by Ishtar, yet merits a special treatment, is one whose name is plausibly conjectured to be read Ninâ. The compound ideogram expressing the deity signifies 'house of the fish.' The word 'house' in Semitic parlance is figuratively extended to convey the idea of 'possessing or harboring.' Applied to a settlement, the ideogram would be the equivalent of our 'Fishtown.' It is with this same ideogram that the famous capitol of Assyria, Nineveh, is written in the cuneiform texts, and since the phonetic reading for the city, Ni-na-a, also occurs, it is only legitimate to conclude that the latter is the correct reading for the deity as well. As a matter of course, if the goddess bears a name identical with that of a city, it cannot be the Assyrian city which is meant in the old Babylonian inscriptions, but some other place bearing the same name. Such a place actually occurs in the inscriptions of Gudea. It is, in fact, one of the three towns that combined with Shirpurla to create the great capitol bearing the latter name; and Jensen[1] has called attention to a passage in one of Gudea's inscriptions in which the goddess is brought into direct association with the town, so that it would appear that Ninâ is the patron of Ninâ, in the same way that Nin-girsu is the protector of Girsu. In keeping with this we find the mention of the goddess limited to the rulers of Lagash. Several of them — En-anna-tuma, Entemena, and Gudea — declare themselves to have been chosen by her. She is said to regard Gudea with special favor. She determines destinies. Another king, Ur-Ninâ, embodies the name of the goddess in his own, and devotes himself to the enlargement of her

---

[1] *Keils Bibl.* 3, 1, 72, note. Some scholars, as Hommel (*Gesch. d. alt. Morgenlandes*, p. 68), propose to identify this place with the Assyrian Nineveh, but the conjecture lacks proof and is altogether improbable.

temple. From the manner in which she is associated with Nin-girsu, aiding the latter in guarding his temple E-ninnu, and uniting with the god in granting the sceptre to Gudea, one is tempted to conclude that the two towns, Girsu and Ninâ, were amalgamated before their absorption into Lagash, so that the god and goddess acquired the relationship to one another of husband and consort. As for the connection between this Babylonian Ninâ and the late Assyrian capital, it is quite possible that the origin of the latter is to be traced to a settlement made by inhabitants of the former, although it should be added that there is no positive evidence that can be adduced in support of this proposition. It accords, however, with the northward movement of culture and civilization in Mesopotamia. If this connection between the two Ninevehs be accepted, the question suggests itself whether, in time, Ninâ did not become merely another form of Ishtar. The Assyrian capital is frequently spoken of as the 'beloved city' of Ishtar, and unless it be supposed that this epithet simply reflects the comparatively late popularity of the distinctively Assyrian Ishtar, the most natural explanation would be to propose the equation Ninâ = Ishtar.

In the incantation texts, Ninâ is frequently appealed to as the daughter of Ea, — the god of the deep. This relationship, as well as the interpretation of the ideogram above set forth, points to the original character of the goddess as a water-deity. This goddess, therefore, would be of an entirely different form from the ones discussed in the previous paragraphs. Instead of being a member of the heavenly pantheon, her place is with the kingdom over which Ea presides, and whose dwelling-place is the watery deep. In any case, Ninâ is originally distinct from Ishtar, Nanâ, and Anunit; and she retains an independent existence to a later period than most of the other great goddesses that have been discussed. In an inscription of the days of Belnâdinaplu (c. 1100 B.C.), published by Hilprecht,[1] Ninâ appears as the patron deity of Dêr,—a city of Southern Babylonia. There too she is called the 'daughter of Ea,' the creator of everything. She is 'the mistress of goddesses.' Attached to her temple there are lands that having been wrongfully wrested from the priests are returned upon royal command, under solemn invocation of the goddess. How her worship came to be transferred to Dêr we do not know. She appears in the inscription in question by the side of a goddess who — following Hommel — is none other than Bau. Dêr is called the city of the god Anu, and we can only suppose that it must at one time have risen to sufficient importance to harbor in its midst a number of deities. It is presumably[2] the place whence Nebuchadnezzar I. sets out in the twelfth century to drive the Cassites off the throne of Babylonia. May it be that, during the days of the foreign rule, priests attached to the service of various of the old gods and goddesses transferred the worship of these deities to places more secure from interference?

Be this as it may, if our Ninâ has any connection with the goddess of Nineveh, it is certain that Ishtar has retained none of Ninâ's traits. The fusion in this case has been so complete that naught but the faintest tradition of an original and independent Ninâ has survived in the North.

Anu.

This god, who, from a theoretical point of view (as will be shown in a subsequent chapter), was regarded as standing at the head of the organized Babylonian pantheon, figures only incidentally in the inscriptions prior to the days of Hammurabi. Ur-Gur of the second dynasty of Ur, in invoking Nannar, calls

---

[1] *Old Babylonian Inscriptions*, I. pls. 30, 31. (See now Peiser, *Keils Bibl.* 4, pp. 64–66.)
[2] Questioned by Peiser, *ib.*

the latter 'the powerful bull of Anu.' The reference is interesting, for it shows that already in these early days the position of Anu, as the god of the heavenly expanse, was fixed. The moon appearing in the heavens, and the resemblance of its crescent to a bull's horn,[1] are the two factors that account for the expressive epithet used by Ur-Bau. That the worship of the god of heaven *par excellence* should not have enjoyed great popularity in the early days of the Babylonian religion might seem strange at first sight. A little reflection, however, will make this clear. A god of the heavens is an abstract conception, and while it is possible that even in an early age, such a conception may have arisen in some minds, it is not of a character calculated to take a popular hold. As we proceed in our attempt to trace the development of the Babylonian religion, we will find the line of demarcation separating the theological system, as evolved by the schoolmen, from the popular phases of the religion, becoming more marked. In the inscriptions of the old Babylonian rulers, comparatively little of the influence of the Babylonian theologians is to be detected. Even the description of the moon as the bull of heaven falls within the domain of popular fancy. It is different in the days after Hammurabi, when political concentration leads to the focussing of intellectual life in the Euphrates Valley, with all the consequences that the establishment of a central priesthood, with growing powers over ever-increasing territory, involves. It is to be noted, moreover, that the manner in which in the old Babylonian inscriptions *Anu* is written,[2] indicates that the abstraction involved in the conception of a god of heaven had not yet been reached, though some measure of personification was of course inevitable at a time when animistic

---

[1] Among many nations the moon is pictured as a horned animal. See Robert Brown's interesting monograph on *The Unicorn*, pp. 27 *seq. et passim;* also above, p. 76.

[2] Simply the sign AN (= god, heaven) and the phonetic complement *na*.

notions still held sway. A direct indication of this personification of heaven without the deification appears in the epithet 'child of Anu,' bestowed upon the goddess Bau. The reference to the heavens in this connection is an allusion to Bau's position as the patroness of that quarter of Lagash known as the 'brilliant town,'[1] and where Bau's temple stood. The transference of the quality of 'brilliancy' from the town to the goddess would be expressed by calling the latter the offspring of that part of visible nature which is associated in the mind with 'brilliancy.' Somewhat mysterious, and still awaiting a satisfactory explanation, is the title 'sacrificer,' or 'priest of Anu,' which one of the rulers of Lagash, Ur-Nin-girsu, assumes. It is scarcely possible that the god of heaven can be meant; and, on the other hand, if we are to assume merely a personification of heaven, we encounter fresh difficulties. It seems to me that the use of Anu[2] here is purely metaphorical for 'high' or 'lofty,' and that the king merely wishes to emphasize the dignity of his station by declaring himself to be the heavenly priest, somewhat as we should say 'priest by divine grace,' or 'supreme priest.'

$\text{Nin-si}^3\text{-a}$.

Ur-Bau and Gudea alone of the ancient rulers refer to this god. The former erects a temple in honor of the god in some quarter of his capitol city, while the latter emphasizes the strength that the god has given him. These references, however, show that the god must have been of considerable importance, and in this case, his disappearance from the later pantheon is probably due to the absorption of his rôle by the

---

[1] See above, p. 59.

[2] Written An-na, without the determinative for deity. De Sarzec, *Découvertes en Chaldée*, pl. 37, no. 8.

[3] The second element may also be read *dar*. See Jensen, *Keils Bibl.* 3, 1, p. 24, note 1.

greater god of Lagash, — Nin-girsu. Like Nin-girsu, Nin-si-a was a god of war, and his worship, imported perhaps from some ancient site to Lagash, falls into desuetude, as the attribute accorded to him becomes the distinguishing trait of the chief deity of the place.

GAL-ALIM.

Among the various deities to whom Gudea gives praise for the position and glory which he attains is Gal-alim.[1] From him he has received great rule and a lofty sceptre. The phrase is of a very general nature and reveals nothing as to the special character of the god in question. An earlier king, Uru-kagina, refers to the temple of the god at Lagash. Gal-alim may have been again a merely local deity belonging to one of the towns that fell under Gudea's rule, and whose attributes again were so little marked that this god too disappeared under the overshadowing importance of Nin-girsu. He and another god, Dun-shagga, are viewed as the sons of Nin-girsu.

Coming to some of the deities that we may designate as minor, it is to be noted that in the case of certain ones, at least, it will be found that they may be identified with others more prominent, and that what seem to be distinct names are in reality descriptive epithets of gods already met with. This remark applies more particularly to such names as begin with the element Nin, signifying either 'lord' or 'lady,' and which, when followed by the name of a place, always points to its being a title, and, when followed by an ideographic compound, only diminishes that probability to a slight degree. We have already come across several instances; thus Nin-girsu, the

[1] Inscription B, col. ii. 19.

lord of Girsu, has been shown to be a form of Ninib, itself an ideogram, the reading of which, it will be recalled, is still uncertain; and again, Nin-khar-sag has been referred to, as one of the titles of the great goddess Belit. Similarly, Nin-gish-zida, whose name signifies 'the lord of the right-hand (or propitious) sceptre,' becomes a title and not a name, and when Gudea speaks of this god as the one who leads him to battle, and calls him 'king,' he is simply describing the same god who is elsewhere spoken of as Nin-girsu. By the side of Nin-girsu and Nin-gish-zida appears Nin-shakh, who, as Oppert[1] has shown, is like Nin-girsu the prototype of the well-known god of war, Ninib. However, Nin-shakh occupies, in contradistinction to Nin-gish-zida and others, a position in the old Babylonian pantheon of an independent character, so that it is hardly justifiable, in such a case, to identify him completely with Ninib, and place the name on a par with the epithets just referred to. The dividing line between the mere title and an independent god thus becomes at times very faint, and yet it is well to maintain it whenever called for. In the following enumeration of the minor gods of the old Babylonian pantheon, the attempt will be made to bring out this distinction in each instance.

Beginning with

NIN-SHAKH

the element *Nin*, as has several times been mentioned, points to an ideographic form. The second element signifies 'wild boar,' and from other sources we know that this animal was a sacred one in Babylonia, as among other Semitic nations.[2] Its flesh, on certain days of the Babylonian calendar, was

---

[1] See Hommel, *Semitische Kulturen*, p. 389.

[2] For the sacred character of the swine among the Semites, see W. Robertson Smith's *The Religion of the Semites*, pp. 201, 272, 332, 457. Rawlinson, iii. 68, 22, occurs a deity, 'swine of the right hand,' *i.e.*, propitious.

forbidden to be eaten, from which we are permitted to conclude that these days were dedicated to the animal, and the prohibition represents perhaps the traces of some old religious festival. May Nin-shakh therefore have been a 'swine deity,' just as Nergal is symbolized by the 'lion'? In both cases the animal would be a symbol of the violent and destructive character of the god.

The ferocious character of the 'swine' would naturally result in assigning to Nin-shakh warlike attributes; and as a matter of fact he is identified at times with Ninib. His subordinate position, however, is indicated by his being called the 'servant,' generally of En-lil, occasionally also of Anu, and as such he bears the name of Pap-sukal,[1] *i.e.*, 'divine messenger.' Rim-Sin builds a temple to Nin-shakh at Uruk, and from its designation as his 'favorite dwelling place' we may conclude that Rim-Sin only restores or enlarges an ancient temple of the deity. In the light of this, the relationship above set forth between Nin-girsu, Nin-gish-zida, and Nin-shakh becomes somewhat clearer. The former, the local deity of Girsu, would naturally be called by the kings 'the lord of the true sceptre,' while the subordination of Girsu as a quarter of Lagash finds its reflection in the relationship of master and servant pictured as existing between En-lil and Nin-girsu. Again, the warlike character of the patron deity of Girsu would lead to an identification with Nin-shakh of Uruk, possessing the same traits; and the incorporation of Uruk as a part of the same empire which included Lagash and its quarters, would be the last link bringing about the full equation between the three. With Ninib — the solar deity — coming into prominence as the god of war, all three names, Nin-girsu, Nin-gish-zida, and Nin-

---

[1] Rawlinson, II. 59, 23. The second element in Pap-sukal is the common Babylonian word for 'servant,' or 'messenger'; other deities therefore standing in a subsidiary position are also called Pap-sukal. So *e.g.*, Nebo and Nusku. See further on and compare Hommel, *Semiten*, pp. 479, 480.

shakh, would be regarded by a later age as merely descriptive of one and the same god.

DUN-SHAGGA.

Gudea makes mention in one of his inscriptions, by the side of Nin-gish-zida, of a god Dun-shagga,[1] whose name signifies the 'chief hero,' but the phonetic reading of which it is impossible to determine.[2] Like Nin-gish-zida, he is a warlike god, and from that one might suppose that he too is only another form of Nin-girsu-Ninib. At all events, he did not differ materially from the latter. It is from him, that Gudea again declares his power to be derived, just as elsewhere he accords to Nin-girsu this distinction. The element 'Dun,' which is very much the same as 'Nin,' speaks in favor of regarding Dun-shagga as a title; but, in default of positive evidence, it will not be out of place to give him an independent position, and to regard his identification with Nin-girsu as a later phase due to the extension of Nin-girsu's jurisdiction and his corresponding absorption of a varying number of minor gods. This tendency on the part of the greater gods to absorb the minor ones is as distinctive a trait in the development of the Babylonian religion, as is the subordination of one god to the other, whether expressed by making the subordinate god the consort, the chief, or the servant of a superior one. We have seen that such terms of relationship correspond to certain degrees of political conditions existing between the conquering and the conquered districts. Amalgamation of two cities or districts is portrayed in the relation of the two patron deities as husband and wife, the stronger of the two being the former, the

---

[1] Inscription B, col. III. 2.
[2] Uru-kagina, earlier than Gudea (de Sarzec, pl. 32), appears to have built a temple to Dun-shagga, but the passage is not altogether clear. The element also appears in the name of the ruler of Ur, *Dungi, i.e.,* 'the legitimate hero,' as Sargon is the 'legitimate king.'

more subservient pictured as the latter. The more pronounced superiority of the one place over the other finds expression in the relation of father to child, while that of master and servant emphasizes the complete control exercised by the one over the other. Lastly, the absorption of one deity into another, is correlative either with the most perfect form of conquest, or the complete disappearance of the seat of his worship in consequence of the growing favor of one possessing sufficiently similar qualities to warrant identification with the other.

Lugal-banda.

Sin-gashid of the dynasty of Uruk makes mention of this deity at the beginning of one of his inscriptions. To him and to his consort, Nin-gul, a temple as 'the seat of their joy' at that place is devoted. This association of the god with the town points again to a local deity, but possessing a character which leads to the absorption of the god in the solar god, Nergal, whom we have already encountered, and who will occupy us a good deal when we come to the period after Hammurabi. The identification of the two is already foreshadowed in an inscription of another member of the same dynasty, Sin-gamil, who places the name of Nergal exactly where his predecessor mentions Lugal-banda. The first element in his name signifies 'king,' the second apparently 'strong,' so that in this respect, too, the god comes close to Nergal, whose name likewise indicates 'great lord.' The consort of Lugal-banda is

Nin-Gul.

Her name signifies 'the destructive lady,'—an appropriate epithet for the consort of a solar deity. It is Sin-gashid again who associates Ningul with Lugal-banda, and emphasizes his affection for the goddess by calling her his mother. In one inscription, moreover, Sin-gashid addresses himself exclusively to the goddess, who had an equal share in the temple at Uruk.

Dumuzi-zu-aba.

Among the deities appealed to by Ur-Bau appears one whose name is to be interpreted as the 'unchangeable child of the watery deep.' The great god of the deep we have seen is Ea. Dumuzi-zu-aba therefore belongs to the water-deities, and one who, through his subordinate rank to Ea, sinks to the level of a water-spirit. Ur-Bau declares himself to be the darling of this deity, and in the town of Girsu he erects a temple to him. Girsu, however, was not the patron city of the god, for Ur-Bau gives Dumuzi-zu-aba, the appellation of 'the lord of Kinunira,'[1] a place the actual situation of which is unknown. Dumuzi-zu-aba, accordingly, is to be regarded as a local deity of a place which, situated probably on an arm of the Euphrates, was the reason for the watery attributes assigned to the god. The comparative insignificance of the place is one of the factors that accounts for the minor importance of the god, and the second factor is the popularity enjoyed by another child of the great Ea, his child *par excellence*, Marduk, who is best known as the patron god of the city of Babylon. By the side of Marduk, the other children of Ea, the minor water-deities, disappear, so that to a later generation Dumuzi-zu-aba appears merely as a form of Marduk. With Dumuzi-zu-aba, we must be careful not to confuse

Dumu-zi,

who in the old Babylonian inscriptions is mentioned once by Sin-iddina,[2] in connection with the sun-god. Dumu-zi, signifying 'child of life,' has a double aspect — an agricultural deity

---

[1] Signifying, according to Jensen, *Keils Bibl.* 3, 1, p. 25, 'fighting-place.'
[2] Published by Delitzsch, *Beiträge zur Assyr.* I. 301-311.

and at the same time a god of the lower world. He plays an important part in the eschatological literature of the Babylonians, but hardly none at all in the historical and incantation texts. A fuller treatment may therefore be reserved for a future chapter.

LUGAL-ERIMA.

A purely local deity, if the reading and interpretation offered by Jensen, 'King of the city Erim,' is correct. The mention of the deity in an inscription of Ur-Bau, who calls himself the 'beloved servant' of this god, would be due to the circumstance that the district within which the city in question lay was controlled by the rulers of Lagash. To invoke as large a number of deities as possible was not only a means of securing protection from many sides, but was already in the early days of Babylonian history indulged in by rulers, as a means of emphasizing the extent and manifold character of their jurisdiction.

NIN-E-GAL AND NINGAL.

A temple was erected to Nin-e-gal by the wife of Rim-Sin, of the dynasty ruling in Larsa. Her name as interpreted in the tablet dedicated to her, signifies again, as in several cases already noted, 'great lady.' She was probably therefore only the consort of some patron deity; and Nannar being the most prominent god invoked by Rim-Sin, it would seem that the goddess to whom the queen pays her respects is again one of the consorts of the moon-god.[1] This conclusion is supported by the direct association of Nannar of Ur and Ningal in an inscription emanating from an earlier member of the same dynasty to which Rim-Sin belongs. Nur-Rammân speaks of building temples to these deities in the city of Ur. Hence the goddess is also represented as interceding with

[1] So also Jensen, *Kosmologie* p. 14, note 3.

Sin on behalf of those who appeal to her. The form Nin-e-gal is but a variant of Nin-gal, so that the identification of the two lies beyond doubt, and it may very well be that the temple erected by the consort of Rim-Sin is the same as the one referred to by Nur-Rammân. In a land where polygamy was a prevailing custom, the gods too might be represented as having a number of consorts. There would of course be, just as in human relations, one chief consort, but there might be others ranged at the side of the latter.[1] Some of these may have been consorts of other minor deities, worshipped in the same district, and who were given to the more important divinity as he gradually overshadowed the others. In this way, we may account for the large variety of 'ladies' and 'great ladies' met with in the Babylonian pantheon, and who, being merely 'reflections' of male deities, with no sharply marked traits of their own, would naturally come to be confused with one another, and finally be regarded as various forms of one and the same goddess. A member of the dynasty ruling in Isin, En-anna-tuma, earlier even than Nur-Rammân, invokes Nin-gal in an inscription found in the ancient capital, Ur. Here, too, the goddess appears in association with Nannar; but, curiously enough, she is designated as the mother of Shamash. It will be borne in mind that in the city of Ur, the sun-god occupied a secondary place at the side of the moon-god. This relationship is probably indicated by the epithet 'offspring of Nin-gal,' accorded to Shamash in the inscription referred to. The moon being superior to the sun, the consort of the moon-god becomes the mother of the sun-god.

Reference has several times been made to

---

[1] So Anu appears to have concubines.

Nin-gish-zida,

who, originally a distinct solar deity, becomes scarcely distinguishable from Nin-girsu, and is eventually identified with the great Nin-ib.[1] It is noticeable that these four deities, Nin-girsu, Nin-shakh, Nin-gish-zida, and Nin-ib, who are thus associated together, all contain the element *Nin* in their names, — a factor that may turn out to be of some importance when more abundant material shall be forthcoming for tracing their development in detail. One of Gudea's inscriptions[2] begins with the significant statement, 'Nin-gish-zida is the god of Gudea'; and elsewhere when speaking of him, he is 'my god,' or 'his god.' None of the ancient Babylonian rulers make mention of him except Gudea, though in the incantation texts he is introduced and significantly termed 'the throne-bearer' of the earth. The purely local character of the deity is, furthermore, emphasized by the reference to his temple in Girsu, on a brick and on a cone containing dedicatory inscriptions, inscribed by Gudea in honor of the god.[3]

Shul(or Dun)-pa-uddu.

The wife of the famous Gudea, Gin-Shul-pa-uddu, bears a name in which one of the elements is a deity, the phonetic reading of whose name is still uncertain.[4] The elements comprising it, namely, 'lord' (?), 'sceptre,' and 'radiant,' leave little doubt as to the solar character of the god. Besides Gudea's wife, a ruler, Ur-Shul-pa-uddu,[5] belonging apparently to a somewhat earlier period, embodies this deity in his name. The worship of the deity, therefore, belongs to a very early epoch, and

---

[1] See above, pp. 92, 93. [2] Inscription C.
[3] De Sarzec, pl. 37, no. 5; *Trans. Soc. Bibl. Arch.* vi. 279.
[4] Jensen, *Kosmologie*, p. 127, proposes to read Umun-pauddu.
[5] Hilprecht, *Old Babylonian Inscriptions*, i. 2, no. 93. The name also appears in syllabaries as Shul-pa-ud-du-a. For the element *pa-udda*, see p. 103. In Nergal's name Shid-lam-ta-uddu-a (p. 65), the same final elements are found which appear to be characteristic epithets of solar deities. The first element in the name has also the value Dun (as in Dun-gi).

appears at one time to have enjoyed considerable popularity within a certain district of Babylonia. To what region of Babylonia he belongs has not yet been ascertained. Judging from analogous instances, he represented some phase of the sun worshipped in a particular locality, whose cult, with the disappearance of the place from the surface of political affairs, yielded to the tendency to concentrate sun-worship in two or three deities, — Shamash and Ninib more especially. In the astronomy of the Babylonians the name survived as a designation of Marduk-Jupiter.[1]

Nin-Mar.

A local deity, designated as the lady of Mar, is invoked by Ur-Bau, from whom we learn that she was the daughter of Ninâ. *Mar*, with the determinative for country, *Ki*, appears to have been the name of a district extending to the Persian Gulf.[2] The capital of the district is represented by the mound Tel-Id, not far from Warka. Her subsidiary position is indicated in these words, and we may conclude that Nin-Mar at an early period fell under the jurisdiction of the district in which Ninâ was supreme. For all that, Nin-Mar, or the city in which her cult was centralized, must have enjoyed considerable favor. Ur-Bau calls her the 'gracious lady,' and erects a temple, the name of which, Ish-gu-tur,[3] *i.e.*, according to Jensen's plausible interpretation, 'the house that serves as a court for all persons,' points to Mar as a place of pilgrimage to which people came from all sides. Gudea, accordingly, does not omit to include 'the lady of Mar' in his list of the chief deities to whom he pays his devotions; and on the assumption of the general favor in which the city of Mar stood as a sacred town, we may account for the fact that a much later ruler, Dungi, of the dynasty of Ur,[4] erects a temple to her honor.

---

[1] Jensen, *Kosmologie*, pp. 125, 126.
[2] See *Journal Asiatique*, September–October, 1895, p. 393.
[3] De Sarzec, pl. 8, col. v. ll. 8–12.   [4] IR. pl. 2, no. 4.

Pa-sag.

A deity, the phonetic reading of whose name is unknown, or at all events uncertain,[1] is mentioned once by Gudea in the long list of deities that has been several times referred to. The ideographs with which his name is written designate him as a chief of some kind, and in accord with this, Gudea calls him 'the leader of the land.' Pa-sag is mentioned immediately after the sun-god Utu, and in view of the fact that another solar deity, I-shum, whom we shall come across in a future chapter, is designated by the same title[2] as Pa-sag, it seems safe to conclude that the latter is likewise a solar deity, and in all probability, the prototype of I-shum, if not indeed identical with him.

Nisaba (or Nidaba).

In a dream which the gods send to Gudea, he sees among other things, a goddess, whose name may be read Nisaba or Nidaba.[3] Ninâ, who interprets the dream to the ruler of Shirpurla, declares that Nisaba is her sister. In a text belonging to a still earlier age, the deity is mentioned as the begetter of a king whose name is read Lugal-zaggisi.[4] From the manner in which the name of the goddess is written, as well as from other sources, we know that Nisaba is an agricultural deity. In historical texts she plays scarcely any rôle at all, but in incantations she is often referred to; and from the fact that Nisaba is appealed to, to break the power of the demons in conjunction with Ea, it would appear that the position once occupied by her was no insignificant one. Nin-girsu, it will

---

[1] Jensen regards Pa-sag as a possible phonetic form, but his view is hardly tenable.
[2] See Zimmern, *Busspsalmen*, pp. 60, 61.
[3] Cylinder A, cols. iv. and v. Amiaud read the name *Nirba*.
[4] Just published by Hilprecht, *Old Babylonian Inscriptions*, i. 2, pls. 38–42. *Cf.* p. 52.

be recalled, has also traits which connect him with agricultural life, and Ninâ being the daughter of Nin-si-a, one of the forms under which Ningirsu-Ninib appears, we may connect Nisaba directly with the cults of which Lagash formed the center. Nisaba must have been the consort of one of the agricultural gods, whose jurisdiction falls within Gudea's empire. Lugalzaggisi, as the king of Uruk, assigns to the goddess a first place. Her origin must, therefore, be sought in this region. In later days the name of the goddess is used to describe the fertility of the soil in general. So Ashurbanabal, describing the prosperity existing in his days, says that grain was abundant through the 'increase of Nisaba.'[1]

KU(?)-ANNA.

A goddess of this name — reading of the first sign doubtful — is mentioned by Ur-Bau, who builds a temple to her in Girsu. If Amiaud is correct in his reading of the first sign, the goddess was identified at one time by the Babylonians with the consort of Ramman — the storm-god. This would accord with the description that Ur-Bau gives of the goddess. She is the one who deluges the land with water — belonging therefore to the same order as Bau.

In a list of deities enumerated by a ruler of Erech, Lugalzaggisi,[2] are found (1) a local goddess,

UMU,

designated as the 'priestess of Uruk,'[3] and occupying an inferior rank to (2) a goddess,

---

[1] V R. col. I. 48.
[2] See at close of chapter vi.
[3] Hilprecht, *ib.* no. 87, col. i. 30.

NIN-AKHA-KUDDU,[1]

who is called 'the mistress of Uruk.' The importance of Erech in the early history of Babylonia is emphasized by the inscriptions from Nippur, recently published by Dr. Hilprecht. It is natural, therefore, to find several deities of a purely local type commemorated by kings who belong to this region. The goddess Umu is not heard of again. The great goddess of Uruk, Nanâ, absorbs the smaller ones, and hence Nin-akha-kuddu survives chiefly in incantation texts as 'the lady of shining waters,' of 'purification,' and of 'incantations.'[2]

Lastly, a passing reference may be made to several deities to whom sanctuaries are erected by Uru-Kagina in the great temple of Bau at Uru-azaga, and whom Amiaud regards as sons of Bau.

Uru-Kagina enumerates three, Za-za-uru, Im-pa-ud-du, and Gim-nun-ta-ud-du-a.[3] The element *ud-du* in the last two names signifies 'radiant' or 'rising up'; while *pa-ud-du* (like in Shul-pa-ud-du, p. 99) means 'radiant sceptre.' If to this, we add that *Im* is 'storm,' it will appear plausible to see in the second name a form of a raging solar deity and perhaps also in the third; *gim nun* in the latter name may mean 'creating lord.' To these Amiaud[4] adds from other sources, Khi-gir-nunna, Khi-shaga, Gurmu, and Zarmu. He takes these seven deities as sons of Bau, but he offers no conclusive evidence for his theory. Some of these deities may turn out to be synonymous with such as have already been met with.

[1] *Ib.* i. 32. Hilprecht reads Nin-a-gid-kha-du, but this can hardly be correct.
[2] The two ideas, 'water' and 'incantation,' are correlated. The 'waters' meant are those used for purification purposes in connection with the magic formulas.
[3] De Sarzec, pl. 32, col. ii. 9-11.
[4] *Records of the Past*, N.S., i. 59. Amiaud reads the second name Im-gbud-êna and the third Gim (or Ur)-nun-ta-êna. The publication in De Sarzec favors my readings.

CHAPTER V.

THE CONSORTS OF THE GODS.

ATTENTION has already been directed to the comparatively small number of female deities that appear in the inscriptions of the first period of Babylonian history. We must, however, not conclude from this, that such deities did not exist in larger numbers. On the contrary, we may feel certain that every god had his consort, and in some cases more than one. Several instances of such consorts have been furnished in this chapter; but if the consorts of the larger number of these gods are unknown, it is because of the insignificant rôle that these consorts played. The goddesses of Babylonia, with few exceptions, become mere shadowy reflections of the gods, with but little independent power, and in some cases none at all. They owe what popularity they enjoyed to their association with their male companions. In consequence of this inferior rôle played by the female deities, the tendency becomes more pronounced, as we pass from the first to the second period of Babylonian history, to reduce by assimilation the small number that have independent attributes, until we reach a condition in which we have practically only one goddess, appearing under many forms. It is only in the religious texts, and in some phases of the popular beliefs, that goddesses retain a certain degree of prominence. So, a goddess Allat, as we shall see, plays an important part as the chief goddess of the subterranean cave that houses the dead. Allat appears to have been originally a consort of the famous Bel of Nippur, but through association with Nergal, who becomes the chief god of the lower world, almost all traces of the original character of the goddess disappear. Again,

Gula, the consort of Nin-ib, while occasionally mentioned in the historical texts of the second and third period, and under the form Ma-ma, as an element in a proper name belonging to the oldest period,[1] is more frequently invoked in incantations as the healer of disease. The same is the case with other goddesses; so that we may conclude that from the earliest times, the Babylonian religion shared the trait so marked in all Semitic cults, of a combination of the male and female principle in the personification of the powers that controlled the fate of man. In part, no doubt, the minor importance of women, so far as the outward aspects of social and political life were concerned, is a factor in the altogether secondary importance attaching to the consorts of the gods; but we may feel certain that there was no god, however restricted in his jurisdiction, or however limited in the number of his worshippers, who had not associated with him a female companion, who follows him as the shadow follows the substance.

[1] According to Hilprecht, *ib.* p. 48, note 6. For *Ma-ma* and *Me-me*, as names of Gula, see chapter viii.

CHAPTER VI.

GUDEA'S PANTHEON.

GUDEA manifests a fondness for giving to his pantheon as large a compass as possible. In this respect, he follows earlier examples, and also sets an example which is followed by many of the rulers of Babylonia and Assyria, who felt that the larger the number of gods invoked by them, the more impressive would their own position appear in the eyes of their subjects. Moreover, by incorporating in their pantheon the gods associated with districts that they controlled, they would not only secure the protection of these deities, but would emphasize their own claim to an extended sovereignty. The beginning and the close of dedicatory and commemorative inscriptions were the favorite opportunities, seized upon by the kings, for parading the list of the powers under whose patronage they wished to appear. These lists are both interesting and valuable, as furnishing in a convenient form a summary of the chief gods included in the Babylonian pantheon at the various historical periods. At the close of one of his inscriptions,[1] Gudea furnishes a list of no less than eighteen deities. In rapid succession he enumerates Anu, En-lil (Bel), Nin-khar-sag, En-ki (Ea), En-zu (Sin), Nin-girsu, Ninâ, Nin-si-a, Ga-tum-dug, Bau, Ninni, Utu (Shamash), Pa-sag, Gal-alim, Dun-shagga, Nin-Mar, Dumuzi-zuaba, Nin-gish-zida. These deities may be taken as indicative of the territorial extent of Gudea's jurisdiction. They are called upon to punish him who attempts to alter the decrees of the ruler, or to efface the memory of his deeds. Again, at the beginning of one of his inscriptions, he appeals to Nin-girsu, En-lil, Ninâ,

[1] Inscr. B, cols. viii. ix.

Bau, Ga-tum-dug, Gal-alim, and Dun-shagga. He recounts what he has done to promote the cults of these deities, and upon his conduct he grounds his hope that they will aid him in his undertakings. The lists, as will be observed, vary in the number and in the order of the gods enumerated. In the second list, the position of Nin-girsu at the head is due to the fact that the inscription commemorates the dedication of a sanctuary to that god. But Nin-girsu, despite his rank as the chief god of Lagash, belongs to a second class of deities. Standing far above him is the triad, Anu, Bel, and Ea, the gods that personify, as we have seen, the great divisions of the universe, — heaven, earth, and water. These gods, accordingly, take precedence of Nin-girsu in the first list. In a succeeding chapter, the significance of this triad for the Babylonian religion will be fully set forth. For the present, it is sufficient to note that the systematization of popular beliefs, involved in the distinctions thus emphasized in the groupings of deities into classes, begins at so early a period. This systematization, however, has not yet assumed final shape. True, the moon-god has already been given the place, immediately following upon the triad, that he will hold in the developed form of Babylonian theology; but while, as we have seen, Sin properly takes precedence of the sun-god, the latter should follow in the wake of his associate. Not only, however, does Nin-girsu precede, but two other deities who are closely related in general character to the 'warrior deity' of Gudea's dominion. Then the two great goddesses, Bau and Ninni, are introduced, and it is not until they are disposed of that the sun-god, together again with Pa-sag as a kind of lieutenant,[1] is invoked. In the arrangement of the five remaining deities, no special principle can be recognized. They, evidently, occupy a minor rank. It is possible, then, to distinguish no less than four classes in the old Babylonian pantheon: (1) the great triad, Anu, Bel, and Ea;

---

[1] See above, p. 101.

(2) a second group, as yet incomplete, but which will eventually include Sin, Shamash, and Ramman, representing the great powers of nature—moon, sun, and storm; (3) the great gods, the patron deities of the more important political centers of the country; and (4) the minor ones, representing the local cults of less important places. Naturally, the dividing line between the two last-named classes is not sharply marked, and in accordance with the ever-varying political kaleidoscope, local deities will rise from the rank of minor gods to a higher place in the pantheon; while such as once enjoyed high esteem will, through decline in the political fortunes of their worshippers, be brought down from the higher to an inferior rank.[1] It is this constant interaction between the political situation and the relationship of the gods to one another, that constitutes one of the most striking features of the religion of Babylonia and Assyria. In the course of time, as an organized pantheon leads to greater stability in the domain of theological speculation, the influence of the politics of the country on the religion becomes less marked, without, however, disappearing altogether. The various classes into which the gods are divided, are definitely fixed by the schools of theology that, as we shall see, take their rise in the Euphrates Valley. The rivalry, on the one hand, between the Babylonian empire united under one head, and the Assyrian empire on the other, alone remains to bring about an occasional exchange of places between the two gods who stand at the head of the great gods of the Babylonian and Assyrian pantheon respectively. The attempt has been made by Amiaud[2] to arrange the pantheon of this oldest period in a genealogical order. In Gudea's long list of deities, he detects three generations,—the three chief gods and one goddess, as the progenitors of Sin, Shamash, Nin-girsu, Bau, and others.

---

[1] See Winckler's excellent remarks on the relationship between the city and the god in ancient Babylonia (*Altorientalische Forschungen*, III. 232-235).
[2] *Records of the Past*, N.S., i. 57-59.

The gods of this second division give rise to a third class, viewed again as the offspring of the second. Professor Davis, taking up this idea of Amiaud, has quite recently maintained[1] that the family idea must form our starting-point for an understanding of the pantheon of Lagash. The theory, however, does not admit of consistent application. There are gods, as Amiaud recognized, who cannot be brought under his scheme, so far at least as present testimony is concerned; and others can only by an arbitrary assumption be forced into accord with the theory. Moreover, we should expect to find traces of this family idea in the later phases of the Assyro-Babylonian pantheon. Such, however, is not the case. A more reasonable and natural explanation of the relationship existing between many — not all — of the gods of Gudea's pantheon has already been suggested. In part, we must look to the development of a theological system of thought in the Euphrates Valley to account for the superior position accorded to certain gods, and in part, political conditions and political changes afford an explanation for the union of certain deities into a family group. So far, indeed, Amiaud is correct, that the relationship existing between the various deities, was as a rule expressed in terms applicable to human society. The secondary position occupied, *e.g.*, by Sin when compared with a god whose domain is the entire 'lower regions,' would be aptly expressed by calling the moon-god the eldest son of En-lil or Bel; and, similarly, a goddess like Bau would be called the daughter of Anu. It is a mistake, however, to interpret the use of 'daughter' and 'son' literally. Such terms are employed in all Semitic languages in a figurative sense, to indicate a dependent position of some sort. Again, we have seen that the union of a number of cities or states under one head would be followed by a union of the deities proper to these cities or states. That union would

[1] In a paper on "The Gods of Shirpurla," read before the American Oriental Society in April, 1895. (*Proceedings*, ccxiii–ccxviii.)

be expressed, according to circumstances, either by placing the deities on a footing of equality — in which case they would be consorts, or brothers and sisters, *offsprings* therefore of one and the same god — or, the superior rank of one patron god would be indicated by assigning to the god of a conquered or subordinate territory the rank of offspring or attendant.

In studying such a list as that presented by Gudea, we must, therefore, make due allowance for what may be called local peculiarities and local conditions. It is only by comparing his list with others that we can differentiate between the general features of Babylonian cults and the special features due to political and local associations. We are in a position now to institute this comparison for a period which is certainly some centuries earlier than Gudea. The date of the reign of Lugal-zaggisi, king of Uruk, who has been several times referred to in a previous chapter, is fixed by Hilprecht at *c.* 4500 B.C., but it is doubtful whether so high an age will be accepted by scholars. The chronology for the period beyond Gudea is still in a very uncertain condition. Lugal-zaggisi, in a long list of deities at the beginning of an important inscription, enumerates in succession Anu, the goddess Nisaba, the gods En-lil (or Bel), En-ki (=Ea), En-zu (Sin), Utu (the sun-god), the goddess Ninni (or Nanâ[?]), Nin-khar-sag, Umu, and Nin-akha-kuddu. As for Anu, the king introduces the name, as Ur-Ningirsu of Lagash does (see above, p. 90), in calling himself 'priest of Anu,' and which, according to the explanation suggested, means simply 'divine priest.'

Bel, Ea, Sin, and Shamash (or Utu) are common to Gudea and Lugal-zaggisi. These constitute, then, the great gods whose worship is no longer limited to any particular district. They have become common property, in part through the sanctity attached to the places where the gods were worshipped, in part through the antiquity of these places, and in part, no doubt, as the result of a political development lying behind the period under consideration. The prominence given by Lugal-zaggisi to Nisaba is rather surprising. He calls himself and also his father, 'hero' of Nisaba. If, however, it be borne in mind that of the goddesses at least two, Umu and Nin-akha-kuddu, are of a local character, the conclusion appears justified that Nisaba was a goddess associated more particularly with the district in which Uruk lay. The goddess Ninni (written simply as 'the goddess') is no doubt identical with the great Nanâ of Uruk, and Nin-khar-sag is introduced as the consort of En-lil.

As a result of this comparison, we may note the tendency towards a general recognition of certain great gods, which is more fully developed in the period of Hammurabi. At the same time, the loyalty of the rulers to the gods, peculiar to their own district, is manifested by the prominent place assigned in the several cases to gods who otherwise play an insignificant rôle, and who eventually are absorbed by others; and lastly, as between Lugal-zaggisi and Gudea, the observation may be made of the disposition to emphasize local gods, less for their own sake, than because of the éclat furnished by the enumeration of a large pantheon, which shall be coequal in extent and dignity to the district claimed by the rulers and to the rank assumed by them.

CHAPTER VII.

SUMMARY.

We have thus passed in review the old Babylonian pantheon, so far as the discovered texts have revealed their names and epithets. The list does not claim to be exhaustive. That future texts will add to its length, by revealing the existence at this early period of many known to us at present only from later texts or from the religious literature,[1] is more than likely. The nature of the old Babylonian religion entails, as a necessary consequence, an array of gods that might be termed endless. Local cults would ever tend to increase with the rise of new towns, and while the deities thus worshipped would not rise to any or much importance, still their names would become known in larger circles, and a ruler might, for the sake of increasing his own lustre, make mention of one or more of them, honoring them at the same time by an epithet which might or might not accurately define their character. As long as the various districts of Babylonia were not formally united under one head, various local cults might rise to equally large proportions, while the gods worshipped as the special patrons of the great centers, as Lagash, Ur, Uruk, Nippur, and the like, would retain their prominence, even though the political status of the cities sacred to them

[1] Quite recently there have been found at Telloh some thirty thousand clay tablets, chiefly lists of sacrifices, temple inventories, and legal documents. These tablets will probably furnish additional names of deities, and perhaps throw further light on those known. Further excavations at Nippur will likewise add to the material. But after all, for our main purpose in this chapter, which is the illustration of the chief traits of the Babylonian pantheon in early days, these expected additions to the pantheon will not be of paramount significance.

suffered a decline. The ruler of the district that claimed a supremacy over one that formerly occupied an independent position, would hasten to emphasize this control by proudly claiming the patron deity as part of his pantheon. The popularity of Sin at Ur suffered no diminution because the supremacy of Ur yielded to that of Uruk. On the contrary, the god gained new friends who strove to rival the old ones in manifestations of reverence; and when, as happened in several instances, the patron deities were personifications of natural phenomena, whose worship through various circumstances became associated with particular localities, there was an additional reason for the survival, and, indeed, growing importance of such local cults, quite independent of the political fortunes that befell the cities in which the gods were supposed to dwell.

As a consequence, there are a considerable number of deities who are met with both at the beginning and at the end of the first period of Babylonian history — a period, be it remembered, that, so far as known, already covers a distance of 2,000 years. These are of two classes, (*a*) deities of purely local origin, surviving through the historical significance of the places where they were worshipped, and (*b*) deities, at once local in so far as they are associated with a fixed spot, but at the same time having a far more general character by virtue of being personifications of the powers of nature. The jurisdiction of both classes of deities might, through political vicissitudes, be extended over a larger district than the one to which they were originally confined, and in so far their local character would tend to be obscured. It would depend, however, upon other factors, besides the merely political ones, whether these cults would take a sufficiently deep hold upon the people to lead to the evolution of deities, entirely dissociated from fixed seats, who might be worshipped anywhere, and whose attributes would tend to become more and more abstract in character. Such a process, however, could not be completed by the silent working of what, for want of a better name, we call the genius of the people. It requires the assistance, conscious and in a measure pedantic, of the thinkers and spiritual guides of a people. In other words, the advance in religious conceptions from the point at which we find them when the union of the Babylonian states takes place, is conditioned upon the infusion of the theological spirit into the mass of beliefs that constituted the ancient heritage of the people.

On the other hand, various circumstances have already been suggested that coöperated, already prior to the days of Hammurabi, in weeding out the superfluity of deities, at least so far as recognition of them in the official inscriptions of the rulers were concerned. Deities, attached to places of small and ever-diminishing importance would, after being at first adopted into the pantheon by some ruler desirous of emphasizing his control over the town in question, end in being entirely absorbed by some more powerful god, whose attributes were similar to those of his minor companion. Especially would this be the case with deities conceived as granting assistance in warfare. The glory of the smaller warrior gods would fade through the success achieved by a Nin-girsu. The names and epithets would be transferred to the more powerful god, and, beyond an occasional mention, the weaker would entirely pass out of consideration. Again, the worship of the moon or of the sun, or of certain aspects of the sun, — the morning sun, the noonday sun, and the like, — at localities of minor importance, would yield to the growing popularity of similar worship in important centers. As a consequence, names that formerly designated distinct deities or different phases of one and the same deity, would, by being transferred to a single one, come to be mere epithets of this one. The various names would be used interchangeably, without much regard to their original force.

All the essential elements of the Babylonian religion are already to be found in the conditions prevailing during the period that we have been considering. Some new deities are met with in the periods that followed, but there is no reason to believe that any profound changes in the manner of worship, or in the conceptions regarding the gods, were introduced. The relations, however, which the gods bear to one another are considerably modified, their attributes become more sharply defined, the duties and privileges pertaining to each are regulated. Hand in hand with this systematization, the organization of the cult becomes more perfect, the ritual enters upon further phases of development, speculations regarding the unknown have their outcome in the establishment of dogmas. Finally the past, with its traditions and legends, is viewed under the aspect of later religious thought. The products of popular fancy are reshaped, given a literary turn that was originally foreign to them, and so combined and imbued with a meaning as to reflect the thoughts and aspirations of a comparatively advanced age. What may be called the flowering of the theological epoch in the history of the Babylonian religion, viewed as a unit, is so directly dependent upon the political union of the Babylonian states, brought about by Hammurabi (*c.* 2300 B.C.), that it may be said to date from this event.

CHAPTER VIII.

THE PANTHEON IN THE DAYS OF HAMMURABI.

MARDUK.

THE immediate result of Hammurabi's master-stroke in bringing the various states of the Euphrates Valley under a single control, was the supremacy secured for his capital, of the city of Babylon over all other Babylonian cities, and with this supremacy, the superior position henceforth assumed by the patron deity of the capital, Marduk.[1] It is needless for our purposes to enter upon the question as to the age of the city of Babylon,[2] nor as to its political fortunes prior to the rise of the dynasty of which Hammurabi was the sixth member. That its beginnings were modest, and that its importance, if not its origin, was of recent date in comparison with such places as Eridu, Nippur, Lagash, Ur, and the like, is proved by the absence of the god Marduk in any of the inscriptions that we have been considering up to this point. The first mention of the god occurs in the inscriptions of Hammurabi, where he appears distinctly as the god of the city of Babylon. No doubt the immediate predecessors of Hammurabi regarded Marduk in

[1] The name is also written Ma-ru-duk, which points to its having been regarded (for which there is other evidence) as a compound of *maru*, 'son,' and an element, *duk(u)*, which in religious and other texts designates the 'glorious chamber' in which the god determines the fate of humanity. Such an 'etymology' is, however, merely a play upon the name, similar to the plays upon proper names found in the Old Testament. The real etymology is unknown. The form Marduk is Semitic, and points to an underlying stem, *rdk*. Marduk appears under a variety of names which will be taken up at their proper place. See Schrader's *Assyrisch-Babyl. Keilschriften*, p. 129; and the same author's *Cuneiform Inscrip. and the O. T.* (p. 422) for other etymologies.

[2] Hommel's view that Gish-galla, in Gudea's inscriptions, is Babylon lacks convincing evidence, but the city may be as old as Gudea's days for all that.

the same light as the great conqueror, so that we are justified in applying the data, furnished by the inscriptions of Hammurabi to such of his predecessors, of whom records are still lacking. It is to Marduk, that Hammurabi ascribes his success. The king regards himself as the beloved of Marduk. The god rejoices his heart and gives him power and plenty. Even when paying his homage at the shrines of other deities, he does not forget to couple the name of Marduk with that of the deity whose protection he invokes. So at Sippar, sacred to Shamash, and where the king deposits a cylinder recording the improvements that he instigated in the city, he associates the sun-god with Marduk, whereas in contradistinction to the rulers of the old Babylonian cities or states, when addressing Marduk, he does not find it necessary to make mention at the same time of an entire pantheon. Marduk's protection suffices for all purposes. This, of course, does not exclude the worship of other gods. A reference has already been made to the king's care for the city of Shamash. In this respect, he was but following the example of his predecessors, who, while regarding Babylon as their capital, were zealous in doing honor to ancient centers of worship. So one of these predecessors, Zabu, restores the temple of Shamash at Sippar, and that of Anunit at Agade. Hammurabi, besides his work at Sippar, builds a temple to Innanna at Hallabi.[1] Babylon, however, is the beloved city of Marduk, and upon its beautification and improvement Hammurabi expends his chief energy. Such are the endearing terms in which he speaks of his god, as to give one the impression that, when thinking of Marduk, the king for the moment loses sight of the existence of other gods. The most striking tribute, however, that is paid to Marduk in the period of Hammurabi is his gradual assumption of the rôle played by the old En-lil or Bel of Nippur, once the head of the Babylonian pantheon. This identification is

---

[1] Near Sippar.

already foreshadowed in the title *bêlu rabu*, *i.e.*, 'great lord,' which Hammurabi is fond of bestowing upon Marduk. It is more clearly indicated in an inscription of his son, Samsu-iluna, who represents Bel, 'the king of heaven and earth,' as transferring to Marduk, the 'first-born son of Ea,' rulership over 'the four regions,' — a phrase that at this time had already assumed a much wider meaning than its original portent. In the religious literature of this age, which reflects the same tendency, Bel expressly transfers his title 'lord of the lands'[1] to Marduk, while Ea likewise pays homage to his son, declaring that the latter's 'name' shall also be Ea. The transference of the name, according to Babylonian notions, is equivalent to a transference of power. As a consequence, Bel and Marduk are blended into one personage, Marduk becoming known as Bel-Marduk, and finally, the first part of the compound sinking to the level of a mere adjective, the god is addressed as 'lord Marduk,' or 'Marduk, the lord.' The old Bel is entirely forgotten, or survives at best in conventional association with Anu and Ea, as a member of the ancient triad.

It has been satisfactorily shown[2] that Marduk was originally a solar deity. His association with Babylon, therefore, must be viewed in the same light as the association of Sin, the moon-god, with the city of Ur, and the association of Shamash, the sun-god, with Larsa and Sippar. Just as in the latter places, other cults besides that of the patron deity prevailed, so in Babylon it was merely the prominence which, for some reason, the worship of the sun-god acquired, that led to the closer identification of this particular deity with the city, until he became viewed as the god *par excellence* of the city, and the city itself as his favorite residence. As long as Larsa and Sippar retained a prominence overshadowing that of Babylon,

---

[1] *Bêl matâti*.
[2] Sayce, *Religion of the Ancient Babylonians*, pp. 98 *seq.*; Jensen, *Kosmologie der Babylonier*, p. 88.

the sun cult at the latter place could attract but little attention. Only as Babylon began to rival, and finally to supersede, other centers of sun-worship, could Marduk be brought into the front rank of prevailing cults. It may appear strange, in view of this original character of Marduk, that neither in the inscriptions of Hammurabi, nor in those of his successors, is there any direct reference to his qualities as a solar deity. However, in the ideographs composing his name, which are to be interpreted as 'child of the day,'[1] and in the zodiacal system, as perfected by the Babylonian scholars, there lurk traces of the god's solar origin, and beyond this, perhaps, in certain set phrases, surviving in prayers addressed to him. The explanation for this absence of solar traits is to be sought in the peculiar political conditions that resulted in bringing Marduk into such prominence. Hammurabi was preëminently a conquering king. He waged war on all sides, and carried on his campaigns for many years. When he finally succeeded in bringing both North and South Babylonia under his sway, it still required constant watching to keep his empire together. His patron god, therefore, the protector of the city, whose jurisdiction was thus spread over a larger extent of territory than that of any other deity, must have appeared to Hammurabi and his followers, as well as to those vanquished by him, essentially as a warrior. It is he who hands over to kings the land and its inhabitants. The fact that he was a solar deity would become obscured by the side of the more potent fact that, as god of the city of Babylon, his sway was supreme. He therefore became Marduk, the 'great lord.' The epithets bestowed upon him naturally emphasized the manner in which he manifested himself, and these epithets, therefore, referred to his power, to his supremacy over other gods, to his favor shown to his worship-

---

[1] So Delitzsch, *Beiträge zur Assyriologie*, ii. 623. The first part of the name is also used to designate the 'young bullock,' and it is possible, therefore, that the god was pictured in this way, as both Anu and Sin are occasionally called 'bulls.'

pers by granting them unprecedented glory; and since the political supremacy remained undisputed for many centuries, no opportunity was afforded for ever reverting to the attributes of the god as a solar deity. He remained — if one may so express it — a political deity. The political significance of Babylon permitted only one phase of his nature to be brought forward.

In the religious texts, however, preserving as they do the more primitive conceptions by the side of the most advanced ones, some traces of other attributes besides prowess in war are found. By virtue of his character as a solar deity, Marduk, like the orb personified through him, is essentially a life-giving god. Whereas Shamash is viewed as the 'judge of mankind,' Marduk becomes the god who restores the dead to life, though he shares this power with Shamash, Gula, Nebo, and Nergal. But after all, even in the religious texts, his more prominent rôle is that of a ruler, — a magnified king. He protects the weak, releases the imprisoned, and makes great the small. He controls by his powerful hand the mountains and rivers and fountains. He is the counsellor who guides the decrees, even of the great gods, Anu and Bel. On his head rests a crown with high horns, as the symbol of rulership. As the supreme ruler, life and death are in his hands. Blessings flow from him; and of awe-inspiring appearance, his wrath inflicts severe punishment on the evil-doer.

It is a noteworthy circumstance, and characteristic of the phase of the Babylonian religion which we are considering, that the extension of Marduk's political sway did not lead to the establishment of Marduk cults outside of Babylon. One reason for this was that, in accordance with the political conceptions, dwelt upon in the introductory chapter, the empire of Babylonia was regarded simply as an extension of the city of Babylon. Babylonia, therefore, being identified in theory with the city of Babylon, there was no need of emphasizing the power of Marduk by establishing his cult elsewhere. Within the limits of Babylon, however, there might be more than one shrine to Marduk, and accordingly, when the city was extended so as to include the place known as Borsippa, a temple to Marduk was also erected there. The temple on the east side of the Euphrates, known as E-Sagila, 'the lofty house,' was the older, and dates probably from the beginnings of Babylon itself; that in Borsippa, known as E-Zida, 'the true house,' seems to have been founded by Hammurabi.[1] While it was not in accord with the dignity attaching to Marduk that his cult should be established outside of the precincts of the city of Babylon, it would only add to his glory to have the worship of other deities grouped around his own sanctuary. Such a course would emphasize the central position of Marduk among the gods, and accordingly, we find that the chief gods of Babylonia are represented by shrines within the sacred precincts of his great temples at Babylon and Borsippa. First among these shrines is that of Marduk's consort,

SARPANITUM.

Neither Hammurabi nor his immediate successor make mention of Sarpanitum, and at no time does she appear independently of Marduk. The glory of Marduk did not permit of any rival, and so his consort becomes merely his shadow,— less significant than most of the consorts of the male deities. Her name, signifying the 'silvery bright one,' evidently stands in some connection with the solar character of her consort. Popular etymology, by a play upon the name, made of Sarpanitum (as though Zer-banit) the 'offspring-producing' goddess. She had her shrine within the precincts of the great temple E-Sagila, but we are not told of any special honors being paid her, nor do we find her invoked to any extent in incantations or in votive inscriptions. Agumkakrimi, or Agum (as he is also called),

[1] Louvre Inscription II, col. ii. ll. 12-17.

who rules about five centuries after Hammurabi, speaks of having recovered the image of Sarpanitum, and that of Marduk, out of the hands of a mountainous people living to the northwest of Babylonia, in the district between the Bay of Iskenderun and the Euphrates. The capture of the statues of the patron gods points to a great humiliation which Babylon must have encountered. Upon receiving a favorable omen from the sungod, Agum undertakes the task of bringing Marduk and Sarpanitum back to their seats. Their temples, too, at Babylon appear to have suffered damage during the invasion of the city, and accordingly the statues are placed in the temple of Shamash pending the restoration of E-Sagila. Agum dwells at length upon the handsome garments and head-dress, studded with precious stones, that he prepared for the god and his consort. In all this description, one feels that it is Marduk for whom the honors are intended, and that Sarpanitum is of less than secondary importance, — shining merely by the reflected glory of her great liege, whose presence in Babylon was essential to a restoration of Babylon's position.

There are reasons for believing, however, that Sarpanitum once enjoyed considerable importance of her own, that prior to the rise of Marduk to his supreme position, a goddess was worshipped in Babylon, one of whose special functions it was to protect the progeny while still in the mother's womb. A late king of Babylon, the great Nebuchadnezzar, appeals to this attribute of the goddess. To her was also attributed the possession of knowledge concealed from men. Exactly to what class of deities she belonged, we are no longer able to say, but it is certain that at some time, probably about the time of Hammurabi, an amalgamation took place between her and another goddess known as Erua,[1] — a name that etymologically suggests the idea

---

[1] There is also a goddess *Eria* worshipped in Elam, who may be identical with Erua. The scribes in the days of Nebuchadnezzar (*c.* 1140 B.C.), at least, appear to have thought so, for they associate her with Bel, just as Sarpanitum is associated with Bel-Marduk. (See the Inscription V R. 57, col. ii. ll. 11, 12.)

of 'begetting.'[1] She is represented as dwelling in the temple of E-Zida at Borsippa, and was originally the consort of Nabu, the chief god of this place.[2] A late ruler of Babylon — Shamash-shumukin — calls her the queen of the gods, and declares himself to have been nominated by her to lord it over men.

A factor in this amalgamation of Erua and Sarpanitum was the close association brought about in Babylon between Marduk and a god whose seat was originally at the Persian Gulf — Ea. The cult of this god, as we shall see, survived in Babylonia through all political vicissitudes, and so did that of some other minor water-deities that belong to this region. Among these was Erua, whose worship centered in one of the islands in or near the gulf. Wisdom and the life-giving principle were two ideas associated in the Babylonian mind with water. As inferior in power to Ea, Erua appears to have been regarded as the daughter of Ea, and such was the sway exercised by Ea over men's minds, that even the Babylonian schoolmen did not venture to place Marduk over Ea, but pictured him as Ea's son. Erua, however, was not prominent enough to become Marduk's mother, and so she was regarded as his consort. In this capacity she was associated with Sarpanitum, and the two were merged into one personality. It rarely happens that all the links in such a process are preserved, but in this case, the epithets borne by Sarpanitum-Erua, such as 'lady of the deep,' 'mistress of the place where the fish dwell,' 'voice of the deep,' point the way towards the solution of the problem involved in the amalgamation of Erua and Sarpanitum.[3]

---

[1] Whether, however, this was the real meaning of the name is doubtful, for the name of the goddess is also written Aru and Arua, which points to a different verbal stem.

[2] See below under Tashmitum.

[3] There are indications also of an arrested amalgamation of Erua-Sarpanitum with Tashmitum, the wife of Nabu. (See Sayce, *Hibbert Lectures*, p. 112.)

NABU.

The god Nabu (or Nebo) enjoys a great popularity in the Babylonian cult, but he owes his prestige to the accident that, as god of Borsippa, he was associated with Marduk. Indeed, his case is a clear instance of the manner in which Marduk overshadows all his fellows. Only as they are brought into some manner of relationship with him do they secure a position in the pantheon during this second period of Babylonian history. Since Nabu's position in the pantheon, once established, incurs but little change, it will be proper, in treating of him, to include the testimony furnished by the historical records of the Assyrian kings. The most prominent attribute of Nabu, at least in the later phases of the Babylonian religion, is that of wisdom. He is the wise, the all-knowing. He embodies in his person all the wisdom of the gods. To him the Assyrian kings are particularly fond of ascribing, not merely the understanding that they possess, but the thought of preserving the wisdom of the past for future ages; and in doing this the Assyrians were but guided by examples furnished by the south. Wisdom being associated, in the minds of the Babylonians, with the watery deep, one is tempted to seek an aqueous origin for Nabu. Such a supposition, although it cannot be positively established, has much in its favor. It is not necessary, in order to maintain this proposition, to remove Nabu from Borsippa. The alluvial deposits made by the Euphrates yearly have already demonstrated that Babylon lay much nearer at one time to the Persian Gulf than it does at present. The original seat of Ea, whose worship continued through all times to enjoy great popularity at Babylon, was at Eridu, which, we know, once lay on the Persian Gulf, but does so no longer. The similarity of the epithets bestowed in various texts upon Ea and Nabu point most decidedly to a similar starting-point for both; and since in a syllabary[1] we find the god actually identi-

[1] Rawlinson, ii. 60, 30.

fied with a deity of Dilmun, — probably one of the islands near Bahrein, — there are grounds for assuming that a tradition survived among the schoolmen, which brought Nabu into some connection with the Persian Gulf. Sayce[1] has already suggested that Borsippa may have originally stood on an inlet of the Persian Gulf. Nabu is inferior to Ea, and were it not for the priority of Marduk, he would have become in Babylonian theology, the son of Ea. Since this distinction[2] is given to Marduk, no direct indication of an original relationship to Ea has survived.

But besides being the god of wisdom and intelligence, Nabu is a patron of agriculture, who causes the grain to sprout forth. In religious and historical texts, he is lauded as the deity who opens up the subterranean sources in order to irrigate the fields. He heaps up the grain in the storehouses, and on the other hand, the withdrawal of his favor is followed by famine and distress. Jensen[3] would conclude from this that he was originally (like Marduk, therefore) a solar deity. This, however, is hardly justified, since it is just as reasonable to deduce his rôle as the producer of fertility from his powers as lord of some body of water. However this may be, in the case of Nabu, there are no grounds for supposing that he represents the combination of two originally distinct deities. A later — chiefly theoretical — amalgamation of Nabu with a god Nusku will be discussed in a subsequent chapter.[4] Hammurabi and his immediate successors, it is noteworthy, do not make mention of Nabu. A sufficient number of inscriptions of this period exists to make it probable that this omission is not accidental. This dynasty was chiefly concerned in firmly establishing the position of Marduk. Other deities could, indeed, be tolerated at his side, provided they were subservient to him; but Nabu, the god of a place so near Babylon, might prove a dangerous rival because

[1] *Hibbert Lectures*, p. 117.
[2] See further on, *sub* Ea.
[3] *Kosmologie*, p. 239.
[4] *Sub* Nusku, chapter xiii.

of this proximity. The city on the west bank of the Euphrates was probably as old as that on the east, if not, indeed, older. It did not seem consistent with this devotion to Marduk that Hammurabi and his successors should also recognize Nabu. Policy dictated that Nabu should be ignored, that the attempt must be made to replace his worship, even in Borsippa, by that of Marduk. Viewed in this light, Hammurabi's establishment of the Marduk cult in Borsippa assumes a peculiar significance. It meant that Borsippa was to be incorporated as part of Babylon, and that Marduk was henceforth to take the place occupied by Nabu. In order to emphasize this, Hammurabi actually transfers the name of Nabu's temple in Borsippa, E-Zida, to the one erected by him at that place to Marduk. Did he perhaps entirely suppress the worship of Nabu at Borsippa? It would almost appear so from Agum's utter omission of Nabu. Only the statues of Marduk and Sarpanitum seem to have been robbed by the Hani. Not a word is said as to Nabu. Either there was no statue at the time at Borsippa, or the cult was of such insignificance that the capture of the god was not considered of sufficient moment to occupy the thoughts of the enemy, as little as it did that of the rulers of Babylon at the time. In the inscription in which Hammurabi recounts the building of E-Zida in Borsippa, there are certain expressions which go to substantiate the proposition that Nabu is intentionally ignored.[1] He calls Marduk the lord of E-Sagila and of E-Zida; he speaks of Borsippa as the beloved city of Marduk, just as though it were Babylon. Taking unto himself the functions of Nabu, he even appears to play upon the name, which signifies 'pro-

---

[1] Tiele, *Geschichte d. Religion i. Alterthum*, i. 171 and 188, is of the opinion that Nabu is a late deity whose worship dates from a period considerably subsequent to Hammurabi. This conclusion from the non-occurrence of the god in early inscriptions is not justified. There is no reason why Nabu should have been added as a deity in later times, and in general we must be on our guard against assuming new deities subsequent to Hammurabi. It is much more plausible to assume the restored popularity of very old ones.

claimer,' and styles himself the *nabiu Anu*, 'the proclaimer of Anu.' However this may be, the attempt to suppress Nabu did not succeed,—a proof that in early times he had gained popular favor. He had to be readmitted into the Babylonian pantheon, though in a subordinate position to Marduk. He took his place in the theological system as the son of Marduk, and on the great festival—the New Year's day—celebrated in honor of the great god of Babylon, the son shared some of the honors accorded to the father. In time, his sanctuary at Borsippa was again recognized. The former rivalry gave way to a cordial *entente*. Nabu was even granted a chapel in E-Sagila at Babylon, to which likewise the name of E-Zida was given. Every New Year's day the son paid a visit to his father, on which occasion the statue of Nabu was carried in solemn procession from Borsippa across the river, and along the main street of Babylon leading to the temple of Marduk; and in return the father deity accompanied his son part way on the trip back to E-Zida. In this way, due homage was accorded to Marduk, and at the same time the close and cordial bonds of union between Babylon and Borsippa found satisfactory illustration. E-Sagila and E-Zida become, and remain throughout the duration of the Babylonian religion, the central sanctuaries of the land around which the most precious recollections cluster, as dear to the Assyrians as to the Babylonians. The kings of the northern empire vie with their southern cousins in beautifying and enlarging the structures sacred to Marduk and Nabu.

In view of the explanation offered for the silence maintained by Hammurabi and his successors regarding Nabu, we are justified in including Nabu in the Babylonian pantheon of those days. In later times, among the Assyrians, the Nabu cult, as already intimated, grows in popularity. The northern monarchs, in fact, seem to give Nabu the preference over Marduk. They do not tire of proclaiming him as the source of wisdom. The staff is his symbol, which is interpreted in a double sense, as the writer's stylus and as the ruler's sceptre. He becomes, also, the bestower of royal power upon his favorites. Without his aid, order cannot be maintained in the land. Disobedience to him is punished by the introduction of foreign rule. Political policy may have had a share in this preference shown for the minor god of Babylon. The Assyrian kings were always anxious to do homage to the gods of Babylon, in order to indicate their control over the southern districts. They were particularly proud of their title 'governor of Bel.'[1] On the other hand, they were careful not to give offence to the chief of the Assyrian pantheon, — the god Ashur, — by paying too much honor to Marduk, who was in a measure Ashur's rival. In consequence, as Hammurabi and his successors endeavored to ignore Nabu, the Assyrian rulers now turned the tables by manifesting a preference for Nabu; and obliged as they were to acknowledge that the intellectual impulses came from the south, they could accept a southern god of wisdom without encroaching upon the province of Ashur, whose claims to homage lay in the prowess he showed in war. Marduk was too much like Ashur to find a place at his side. Nabu was a totally different deity, and in worshipping him who was the son of Marduk, the Assyrian kings felt that they were paying due regard to the feelings of their Babylonian subjects. The cult of Nabu thus became widely extended in Assyria. Statues of the god were erected and deposited in shrines built for the purpose, although the fact was not lost sight of that the real dwelling-place of the god was in Borsippa. At the end of the ninth century B.C. this cult seems to have reached its height. We learn of a temple at Calah, and of no less than eight statues of the god being erected in the days of Ramman-nirari III., and the terms in which the god is addressed might lead one to believe that an attempt was made to concentrate the

---

[1] Bel being Marduk, the title was equivalent to that of 'governor of Babylonia.'

cult in Assyria on him.[1] This, however, was an impossibility. As long as Assyria continued to play the rôle of the subduer of nations, Ashur — the god of war *par excellence* — necessarily retained his position at the head of the Assyrian pantheon. The popularity of Nabu, which continued to the end of the Assyrian empire, and gained a fresh impetus in the days of Ashurbanabal, who, as a patron of literature, invokes Nabu on thousands of the tablets of his library as 'the opener of ears to understanding,' reacted on his position in the Babylonian cult. In the new Babylonian empire, which continued to so large a degree the traditions of Assyria, it is no accident that three of the kings — Nabupolassar, Nebuchadnezzar, and Nabonnedos — bear names containing the deity as one of the elements. While paying superior devotion to Marduk, who once more became the real and not merely the nominal head of the pantheon, they must have held Nabu in no small esteem; and indeed the last-named king was suspected of trying actually to divert the homage of the people away from Marduk to other gods, though he did not, as a matter of course, go so far as to endeavor to usurp for the son, the position held by the father. It is probably due to Assyrian influence that even in Babylonia, from the eighth century on, Nabu is occasionally mentioned before Marduk. So Marduk-baladan II. (721–710) calls himself the "worshipper of Nabu and Marduk," and similarly others. In official letters likewise, and in astronomical reports, Nabu is given precedence to Marduk, but this may be due to Nabu's functions, as the god of writing and the patron of science.

The Neo-Babylonian kings are not sparing in the epithets they bestow on Nabu, though they emphasize more his qualities as holder of the 'sceptre' than as lord of the 'stylus.' So Nebuchadnezzar declares that it is he 'who gives the sceptre of sovereignty to kings to rule over all lands.' In this capacity

---

[1] So, Tiele, *Geschichte d. Religion i. Alterthum*, i. 191.

he is 'the upholder of the world,' 'the general overseer,' and his temple is called 'the house of the sceptre of the world.'

His name signifies simply the 'proclaimer,' or herald, but we are left in doubt as to what he proclaims, — whether wisdom or sovereignty. Sometimes he appears as the 'herald' of the gods. In this rôle he receives the name of Papsukal (*i.e.*, supreme or sacred messenger), and it may be that this function was a very old one. But, again, as god of fertility he could also be appropriately termed the 'proclaimer.' The question must, accordingly, be left open as to the precise force of the attribute contained in his name. Finally, an interesting feature connected with Nabu, that may be mentioned here, is that in the name borne by a famous mountain in Moab, Nebo, where Moses — himself a 'proclaimer'[1] — died, there survives a testimony that the worship of this popular deity extended beyond the Euphrates and the Tigris, to Semites living considerably to the west. To Nabu, as to Marduk, a consort was given. Her name was

Tashmitum.

The name Tashmitum appears for the first time in the days of Hammurabi. Attention has already been called to the king's ignoring of the god of Borsippa. While his attempt to suppress the cult of Nabu was not successful, he did succeed in causing the old consort of Nabu to disappear. This consort appears to have been no other than Erua. It will be recalled that up to very late times the tradition survived that her dwelling-place was Borsippa.[2] This is never said of Sarpanitum. Despite, therefore, the amalgamation of Sarpanitum and Erua, the association of the latter with Nabu's dwelling-place remains

---

[1] The Hebrew word for prophet, *nabi*, is of the same stem as the Assyrian Nabu, and the popular tradition in placing the last scene in the life of Moses on Mt. Nebo is apparently influenced by the fact that Moses was a *nabi*.

[2] See above, p. 123.

impressed upon the memory of the Babylonian scholars, at least. Nabu's consort having thus been transferred to Marduk, a new mate had to be found for the former, when once his rivalry was no longer to be dreaded, and his cult again rose to prominence. 'Tashmitum' is an abstract noun in Assyrian, signifying 'revelation.' As such, it is bestowed in historical texts upon Nabu himself, who is called *ilu tashmêti*, 'god of revelation.' Nabu is, above all, a 'revealing' god, — revealing knowledge, the art of writing, and the method of ruling. The appellation is therefore a most appropriate one, and there seems little reason to question that Tashmitum was originally nothing but one of the terms by which Nabu was designated, just as he was called Papsukal in his rôle as 'messenger' of the gods, — the messenger of his father Marduk and of his grandfather Ea, in particular. But Tashmitum, being feminine in gender, as an abstract noun, seemed appropriate as the designation of a goddess. It would appear, then, that 'Revelation,' from being so constantly associated with Nabu, was personified, dissociated from him, as it were, through the conception of a distinct goddess bearing the name of 'Tashmitum.' This process of thought, in giving rise to a new goddess, may have been, in part, a popular one. The translation of a metaphor into reality is a phenomenon that may be observed in almost all religions of antiquity. But the process, whatever its course in detail may have been, was not uninfluenced by the theological dogma whereby a god was supposed to have a 'reflection' who was pictured as his consort. Through this conception, as we have already seen, many a goddess once ruling in her own right, and enjoying an independent existence, degenerated into a mere shadow of some male deity, though, on the other hand, it must be borne in mind that these female deities would have disappeared altogether but for the opportunity thus afforded them of becoming 'attachées' to some male deity. This theory of the *quasi*-artificial character and origin of Tashmit finds support in the manner in which the mention of her name is entwined with that of Nabu. Sarpanitum, bound up as the goddess is with Marduk, has at least a shrine of her own, and occasionally she is spoken of in the texts without her husband Marduk.[1] The mention of Tashmitum, however, invariably follows that of Nabu. It is always 'Nabu and Tashmitum,' and it is never Tashmitum without Nabu. While the creation of Tashmitum may be a product of Babylonian religious thought, it is in Assyrian texts that her name is chiefly found. The great Ashurbanabal, in the conventional subscript attached to his tablet, is particularly fond of coupling Tashmitum with Nabu, as the two deities who opened his ears to understanding and prompted him to gather in his palace the literary treasures produced by the culture that flourished in the south. Tashmit has no shrine or temple, so far as known, either in Borsippa or in any of the places whither the Nabu cult spread. She has no attributes other than those that belong to Nabu, and, what is very remarkable, the later Babylonian kings, such as Nebuchadnezzar II., when they deem it proper to attach a consort to Nabu call her Nanâ,[2] *i.e.*, simply the lady, and not Tashmitum, a proof, how little hold the name had taken upon the Babylonian populace. If to this it be added, that in by far the greater number of instances, no reference whatsoever to a consort is made when Nabu is spoken of, an additional reason is found for the unreal, the shadowy character of this goddess.

Ea.

In treating of the position occupied by Ea in the oldest period of Babylonian history (see above, pp. 61–64), it has already been mentioned that he grows to much larger proportions under the influence of a more fully developed theological system. Indeed, there is no god who shows such profound

---

[1] So in the cylinder of Shamash-shum-ukin (Lehmann's publication, pls. viii. *seq.*).
[2] *E.g.*, in the so-called Grotefend Cylinder, col. ii. 34.

traces of having been submitted to a theological treatment, and indirectly, therefore, furnishes so distinct a proof of the existence of theological schools in the ancient centers of Babylonian culture, as Ea. The question may with propriety be here discussed, to what period we are to attribute the completion of the process, which, to summarize his position, made Ea the special god of humanity, the father of Marduk, the third in a great triad, of which the other two members were Anu, the god of heaven, and Bel, the god of earth. Already, in the days preceding the union of the Babylonian states under one head, we have had occasion to see traces of an attempt to systematize the relations existing between the gods. A high degree of culture, such as the existence of a perfected form of writing, an advanced form of architecture, and commercial enterprise reflect, cannot be dissociated from a high degree of activity in the domain of philosophic or religious thought. Accordingly, we are in no danger of attributing too great an antiquity to the beginnings of theological speculation in Babylonia. Be it remembered that from the earliest to the latest days, the priests were the scribes and that in their capacity as writers of the texts, they would be enjoying the advantages of an intellectual impulse. But they were also the composers of the texts, as well as the writers, and the prominence given to the gods in texts of whatever description, would inevitably lead their thoughts to speculations regarding the attributes of the gods. The attempt would at an early period be made to find some unifying principles in the tangled mass of gods. By the time that Hammurabi appears on the scene, we have every reason to believe that some of the ancient libraries of the south, whither Ashurbanabal sent his scribes, were already well stocked, and that a goodly portion of the Babylonian literature known to us already existed. What these portions were, we will have occasion to point out when we come to discuss the literature of Babylonia. On the other hand, this literature would not only necessarily increase as long as any degree of intellectual activity existed in the country, but this activity would also manifest itself in transforming this literature, so as to adapt it to the thoughts and aspirations of a later age. Especially would this be the case in the purely religious divisions of literature. The ancient traditions, legends, and myths, once committed to writing, would serve as a point of departure for further speculations. The existence of a text to which any measure of value is attached, is bound to give rise to various attempts at interpretation, and if this value be connected with the religion of a people, the result is, invariably, that the ancient words are invested with a meaning conformable to a later age. Each generation among a people characterized by intellectual activity has a signature of its own, and it will seek to give to the religious thoughts of the time its own particular impress. Since, however, the material upon which any age works is not of its own making, but is furnished by a preceding one, it follows that much of the intellectual activity of an age manifests itself in a transformation of its literary or speculative heritage. This process was constantly going on in Babylonia, and had we more material — and older material — at our disposal, we would be able to trace more clearly than we can at present, the various stages that led to the system of theology, as embodied in the best productions of the ancient Babylonian schoolmen.

The days of Hammurabi, as they were politically of great importance, also appear to have ushered in a new era in the religious life of the people. Stirring political events are always apt to bring in their wake intellectual movements, and in a country like Babylonia, where politics react so forcibly on religious conditions, the permanent establishment of the supremacy of the city of Babylon would be fraught with important consequences for the cult. The main change brought about by this new epoch of Babylonian history was, as we have seen, the superior position henceforth accorded in the pantheon to Marduk as the patron deity of Babylon; but this change entailed so many others, that it almost merits being termed a revolution. In order to ensure Marduk's place, the relations of the other deities to him had to be regulated, the legends and traditions of the past reshaped, so as to be brought into consistent accord with the new order of things, and the cult likewise to be, at least in part, remodelled, so as to emphasize the supremacy of Marduk. This work, which was an inevitable one, was primarily of an intellectual order. We are justified, then, in looking for traces of this activity in the remains that have been recovered of ancient Babylonian literature. We know from direct evidence that the commercial life of Babylonia had already, in the period preceding Hammurabi, led to regulated legal forms and practices for the purpose of carrying out obligations and of settling commercial and legal difficulties. The proof has been furnished by Dr. Meissner[1] that syllabaries prepared for the better understanding of the formulas and words employed in preparing the legal and commercial tablets, date, in part, from the period which we may roughly designate as that of Hammurabi, — covering, say, the three centuries 2300 to 2000 B.C. With this evidence for the existence of pedagogues devoted to the training of novices in the art of reading and writing, in order to fit them for their future tasks as official scribes, we are safe in assuming that these same schoolmen were no less active in other fields of literature. If, in addition to this, we find that much of the religious literature, in the shape that we have it, reflects the religious conditions such as they must have shaped themselves in consequence of the promotion of Marduk to the head of the pantheon, the conclusion is forced upon us that such literary productions date from this same epoch of Hammurabi. This influence of the schoolmen while centering, as repeatedly pointed out, around the position of Marduk, manifests itself in a pro-

[1] *Wiener Zeitschrift für die Kunde d. Morgenlandes*, iv. 301–307.

nounced fashion, also, in the changed position henceforth accorded to the god Ea. It will be recalled that in the earliest period of Babylonian history, Ea does not figure prominently. At the same time we must beware of laying too much stress upon the negative testimony of the historical texts. Besides the still limited material of this character at our disposal, the non-mention of a deity may be due to a variety of circumstances, that may properly be designated as accidental. The gods to whom the kings of the ancient Babylonian states would be apt to appeal would be, in the first instance, the local deities, patrons of the city that happened to be the capital of the state; in the second instance, the gods of the vanquished towns; and thirdly, some of the great deities worshipped at the sacred centers of the Euphrates valley, and who constituted, as it were, the common heritage of the past. Ea, as the god of the Persian gulf, the region which forms the starting-point of Babylonian culture, and around which some of the oldest and most precious recollections center, would come within the radius of the third instance, since, in the period we have in mind, Eridu no longer enjoyed any political importance. We may be sure, then, despite the silence of the texts, that Ea was always held in great esteem, and that even the absence of temples in his honor, did not affect the reverence and awe that he inspired. As for the epoch of Hammurabi, the historical spirit that is never absent in a truly intellectual age would be certain to restore Ea to his proper prestige, assuming that a previous age had permitted him to fall into neglect. Next to Marduk, there is no deity who is given such distinction in Babylonia, after the union of the Babylonian states, as Ea. In the religious literature, moreover, as reshaped by the schoolmen of the time, his rôle is even more prominent than that of Marduk. As a water-god, and more particularly as the god to whom the largest body of water known to the Babylonians was sacred, Ea was regarded as the source and giver of wisdom.

Fountains everywhere were sacred to him; and so he becomes also the giver of fertility and plenty. Berosus tells us of a mystic being, half man, half fish, who spent his nights in the waters of the gulf, but who would come out of the waters during the day to give instruction to the people, until that time steeped in ignorance and barbarism. This 'Oannes,' as Berosus is said[1] to have called him, was none other than Ea. As the great benefactor of mankind, it is natural that Ea should have come to be viewed as the god whose special function it is to protect the human race, to advance it in all its good undertakings, to protect it against the evil designs of gods or demons. In this rôle, he appears in the religious literature — in the epics, the cosmogony, and the ritual — of Babylonia. There is no god conceived in so universal a manner as Ea. All local connection with Eridu disappears. He belongs to no particular district. His worship is not limited to any particular spot. All of Babylonia lays claim to him. The ethical import of such a conception is manifestly great, and traces of it are to be found in the religious productions. It impressed upon the Babylonians the common bond uniting all mankind. The cult of Ea must have engendered humane feelings, softening the rivalry existing among the ancient centers of Babylonian power, and leading the people a considerable distance, on the road to the conception of a common humanity. When the gods decide to destroy mankind, it is Ea who intercedes on behalf of humanity; when the demon of disease has entered a human body, it is to Ea that, in the last resort, the appeal is made to free the sufferer from his pain. Ea is the god of the physicians. Nay, more, it is Ea who presided at the birth of humanity, so that

[1] We only know the name through Eusebius' extract from Alexander Polyhistor's digest of Berosus. The form, therefore, cannot be vouched for. The various modern attempts to explain the name have failed (see *e.g.*, Lenormant's *Magie und Wahrsagekunst der Chaldaer*, 2d German edition, pp. 376–379). There may be some ultimate connection between Oannes and Jonah (see Trumbull in *Journal of Bibl. Liter.* xi. 58, note).

his protection reaches far back, beyond even the beginnings of civilization, almost to the beginning of things. Lastly, as the god of civilization, it is to him that the great works of art are ascribed. He is the god of the smithy, the patron of the gold- and silversmiths, of workers in lapis-lazuli, and all kinds of precious stones. He is the god of sculpture. The great bulls and lions that guarded the approaches to the temple and palace chambers, as well as the statues of the gods and kings, were the work of his hands. Furthermore, he is the patron of weavers, as of other arts. This conception may have been perfected in a general way, and in all probability was perfected before the days of Hammurabi, though perhaps not prominently brought forward; but important modifications were introduced into it, through the compromise that had to be arranged between the position of Ea and that of Marduk. Of course, neither the rulers nor the priests of Babylon could have permitted the reverence for Ea to have gone to the length of throwing Marduk into the shade. Many of the functions assigned to Ea seemed to belong of right to Marduk, who, as the patron of Babylon, presided over the destinies of what to the Babylonians was the essential part of mankind, — namely, themselves. Moreover, Babylon being the seat of culture as well as of power, in the period following upon Hammurabi, Marduk was necessarily conceived as possessing the same wisdom that distinguishes Ea. As a consequence, the attributes of Ea were transferred in a body to Marduk. An amalgamation of the two, however, such as took place in the case of other deities, was neither possible, nor, indeed, desirable. It was not possible, because of the antiquity of the Ea cult and the peculiar position that he, as a common heirloom of all Babylonia, occupied; nor was it desirable, for to do so would be to cut off completely the bond uniting Babylon to its own past and to the rest of Babylonia. The solution of the problem was found in making Ea, the father of Marduk —

the loving and proud father who willingly transfers all his powers and qualities to his son, who rejoices in the triumph of his offspring, and who suffers no pangs of jealousy when beholding the superior honors shown to Marduk, both by the gods and by men.

Ea and Marduk.

The combination of the two gods is particularly frequent in the so-called incantation texts. Marduk becomes the mediator between Ea and mankind. The man smitten with disease, or otherwise in trouble, appeals to Marduk for help, who promptly brings the petition to his father Ea. The latter, after modestly declaring that there is nothing that he knows which his son Marduk does not know, gives Marduk the necessary instructions, which in turn are conveyed to the one crying for divine succor. It is clear that these texts have been reshaped with the intention of adding to the glory of Marduk. They must, therefore, have been remodelled at a time when the Marduk cult was in the ascendancy. This was after the days of Hammurabi, and before the subjugation of Babylonia to Assyrian rule. The limits thus assigned are, to be sure, broad, but from what has above been said as to the intellectual activity reigning in the days of Hammurabi, we need not descend far below the death of the great conqueror to find the starting-point for the remodelling of the texts in question. Not all of them, of course, were so reshaped. There are quite a number in which Ea is alone and directly appealed to, and these form a welcome confirmation of the supposition that those in which Ea is joined to Marduk have been reshaped with a desire to make them conform to the position of Marduk in the Babylonian pantheon. Again, there are incantations in which the name of Marduk appears without Ea. Such are either productions of a later period, of the time when Marduk had already assumed his superior position, or what is also possible, though less probable, old compositions in which the name of Ea has been simply replaced by that of Marduk. An especially interesting example of the manner in which ancient productions have been worked over by the Babylonian theologians, with a view to bringing their favorite Marduk into greater prominence, appears in one of the episodes of the Babylonian cosmogony. Prior to the creation of man a great monster known as Tiamat had to be subdued. The gods all shrink in terror before her. Only one succeeds in conquering her. In the form of the story, as we have it, this hero is Marduk, but it is quite evident[1] that the honor originally belonged to an entirely different god, one who is much older, and who stands much higher than the god of Babylon. This was Bel, — the old god of Nippur who was conceived as the god of earth *par excellence*, and to whom therefore the task of preparing the earth for the habitation of mankind properly belonged. How do the Babylonian theologians, who stand under the influence of the political conditions prevailing in Babylonia after the union of the Babylonian states, reconcile this older and true form of the episode with the form in which they have recast it? The gods who are called the progenitors of Marduk are represented as rejoicing upon seeing Marduk equipped for the fray. In chorus they greet and bless him, "Marduk be king." They present him with additional weapons, and encourage him for the contest. Upon hearing of his success the gods vie with one another in conferring honors upon Marduk. They bestow all manner of glorious epithets upon him; and, to cap the climax, the old Bel, known as 'father Bel,' steps forward and transfers to him his name, *bêl matâti*,[2] 'lord of lands.' To bestow the name was equivalent to transferring Bel's powers to Marduk; and so Marduk is henceforth

---

[1] For fuller proof, see the chapter on "The Cosmology of the Babylonians."

[2] This, it will be remembered (see above, p. 118), is one of the titles of Marduk in one of Hammurabi's inscriptions, — an important point for the date of the episode in its present form.

known as *Bel*. But Ea must be introduced into the episode. It is not sufficient that Bel, the original subduer of Tiamat, should pay homage to Marduk; Ea also greets his son, and bestows his name upon him,[1] — that is, transfers his powers to his son. There is a special reason for this. The overthrow of Tiamat is followed by the creation of man. This function properly belongs to Bel, both as the god of earth and as the subduer of Tiamat. According to one — and probably the oldest — version of this part of the Babylonian cosmogony which was embodied in the work of Berosus,[2] it is Bel who creates mankind. The substitution of Marduk for Bel necessitated the transference of the rôle of creator to Marduk likewise, and yet the latter could not take this upon himself without the consent of his father Ea, who had become the god of humanity *par excellence*. Ea could interpose no objection against Bel being replaced by Marduk in vanquishing the monster, but when it came to drawing the conclusion and replacing Bel by Marduk also in the creation of man, the case was different. If Bel was to be replaced, Ea had a prior claim. Marduk could only take the new functions upon himself after receiving the powers of Ea. That is the force of Ea's saying that Marduk's name also shall be Ea just as his. This transference of the name of Ea to Marduk is in itself an indication that there must have existed a second version in Babylonia — probably of later origin than the other — of the creation of man, according to which Ea, and not Bel, was the creator. We shall have occasion to see, in a future chapter, that there were at least two different versions current in Babylonia of the creation of the gods and of the universe. The opening chapters in Genesis form an interesting parallel to show the manner in which two different versions of one and the same subject may be combined. There is, therefore,

---

[1] Literally, 'Ea shall be his name, his as mine.'

[2] According to Syncellus. In cuneiform texts the old Bel is at times invoked as the creator of mankind.

nothing improbable in the supposition that a later version, reflecting a period when Bel had sunk into comparative insignificance, made Ea the creator of mankind instead of Bel, and that still later a solution of the apparent inconsistency involved in transferring only part of Bel's powers to Marduk was found by securing Ea's consent to the acknowledgment of Marduk not merely as creator of mankind but of the heavenly vault as well. Jensen[1] has brought other evidence to show that Ea was once regarded as the creator of mankind. One of his titles is that of 'potter,' and mankind, according to Babylonian theories, was formed of 'clay.' Moreover, in a Babylonian myth that will be set forth in its proper place, Ea expressly figures in the rôle of creating a mysterious being, *Uddushu-namir*, whose name signifies 'his light shines.' Such a proper name, too, as "Ea-bani," *i.e.*, 'Ea creates,' points in the same direction.

In other literary productions of Babylonia, such as, *e.g.*, the so-called Izdubar epic, Ea again appears without Marduk, showing that this story has not been remodeled, or that the later version, in which the traces of a recasting may have been seen, has not been discovered. In the deluge story, which forms part of the Izdubar epic, Ea alone is the hero. It is he who saves humanity from complete annihilation, and who pacifies the angered Bel. Marduk's name does not appear in the entire epic. We have found it necessary to dwell thus at length upon these evidences of the recasting of the literary products of ancient Babylonia under the influence of changed conceptions of the gods and of their relations to one another, for upon the understanding of these changes, our appreciation of the development of religious beliefs in Babylonia, and all connected with these beliefs, hinges. The epoch of Hammurabi was a crucial one for Babylonia from a religious as well as from a political point of view.

[1] *Kosmologie*, pp. 293, 294.

DAMKINA.

The consort of Ea figures occasionally in the historical texts of Hammurabi's successors. Agumkakrimi invokes Ea and Damkina, asking these gods, who 'dwell in the great ocean' surrounding the earth, to grant him long life. In addition to this, the antiquity of the literary productions in which her name appears justifies us in reckoning her among the gods of Babylonia of Hammurabi's time. Her name signifies 'lady of the earth,' and there is evidently a theoretical substratum to this association of Ea, the water-god, with an earth-goddess. The one forms the complement to the other; and Marduk, as the son of water and earth, takes his place in the theory as the creator of the world. In this form the 'natural philosophy' of Babylonia survived to a late period. Nicolas of Damascus still knows (probably through Berosus) that Ea and Damkina[1] had a son Bel (*i.e.*, Marduk). The survival of the name is a proof that, despite the silence of the historical texts, she was a prominent personage in Babylonian mythology, even though she did not figure largely in the cult. She appears in the magical texts quite frequently at the side of Ea. In a hymn[2] where a description occurs of the boat containing Ea, Damkina his wife, and Marduk their son, together with the ferryman and some other personages sailing across the ocean, we may see traces of the process of symbolization to which the old figures of mythology were subjected.

SHAMASH.

Passing on, we find Hammurabi as strongly attached to the worship of the old sun-god as any of his predecessors. Next to Babylon, he was much concerned with making improvements in Sippar. The Temple of Shamash at Larsa also was

---

[1] *Aos* and *Dauke*.   [2] Rawlinson, iv. 25.

improved and enlarged by him. Hammurabi's example is followed by his successors. Agumkakrimi invokes Shamash as 'warrior of heaven and earth'; and it is likely that the precedent furnished by these two kings, who considered it consistent with devotion to Marduk to single out the places sacred to Shamash for special consideration, had much to do in maintaining the popularity of sun-worship in Babylonia and Assyria. Kara-indash, of the Cassite dynasty (c. 1450 B.C.), restores the temple of Shamash at Larsa, and Mili-shikhu, two centuries later, assigns to Shamash the second place in his pantheon, naming him before Marduk. Foreign rulers were naturally not so deeply attached to Marduk as were the natives of Babylon. In the Assyrian pantheon Shamash occupies the third place, following immediately upon the two special deities of Assyria. One of the greatest of the northern kings erects a temple in honor of the god, and the later Babylonian kings vie with one another in doing honor to the two oldest sanctuaries of Shamash, at Sippar and Larsa. Perhaps the pristine affinity between Marduk, who, as we saw, was originally a sun-deity, and Shamash, also had a share in Hammurabi's fondness for coupling these two gods. When describing his operations at Sippar he speaks of himself as 'doing good to the flesh of Shamash and Marduk.' Hammurabi felt himself to be honoring Marduk, through paying homage to a deity having affinity with the patron protector of Babylon.

INNANNA.

We have already come across a deity of this name in a previous chapter.[1] Hammurabi tells us, in one of his inscriptions, that he has restored the temple in honor of Innanna at Hallabi — a town near Sippar.[2] Innanna, or Ninni, signifying

---

[1] See p. 79.
[2] See Jensen, *Keils Bibl.* 3, 1, p. 108, note 5. Tiele, *Gesch.* p. 126, apparently identifies Innanna of Hallabi with Tashmit, but, so far as I can see, without sufficient reason.

merely 'lady,' or 'great lady,' appears to have become a very general name for a goddess, hence the addition 'of Hallabi,' which Hammurabi is careful to make. At the same time the designation 'lady of Hallabi' points to her being a consort of a male deity who was the patron of the place. May this have been the moon-god again, as in the case of the other Innanna? Our knowledge of this goddess is confined to what the king tells us about her. For him she is the mistress whose glory fills heaven and earth, but when he adds that she has placed in his hands the reins of government, this only means that the goddess recognizes his right to supreme authority over the Babylonian states — not that he owes his power to her. It is after he has succeeded in making Babylon the capital of a great kingdom that he proceeds to improve the temple of Innanna.

BEL AND THE TRIAD OF BABYLONIAN THEOLOGY.

Among the literary remains of Hammurabi's days we have a hymn in which the chief gods worshipped by the king are enumerated in succession. The list begins with Bel, and then mentions Sin, Ninib, Ishtar, Shamash, and Ramman. We should expect to find at the head of the list Marduk. The hymn may be older than Hammurabi, who, perhaps, is quoting or copying it; and since the Bel who is here at the head of the pantheon is the god of Nippur, the hymn may originally have belonged to the ritual of that place. For Hammurabi the highest 'Bel,' or lord, is Marduk, and there is hardly room for doubt that in using this hymn as a means of passing on to singing his own praises, with which the inscription in question ends, Hammurabi has in mind the patron god of Babylon when speaking of Bel.[1] It is this amalgamation of the old Bel with Marduk that marks, as we have seen, the transition to the use of Bel's name as a mere title of Marduk. Elsewhere, however,

---

[1] Here written En-lil, as the Bel of Nippur.

Hammurabi uses Bel to designate the old god. So when he calls himself the proclaimer of Anu and Bel[1] the association with Anu makes it impossible that Marduk should be meant. At times he appears to refer in the same inscription, now to the old Bel and again to Bel-Marduk, under the same designation. When Kurigalzu, a member of the Cassite dynasty (c. 1400 B.C.), speaks of 'Bel, the lord of lands,' to whom he erects a temple in the new city, Dur-Kurigalzu — some forty miles to the northeast of Babylon — it is the old Bel who is again meant. While acknowledging Marduk as one of the chief gods, these foreign rulers in Babylonia — the Cassites — did not feel the same attachment to him as Hammurabi did. They gave the preference to the old god of Nippur, and, indeed, succeeded in their attempt to give to the old city of Nippur some of its pristine glory. They devoted themselves assiduously to the care of the great temple at Nippur. There are some indications of an attempt made by them to make Nippur the capital of their empire. In the case of Hammurabi's immediate successor, as has been pointed out, the equation Bel-Marduk is distinctly set down, but, for all that, the double employment of the name continues even through the period of the Assyrian supremacy over Babylonia. The northern rulers now use Bel to designate the more ancient god, and, again, merely as a designation of Marduk. Tiglathpileser I. (see note 1, below) expressly adds 'the older' when speaking of Bel. When Sargon refers to Bel, 'the lord of lands, who dwells on the sacred mountain of the gods,' or when Tiglathpileser I. calls Bel 'the father of the gods,' 'the king of the group of spirits' known as the Anunaki, it is

---

[1] Attached to the name here (Rawlinson, I. 4, no. xv–9), which is written ideographically En-Lil, is the designation *da-gan-ni*, which has occasioned considerable discussion. See Jensen, *Kosmologie*, pp. 449–456. It seems to me that the addition which emphasizes this identity of Bel with another god, Dagan, is to indicate that the Bel of the triad, and not Bel-Marduk, is here meant. Somewhat in the same way Tiglathpileser I. (Rawlinson, i. 14, vi. 87) distinguishes the older Bel by calling him 'Bel labara,' *i.e.*, 'Bel the older.'

of course only the old Bel, the lord of the lower region, or of the earth, who can be meant; but when, as is much more frequently the case, the kings of Assyria, down to the fall of the empire, associate Bel with Nabu, speak of Bel and the gods of Akkad (*i.e.*, Babylonia), and use Bel, moreover, to designate Babylonia,[1] it is equally clear that Marduk is meant. In the Neo-Babylonian empire Marduk alone is used.

The continued existence of a god Bel in the Babylonian pantheon, despite the amalgamation of Bel with Marduk, is a phenomenon that calls for some comment. The explanation is to be found in the influence of the theological system that must have been developed in part, at least, even before the union of the Babylonian states.[2] Bel, as the god of earth, was associated with Anu, as the god of heaven, and Ea, as the god of the deep, to form a triad that embraced the entire universe. When, therefore, Anu, Bel, and Ea were invoked, it was equivalent to naming all the powers that influenced the fate of man. They embraced, as it were, the three kingdoms of the gods, within which all the other gods could be comprised. The systematization involved in the assumption of a triad of gods controlling the entire pantheon can hardly be supposed to have been a popular process. It betokens an amount of thought and speculation, a comprehensive view of the powers of nature, that could only have arisen in minds superior to the average intelligence. In other words, the conception of the triad Anu, Bel, and Ea is again an evidence of the existence of schoolmen and of schools of religious thought in the days of the ancient empire. So far, however, as Hammurabi is concerned, he only refers to a duality — Anu and Bel — which, for him, comprises all the other gods. He is the 'proclaimer of Anu and Bel.' It is Anu and Bel who give him sovereignty over the land. In

---

[1] 'Governor of Bel' for governor of Babylonia, and ' subjects of Bel' for subjects of Babylonia.
[2] See p. 89 and chapter vii.

the texts of the second period the triad does not occur until we come to the reign of a king, Mili-shikhu, who lives at least eight centuries after Hammurabi. Ea, in fact, does not occur at all in those inscriptions of the king that have as yet been discovered. If any conclusion is to be drawn from this omission, it is certainly this, — that there are several stages in the development of the ancient theological system of Babylonia. At first a duality of kingdoms — the kingdom of what is above and below — was conceived as comprising all the personified powers of nature, but this duality was replaced by a triad through the addition of the god who stands at the head of all water-deities. Of course the assumption of a duality instead of a triad may have been due to a difference among existing schools of thought. At all events, there seems to be no political reason for the addition of Ea, and it is difficult to say, therefore, how soon the conception of a triad standing at the head of the pantheon arose. We have found it in Gudea's days, and it must, therefore, have existed in the days of Hammurabi, without, perhaps, being regarded as an essential dogma as yet. A direct and natural consequence of Bel's position in the triad was that, by the side of Bel-Marduk, the older Bel continued to be invoked in historical inscriptions. Since Anu and Ea were appealed to by themselves, the former occasionally, the latter more frequently, there was no reason why a ruler should not at times be prompted to introduce an invocation to Bel, without the direct association with Anu and Ea. The confusion that thus ensues between the two Bels was not of serious moment, since from the context one could without difficulty determine which of the two was meant; and what we, with our limited knowledge of ancient Babylonia, are able to do, must have been an easy task for the Babylonians themselves.[1]

[1] Occasionally a king (so *e.g.* Nabubaliddin, *c.* 883 B.C.) associates Anu with Ea, and omits Bel (Rawlinson, v. 60, ii. 21), as though with the intent of avoiding confusion.

It is tempting to suppose that the first command of the Decalogue (Exodus, xx) contains an implied reference to the Babylonian triad.

Anu, Bel, and Ea.

The theory of the triad succeeds in maintaining its hold upon Babylonian minds from a certain period on, through all political and intellectual vicissitudes. To invoke Anu, Bel, and Ea becomes a standing formula that the rulers of Babylonia as well as of Assyria are fond of employing. These three are the great gods *par excellence.* They occupy a place of their own. The kings do not feel as close to them as to Marduk, or to Ashur, or even to the sun-god, or to the moon-god. The invocation of the triad partakes more of a formal character, as though in giving to these three gods the first place, the writers felt that they were following an ancient precedent that had more of a theoretical than a practical value for their days. So among Assyrian rulers, Ashur-rish-ishi (*c.* 1150 B.C.) derives his right to the throne from the authority with which he is invested by the triad. Again, in the formal curses which the kings called down upon the destroyers of the inscriptions or statues that they set up, the appeal to Anu, Bel, and Ea is made. Ashurnasirbal calls upon the triad not to listen to the prayers of such as deface his monuments. Sargon has an interesting statement in one of his inscriptions, according to which the names of the months were fixed by Anu, Bel, and Ea. This 'archaeological' theory illustrates very well the extraneous position occupied by the triad. The months, as we shall see, are sacred, each to a different god. The gods thus distinguished are the ones that are directly concerned in the fortunes of the state, — Sin, Ashur, Ishtar, and the like. Anu, Bel, and Ea are not in the list, and the tradition, or rather the dogma according to which they assign the names is evidently an attempt to make good this omission by placing them, as it were, beyond the reach of the calendar. In short, so far as the historical texts are concerned which reflect the popular beliefs, the triad represents a theological doctrine rather than a living force. In combination, Anu, Bel, and Ea did not mean as much, nor the same thing, to a Babylonian or an Assyrian, as when he said Marduk, or Nabu, or Ashur, or Sin, as the case might be. It was different when addressing these gods individually, as was occasionally done. The Assyrians were rather fond of introducing Anu by himself in their prayers, and the Babylonians were prompted to a frequent mention of Ea by virtue of his relationship to Marduk, but when this was done Anu and Ea meant something different than when mentioned in one breath along with Bel.

Belit.

One might have supposed that when Bel became Marduk, the consort of Bel would also become Marduk's consort. Such, however, does not appear to be the case, at least so far as the epoch of Hammurabi is concerned. When he calls himself 'the beloved shepherd of Belit,' it is the wife of the old Bel that is meant, and so when Agumkakrimi mentions Bel and Belit together, as the gods that decree his fate on earth, there is no doubt as to what Belit is meant. In later days, however, and in Assyria more particularly, there seems to be a tendency towards generalizing the name (much as that of Bel) to the extent of applying it in the sense of 'mistress' to the consort of the chief god of the pantheon; and that happening to be Ashur in Assyria accounts for the fact, which might otherwise appear strange, that Tiglathpileser I. (*c.* 1140 B.C.) calls Belit the 'lofty consort and beloved of Ashur.' Ashurbanabal (668-626 B.C.) does the same, and even goes further and declares himself to be the offspring of Ashur and Belit. On the other hand, in the interval between these two kings we find Shalmaneser II. (860–825 B.C) calling Belit 'the mother of the great gods' and 'the wife of Bel,' making it evident that the old Belit of the south is meant, and since Ashurbanabal on one occasion also calls the goddess 'the beloved of Bel,'[1] it follows that in his days two Belits were still recognized, or perhaps it would be more accurate to say two uses of the term, — one specifically for the consort of the Babylonian Bel, the god of the earth, with his ancient seat at Nippur; the other of a more general character, though still limited as 'lady' to the consort of the *chief* gods, just as 'Bel,' while acquiring the general sense of 'lord,' was restricted in actual usage to the *greatest* 'lords' only. An indication of this distinction, somewhat parallel to the addition of Dagan to Bel, to indicate that the old Bel was meant,[2] appears in the sobriquet 'of Babylonia,'[3] which Ashurbanabal gives to the goddess in one place where the old Belit is meant. Under the influence of this Assyrian extension of the term, Nabopolassar, in the Neo-Babylonian period, applies the title to the consort of Shamash at Sippar, but he is careful to specify 'Belit of Sippar,' in order to avoid misunderstanding. Besides being applied to the consorts of Ashur and of Shamash, 'Belit,' in the general sense of 'mistress,' is applied only to another goddess, the great Ishtar of the Assyrian pantheon — generally, however, as a title, not as a name of the goddess. The important position she occupied in the Assyrian pantheon seemed to justify this further modification and extension in the use of the term. Occasionally, Ishtar is directly and expressly called 'Belit.' So, Ashurbanabal speaks of a temple that he has founded in Calah to 'Belit mâti,'[4] 'the Belit (or lady) of the land,' where the context speaks in favor of identifying Belit with the great goddess Ishtar. Again

---

[1] Rassam, Cylinder ix. 75.

[2] See chapter xii., "The Assyrian Pantheon," p. 208.

[3] Rassam, Cylinder viii. 98, 99. 'Belit of Babylonia, honored among the great gods.'

[4] *Annals*, lii. 135.

Ashurbanabal, in a dedicatory inscription giving an account of improvements made in the temple of Ishtar, addresses the goddess as Belit 'lady of lands, dwelling in E-mash-mash.'[1]

ANU AND ANATUM.

In the second period of Babylonian history the worship of the supreme god of heaven becomes even more closely bound up with Anu's position as the first member of the inseparable triad than was the case in the first period. For Hammurabi, as has been noted, Anu is only a half-real figure who in association with Bel is represented as giving his endorsement to the king's authority.[2] The manner in which Agumkakrimi introduces Anu is no less characteristic for the age of Hammurabi and his successors. At the beginning of his long inscription,[3] he enumerates the chief gods under whose protection he places himself. As a Cassitic ruler, he assigns the first place to the chief Cassite deity, Shukamuna, a god of war whom the Babylonian scholars identified with their own Nergal.[4] Shukamuna is followed by the triad Anu, Bel, and Ea. Marduk occupies a fifth place, after which comes a second triad, Sin, Shamash "the mighty hero," and Ishtar[5] "the strong one among the gods." The inscription is devoted to the king's successful capture of the statues of Marduk and Sarpanitum out of the hands of the Khani, and the restoration

---

[1] The name of the temple. See IIR. 66, ll. 1 and 10. The title 'belit matâti,' 'lady of the lands' is evidently introduced in imitation of 'bel matâti,' 'lord of lands,' belonging to Bel and then to Marduk.

[2] Sayce's view (*Hibbert Lectures*, p. 186), according to which Anu was originally the local god of Erech, is erroneous.

[3] VR. pl. 33.

[4] Delitzsch, *Die Kossaer*, pp. 25, 27.

[5] The omission of Ramman here, though invoked at the close of the inscription, is noticeable. Ishtar takes the place that in the more developed system belongs to the god of storms, who with the moon-god and sun-god constitutes a second triad. See p. 163.

of the shrines of these deities at Babylon. At the close, the king Agumkakrimi appeals to Anu and his consort Anatum,[1] who are asked to bless the king in heaven, to Bel and Belit who are asked to fix his fate on earth, and to Ea and Damkina, inhabiting the deep,[2] who are to grant him long life. As in the beginning of the inscription, the thought of the triad — Anu, Bel, Ea — evidently underlies this interesting invocation, but at the same time the association of a consort with Anu brings the god into closer relationship with his fellows. He takes on — if the contradiction in terms be permitted — a more human shape. His consort bears a name that is simply the feminine form to Anu, just as Belit is the feminine to Bel. 'Anu,' signifying 'the one on high,' — a feminine to it was formed, manifestly under the influence of the notion that every god must have a consort of some kind. After Agumkakrimi no further mention of Anatum occurs, neither in the inscriptions of Babylonian nor of Assyrian rulers. We are permitted to conclude, therefore, that Anatum was a product of the schools, and one that never took a strong hold on the popular mind. Among the Assyrian kings who in other respects also show less dependence upon the doctrines evolved in the Babylonian schools, and whose inscriptions reflect to a greater degree the purely popular phases of the faith, we find Anu mentioned with tolerable frequency, and in a manner that betrays less emphasis upon the position of the god as a member of the triad. Still, it is rather curious that he does not appear even in the inscriptions of the Assyrian kings by himself, but in association with another god. Thus Tiglathpileser I. (c. 1130 B.C.) gives an elaborate account of an old temple to Anu and

---

[1] Written with the sign *An*, and the feminine ending *tum*, but probably pronounced Anatum. The form Anat (without the ending) is used by many scholars, as Sarpanit and Tashmit are used instead of Sarpanitum and Tashmitum. I prefer the fuller forms of these names. Anum similarly is better than Anu, but the latter has become so common that it might as well be retained.

[2] V R. 33, vii. 34-44.

Ramman in the city of Ashur that he restores to more than its former grandeur.[1] This dedication of a temple to two deities is unusual. Ramman is the god of thunder and storms, whose seat of course is in the heavens. He stands close, therefore, to Anu, the supreme god of heaven. In the religious productions, this relationship is expressed by making Ramman the son of Anu. From a passage descriptive of this temple it would appear that the old temple founded by King Samsi-Ramman, who lived several centuries before Tiglathpileser, was dedicated to Ramman. It looks, therefore, as though the association of Anu with Ramman was the work of the later king. What his motive was in thus combining Anu with Ramman it is difficult to say, but in his account of the restoration of the sanctuary, he so consistently mentions Anu and Ramman together,[2] designating them unitedly as 'the great gods my lords,' that one gains the impression that the two were inseparable in his mind, Ramman being perhaps regarded simply as a manifestation of Anu. The supposition finds some support in the closing words of the inscription, where, in hurling the usual curses upon those who should attempt to destroy his monuments, he invokes Ramman alone, whom he asks to punish the offender by his darts, by hunger, by distress of every kind, and by death.

Elsewhere Anu appears in association with Dagan, of whom we shall have occasion to speak in the chapter on the Assyrian pantheon. Suffice it to say here that Dagan in this connection is an equivalent of Bel. When, therefore, Ashurbanabal and Sargon call themselves 'the favorite of Anu and Dagan,' it is the same as though they spoke of Anu and Bel. Apart from this, Anu only appears when a part or the whole of the Assyrian pantheon is enumerated. Thus we come across Anu, Ramman, and Ishtar as the chief gods of the city of Ashur,[3] and again

---

[1] IR. pl. 15, col. vii. 71 – pl. 16, col. viii. 88.   [2] No less than nine times.
[3] Tiglathpileser I.

Anu, Ashur, Shamash, Ramman, and Ishtar.[1] Finally, Sargon who names the eight gates of his palace after the chief gods of the land does not omit Anu, whom he describes as the 'one who blesses his handiwork.' Otherwise we have Anu only when the triad Anu, Bel, and Ea is invoked. Once Ramman-nirari I. (c. 1325 B.C.) adds Ishtar to the triad. After Sargon we no longer find Anu's name at all among the deities worshipped in Assyria. On the whole, then, Anu's claim to reverence rests in Assyria as well as in Babylonia upon his position in the triad, and while Assyria is less influenced by the ancient system devised in Babylonia whereby Anu, Bel, and Ea come to be the representatives of the three kingdoms among which the gods are distributed, still Anu as a specific deity, ruling in his own right, remains a rather shadowy figure. The only temple in his honor is the one which he shares with Ramman, and which, as noted, appears to have been originally devoted to the service of the latter. One other factor that must be taken into account to explain the disappearance of Anu is the gradual enforcement of Ashur's claim to the absolute headship of the Assyrian pantheon. Either Anu or Ashur had to be assigned to this place, and when circumstances decided the issue in favor of Ashur, there was no place worthy of Anu as a specific deity. Ashur usurps in a measure the rôle of Anu. So far as Babylonia was concerned, there was still in the twelfth century B.C. a city 'Der' which is called the 'city of Anu.' The city is probably of very ancient foundation, and its continued association with Anu forms an interesting survival of a local conception that appears to have been once current of the god.

In the religious literature, especially in that part of it which furnishes us with the scholastic recastings of the popular traditions, Anu is a much more prominent figure than in the historical texts. From being merely the personification of the heavens, he is raised to the still higher dignity of symbolizing,

[1] Ramman-nirari I.

as Jensen puts it,[1] the abstract principle of which both the heavens and earth are emanations. All the earliest gods conceived of by popular tradition as existing from the beginning of things are viewed as manifestations of Anu, or of Anu and Anatum in combination. He gives ear to prayers, but he is not approached directly. The gods are his messengers, who come and give him report of what is going on.[2] He is a god for the gods rather than for men. When his daughter Ishtar is insulted she appeals to her father Anu; and when the gods are terrified they take refuge with Anu. Armed with a mighty weapon whose assault nothing can withstand, Anu is surrounded by a host of gods and powerful spirits who are ready to follow his lead and to do his service.

RAMMAN.

With Ramman we reach a deity whose introduction into the Babylonian pantheon and whose position therein appears to be entirely independent of Marduk.

The reading of the name as Ramman (or Rammanu) is provisional. The ideograph *Im* with which the name is written designates the god as the power presiding over storms; and while it is certain that, in Assyria at least, the god was known as Ramman, which means 'the thunderer,' it is possible that this was an epithet given to the god, and not his real or his oldest name. It is significant that in the El-Amarna tablets (*c.* 1500 B.C.), where the god *Im* appears as an element in proper names, the reading *Addu* is vouched for, and this form has been justly brought into connection with a very famous solar deity of Syria,— Hadad. The worship of Hadad, we know, was widely spread in Palestine and Syria, and there is conclusive evidence that Hadad (or Adad), as a name for the god *Im*, was known in Babylonia. Professor Oppert is of the opinion

---

[1] *Kosmologie*, p. 274.   [2] See the list IIIR. 68, 26 *seq.*

that Adad represents the oldest name of the god. Quite recently the proposition has been made that the real name of the deity was *Immeru*.[1] The ideograph in this case would arise through the curtailment of the name (as is frequently the case in the cuneiform syllabary), and the association of *Im* with 'storm' and 'wind' would be directly dependent upon the nature of the deity in question. The material at hand is not sufficient for deciding the question. Besides Immeru, Adad, and Ramman, the deity was also known as *Mer* —connected apparently with Immeru.[2] So much is certain, that Ramman appears to have been the name currently used in Assyria for this god. Adad may have been employed occasionally in Babylonia, as was *Mer* in proper names, but that it was not the common designation is proved by a list of gods (published by Bezold[3]) in which the *foreign* equivalent for *Im* is set down as Adad. We may for the present, therefore, retain Ramman, while bearing in mind that we have only proof of its being an epithet applied to the god, not necessarily his real name and in all probabilities not the oldest name.

We meet with the god for the first time in the hymn to which reference has already been made,[4] and where the god is mentioned together with Shamash. If the suggestion above thrown out is correct, that the hymn is older than the days of Hammurabi, Ramman too would be older than his first mention in historical texts. However, it is worthy of note that in this hymn each of the other gods mentioned receives a line for himself, and that Ramman is the only one who is tacked on to another deity. It is not strange that in making copies of older

---

[1] Thureau-Dangin, *Journal Asiatique*, 1895, pp. 385-393. The name of this deity has been the subject of much discussion. For a full discussion of the subject with an account of the recent literature, see an article by the writer in *The American Journal of Semitic Languages and Literatures*, xii. 159-162.

[2] Arising perhaps after *Im* came into use as the ideographic form.

[3] *Proc. Soc. Bibl. Arch.*, xi. 173-174 and pl. 1, col. i. 7.

[4] See p. 145 and also p. 161.

texts, especially those of a religious character, the scribes should have introduced certain modifications. At all events, the god does not acquire any degree of prominence until the days of Hammurabi; so that whatever his age and origin, he belongs in a peculiar sense to the pantheon of Hammurabi rather than to that of the old Babylonian period. The successor of Hammurabi, Samsu-iluna, dedicates a fort, known as Dur-padda, to Ramman whom he addresses as his 'helper,' along with several other gods. Despite this fact, his worship does not appear to have been very firmly established in Babylonia, for Agum-kakrimi, who follows upon Samsu-iluna, does not make mention of Ramman. During the reign of the Cassite dynasty, however, the worship of Ramman appears to have gained a stronger foothold. Several kings of this dynasty have incorporated the name of this deity into their own names, and in an inscription dealing with events that transpired in the reign of one of these kings, Ramman occupies a prominent place. Immediately after the great triad, Anu, Bel, and Ea, there is enumerated a second, Sin, Shamash, and Ramman, and only then there follows Marduk.[1] More than this, Ramman is introduced for a second time in conjunction with Shamash, as in the hymn of Hammurabi. The two are appealed to as 'the divine lords of justice.' The conqueror of the Cassites, Nebuchadnezzar I., also holds Ramman in high esteem. For him, Ramman is the god of battle who in companionship with Ishtar abets the king in his great undertakings. He addresses Ramman as the great lord of heaven, the lord of subterranean waters and of rain, whose curse is invoked against the one who sets aside the decrees of Nebuchadnezzar or who defaces the monument the king sets up. While acknowledging the supremacy of Marduk, upon whose appeal he proceeds to Babylonia to rid the country of its oppressors, Nebuchadnezzar nevertheless

---

[1] Belser in Haupt and Delitzsch, *Beiträge zur Assyriologie*, ii. 187 *seq.*, col. vi. l. 3 *seq.*

shows remarkable partiality for Ramman, perhaps as a matter of policy to offset the supposed preference shown by Ramman towards the previous dynasty. Ramman with Nergal and Nanâ are also enumerated as the special gods of Namar — a Babylonian district which caused the king considerable annoyance, and which may have been one of the strongholds whence the Cassitic kings continued their attacks upon Nebuchadnezzar.

In order to determine more precisely the nature of this deity, it is necessary to turn to Assyria, where his worship dates from the very earliest times, and where he appears consistently in a single rôle, — that of the god of storms, more particularly of thunder and lightning. The oldest Assyrian ruler known to us is Samsi-Ramman (*c.* 1850 B.C.), whose name, containing the god as one of its elements, points to the antiquity of the cult of Ramman in the north. Another king who has frequently been mentioned, Ramman-nirari (*i.e.*, Ramman is my helper), bears evidence to the same effect, and Tiglathpileser I. speaks of a temple to Ramman whose foundation carries us back several centuries beyond the period of these two kings — almost to the days of Hammurabi. The theory has accordingly been advanced that the worship of Ramman came to Babylonia from the north, and since the cult of this same god is found in Damascus and extended as far south as the plain of Jezreel, the further conclusion has been drawn that the god is of Aramaic origin and was brought to Assyria through Aramaic tribes who had settled in parts of Assyria. The great antiquity of the Ramman cult in Assyria argues against a foreign origin. It seems more plausible to regard the Ramman cult as indigenous to Assyria; but reverting to a time when the population of the north was still in the nomadic state of civilization, the cult may have been carried to the west by some of the wandering tribes who afterwards established themselves around Damascus. Up to a late period Aramaic hordes appear from time to time in western Assyria; and in a higher stage of culture, contact between Aramaeans and Assyrians was maintained by commercial intercourse and by warfare. Since the earliest mention of Ramman's cult is in the city of Ashur, it may be that he was originally connected with that place. As already intimated, he was essentially a storm-god, whose manifestation was seen in the thunder and lightning, and the god was known not merely as 'the thunderer,' but also as Barku, *i.e.*, lightning. Perhaps it was because of this that he was also brought into association with the great light of heaven, — the sun-god. In many mythologies, the sun and lightning are regarded as correlated forces. At all events, the frequent association of Shamash and Ramman cannot have been accidental. This double nature of Ramman — as a solar deity representing some particular phase of the sun that escapes us and as a storm-god — still peers through the inscription above noted from the Cassite period where Ramman is called 'the lord of justice,' — an attribute peculiar to the sun-god; but in Assyria his rôle as the thunder- and storm-god overshadows any other attributes that he may have had.

There are two aspects to rainstorms in Babylonia. The flooding of the fields while committing much havoc is essential to the fertility of the soil. Ramman is therefore the carrier of blessings to the cities, the one who supplies wells and fields with water; but the destructive character of the rain and thunder and lightning are much more strongly emphasized than their beneficent aspects. Even though the fields be flooded, Ramman can cause thorns to grow instead of herbs. The same ideograph *Im* that signifies Ramman also means distress. When the failure of the crops brings in its wake hunger and desolation, it is the 'god of the clouds,' the 'god of rain,' the 'god of the overflow,' whose wrath has thus manifested itself. It is he who (as a hymn puts it) 'has eaten the land.' No wonder that the 'roar' of the god is described as 'powerful,' and that he is asked to stand at the right side of the petitioner and grant protection. When Ramman lets his voice resound, misfortune is at hand. It was natural that he who thus presided over the battle of the elements should come to be conceived essentially as a god of war to a people whose chief occupation grew to be conquest. As such he appears constantly in the inscriptions of Assyrian kings, and to such a degree as to be a formidable rival, at times, to the head of the Assyrian pantheon. The final victory of the Assyrian arms is generally attributed to Ashur alone, but just before the battle and in the midst of the fray, Ramman's presence is felt almost as forcibly as that of Ashur. He shares with the latter the honor of invocations and sacrifices at such critical moments. In this capacity Ramman is so essentially an Assyrian god that it will be proper to dwell upon him again in the following chapter, when the specially Assyrian phases of the religion we are investigating will be taken up. The consort of Ramman also, the goddess Shala, will best be treated of in connection with the Assyrian phases of the Ramman cult.

Of the other gods whose names occur in the inscriptions of Hammurabi, but little of a special character is to be noted. The attributes that he gives them do not differ from those that we come across in the texts of his predecessors. It is sufficient, therefore, to enumerate them. The longest list is furnished by the hymn which has already been referred to. The text is unfortunately fragmentary, and so we cannot be sure that the names embrace the entire pantheon worshipped by him. The list opens with Bel (who, as we have seen, is the old Bel of Nippur); then follow Sin, Ninib, Ishtar, Shamash, Ramman. Here the break in the tablet begins and, when the text again becomes intelligible, a deity is praised in such extravagant terms that one is tempted to conclude that Hammurabi has added to an old hymn a paean to his favorite Marduk.[1] To Bel is given

[1] The character of this part of the hymn is quite different from that which precedes.

the honor of having granted royal dignity to the king. Sin has given the king his princely glory; from Ninib, the king has received a powerful weapon; Ishtar fixes the battle array, while Shamash and Ramman hold themselves at the service of the king. With this list, however, we are far from having exhausted the pantheon as it had developed in the days of Hammurabi. From the inscriptions of his successors we are permitted to add the following: Nin-khar-sag, Nergal, and Lugal-mit-tu, furnished by Samsu-iluna; Shukamuna, by Agumkakrimi; and passing down to the period of the Cassite dynasty, we have in addition Nin-dim-su, Ba-kad, Pap-u, Belit-ekalli, Shumalia.[1]

During the Cassitic rule, Marduk does not play the prominent part that he did under the native rulers, but he is restored to his position by Nebuchadnezzar I., who, it will be recalled, succeeds in driving the Cassites out of power. But besides Marduk, Nebuchadnezzar invokes a large number of other deities. For purposes of comparison with the pantheon of Hammurabi, and of his immediate successors, I give the complete list and in the order mentioned by him in the only inscription that we have of this king. They are Ninib, Gula, Ramman, Shumalia, Nergal, Shir, Shubu, Sin, Belit of Akkad. Moreover, Anu is referred to as the especial god of Der, and a goddess Eria[2] is worshipped in Elam. Passing still further down, we obtain as additional names, Malik and Bunene, from the inscription of Nabubaliddin (c. 883-852 B.C.).[3]

We may divide this long period from Hammurabi down to the time that the governors of Babylonia became mere puppets of the Assyrian rulers into three sections: (1) Hammurabi and his successors, (2) the Cassite dynasty, (3) the restoration of native rulers to the throne. A comparison of the names furnished by the inscriptions from these three sections shows that

---

[1] For further notices of these gods, see chapter x.   [2] See above, p. 122.
[3] One might include in the list also Nin-igi-nangar-bu, Gushgin-banda, Nin-kurra, Nin-zadim (from Nabubaliddin's inscription), but these are only so many epithets of Ea or various *forms* under which the god came to be worshipped. See p. 177.

the gods common to all are Marduk, Bel, Shamash, Ramman. But, in addition, our investigations have shown that we are justified in adding the following as forming part of the Babylonian pantheon during this entire period: Sarpanitum, Belit, Tashmitum, Sin, Ninib, Ishtar, Nergal, Nin-khar-sag, and the two other members of the triad, Anu and Ea, with their consorts, Anatum and Damkina. All these gods and goddesses are found in the texts from the first and third section of the period, and the absence of some of them from texts of the second section is simply due to the smaller amount of material that we have for the history of the Cassite dynasty in Babylonia. Some of the deities in this list, which is far from being exhaustive,[1] are foreign, so *e.g.*, Shukamuna and Shumalia, who belong to the Cassitic pantheon; others are of purely local significance, as Shir and Shubu.[2] As for Sin, Ninib, and Ishtar, the worship of none of these deities assumes any great degree of prominence during this period. No doubt the local cult was continued at the old centers much as before, but except for an occasional invocation, especially in the closing paragraphs of an inscription, where the writers were fond of grouping a large array of deities so as to render more impressive the curses upon enemies and vilifiers, with which the inscriptions usually terminated, they do not figure in the official writings of the time. Of Sin, it is of some importance to note that under the Cassite dynasty he stands already at the head of a second class of triads which consists of Sin, Shamash, and Ramman, or Ishtar (see note 3 on page 152), and that through the inscription of Nebuchadnezzar I., we learn of an additional district of Babylonia,—that of Bit-Khabban, where in association with Belit of Akkad, the consort of the older Bel, he was worshipped as the patron deity. Nebuchadnezzar himself does not enu-

[1] We may now look forward to finding many more gods in the rich material for this period unearthed by the University of Pennsylvania Expedition to Niffer.
[2] See chapter x.

merate Sin among the chief gods. Ninib appears in the familiar rôle as a god of war. After Hammurabi he is only mentioned once in inscriptions of the Cassitic period and then again in the days of Nebuchadnezzar I., who assigns a prominent place to him. It is Ninib who, with the title 'king of heaven and earth,' leads off in the long list of gods whose curses are invoked upon the king's opponents. Similarly, the belligerent character of Ishtar is the only phase of the goddess dwelt upon during this period. While for Agumkakrimi, she still occupies a comparatively inferior rank, coming seventh in his list, Nebuchadnezzar places her immediately after Anu and before Ramman and Marduk. This advance foreshadows the superior rôle that she is destined to play in the pantheon during the period of Assyrian supremacy. The cult of Nergal does not figure prominently during this period. In fact, so far as the historical texts go, he disappears from the scene till the time of Nebuchadnezzar I., when he is incidentally invoked in a group with Ramman and Nanâ as the gods of a district in Babylonia known as Namar. Exactly where Namar lay has not yet been ascertained. Since Nergal, as was shown in the previous chapter, was the local patron of Cuthah, it may be that the latter city was included in the Namar district. At all events, we may conclude from the silence of the texts as to Nergal, that Cutha played no conspicuous part in the empire formed of the Babylonian states, and that the cult of Nergal, apart from the association of the deity in religious texts with the lower world, did not during this entire period extend beyond local proportions. Lastly, it is interesting to note that Samsu-iluna, the son of Hammurabi, refers to Belit of Nippur as Nin-khar-sag, which we have seen was one of her oldest titles.

CHAPTER IX.

THE GODS IN THE TEMPLE LISTS AND IN THE LEGAL AND COMMERCIAL DOCUMENTS.

BESIDES the historical texts in the proper sense, there is another source for the study of the Babylonian pantheon.

Both for the first and for the second periods we now have a large number of lists of offerings made to the temples of Babylonia and of thousands of miscellaneous legal documents. De Sarzec found a number of such documents at Telloh some years ago, and quite recently some thirty thousand tablets of the temple archives have come to light.[1] At Tell-Sifr, Abu-Habba, and elsewhere, many thousands also have been found, belonging chiefly to the second period. A feature of these documents is the invocation of the gods, introduced for various purposes, at times in connection with oaths, at times as a guarantee against the renewal of claims. Again, certain gods are appealed to as witnesses to an act, and in the lists of temple offerings, gods are constantly introduced. Since many of the commercial transactions recorded in these documents, moreover, concern the temples of Babylonia, further occasions were found for the mention of a god or gods. The proper names occurring in these documents, compounded as these names in most cases are with some deity,[2] furnish some

---

[1] The museums of Europe and America have secured a large proportion of these through purchase.

[2] The longer names consist of three elements: subject, verb, and object. The deity is generally the subject; *e.g.*, Sinacherib = Sin-akhe-lrba, *i.e.*, may the god Sin increase the brothers. But there are many variations. So the imperative of the verb is often used, and in that case, the deity is in the vocative case. Instead of three elements, there are frequently only two, a deity and a participle or an adjective; *e.g.*,

additions to the pantheon of Babylonia. Naturally, a distinction is to be made between deities introduced in temple lists and in the course of legal proceedings, and such as are merely known through forming an element in proper names. The former constitute a part of what might be called the 'active' pantheon of the time. Deities that are actually invoked by contracting parties for whatever purpose are such as are endowed with real significance; and if any of these are not mentioned in the historical texts proper, the omission is due to the lack of material. The testimony of the legal documents in this respect is fully as valid as is that of the historical texts. In proper names the case is different. Custom being a prominent, if not a controlling, factor in the giving of names, it may happen that the deity appearing as an element in a name is one who, for various reasons, is no longer worshipped, or whose worship has diminished in significance at the time we meet with the name. Again, deities of very restricted local fame, deities that occupy the inferior rank of mere spirits or demons in the theological system of the Babylonians, may still be incorporated in proper names. Lastly, in view of the descriptive epithets by which some deities are often known, as much as by their real names, it frequently happens in the case of proper names that a deity otherwise known is designated by one of his attributes. Thus we find in legal documents of the second period a goddess, Da-mu-gal, who is none other than the well-known Gula, the great healing deity; Ud-zal, who is identical with Ninib, and so written as the god of 'the rising sun';[1] and Mar-tu (lit., 'the west god'), which is a designation of Ramman.[2]

Sin-magir, *i.e.*, Sin is favorable, or a person is called 'the son' or 'the servant' of a god. The name of the deity alone may also constitute a proper name; and many names of course do not contain the mention of a deity at all, though such names are often abbreviations from longer ones in which some god was introduced.

[1] Jensen, *Kosmologie*, p. 458.

[2] Arnold, *Ancient Babylonian Temple Records*, p. 5, is of the opinion that Id-nik-mar-tu is also a designation of Ramman. His view is plausible, but it still remains to be proved.

Bearing in mind all these considerations, we find in the tablets of the first period, so far as published,[1] the same deities that are met with in the historical inscriptions: En-lil, Bau, En-zu (or Sin), Nin-girsu, Nin-gish-zida, Nin-mar, Nanâ, Ninâ, Shul-pa-uddu, and others. No doubt a complete publication of the Telloh archives will furnish some—not many—new deities not occurring in the historical texts of this period. A rather curious feature, illustrated by these temple archives, and one upon which we shall have occasion to dwell, is the divine honors that appear to have been paid towards the end of the first period of Babylonian history to some of the earlier rulers, notably Gudea and Dungi.[2] Alongside of wine, oil, wheat, sheep, etc., offered to Bau, Nin-gish-zida, and Shul-pa-uddu, the great kings and *patesis* of the past are honored. More than this, sanctuaries sacred to these rulers are erected, and in other respects they are placed on a footing of equality with the great gods of the period. Passing on to the lists and the legal documents of the second period,[3] we may note that the gods in whose name the oath is taken are chiefly Marduk, Shamash,[4] Â, Ramman, and Sin. Generally two or three are mentioned, and often the name of the reigning king is added to lend further solemnity to the oath. Other gods directly introduced are Nanâ, Ishtar, Nebo, Tashmitum, and Sarpanitum, after whom the years are at times designated, probably in consequence of some special honors accorded to the gods. The standing phrase is 'the year of the throne,' or simply 'the year' of such and such a deity. Nin-mar

---

[1] Scheil, "Le Culte de Gudea sous le IIe Dynastie d'Ur" (*Recueil des Travaux, etc.* xviii. 64–74). W. R. Arnold, *Ancient Babylonian Temple Records* (New York, 1896). The Telloh tablets appear to be largely lists of offerings made to the temples at Lagash, and temple accounts. [See now Reisner, Tempelurkunden aus Telloh (Berlin, 1901).]

[2] See besides Scheil's article (above), Lehmann's note, *Zeits. für Assyr.* x. 381.

[3] Our knowledge of the documents of this period is due chiefly to Strassmaier and Meissner.

[4] At times under rather curious forms, *e.g.*, Shush-sha; Strassmaier, Warka, no. 30, l. 21. The form Sha-ash-sha also occurs in nos. 43 and 105 (*cf.* Meissner's note, *Beiträge zum Altbabylonischen Privatrecht*, p. 156).

appears in the days of Hammurabi as the daughter of Marduk. Among gods appearing for the first time are Khusha,[1] Nun-gal, and Zamama. Mentioned in connection with the gates of the temple where the judges held court, the association of Khusha with Marduk, Shamash, Sin, and Nin-mar points to a considerable degree of prominence enjoyed by this deity. Of his nature and origin, however, we know nothing. Nun-gal signifies the 'great chief.' His temple stood in Sippar,[2] and from this we may conclude that he was one of the minor gods of the place whose original significance becomes obscured by the side of the all-powerful patron of Sippar — the sun-god. A syllabary describes the god as a 'raging' deity, a description that suggests solar functions. Nun-gal appears, therefore, to be the ideograph proper to a deity that symbolized, like Nergal, Ninib, and Â, some phase of the sun. The disappearance of the god would thus be naturally accounted for, in view of the tendency that we have found characteristic of the religion, whereby powerful gods absorb the functions of weaker ones whose attributes resemble their own. But while the god disappears, the name survives. Nun-gal with the plural sign attached becomes a collective designation for a group of powerful demons.[3] In this survival and use of the name we have an interesting example of the manner in which, by a species of differentiation, local gods, unable to maintain themselves by the side of more powerful rivals, sink to the lower grade of demons, either beneficent or noxious. In this grade, too, distinctions are made, as will be pointed out at the proper place. There is a 'pantheon' of demons as well as of gods in the Babylonian theology. Nun-gal accordingly recovers some of his lost dignity by becoming an exceptionally powerful demon — so powerful as to confer his name upon an entire class. The god Zamama appears in connection with a date attached to a legal document

---

[1] Meissner, no. 42. Also in a proper name, Khusha-ilu, *i.e.*, ' Khusha is god.'
[2] Meissner, nos. 40 and 118.   [3] See chapter xl.

of the days of Hammurabi. The building of a sanctuary in honor of this deity and his consort was of sufficient importance to make the year known by this event. Zamama is occasionally mentioned in the religious hymns. He belongs to the deities that form a kind of court around Marduk. From syllabaries, we learn that he was a form of the sun-god, worshipped in the city of Kish in northern Babylonia, and it also appears that he was identified at one period with Ninib. The temple to Zamama —perhaps only a shrine—stood in the city of Kish, which was remodeled by Hammurabi. The shrine, or temple, bore the significant name 'house of the warrior's glory.' The warrior is of course the god, and the name accordingly shows clearly the character of the god in whose honor the sanctuary was built. Elsewhere, he is explicitly called a 'god of battle.' Associated with Zamama of Kish was his consort, who, however, is merely termed again in a general way, 'Ninni,' i.e., 'the lady.' In the case of such a deity as Zamama, it is evident that the absence of the name in historical texts is accidental, and that we may expect to come across it with the increase of historical material. In the proper names, all of the prominent deities discussed in this and the previous chapters are found, though with some notable exceptions. Anu, e.g., is not met with as an element in proper names, but among those occurring may be mentioned Shamash, Â, Ishtar, Ramman (also under the forms Im-me-ru and Mar-tu), Marduk, sometimes called Sag-ila after his temple in Babylon, Nabu, Ishum, Shala, Bau, Nin-ib, Nin-gir-su, Sin, Bunene, Annuit, and Ea. Among gods appearing for the first time in connection with the names, it is sufficient to record a goddess Shubula, who from other sources[1] we know was the local patron of the city Shumdula, a goddess Bashtum,[2] a goddess Mamu (a form of Gula), Am-na-na, Lugal-ki-mu-na,

---

[1] IIR. 60, 18a Pinches (*Journal Victoria Institute*, xxviii. 36, reads Shu-gid-la; Hommel, *ib.* 36, Shu-sil-la).

[2] For this deity, see a paper by the writer, "The Element *Bosheth* in Hebrew Proper Names," in the *Journal of Bibl. Liter.* xiii. 20–30.

E-la-li (perhaps an epithet for the fire-god Gibil), Ul-mash-shi-tum, and a serpent god Sir. Most of these may be safely put down as of purely local origin and jurisdiction, and it is hardly likely that any of them embody an idea not already covered by those which we have discussed. From the lists of gods prepared by the Babylonian scholars, it is clear that the number of local deities whose names at least survived to a late period was exceedingly large, ranging in the thousands; and since, as seems likely, these lists were prepared (as so much of the lexicographical literature) on the basis of the temple lists and of the commercial and legal documents, we may conclude that all, or at any rate most, of these deities were in use as elements in proper names, without, however, having much importance beyond this incorporation.

CHAPTER X.

THE MINOR GODS IN THE PERIOD OF HAMMURABI.

COMING back now to the historical texts and placing the minor deities together that occur in the inscriptions of Hammurabi and his successors down through the restoration of native rulers on the throne of Babylonia, we obtain the following list: Zakar, Lugal-mit-tu (?), Nin-dim-su, Ba-kad, Pap-u, Belit-ekalli, Shumalia, Shukamuna, Gula, Shir, Shubu, Belit of Akkad, Malik, Bunene, Nin-igi-nangar-bu, Gushgin-banda, Nin-kurra, Nin-zadim. In view of the limited amount of historical material at our disposal for the second period of Babylonian history, the list of course does not permit us to form a definite notion of the total number of minor gods that were still occasionally invoked by the side of the great gods. By comparison, however, with the pantheon so far as ascertained of the first period, the conclusion is justified that with the systematization of cults and beliefs characteristic of the Hammurabi, a marked tendency appears towards a reduction of the pantheon, a weeding out of the numerous local cults, their absorption by the larger ones, and the relegation of the minor gods of only local significance to a place among the spirits and demons of the Babylonian religion. Brief statements of these minor gods will suffice to indicate their general character. Of most of the gods in this list there is but little we know as yet beyond the name. Some of them will occur again in the Assyrian and Neo-Babylonian historical texts, others in the hymns and incantations; some are only found in the period we are considering, though with the material constantly increasing we must beware of drawing any conclusions from the fact of a single mention. 'Zakar,' signifying, probably, 'heroic,' appears to have been worshipped in Nippur, where a wall known as the 'wall of Zakar' was built by Samsu-iluna. From the fact that this wall was sacred to Nin-khar-sag or Belit, we may, perhaps, be permitted to conclude that 'Zakar' stood in close relationship to Bel and Belit of Nippur, — possibly a son, — or, at all events, belonged to the inner circle of deities worshipped in the old city sacred to the great Bel.

Another wall in Nippur was dedicated by this Samsu-iluna to a god whose name is provisionally read by Winckler, Lugal-mit-tu.[1] Lugal, signifying 'king,' is an element that enters as an ideograph in the composition of the names of several deities. Thus we have Lugal-edinna, 'king of the field,' which is the equivalent of Nergal, and again for the same god, the combination Lugal-gira, which is, as Jensen[2] has shown, 'raging king,' and a title of Nergal in his character as the god of pestilence and war. Nin-dim-su, Ba-kad, Pap-u, Belit-ekalli, Shumalia, and Shukamuna occur at the close of the inscription of Melishikhu, among the gods asked to curse the transgressors of the royal decree.[3] That some of these are Cassite deities imported into Babylonia, and whose position in the pantheon was therefore of a temporary character, there seems little reason to question. Bakad may, and Shumalia quite certainly does, belong to this class. As for Shukamuna, the fact that Agumkakrimi, who places his title, 'king of Cassite land,' before that of Akkad and Babylon, opens his inscription with the declaration that he is the glorious offspring of Shukamuna, fixes the character of this god beyond all doubt; and Delitzsch has shown[4] that this god was regarded by the Babylonian schoolmen as the equivalent of their own Nergal. Shukamuna, accordingly, was the Cassite god of

---

[1] The text is defective at the point where the god's name is mentioned. See *Keils Bibl.* 3, 1, p. 133. King reads, Lugal-diri-tu-gab.

[2] *Kosmologie*, pp. 481 *seq.*

[3] Belser, *Beiträge zur Assyr.* ii. 203, col. vi.

[4] *Kossaer*, pp. 25–27.

war, who, like Nergal, symbolized the mid-day sun, — that is, the raging and destructive power. Shumalia is the consort of Shukamuna,[1] and is invoked as the 'lady of the shining mountains.' Nin-dim-su is a title of Ea, as the patron of arts. Belit-ekalli—*i.e.*, Belit of the palace—appears as the consort of Ninib, the epithet 'ekalli' being added to specify what Belit is meant, and to avoid confusion with the consort of Bel. At the same time it must be confessed that the precise force of the qualification of 'Belit of the palace' (or temple) escapes us. Ninib's consort, as we know from other sources, was Gula.[2] This name is in some way connected with an Assyrian stem signifying 'great,' and it is at least worthy of note that the word for palace is written by a species of punning etymology with two signs, $e=$ house and $gallu=$ large. The question suggests itself whether the title 'Belit-ekalli' may not have its rise in a further desire to play upon the goddess's name, just as her title Kallat-Eshara (bride of Eshara, or earth) rests upon such a play. Such plays on names are characteristic of the Semites, and indeed in a measure are common to all ancient nations, to whom the name always meant much more than to us. Every *nomen*, as constituting the essence of an object, was always and above all an *omen*. It is, therefore, plausible to suppose that titles of the gods should have been chosen in part under the influence of this idea.[3] A further suggestion that I would like to offer is that 'ekallu,' as temple or palace (lit., large house), may be one of the numerous names of the nether world. A parallel would be furnished by Ekur, which signifies both 'temple' and 'earth,'[4] and is also one of the names of the gathering-place of the dead. Gula, being the goddess of the

[1] Delitzsch, *Kossaer*, p. 33.

[2] See above, p. 105.

[3] Examples of punning etymologies on names of gods are frequent. See Jensen's discussion of Nergal for examples of various plays upon the name of the god. *Kosmologie*, pp. 185 *seq.*

[4] Jensen, *Kosmologie*, pp. 185 *seq.* and p. 218.

nether world who restores the dead to life, would be appropriately called 'the lady of the nether world.' One should like to know more of Pap-u (the phonetic reading unknown), who is called the offspring of Eshara, and 'the lord of the boundary.' Eshara, as Jensen has shown,[1] is a poetical name for earth. The god Ninib, in his capacity as a god of agriculture, is called the 'product of Eshara.'[2] Pap-u, therefore, must be a god somewhat of the same character — a conclusion which is borne out by the description given of him as the protector of the boundary. He is probably one of the numerous forms of boundary gods that are met with among all nations. That we do not encounter more in Babylonia is due to the decided tendency that has been noted towards a centralization of power in a limited number of deities. Instead of gods of boundaries, we have numerous demons and spirits in the case of the developed Babylonian religion, into whose hands the care of preserving the rights of owners to their lands is entrusted. Symbols of these spirits — serpents, unicorns, scorpions, and the like — are added on the monuments which were placed at the boundaries, and on which the terms were specified that justified the land tenure. To this class of monuments the name of 'Kudurru,' or 'boundary' stones, was given by the Babylonians themselves. The inscription on which the name of Pap-u occurs belongs to this class; and he is invoked, as already said, along with many other gods — in fact, with the whole or a goodly portion of the pantheon. It would seem, therefore, that we have in Pap-u a special boundary god who has survived in that rôle from a more primitive period of Babylonian culture. He occupies a place usually assigned to the powerful demons who are regarded as the real owners of the soil.[3]

[1] *Kosmologie*, p. 195.   [2] Rawlinson, i. 29, 16.
[3] This notion that the ground belongs to the gods, and that man is only a tenant, survives to a late period in Semitic religions. The belief underlies the Pentateuchal enactments regarding the holding of the soil, which is only to be temporary. See W. R. Smith, *Religion of the Semites*, pp. 91 *seq.*

Perhaps the most interesting of the minor deities during this second period is

GULA.

As has just been stated, she is the consort of Ninib. She is not mentioned in any of the inscriptions of this period till we come to the days of Nebuchadnezzar I., who invokes her as the bride of Eshara,—*i.e.*, of the earth.[1] We also meet with her name in that of several individuals, Balatsu-Gula[2] and Arad-Gula,[3] and we have seen that she is also known as *Damu* and *Mamu*, or *Meme*. We have a proof, therefore, of her cult being firmly established at an early period of Babylonian history. Her rôle is that of a 'life-giver,' in the widest sense of the word. She is called the 'great physician,' who both preserves the body in health and who removes sickness and disease by the 'touch of her hand.' Gula is the one who leads the dead to a new life. She shares this power, however, with her husband Ninib. Her power can be exerted for evil as well as for good. She is appealed to, to strike the enemy with blindness; she can bring on the very diseases that she is able to heal, and such is the stress laid upon these qualities that she is even addressed as the 'creator of mankind.' But although it is the 'second' birth of mankind over which she presides, she does not belong to the class of deities whose concern is with the dead rather than the living. The Babylonians, as we shall have occasion to point out, early engaged in speculations regarding the life after death, and, as a result, there was developed a special pantheon for the nether world. Gula occupies a rather unique place intermediate, as it were, between the gods of the living and the gods of the dead.

---

[1] In Babylonian, *Kallat Eshara*, with another play upon her name. See above, p. 173.

[2] *I.e.*, [Protect] his life, O Gula.

[3] Servant of Gula.

Of the other deities occurring in the inscription of this same Nebuchadnezzar I. it is sufficient to note that two, Shir and Shubu, are enumerated among the gods of Bit-Khabban. They were, therefore, local deities of some towns that never rose to sufficient importance to insure their patrons a permanent place in the Babylonian pantheon. 'Belit of Akkad,' whom Nebuchadnezzar invokes, is none other than the great Belit, the consort of Bel. 'Akkad' is here used for Babylonia, and the qualification is added to distinguish her from other 'ladies,' as, *e.g.*, 'Belit-ekalli,' who, we have seen, was Gula.

Malik and Bunene.

Upon reaching so late a period as the days of Nabubaliddin (*c.* 850 B.C.), it becomes doubtful whether we are justified in including the additional deities occurring in his inscription among the Babylonian pantheon of the second period. The occurrence of some of these gods in the religious literature is a presumption in favor of regarding them as ancient creations, rather than due to later influences. Certainly this appears to be the case with Malik and Bunene, who, with Shamash, form a triad that constitutes the chief object of worship in the great temple E-babbara at Sippar, to whose restored cult Nabu-baliddin devotes himself. Both names, moreover, occur as parts of proper names in the age of Hammurabi. Malik—*i.e.*, ruler—is one of the names frequently assigned to Shamash, just as the god's consort was known as Malkatu, but for all that Malik is not the same as Shamash. Accompanying the inscription of Nabubaliddin is a design[1] representing the sun-god seated in his shrine. Before him on a table rests a wheel, and attached to the wheel are cords held by two figures, who are evidently directing the course of the wheel. These two figures are Malik

---

[1] See VR. pl. 60.

and Bunene, a species of attendants, therefore, on the sun-god, who drive the fiery chariot that symbolized the great orb. Bunene, through association with Malik, becomes the latter's consort, and it is interesting to observe the extent to which the tendency of the Babylonian religion to conceive the gods in pairs goes. Bunene is not the only instance of an originally male deity becoming through various circumstances the female consort to another. Originally, Malik may have been a name under which the sun-god was worshipped at some place, for the conception that makes him the chariot-driver to Shamash appears to be late. The absorption by the greater sun-cults (at Sippar and Larsa more particularly) of the lesser ones leads to the complete transfer of the names of minor sun-deities to the great Shamash, but in some instances the minor deities continue to lead a shadowy existence in some rôle of service to the greater ones.

Nin-igi-nangar-bu, Gushgin-banda, Nin-kurra, and Nin-zadim.

We have seen that Ea, among other powers assigned to him, was regarded as the god of fine arts, — in the first instance as the god of the smithy, because of the antiquity and importance of the smith's art, and then of art in general, including especially the production of great statues. In accordance with this conception, Nabubaliddin declares that it was through the wisdom of Ea that he succeeded in manufacturing the great image of Shamash that was set up by him in the temple at Sippar. But in the days of Nabubaliddin the arts had been differentiated into various branches, and this differentiation was expressed by assigning to each branch some patron god who presided over that section. In this way, the old belief that art comes to men from the gods survived, while at the same time it entered upon new phases.[1] Accordingly, Nabu-baliddin assigns several deities who act the part of assistants to Ea. The names of these deities point to their functions. Nin-igi-nangar-bu is the 'lord who presides over metal-workers'; Gushgin-banda, 'brilliant chief,' is evidently the patron of those skilled in the working of the bright metals; Nin-kurra, 'lord of mountain,' the patron of those that quarried the stones; while Nin-zadim is the patron of sculpture. Ea stands above these as a general overseer, but the four classes of laborers symbolized by gods indicate the manner of artistic construction in the advanced state of Babylonian art, and of the various distinct professions to which this art gave birth. In a certain sense, of course, these four gods associated with Ea belong to the Babylonian pantheon, but not in the same sense in which Ea, for example, or the other gods discussed in this chapter, belong to it. They cannot even be said to be gods of a minor order — they are hardly anything more than personifications of certain phenomena that have their source in the human intellect. In giving to these personified powers the determinative indicative of deity, the Babylonian schoolmen were not conscious of expressing anything more than their belief in the divine origin of the power and skill exercised by man. To represent such power as a god was the only way in which the personification could at all be effected under the conditions presented by Babylonian beliefs. When, therefore, we meet with such gods as Nin-zadim, 'lord of sculpture,' it is much the same as when in the Old Testament we are told that Tubal-cain was the 'father' of those that work in metals, and where similarly other arts are traced back to a single source. 'Father' in Oriental hyperbole signifies 'source, originator, possessor, or patron,' and, indeed, includes all these ideas. The Hebrew writer, rising to a higher level of belief, conceives the arts to

[1] To this day in the Orient, fine productions of man's skill are attributed to the influence of hidden spirits, good or bad, as the case may be.

have originated through some single personage endowed with divine powers;[1] the Babylonian, incapable as yet of making this distinction, ascribes both the origin and execution of the art directly to a god. In this way, new deities were apparently created even at an advanced stage of the Babylonian religion, but deities that differed totally from those that are characteristic of the earlier periods. The differentiation of the arts, and the assignment of a patron to each branch, reflect the thoughts and the aspirations of a later age. These views must have arisen under an impulse to artistic creation that was called forth by unusual circumstances, and I venture to think that this impulse is to be traced to the influence of the Assyrian rulers, whose greatest ambition, next to military glory, was to leave behind them artistic monuments of themselves that might unfold to later ages a tale of greatness and of power. Sculpture and works in metal were two arts that flourished in a special degree in the days when Assyria was approaching the zenith of her glory. Nabubaliddin's reign falls within this period; and we must, therefore, look from this time on for traces of Assyrian influence in the culture, the art, and also to some extent in the religious beliefs of the southern district of Mesopotamia.

[1] This position does not, of course, exclude the fact that in the original form of the tradition, Tubal-cain, Naamah, and other personages in the fourth chapter of Genesis were deities.

CHAPTER XI.

SURVIVALS OF ANIMISM IN THE BABYLONIAN RELIGION.

The Assyrian influence however was only one factor, and a minor factor at that, in maintaining the belief in countless spirits that occupied a place of more or less importance by the side of the great and lesser gods. That conservatism which is a distinguishing trait of the popular forms of religion everywhere, served to keep alive the view that all the acts of man, his moods, the accidents that befell him, were under the control of visible or invisible powers. The development of a pantheon, graded and more or less regulated under the guidance of the Babylonian schoolmen, did not drive the old animistic views out of existence. In the religious literature, and more especially in those parts of it which reflect the popular forms of thought, the unorganized mass of spirits maintain an undisputed sway. In the incantation texts, which will be discussed at length in a subsequent chapter, as well as in other sections of Babylonian literature embodying both the primitive and the advanced views of the Babylonians regarding the origin of the universe, its subdivisions, and its order of development, and, thirdly, in the legends and epics, hundreds of spirits are introduced, to which some definite function or functions were assigned. In many, indeed in the majority of cases, the precise character of these functions still escapes us. The material at our disposal is as yet inadequate for any satisfactory treatment of this phase of Babylonian belief, and we must content ourselves for the present with some generalizations, or at the most with some broad classifications. Besides the texts themselves, we have proper names containing a spirit as an element, and also lists of those spirits prepared by the schoolmen on the basis of the texts. When, as sometimes happens, these lists contain explanatory comments on the spirits enumerated, we are able to take some steps forward in our knowledge of the subject.

In the first place, then, it is important to bear in mind that the numerous spirits, when introduced into the religious and other texts, are almost invariably preceded by a sign — technically known as a determinative — which stamps them as divine. This sign being the same as the one placed before the names of the gods, it is not always possible to distinguish between deities and spirits. The use of a common sign is significant as pointing to the common origin of the two classes of superior powers that thus continue to exist side by side. A god is naught but a spirit writ large. As already intimated in a previous chapter, a large part of the development of the Babylonian religion consists in the differentiation between the gods and the spirits, — a process that, beginning before the period of written records, steadily went on, and in a certain sense was never completed. In the historical texts, the gods alone, with certain exceptions, find official recognition, and it is largely through these texts that we are enabled to distinguish between the two classes of powers, the gods and the spirits; but as a survival of a primitive animism, the demons, good, bad, and indifferent, retain their place in the popular forms of religion. Several hundred spirits occur in the incantation texts, and almost as many more in other religious texts. We may distinguish several classes. In the first place, there are the demons that cause disease and all manner of physical annoyances. The chief of these will be considered when we come to the analysis of the incantation texts. Against these demons the sufferer seeks protection by means of formulas, the utterance of which is invested with peculiar power, and again by means of certain rites of an expiatory or purificatory character. Next, we have the demons supposed to inhabit the fields, and to whom the ground is supposed to belong. These were imaged under various animal forms, serpents and scorpions being the favorite ones. When possession was taken of the field, the spirits inhabiting it had to be propitiated. The owner placed himself under their protection, and endeavored to insure his rights against wrongful encroachment by calling upon the demons to range themselves on his side. It was customary, especially in the case of territory acquired by special grant of the monarch, or under extraordinary circumstances, to set up a so-called boundary stone,[1] on which the owner of the field detailed his right to possession, through purchase or gift, as the case may be. This inscription closed with an appeal to various gods to strike with their curses any intruder upon the owner's rights. In addition to this, the stones are embellished with serpents, scorpions, unicorns, and various realistic or fantastic representations of animal forms. These, it would seem, symbolize the spirits, the sight of which, it was hoped, might act as a further and effectual warning against interference with the owner's rights.[2]

A special class of demons is formed by those which were supposed to infest the resting-places of the dead, though they stand in a certain relationship to the demons that plague the living. A remarkable monument found a number of years ago,

---

[1] The technical name for this class of monuments was *Kudurru*, i.e., mark, and then used like the German word *Mark* both for boundary and for the territory included within the bounds. A notable contribution to the interpretation of the Kudurru monuments was made by Delser, in the *Beiträge zur Assyriologie*, ii. 111–203.

[2] The question has been raised (see Delser, *ib.* p. 111) by Pinches whether these representations are not the symbols of the zodiac, but, as Delser justly remarks, the attempt to interpret the pictures in this way has not been successful. It still seems most plausible to regard the pictures as symbols of spirits or demons. Such an interpretation is in accord with the Babylonian and general Semitic view of land ownership. At the same time, it must be confessed that we are still in the dark as to the motives underlying the choice of the animals portrayed. There may be some ultimate connection with *some* of the signs of the zodiac, — so Hommel believes, — but such connection would have to be judged from the earlier forms that animism takes on, and not in the light of an advanced theology such as appears in the zodiacal system of the Babylonians.

and which will be fully described in a subsequent chapter, affords us a picture of some of these demons whose sphere of action is more particularly in the subterranean cave that forms the gathering-place of the dead. They are represented as half human, half animal, with large grotesque and terror-inspiring features.[1] Their power, however, is limited. They are subject to the orders of the gods whose dominion is the lower world, more particularly to Nergal and his consort Allatu. In the advanced eschatology of the Babylonians the demons play a minor part. It is with the gods that the dead man must make his peace. Their protection assured, he has little to fear ; but the demons of the lower world frequently ascend to the upper regions to afflict the living. Against them precautions must be taken similar to the means employed for ridding one's self of the baneful influence of the disease- and pain-bringing spirits. Reference has already been made to the spirits that belong to the higher phases of Mesopotamian culture, — those that have a share in the production of works of skill and art. We have seen that in accounting for these we are justified in assuming a higher phase of religious belief. The dividing line between god and spirit becomes faint, and the numerous protecting patrons of the handicrafts that flourished in Babylonia and Assyria can hardly be placed in the same category with those we have so far been considering. Still, to the popular mind the achievements of the human mind were regarded as due to the workings of hidden forces. Strange as it may seem, there was an indisposition to ascribe everything to the power of the gods. Ea and Nabu, although the general gods of wisdom, did not concern themselves with details. These were left to the secondary powers, — the spirits. Hence it happens that by the side of the great gods, we have a large number of minor powers who preside over the various branches of human handiwork and control the products of the human mind.

---

[1] See Perrot and Chipiez, *History of Art in Chaldaea and Assyria*, I. 351.

Reserving further details regarding the several classes of demons and spirits enumerated, it will suffice to say a few words about one particular group of spirits whose rôle was peculiarly prominent in both historical, liturgical, and general religious texts. The tendency to systematize the beliefs in spirits manifests itself in Babylonia, equally with the grouping of the gods into certain classes. In consequence of this general tendency, the conception arose of a group of spirits that comprised the associated secondary powers of earth and heaven, somewhat as Anu, Bel, and Ea summed up the quintessence of the higher powers or gods. This group was known as the

ANUNNAKI AND IGIGI.

Regarding these names it may be said that the former has not yet been satisfactorily interpreted. On the assumption that the union of the syllables A-nun-na-ki[1] represents a compound ideograph, the middle syllable *nun* signifies 'strength,' whereas the first is the ordinary ideograph for 'water.' Hommel[2] proposed to interpret the name therefore as 'gods of the watery habitation.' The artificiality of this manner of writing points, as in several instances noted, to a mere 'play' upon the real name. *Anunna* reminds one forcibly of the god *Anu* and of the goddess *Anunit*, and the element *ak* is quite a common afformative in Babylonian substantives, conveying a certain emphatic meaning to the word. If therefore we may compare Anun with the name of the god of heaven, the name *Anunnak* embodying, as it does in this case, the idea of power, would be an appropriate designation for the spirits, or a group of spirits collectively. Be it understood that this explanation is offered merely as a conjecture, which, however, finds support in the meaning attached to the term 'Igigi.' This, as

---

[1] The element *ki* is sometimes omitted. The force of *na* is not clear, unless it be a phonetic complement merely.
[2] *Semitische Völker*, p. 369.

Halevy and Guyard have recognized, is a formation of a well-known stem occurring in Babylonian, as well as in other Semitic languages, that has the meaning 'strong.' The ideographic form of writing the name likewise designates the spirits as 'the great chiefs.' The 'Igigi,' therefore, are 'the strong ones,' and strength being the attribute most commonly assigned to the Semitic deities,[1] there is a presumption, at least, in favor of interpreting Anunnak, or Anunnaki,[2] in the same way. The 'Igigi' are at times designated as the seven gods, but this number is simply an indication of their constituting a large group. Seven is a round number which marked a large quantity. At an earlier period five represented a numerical magnitude, and hence the Anunnaki are at times regarded as a group of five.[3] The Anunnaki and Igigi appear for the first time in an historical text in the inscription of the Assyrian king Rammannirari I., who includes them in his appeal to the great gods. He designates the Igigi as belonging to heaven, the Anunnaki as belonging to the earth. The manner in which he uses the names shows conclusively that, at this early period, the two groups comprehended the entire domain over which spirits, and for that matter also the gods, exercised their power. Indeed, it would appear that at one time the two names were used to include the gods as well as the spirits. At least this appears to be the case in Assyria, and the conclusion may be drawn, from the somewhat vague use of the terms, that the names belong to a very early period of the religion, when the distinction between gods and spirits was not yet

---

[1] Very many of the names of the Semitic gods and heroes signify strong, *e.g.*, *El, Adon, Baal, Etana, Kemosh*, etc.

[2] The final vowel *i* would, on the basis of the explanation offered, be paralleled by the *i* of Igigi — an indication of the plural. See Delitzsch, *Assyr. Gram.* § 67, 1.

[3] The Igigi are designated ideographically as v plus ii, and Hommel (*Semitische Völker*, p. 491) properly suggests that this peculiar writing points to an earlier use of five as constituting the group. Hommel, however, does not see that neither five nor seven are to be interpreted literally, but that both represent a large round number, and, therefore, also a holy one.

clearly marked. However that may be, in Babylonian hymns and incantations the Igigi and Anunnaki play a very prominent part. Anu is represented as the father of both groups. But they are also at the service of other gods, notably of Bel, who is spoken of as their 'lord,' of Ninib, of Marduk, of Ishtar, and of Nergal. They prostrate themselves before these superior masters, and the latter at times manifest their anger against the Igigi. They are sent out by the gods to do service. Their character is, on the whole, severe and cruel. They are not favorable to man, but rather hostile to him. Their brilliancy consumes the land. Their power is feared, and Assyrian kings more particularly are fond of adding the Igigi and Anunnaki to the higher powers — the gods proper — when they wish to inspire a fear of their own majesty. At times the Igigi alone are mentioned, but generally the Igigi and Anunnaki appear in combination. To the latest period of Babylonian history these two groups continue to receive official recognition. Nebuchadnezzar II.[1] dedicates an altar, which he erects at the wall of the city of Babylon, to the Igigi and Anunnaki. The altar is called a structure of 'joy and rejoicing,' and on the festival of Marduk, who is the 'lord of the Anunnaki and Igigi,' sacrifices were offered at this altar. In the great temple of Marduk there was a fountain in which the gods and the Anunnaki, according to a Babylonian hymn, 'bathe their countenance'; and when to this notice it be added that another hymn praises them as the 'shining chiefs' of the ancient city of Eridu, it will be apparent that the conceptions attached to this group span the entire period of Babylonian-Assyrian history.

Besides the Igigi and Anunnaki there is still a third group of seven spirits, generally designated as the 'evil demons,' who represent the embodiment of all physical suffering to which man is subject. They appear, however, only in the incantation texts, and we may, therefore, postpone their consideration

[1] IR. 55, col. iv. ll. 7-13.

until that subject is reached. The point to be borne in mind, and which I have attempted to emphasize in this place, is the close relationship existing in the *popular* forms of the Babylonian religion between the gods and the spirits. The latter belong to the pantheon as much as the former. Primitive animism continues to enchain the minds of the people, despite the differentiation established between the higher and the secondary powers, and despite the high point of development reached by the schoolmen in their attempts to systematize and, in a measure, to purify the ancient beliefs.

CHAPTER XII.

THE ASSYRIAN PANTHEON.

We have now reached a point where it will be proper to set forth the phases that the Babylonian religion assumed during the days of Assyrian supremacy.

An enumeration of the gods occurring in the inscriptions of the rulers of Assyria from the earliest days to the close of the empire, so far as published, will show better than any argument the points of similarity between the Babylonian and the Assyrian pantheon. These gods are in alphabetical order:[1] Anu, Ashur, Bel, Belit, Gaga, Gibil, Gamlat, Gula, Dibbarra, Dagan, Damkina, Ea, Ishtar, Kadi, Khani, Marduk, Nabu, Nanâ, Nin-gal, Nergal, Ninib, Nusku, Ramman, Sin, Shala, Shalman, Shamash, Shanitka(?), Tashmitum. Of these quite a number are only mentioned incidentally, and in a manner that indicates that they do not belong to the pantheon in the strict sense. Others, like Khani[2] and Gamlat,— *i.e.*, 'the merciful one,'[3] — may turn out to be mere epithets of deities otherwise known; and it would hardly be legitimate to extend the list by including deities that have not yet been identified,[4] and which may similarly be only variant forms, descriptive of such as are already included. But however much this list may be extended and modified by further publications and researches, the historical material at hand for the Assyrian period of the religion is sufficient to warrant us in setting up two classes of the pantheon,— one class constituting the active pan-

---

[1] Semitic alphabet.
[2] A form of Nebo, according to Meissner-Rost, *Bauinschriften Sanherib's*, p. 105.
[3] See Meissner-Rost, *ib.* p. 108.
[4] As *e.g.*, En-e-ia-pal (Meissner-Rost, *ib.* p. 76). Sherua and Azag-sir (*ib.* p. 101). For further lists of deities, see pp. 234, 238.

theon, the other, deities introduced by the kings merely for purposes of self-glorification, or to give greater solemnity to the invocations and warnings that formed a feature of all commemorative and dedicatory inscriptions, as well as of the annals proper. The future additions to the list, it is safe to assert, will increase the second class and only slightly modify, if at all, the first class. Bearing in mind this distinction we may put down as active forces in Assyria the following: Anu, Ashur, Bel, Belit, Gula, Dagan, Ea, Khani, Ishtar, Marduk, Nabu, Nergal, Ninib, Nusku, Ramman, Sin, Shala, Shamash, Tashmitum.

Comparing both the fuller and the restricted list with the Babylonian pantheon during the two periods treated of in the preceding chapters, we are struck by three facts: (1) the smaller compass of the Assyrian pantheon; (2) the more restricted introduction of what, for want of a better term, we may call minor deities; and (3) the small number of new deities met with. To take up the latter point, the only gods in the above list that are not found in Babylonian inscriptions are Ashur, Gibil, Gamlat, Dibbarra, Kadi, Nusku, Shala, Shanitka. Of these it is purely accidental that Gibil, Dibbarra, Nusku, and Shala are not mentioned, for, except those that are foreign importations, they belong to Babylonia as much as to Assyria and fall within the periods of the Babylonian religion that have been treated of. Kadi is a foreign deity.[1] Shanitka(?) may only be a title of some goddess, and Shalman (or Shalmannu) occurs only in proper names, and may likewise be only a title of some god.[2] There remains, as the only god peculiar to Assyria, the god Ashur. But for this god, the Babylonian and the Assyrian pantheon are identical.

---

[1] The Assyrian kings are fond of mentioning foreign deities, and of adding them to their pantheon. In his annals (VR. col. vi. ll. 30-43) Ashurbanabal gives a list of twenty Elamitic deities captured by him.
[2] Tiele (*Babyl.-Assyr. Geschichte*, p. 519) suggests Ea.

When we come, however, to the position held by the gods in the pantheon, their relationship to one another, and the traits which secured for them popular and royal favor, the differences between the Babylonian and the Assyrian phases of the religion will be found to be more accentuated.

As for the smaller compass of the Assyrian pantheon, we may recognize in this a further advance of the tendency already noted in the second period of the Babylonian religion. There, too, we found the minor local cults yielding to the growing influence and favor of certain gods associated with the great centers of Babylonian life, or possessing attributes that accorded more with the new political order and the general advance of culture. One of the chief factors in this tendency towards centralization was, as we saw, the supremacy accorded to Marduk in the new empire as the patron god of the capital, and that not only led to his absorbing the rôle of other deities,[1] but resulted also in strengthening the belief that there were only a limited number of deities upon whose power and willingness to aid dependence could be placed. This tendency was in a measure offset by the pride that the rulers of the second Babylonian period still took in parading at times, as large a number as possible of deities under whose protection they claimed to stand. As we pass from one age to the other, the number of minor deities thus invoked also tends to diminish, and the occasions likewise when they are invoked become limited to the more solemn invocations at the beginning and the close of inscriptions. Now, in Assyria we have

[1] An interesting example of this tendency is furnished by a tablet published by T. G. Pinches (*Journal of the Victoria Institute*, xxviii. 8-10), in which the name Marduk is treated almost as a generic term for deity. Nergal is called 'the Marduk of warfare'; Nebo, 'the Marduk of earthly possessions'; Ninib, 'the Marduk of strength'; En-lil, 'the Marduk of sovereignty'; and so on, in a long enumeration, the gods are regarded as so many forms of Marduk. Pinches' conclusion that the list points to monotheistic beliefs is, however, unwarranted. The list only illustrates a tendency towards a centralization of divine powers in Marduk, that accompanies the political centralization of the period.

much the same political conditions as in Babylonia, only intensified. Here, too, we have one god towering above the others, only to a still greater degree even than Marduk in Babylonia. Marduk, while absorbing the rôle of the old Bel, is still bound to acknowledge the fathership of Ea. For a time he has to fear the rivalry of Nabu, and we have seen that during the Cassitic rule, the glory of Marduk is somewhat dimmed. The god who comes to stand at the head of the Assyrian pantheon — Ashur — suffers from none of these restrictions. He is independent of other gods and is under no obligations to any of his fellows, and his rule once acknowledged remains supreme, with, perhaps, one short period excepted,[1] throughout all the vicissitudes that the empire undergoes. As a consequence of this unique position, Ashur is so completely identified with Assyria, that with the fall of the empire he, too, disappears, — whereas the Marduk cult survives the loss of Babylonian independence, and is undisturbed even by the final absorption of Babylonia into the empire of Cyrus. The tendency towards centralization of the cult is even more pronounced, therefore, in Assyria than in Babylonia. Marduk is a leader who has many gods as followers, but all of whom have their distinct functions. Ashur is a host in himself. He needs no attendants. His aid suffices for all things, and such is the attachment of his subjects to him that it would almost appear like an insult to his dignity to attach a long array of minor gods to him. For the Assyrian kings the same motives did not exist as for the Babylonians to emphasize their control over all parts of their empire by adding the chief gods of these districts to the pantheon. Assyria was never split up into independent states like Babylonia before the days of Hammurabi. The capital, it is true, changed with considerable frequency, but there was always only one great center of political power. So far as Assyrian

---

[1] See below, pp. 228, 229.

control over Babylonia was concerned, it was sufficient for the purposes of the Assyrian rulers to claim Marduk as their patron and protector, and, as we shall see, they always made a point of emphasizing this claim. Hence we have only 'great gods,'[1] and no minor deities, in the train of Ashur. These 'great gods' could not be expunged from the pantheon without a complete severance of the ties that bound the Assyrians to their past. Kings of great empires seldom favor religious revolutions. But by the side of Ashur these great gods pale, and in the course of time the tendency becomes more marked to regard them merely as formal members of a little court with few functions of their own, beyond that of adding by their presence to the majesty and glory of Ashur. One receives the impression that in Assyria only a few of the gods invoked by the kings at the side of Ashur exert any real influence on the lives of the people; and such as do, gain favor through possessing in some measure the chief attribute that distinguished Ashur, — prowess in war. They are little Ashurs, as it were, by the side of the great one. The position of Ashur in the Assyrian pantheon accounts for the general tendencies manifested by the religion of the northern empire, and upon a clear conception of the character of Ashur depends our understanding of the special points that distinguish the other gods from what we have learned of their character and traits in the southern states. The beginning, therefore, of an account of the Assyrian pantheon is properly to be made with Ashur.

ASHUR.

The starting-point of the career of Ashur is the city of Ashur, situated on the west bank of the Tigris, not far from the point where the lower Zab flows into the Tigris. Ashur is

---

[1] So the gods of the Assyrian pantheon are generally termed in the inscriptions of the kings.

therefore distinctly a local deity, and so far as the testimony of the texts goes, he was never regarded in early days in any other light than as the local patron of the city to which he has given his name. He was never worshipped, so far as can be ascertained, as a manifestation of any of the great powers of nature, — the sun or the moon; though, if anything, he was originally a solar deity.[1] Nor was he a symbol of any of the elements, — fire or water. In this respect he differs from Sin, Shamash, Nusku,[2] and Ea, whose worship was localized, without affecting the *quasi*-universal character that these deities possessed. As a local deity his worship must have been limited to the city over which he spread his protecting arm; and if we find the god afterwards holding jurisdiction over a much larger territory than the city of Ashur, it is because in the north, as in the south, a distinct state or empire was simply regarded as the extension of a city. Ashur became the god of Assyria as the rulers of the city of Ashur grew in power, — in the same way that Marduk, upon the union of the Babylonian states under the supremacy of the city of Babylon, became the god of all Babylonia. But a difference between the north and the south is to be noted. Whereas Marduk, although the god of Babylonia, was worshipped only in the city of Babylon where he was supposed to have his seat, temples to Ashur existed in various parts of the Assyrian empire. The god accompanied the kings in their wars, and wherever the rulers settled, there the god was worshipped. So in the various changes of official residences that took place in the course of Assyrian history from Ashur to Calah, and from Calah to Nineveh, and from Nineveh to Khorsabad, the god took part, and his central seat of worship depended upon the place that the kings chose for their official residence. At the same time, while the cult in the various temples that in the course of time were erected in his honor probably continued

[1] See below, p. 195.   [2] See below, p. 220.

without interruption, there was always one place — the official residence — which formed the central spot of worship. There the god was supposed to dwell for the time being. One factor, perhaps, that ought to be taken into consideration in accounting for this movable disposition of the god was that he was not symbolized exclusively by a statue, as Marduk and the other great gods were. His chief symbol was a standard that could be carried from place to place, and indeed was so made that it could be carried into the thick of the fray, in order to assure the army of the god's presence. The standard consisted of a pole surrounded by a disc enclosed within two wings, while above the disc stood the figure of a warrior in the act of shooting an arrow.[1] The statues of the gods were deposited in shrines, and after being carried about, as was done on festive days or other occasions, they would be replaced in their shrines. The military standard, however, followed the camp everywhere, and when the kings chose to fix upon a new place for their military encampment — and such the official residences of the Assyrian warrior-kings in large measure were — the standard would repose in the place selected. How this standard came to be chosen, and when, is another question, and one more difficult to answer. It may be that the representation of the god by a standard was a consequence of the fondness that the rulers of Ashur manifested for perpetual warfare; or, in other words, that the god Ashur was represented by a standard so that he might be carried into the battle and be moved from place to place. At all events, the two things — the standard and the warlike character of the subjects of Ashur — stood in close relationship to one another, and the further conclusion is justified that when a military standard came to be chosen as the symbol of Ashur, the god was recog-

---

[1] A description of this symbol occurs in a text of Sennacherib (Meissner-Rost, *Bauinschriften Sanherib's*, p. 94). The symbol itself is found on sculptured slabs and on seal cylinders.

nized distinctly as a god of war. The symbols accompanying the standard are of importance as enabling us to determine something more regarding the character of Ashur. In the first place, the fact that it contained a figure may be taken as an indication that the god was at one time represented by a statue, — as indeed we know from other evidence,[1] — and that the change of his symbol from a statue to a standard is a result of the military activity of the Assyrians. The winged disc is so general a symbol of the sun in the religious system of various ancient nations[2] that one cannot escape the conclusion that the symbol must be similarly interpreted in the case before us. Is it possible, therefore, that in a period lying beyond that revealed by the oldest inscriptions at our disposal, Ashur was worshipped as a solar deity? One is bound to confess that the evidence does not warrant us in regarding Ashur as anything but the patron of the city of Ashur. Nowhere do we find any allusion from which we are justified in concluding that he originally represented some elemental power or phenomenon. Tiele[3] is of the decided opinion that Ashur was at his origin a nature god of some kind, and he goes so far as to suggest, though with due reserve, the possible identification of Ashur with Sin. No doubt Tiele is prompted to this view by the example of the great god of the south, Marduk, who is originally a solar deity, and by all the other great gods who represent, or represented, some power of nature. Analogy, however, is not a sufficiently reliable guide to settle a question for the solution of which historical material is lacking. So much, however, may be said, that if we are to assume that Ashur personified originally some natural power, the symbol of the winged disc lends a strong presumption in favor of supposing

---

[1] So Sennacherib still speaks of images of Ashur, and of the great gods erected by him (Meissner-Rost, *Bauinschriften Sanherib's*, p. 94).

[2] See Stevenson, "The Feather and the Wing in Mythology," *Oriental Studies of the Phila. Oriental Club*, pp. 236–239.

[3] *Babyl.-Assyr. Geschichte*, p. 533.

him to have been some phase of the sun. So much, then, for the general character of Ashur. Before passing on to a specification of his rôle and his traits, as revealed by the historical texts, a word remains to be said as to the etymology and form of the name. Ashur is the only instance that we have of a god expressly giving his name to a city, for the name of the city can only be derived from that of the god, and not *vice versa*. The identification of the god with his favorite town must have been so complete that the town, which probably had some specific name of its own, became known simply as the 'city of the god Ashur.' From such a designation it is but a small step to call the city simply, Ashur. The difference between the god and the city would be indicated by the determinative for deity, which was only attached to the former, while the latter was written with the determinative attached to towns. When this city of Ashur extended its bounds until it became coequal with the domain of Assyria, the name of the god was transferred to the entire northern district of Mesopotamia, which, as the country of the god Ashur, was written with the determinative for country.[1] The ideographs which the Assyrian scribes employed in writing the name of the god reveal the meaning they attached to it. He is described ideographically as the 'good god.' This interpretation accords admirably with the general force of the verbal stem underlying the name. In both Hebrew and Assyrian *a-sh-r* signifies 'to be gracious, to grant blessing, to cause to prosper.' Ashur, therefore, is the god that blesses his subjects, and to the latter he would accordingly appear as the 'good god' *par excellence*. If the tempting etymology of our own word 'god,' which connects it with 'good,' be correct, 'god' would be almost the perfect equivalent of Ashur. It is not necessary to conclude, as Tiele does,[2]

---

[1] For the sake of convenience it is customary to distinguish between Ashur the god, and the country by writing the latter with a double *sh* — Ashshur.

[2] *Geschichte*, p. 533.

that Ashur, as the 'good one,' is an ethical abstraction, but certainly a designation of a god as 'a good one' sounds more like a descriptive epithet than like a name. The supposition that Ashur was not, therefore, the original name of the god receives a certain measure of force from this consideration. Moreover, there are indications that there actually existed another form of his name, namely, Anshar.[1] This form Anshar would, according to the phonetic laws prevailing in Assyria, tend to become Ash-shar.[2] Ashur — the 'good one' — would thus turn out to be an epithet of the god, chosen as a 'play' suggested by Ash-shar, just as we found Gula called the lady of *Ekalli*, and again *Kallat* (bride).[3] The etymology of Anshar is as obscure as that of most of the ancient gods of Babylonia, — as of Sin, Marduk, Ishtar, and many more. But before leaving the subject, it will be proper to call attention to the rôle that a god Anshar plays in the Babylonian-Assyrian cosmological system. *Anshar* and *Kishar* are the second pair of deities to be created, the first pair being *Lakhmu* and *Lakhamu*. In the great fight of the gods against the monster Tiamat, it would appear that, according to one version at least, Anshar sends Anu, Ea, and finally Bel-Marduk, in turn to destroy the monster. He appears, therefore, to have exercised a kind of supremacy over the gods. Assuming the correctness of the deductions, according to which Ashur is an epithet arising by a play upon Ash-shar (from an original Anshar), it is hardly open to doubt that this Anshar is the same as the one who appears in the cosmology. On the other hand, it is difficult to suppose that Anshar should have played so significant a part in Babylonian traditions and yet find no mention in the text of the rulers of Babylonia. Bearing in mind what has been said as to the manner in which ancient

---

[1] See Jensen, *Zeits. für Assyr.* i. 1 *seq.* and Delitzsch, *Das Babylonische Weltschöpfungsepos*, p. 94.

[2] By the assimilation of the *n* to the following consonant.

[3] See above, pp. 173, 175.

traditions and myths were remodeled by the schoolmen to conform to later ideas, — we have seen how in this process the popularity of Marduk led to his assuming the rôle originally played by Bel, — may not the recognition given to Anshar be a concession, made at the time that Assyria had begun her glorious career (*c.* 1400 B.C.), to the chief god of the northern empire?

That such tendencies to glorify Ashur may justly be sought for in part of the religious literature is proved by a version of one of the series of tablets giving an account of the creation, and which assigns to Anshar the work of building Esharra, — *i.e.*, the earth, — that, according to another version, belongs to Marduk.[1] Evidently, then, just as the Babylonian theologians sought to glorify Marduk at the expense of Bel, so Assyrian theologians, or such as stood under Assyrian influences, did not hesitate to replace Marduk by their own favorite, Anshar. In the chapter on the 'Cosmology' we will have occasion to come back to this point. For present purposes it is sufficient to have shown that the position of Anshar in the remodeled traditions is an argument in favor of regarding Anshar as the real name of the god who stands at the head of the Assyrian pantheon.

In the oldest Assyrian inscription known to us, the god Ashur is mentioned. Samsi-Ramman, who does not yet assume the title of king, but only *patesi*, — *i.e.*, 'religious chief,'[2] — prides himself upon being 'the builder of the temple of Ashur.' The phrase does not mean that he founded the temple, but only that he undertook building operations in connection with it. The date of this ruler may be fixed roughly at 1850 B.C., and since the two inscribed bricks that we have of Samsi-Ramman were found in the ruins of Kalah-Shergat, — the site of the ancient city of Ashur, —

---

[1] Jensen, *Kosmologie*, p. 275.

[2] The combination of religious supremacy with political power, which characterizes the social state of ancient Babylonia and Assyria, gives to the title *patesi* a double significance. In Babylonia, moreover, it acquires the force of vassal-king.

there can, of course, be no doubt that the temple at that place is referred to.

The rulers of Assyria, even after they assumed the title of 'king' (c. 1500 B.C.), were still fond of calling themselves the 'priest' of the god Ashur, and frequently gave this title the preference over others. In the fourteenth century the temple of Ashur seems to have suffered at the hands of the Cassites, who attempted to extend their power to the north. This plan was, however, frustrated by Ramman-nirari I., who forces the Cassites to retreat, successfully opposes other enemies of Assyria, and restores the injured parts of Ashur's temple. From this time on, and for a period of several centuries, Assyria assumes an aggressive attitude, and as a consequence the dependency upon the god is more keenly felt than before. The enemies against whom the kings proceed are called 'the enemies of Ashur,' the troops of the king are the troops of Ashur, and the weapons with which they fight are the weapons of Ashur. It is he who causes the arms of Tiglath-pileser I. to strike down his foes. The nations cannot endure the awful sight of the god. His brilliancy — the reference being no doubt to the shining standard as it was carried into the fray — inspires on every side a terror that casts all enemies to the ground. All warfare is carried on in the name of Ashur. The statement may be taken literally, for an oracle was sought at critical moments to determine the course that was to be pursued. The fight itself takes place with the help of the god, — again to be taken literally, for the god, represented by his symbol, is present on the battlefield. The victory, accordingly, belongs to the god in the first instance, and only in a secondary degree to the king. The nations are vanquished by Ashur, the conquered cities become subject to Ashur, and when the tribute is brought by the conquered foe, it is to Ashur that it is offered by the kings. Proud and haughty as the latter were, and filled with greed for glory and power, they never hesitated to humble themselves before their god. They freely acknowledged that everything they possessed was due to Ashur's favor. It was he who called them to the throne, who gave them the sceptre and crown, and who firmly established their sovereignty. Through Ashur, who gives the king his invincible weapon, — the mighty bow, — the kingdom is enlarged, until the kings feel justified in saying of themselves that, by the nomination of Ashur, they govern the four quarters of the world. Nay, the rulers go further and declare themselves to be the offspring of Ashur. It is not likely that they ever desired such an assertion also to be interpreted literally. The phrase is rather to be taken as the strongest possible indication of the attachment they felt for their chief god. Everything that they possessed coming directly from their god, how could this be better expressed than by making the god the source of their being? The phrase, at all events, is interesting as showing that the element of love was not absent in the emotions that the thought of Ashur aroused in the breasts of his subjects. The kings cannot find sufficient terms of glorification to bestow upon Ashur. Tiglathpileser I. calls him 'the great lord ruling the assembly of gods,' and in similar style, Ashurnasirbal invokes him as 'the great god of all the gods.' For Ramman-nirari III., he is the king of the Igigi — the heavenly host of spirits. Sargon lovingly addresses him as the father of the gods. Sennacherib calls him the great mountain or rock, — a phrase that recalls a Biblical metaphor applied to the deity, — and Esarhaddon speaks of him as the 'king of gods.' Frequently Ashur is invoked together with other gods. He is 'the guide of the gods.' There is only one instance in which he does not occupy the first place. Ramman-nirari I., to whom reference has above been made, gives Anu the preference over Ashur in a list of gods,[1] to whom conjointly he ascribes his victories. We have already had occasion (see

---

[1] The full list is Anu, Ashur, Shamash, Ramman, and Ishtar.

pp. 153–155) to note the antiquity of Anu worship in Assyria, the foundation of whose temple takes us beyond the period of Samsi-Ramman. Ashur's importance begins only with the moment that the rulers of his city enter upon their career of conquest. Before that, his power and fame were limited to the city over which he presided. Those gods who in the south occupied a superior rank were also acknowledged in the north. The religion of the Assyrians does not acquire traits that distinguish it from that of Babylonia till the rise of a distinct Assyrian empire. Here, as in Babylonia, the religious conceptions, and in a measure the art, are shaped by the course of political events. Anu, accordingly, takes precedence to Ashur previous to the supremacy of the city of Ashur. This superior rank belongs to him as the supreme god of heaven. Ramman-nirari's reign marks a turning-point in the history of Assyria. The enemies of Ashur, who had succeeded for a time in obscuring the god's glory through the humiliation which his land endured, were driven back, but neither the people nor the rulers had as yet become conscious of the fact that it was solely to Ashur that the victory was due. Hence, other gods are associated with Ashur by Ramman-nirari, and the old god Anu is accorded his proper rank. After the days of Ramman-nirari, however, Ashur's precedence over all other gods is established. Whether associated with Bel or with Ramman, or with Shamash and Ramman, or with a larger representation of the pantheon, Ashur is invariably mentioned first.

From what has been said of the chief trait of Assyrian history, it follows, as a matter of course, that the popularity of Ashur is due to the military successes of the Assyrian armies; and it follows, with equal necessity, that Ashur, whatever he may originally have been, becomes purely a god of war, from the moment that Assyria enters upon what appeared to be her special mission. All the titles given to Ashur by the kings may be said to follow from his rôle as the god who presides over the fortunes of the wars. If he is the 'ruler of all the gods,' and their father, he is so simply by virtue of that same superior strength which makes him the 'law-giver' for mankind, and not because of any ancient traditions, nor as an expression of some nature-myth. He lords it over gods and spirits, but he lords it solely because of his warlike qualities. Ashur is the giver of crown and sceptre, and the kings of Assyria are the *patesis* of the god, his lieutenants. He is the god that embodies the spirit of Assyrian history, and as such he is the most characteristic personage of the Assyrian pantheon — in a certain sense the only characteristic personage. So profound is his influence that almost all the other gods of the pantheon take on some of his character. Whenever and wherever possible, those phases of the god's nature are emphasized which point to the possession of power over enemies. The gods of the Assyrian pantheon impress one as diminutive Ashurs by the side of the big one, and in proportion as they approach nearer to the character of Ashur himself, is their hold upon the royal favor strengthened.

Ishtar.

Second in rank to Ashur during the most glorious part of Assyrian history stands the great goddess Ishtar. That the Assyrian Ishtar is identical with the great goddess of the Babylonian pantheon is beyond reasonable doubt. She approaches closest to Nanâ, — the Ishtar of Erech; but just as we found the Babylonian Ishtar appearing under various names and forms, so there are no less than three Ishtars in Assyria, distinguished in the texts as Ishtar of Nineveh, Ishtar of Arbela, and Ishtar who presides over the temple known as Kidmuru and who for that reason is generally called 'the queen of Kidmuru.' The seat of the latter was in Nineveh, as was of course also the seat of Ishtar of Nineveh. The third Ishtar had her cult at Arbela,[1] a town lying to the east of Calah about midway between the upper and lower Zab. It is not easy to determine which of these three Ishtars is the oldest. The Assyrians themselves seem to have been aware of the Babylonian origin of Ishtar, for Tiglathpileser I. is at pains to emphasize that the temple he builds to Ishtar in his capital is dedicated to the 'Assyrian Ishtar.'[2] This being the oldest mention of Ishtar in Assyrian texts, we are perhaps warranted in concluding that the cult of the goddess was transferred with the seat of government to Nineveh. This would not necessarily make Ishtar of Nineveh the oldest of the three, but accounts for the higher rank that was accorded to her, as against the other two. Ishtar of Arbela and the queen of Kidmuru do not make their appearance so far as the historical texts are concerned till the time of Esarhaddon (681, B.C.) — a comparatively late date. Tiele[3] suggests that Arbela became the seat of a school of prophets in the service of Ishtar. The curious name of the place, the 'four-god' city, certainly speaks in favor of supposing Arbela to have been a great religious center, but until excavations shall have been conducted on the modern site of the town, the problems connected with the worship of Ishtar of Arbela cannot be solved. It is quite possible, if not probable, that the three Ishtars are each of independent origin. The 'queen of Kidmuru,' indeed, I venture to think, is the indigenous Ishtar of Nineveh, who is obliged to yield her place to the so-called 'Assyrian Ishtar' upon the transfer of the capitol of Assyria to Nineveh, and henceforth is known by one of her epithets to distinguish her from her formidable rival. The cult of Ishtar at Arbela is probably, too, of ancient date; but special circumstances that escape us appear

---

[1] More precisely Arba-ilu, signifying 'city of the fourfold divinity' or 'four-god' city. *Cf.* the Palestinian form Kiryath-Arba, "four city," — originally perhaps, likewise, a city of four gods, rather than four roads or four quarters, as commonly explained.

[2] IR. 14, l. 86.   [3] *Babyl.-Assyr. Geschichte*, p. 85.

to have led to a revival of interest in their cults during the period when Assyria reached the zenith of her power. The important point for us to bear in mind is that no essential distinctions between these three Ishtars were made by the Assyrians. Their traits and epithets are similar, and for all practical purposes we have only one Ishtar in the northern empire. Next to Ashur, or rather by the side of Ashur, Ishtar was invoked as the great goddess of battle and war. This trait, however, was not given to her by the Assyrians. Hammurabi views the goddess in this light,[1] and in the Izdubar or Gilgamesh epic, as already pointed out, she appears at times in the rôle of a violent destroyer. The warlike phase of the goddess's nature is largely accentuated in the Assyrian pantheon and dwelt upon to the exclusion of that softer and milder side which we have seen characterized her as 'the mother of mankind.' Her rôle as the goddess of war grows in prominence as the Assyrian rulers proceed in their triumphal careers. Ashurrishishi (c. 1150 B.C.) invokes her simply as the superior goddess, but for Tiglathpileser I. and from his days on, she is primarily the lady of war, who arranges the order of battle and encourages her favorites to fight. She appears in dreams at critical moments, and whispers words of cheer to King Ashurbanabal. When danger threatens, it is to her that the great king spreads his hands in prayer. She is not merely the goddess of the kings, but of the people as well. The latter are instructed to honor her. No deity approaches her in splendor. As Ashur rules the Igigi, so Ishtar is declared to be 'mighty over the Anunnaki.' Her commands are not to be opposed. Her appearance is that of a being clothed with fiery flames, and streams of fire are sent down by her upon the enemies of Ashurbanabal — a description that expresses admirably the conception formed by the Assyrians of a genuine goddess of war. Like Ashur, she is given a supreme rank among the

[1] See above, p. 83.

gods. Shalmaneser II. calls her the first-born of heaven and earth, and for Tiglathpileser I., she is the first among the gods. Her milder attributes as the gracious mother of creation, the giver of plenty, and the hearer of the supplications of the sinner, so prominent in the religious literature,[1] are not dwelt upon in the historical texts. Still, an element of love also enters into the relationship with her subjects. Ashurnasirbal (885-860 B.C.) speaks of her as the lady who 'loves him and his priesthood.' Sennacherib similarly associates Ishtar with Ashur as the lover of his priesthood. As a goddess of war she is of course 'perfect in courage,' as Shalmaneser II. declares. Temples are erected to her in the city of Ashur, in Nineveh and Arbela. Ashurbanabal distinguishes carefully between the two Ishtars, — the one of Nineveh and the one of Arbela; and, strange enough, while terming Nineveh the favorite city of Ishtar, he seems to give the preference to Ishtar of Arbela. It is to the latter[2] that when hard pressed by the Elamites he addresses his prayer, calling her 'the lady of Arbela'; and it is this Ishtar who appears to the royal troops in a dream. The month of Ab — the fifth month of the Babylonian calendar—is sacred to Ishtar. Ashurbanabal proceeds to Arbela for the purpose of worshipping her during this sacred period. Something must have occurred during his reign, to bring the goddess of Arbela into such remarkable prominence, but even Ashurbanabal does not go so far as to place Ishtar of Arbela before Ishtar of Nineveh, when enumerating the gods of the pantheon. One point still remains to be mentioned before passing on. Ashurbanabal calls Ishtar — he is speaking of Ishtar of Nineveh — the wife of Bel.[3] Now Ishtar never appears in this capacity in the Baby-

---

[1] See above, pp. 83, 84.

[2] Cylinder B, col. v. ll. 30 *seq.*; elsewhere (Rassam Cylinder, col. ii. ll. 115 *seq.*) he prays to Ashur and Ishtar.

[3] Rassam Cylinder, col. viii. l. 92. Elsewhere, Cylinder B, col. v. 17, Ishtar is called the daughter of Bel. This, however, must be an error; either Sin must be read for Bel, or *khirat* (consort) for *marat* (daughter).

lonian inscriptions. If there is one goddess with whom she has nothing in common, it is Belit of Nippur. To account for this curious statement on the part of the Assyrian scribes, it is only necessary to bear in mind that the name Belit signifies 'lady,' and Ishtar is constantly spoken of as the Belit or lady of battle. Much the same train of thought that led to regarding Bel in the sense of 'lord,' merely as a title of Marduk, gave rise to the use of 'Belit,' as the title of the great 'lady' of the Assyrian pantheon.[1] From this it is but a small — but of course erroneous — step, to speak of Belit-Ishtar as the consort of Bel. Whether the error is due only to the scribe, or whether it actually made its way into the Assyrian system of theology, it is difficult to say. Probably the former; for the distinguishing feature of both the Babylonian and the Assyrian Ishtar is her independent position. Though at times brought into close association with Ashur, she is not regarded as the mere consort of any god — no mere reflection of a male deity, but ruling in her own right on a perfect par with the great gods of the pantheon. She is coequal in rank and dignity with Ashur. Her name becomes synonymous with goddess, as Marduk becomes the synonym for god. The female deities both native and foreign come to be regarded as so many forms of Ishtar. In a certain sense Ishtar is the only *real* goddess of the later Assyrian pantheon, the only one taking an active part in the religious and political life of the people. At the same time it is to be noted that by the side of the Assyrian Ishtar, the Babylonian Ishtar, especially the one associated with Erech (or Warka) is also worshipped by the monarchs of the north. Esarhaddon devotes himself to the improvement of the old temple at Erech, and Ashurbanabal prides himself upon having rescued out of the hands of the Elamites a statue of Ishtar or Nanâ of Erech that had been captured 1635 years previous.[2]

[1] See above, p. 151.
[2] See Barton, "The Semitic Ishtar Cult" (*Hebraica*, x. 9–12).

Anu.

Reference has already been made to the antiquity of the Anu cult in Assyria, and that prior to the time that the city of Ashur assumes the rôle of mistress of the northern district, Anu stood at the head of the pantheon, just as theoretically he continued to occupy this place in the pantheon of the south. What is especially important, he had a temple in the very city of Ashur, whose patron god succeeded in usurping the place of the old 'god of heaven.' The character of Anu in the north differs in no way from the traits assigned to him in the south. He is the king of the Igigi and Anunnaki, that is, of all the heavenly and earthly spirits, and he is this by virtue of being the supreme god of heaven. His cult, however, appears to have suffered through the overshadowing supremacy of Ashur. Even in his old temple at Ashur, which Tiglathpileser I. on the occasion of his rebuilding it, tells us was founded 641 years before this restoration,[1] he is no longer accorded sole homage. Ramman, the god of thunder and of storms, because correlated to Anu, is placed by the side of the latter and permitted to share the honors with Anu.[2] Anu survives in the Assyrian as in the Babylonian pantheon by virtue of being a member of the theological triad, composed as we have seen of Anu, Bel, and Ea. Tiglathpileser I. still invokes Anu as a deity of practical importance. He associates him with Ramman and Ishtar as the great gods of the city of Ashur or with Ramman alone, but beyond an incidental mention by Ashurnasirbal, who in a long list of gods at the beginning of his annals emphasizes the fact of his being the favorite of Anu, he appears only in combination with Bel and Ea. The same degree of reverence, however, was shown to the old triad in Assyria as in Babylonia. The three gods are asked not to listen to the prayers of the one who destroys

---

[1] *Ie.*, c. 1800 B.C. [2] See p. 154.

the monuments set up by the kings. Sargon tells us that it is Anu, Bel, and Ea who fix the names of the months,[1] and this same king when he comes to assign names to the eight gates of his great palace, does not forget to include Anu in the list of deities,[2] describing him as the god who blesses his handiwork.

DAGAN.

Coequal in antiquity with the cult of Anu in Assyria is that of Dagan. Although occurring in Babylonia as early as the days of Hammurabi, and indeed earlier,[3] it would appear that his worship was imported from the north into the south.[4] At all events, it is in the north that the cult of Dagan rises to prominence. The name of the god appears as an element in the name of Ishme-Dagan (the father of Samsi-Ramman II.),[5] whose date may be fixed at the close of the nineteenth century B.C. The form Dagan is interesting as being almost identical with the name of the chief god of the Philistines, Dagon,[6] who is mentioned in the Book of Judges. The resemblance can hardly be entirely accidental. From other sources we know that Dagan was worhipped in Palestine as early as the fourteenth or fifteenth century, and the form Dagan, if derived from *Dag*, contains an afformative element which stamps the word as non-Assyrian. The proposition has much in its favor which regards Dagan as a god whose worship was introduced into Assyria at a very early period through the influence of Aramaean hordes, who continue throughout Assyrian history to skirt the eastern shores of the Tigris. Once introduced, however, into Assyria, Dagan assumes a different form from

---

[1] See above, p. 149.
[2] See below, p. 237.
[3] A king of Nippur (*c.* 2500 B.C.) bears the name Ishme-Dagan.
[4] See above, p. 154; Tiele, *Geschichte der Religion im Alterthum*, I. 172.
[5] See Hommel, *Geschichte*, p. 490. How much earlier Samsi-Ramman I. reigned is not known — perhaps only 40 or 50 years.
[6] The *ð* of Dagon would be represented by *d* in cuneiform writing.

the one that he receives among the Philistines. To the latter he is the god of agriculture, while in Assyria he rises to the rank of second in the pantheon, and becomes the associate of Anu. The latter's dominion being the heavens, Dagan is conceived as the god of earth. Hence, there results the fusion with the Babylonian Bel, which has already been noted,[1] and it is due to this fusion that Dagan disappears almost entirely from the Assyrian pantheon. Ashurnasirbal invokes Dagan with Anu. Two centuries later, Sargon, whose scribes, as Jensen has noticed, manifest an 'archaeological' fondness for the earlier deities, repeats the phrase of Ashurnasirbal, and also calls his subjects 'troops of Anu and Dagan'; but it is important to observe that he does not include Dagan among the deities in whose honor he assigns names to the gates of his palace. We may, therefore, fix upon the ninth century as the terminus for the Dagan cult in Assyria. Proper names compounded with Dagan do not occur after the days of Ashurnasirbal.[2]

SHAMASH.

Besides the testimony furnished by the name of the king, Samsi-Ramman, we have a proof for the antiquity of the Shamash cult in Assyria in the express statement of Pudilu (c. 1350 B.C.) that he built a temple to the sun-god in the city of Ashur. He calls Shamash the 'protecting deity,' but the protection vouchsafed by Shamash is to be understood in a peculiar sense. Shamash does not work by caprice. He is, as we have seen, preëminently a god of justice, whose favors are bestowed in accordance with unchangeable principles. So far as Assyria is concerned, the conceptions regarding Shamash reach a higher ethical level than those connected with any other deity. Ashur and Ishtar are partial to Assyria, and uphold

---

[1] See p. 154.

[2] An eponym in his days bears the name Daganbelusur.

her rulers at any cost, but the favors of Shamash are bestowed upon the kings because of their righteousness, or, what is the same thing, because of their claim to being righteous. For Tiglathpileser I., great and ruthless warrior as he is, Shamash is the judge of heaven and earth, who sees the wickedness of the king's enemies, and shatters them because of their guilt. When the king mercifully sets certain captives free, it is in the presence of Shamash that he performs this act. It is, therefore, as the advocate of the righteous cause that Tiglathpileser claims to have received the glorious sceptre at the hands of Shamash; and so also for the successors of Tiglathpileser, down to the days of Sargon, Shamash is above all and first of all the judge, both of men and of the gods. There is, of course, nothing new in this view of Shamash, which is precisely the one developed in Babylonia; but in Assyria, perhaps for the reason that in Shamash is concentrated almost all of the ethical instinct of the northern people, the judicial traits of Shamash appear to be even more strongly emphasized. Especially in the days of Ashurnasirbal and Shalmaneser II. — the ninth century — does the sun-cult receive great prominence. These kings call themselves the *sun* of the world. The phrase,[1] indeed, has so distinctly an Egyptian flavor, that, in connection with other considerations, it seems quite plausible to assume that the influence of Egyptian reverence for *Ra* had much to do with the popularity of the sun-cult about this time. Shalmaneser bestows numerous epithets upon Shamash. He is the guide of everything, the messenger of the gods, the hero, the judge of the world who guides mankind aright, and, what is most significant, the lord of law. The word used for law, *têrtu*, is identical with the Hebrew term *tôrâ* that is used to designate the Pentateuchal legislation. No better testimony could be desired to show the nature of the conceptions that

---

[1] In the El-Amarna tablets (*c.* 1400 B.C.) the governors of the Palestinean states generally address their Egyptian lord as 'my sun.'

must have been current of Shamash. Sargon, again, who is fond of emphasizing the just principles that inspire his acts, goes to the length of building a sanctuary[1] for Shamash far beyond the northern limits of Assyria. But the kings, in thus placing themselves under the protection of the great judge, were not oblivious to the fact that this protection was particularly desired on the battlefield. War being uppermost in their thoughts, the other side of Shamash's nature — his power and violence — was not overlooked. Tiglathpileser invokes him also as the warrior, — a title that is often given to Shamash in the religious literature. There can be little doubt that a nation of warriors whose chief deities were gods of war, was attracted to Shamash not merely because he was the judge of all things, but also, and in a large degree, because he possessed some of the traits that distinguished Ashur and Ishtar.

Ramman.

The association of Ramman with Shamash in the name of the old ruler of Assyria, Samsi-Ramman, is not accidental or due to mere caprice. Only such deities are combined in proper names that are, or may be, correlated to one another. Ramman, as the god of storms, is naturally viewed as a power complementary to the great orb of light.[2] The two in combination, viewed as the beneficent and the destructive power, constitute the most powerful elements of nature, whose good will it was most important, especially for a nation of warriors, to secure. Some such thought surely underlies this association of Shamash with Ramman. The Assyrian Ramman differs in no way from the Ramman of Babylonia, but he is much more popular in the north than in the south. The popularity of the god is but a reflection of the delight that the Assyrians took

---

[1] Exactly of what nature we do not know. The Assyrian word used, Cylinder, l. 43, is obscure.
[2] See p. 160.

in military pursuits. Ramman is hardly anything more than another Ashur. Tiglathpileser I., who once calls the god Mar-tu, *i.e.*, "the West god,"[1] has left us an admirable description of him. He is the hero who floods the lands and houses of the country's enemies. The approach of the Assyrian troops is compared to an onslaught of Ramman. His curses are the most dreadful that can befall a nation or an individual, for his instruments of destruction are lightning, hunger, and death. Reference has several times been made to the manner in which Tiglathpileser honors Ramman by making him a partner of Anu in the great temple of the latter at Ashur. But the successors of Tiglathpileser are no less zealous in their reverence for Ramman. It is to Ramman that the kings offer sacrifices during the campaign, and when they wish to depict in the strongest terms the destruction that follows in the wake of an onslaught of the Assyrian troops, they declare that they swept over everything like Ramman. It is natural, in view of this, that Ramman should have been to the Assyrians also the 'mightiest of the gods.'[2] Through the Assyrian inscriptions we learn something of the consort of Ramman.

Shala.

Sennacherib tells us that in the course of his campaign against Babylonia he removes out of the city of Babylon, and replaces in Ekallâte[3] the statues of Ramman and Shala. This, he says, he did 418 years after the time that they had been carried captive from Ekallâte to Babylon by Marduknadinakhi.[4] We know nothing more of this Ekallâte except that it lay in Assyria, — probably in the southern half, — and that Ramman

---

[1] IR.8, col. I. 85. See above, p. 166.

[2] Ashurnasirbal calls him so in his annals, *e.g.*, col. iii. l. 130.

[3] Davian Inscription, ll. 48-50. See also Meissner-Rost, *Bauinschriften Sanherib's*, p. 102. The reading of the name of the city is not certain. It signifies 'city of palaces.'

[4] c. 1120 B.C.

and Shala are called the gods of the city. The name 'Shala' appears to signify 'woman.' It reminds us, therefore, of 'lady' (Ninni, Nanâ, etc.), which we have found to be the designation for several distinct goddesses. It is possible that Shala, likewise, being a name of so indefinite a character, was applied to other goddesses. A 'Shala of the mountains,' who is stated to be the wife of Marduk, is mentioned in a list of gods.[1] The wife of Bel, too, is once called Shala, though in this case the confusion between Marduk and Bel may have led to transferring the name from the consort of one to the consort of the other. Too much importance must not be attached to the data furnished by these lists of gods. They represent in many cases purely arbitrary attempts to systematize the Babylonian and Assyrian pantheon, and in other cases are valuable only as reflecting the views of the theologians, or rather of certain schools of theological thought, in Babylonia. In the religious hymns, too, the consort of Ramman finds mention, and by a play upon her name is described as the 'merciful one.' The attribute given to her there is the 'lady of the field,' which puts her in contrast to Ramman, rather than in partnership with him. Since we hear little of her worship in Assyria, beyond the notices of Sennacherib, we may conclude that, like so many goddesses, Shala dwindled to the insignificant proportions of a mere pale reflection of the male deity.

Nin-ib.

Another god, who by virtue of his violent traits enjoys the favor of the Assyrian rulers, is the old Babylonian deity whose name is provisionally read Nin-ib. In the very first mention of him, in the inscription of Ashurrishishi (c. 1150 B.C.), he is called the 'mighty one of the gods.' Through the protection of Nin-ib, Ashurrishishi secures victory over his enemies on

[1] II Rawlinson, 57, 33.

all sides. Similarly, other of the Assyrian rulers emphasize the strength of Nin-ib. Tiglathpileser I. calls him the courageous one, whose special function is the destruction of the king's enemies. In doing so he becomes the god 'who fulfills the heart's desire.' The unmistakable character of the god as a god of war is also shown by his association with Ashur.[1] If Ashur is the king of Igigi and Anunnaki, Nin-ib is the hero of the heavenly and earthly spirits. To him the rulers fly for help. Of all the kings, Ashurnasirbal seems to have been especially devoted to the service of Nin-ib. The annals of this king, instead of beginning, as is customary, with an invocation of all or many of the gods, starts out with an address to Nin-ib, in which the king fairly exhausts the vocabulary of the language in his desire to secure the favor of this powerful deity. Almost all the attributes he assigns to him have reference to the god's powers in war. Dwelling in the capital Calah, he is 'the strong, the mighty, the supreme one,' the perfect hero, who is invincible in battle, the 'destroyer of all opposition, who holds the lock of heaven and earth, who opens the deep; the strong one, endowed with youthful vigor, whose decree is unchangeable, without whom no decision is made in heaven or on earth, whose attack is like a flood, who sweeps away the land of his enemies,' and so forth, through a bewildering array of epithets. The inscriptions of the Assyrian kings, especially in the introductions, manifest little originality. One king, or rather his scribe, frequently copies from earlier productions, or imitates them. Hence, it happens that the grandson of Ashurnasirbal, Shamshi-Ramman (c. 825–812 B.C.), furnishes us with an almost equally long array of epithets, exalting the strength and terror of Nin-ib. Like Ashurnasirbal, he declared himself to have been chosen by this god to occupy the throne. A comparison of the two lists makes it evident that the later one is modeled upon the earlier produc-

[1] So Tiglathpileser associates Ashur and Nin-ib, as those 'who fulfill his desire.'

tion. The conclusion is justified that in the century covered by the reigns of Ashurnasirbal[1] and Shamshi-Ramman, the cult of Nin-ib must have acquired great popularity, though suffering, perhaps, an interruption during the reign of Shalmaneser II., — midway between these two kings, — whose favorite we have seen was Shamash. The great temple of Nin-ib stood in Calah, which Ashurnasirbal chose as his official residence, and it was in this temple that the king deposited a long inscription commemorating his deeds. In the temple, he also places a colossal statue of the god. Upon the completion of the edifice, he dedicates it with prayer and sacrifices. The special festivals of the god are fixed for the months of Shabat and Ulul, — the eleventh and sixth months, — and provision is made for the regular maintenance of the cult. It must, of course, not be supposed that, because Nin-ib appears to be a favorite of the king, the latter concentrates his attentions upon this god. He appears to have been specially fond of temple building, and, besides the one to Nin-ib, he tells us of sanctuaries to 'Belit of the land,' *i.e.*, Ishtar,[2] Sin, Gula, Ea, and Ramman, — that he erects or improves. One might be led to regard it as strange that a god like Nin-ib, or Shamash, should claim so large a share of the attention of the Assyrian rulers, to the apparent neglect of Ashur, but it must be borne in mind that the position of Ashur was so assured as to be beyond the reach of rivalry. The fact also that Ashur's popular symbol was the movable standard was no doubt a reason why so few temples were erected to him. He did not stand in need of temples. For the very reason that Ashur was the universally acknowledged master of everything, the kings felt called upon to choose, by the side of Ashur, some additional deity, — a patron under whose special protection they placed themselves. The natural desire for novelty — together with

---

[1] Ashurnasirbal's father bears the name Tukulti-Ninib.
[2] See above, pp. 151, 206.

other circumstances that escape us — led one to choose Ramman, another Nin-ib, a third Shamash, and a fourth, as we shall see, Nabu. In doing so they were not conscious of any lack of respect towards Ashur, of whose good will they always felt certain.

Besides the service rendered by Nin-ib in war, his aid was also invoked by the kings in their recreations, which partook of the same violent character as their vocation. Their favorite sport was hunting, especially of lions, wild horses, elephants, stags, boars, and bulls. They either proceeded to districts where these animals were to be found, or they had large parks laid out near their residences, which were then stocked with material for the chase. Ashurnasirbal does not shun a long journey to distant mountainous regions to seek for sport, and it is Nin-ib whom he invokes, together with Nergal. These two, he declares, who, like Ashur and Ishtar, "love his priesthood," are the ones that convey into his hands the hunting spoils. Tiglathpileser I. was especially fond of lion and elephant hunting. He declares that on one occasion he killed 10 elephants and 920 lions in various parts of northwestern Mesopotamia; and he ascribes his success to Nin-ib, who loves him, and who, again, in association with Nergal, and Ashur, has placed in the king's hands the mighty weapons and the glorious bow. After the days of Shamshi-Ramman we hear of Nin-ib chiefly in the formal lists of gods which the later kings of Assyria, from Sargon[1] on, are fond of placing at the beginning and end of their inscriptions. These lists, again, copied the one from the other, are of value only as indicating the chief gods of the pantheon, but warrant no conclusions as to the activity reigning in the cults of the gods there mentioned. Before leaving Nin-ib a few words need be said as to his relations to the other gods. In the chapter on the pantheon before Hammurabi,[2] the identity of Nin-ib with the chief god

---

[1] One of the gates of Sargon's palace is called after Nin-Ib. [2] See above, p. 57.

of Gudea's district, Nin-girsu, has been pointed out. The solar character of the latter being clear, it follows that Nin-ib, too, is originally a personification of the sun, like Nin-gish-zida and Nin-shakh, whose rôles are absorbed by Nin-ib.[1] This has long been recognized, but it is the merit of Jensen[2] to have demonstrated that it is the east sun and the morning sun which is more especially represented by Nin-ib. On this supposition, some of the titles given to him in the inscriptions of Ashurnasirbal and Shamshi-Ramman become perfectly clear. Like Marduk, who, it will be remembered, is also originally a phase of the solar deity, Nin-ib is called the first-born of Ea; and as the rising sun he is appropriately called the offspring of Ekur,—*i.e.*, the earth,—in allusion to his apparent ascent from a place below the earth. Ekur and Eshara being employed as synonyms, Shamshi-Ramman replaces Ekur by Eshara, and since Bel is the lord of Ekur-Eshara, Nin-ib also becomes the first-born son of Bel. Other epithets, such as 'the light of heaven and earth,' 'the one who pursues his path over the wide world,'[3] are all in keeping with the solar character of the deity, and date, therefore, from a period when the more purely 'nature' phases of the god were dwelt upon. But just as in the case of Shamash and Nergal (also, as we have seen, a solar deity), so in that of Nin-ib, the violent, fiery, and destructive character that the sun has in a climate like that of Babylonia brought it about that Nin-ib was viewed as a destructive force, whose assistance was of great value in military strife. He becomes the god of the cloud storm, before whom, as he passes along, heaven and earth tremble. By his strong weapon he humiliates the disobedient, destroys the enemies of the kings, and grants all manner of protection to his favorites. Only in the religious literature are other qualities

---

[1] See above, pp. 92-94.   [2] *Kosmologie*, pp. 457-475.

[3] He is also called the offspring of a goddess, Ku-tu-shar, but this reference is not clear. See Jensen, *Kosmologie*, p. 468, note 5.

dwelt upon, such as his 'holiness.'[1] For Hammurabi, it will be recalled, Nin-ib is already the god of war, and it is natural that in a country like Assyria this side of the god's nature should become accentuated to the point of obscuring all others, until nothing more is left of his solar character than is indicated by stray bits of mythological phrases, perhaps only half understood, and introduced to add to the imposing array of epithets that belong to the terrible god of war. As the consort of Nin-ib, the Assyrians recognized

GULA.

She is only occasionally invoked by the Assyrian rulers. A sanctuary to Gula, as the consort of Nin-ib, is erected by Ashurnasirbal, and a festival in honor of the goddess is referred to by Ashurbanabal.

NERGAL.

Nergal not only shares with Nin-ib, as already mentioned, the honor of being the god under whose auspices the royal chase is carried on, but he is also, like Nin-ib, invoked in that other sport of which the Assyrian rulers were so fond, — war. He is scarcely differentiated from Nin-ib. Like the latter he is the perfect king of battle, who marches before the monarch together with Ashur, and he is pictured as carrying the mighty weapons which Ashur has presented to the king. In an inscription of Shalmaneser II.[2] there is an interesting reference to the city sacred to Nergal — Cuthah. The king, who in the course of his campaign against Babylonia reaches Cuthah, brings sacrifices to Nergal, whom he speaks of as 'the hero of the gods, the supreme raging sun.' A later king, Sargon, also honors the god by giving a fortress in the distant land of Nairi, to the northeast of Assyria, the name of Kar[3]-

---

[1] In a religious text he is addressed as 'holy, holy, holy.'
[2] Balawat, col. v. ll. 4, 5.   [3] Kar = fortress.

Nergal. It would seem as though, through the influence of Sargon, a revival of the Nergal cult took place. His successor, Sennacherib, erects a temple in honor of the god at Tarbisu, a suburb to the north of Nineveh proper, and Ashurbanabal, who dwells at Tarbisu for a while, is engaged in adding to the beauty of the edifice, — an indication of the honor in which the god continued to be held. Nergal's consort is Laz, but she is not referred to by the Assyrian rulers.

SIN.

The old Babylonian moon-god plays a comparatively insignificant rôle in Assyria. Ashurnasirbal speaks of a temple that he founded in Calah — perhaps only a chapel — in honor of Sin. It could not have been of much importance, for we learn nothing further about it. Sargon, too, who manifests a great fondness for reviving ancient cults, erects sanctuaries to Sin along with a quantity of other gods in his official residence at Khorsabad and beyond the northeastern confines of Assyria at Magganubba. But when invoked by the kings, Sin shows traces of the influence which the conceptions current about Ashur exerted upon his fellow deities. He takes on, as other of the gods, the attributes of the war-god. Instead of being merely the lord of the crescent, as in Babylonia, and one of the sources of wisdom because of the connection of astrology with lunar observations, he is pictured as capable of inspiring terror. At the same time he is also the lord of plenty, and in his capacity as the wise god he is regarded as the lord of decisions. But by the side of new epithets that are attached to him in the Assyrian inscriptions, there is one which, just as in the case of Nin-ib, connects the Assyrian Sin cult with the oldest phase of moon-worship in the south. It is one of the last kings of Assyria, Ashurbanabal, who calls Sin 'the firstborn son of Bel.' He appears in this relationship to Bel in the religious texts of Babylonia. The Bel here meant can only be the great god of Nippur, and the title 'son of Bel' accordingly shows that the moon-worship of Assyria is ultimately derived from that which had its seat in the south. Sin's secondary position is indicated by making him a son of Bel. The rise of the science of astronomy in connection with astrology, was, as already suggested, an important factor in spreading and maintaining the Sin cult in the south, while the lack of intellectual originality in Assyria would equally account for the comparatively subordinate position occupied by Sin in the Assyrian pantheon.

NUSKU.

That Nusku is a Babylonian god, meriting a place in the pantheon of Hammurabi, if not of the days prior to the union of the Babylonian states, is shown by the fact (1) that he had a shrine in the great temple of Marduk at Babylon, along with Nebo, Tashmitum, and Ea;[1] and (2) that he appears in the religious texts. In view of this it might appear strange that we find no reference to the god in historical texts till we reach the Assyrian period. The reason, or at least one reason, is that Nusku is on the one hand amalgamated with Gibil, the fire-god, and on the other identified with Nabu. The compound ideogram with which his name is written includes the same sign — the stylus or sceptre — that is used to designate Nabu, the second part of the ideogram adding the idea of 'force and strength.' Whether this graphical assimilation is to be regarded as a factor in bringing about the identification of Nusku and Nabu, or is due to an original similarity in the traits of the two gods, it is difficult to say. Hardly the latter, for Nusku is a solar deity, whereas, as we have tried to show, Nabu is originally a water-deity.[2] But however we may choose to account for it,

---

[1] See Sayce, *Hibbert Lectures*, p. 438, and Jensen's important note, *Kosmologie*, pp. 492–494. [2] See pp. 124, 125.

the prominence of Nusku is obscured by Nabu. As a solar deity, it is easy to see how he should have been regarded as a phase of the fire-god, and if the various other solar deities were not so regarded, it is because in the course of their development they were clothed with other attributes that, while obscuring their origin, saved them from the loss of their identity. Apart from the formal lists of gods drawn up by Sargon and his successors, Shalmaneser II. and Ashurbanabal are the only kings who make special mention of Nusku. The former calls him the bearer of the brilliant sceptre, just as Nabu is so called; and again, just as Nabu, he is termed the wise god. The two phases of the ideogram used in his name — the sceptre and the stylus — are thus united in the personage of Nusku precisely as in Nabu. On the other hand, the manner in which Ashurbanabal speaks of him reflects the mythological aspect of Nusku. In the religious literature Nusku is the messenger of Bel-Marduk, who conveys the message of the latter to Ea. From being the messenger of Bel, he comes to be viewed as the messenger of the gods in general, and accordingly Ashurbanabal addresses him as 'the highly honored messenger of the gods,' but, combining with the mythological the more realistic aspect of Nusku, refers to him also as the one who glorifies sovereignty and who, at the command of Ashur and Belit, stands at the king's side to aid in bringing the enemies to fall. As for the fire-god Gibil, with whom Nusku is identified, we have merely a reference to a month of the year sacred to the servant of Gibil in a passage of the inscriptions of Sargon.[1]

Bel–Marduk.

From the time that the Assyrian rulers claimed a greater or small measure of control over the affairs of Babylonia, that is, therefore, from about the twelfth century, they were anxious to

[1] Cylinder, L 61.

make good their claim by including in their pantheon the chief god of Babylonia. The Assyrian inscriptions prove that, as early as the twelfth century, the theoretical absorption on the part of Marduk, of the rôle taken by the old god Bel of Nippur, which was enlarged upon in a preceding chapter,[1] had already taken place. Marduk is not only frequently known as Bel, but what is more, Babylonia is the country of Bel, or simply Bel, and the Babylonians are referred to as 'the subjects of Bel,' or the 'humanity of Bel.' There can be no doubt that in all these cases Bel-Marduk is meant and not the older Bel. In the days of Ashurrishishi we already come across the title 'governor of Bel,' that to the latest days remains the official designation for political control over the southern empire. So general is this use of Bel for Marduk that the latter name does not occur until we reach Shalmaneser II., *i.e.*, the ninth century. There seems to be no reason to question, therefore, that even when Tiglath-pileser I. applies to Bel titles that certainly belong to the older Bel, such as 'father of the gods,' 'king of all the Anunnaki,' 'who fixes the decrees of heaven and earth,' he means Marduk, a proof for which may be seen in the epithet *bêl matâti*, 'lord of lands,' which follows upon these designations and which, as we saw, is a factor in the evolution of Marduk into Bel-Marduk.[2] The importance that Tiglathpileser I., and therefore also his successors, attached to their control over the old southern district, is shown by his according to Bel the second place in the pantheon, invoking him at the beginning of his inscriptions immediately after Ashur. The control over Babylonia was an achievement that stirred the pride of the Assyrian rulers to the highest degree. Its age and its past inspired respect. Besides being the source of the culture that Assyria possessed, Babylonia had sacred associations for the Assyrians, as the original

---

[1] See pp. 117 *seq.*

[2] We may therefore expect, some day, to come across the name Marduk in Assyrian texts earlier than the ninth century.

dwelling-places of most of the gods worshipped by them. The old sacred centers like Ur, Nippur, Uruk, Sippar, with their great temples, their elaborate cults, their great storehouses of religious literature, and their great body of influential priests and theologians and astrologers were as dear to the people of the north as to those of the south; and in proportion as these old cities lost their political importance, their rank as sacred centers to which pilgrimages were made on the occasion of the festivals of the gods was correspondingly raised. Hence the value that the Assyrian rulers attached to the possession of Babylonia. They do not like to be reminded that they rule the south by force of arms. They prefer, as Tiglathpileser I. declares, to consider themselves 'nominated by the gods to rule over the land of Bel.' They want to be regarded as the favorites of Bel, and they ascribe to him the greatness of their rule. It is he who fulfills the wishes of the kings; and when the kings enter upon a campaign against Babylonia, as they frequently did to quell the uprisings that were constantly occurring in the one or the other of the southern districts, they emphasize, as Shalmaneser II. does, that he enters upon this course at the command of Marduk. They set themselves up as Marduk's defenders, and it must be said for the Assyrian rulers that they were mild and sparing in their treatment of their southern subjects. They do not practise those cruelties — burning of cities, pillage, and promiscuous slaughter — that form the main feature in their campaigns against the nations to the northeast and northwest, and against Elam. They accord to the Babylonians as much of the old independence as was consistent with an imperial policy. The internal affairs continue for a long time to be regulated by rulers who are natives of Babylonia, and it is not until a comparatively late day — the time of Sennacherib — that in consequence of the endless trouble that these native rulers gave the Assyrians through their constant attempt to make themselves independent, it became customary for the

Assyrian kings to appoint a member of the royal house — a son or brother — to the lieutenancy over Babylonia. As for the cult, the Assyrian kings were at great pains to leave it undisturbed, or where it had been interrupted to restore it, and thus secure the favor of the southern gods. So Shalmaneser II. upon the completion of his campaign enters Marduk's great temple at Babylon, E-sagila, and offers prayers and sacrifices to Bel and Belit, *i.e.*, Marduk and Sarpanitum. From E-sagila he crosses over to Borsippa, and pays homage to Nabu and to Nabu's consort, whom he calls Nanâ.[1] The kings are fond, especially when speaking of the Babylonian campaigns, of slipping in the name of Marduk after that of Ashur. With the help of Ashur and Marduk their troops are victorious. Marduk shares Ashur's terrible majesty. At times Shamash, or Shamash and Ramman, are added to form a little pantheon whose assistance is invoked in the Babylonian wars. From being used in restricted application to Babylonian affairs, Ashur and Marduk came to be invoked in a general way. Esarhaddon expressly sets up the claim of being the savior of Marduk's honor, as a kind of apology for proceeding against Babylonia with his armies. Sargon, to emphasize his legitimate control over Babylonia as well as Assyria, says that he has been called to the throne by Ashur and Marduk, but Ashurbanabal goes further even than his predecessors. He proceeds to Babylon on the occasion of the formal installation of his brother Shamashshumukin as viceroy of the district, enters the temple of Marduk, whom he does not hesitate to call 'the lord of lords,' performs the customary rites, and closes the ceremonies by a fervent prayer to Marduk for his continued good will and blessing.[2] The great gods Nergal, Nabu, and Shamash come from their respective shrines to do homage to Marduk. Ashurbanabal's

---

[1] See p. 132.
[2] So also Shalmaneser II., Obelisk, l. 179, unless Marduk here is an error for Ramman, *cf.* l. 175.

brother Shamashshumukin, when he attempts as governor of
Babylon to make himself independent of his brother, endeavors
by means of sacrifices and other devices to secure the favor of
Marduk, well aware that in this way he will also gain the support of the Babylonians. On another occasion, incidental to a
northern campaign, Ashurbanabal mentions that the day on
which he broke up camp at Damascus was the festival of Marduk,—an indication that the Babylonian god was in his thoughts,
even when he himself was far away from Babylonia. Esarhaddon and Ashurbanabal, when approaching the sun-god to obtain
an oracle, make mention of Marduk by the side of Shamash.
There are, however, a number of passages in the Assyrian
inscriptions in which when Bel is spoken of, not Marduk but
the old god Bel is meant.

BEL.

Tiglathpileser I. tells us that he rebuilt a temple to Bel in
the city of Ashur, and he qualifies the name of the god by
adding the word 'old' to it. In this way he evidently distinguished the god of Nippur from Bel-Marduk, similarly as Hammurabi in one place adds Dagan to Bel,[1] to make it perfectly
clear what god he meant. Again, it is Sargon who in consistent accord with his fondness for displaying his archaeological
tastes, introduces Bel, the 'great mountain,' 'the lord of countries,' who dwells in E-khar-sag-kurkura, *i.e.*, the sacred mountain on which the gods are born, as participating in the festival that takes place upon the dedication of the king's palace
in Khorsabad. The titles used by the king are applicable only
to the old Bel, but whether he or his scribes were fully conscious
of a differentiation between Bel and Bel-Marduk, it is difficult
to say. Bel is introduced in the inscription in question[2] immediately after Ashur, and one is therefore inclined to suspect

---

[1] See above, p. 146.
[2] The so-called *Prunkinschrift*, ll. 174 *seq.*

that Sargon's archaeological knowledge fails him at this point in speaking of the old Bel, whereas he really meant to invoke the protection of Bel-Marduk as the chief god of his most important possession next to Assyria.[1] Besides this, the old Bel is of course meant, when associated with Anu, as the powers that, together with Belit, grant victory,[2] or as a member of the old triad, Anu, Bel, and Ea, whose mention we have seen is as characteristic of the Assyrian inscriptions as of the Babylonian. Lastly, Sargon calls one of the gates of his palace after Bel, whom he designates as the one who lays the foundation of all things. In this case, too, the old Bel is meant.

BELIT.

In the case of Belit a curious species of confusion confronts us in the Assyrian inscriptions. At times Belit appears as the wife of Bel, again as the consort of Ashur, again as the consort of Ea, and again simply as a designation of Ishtar.[3] To account for this we must bear in mind, as has already been pointed out, that just as Bel in the sense of lord came to be applied merely as a title of the chief god of Babylonia, so Belit as 'lady' was used in Assyria to designate the chief goddess. This was, as the case may be, either Ishtar or the pale 'reflection' associated with Ashur as his consort. Now this Belit, as the wife of Ashur, absorbs the qualities that distinguish Belit, the wife of Bel-Marduk. The temple in the city of Ashur, which Tiglathpileser I.[4] enriches with presents consisting of the images of the deities vanquished by the king, may in reality have been sacred to the Belit of Babylonia, but Tiglathpileser, for whom Bel becomes merely a designation of Marduk, does not feel called upon to pay his devotions to the Babylonian Sarpanitum,

---

[1] Note the frequent use of Ashur and Bel for Assyria and Babylonia.
[2] Ashurbanabal, Rassam Cylinder, col. ix. ll. 76, 77.
[3] See above, p. 205.
[4] IR. II. col. Iv. ll. 34, 35.

and so converts the old Belit into 'the lofty wife, beloved of Ashur.' Sargon, on the other hand, who calls one of the gates of his palace *Belit ilâni*, 'mistress of the gods,' seems to mean by this, the consort of Ea.[1] Similarly, Ashurbanabal regards Belit as the wife of Ashur, and himself as the offspring of Ashur and Belit. At the same time he gives to this Belit the title of 'mother of great gods,' which of right belongs to the consort of the Babylonian Bel. In the full pantheon as enumerated by him, Belit occupies a place immediately behind her consort Ashur. Ashurbanabal, however, goes still further, and, influenced by the title of 'Belit' as applied to Ishtar, makes the latter the consort of Ashur. This at least is the case in an inscription from the temple of Belit at Nineveh,[2] known as E-mash-mash, and in which Ashurbanabal alternately addresses the goddess as Belit and as Ishtar, while elsewhere[3] this same Belit, whose seat is in E-mash-mash, is termed the consort of Ashur. How Ashurbanabal or his scribes came to this confusing identification we need not stop to inquire. In part, no doubt, it was due to the general sense of 'goddess,' which Ishtar began to acquire in his days.[4] At all events, Ashurbanabal's conception marks a contrast to the procedure of Shalmaneser II., who correctly identifies the mother of the great gods with the wife of Bel.[5] On the other hand, the confusion that took place in Ashurbanabal's days is foreshadowed by the title of 'Bêlit mâti,' *i.e.*, 'mistress of the land,' by which Ashurbanabal appears to designate some other than Ishtar.[6] Lastly, it is interesting to note that Ashurbanabal recognizes by the side of Belit-Ishtar, the wife of Ashur, the older Belit, the wife of the Bel of Nippur, to whom, in associa-

---

[1] See below, pp. 231, 237.
[2] Rawlinson, ii. 66.
[3] Rassam Cylinder, col. x. ll. 25–27.
[4] See Tiele, *Babyl.-Assyr. Geschichte*, p. 127.
[5] Obelisk, l. 52.
[6] Annals, col. ii. l. 135.

tion with Anu and Bel, he attributes his victory over the Arabs.[1]

SARPANITUM.

The consort of Marduk is only incidentally referred to: once by Sargon,[2] who groups Bel with Sarpanitum and Nabu and Tashmitum, at the head of the gods of Babylonia; and similarly by Tiglathpileser III., on the occasion of his enumerating the chief gods of the Babylonian pantheon.

NABU.

The intimate association of Nabu with Marduk in the city of Babylon leads as a natural consequence to a similar association in Assyria, when once the Marduk cult had for political reasons become established in the north. The kings invoke the favor of Bel (meaning Marduk) and Nabu, especially when dealing with the affairs of Babylonia,[3] as they invoke Ashur and Ishtar. Just as we have certain kings devoted to Nin-ib and Shamash by the side of Ashur, so there are others whose special favorite is Nabu. In the days of Ramman-nirari III. (812–783 B.C.) the Nabu cult reached its highest point of popularity in Assyria. From the manner in which the king speaks of the god, one might draw the conclusion that he attempted to concentrate the whole Assyrian cult upon that god alone. He erects a temple to the god at Calah, and overwhelms the deity with a great array of titles. The dedicatory inscription which the king places on a statue of Nebo closes with the significant words, 'O Posterity! trust in Nabu. Trust in no other god.'[4] Still we must not press such phrases too hard. Ramman-nirari III. had no intention of suppressing Ashur worship, for he

---

[1] Rassam Cylinder, col. x. l. 75.
[2] *Prunkinschrift*, l. 143.
[3] Esarhaddon, IR. 46, col. II. l. 48; Rawlinson, iii. 16, col. III. l. 24.
[4] IR. 35, no. 2, l. 12.

mentions the god elsewhere, and assigns to him the same rank as the other kings do, but so much we are justified in concluding, that next to Ashur and Ishtar he feels most strongly attached to Nabu. That the Babylonian Nabu is meant, is clear from such designations as 'the offspring of E-sagila, the favorite of Bel,' 'he who dwells at E-zida,' which appear among the epithets bestowed upon the god; and the temple in Calah, which one of the last kings of Assyria, Ashuretililani,[1] is engaged in improving, bears the same name E-zida, as Nabu's great temple at Borsippa. We have already set forth the reasons[2] for the popularity of the Nabu cult in Assyria. Suffice it to recall that the peculiar character of the god as the patron of wisdom placed him beyond the reach of any jealousy on the part of the other members of the pantheon. So Ramman-nirari III. extols Nabu as the protector of the arts, the all-wise who guides the stylus of the scribe, and the possessor of wisdom in general. He is not merely the originator of writing, but the source of all wisdom, and for this reason he is spoken of as the son of Ea. Attributes of mere brutal force are rarely assigned to Nabu, but as befits a god of wisdom, mercy, nobility, and majesty constitute his chief attractions. By virtue of his wisdom, Sargon calls him 'the clear seer who guides all the gods,' and when the last king of Assyria — Saracus, as the Greek writers called him — invokes Nabu as the 'leader of forces,' he appears to have in mind the heavenly troops rather than earthly armies. Such patrons of learning as Sargon and Ashurbanabal were naturally fond of parading their devotion to Nabu. The former significantly calls him the 'writer of everything,' and as for Ashurbanabal, almost every tablet in the great literary collection that he made at Nineveh closes with a solemn invocation to Nabu and his consort Tashmitum, to whom he offers thanks for having opened his ears to receive wisdom, and who persuaded him

---

[1] IR. 8, no. 3, ll. 5 *seq.*
[2] See above, p. 126.

to make the vast literary treasures of the past accessible to his subjects.

Tashmitum.

The consort of Nabu was permitted to share the honors in the temple of Nabu at Calah, but beyond this and Ashurbanabal's constant association of Tashmitum with Nabu in the subscript to his tablets, she appears only when the kings of Assyria coming to Babylonia as they were wont to do,[1] in order to perform sacrifices, enumerate the chief gods of the Babylonian pantheon.

Ea.

Ea takes his place in the Assyrian pantheon in the double capacity of god of wisdom and as a member of the old triad. Ashurnasirbal makes mention of a sanctuary erected to the honor of Ea in Ashur. A recollection of the rôle that Ea plays in Babylonian mythology survives in the titles of 'creator' and 'king of the ocean,' which Shalmaneser gives him,[2] and of the 'one who opens the fountains' as Ashurbanabal declares.[3] He is also, as in Babylonia, the one who determines the fates of mankind. As the one who has a care for the arts, he is the wise god, just as Nabu, and under various titles, as Nu-gim-mud,[4] Nin-igi-azag, and Igi-dug-gu,[5] all emphasizing his skill, he is the artificer who aids the kings in their building operations. The similarity of the rôles of Nabu and Ea, as gods of wisdom and the arts, might easily have led to a confusion.

---

[1] *E.g.*, Tiglathpileser III., Nimrud inscription (Layard, pl. 17, L 12).
[2] Obelisk, l. 5.
[3] Kassam Cylinder, col. i. L 45.
[4] Delitzsch (*Das Babylonische Weltschöpfungsepos*, p. 99) questions whether Nu-gim-mud (or Nu-dim-mud) was originally a designation of Ea. Nu-dim-mud being an epithet might, of course, be applied to other gods, but there can be no doubt that it was used to designate more particularly Ea as the artificer. See my remarks, pp. 138, 177 *seq.*
[5] Meissner-Rost, *Bauinscriften Sanherib's*, p. 105.

Fortunately, the grandiloquent and all-embracing titles accorded to the former did not alter his character as essentially the god who presides over the art of writing, while Ea retains the control over the architectural achievements, — the great colossi, in the first instance, that guarded the approach of palaces, the images of the gods in the second, and the temples and palaces in general as his third function.

DAMKINA.

Of the consort of Ea, it is sufficient to note that she is occasionally referred to in the historical texts of the Assyrian period. In the inscriptions of Sargon she appears under the rather strange title of 'Belit ilâni,' *i.e.*, the mistress of the gods.[1] This 'mistress' cannot be, as might at first blush appear, Ishtar or the old Belit, for elsewhere[2] Ishtar, Belit, and Belit ilâni occur side by side. Sargon declares that he owes his wisdom to Ea and Belit ilâni. In naming the gates of his palace, he again associates Ea with ' the mistress of the gods,' from which it is clear that the epithet is used of Ea's consort.

NIN-GAL.

A sanctuary to the old Babylonian goddess Nin-gal is included by Sargon among the holy edifices erected by him in his official residence.[3]

DIBBARRA.

We have pointed out in a previous chapter how faint the dividing line sometimes becomes between gods and spirits. Among the minor deities, ranking hardly above demons, is the

---

[1] Cylinder, l. 48, ideographically as Nin-men-an-na, ' lady of the heavenly crown.' In the parallel passage, however, as Lyon (*Sargontexte*, p. 71) points out, *Belit ilâni* is used.

[2] Cylinder, l. 70.

[3] Cylinder, l. 68.

plague-god, whose name may provisionally be read Dibbarra.[1] The god plays a rôle in some of the ancient legends of Babylonia. Remains have been found of a kind of epic in which Dibbarra is the chief personage.[2] In the historical texts he is once incidentally mentioned by Ashurbanabal, who in the course of his campaign against Babylonia[3] describes how the corpses of those killed by Dibbarra, *i.e.*, through hunger and want, filled the streets of the cities. Evidently Dibbarra here is a mere personification of the dreadful demon of want that so often follows in the wake of a military destruction. Still there can be no doubt that at one time he was regarded as a real deity, and not merely a spirit or demon. Dibbarra is identified in the theological system of Babylonia with Nergal.

Damku, Sharru-ilu, and Sha-nit(?)-ka.

In an interesting passage recounting the restoration of the city Magganubba, Sargon[4] says that he prayed to Damku, *i.e.*, 'grace,' Sharru-ilu, *i.e.*, 'king-god,' and Sha-nit(?)-ka. The two former he calls the judges of mankind. That Damku and Sharru-ilu are titles and not names is evident from the meaning of the words, but at present it is impossible to say what gods are meant.[5] Perhaps that these are the translations of names of the old deities of Magganubba. We have at least one other example of a foreign deity introduced into the Assyrian pantheon. At Dur-ilu, a town lying near the Elamitic frontier, there flourished the cult of Ka-di,[6] evidently a god imported into the Assyrian pantheon from Elam or some other eastern district. Sargon's scribes are fond of translating foreign names

---

[1] Jensen, *Kosmologie*, p. 445, reads the name *Gira*. See pp. 527-28.
[2] See the author's work on *A Fragment of the Dibbarra Epic*. (Ginn & Co., Boston, 1891).
[3] Rassam Cylinder, col. iv. ll. 79 *seq.*   [4] Cylinder, ll. 44-53.
[5] Delitzsch's supposition (see Lyon, *Sargontexte*, p. 71) that Sharru-ilu is Izdubar is untenable.
[6] *Babyl. Chronicle*, col. iii. l. 44.

and words, and they may have done so in this case, and thus added two new deities to the glorious pantheon protecting their royal chief. As for Sha-nit(?)-ka,[1] were it not that she is called the mistress of Nineveh, one would also put her down as a foreign goddess. In view of this, however, it may be that Sha-nit(?)-ka is an ideographic designation of Ishtar.

Before leaving the subject, a word needs to be said regarding the relation between the active Assyrian pantheon and the long lists of deities prepared by the schoolmen of Babylonia and Assyria. Reference has already been made to these lists.[2] They vary in character. Some of them furnish an index of the various names under which a god was known,[3] or the titles assigned to him. These names and titles are frequently indications that some great god has absorbed the attributes of smaller ones, whose independence was in this way destroyed. Other lists[4] are simple enumerations of local deities, and when to these names some indications are added, as to the locality to which the gods belong,[5] their importance is correspondingly increased. There can be no doubt that most of these lists were prepared on the basis of the occurrence of these gods in texts, and it seems most plausible to conclude that the texts in question were of a religious character. References to local cults are numerous in the incantations which form a considerable proportion of the religious literature, while in hymns and prayers, gods are often referred to by their titles instead of their names. In some respects, however, these lists of gods are still obscure. It is often difficult to determine whether we are dealing with gods or spirits, and the origin and meaning of many of the names and epithets assigned to gods are similarly in-

---

[1] May also be read Sha-ush-ka.
[2] See above, pp. 13, 170.
[3] *E.g.*, IIR. 58, no. 5, titles of Ea; IIR. 60, no. 2, titles of Nabu.
[4] *E.g.*, IIR. 60, no. 1.
[5] *E.g.*, IIIR. 66, lists of gods worshipped in various temples of Assyria and also of Babylonia.

volved in doubt. Use has been made of these lists in determining the character of the gods included in this survey of the Babylonian and Assyrian pantheon, but it would be manifestly precarious to make additions to this pantheon on the basis of the lists alone. Despite the tendency towards centralization of divine power in a limited number of gods, local cults, no doubt, continued to enjoy some importance in Assyria as well as Babylonia; but, in the present stage of our knowledge, we have no means of determining either the number or the character of these local cults. While, therefore, a complete treatment of the pantheon of Babylonia and Assyria would include all the minor local cults, we may feel quite certain that these local cults furnish few, if any, additions to the concepts connected with these gods which we have discussed. I have therefore contented myself with some illustrations, in each of the three divisions under which the pantheon has been surveyed, of some of the minor deities chosen, such as actually occur in historical, commercial, or religious texts. For the Assyrian pantheon, we may place Nin-gal and most of the consorts of the gods among the minor gods, and also such deities as Ka-di, Khani, Gaga, Dibbarra, Sherua, and Azag-sir, who are merely incidentally referred to.[1] These illustrations suffice for placing clearly before us the distinction to be made in the pantheon between gods whose worship was actively carried on, and those who occupy more of a theoretical position in the system perfected by the schoolmen, standing under the political and social influences of their days. With this distinction clearly impressed upon us, we will be prepared for such modifications of our views of the Babylonian-Assyrian pantheon as further researches and discoveries may render necessary.

[1] See pp. 189, 238.

CHAPTER XIII.

THE TRIAD AND THE COMBINED INVOCATION OF DEITIES.

The Assyrian kings, in imitation of the example set by their Babylonian predecessors, are fond of introducing into their inscriptions, a series of gods under whose protection they place themselves. They do not do this as the earlier Babylonian rulers did, to emphasize the extent of their jurisdiction by adding to their pantheon the deities of towns or districts vanquished by them. The day of independent states being over, the importance of merely local deities had ceased. The theological system evolved in Babylonia in combination with the popular instinct had led to a selection out of the mass of deities of a limited number, each with tolerably definite attributes, and who together embraced all the forces under whose power mankind stood. Of these deities again, as we have seen, some acquired greater favor in Assyria than others, but for all that, the kings especially of the later period of Assyrian history were fond of including in an enumeration of the pantheon, even those who had no special significance. Policy and the meaningless imitation of earlier examples played an equal part in thus giving to the lists an aspect of formality that deprives them of the impression that they might otherwise make.

The combined invocations are found usually at the beginning and at the end of the inscriptions — at the beginning for invoking the aid of the gods, at the close for invoking their curses upon those who would attempt to destroy the ambitious monuments set up by the kings. Often, however, the narrative is interrupted for the purpose of making acknowledgment to a larger or smaller series of gods for victory, granted or hoped for.

In these combined references a separate place belongs to the triad, Anu, Bel, and Ea. While not occupying the prominent position they have in Babylonian inscriptions, still the kings often mention Anu, Bel, and Ea separately, or Anu and Bel alone, ascribing victory to them, putting them down as the originators of the calendar system, and declaring themselves to have been nominated by them to rule over Assyria. Sargon, with his antiquarian zeal, appears to have made an effort to reinstate the triad as a special group in the pantheon. In general, however, they take their place with other gods. So Ramman-nirari I. invokes the curse of Ashur, Anu, Bel, Ea, and Ishtar, together with the Igigi and Anunnaki; but, what is more important, already at an early period the triad disappears altogether from the pantheon, except for the artificial attempts of Sargon to revive interest in them. In both the longer and shorter lists of gods enumerated by the kings from the time of Tiglathpileser, the triad is conspicuous for its absence.

As for the other gods, it is to some extent a matter of caprice which ones happen to be invoked, though just as frequently we see the motive for selecting certain ones of the pantheon. Thus, when proceeding to Babylonia for war or sacrifices, the gods of Babylonia are invoked, either Marduk and Nabu alone, as the chief gods, or Bel (*i.e.*, Marduk), Sarpanitum, Nabu, Tashmitum, Nanâ, Nergal, with Ashur, or Ashur and Marduk, or Marduk and Nabu in combination with Ashur. At other times it depends upon the gods to whom certain kings may be especially attached, or with whom they may have special dealings in their inscriptions. Thus Tiglathpileser I., when speaking of the temple of Anu and Ramman, contents himself with invoking these two gods alone at the close of his great inscription. Elsewhere, when referring to the special gods of his city, he combines Anu and Ramman with Ishtar; but again, for no special reason, his prayer is addressed to Ashur, Shamash, and Ramman. The pantheon of Ramman-nirari I.

consists either of the longer one above enumerated, or of Anu, Ashur, Shamash, Ramman, and Ishtar. As we proceed down the centuries, the formal lists at the beginning of inscriptions have a tendency to grow larger. Ashurnasirbal's pantheon consists of Bel and Nin-ib, Anu and Dagan, Sin, Anu, Ramman, and, of course, Ashur, though on special occasions, as when speaking of his achievements in the chase, he contents himself with a mention of Nin-ib and Nergal. He loves, too, to vary the style of his inscriptions by naming various groups of deities in pairs: now Ashur and Shamash, again Ashur and Nin-ib, or Ashur and Bel; then Shamash and Ramman, or a group of three deities, Ashur, Shamash, and Ramman, or Sin, Anu, and Ramman. His successors imitate this example, though each one chooses his own combinations. Shalmaneser II.'s pantheon embraces Ashur, Anu, Bel, Ea, Sin, Shamash, Nin-ib, Nergal, Nusku, Belit, and Ishtar — eleven in all. Sargon's practice varies. The best list is furnished by his account of the eight gates of his palace and of two walls, which he names after the gods in the following order:[1]

Shamash, who grants victory.
Ramman, who brings superabundance. } As the names for the eastern gates.

Bel, who lays foundations.
Belit, who brings fertility. } For the northern gates.

Anu, who blesses handiwork.
Ishtar, who causes the inhabitants to flourish. } For the western gates.

Ea, who unlocks fountains.
Belit ilâni,[2] who increases the offspring. } For the southern gates.

Ashur, who permits the king to grow old, and protects the troops. — For the inner wall.

Nin-ib, who lays the foundations of the city. — For the outer wall.

The order here is dictated by the directions of the gates. Elsewhere he sets up the group Ea, Sin, Shamash, Nabu, Ramman, Nin-ib, and their consorts.

[1] Cylinder, ll. 67–73. [2] Ea's consort; see above, p. 231.

Sennacherib's fuller group consists of Ashur, Sin, Shamash, Bel (*i.e.*, Marduk), Nabu, Nergal, Ishtar of Nineveh, and Ishtar of Arbela — only eight. But at the close of one of his building inscriptions[1] he invokes some twenty deities, adding to these eight, Nusku, Khani, Gaga, Sherua, Nin-gal, a god Azag-sir, and Nin-ib under three different forms; but it is evident that most of these are added to give effect and solemnity. They do not form part of the active pantheon. His successor, Esarhaddon, sets up various groups. At one time he enumerates Ashur, Sin, Shamash, Nabu, Marduk, Ishtar of Nineveh, Ishtar of Arbela; at another he prefers different combinations of these gods. Ashurbanabal is more consistent than most of the Assyrian rulers, and furnishes at the same time the best list. While he, too, frequently mentions only a few deities, grouping three or four together, his longer series consists, with but one or two exceptions, invariably of the following, and who always occur in the same order: Ashur, Belit, Sin, Shamash, Ramman, Bel (*i.e.*, Marduk), Nabu, Ishtar of Nineveh, the queen of Kidmuru, Ishtar of Arbela, Nin-ib, Nergal, and Nusku — thirteen in all. Of these, as we have seen, only some were actively worshipped at all times in Assyria; as for the others, the popularity of their cult varied from age to age, now being actively carried on under the stimulus afforded by the erection or improvement of an edifice sacred to the god, and again falling into comparative insignificance; but formally, at least, all these gods were regarded at all times as forming part of the pantheon of the 'great gods.' The testimony of Ashurbanabal thus becomes valuable as a proof that to the latest days of the Assyrian monarchy, the attachment to these gods was still strong enough to merit the formal acknowledgments of the king to them on all occasions, and that through their combined aid the glorious achievements of the past and present were attained.

---

[1] Meissner-Rost, *Bauinschriften Sanherib's*, p. 99.

CHAPTER XIV.

THE NEO-BABYLONIAN PERIOD.

WHEN upon the fall of the Assyrian empire, in 606 B.C., Babylonia regained her full measure of independence, Marduk once more obtained undisputed sway at the head of the pantheon. True, so far as Babylonia was concerned, Marduk was always the acknowledged head, but during the period that Assyria held Babylonia in a more or less rigid form of subjection it was inevitable that Ashur should lower the prestige of Marduk. When the kings of Assyria paid their respects to Marduk, it was always as second in rank to Ashur; and, what is more, they claimed Marduk and the other gods of Babylonia as their own, and as upholders of their own sovereignty. When the kings feel impelled to invade the southern districts, they not only claim to be under the protection of the Babylonian gods, but they carry these gods with them into the land to be invaded. 'Bel and the gods of Akkad leave Assyria and go to Babylonia' is the official term in which a campaign against Babylonia is described.[1] In the eyes of the Babylonians such a haughty assumption on the part of the Assyrians must have been regarded as humiliating to Marduk, Nabu, and their associates.

The state of affairs changed when Nebopolassar at the end of the seventh century once more claimed independent control over Babylonia. Marduk triumphs over Ashur. He is once more the great god, lord of gods, supreme king of the Igigi, the father of the Anunnaki — all titles that the Assyrians were fond of heaping upon Ashur. One feels the anxiety of Nebo-

[1] Babylonian Chronicle B, col. iv. ll. 34, 35.

polassar to emphasize the new order of things by attributing once more to Marduk what was formerly claimed for Ashur. The successor of Nebopolassar, the great Nebuchadnezzar, continues the policy of his father. He neglects no opportunity for exalting Marduk as the king, the creator, the leader of the gods, the lord of everything, the merciful one, the light of the gods, the all-wise. Nabu shares the honors with Marduk. Nebopolassar, indeed, accords to Nabu an equal share, and he does not hesitate at times to place the name Nabu before that of Marduk.[1] He does not speak of Nabu as the son of Marduk, and seems to be at particular pains to emphasize the equality of Nabu with Marduk. In this respect Nebopolassar presents a contrast to Hammurabi, who, it will be recalled, made an attempt to suppress the Nabu cult.[2] Nebopolassar, however, does not go to the extent of endeavoring to make Nabu supersede Marduk. He contents himself with manifesting his partiality for the former, and it is probably no accident that both his official name and that of his son contain the god Nabu as one of their elements, and not Marduk. One is inclined to suspect that this popularity of the Nabu cult is a trace of Assyrian influence. But whatever may have been Nebopolassar's intention in exalting Nabu at the cost of Marduk, Nebuchadnezzar restores the old relationship between the two. For him Nabu is again merely the son of Marduk, and he honors Nabu in this capacity. Like the Assyrian Nabu, the god places the sceptre in the king's hands, but he is, after all, only the supreme messenger of Marduk. In the closing days of the Babylonian monarchy a more serious attempt, it would appear, was made to displace Marduk. Nabonnedos formed the design of replacing both Marduk and Nabu by the cult of Shamash. He incurs the ill-will of the priests by paying much more attention to the restoration of the various Shamash temples in Babylonia than

---

[1] *Zeitschrift für Assyriologie*, II. 72, col. I. ll. 2, 3.
[2] See above, p. 127.

would appear to be consistent with devotion to Marduk. Cyrus, therefore, in his conquest of Babylonia, sets up the claim of being the savior of Marduk's honor.[1]

The Neo-Babylonian period may properly be designated as a religious age. The rulers, anxious to manifest their gratitude to the gods, and prompted in part, no doubt, by the desire to emulate the glorious architectural achievements of the Assyrian monarchs, devote themselves assiduously to the improvement of the great temples of the city of Babylon, and to the restoration or enlargement of those scattered throughout the country. Nebopolassar sets the example in this respect, which is considerably improved upon by Nebuchadnezzar. Over forty temples and shrines are mentioned in the latter's inscriptions as having been improved, enlarged, or restored by him; and the last king of Babylonia, Nabonnedos, endeavors to continue this royal policy of temple-building. In this respect the Neo-Babylonian rulers present a contrast to the Assyrian rulers, who were much more concerned in rearing grand edifices for themselves. While the gods were not neglected in Assyria, one hears much more of the magnificent palaces erected by the kings than of temples and shrines. In fact, as compared with Babylonia, Assyria was poor in the number of her temples. The chief sanctuaries to which the Neo-Babylonian kings devoted themselves were, in the first instance, E-sagila of Babylon and E-zida of Borsippa. Nebopolassar and his successors are fond of giving themselves the title of 'beautifier of E-Sagila and E-zida.' In these great temples sacred to Marduk and Nebo, there were shrines to Sarpanitum, Tashmitum, Nusku, Ea and others, which also engaged the energies of the rulers.

After Babylon came the old sanctuaries in the ancient religious centers of the south, — the temples to Shamash and his consort at Sippar and Larsa, the temples to Sin at Ur and Har-

---

[1] See a paper by Tiele, on "Cyrus and the Babylonian Religion," in the *Proceedings of the Amsterdam Academy*, 1896.

ran, to the old Ishtar or Anunit at Agade, to Nanâ in Erech. Thirdly, the cities of Babylon and Borsippa, to which the kings, especially Nebuchadnezzar, are deeply attached, were enriched with many sanctuaries more or less imposing, sacred to a variety of deities. So Shamash, Sin, Nin-makh, — *i.e.*, the great lady, or Ishtar, — Nin-khar-shag, Gula, also appearing as Nin-Karrak,[1] have their temples in Babylon, while Ramman has one in Borsippa, and Gula no less than three sanctuaries — perhaps only small chapels — in Borsippa. Fourthly, there are sanctuaries of minor importance in other quarters of Babylonia. Among these we find mention of the improvement of sanctuaries to the local deity of Marad, whom Nebuchadnezzar simply calls Lugal-Marad a, *i.e.*, king of Marad, to Bel-sarbi, or Shar-sarbi, in Baz, — perhaps a title of Nergal, — to Nin-ib in Dilbat, to Ramman in Kumari(?).

Most of these sanctuaries are referred to in the inscriptions of Nebuchadnezzar — a circumstance which, in connection with the many other gods whom he invokes on various occasions, points to a great revival of ancient cults in his days. Some of these cults had never reached any degree of importance prior to his time. Hence it happens that we come across deities in his inscriptions of whom no mention is found elsewhere. It is probable that such gods were purely local deities, some of them, if not many, being at the same time personifications of the powers or phenomena of nature, while others may be familiar gods, masquerading under strange attributes. Unfortunately most of these gods are written in ideographic fashion, so that we cannot be certain of the reading of their names. Among these are Nin-lil-anna, a goddess called by Nebuchadnezzar 'the lady who loves me,'[2] and Tur-lil-en,[3] a god who is described as

---

[1] For the identity of Nin-Karrak and Gula, see the 'Shurpu' Incantation Series, iv. l. 86 (ed. Zimmern), where the former is called the 'great physician,' — the epithet peculiar to Gula.   [2] East India House Inscription, col. iv. L 44.

[3] VR. 34, col. ii. l. 26, or simply Tur-lil (East India House Inscription, col. iv. l. 49, not Tur-e, as Winckler, *Keils Bibl.* 3, 2, 18, reads).

'breaking the weapons of enemies.' As for Bel-sarbi, or Shar-sarbi, the god of Baz,[1] they appear to be titles rather than names. Dibbarra, Nergal and his consort Laz, and Zamama are also included in the pantheon of Nebuchadnezzar.

In regard to none of these deities do we find any conceptions different from those developed in the period of Hammurabi, any more than in the conceptions of those gods who occupy a more prominent place in the pantheon. Shamash is the judge, Sin is the wise one, Ramman the thunderer, and so on throughout the list. It was not a period favorable to the production of new religious thought, but only to the more or less artificial revival of old cults.

With the conquest of Babylonia by Cyrus in 539 B.C., we reach the close of the period to be embraced in a history of the Babylonian-Assyrian religion. True, the Marduk and Nabu cults were upheld by the Persian rulers, and the policy of the latter in not disturbing the religious status was continued by the Greeks when they in turn succeeded the Persians in their control of Babylonia, but the presence of strange civilizations with totally different religious trains of thought was bound to affect the character of the old faith, and in time to threaten its existence. At all events, it ceases to have any interest for us. There are no further lines of development upon which it enters. The period of decay, of slow but sure decay, has set in. The cuneiform writing continues to be used till almost the beginning of our era, and so the religious cults draw out their existence to a late period; but as the writing and the civilization yield before new forces that entirely alter the character of Oriental culture, so also the religion, after sinking ever

---

[1] *Ie.*, king or lord of Sarbi. Pognon (*Les Inscriptions Babyloniennes de Wadi Brissa*), p. 46, is of the opinion that *sarbi* is the palm, but he fails to bring sufficient proof, and his theory is improbable. The stem *sarabu* means to burn, and the "fiery lord" is certainly an epithet belonging to some solar deity.

lower into the bogs of superstition, disappears, much as the canals and little streams of the Euphrates valley, through the neglect which settled over the country, become lost in the death-breeding swamps and marshes.

CHAPTER XV.

THE RELIGIOUS LITERATURE OF BABYLONIA.

The pantheon of a religion presents us with the external phases of the religion in question. In order to penetrate further towards the core of the religion, and to see it at its best, the religious thought as manifested in the national literature constitutes our most valuable guide. The beginnings of Babylonian literature are enveloped in obscurity. We have seen that we are justified in passing beyond the period of Hammurabi[1] for these beginnings, but exactly when and precisely how the literary spirit first manifested itself in Babylonia will probably remain for a long time, if not for always, a matter of conjecture. The great political and religious centers of Babylonia, such as Ur, Sippar, Agade, Eridu, Nippur, Uruk, perhaps also Lagash, and later on Babylon, formed the foci of literary activity, as they were the starting-points of commercial enterprise. This intimate connection of religion with literature left its impress upon all branches into which the Babylonian literature was in the course of time differentiated. In a certain sense all the literature of Babylonia is religious. Even the legal formulas, as embodied in the so-called contract tablets, have a religious tinge. The priests being the scribes, a contract of any kind between two or more parties was a religious compact. The oath which accompanied the compact involved an invocation of the gods. The decree of the judges in a disputed suit was confirmed by an appeal to the gods. The terms in which the parties bound themselves consisted largely of religious phrases, and finally the dating of the tablet often contained a reference to some religious festival or to some event

[1] See above, pp. 72, 114, 133 *seq.*

of religious import — such as the building of a sanctuary. Science, so far as it existed in Babylonia, never loosened the leading-strings that bound it to the prevailing religious thought. The observation of the stars was carried on under the belief of the supposed influence exerted by the heavenly bodies upon the fate of man; and surprising as we find the development of astronomical calculations and forecasts to be, mathematics does not pass beyond the limits of astrology. Medicine was likewise the concern of the priests. Disease was a divine infliction supposed to be due to the direct presence in the body, or to the hidden influence, of some pernicious spirit. The cure was effected by the exorcising of the troublesome spirit through prescribed formulas of supposed power, accompanied by symbolical acts. There is indeed no branch of human knowledge which so persistently retains its connection with religious beliefs among all peoples of antiquity as the one which to-day is regarded as resting solely upon a materialistic basis. As a consequence the Babylonians, although they made some progress in medicinal methods, and more especially in medical diagnosis, never dissociated medicinal remedies from the appeal to the gods. The recital of formulas was supposed to secure by their magic force the effectiveness of the medical potions that were offered to the sufferer.

As for the historical texts, the preceding chapters have illustrated how full they are of religious allusions, how at every turn we meet with the influence exerted by the priests as the composers of these texts. Almost all occurrences are given a religious coloring. That these texts furnish us with such valuable material, and such a quantity of it, is indeed to be traced directly to the fact that the historical literature is also the direct production of the religious leaders and guides of the people, acting at the command of rulers, who were desirous of emphasizing their dependence upon the gods of the country, and who made this dependence the basis of the authority they exerted.

Such being the general aspect of Babylonian literature, it is not always possible to draw a sharp line separating religious productions from such as may properly be termed secular. For example, the zodiacal system of the Babylonians, which we shall have occasion to discuss, although presenting a scientific aspect, is in reality an outcome of the religious thought; and so at other points it is necessary to pass over into the region of secular thought for illustrations of the religious beliefs. Bearing this in mind, we may set up a fivefold division of the religious literature of the Babylonians in the stricter sense: (1) the magical texts, (2) the hymns and prayers, (3) omens and forecasts, (4) the cosmology, (5) epics and legends. It will be apparent that the first three divisions represent a practical part of the literature, while the two latter are of a more purely literary character. The magical texts, as well as the hymns and prayers and omens, we can well imagine were produced as circumstances called them forth, and one can also understand how they should, at an early age, have been committed to writing. The incantations serving the practical purpose already referred to of securing a control over the spirit, it will be readily seen that such as had demonstrated their effectiveness would become popular. The desire would arise to preserve them for future generations. With that natural tendency of loose custom to become fixed law, these incantations would come to be permanently associated with certain temples. Rituals would thus arise. The incantation would be committed to writing so that one generation of priests might be certain of furnishing orthodox instruction to the other; and, once written, they would form part of the temple archives, finding a place in these archives by the side of the contract tablets, for which the sacred edifices of the country also served as depositories. The large quantity of incantation texts that have been found in Ashurbanabal's library,[1] as well as the variations and contrasts they present

---

[1] See pp. 12-14.

when compared with one another, are probably due to the various sources whence the scribes of the king, who were sent to the libraries of the south, collected their material. It is only reasonable to suppose that each great temple acquired in the course of time a ritual of its own, which, while perhaps not differing in any essential points from that introduced in another place, yet deviated from it sufficiently to impart to it a character of its own. In the case of some of the texts that have been preserved, it is still possible to determine through certain traits that they exhibit in what religious center they were produced. With considerable more guarantee of accuracy can this be done in the case of the hymns and prayers. Addressed as the latter were to certain deities, it stands to reason that they were written for use in the temples sacred to those deities, or, if not to be used, at least composed in honor of certain sanctuaries that contained the images of the deities thus exalted. Again, in the historical inscriptions of the Assyrian and Neo-Babylonian periods, prayers are introduced, and we are as a general thing expressly told on what occasion they were composed and in what sanctuary they were uttered. We may therefore conclude that those which have been preserved independently also served a practical purpose, and were written, not merely for certain occasions, but for certain places. The practical purpose served by texts containing omens and forecasts derived from the observation of the planets and stars, from monstrosities — human and animal — from strange occurrences, accidents, and the like, is too obvious to require demonstration. But while duly emphasizing the practical purpose that gave rise to the incantation texts, the hymns, the prayers and omens, we must be careful not to press this point too far. The rituals of the various temples once being fixed, the impulse to literary composition would still go on in an age marked by intellectual activity. The practical purpose would be followed by the pure love of composition. The attachment to certain sanctuaries or certain deities would inspire earnest and gifted priests to further efforts. Accordingly, while we cannot be certain that among the actual remains of magical texts and hymns we may not have specimens that belong to this class, there is no reason to question that such must have been produced. The guarantee for this hypothesis is furnished by the compositions that reflect the cosmological beliefs, the epics and legends that form the second half of the religious productions of Babylonia.

Speculation regarding the origin of the universe belongs to an early period in the development of culture. There are few people, however primitive their culture, who are not attracted by the spirit of curiosity to seek for some solution of the mysteries which they daily witness; but the systematization of these speculations does not take place until a body of men arises among a people capable of giving to the popular fancies a logical sequence, or the approach at least to a rational interpretation. This process, which resulted in producing in Babylonia compositions that unfold a system of creation, is one of long duration. It proceeds under the influence of the intellectual movements that manifest themselves from time to time with the attendant result that, as the conceptions become more definite and more elaborate, they reflect more accurately the aspirations of the various generations engaged in bringing these conceptions to their final form. When finally these beliefs and speculations are committed to writing, it is done in part for the purpose of assuring them a greater degree of permanence, and in part to establish more definitely the doctrines developed in the schools — to define, as it were, the norm of theological and philosophical thought.

In examining, therefore, the cosmological speculations of the Babylonians as they appear in the literary productions, we must carefully distinguish between those portions which are the productions of popular fancy, and therefore old, and those parts which give evidence of having been worked out in the schools. In a general way, also, we must distinguish between the contents and the form given to the speculations in question. We shall see in due time that a certain amount of historical tradition, however dimmed, has entered into the views evolved in Babylonia regarding the origin of things, inasmuch as the science of origins included for the Babylonians the beginning, not merely of gods, men, animals, and plants, but also of cities and of civilization in general. Still more pronounced is the historical spirit in the case of the epics and legends that here, as everywhere else, grew to even larger proportions, and were modified even after they were finally committed to writing. The great heroes of the past do not perish from the memory of a people, nor does the recollection of great events entirely pass away. In proportion as the traditions of the past become dimmed, the more easily do they lend themselves to a blending with popular myths regarding the phenomena of nature. To this material popularly produced, a literary shape would be given through the same medium that remodeled the popular cosmological speculations. The task would have a more purely literary aspect than that of systematizing the current views regarding the origin and order of things, since it would be free from any doctrinal tendency. The chief motive that would prompt the *literati* to thus collect the stories of favorite heroes and the traditions and the legends of the past would be — in addition, perhaps, to the pure pleasure of composition — the desire to preserve the stories for future generations, while a minor factor that may have entered into consideration would be the pedagogical one of adding to the material for study that might engage the attention and thoughts of the young aspirants to sacred and secular lore. While the ultimate aim of learning in Babylonia remained for all times a practical one, namely, the ability to act as a scribe or to serve in the cult, to render judicial decisions or to observe the movements of the stars, to interpret the signs of nature and the like, it was inevitable that through the intellectual activity thus evoked there would arise a spirit of a love of learning for learning's sake, and at all events a fondness for literary pursuits independent of any purely practical purposes served by such pursuits.

In this way we may account for the rise of the several divisions of the religious literature of Babylonia. Before turning to a detailed exposition of each of these divisions, it only remains to emphasize the minor part taken in all these literary labors by the Assyrians. The traditions embodied in the cosmological productions, the epics and legends of Babylonia, are no doubt as much the property of the Assyrians as of their southern cousins, just as the conceptions underlying the incantation texts and the hymns and prayers and omens, though produced in the south, are on the whole identical with those current in the north. Whatever differences we have discovered between the phases of the Babylonian-Assyrian religion, as manifested in the north and in the south, are not of a character to affect the questions and views involved in the religious literature. The stamp given to the literary products in this field, taken as a whole, is distinctly Babylonian. It is the spirit of the south that breathes through almost all the religious texts that have as yet been discovered. Only in some of the prayers and oracles and omens that are inserted in the historical inscriptions of Assyrian kings, or have been transmitted independently, do we recognize the work of Assyrian *literati*, imbued with a spirit peculiar to Assyria. Perhaps, too, in the final shape given to the tales connected with the creation of the gods and of men we may detect an Assyrian influence on Babylonian thought, some concession made at a period of Assyrian supremacy to certain religious conceptions peculiar to the north. But such influences are of an indirect character, and we may accept the statement of Ashurbanabal as literally true that the literature collected by him is a copy of what was found in the great literary archives of the south — and not only found, but produced there. In imitation of the example set by the south, schools were of a certainty established in Nineveh, Arbela, and elsewhere for the education of priests, scribes, and judges; but we have no evidence to show that they ever developed to the point of becoming intellectually independent of Babylonian *models*, except perhaps in minor particulars that need not enter into our calculations. This relationship between the intellectual life of Babylonia and Assyria finds its illustration and proof, not merely in the religious literature, but in the religious art and cult which, as we shall see, like the literature, bear the distinct impress of their southern origin, though modified in passing from the south to the north.

CHAPTER XVI.

THE MAGICAL TEXTS.

Turning to the first subdivision of Babylonian religious literature, we find remains sufficient to justify us in concluding that there must have been produced a vast number of texts containing formulas and directions for securing a control over the spirits which were supposed at all times to be able to exercise a certain amount of power over men. By virtue of the aim served by these productions we may group them under the head of magical texts, or incantations. We have already indicated the manner in which these incantations grew into more or less rigid temple rituals. This growth accounts for the fact that the incantations generally framed in by ceremonial directions, prayers, and reflections, were combined into a continuous series (or volume, as we would say) of varying length, covering nine, ten, a dozen, twenty tablets or more. It has been generally assumed that these incantation texts constitute the oldest division of the religious literature of the Babylonians. The assertion in an unqualified form is hardly accurate, for the incantation texts, such as they lie before us, give evidence of having been submitted to the influences of an age much later than the one in which their substance was produced. Conceptions have been carried into them that were originally absent, and a form given to them that obliges us to distinguish between the underlying concepts, and the manner in which these concepts have been combined with views that reflect a later and, in many respects, a more advanced period. The incantation texts are certainly no older than texts furnishing omens. Some of the incantation texts indeed may not be any older than portions of the creation epic, and in the latter, as in other parts of the religious literature, there are elements as ancient and as primitive as anything to be found in the omens or incantations. So much, however, is true, that the incantations represent the earliest ritual proper to the Babylonian cult, and that the conceptions underlying this ritual are the emanation of popular thought, or, if you choose, of popular fancy of a most primitive character. It is also true that, on the whole, the incantation texts retain more traces of primitive popular thought than other divisions of the religious literature with the exception of the omens. The remodeling to which they were subjected did not destroy their original character to the extent that might have been expected — a circumstance due in the first instance to the persistency of the beliefs that called these texts forth.

Many of the texts containing incantations were found by the modern explorers in so mutilated a condition, that one can hardly hazard any generalizations as to the system followed in putting the incantations together. From the fact, however, that in so many instances the incantations form a series of longer or shorter extent, we may, for the present at least, conclude that the serial form was the method generally followed; and at all events, if not the general method, certainly a favorite one. Deviating from the ordinary custom of calling the series according to the opening line of the first tablet, the incantation texts were given a distinct title, which was either descriptive or chosen with reference to their general contents. So one series which covered at least sixteen tablets was known by the very natural name of the 'evil demon'; the incantations that it contained being intended as a protection against various classes of demons. Another is known as the series of 'head sickness,' and which deals, though not exclusively, with various forms of derangements having their seat in the brain. It covered no less than nine tablets. Two others bear names that are almost synonymous, — "Shurpu" and "Maklu," both signifying 'burning,' and so called from the chief topic dealt with in them, the burning of images of the sorcerers, and the incantations to be recited in connection with this symbolical act. The "Maklu" series embraced eight tablets and contained, according to Tallqvist's calculations,[1] originally about 1550 lines, or upwards of 9000 words. The "Shurpu" series, although embracing nine tablets, appears to have been somewhat shorter. In view of the extensive character of these series we are justified in speaking of incantation 'rituals.' The texts were evidently prepared with a practical purpose in view. The efficacy of certain formulas having been demonstrated, it was obviously of importance that their exact form should be preserved for future reference. But a given formula was effective only for a given case, or at most for certain correlated cases, and accordingly it became necessary to collect as many formulas as possible to cover all emergencies. The priests, acting as exorcisers, would be the ones interested in making such collections, and we may assume, as already suggested, that each temple would develop a collection of its own, — an incantation code that served as a guide for its priests. The natural tendency would be for these codes to increase from generation to generation, perhaps not rapidly, but steadily. New cases not as yet provided for would arise, and new formulas with new instructions would be produced; or the exorcisers at a certain temple would learn of remedies tried elsewhere, and would embody them in their own special code. In short, the growth of these incantation 'rituals' was probably similar to the manner in which, on the basis of actual practice, religious codes grew up around the sanctuaries of ancient Israel, — a process that terminated in the production of the various codes and rituals constituting the legal documents embodied in the Pentateuch.

The prominence given to Ea and to his favorite seat, the city of Eridu, in the incantations suggests the theory that many

[1] *Die Assyrische Beschwörungsserie, Maqlû*, p. 14.

of our texts are to be ultimately traced to the temple of Ea, that once stood at Eridu. In that case an additional proof would be furnished of the great antiquity of the use of incantations in Babylonia. We must sharply distinguish however, as already emphasized, between the origin and the present form of the rituals. Again, those parts of a ritual in which Gibil, or Nusku, appears prominently would most naturally be produced by priests connected with a temple sacred to the one or the other of these gods. The practice of incantation, however, being common to all parts of Babylonia, we can hardly suppose that any temple should have existed which did not have its exorcising formulas. In the combination of these formulas into a ritual, due consideration would naturally be had to the special gods invoked, the obvious result of which would be to produce the long lists of deities that are often embodied in a single incantation. The details of this process can of course no longer be discerned, but the inevitable tendency would be towards increasing complications. The effort would be made to collect everything, and from all known quarters. Hence the heterogeneous elements to be detected in the texts, and which, while adding to their interest, also increase the difficulty of their interpretation. In consequence of the presence of such heterogeneous elements, it is difficult to determine within an incantation series any guiding principles that prompted the collectors. Still we can often distinguish large groups in a series that belong together. So we have whole series of addresses to the fire-god ending with incantations, and again a series of descriptions of the group of seven spirits serving a similar purpose as introductions to incantations, but we cannot see on what grounds the transition from one subject to the other takes place. Indeed the transitions are generally marked by their abruptness.

The only legitimate inference is that the main purpose of the collectors of incantation texts was to exhaust the subject so far as lay in their power. They included in their codes as much as possible. The exorciser would have no difficulty in threading his way through the complicated mass. He would select the division appropriate to the case before him without much concern of what preceded or followed in the text. Moreover, these divisions in the texts were clearly marked by dividing lines, still to be seen on the clay tablets. These divisions correspond so completely to divisions in the subject-matter that the purely practical purpose they served can hardly be called into question, while at the same time they furnish additional proof for the compiled character of the texts.

As for the date of the composition of the texts, the union of the Babylonian states under Hammurabi, with its necessary result, the supremacy of Marduk, that finds its reflection in the texts, furnishes us with a terminus *a quo* beyond which we need not proceed for the *final* editing. On the other hand, there are indications in the language which warrant us in not passing below 2000 B.C. as the period when many of the incantation texts received their present form, and the editions were completed from which many centuries afterwards the Assyrian scribes prepared their copies for their royal masters.

There is, of course, no reason for assuming that all our texts should be of one age, or that the copying and, in part, the editing should not have gone on continually. Necessity for further copies would arise with the steady growth of the temples. Priests would be engaged in making copies for themselves, either for their edification as a pious work, or for real use; and accordingly, in fixing upon any date for the texts, one can hardly do more than assign certain broad limits within which the texts, so far as their present contents are concerned, may have been completed. The *copies* themselves may of course belong to a much later period without, for that reason, being more recent productions.

Attention must also be directed to the so-called 'bilingual' form, in which many of the incantation texts are edited; each line being first written in the ideographic style, and then followed by a transliteration into the phonetic style.[1] The use of the ideographic style is a survival of the ancient period when all texts were written in this manner, and the conservatism attaching to all things religious accounts for the continuation of the ideographic style in the religious rituals down to the latest period, beyond the time when even according to those who see in the ideographic style a language distinct from Babylonian, this supposed non-Semitic tongue was no longer spoken by the people, and merely artificially maintained, like the Latin of the Middle Ages. The frequent lack of correspondence in minor points between the ideographic style and the phonetic transliteration shows that the latter was intended merely as a version, as a guide and aid to the understanding of the 'conservative' method of writing. It was not necessary for a transliteration to be accurate, whereas, in the case of a translation, the greatest care would naturally be taken to preserve the original sacred text with all nicety and accuracy, since upon accuracy and nicety the whole efficacy of the formulas rested. The redaction of the incantation texts in the double style must not be regarded as a necessary indication of high antiquity, but only as a proof that the oldest incantation texts were written in the ideographic style, and that for this reason the custom was continued down to the latest period. On the other hand, the addition of the transliteration points to a period when the old style could no longer be read by the priests with facility without some guide, and incidentally proves again that the texts have gone through an editing process. But in the course of time, additions to the ritual were made, written in the phonetic style; and then it would happen, as a concession to religious conservatism, that the text would be translated back into the ideographic form. We would then have a "bilingual" text,

---

[1] There are some preserved solely in the ideographic style, and others of which we have only the phonetic transliteration.

consisting of Babylonian and an artificial "Sumero-Akkadian." That incantations were also composed in pure Babylonian without reference to any "Sumero-Akkadian" original is conclusively shown by the metrical traits frequently introduced. Many of the sections — by no means all — can be divided into regular stanzas of four, six, or eight lines, and frequently to the stanza is added a line which forms what Professor D. H. Müller[1] calls the "response." The same metrical traits being found in other parts of the Babylonian literature, — so, *e.g.*, in the creation epic, — their occurrence in the incantation texts is of course not accidental. When, therefore, we come across a ritual as the "Maklu" series, written exclusively in the phonetic style, and giving evidence of being in part a metrical composition, we are justified in assuming this to have been the original form. Again, in the case of another series, — the "Shurpu," in part Babylonian, in part bilingual,[2] — since the Babylonian section shows the metrical form, it is likely that the ideographic style represents a transliteration of a phonetic, or pure Babylonian, original.

The chief value of the incantation texts lies, naturally, in the insight they afford into the popular beliefs. As among other nations, so among the Babylonians, the use of certain formulas to secure release from ills, pains, and evils of any kind, either actual or portending, rests upon the theory that the accidents and misfortunes to which man is heir are due largely to the influence of more or less powerful spirits or demons, acting independently or at the command of higher powers, — the gods.

Through the incantation rituals we are enabled to specify the traits popularly ascribed to these demons and the means employed to rid oneself of their baneful grasp.

---

[1] *Die Propheten in ihrer ursprünglichen Form*, pp. 1, 6. This work is a valuable investigation of the oldest form of the poetic compositions of the Semites.

[2] The fifth and sixth tablets of the series. It is probable that several editions were prepared, — some wholly Babylonian, others bilingual.

Demons.

The demons were of various kinds and of various grades of power. The names of many of them, as *utukku*, *shedu*, *alu*, *gallu*, point to 'strength' and 'greatness' as their main attribute; other names, as *lilu*, 'night-spirit,' and the feminine form *lilitu*, are indicative of the moment chosen by them for their work; while again, names like *ekimmu*, the 'seizer,' *akhkhazu*, the 'capturer,' *rabisu*, 'the one that lies in wait,' *labartu*, 'the oppressor,' and *labasu*, 'the overthrower,' show the aim that the demons have in view. Putting these names together, we may form a general idea of the conceptions connected with the demons. They lurk in hidden or remote places, in graves, in the shadow of ruins, on the tops of mountains, in the wilderness. Their favorite time of activity is at dead of night. They glide noiselessly like serpents, entering houses through holes and crevices. They are powerful, but their power is directed solely towards evil. They take firm hold of their victims and torture them mercilessly.

To these demons all manner of evil is ascribed. Their presence was felt in the destructive winds that swept the land. The pestilent fevers that rise out of the marshes of the Euphrates valley and the diseases bred by the humid heat of summer were alike traced to demons lurking in the soil. Some of these diseases, moreover, were personified, as *Namtar*, the demon of 'plague,' and *Ashakku*, the demon of 'wasting disease.' But the petty annoyances that disturb the peace of man — a sudden fall, an unlucky word, a headache, petty quarrels, and the like — were also due to the instigation of the demons; while insanity and the stirring up of the passions — love, hatred, and jealousy — were in a special sense indicative of the presence and power of the demons. Men and women stood in constant danger of them. Even the animals were not safe from their attacks. They drive the birds out of their nests, strike down lambs and bulls. It was impossible to forestall their attacks. They enter a man's dwelling, they wander through the streets, they make their way into food and drink. There is no place, however small, which they cannot invade, and none, however large, that they cannot fill. In a text which furnishes the sacred formulas by means of which one can get rid of the demoniac influence, a description is given of the demons which may serve as an illustration of what has just been said. The incantation is directed against a variety of the demons :[1]

> The *utukku* [2] of the field and the *utukku* of the mountain,
> The *utukku* of the sea and the one that lurks in graves,
> The evil *shedu*, the shining *alu*,
> The evil wind, the terrible wind,
> That sets one's hair on end.

Against these the spirits of heaven and earth are invoked. The text proceeds :

> The *utukku* that seizes hold of a man,
> The *ekimmu* that seizes hold of a man,
> The *ekimmu* that works evil,
> The *utukku* that works evil.

And after invoking against these demons, likewise, the spirits of heaven and earth, the text passes on to an enumeration of a long list of physical ills : sickness of the entrails, of the heart, of the head, of the stomach, of the kidneys, of the limbs and muscles, of the skin, and of the senses, which are all ascribed to the influence of the demons.

Apart from the demons that are naught but the personification of certain diseases, it does not appear that the demons were limited in their power to one specific kind of action. In other words, sharp distinctions between the demons do not appear to have been drawn. As appears from the extracts above

---

[1] Haupt, *Akkadische und Sumerische Keilschrifttexte*, p. 83, col. I. ll. 1-10.

[2] Wherever feasible, the Babylonian name of the demon will be used in the translations.

translated, the *utukku*, *shedu*, *alu*, and *ekimmu* were grouped together, and hardly regarded as anything more than descriptive epithets of a general class of demons. At the same time it appears likely that at one time they were differentiated with a greater degree of preciseness. So the *ekimmu* appears to be the shadowy demon that hovers around graves, a species of ghost or vampire that attacks people in the dead of night and lays them prostrate. *Lilu* and *lilitu* are the spirits that flit by in the night. Of a specific character likewise are the conceptions connected with a demon known as *ardat lili*, 'maid of the night,' a strange female 'will-o'-the-wisp,' who approaches men, arouses their passions, but does not permit a satisfaction of them. Great importance being attached by the Babylonians to dreams, the belief in a 'maid of the night' was probably due to the unchecked play of the imagination during the hours of sleep. Bad dreams came at the instigation of the demons, and such a demon as the *rabisu* or the *labartu* appears to have been especially associated with the horrible sensations aroused by a 'nightmare.'[1] Again the *utukku* is represented at times as attacking the neck of man; the *gallu* attacks the hand, the *ekimmu* the loins, the *alu* the breast. But these distinctions count for little in the texts. *Utukku* becomes a general name for demon, and *gallu*, *alu*, and *shedu* are either used synonymously with *utukku* or thrown together with the latter in a manner that clearly shows the general identity of the conceptions ultimately connected with them. The same is the case with the *rabisu* and *gallu*, with the *labartu*, *akhkhazu*, and *ekimmu*.

The demons were always given some shape, animal or human, for it was a necessary corollary of the stage of religious thought to which the belief in demons belongs, that the demon must not only be somewhere, though invisible to mankind, but

---

[1] Our word 'nightmare' still embodies the same ancient view of the cause of bad dreams as that found among the Babylonians.

also *in* something that manifests life. Among animals, those calculated to inspire terror by their mysterious movements were chosen, as serpents appearing and disappearing with startling suddenness, or ugly scorpions, against whom it was difficult to protect oneself, or the fabulous monsters with which graves and pestiferous spots were peopled. Regions difficult of access — the desert, the deep waters, the high mountains — were the favorite haunts of the demons. Some of these demons were frequently pictured in the boundary stones between fields, in order to emphasize the curses hurled upon the head of him who should trespass on the lawful rights of the owner of the land.[1] It is to such demons embodied in living form that epithets such as the 'seizer,' the 'one that lurks,' and the like apply with peculiar aptness. In a tablet belonging to a long series of incantations,[2] we find references to various animals — the serpent, the scorpion, monsters — that are regarded as the embodiment of demons.

In the distinctively religious art, the evil spirits are often pictured as ugly monsters that were to inspire terror by their very aspect. Depicted on the monuments, singly or in groups,[3] the shape of wild animals was given to the head, while the remainder of the body was suggestive of a human form. With gaping mouths and armed with some weapon, they stand ready to make an attack. The Assyrian kings, up to the latest period, acknowledged the power of the demons by making huge representations of them, which they placed at the approaches, entrances, and divisions of their temples and palaces, in the hope of thus securing their protection. The great bulls and lions with human heads — so familiar to every one — are but another form of the same idea. These colossal statues were actually known by the name *shedu*, which we have seen is

---

[1] See above, p. 182.
[2] IV R. pl. 5.
[3] See Perrot and Chipiez, *History of Art in Chaldaea and Assyria*, i. 61, 62; ii. 81 for illustrations.

one of the general terms for 'demon.' But as a general thing, this personal phase of the demon's existence is lost sight of. Even though embodied in animal form, the demons could make themselves invisible to man; and since most of their actions were performed in secret, so that people were totally at their mercy, the differentiation of the demons became a factor of minor importance. With so large a quantity of demons at command, it was difficult to hit upon the one who was manifesting himself by some evil at any given moment. Accordingly, instead of a single mention, a number or a group were enumerated, and the magic formulas pronounced against them in concert. We have one such group of seven to whom quite a number of references are found in the incantation texts. A section in one of these texts gives a vivid description of them:[1]

> Seven are they, they are seven,
> In the subterranean deep, they are seven,
> Perched (?) in the sky, they are seven,
> In a section of the subterranean deep they were reared,
> They are neither male nor are they female,
> They are destructive whirlwinds,
> They have no wife, nor do they beget offspring.
> Compassion and mercy they do not know,
> Prayer and supplication they do not hear,
> Horses bred on the mountains, are they
> Hostile to Ea[2] are they,
> Powerful ones among the gods are they.
> To work mischief in the street they settle themselves in the highway.
> Evil are they, they are evil,
> Seven are they, they are seven, seven, and again seven[3] are they.

These seven spirits, who are elsewhere compared to various animals, have power even to bewitch the gods. The eclipse of the moon was attributed to their baneful influence. The num-

[1] IV R. 2, col. v. ll. 30–60.
[2] The god of humanity. The phrase is equivalent to saying that the spirits are hostile to mankind.
[3] Literally, 'to their second time,' i.e., repeat 'seven are they.'

ber seven is probably not to be taken literally. As among so many nations,[1] seven had a sacred significance for the Babylonians; but largely, if not solely, for the reason, as I venture to think, because seven was a large number. In the Old Testament seven is similarly used to designate a large number. A group of seven spirits, accordingly, meant no more than a miscellaneous mass of spirits, and we may therefore regard this 'song of the seven' as a general characterization of the demons who, according to this view, appear to move together in groups rather than singly. Elsewhere[2] we are told of this same group of spirits 'that they were begotten in the mountain of sunset,' *i.e.*, in the west, 'and were reared in the mountain of sunrise,' *i.e.*, the east; 'that they dwell in the hollow of the earth, and that they are proclaimed on the mountain tops.' Evidently a description of this kind is intended to emphasize the universal presence of the spirits. There is no place where they are not found; and when we are furthermore told (apparently in contradiction to what has just been said) 'that neither in heaven nor earth is their name pronounced (*i.e.*, are they known to be), that among the gods of the earth (*i.e.*, the pantheon) they are not recognized, that neither in heaven nor earth do they exist,' this is but the reverse of the picture intended to illustrate the capability of the spirits to disappear without leaving any trace of their presence. They are everywhere and yet invisible. They come and they go, and no one knows their place. Nothing is proof against their approach. Of all the demons it is true, as of this group, that they slip through bolts and doorposts and sockets, gliding, as we are told, 'like snakes.' Such are the demons against whom man must seek to protect himself.

The relationship of the demons or spirits to the gods of the pantheon has been touched upon in a previous chapter.[3] It is

---

[1] See Hopkins, *The Holy Numbers in the Rig-Veda* (Oriental Studies), pp. 144–147.
[2] IVR. 15, col. II. 21 *seq.*   [3] See chapter xi.

sufficient here to emphasize the fact that the dividing line between the two becomes at times exceedingly faint. A deity, we have seen, is a spirit writ large; but often the demon assumes dimensions and is clothed with power that makes him 'little short of divine.' Strength is the attribute of the demons as it is the chief feature of the gods. Both classes of powers influence man's career. The names of the demons are preceded by the same determinative that is used for the gods. As a matter of fact, many of the spirits were originally worshipped as local deities in some restricted territory, which, losing its importance, bequeaths the name of its protective genius to posterity. In the realm of religious belief, as in the domain of nature, absolute loss of something that once had existence does not take place. Something remains. Hundreds of old local gods of Babylonia thus survived in the literature as spirits or demons. The tendency towards making a selection out of the great mass of gods goes hand in hand with the multiplication of spirits that might, as occasion presented itself, be invoked. In general, the larger affairs of life were consigned into the hands of the gods; the petty annoyances — accidents, pains, ill luck, and the like — were put down to the account of the spirits. The gods were, on the whole, favorably disposed towards man. They were angry at times, they sent punishments, but they could be appeased. The spirits were, on the whole, hostile; and although the Babylonians also invoked favorable and kind spirits, when a spirit was hostile there was only one method of ridding oneself of the pernicious influence, — to drive it out by means of formulas, and with the help of a priest acting as exorciser.

Sorcerers and Sorceresses.

A widespread and apparently very ancient belief among the Babylonians and Assyrians was that certain human beings possessed demoniac power, and could exercise it for evil purposes over whomsoever they pleased. This belief may have originated in the abnormal appearance presented by certain individuals in consequence of physical deformities or peculiarities. The uncanny impression made by dwarfs, persons with misshapen limbs, with a strange look in their eyes, and, above all, the insane would give rise to the view that some people, for the very reason of their variation from the normal type, possessed peculiar powers. But by the side of such as were distinguished by bodily defects, those who outranked their fellows by virtue of their prowess or of natural gifts, by keenness of intellect or cunning, would also be supposed to have received their power through some demoniac source. With the giant and the artificer there would thus be associated ideas of sorcery and witchcraft, as with dwarfs, the deformed, and insane. The sorcerers might be either male or female, but, for reasons which are hard to fathom, the preference was given to females. Accordingly, it happens that among the Babylonians, as in the Middle Ages, the witch appears more frequently than the male sorcerer. The witches have all the powers of the demons, and in the incantation texts the two are often thrown together. Just as the demons, so the witches take away the breath of man, defile his food and drink, or close up his mouth. They are able to penetrate into the body of men, and thus produce similar physical and mental disturbances as the animalic demons. In view of this close relationship between witches and demons, we are justified in regarding the two as varying aspects of one and the same belief. The witch appears to be merely the person through whom the hitherto 'invisible' demon has chosen to manifest itself. From being identical in character with the demons, the witches reached a stage which made them superior to the former. They could not only do everything that the demons did, but they could also control the latter, whereas the demons had no power over witches. Witches could invoke the demons at their will and bring such persons as they chose within the demons' power.

Various means were at their disposal for bringing this about. The glance of a witch's 'evil eye' was supposed to have great power.[1] Terrible were the sufferings of the one on whom a witch threw the glance that kept the person under her spell. The 'evil word,' as it was called, and by which the use of certain magic formulas was meant, was another effective means at her command for inflicting all manner of evil. Magical potions, too, compounded of poisonous weeds, appear to have been prepared by them, and which, entering the body of those whom they desired to punish, had a disastrous effect. Such means might be denominated as direct. There were others indirect which were even more effective, and which rested upon the principle commonly known as 'sympathetic magic.'[2] Under the notion that the symbolical acts of the sorcerers would have their effect upon the one to be bewitched, the male sorcerer or the witch, as the case might be, would tie knots in a rope. Repeating certain formulas with each fresh knot, the witch would in this way symbolically strangle the victim, seal his mouth, wrack his limbs, tear his entrails, and the like.

Still more popular was the making of an image of the desired victim of clay or pitch, honey, fat, or other soft material,[3] and either by burning it inflict physical tortures upon the person represented, or by undertaking various symbolical acts with it, such as burying it among the dead, placing it in a coffin, casting it into a pit or into a fountain, hiding it in an inaccessible place, placing it in spots that had a peculiar significance, as the doorposts, the threshold, under the arch of gates, would prognosticate in this way a fate corresponding to one of these acts for the unfortunate victim.

[1] For the general views connected with the evil eye among all nations, see Elworthy's recent volume, *The Evil Eye.* (London, 1896.)

[2] For illustrations taken from various nations, see Fraser, *The Golden Bough*, ii. 9-12; ii. 85-89.

[3] See for illustrations of similar practices among Egyptians and Greeks, Budge, *Life and Exploits of Alexander the Great* (London, 1896), pp. xii-xvii.

The Exorcisers.

As a protection against the demons and witches, small images of some of the protecting deities were placed at the entrances to houses, and amulets of various kinds were carried about the person. Tablets, too, were hung up in the house, — probably at the entrance, — on which extracts from the religious texts were inscribed. These texts by virtue of their sacred character assured protection against the entrance of demons.[1] But when once a person had come under the baneful power of the demons, recourse was had to a professional class of exorcisers, who acted as mediators between the victims and the gods to whom the ultimate appeal for help was made. These exorcisers were of course priests, and at an early period of Babylonian culture it must have been one of the main functions of priests to combat the influence of evil spirits. It was for this purpose chiefly that the people came to the temples, and in so far we are justified in regarding incantation formulas as belonging to the oldest portion of the Babylonian temple rituals. In the course of time, as the temples in the great religious centers developed into large establishments, the priests were divided into classes, each with special functions assigned to them. Some were concerned with the sacrifices, others presided over the oracles, others were set aside for the night and day watches which were observed in the temple, and it is likely that the scribes formed a class by themselves. To this age of differentiation in priestly functions belongs the special class who may be regarded as the forerunners of the eastern *magi* or magicians, and who by powers and methods peculiar to them could ward off the dangerous attacks

---

[1] Mr. L. W. King describes (*Zeits. für Assyr.* xl. 50–62) interesting fragments of the Dibbarra (or 'plague-god') legend found on tablets which were evidently intended to be hung up. Mr. King suggests that such tablets were hung up in the houses of the Babylonians whenever a plague broke out. One is reminded of the *mezuzoth*, the metallic or wooden cases, attached to the doorposts of their houses by the Jews, and which originally served a similar purpose.

of the demons and witches. The means employed by them may in general be described as forming the complement to those used by the witches, — the reverse side of the picture, — only that they were supposed to be effective against sorcerers, witches, and demons alike. Against the incantation formulas of the witches, incantations of superior force were prescribed that might serve to overcome the baneful influence of the former. The symbolical tying of knots was offset by symbolical loosening, accompanied by formulas that might effect the gradual release of the victim from the meshes of both the witches and the demons; or the hoped-for release was symbolized by the peeling of the several skins of an onion. Corresponding to the images made by the witches, the exorcising priests advised the making of counter images of the witches, and by a symbolical burning, accompanied by certain ceremonies and conciliatory gifts to the gods, hoped to destroy the witches themselves. Since, moreover, the favorite time chosen by the demons and witches for their manifestations was the night, the three divisions of the nights — evening, midnight, and dawn — that correspond to the temple watches were frequently selected as the time for the incantations and the symbolical acts. The address was often made to the gods of night. A series of incantation formulas begins:

> I call upon you, gods of the night,
> With you I call upon the night, the veiled bride,[1]
> I call at evening, midnight, and at dawn.

The formulas themselves, as we shall see, are characterized by their large number rather than by any elements that they have in common. At times they constitute a direct appeal to

---

[1] Tallqvist, *Assyr. Beschwörungsserie Maklu*, p. 115, suggests that the 'veiled bride' may be a name of some goddess of the night. This is improbable. It sounds more like a direct personification of the night, for which an epithet as 'veiled bride' seems appropriate. The name may have arisen in consequence of mythological conceptions affecting the relationship between day and night.

some god or gods, to some particular spirit, or to the associated spirits of heaven and earth, together with a direct indication of what is desired. An incantation addressed to Nusku, the god of fire, closes:

> Fire-god, mighty and lofty one of the gods,
> Who dost overpower the wicked and the hostile,
> Overpower them (the witches) so that I be not destroyed.
> Let me thy servant live, let me
> unharmed stand before thee,
> Thou art my god, thou art my lord,
> Thou art my judge, thou art my helper,
> Thou art my avenger.

Preceding the direct appeal, there is usually a recital more or less detailed of the woes with which one is afflicted. The victim tells of the pains which torture him. Says one bewitched:

> I stand upright, and cannot lie down,
> neither night nor day. The witches have filled my
> mouth with their knots.
> With the aid of *upuntu* weed,[1]
> they have stuffed up my mouth.
> The water that I drink have they diminished,
> My joy is changed to pain, my pleasure to sorrow.

This recital, which is often wearisome by its length, may or may not end in a direct appeal to some god or gods. The narrative of woes, however, is merely introductory to the incantation itself. To prescribe the formula to be used to the one appealing for help, is the special function of the priest acting as exorciser. He recites the formula, which is then repeated by the communicant.

Instead of an appeal to the gods for help, the incantation often embodies threats hurled in the name of the gods at the demons or witches in case they do not release their victim.

[1] A magic potion compounded of this plant. 'Maklu' series, i. ll. 8-12.

Such incantations appear to derive their power chiefly through the personage of the exorciser, who believes himself to be able to control the evil spirits. So in one case, after the sufferer has poured out his troubles, the exorciser replies, threatening the witches with the same evils that they have inflicted:[1]

> They have used all kinds of charms
> to entwine me as with ropes,
> to catch me as in a cage,
> to tie me as with cords,
> to overpower me as in a net,
> to twist me as with a sling,
> to tear me as a fabric,
> to fill me with dirty water as that which runs down a wall (?)
> to throw me down as a wall.

At this point the exorciser takes up the thread and declares:

> But I by command of Marduk, the lord of charms,
> by Marduk, the master of bewitchment,
> Both the male and female witch
> as with ropes I will entwine,
> as in a cage I will catch,
> as with cords I will tie,
> as in a net I will overpower,
> as in a sling I will twist,
> as a fabric I will tear,
> with dirty water as from a wall I will fill,
> as a wall throw them down.

Accompanying these threats, the actions indicated were symbolically performed by the exorciser on effigies of the witches made, in this case, of bitumen covered with pitch.

Corresponding again to the potions prepared by the witches, the priests prepared draughts compounded of various weeds and herbs that were given to the victim, or concoctions that were poured over his body. This constituted the medicinal phase of the priest's labors, and marks the connection between

[1] 'Maklu' series, ii. ll. 148-168.

magic and medicine. Naturally such herbs and weeds were chosen as through experience had proved effective.

The Gods of the Incantation Texts.

A feature of the incantation texts is the appeal to the gods, which is seldom, if ever, wanting. Just as the kings sought, by the enumeration of a large pantheon, to secure the protection of as large a number of powers as possible, so the priests endeavored to strengthen their magic formulas by including the mention of all the chief and a varying number of the minor deities. This invocation of groups of deities, as the invocation of groups of spirits, became more or less conventional, so much so that, instead of mentioning the gods individually, the scribe would content himself with an indication, at the proper point, of the number of gods to be appealed to,—six, ten, fifteen, as the case may be, to as many as fifty.[1] Precisely what gods he had in mind we are no longer in a position to know, but no doubt the chief members of the pantheon were included in the first place. Lists of these deities are often added. The superior triad, Anu, Bel, and Ea, head the list, at times accompanied by their consorts, at times standing alone. The second class of triads, Sin, Shamash, and Ramman, follow, and then the other great gods, Nin-ib, Marduk, Nergal, Nusku, and Gibil; and finally the chief goddesses are added, notably Ishtar, Nin-karrak, or Gula, and Bau.

But besides the chief deities, an exceedingly large number of minor ones are found interspersed through the incantation texts. Some are well known, as Nin-girsu, Zamama, and Papsukal. Many of them are found in other branches of the religious literature or in invocations attached to historical texts, commemorative of some work undertaken and completed

[1] See Reisner, *Sumerisch-Babylonische Hymnen* (Berlin, 1896), p. 15.

by the kings; but a large proportion of these powers, not often distinguishable from mere spirits, only appear once in the literary remains of Babylonia. It is manifestly impossible, under such circumstances, to specify their traits. In most cases, indeed, the phonetic reading is unknown or uncertain. While a considerable proportion may be put down as local gods, enjoying an independent, albeit obscure, existence, at least an equal number will turn out to be mere epithets of gods already known. In all cases where the god's name actually appears as an epithet, we may be certain that such is the case. So when a god is called simply *Dainu*, *i.e.*, Judge, there can be little doubt that Shamash, the sun-god, is meant; a god, 'great mountain,' is none other than Bel; and similarly, such names as 'merciful,' 'hearer of prayer,' 'conqueror of enemy' are manifestly titles belonging to certain well-known deities, and used much as among the Greeks the gods were often referred to by the traits, physical or moral, that distinguished them. As for the residue, who are independent deities, while of course our knowledge of the Babylonian religion would be increased did we know more of them than their names, it is not likely that the worship of these gods, nor the conceptions connected with them, involved any new principle. A mere enumeration would of course be of little use. Moreover, such an enumeration would not be exhaustive, for new deities are found in almost every additional text that is published. Already this list counts considerably over two hundred. At most, such an enumeration would merely illustrate what we already know, — the exceedingly large number of local cults that once existed in Babylonia and Assyria, and disappeared without leaving any trace but the more or less accidental preservation of the name of the deity, who was once regarded as the patron of the place. Lastly it is to be noted that, besides gods, stars are invoked, as well as rivers, temples, and even towns, — in short, anything that has sacred associations.

On a different level from the gods enumerated in groups stand those deities who are introduced into the incantation texts at essential points individually and for a special reason. Such deities are comparatively few, — hardly more than half a dozen. These gods may be called the gods of the incantation texts *par excellence*. Their help is essential to ensure the effectiveness of the exorciser's task. They stand in close and direct connection with the troubles from which relief is prayed for. For physical ills, they act as healers. If the evil for which the individual or the country suffers is due to some natural phenomena, — an eclipse of the moon, of which people stood in great terror, or a deluge or a famine, — the moon-god, the storm-god, some phase of the sun-deity, or an agricultural god would naturally be implored; while in a general way the heads of the pantheon, Marduk in Babylonia and Ashur in Assyria, come in for a large share of attention.

As already intimated in a previous chapter,[1] the god who plays perhaps the most prominent rôle in the incantation texts is Ea. He occupies this rank primarily by virtue of his being the god of humanity; but another factor which enters into consideration, though in an indirect fashion, is his character as a water-god. Water, being one of the means of purification frequently referred to in the texts, acquires a symbolical significance among the Babylonians, as among so many other nations. Ea, therefore, as the water-god of the ancient sacred town, Eridu, acquires additional popularity through this circumstance. The titles that he receives in the texts emphasize his power to heal and protect. He is the great physician who knows all secret sources whence healing can be obtained for the maladies and ills caused by the demons and sorcerers. He is therefore in a peculiar sense 'the lord of the fates' of mankind, the chief exorciser, the all-wise magician of the gods, at whose command and under whose protection, the priest performs his symbolical

[1] See p. 137.

acts. Not only does humanity turn to Ea: the gods, too, appeal to him in their distress. The eclipse of the moon was regarded by the popular faith as a sort of bewitchment of the great orb through the seven evil spirits. All the heavenly bodies are affected by such an event. Anu is powerless. It is only through Ea that Sin is released, just as though he were a human individual. But Ea is rarely approached directly. At his side stands his son Marduk, who acts as a mediator. Marduk listens to the petition addressed to him by the exorcising priest on behalf of the victim, and carries the word to Father Ea. The latter, after first declaring Marduk to be his equal in knowledge, proceeds to dictate the cure. Marduk, accordingly, is given the same titles as his father, Ea. He, too, is the lord of life, the master of the exorcising art, the chief magician among the gods.

The importance thus given to Marduk is an indication of a later period, and must be taken in connection with the supremacy accorded to the god after the union of the Babylonian states. Originally, Ea is the god to whom the direct appeal was made. Marduk is an afterthought that points to the remodeling of the ancient texts after the period of Hammurabi. Damkina, the consort of Ea, is occasionally invoked, but it is significant that Sarpanitum, the consort of Marduk, is rarely mentioned.

The burning of images and witches, or of other objects, being so frequently resorted to as a means of destroying baneful influences, the god of fire occupies a rank hardly secondary to Ea. Here, too, the mystical element involved in the use of fire adds to the effectiveness of the method. Water and fire are the two great sources of symbolical purification that we meet with in both primitive and advanced rituals of the past.[1]

---

[1] Robertson Smith, *Religion of the Semites*, p. 352. Grimm, *Deutsche Mythologie*, I. 508-596. Tylor, *Primitive Culture*, ii. 383 *seq*. See also the article "Hestia" in Roscher's *Ausführliches Lexikon der Griechischen und Römischen Mythologie*.

The fire-god appears in the texts under the double form of Gibil and Nusku. The former occurs with greater frequency than the latter, but the two are used so interchangeably as to be in every respect identical. The amalgamation of the two may indeed be due to the growth of the incantation rituals of Babylon. In some districts Gibil was worshipped as the special god of fire, in others Nusku, much as we found the sun-god worshipped under the names of *Shamas* and *Utu*, and similarly in the case of other deities. On the supposition that the incantation rituals are the result of a complicated literary process, involving the collection of all known formulas, and the bringing of them into some kind of connection with one another, this existence of a twofold fire-god finds a ready explanation. At Babylon we know Nusku was worshipped as the fire-god. Gibil belongs therefore to another section, perhaps to one farther south. He is in all probability the older god of the two, and the preponderating occurrence of his name in the texts may be taken as a proof of the ancient origin of those parts in which it occurs. There being no special motive why he should be supplanted by Nusku, his preëminence was not interfered with through the remodeling to which the texts were subjected. While bearing in mind that Gibil and Nusku are two distinct deities, we may, for the sake of convenience, treat them together under the double designation of Gibil-Nusku.

Gibil and Nusku are called 'sons of Anu'; Gibil, indeed, is spoken of as the first-born of heaven, and the image of his father. The conception is probably mythological, resting upon the belief in the heavenly origin of fire held by all nations. Gibil-Nusku is exalted as the 'lofty one' among the gods, whose command is supreme. He is at once the great messenger of the gods and their chief counsellor. Clothed in splendor, his light is unquenchable. A large variety of other attributes are assigned to him, all emphasizing his strength, his majesty, his brilliancy, and the terror that he is able to inspire. The importance of fire to mankind made Gibil-Nusku the founder of cities, and in general the god of civilization. As the fire-god, Gibil-Nusku is more especially invoked at the symbolical burning of the images of the witches. With a raised torch in one hand, the bewitched person repeats the incantation recited by the exorciser. Frequently the instruction is added that the incantation is to be recited in a whisper, corresponding to the soft tones in which the demons, witches, and ghosts are supposed to convey their messages. The incantations in which the fire-god is exalted in grandiloquent terms belong to the finest productions of this branch of the religious literature. The addresses to Gibil-Nusku are veritable hymns that are worthy of better associations. One of these addresses begins:

> Nusku, great god, counsellor of the great gods,[1]
> Guarding the sacrificial gifts[2] of all the heavenly spirits,
> Founder of cities, renewer of the sanctuaries,
> Glorious day, whose command is supreme,
> Messenger of Anu, carrying out the decrees of Bel,
> Obedient to Bel, counsellor, mountain[3] of the earthly spirits,
> Mighty in battle, whose attack is powerful,
> Without thee no table is spread in the temple.
> Without thee, Shamash, the judge executes no judgment.
> . . . .
> I, thy servant so and so, the son of so and so,[4]
> Whose god is so and so, and whose goddess so and so,[5]
> I turn to thee, I seek thee, I raise my hands to thee,
> I prostrate myself before thee.
> Burn the sorcerer and sorceress,
> May the life of my sorcerer and sorceress be destroyed.
> Let me live that I may exalt thee and proudly pay homage to thee.

This incantation, we are told, is to be recited in a whisper, in the presence of an image of wax. The image is burnt as

---

[1] 'Maklu' series, II. II. 1-17.
[2] A reference to the sacred action of the fire in the burnt offerings.
[3] A favorite title of several gods, Bel, Sin, etc., that emphasizes their strength.
[4] Here the seeker for help inserts his name.
[5] Here the names of special deities are to be inserted.

the words are spoken, and as it is consumed the power of the witch is supposed to wane. The reference to the indispensable presence of the fire-god in the temple is rather interesting. Sacrifice always entailed the use of fire. To whatever deity the offering was made, Gibil-Nusku could not in any case be overlooked. The fire constituted the medium, as it were, between the worshipper and the deity addressed. The fire-god is in truth the messenger who carries the sacrifice into the presence of the god worshipped. Even Shamash, though himself personifying fire, is forced to acknowledge the power of Gibil-Nusku, who, we are told elsewhere, is invoked, even when sacrifices are made to the sun-god.

Besides being the son of Anu, Gibil-Nusku is brought into association with the two other members of the triad, Bel and Ea. He is the messenger of Bel and the son of Ea. The former conception is again mythical. Fire is also the instrument of the gods, and Nusku is particularly called the messenger of Bel because Bel is one of the highest gods. In reality he is the messenger of all the gods, and is frequently so designated. His connection with Ea, on the other hand, seems to be the result of the systematizing efforts of the schoolmen. Ea occupying the chief rank in the incantations, the subsidiary rôle of Gibil-Nusku is indicated by making him, just as Marduk, the son of Ea. In this way, too, the two great means of purification — water and fire — are combined under a single aspect. The combination was all the more appropriate since the fire-god, as the promoter of culture, shared with Ea the protection of humanity. Accordingly, all the titles of Ea are bestowed in one place or the other upon Gibil-Nusku. But, after all, Gibil-Nusku is merely a phase of the solar deity,[1] and hence by the side of this fire-god, Shamash and the other solar deities, though in a measure subsidiary to Gibil-Nusku, are frequently invoked. Shamash, as the great judge, was a personage es-

---

[1] See above, Nusku, p. 220.

pecially appropriate for occasions which involved a decision in favor of the bewitched and against the witches or demons. Gibil-Nusku, like Shamash, is exalted as the great judge who comes to the aid of the oppressed. Similarly, the fire-god receives the attributes belonging to Ninib, Nergal, and the various phases of the latter, such as Lugal-edinna, Lugal-gira, and Alamu. These gods, then, and their consorts, because of their relationship to the fire-god, are introduced into the incantations, and what is more to the point, the various phases of Nergal and Ninib are introduced without any trace of the distinctions that originally differentiated them from one another.[1] Besides the great solar deities, minor ones, as Nin-gish-zida [2] and I-shum, are frequently added in long lists of protecting spirits to whom the appeal for help is directed. The attempt is also made to illustrate their relationship to the great fire-god. So I-shum becomes the messenger of Nusku, while Nin-gish-zida (though in the days of Gudea a male deity[3]) appears to be regarded, as Tallqvist has suggested, as the consort of Nusku.

Night being a favorite time for the recital of the incantations, it was natural that the orb of night, the god Sin, should be added to the pantheon of the exorciser. Though playing a minor rôle, the moon-god is never omitted when a long series of protecting spirits is invoked. But there are occasions when Sin becomes the chief deity invoked. Reference has already been made to the general terror that moon eclipses inspired. The disappearance of the moon was looked upon as a sign of the god's displeasure or as a defeat of the moon in a conflict with other planets. Disaster of some kind — war, pestilence, internal disturbances — was sure to follow upon an eclipse, unless the anger of the god could be appeased or his weakness

[1] See p. 67.
[2] A form of Nusku, according to Tallqvist, *Assyr. Beschwör.* p. 146. It would be more accurate to say a form of Ninib. See p. 92.
[3] See p. 91.

overcome. In the case of such general troubles affecting the whole country, it is the kings themselves who seek out the priests. Rituals were prepared to meet the various contingencies. The king begins the ceremony by a prayer addressed to Sin. One of these prayers begins:[1]

> O Sin, O Nannar! mighty one . . .
> O Sin, thou who alone givest light,
> Extending light to mankind,
> Showing favor to the black-headed ones,[2]
> Thy light shines in heaven . . .
> Thy torch is brilliant as fire;
> Thy light fills the broad earth.
> . . . . . .
> Thy light is glorious as the Sun . . .
> Before thee the great gods lie prostrate;
> The fate of the world rests with thee.
> . . . .

An eclipse has taken place, portending evil to the country, and libations have been poured out on days carefully selected as favorable ones. The king continues:

> I have poured out to thee, with wailing,[3] a libation at night;
> I have offered thee a drink-offering with shouts;
> Prostrate and standing erect[4] I implore thee.

With the prayer to Sin, appeals to other gods and also goddesses are frequently combined, — to Marduk, Ishtar, Tashmitum, Nabu, Ramman, and the like. The incantations themselves, consisting of fervent appeals to remove the evil, actual or portending, are preceded by certain ceremonies, — the burning of incense, the pouring out of some drink, or by symbolical acts, as the binding of cords; and the god is appealed to once more to answer the prayer.

[1] King, *Babylonian Magic*, p. 3.
[2] Humanity.
[3] The reference is to the formal lamentations on the occasion of the death of any one. The moon-god, having disappeared, is bewailed as though dead.
[4] *I.e.*, under all conditions and at all times.

Again, just as Gibil-Nusku entails the invocation of a large variety of solar deities, so Ea, as the water-god, leads to the introduction of various water-gods and spirits. Perhaps the most prominent of these is the god Nâru, whose name, signifying 'river,'[1] is clearly the personification of the watery element, though of the minor bodies of water. Next in order comes the goddess Nin-akha-kuddu.[2] She is invoked as 'goddess of purification.' From her association in several passages with the great deep, and with the city of Eridu — metaphorically used for the great deep — one may be permitted to conclude that she, too, was conceived of as a water-god or a water-spirit. She is 'the lady of spells,' who is asked to take possession of the body of the sufferer, and thus free him from the control of demons or witches. By the side of this goddess, Gula, 'the great physician,' is often appealed to. Again, the demons being in some cases the ghosts of the departed, or such as hover around graves, Nin-kigal, or Allatu, the mistress of the lower world, is an important ally, whose aid is desired in the struggle against the evil spirits. Lastly, it is interesting to note that Izdubar, or Gilgamesh, the famous hero of the great Babylonian epic, occurs also in incantations[3] — a welcome indication of the antiquity of the myth, and the proof, at the same time, that the epic is built on a foundation of myth. From the mythological side, Gilgamesh appears to be a solar deity. The connection of a solar god with fire would account for his appearance in the magical texts. However obscure some of the points connected with the gods of the incantation texts may be, so much is certain, that the two factors of water and fire, and the part played by these elements in the ceremonies, control and explain the choice of most of the gods and god-

[1] The reading Nâru is not altogether certain, but probable. See Tallqvist, *Assyr. Beschwör.* pp. 131, 132, whose suggestion, however, that Nâru may be a female deity, is not acceptable. *Elitti* is probably a scribal error.
[2] See above p. 103.
[3] Tallqvist, l. l. 38.

desses introduced, though — be it expressly noted — not of all occurring in the magical texts.

The Ritual and Formulas.

Coming to the incantations themselves, they can best be characterized as appeals interspersed with words of a more or less mystic character. The force and efficacy of the incantation lie not so much in the meaning of the words uttered, as in the simple fact that they *are* to be uttered. These incantations were combined into a ritual, and indications were given of the occasions on which the incantations were to be used. An analysis of one of these rituals will serve to illustrate this branch of the religious literature of the Babylonians. I choose for this purpose the series known as Maklu, *i.e.*, Burning,[1] the interpretation of which has been so considerably advanced by Dr. Tallqvist's admirable work. The first tablet of the series opens with an invocation to the gods of night. After complaining of his sad condition, the bewitched individual continues as follows:

> Arise ye great gods, hear my complaint;
> Grant me justice, take cognizance of my condition.
> I have made an image of my sorcerer and sorceress;
> I have humbled myself before you and bring to you my cause
> Because of the evil they (*i.e.*, the witches) have done,
> Of the impure things which they have handled,[2]
> May she[3] die! Let me live!
> May her charm, her witchcraft, her sorcery (?) be broken.
> May the plucked sprig (?) of the *binu* tree purify me.
> May it release me; may the evil odor[4] of my mouth be scattered to the winds.
> May the *mashtakal* herb[5] which fills the earth cleanse me.
> Before you let me shine like the *kankal* herb

[1] See above, p. 254.
[2] To bewitch me.
[3] The witch.
[4] From which he suffers through the witches.
[5] The identification of the many herbs mentioned in the texts is as yet impossible. The subject awaits investigation at the hands of one versed in botanical lore.

Let me be as brilliant and pure as the *lardu* herb.
The charm of the sorceress is evil;
May her words return to her mouth,[1] her tongue be cut off.
Because of her witchcraft, may the gods of night smite her,
The three watches of the night [2] break her evil charm.
May her mouth be wax [3] (?), her tongue honey.
May the word causing my misfortune that she has spoken dissolve like wax (?).
May the charm that she has wound up melt like honey,
So that her magic knot be cut in twain, her work destroyed,
All her words scattered across the plains
By the order that the gods have given.

The section closes with the ordinary request of the exorciser to the victim: "Recite this incantation." It will be seen how closely the principle of sympathetic magic is followed. The individual having been bewitched by means of certain herbs concocted probably into potions, other herbs are prepared by the exorciser as an antidote. The emphasis laid upon purification, too, is noteworthy. There are numerous synonyms employed for which it is difficult to find the adequate equivalent in English. The terms reach out beyond the literal to the symbolical purification. The victim wishes to become pure, cleansed of all impurities, so that he may be resplendent as the gods are pure, brilliant, and glorious, pure as the water, brilliant and glorious as the fire.

The length of the formulas varies. Often they consist only of a few lines. So the one immediately following appeals to Gilgamesh in these words:

Earth, Earth, Earth,
Gilgamesh is the master of your witchcraft.
What you have done, I know;
What I do, you know not.
All the mischief wrought by my sorceresses is destroyed, dissolved — is gone.

---

[1] *I.e.*, be ineffective.
[2] *I.e.*, the gods presiding over the watches.
[3] Her words dissolve like wax and honey.

At times the conditions under which the witches are pictured as acting are very elaborate. They are represented as dwelling in places with which mythological conceptions are connected ; they are ferried across the river separating their city from human habitations ; they are protected against attacks by the walls which surround their habitations. To effect a release, the exorcisers, it would appear, made representations by means of drawings on clay of these habitations of the witches. They thereupon symbolically cut off the approaches and laid siege to the towns. This, at least, appears to be the meaning of an incantation beginning:

> My city is Sappan,[1] my city is Sappan ;
> The gates of my city Sappan are two,
> One towards sunrise, the other towards sunset.[2]
> I carry a box, a pot with *mashtakal* herbs ;
> To the gods of heaven I offer water ;
> As I for you secure your purification,
> So do you purify me !

The victim imitates the conduct of the witch, goes about as she does, with a pot in which the potions are made, performs the symbolical act which should purify him of the evil that is in him, and hopes, in this way, to obtain his own release. The description continues :

> I have kept back the ferry, have shut off the wall,[3]
> Have thus checked the enchantment from all quarters.
> Anu and Anatum have commissioned me.
> Whom shall I send to Belit of the field ?[4]
> Into the mouth of the sorcerer and sorceress cast the lock.[5]
> Recite the incantation of the chief of gods, Marduk.[6]
> 'Let them [7] call to thee but answer them not,

---

[1] Supposed to be situated at the northern point of the heavens.
[2] The vault of heaven was pictured as having two gates.
[3] So that the witch cannot leave her habitation.
[4] With the order 'to cast the lock,' etc.
[5] To prevent her from uttering her charms.
[6] The following four lines constitute the incantation.
[7] *Ie.*, the witches.

Let them address thee, but hearken not to them.
Let me call to thee, and do thou answer me,
Let me address thee, and do thou hearken unto me.'
By the command of Anu, Anatum, and Belit, recite the incantation.

The hymns to the fire-god, Nusku (or Girru), of which the 'Maklu' series naturally furnishes many specimens,[1] are all pretty much alike. I choose one which illustrates in greater detail the symbolical burning of the image of the witch:[2]

> Nusku, great offspring of Anu,
> The likeness of his father, the first-born of Bel,
> The product of the deep, sprung from Ea,[3]
> I raise the torch to illumine thee, yea, thee.
> The sorcerer who has bewitched me,
> Through the witchcraft by means of which he has bewitched me, do thou bewitch him.
> The sorceress who has bewitched me,
> Through the witchcraft by means of which she has bewitched me, bewitch thou her.
> The charmer who has charmed me,
> Through the charm with which he has charmed me, charm thou him.
> The witch who has charmed me,
> Through the charm with which she has charmed me, charm thou her.
> Those who have made images of me, reproducing my features,
> Who have taken away my breath, torn my hairs,
> Who have rent my clothes, have hindered my feet from treading the dust,
> May the fire-god, the strong one, break their charm.

Just as the witches were burnt in effigy, so also the demons were supposed to be similarly dispelled. Immediately following the incantation comes one directed against the demons:

---

[1] See above, p. 278, where one has been given.
[2] Maklu, I. 122-143.
[3] The fiery element belongs to all three divisions of the universe,—to heaven, earth, and water.

> I raise the torch, their images I burn,
>   Of the *utukku*, the *shedu*, the *rabisu*, the *ekimmu*,
>   The *labartu*, the *labasi*, the *akhkhasu*,
>   Of *lilu* and *lilitu* and *ardat lili*,
>   And every evil that seizes hold of men.
> Tremble, melt away, and disappear!
> May your smoke rise to heaven,
> May Shamash destroy your limbs,
> May the son of Ea [*i.e.*, may the fire-god],
> The great magician, restrain your strength (?).

The witch who has caused the evil may be unknown. For such a case one of the incantations runs:[1]

> Who art thou, sorceress, who bears her evil word within her heart,
> Through whose tongue my misfortune is produced,
> Through whose lips I have been poisoned,
> In whose footsteps death follows?
> Sorceress, I seize thy mouth, seize thy tongue,
> I seize thy searching eyes,
> I seize thy ever-moving feet,
> I seize thy knees ever active,
> I seize thy hands ever stretched out,
> I tie thy hands behind thee.
> May Sin . . . destroy thy body,
> May he cast thee into an abyss of fire and water.
> Sorceress, as the circle of this seal-ring,[2]
> May thy face grow pale and wan.

Of the same character as this, are a variety of other incantations, all applicable to cases in which the sorceress is unknown. As the last specimen of the 'Maklu' series, I choose an incantation addressed to the demons, which is interesting because of the direct character of the commands it contains:

> Away, away, far away, far away,
> For shame, for shame, fly away, fly away,
> Round about face, go away, far away,
> Out of my body, away,

---

[1] Maklu, III. ll. 89-103.
[2] Many of the seals used by the Babylonians were of white stone or bone.

> Out of my body, far away,
> Out of my body, away for shame,
> Out of my body, fly away,
> Out of my body, round about face,
> Out of my body, go away,
> Into my body, come not back,
> Towards my body, do not approach,
> Towards my body, draw not nigh,
> My body torture not.
> By Shamash the mighty, be ye foresworn.
> By Ea, the lord of everything, be ye foresworn.
> By Marduk, the chief magician of the gods, be ye foresworn.
> By the fire-god, be ye foresworn.
> From my body be ye restrained!

Repetition and variation in the use of certain phrases make up, as will be seen from the specimens given, a large part of the incantation. A curious illustration of the importance attributed to such repetition is furnished by the eighth and last tablet of the 'Maklu' series. It consists of seven divisions, each beginning with a repetition of the headlines of the various sections of the preceding seven tablets; and only after the headlines of each of the tablets have been exhausted, does the real incantation begin. This eighth tablet contains therefore a kind of summary of all the others, the purpose of which is to gather together all the power and influence of the seven others.

The 'Maklu' ritual deals so largely with the fire-god that a specimen from another series, to illustrate the position of Ea and Marduk in the incantations, seems called for. The 'Shurpu' series introduces Ea and Marduk more particularly. The fifth tablet of this series begins:[1]

> The evil curse rests like a *gallu* upon the man,
> The pain-giving voice[2] has settled upon him,
> The voice that is not good has settled upon him,
> The evil curse, the charm that produces insanity,
> The evil curse has killed that man as a sheep,

---

[1] Zimmern's edition, pp. 25–29. [2] *Iz.*, the evil word.

His god has departed from his body,[1]
His goddess has . . . taken her place outside,[2]
The pain-giving voice covers him as a garment and confuses him.
Marduk sees him,
And proceeds to the house of his father Ea and speaks:
" My father, the evil curse as a demon has settled on the man."
He says it for a second time.
" What that man should do, I do not know; by what can he be cured?"
Ea answers his son Marduk:
" My son, can I add aught that thou dost not know?
Marduk, what can I tell thee that thou dost not know?
What I know, also thou knowest.
My son Marduk, take him to the overseer of the house of perfect purification,
Dissolve his spell, release him from the charm, and from the troublesome bodily disease.
Whether it be the curse of his father,
Or the curse of his mother,
Or the curse of his brother,
Or the curse of an unknown,[3]
May the bewitchment through the charm of Ea be peeled off like an onion.
May it be cut off like a date.
May it be removed like a husk.
O power of the spirit of heaven, be thou invoked!
O spirit of earth, be thou invoked!"

The purification by water, which is here only incidentally referred to, is more fully touched upon in other incantations, where Ea tells Marduk that the victim must take

> Glittering water, pure water,
> Holy water, resplendent water,
> The water twice seven times may he bring,
> May he make pure, may he make resplendent.
> May the evil *rabisu* depart,
> May he betake himself outside,

---

[1] His protecting deity has deserted him.
[2] Of his body.
[3] *I.e.*, whoever may have invoked the evil demon to settle upon him.

> May the protecting *shedu*, the protecting *lamassu*,
> Settle upon his body.
> Spirit of heaven, be thou invoked!
> Spirit of earth, be thou invoked![1]

Still other methods of magical cure besides the use of water and of potions were in vogue. In a tablet of the same ritual to which the last extract belongs, and which is especially concerned with certain classes of diseases produced by the demons, the sick man is told to take

> White wool, which has been spun into thread,
> To attach it to his couch[2] in front and at the top,
> Black wool which has been spun into thread
> To bind at his left side.

Then follows the incantation which he is to recite:

> The evil *utukku, alu, ekimmu,*
> The evil *gallu*, the evil god, *rabisu*,
> *Labartu, labasu, akhkhazu,*
> *Lilu* and *lilit* and *ardat lili,*
> Sorcery, charm, bewitchment,
> The sickness, the cruel artifice,
> Their head against his head,
> Their hand against his hand,
> Their foot against his foot,
> May they not place,
> May they never draw nigh.
> Spirit of heaven, be thou foresworn!
> Spirit of earth, be thou foresworn!

It is interesting to note the introduction of ethical ideas into these texts, despite the primitive character of the beliefs upon which the incantations repose. The possibility was considered that the attack of the demons was a punishment sent in some way for committed sins. The incantation series 'Shurpu' furnishes us with a long list of wrongs for which a person may

---

[1] The translation of these lines follows in all but some minor passages the correct one given by Sayce, *Hibbert Lectures*, p. 446.   [2] Of the sick man.

be held enthralled in the power of the demons or sorcerers. The exorciser in petitioning that the ban may be relieved, enumerates at length the various causes for which the evil may have been sent:[1]

> Has he sinned against a god,
> Is his guilt against a goddess,
> Is it a wrongful deed against his master,
> Hatred towards his elder brother,
> Has he despised father or mother,
> Insulted his elder sister,
> Has he given too little,[2]
> Has he withheld too much,
> For "no" said "yes,"
> For "yes" said "no"?[3]
>
> . . . .
>
> Has he used false weights?
>
> . . . .
>
> Has he taken an incorrect amount,
> Not taken the correct sum,
> Has he fixed a false boundary,
> Not fixed a just boundary,
> Has he removed a boundary, a limit, or a territory,
> Has he possessed himself of his neighbor's house,
> Has he approached his neighbor's wife,
> Has he shed the blood of his neighbor,
> Robbed his neighbor's dress?
>
> . . . .
>
> Was he frank in speaking,
> But false in heart,
> Was it "yes" with his mouth,
> But "no" in his heart?[4]

In this way the exorciser proceeds to enumerate an exceedingly long list of sins — no less than one hundred — most of which are ethical misdemeanors, while others are merely ceremonial transgressions. In the third tablet of this series[5] there

---

[1] Zimmern, *Die Beschwörungstafeln Shurpu*, pp. 5, 6.
[2] In mercantile transactions.   [3] *I.e.*, lied.
[4] *I.e.*, did he say one thing, but mean the contrary?
[5] Zimmern, *ib.* pp. 13-20.

is even a longer list of causes for the ban which Marduk, the "chief exorciser" among the gods, is called upon to loosen. Here again we find an equal proportion of moral transgressions placed on a par with errors in performing religious rites or unwillful offences in neglecting conventional methods of doing things.

The ethical features of the texts can, without much question, be put down as the work of the later editors. They belong to a period when already an advanced conception not only of right and wrong, but also of sin had arisen among the religious leaders of the people, and perhaps had made its way already among the masses, without, however, disturbing the confidence in the traditional superstitions. The strange combination of primitive and advanced religious beliefs is characteristic, as we shall have occasion to see, of various divisions of the Babylonian religious literature. The lapse from the ethical strain to the incantation refrain is as sudden as it is common. The priest having exhausted the category of possible sins or mishaps that have caused the suffering of the petitioner, proceeds to invoke the gods, goddesses, and the powerful spirits to loosen the ban. There is no question of retribution for actual acts of injustice or violence, any more than there is a question of genuine contrition. The enumeration of the causes for the suffering constitutes in fact a part of the incantation. The mention of the real cause in the long list — and the list aims to be exhaustive, so that the exorciser may strike the real cause — goes a long way towards ensuring the departure of the evil spirit. And if, besides striking the real cause, the exorciser is fortunate enough in his enumeration of the various gods, goddesses, and spirits to call by name upon the *right* god or spirit, the one who has the power over the demon in question, his object is achieved. Speaking the right words and pronouncing the right name, constitute, together with the performance of the correct ceremony and the bringing of the right sacrifice, the conditions upon which depends the success of the priest in the incantation ritual. Hence the striking features of these texts, the enumeration of long lists of causes for misfortune, long lists of powers invoked, and a variety of ceremonies prescribed, in the hope that the priest will "hit it" at one time or the other.

INCANTATIONS AND PRAYERS.

The incantations naturally shade off into prayers. Frequently they are prayers pure and simple. Powerful as the sacred formulas were supposed to be, the ultimate appeal of the sufferer is to the gods. Upon their favor it ultimately depends whether the mystic power contained in the sacred words uttered shall manifest itself to the benefit of the supplicant or not. While it is proper, therefore, to distinguish incantations from prayers, the combination of the two could scarcely be avoided by the priests, who, rising in a measure superior to the popular beliefs, felt it to be inconsistent with a proper regard for the gods not to give them a superior place in the magical texts. The addition, to the sacred formulas, of prayers directly addressed to certain gods may be put down as due to the adaptation of ancient texts to the needs of a later age; and, on the other hand, the addition of incantations to what appear to have been originally prayers, pure and simple, is a concession made to the persistent belief in the efficacy of certain formulas when properly uttered. Such combinations of prayers and incantations constituted, as would appear, a special class of religious texts; and, in the course of further editing,[1] a number of prayers addressed to various deities were combined and interspersed with incantation and ceremonial directions which were to accompany the prayers.

The incantations accordingly lead us to the next division in the religious literature of the Babylonians, — the prayers and hymns.

[1] For details as to the manner in which this editing was done, see King's admirable remarks in the Introduction to his *Babylonian Magic and Sorcery*, pp. xx-xxiv.

CHAPTER XVII.

THE PRAYERS AND HYMNS.

From what has just been said, it follows that the step from magical formulas to prayers and hymns is but a small one, and does not, indeed, carry with it the implication of changed or higher religious conceptions. While the incantation texts in their entirety may be regarded as the oldest *fixed* ritual of the Babylonian-Assyrian religion, there were occasions even in the oldest period of Babylonian history when the gods were approached in prayer without the accompaniment of magic formulas. Such occasions were the celebration of festivals in honor of the gods, the dedication of temples or of sacred statues, and the completion of such purely secular undertakings as the building of a canal. Gudea, we are told, upon completing a statue to his god Nin-girsu, prayed: 'O King, whose great strength the land cannot endure (?); Nin-girsu! grant to Gudea, who has built this house, a good fate.'[1] As in the earliest, so in the latest, period, the Babylonian kings approach the gods in prayer upon completing their great sacred edifices. The prayers of Nebuchadnezzar are particularly fine — remarkable, indeed, for their diction and elevation of thought. Upon completing the restoration of a temple to Nin-karrak or Gula in Sippar, he prays:[2]

Nin-karrak, lofty goddess, look with favor upon the work of my hands.
Mercy towards me be the command of thy lips,
Long life, abundance of strength,
Health, and joy, grant to me as a gift.

---

[1] Inscription D, col. v. ll. 2–7.
[2] Abel-Winckler, *Keilschrifttexte*, p. 33, col. III. ll. 52–58.

In the presence of Shamash and Marduk cause my deeds to be regarded with favor,
Command grace for me.

A prayer of the same king addressed to Shamash, upon restoring the great temple at Sippar, E-babbara, runs :[1]

O Shamash, great lord, upon entering joyfully into thy glorious temple E-babbara,
Look with favor upon my precious handiwork,
Mercy towards me be thy command ;
Through thy righteous order, may I have abundance of strength.
Long life, and a firm throne, grant to me.
May my rule last forever !
With a righteous sceptre of blissful rulership,
With a legitimate staff, bringing salvation to mankind, adorn my sovereignty forever.
With strong weapons for the fray, protect my soldiers ;
Then, O Shamash, by oracle and dream, answer me correctly !
By thy supreme command, which is unchangeable,
May my weapons advance, and strike and overthrow the weapons of the enemies.

Nebuchadnezzar's inscriptions are characterized by the prayer with which they almost invariably close. Whether erecting a sanctuary or building a canal or improving the walls of Babylon, he does not fail to add to the description of his achievements a prayer to some deity, in which he asks for divine grace and the blessings of long life and prosperity.

There were other occasions, too, in which, both in ancient times and in more modern periods, prayers were sent up to the gods. Kudur-mabuk, of the second dynasty of Ur, informs us that he built a temple, E-nun-makh, to Sin in gratitude to the god for having hearkened to his prayer.

The Assyrian kings pray to Ashur or Ishtar before the battle, and offer thanks after the victory has been gained. "O goddess of Arbela !" says Ashurbanabal,[2] " I am Ashurbanabal, the king of Assyria, the product of thy hands, created by thee in

[1] Ball, *Proc. Soc. Bibl. Arch.* xi. 124 *seq.*
[2] *Annals*, Cylinder B, col. v. ll. 30–46.

the house of my father. To renew the sanctuaries of Assyria, and to enlarge the cities of Babylonia, . . . have I devoted myself to thy dwelling-places, and have steadfastly worshipped thy sovereignty. . . . . Hearken unto me! O thou mistress of mistresses, supreme in battle, mistress of the fray, queen of the gods, . . . who speakest good things in the presence of Ashur, the father, that produced thee. Teumman, king of Elam, has arrayed his army and fixed upon battle, brandishes his weapons to proceed against Assyria. Do thou now, O warrior, like . . . drive him into the midst of the fray, pursue him with a storm, with an evil wind." Ishtar, the narrative tells us, hearkened to the fervent words of the king. "Be not afraid," says the goddess to her royal subject. Elsewhere the same king prays more briefly to Ashur and Ishtar. "May his corpse [viz., of a certain enemy] be cast before his enemy [*i.e.*, before Ashurbanabal], and his remains be carried off."[1]

Upon ascending the throne, we find Nebuchadnezzar addressing a fervent prayer to the great god Marduk:

O Eternal Ruler! Lord of the Universe!
Grant that the name[2] of the king whom thou lovest,
Whose name thou hast mentioned,[3] may flourish as seems good to thee.
Guide him on the right path.
I am the ruler who obeys thee, the creation of thy hand.
It is thou who hast created me,
And thou hast entrusted to me sovereignty over mankind.
According to thy mercy, O lord, which thou bestowest upon all,
Cause me to love thy supreme rule.
Implant the fear of thy divinity in my heart,
Grant to me whatsoever may seem good before thee,
Since it is thou that dost control my life.

The curses also with which so many of the historical texts of Babylonia and Assyria close may be regarded as prayers. We are also justified in assuming that the offering of sacrifices,

---

[1] Without proper burial,— the greatest misfortune that could happen to the dead.
[2] *I.e.*, life. [3] *I.e.*, called to the throne.

which formed at all times an essential feature of the cult, both in Babylonia and Assyria, was always accompanied by some form of prayer addressed to some deity or to a group of deities. In view of all this, no sharp chronological line, any more than a logical one, can be drawn marking off the incantation formulas from the hymns and prayers pure and simple. The conceptions formed of the gods in the incantation texts are precisely those which we have found to be characteristic of them in the period when this phase of the religion reached its highest development. Ea is the protector of humanity, Shamash the lord of justice; and, if certain ideas that in the prayers are attached to the gods — as wisdom to Sin — are absent from the incantations, it may be regarded rather as an accident than as an indication of any difference of conception. The pantheon too, barring the omission of certain gods, is the same that we find it to be in the historical texts, and the order in which the gods are enumerated corresponds quite closely with the rank accorded to them in the inscriptions of the kings. What variations there are are not sufficiently pronounced to warrant any conclusions. All this points, as has been emphasized several times, to the subsequent remodeling of the texts in question. It is true that we find more traces of earlier and purely mythological notions in the incantations than in the hymns and prayers, but such notions are by no means foreign to the latter. Even in those religious productions of Babylonia which represent the flower of religious thought, we meet with views that reflect a most primitive mode of thought. The proper view, therefore, to take of the prayers and hymns is to regard them as twin productions to the magical texts, due to the same conceptions of the power of the gods, an emanation of the same religious spirit, and produced at the same time that the incantation rituals enjoyed popular favor and esteem, and without in any way interfering with the practice of the rites that these rituals involved.

This position does not of course preclude that among the prayers and hymns that have been preserved there are some betraying a loftier spirit, a higher level of religious thought, and more pronounced ethical tendencies than others. Indeed, the one important result of the dissociation of the address to the gods from the purely practical magic rites was to produce the conditions favorable to a development of higher religious thought. An offering of praise to the gods, whether it was for victory granted or for a favor shown, called forth the best and purest sentiments of which the individual was capable. Freed from all lower associations, such an act proved an incentive to view the deity addressed from his most favorable side, to emphasize those phases which illustrated his affection for his worshippers, his concern for their needs, his discrimination, and not merely his power and strength. In short, the softer and the more humane aspects of the religion would thus be brought out. The individual would address his god in terms betraying his affection, and would couple with him attributes that would reflect the worshipper's rather than the god's view of the purpose and aim of existence. Whatever powers of idealization there lay in the worshipper's nature would be brought into the foreground by the intellectual effort involved in giving expression to his best thoughts, when aiming to come into close communion with a power upon which he felt himself dependent. For an understanding, therefore, of the ethical tendencies of the Babylonian religion, an appreciation of the prayers and hymns is of prime importance; and we shall presently see that, as a matter of fact, the highest level of ethical and religious thought is reached in some of these hymns.

The prayers of Nebuchadnezzar represent, perhaps, the best that has been attained in this branch of religious literature. Returning, for a moment, to the dedication prayer to Marduk, addressed by the king on the occasion of his mounting the throne,[1] one cannot fail to be struck by the high sense of the importance of his station with which the king is inspired. Sovereignty is not a right that he can claim — it is a trust granted to him by Marduk. He holds his great office not for purposes of self-glorification, but for the benefit of his subjects. In profound humility he confesses that what he has he owes entirely to Marduk. He asks to be guided so that he may follow the path of righteousness. Neither riches nor power constitute his ambition, but to have the fear of his lord in his heart. Such a plane of thought is never reached in the incantation texts. For all that, the original dependence of the prayers and hymns upon incantation formulas, tinges even the best productions. Some of the finest hymns, in which elevated thoughts are elaborated with considerable skill, reveal their origin by having incantations attached to them. Again, others which are entirely independent productions are full of allusions to sickness, demons, and sorcerers, that show the outgrowth of the hymns from the incantations; and none are entirely free from traces of the conceptions that are characteristic of the incantation texts. The essential difference between these two classes of closely related texts may be summed up in the proposition that the religious thought which produced them both is carried to a higher point of elaboration in the hymns. The prayers and hymns represent the attempt of the Babylonian mind to free itself from a superstitious view of the relationship of man to the powers around him; an attempt, but — it must be added — an unsuccessful one.

It is rather unfortunate that many of the hymns found in the library of Ashurbanabal are in so fragmentary a condition. As a consequence we are frequently unable to determine more than their general contents. The colophons generally are missing, — at least in those hymns hitherto published,[2] — so

---

[1] See p. 296.

[2] The prayers and hymns of the Babylonians are only beginning to receive the attention they deserve at the hands of scholars. Sayce, e.g., in the specimens attached to his

that we are left in the dark as to the special occasion for which the hymn was composed. Without this knowledge it is quite impossible to assign to it any definite date except upon internal evidence. In the course of time, the hymnal literature of the great temples of Babylonia must have grown to large proportions, and, in collecting them, some system was certainly followed by the priests engaged in this work. There is evidence of a collection having been made at some time of hymns addressed to Shamash. Some of these were intended as a salute upon the sun's rising, others celebrated his setting. These hymns convey the impression of having been composed for the worship of the god in one of his great temples — perhaps in E-babbara, at Sippar. We have several hymns also addressed to Marduk, and one can well suppose that at the great temple E-sagila, in Babylon, a collection of Marduk hymns must have been prepared, and so for others of the great gods. But, again, many of the hymns convey the impression of being merely sporadic productions — composed for certain occasions, and without any reference to a possible position in a ritual.

Of the hymns so far published, those to Shamash are probably the finest. The conception of the sun-god as the judge of mankind lent itself readily to an ethical elaboration. Accordingly, we find in these hymns justice and righteousness as the two prominent themes. A striking passage in one of these hymns reads :[1]

> The law of mankind dost thou direct,
> Eternally just in the heavens art thou,
> Of faithful judgment towards all the world art thou.

Hibbert Lectures, pp. 479–520, does not even distinguish properly between pure hymns and mere incantations. Now that Dr. Bezold's great catalogue of the Koujunjik collection of the British Museum is completed, the opportunity is favorable for some one to study the numerous unpublished fragments of hymns in the British Museum, and produce in connection with those that have been published a comprehensive work on the subject. Knudtzon's *Assyrische Gebete an den Sonnengott* may serve as a model for such a work.

[1] IVR. 28, no. 1.

Thou knowest what is right, thou knowest what is wrong.
O Shamash! Righteousness has lifted up its neck (?);
O Shamash! Wrong like a ———— has been cut (?);
O Shamash! The support of Anu and Bel art thou;
O Shamash! Supreme judge of heaven and earth art thou.

After a break in the tablet, the hymn continues:

O Shamash! Supreme judge, great lord of all the world art thou;
Lord of creation, merciful one of the world art thou.

The following lines now reveal the purpose of the hymn. It is a prayer for the life of the king:

O Shamash! on this day purify and cleanse the king, the son of his god.
Whatever is evil within him, let it be taken out.

The next few lines are a distinct echo of the incantation formulas, and show how readily prayer passes from a higher to a lower stage of thought:

Cleanse him like a vessel . . . . .[1]
Illumine him like a vessel of . . . . .[1]
Like the copper of a polished tablet,[2] let him be bright.
Release him from the ban.

The same incantation occurs at the close of another hymn to Shamash, addressed to the sun upon his rising.[3] The colophon furnishes the opening line of the next tablet, which also begins with an address to Shamash. We have here a clear indication of a kind of Shamash ritual extending, perhaps, over a number of tablets, and to which, in all probability, the hymn just quoted also belongs.

The opening lines of the second hymn read:

O Shamash! out of the horizon of heaven thou issuest forth,
The bolt of the bright heavens thou openest,
The door of heaven thou dost open.
O Shamash! over the world dost thou raise thy head.
O Shamash! with the glory of heaven thou coverest the world.

---

[1] Some specification of the kind of vessel meant.

[2] Inscriptions were written on various metals,—gold, silver, antimony, lead, copper, etc.   [3] IVR. 20, no. 2.

It would be difficult to believe, but for the express testimony furnished by the hymn itself, that a production giving evidence of such a lofty view of the sun-god should, after all, be no more than an incantation. The same is the case, however, with all the Shamash hymns so far published. They either expressly or by implication form part of an incantation ritual. Evidently, then, such addresses to Shamash are to be viewed in no other light than the exaltation of Nusku in the 'Maklu' series,[1] and which we have found were in many cases elaborate, beautiful in diction, and elevated in thought. So — to give one more example — a hymn addressed to the sun-god at the setting, and which is especially interesting because of the metaphors chosen to describe the sun's course, is proved by the colophon to be again an incantation. It belongs to a series — perhaps, indeed, to the same as the specimens furnished:[2]

> O sun-god in the midst[3] of heaven at thy setting,
> May the enclosure of the pure heaven greet thee,[4]
> May the gate of heaven approach thee,
> May the directing god, the messenger who loves thee, direct thy way.
> In E-babbara, the seat of thy sovereignty, thy supremacy rises like the dawn.
> May Â, the wife whom thou lovest, come before thee with joy;
> May thy heart be at rest,[5]
> May the glory of thy divinity be established for thee.
> O Shamash! warrior hero, mayest thou be exalted;
> O lord of E-babbara, as thou marchest, may thy course be directed,
> Direct thy path, march along the path fixed for thy course (?).
> O Shamash! judge of the world, director of its laws art thou.

In the previous chapter, the hymns addressed to the moon-god in connection with eclipses have been referred to and short

---

[1] See above, p. 286.
[2] Published by Bertin in the *Revue d'Assyriologie*, no. 4, and translated by Sayce, *Hibbert Lectures*, p. 573. I adopt Sayce's translation, Bertin's publication being inaccessible to me.
[3] Probably 'horizon.'
[4] Lit., speak to thee of peace.
[5] *I.e.*, may thy anger depart.

specimens given. A more elaborate hymn to Sin will further illustrate the conceptions current about this deity:[1]

O lord, chief of the gods, who on earth and in heaven alone is exalted.
Father Nannar,[2] lord of increase, chief of the gods,
Father Nannar, heavenly lord,
Father Nannar, moon-god, chief of the gods,
Father Nannar, lord of Ur, chief of the gods,
Father Nannar, lord of E-gish-shir-gal,[3] chief of the gods,
Father Nannar, lord of the brilliant crescent, chief of the gods,
Father Nannar, whose sovereignty is brought to perfection, chief of the gods,
Father Nannar, who passes along in great majesty,
O strong Bull,[4] great of horns, perfect in form, with long flowing beard[5] of the color of lapus-lazuli.
Powerful one, self-created, a product (?) beautiful to look upon, whose fullness has not been brought forth,[6]
Merciful one, begetter of everything, who among living things occupies a lofty seat,
Father, merciful one and restorer, whose weapon (?) maintains the life of the whole world.
Lord, thy divinity, like the distant heaven and the wide ocean, is full (?) of fear.
Ruler of the land, protector of sanctuaries, proclaimer of their name.
Father, begetter of the gods and of men, establishing dwellings and granting gifts,
Calling to sovereignty, giving the sceptre, who decreest destinies for distant days.
Strong chief, whose wide heart embraces in mercy all that exists,
... beautiful, whose knees do not grow weary, who opens the road (?) for the gods, his brothers,
... who, from the foundation of heaven till the zenith,
Passes along in brilliancy (?), opening the door of heaven,
Preparing the fate (?) of humanity.

---

[1] IVR. 9. [2] 'The illuminator,' one of the names of Sin. See above, p. 75.
[3] The name of Sin's temple at Ur.
[4] A metaphor descriptive of the moon, because of the resemblance of the crescent to a horn.
[5] The moon-god is pictured with a long beard on the seal cylinders. See p. 76.
[6] *Ie.*, unlike other products, the moon's fullness is self-created.

Father, begetter of everything, . . .
Lord, proclaiming the decisions of heaven and earth,
Whose command is not set aside,
. . . and granting water [1] for all that has life.
No god reaches to thy fullness.
In heaven who is exalted? Thou alone art exalted.
On earth who is exalted? Thou alone art exalted.
Thy strong command is proclaimed in heaven, and the Igigi prostrate themselves.
Thy strong command is proclaimed on earth, and the Anunnaki kiss the ground.
Thy strong command on high, like a storm in the darkness, passes along, and nourishment streams forth.
When thy strong command is established on the earth, vegetation sprouts forth.
Thy strong command stretches over meadows and heights, and life is increased.
Thy strong command produces right and proclaims justice to mankind.
Thy strong command, through the distant heavens and the wide earth, extends to whatever there is.
Thy strong command, who can grasp it? Who can rival it?
Lord, in heaven is [thy] sovereignty, on earth is thy sovereignty. Among the gods, thy brothers, there is none like thee.
O King of Kings, who has no judge superior to him, whose divinity is not surpassed by any other ![2]

A more perfect idealization of the mythological notions connected with the moon-god can hardly be imagined. The old metaphors are retained, but interpreted in a manner that reflects higher spiritual tendencies. The moon is still figured as a bull, but it is the idea of strength that is extracted from the picture and dwelt upon. The writer still thinks of the moon as an old man with flowing beard, but he uses the figure to convey the impression of the brilliancy of the great orb. The influence of the moon upon the change of seasons, upon vegetation,—a belief which the Babylonians shared with other

---

[1] A reference perhaps to the supposed influence of the moon on the tides.

[2] The rest of the hymn—some dozen lines—is too fragmentary to warrant translation.

nations, — leads the writer to extol the benign feelings of the god towards mankind. The sun-god, through the glowing heat that he develops, becomes, as we have seen, the warrior and even the destroyer, the consuming force. The moon-god is the benefactor of mankind who restores the energies of man weakened from the heat of the day. Nannar-Sin becomes the giver of life, whose mercies are extended to all. The gods and the spirits follow the example of mankind in prostrating themselves before the great orb of night. The independence of the course that he pursues in the heavens places him beyond the control of the great judge of the world, the mighty Shamash. There is no one superior to Sin, no one to whose command he must bend. With all this, there is a total absence of any allusion to his power of removing the influence of demons and witches. We have here a hymn purified from all association with the incantation texts, and there is every reason to believe that it was composed for use in the great temple at Ur, which is mentioned in the opening lines.

In the alternating question and answer we have also a valuable indication of the manner in which the hymn was to be recited or sung. The whole production appears to be arranged in a dialogue form, the lines to be alternately read by the reciting priest and the chorus of priests or worshippers. The same method is followed in other productions, while in some, as we shall see, the dialogue does not proceed in alternate lines, but is distributed among a varying number of sections. We may see in this style of composition one of the natural outcomes of the method pursued in the incantation texts, where, as will be remembered, the priest first recites the formulas, and then calls upon the individual before him to repeat it once, twice, or oftener, as the case may be. Such a custom leads to recital and responses in the hymns.

Not many of the hymns rise to such a height as the one just quoted. There were certain gods only, and after all not many, whose nature was such as to make an ethical development of the conceptions formed of them possible. Besides Shamash and Sin, Ea as the god of humanity and Nebo as the god of wisdom belong to this class. Of Ea, however, no hymns have as yet been found. This may of course be accidental, and still, if one bears in mind that in the later periods of Babylonian history Ea enjoyed a theoretical popularity rather than a practical one, the absence of Ea hymns might be explained as due to the lack of a fixed ritual in the Ea temples outside of the incantation texts.[1] Ea's position, like that of Nusku, was too marked in the magical texts to encourage a conception of them entirely independent of their power to release victims from the grasp of the demons.

A hymn to Nebo, which unfortunately is preserved only in part, illustrates the extent to which polytheistic conceptions may be spiritualized:[2]

> . . . Lord of Borsippa,
> . . . son of E-sagila.[3]
> O Lord! To thy power there is no rival power,
> O Nebo! To thy power, there is no rival,
> To thy house, E-zida, there is no rival,
> To thy city, Borsippa, there is no rival,
> To thy district, Babylon, there is no rival.
> Thy weapon is U-sum-gallu,[4] from whose mouth the breath does
>   not issue, blood does not flow.[5]
> Thy command is unchangeable like the heavens.
> In heaven thou art supreme.

There are still plenty of mythological allusions in this hymn that take us back to a primitive period of thought, but it is a hymn prompted by the love and reverence that Nebo inspired. Its direct connection with the Nebo cult is shown again by the

---

[1] We have, however, a list (IIR. 58, no. 5) giving many titles and names of Ea that must have been prepared on the basis of Ea hymns.
[2] IVR. 20, no. 3.   [3] *I.e.*, of Marduk.
[4] This weapon plays a part in some of the Babylonian myths.
[5] The weapon is miraculous — it kills instantly, but without causing blood to flow. The reference is to the lightning stroke.

complementary character of each two lines. The whole hymn was probably adapted in this way to public worship.

Marduk, by virtue of his relationship to Ea, and by his independent position as the supreme god of Babylon, occupies a middle ground between Shamash, Ea, and Nusku on the one side, and such gods as Sin and Nebo on the other. Some of the hymns addressed to him end in incantations; others form part of the cult arranged for solemn occasions, when the praises of the god were sung in connection with sacrificial offerings.

In confirmation of the theory as to the relationship between magical texts and hymns above advanced, we find scarcely any difference in the grade of religious thought between these two classes of Marduk hymns. Both are equally distinguished by their fine diction. A hymn which celebrates Marduk as the restorer of the dead to life, and yet forms part of an incantation text, reads:[1]

> O merciful one among the gods!
> O merciful one who loveth to give life to the dead!
> Marduk, king of heaven and earth,
> King of Babylon, lord of E-sagila,
> King of E-zida, lord of E-makh-tila,
> Heaven and earth are thine.
> The whole of heaven and earth are thine,
> The spell affording life is thine,
> The breath of life is thine,
> The pure incantation of the ocean[2] is thine,
> Mankind, the black-headed race,[3]
> The living creatures, as many as there are, and exist on earth,
> As many as there are in the four quarters,
> The Igigi of the legions of heaven and earth,
> As many as there are,
> To thee do they incline (?).
> Thou art the *shedu*, thou art the *lamassu*.
> Thou restorest the dead to life, thou bringest things to completeness (?).
> O merciful one among the gods!

[1] IVR. 29, no. 1.   [2] Perhaps a reference to Ea.
[3] Name for the inhabitants of Babylonia, and then used in general for mankind. *Cf.* p. 281.

One scarcely detects any difference between such a hymn and those to Sin and Nebo. The lines are adapted, like the other specimens, for recitation by two parties. The last line forms a solemn close to a section of this hymn. In the section that follows, the same character is maintained till we approach the close, when the exorciser steps in and asks Marduk to

> Expel the disease of the sick man,
> The plague, the wasting disease . . .

and the various classes of demons, *utukku*, *alu*, etc., are introduced.

Compare this now with some passages in a prayer addressed to Marduk :[1]

A resting-place for the lord (of E-sagila) is thy house.
A resting-place for the lord of E-makh-tila is thy house.
E-sagila, the house of thy sovereignty, is thy house.
May the city speak 'rest'[2] to thee — thy house.
May Babylon speak peace to thee[3] — thy house.
May the great Anu, the father of the gods, tell thee when there will be rest.
May the great mountain, the father of the gods,[4] tell thee when there will be rest.
. . . .
Look favorably upon thy house,
Look favorably upon the city, O lord of rest!
May he restore to his place the bolt Babylon, the enclosure E-sagila, the edifice E-zida,[5]
May the gods of heaven and earth speak to thee, O lord of rest.

Here we have specific references to Marduk. Everything about the city of Babylon is associated with the god. The great gods pay homage to Marduk. The whole hymn, conceived as a royal prayer to the god, clearly formed part of the ritual prepared for the great Marduk temple at Babylon. The

---

[1] IV R. 18, no. 2. Badly preserved.   [3] *I.e.*, salute thee.
[2] *I.e.*, call upon thee to be pacified.   [4] Bel.
[5] The strongly fortified city of Babylon is compared to a bolt and the temple to an enclosure.

hymn closes, as so many others, with a prayer on behalf of the king. The god is asked

> To establish firmly the foundation of the throne of his sovereignty,
> So that he may nourish (?) mankind to distant days.

'Rest,' in the liturgical language, implied cessation of anger. Marduk, as the 'lord of rest,' was the pacified deity; and since it was a necessary condition in obtaining an answer to petitions that the god should be free from anger, the city, the temple, and the gods are represented as unitedly speaking to him — appealing to him to be at 'rest.' The production might, therefore, be called a 'pacification hymn.' The god has shown his anger by bringing on misfortune of some shape. His divine associates are no less anxious than his human subjects to pacify the mighty god.

Passing on to another god, a hymn to the storm-god, Ramman, enables us to specify the great terror that the god, as the general source of disturbances in the heavenly phenomena, inspired. The god is addressed [1] as

> The lord who in his anger holds the heavens in his control,
> Ramman in his wrath the earth has shaken.
> The mighty mountain — thou dost overturn it.
> At his anger, at his wrath,
> The gods of heaven mount up to heaven,[2]
> The gods of earth enter the earth.
> Into the foundation of heaven Shamash[3] enters.

The illustrations adduced will suffice to show the manner in which the Babylonians conceived the relationship between mankind and the gods. The element of fear alternated with that of love, and no matter how near the gods were felt to be, one was never certain of their good will.

Another feature of some of these hymns which calls for special mention is the introduction of the deity as himself or

---

[1] IVR. 28, no. 2.   [2] *I.e.*, fly to a safe place.
[3] *I.e.*, the sun is obscured.

herself taking part in the dialogue. A hymn addressed to Ishtar, as the morning and evening star,[1] belongs to this class.[2] It begins with a glorification of the goddess as the source of light, of being, and of earthly blessings. The worshipper speaks:

> O light of heaven who arises like fire over the earth, who art fixed in the earth,
> Thou art exalted in strength like the earth.
> As for thee, a just path be graciously granted to thee
> When thou enterest the house of man.
> A hyena on the hunt for a young lamb art thou,
> A restless lion art thou.
> A destructive handmaid, the beauty of heaven,
> A handmaid is Ishtar, the beauty of heaven,
> Who causest all being to emanate, O beauty of heaven,
> Associate (?) of the sun, O beauty of heaven!

At this point the goddess speaks, through the officiating priest, who acts as the mediator:

> For determining oracles[3] I have been established, in perfection have I been established.
> For determining oracles of my father Sin, I have been established, in perfection have I been established.
> For determining oracles of my brother Shamash, I have been established, in perfection have I been established.
> Me has my father Sin fixed, to determine oracles I have been established,
> Shining anew in heaven, for determining oracles I have been established, in perfection have I been established.

From the regular repetition of the refrain at the end of each line, one is tempted to conclude that these utterances of the goddess were to be recited by an officiating priest with the assistance of a chorus of priests, to whom the refrain was assigned, or it may be that the lines were alternately recited by

---

[1] See above, p. 84.
[2] Delitzsch, *Assyrische Lesestücke* (3d edition), pp. 134-136.
[3] The portents taken through observation of the position of Ishtar or Venus in the heavens were of especial value.

the priest and the chorus. In the section that follows, this alternative character of the lines is more clearly indicated:

Full of delight is my majesty, full of delight is my supremacy,
Full of delight do I as a goddess walk supreme.
Ishtar, the goddess of morning am I,
Ishtar, the goddess of evening am I,
(I am) Ishtar, — to open the lock of heaven belongs to my supremacy.
Heaven I destroy, earth I devastate,[1] — such is my supremacy.
The destroyer of heaven, the devastator of the earth, — such is my majesty.
To rise up out of the foundation of heaven,
Whose fame shines among the habitation of men, — such is my supremacy.
Queen of heaven that on high and below is invoked, — such is my supremacy.
The mountain I sweep away altogether, — such is my supremacy.
The destroyer of the mountain walls am I, their great foundation am I,
— such is my supremacy.

The hymn closes with a prayer that the anger of the god be appeased:

May thy heart be at rest, thy liver[2] be pacified.
By the great lord Anu, may thy heart be at rest.
By the lord, the great mountain Bel, may thy liver be pacified.
O goddess, mistress of heaven, may thy heart be at rest.
O supreme mistress of heaven, may thy liver be pacified.
O supreme mistress of the E-anna,[3] may thy heart be at rest.
O supreme mistress of the land of Erech, may thy liver be pacified.
O supreme mistress of the shining Erech, may thy heart be at rest.
O supreme mistress of the mountain of the universe, may thy liver be pacified.
O supreme mistress, queen of E-tur-kalama,[4] may thy heart be at rest.
O supreme mistress, queen of Babylon, may thy liver be pacified.
O supreme mistress, whose name is Nanâ, may thy heart be at rest.
O mistress of the house, lady of the gods, may thy liver be pacified.

---

[1] Phrases introduced to illustrate the power, not the function, of Ishtar.
[2] The liver as the seat of the emotions.
[3] *I.e.*, house of heaven. Name of Ishtar's temple at Erech.
[4] *I.e.*, court of the universe. Name of one of Ishtar's temples.

CHAPTER XVIII.

PENITENTIAL PSALMS.

It will be recalled that both in the Ishtar hymn and in the one to Marduk above quoted, great stress is laid upon pacifying the deity addressed. Starting from the primitive conception that misfortunes were a manifestation of divine anger, the Babylonians never abandoned the belief that transgressions could be atoned for only by appeasing the anger of the deity. But within this limitation, an ethical spirit was developed among the Babylonians that surprises us by its loftiness and comparative purity. Instead of having recourse merely to incantation formulas, the person smitten with disease or pursued by ill fortune would turn in prayer to some god at whose instigation the evil has come and appeal for the pacification of the divine wrath. But while the origin of the so-called penitential psalms is thus closely bound up with the same order of thought that gave rise to the incantation texts, no less significant is the divorce between the two classes of compositions that begins already at an early stage of the literary period. The incantations, it is true, may be combined with compositions that belong to a higher order of religious thought. We have seen that they have been so combined, and yet the dividing line between the two is also sharply marked. Zimmern, to whom, more than to any one else, the interpretation of these penitential psalms is due, has suggested[1] that national misfortunes rather than private grievances may have given an impetus to this class of literary productions. It is true that historical references are found in some of the hymns, and it is also signifi-

---

[1] *Babylonische Busspsalmen*, pp. 1, 2.

cant that not only do these psalms occasionally embody a prayer for the king, — thus giving to them a national rather than a personal character, — but the kings are called upon in times of distress to accompany their libations to the gods with the recitation of a 'lament to quiet the heart,'[1] as the Babylonians called this class of hymns.

One can easily see how such events as defeat in war would be ascribed to divine wrath, and not to the workings of evil spirits or witches; and while the personal tone that pervades most of the penitential psalms makes them applicable to conditions affecting the individual as well as the nation, the peculiar fitness of such psalms for occasions of national importance was a powerful factor in bringing about their sharp separation from the incantation formulas.

Just as in the hymns we found that the mere contemplation of the attributes of the gods, apart from the manifestation of these attributes in any particular instance, led to a loftier interpretation of the relationship existing between the gods and mankind, so the thought that evil was due in the last instance to the anger of some god led to greater emphasis being laid upon this relationship. The anger of the god prompted both the individual and the nation to greater zeal in securing the deity's love. To an even greater extent than in the hymns is the element of love introduced into the penitential psalms, and when not directly expressed, is so clearly implied as to form the necessary complement to the conception of the divine wrath. These psalms indeed show the religious and ethical thought of Babylonia at its best. Their ethical phase manifests itself more particularly in the conception of sin which is unfolded in them. The misfortunes of life, more especially those which could not so readily be ascribed to the presence of evil spirits, filled the individual with his sense of guilt. In some way, known or unknown to him, he must have

[1] *I.e.*, of the deity.

offended the deity. The thought whether the deity was justified in exercising his wrath did not trouble him any more than the investigation of the question whether the punishment was meted out in accordance with the extent of the wrong committed. It was not necessary for the deity to be just; it was sufficient that some god felt himself to be offended, whether through the omission of certain rights or through an error in the performance of rites or what not. The two facts which presented themselves with overpowering force to the penitent were the anger of the deity and the necessity of appeasing that anger. Beyond this conclusion the Babylonians and Assyrians did not go, but this reasoning also sufficed to bring the conviction home to him that his misfortunes were the result of some offence. The man afflicted was a sinner, and the corollary to this position was that misfortunes come in consequence of sin. Through the evils alone which overtook one, it became clear to an individual that he had sinned against the deity. Within this circle of ideas the penitential psalms of Babylonia move. They do not pass wholly outside of the general Semitic view that sin is a 'missing of the mark,'—a failure, whether voluntary or involuntary, to comply with what was demanded by the deity under whose protection one stood. But one became conscious of having 'missed the mark' only when evil in some form — disease, ill luck, deluge, drought, defeat, destruction, storms, pecuniary losses, family discords, the death of dear ones — came to remind the individual or the nation of the necessity of securing the favor of the deity again. Still within this sphere there were great possibilities of ethical progress, and some of the Babylonian psalms breathe a spirit and are couched in a diction that have prompted a comparison with the Biblical psalms.[1] Thrown, as the sinner felt himself to be, upon the mercy of the angry deity, it mattered little what had

---

[1] See an article by Francis Brown, "The Religious Poetry of Babylonia," *Presbyterian Review*, 1888.

called forth this wrath or whether the deity was conceived as acting in accordance with just ideas. The thought that would engage the entire attention of the penitent would be the appeasement of his god. To effect this, he would not stop short at exaggerating his own guilt. He would manifest a contrition of spirit that would not be the less sincere for being, perhaps, out of proportion to the character of his sin when judged by our standards.

Corresponding to the humiliation of mind to which he would be brought, his longing to be reconciled to the offended deity would be intensified. He would address this deity in terms of strong endearment, magnify his or her powers, as the case may be, and belittle himself and his own worth. The result of such a mental discipline could not but react healthfully on the mind of the penitent. The penitent would arise from his prayer with a more spiritual conception of the relationship existing between himself and his god. Not appealing for any material benefits for the time being, but concerned only with appeasing the divine wrath, the single burden of his prayer "that the heart of the offended god might be ' at rest'" would be marked by an intensity all the stronger for being at least comparatively pure of grosser associations.

All these features combined serve to make the penitential psalms the flower of the religious literature of Babylonia. The productions not only represent the highest stage which religious thought reached in the Euphrates Valley, but, in a certain sense, constitute the only productions in cuneiform literature that have a permanent literary value.

We find these compositions marked by a third feature which, however, as we have already seen, is not peculiar to them, — the dialogue form. In order to bring about a reconciliation with an angered god, three personages were necessary in the drama, — the god, the penitent, and, thirdly, the priest, acting as mediator between the sinner and his deity. The deity, according to Babylonian notions, could not be approached directly, but only through his chosen messengers, — the priests. This idea of mediation, as against the immediate approach, was so pronounced as to lead, as we have seen, to the frequent association with a god of a second divine personage, — his son or his servant, — through whom the petitions of mankind were brought to the throne of grace.[1] The priest was similarly conceived as the messenger of the god, and, by virtue of this office, endowed with a certain measure, at least, of divine power. He was, in the full sense, the god's vicar on earth, — his representative, who could, as we saw in the Ishtar hymn, speak in the first person on behalf of the god.[2] The more manifest mission of the priest, however, was to intercede on behalf of the mass of mankind. Accepting the sacrifices offered by the laity, it was he that secured their gracious acceptance on the part of the deity. It was the priest, as we have seen, who instructed the individual to pronounce the magic formulas that would be appropriate to his case; and just as in the incantation texts the priest accompanied the recitation of the formulas with an appeal of his own, so in the penitential psalms, he stood at the penitent's side, instructing him what to say, and emphasizing the confessions of the penitent by an assurance to the deity of the sincerity of the penitent, coupled with a fervent request that the prayer for 'appeasement,' which involved all that we mean by forgiveness, be graciously answered.

It is unfortunate that the text of none of the penitential psalms is perfectly preserved. We must, therefore, content ourselves in our illustrations with more or less imperfect extracts. It is to be noted, too, that often the exact meaning

---

[1] Compare the relationship existing between Ea and Marduk, noted above, p. 276. Similarly, Nusku was the messenger to Bel. See p. 279.
[2] On the wider aspects of this conception of the priest among ancient nations, see Frazer, *The Golden Bough*, passim.

of the lines escapes us, owing to the obscurity of terms employed or to the gaps in the texts themselves. With few exceptions the psalms appear in the double style characteristic of so large a section of the religious literature of the Babylonians, the 'ideographic' composition being accompanied by a phonetic transliteration. The fact, however, that we have at least one text (IVR. 59, no. 2) in the phonetic style alone, is sufficient to show that no *special* weight is to be attached to the supposed 'bilingual' character of the others. This double style is not a feature that need be taken into account in determining the age of this class of compositions. The historical references in some of them have prompted Zimmern to give his partial assent to the opinion which would assign them, or some of them, to the age of Hammurabi. Beyond such references, which are not as clear as they might be, we have no data through which their age can be determined; but so far as the ideas which they convey and the religious spirit manifested in them are concerned, there is no reason why they should not be assigned to as early a period as some of the incantation texts. It is characteristic of the Babylonian, as, in a measure, of all religions, that the old and the new go hand in hand; that more advanced conceptions, so far from setting aside primitive ones, can live and thrive in the same atmosphere with the latter. We may, therefore, assume that penitential psalms existed as early as 2000 B.C. Whether any of these that have been preserved go back to that period is another question. One gains the impression from a careful study of them that most of these, if not all, belong to a somewhat later period, nearer to the first millenium than to the second millenium before our era. The Assyrians adopted these psalms, as they did the other features of the religious literature of the Babylonians, and enriched the collection by productions of their own which, however, follow closely the Babylonian models.

A particularly beautiful psalm, judging from the portion preserved, represents the penitent addressing his goddess — probably Ishtar — as follows :[1]

> I, thy servant, full of sighs, call upon thee;
> The fervent prayer of him who has sinned do thou accept.
> If thou lookest upon a man, that man lives.
> O all-powerful mistress of mankind,
> Merciful one, to whom it is good to turn, who hears[2] sighs!

At this point the priest takes up the thread to emphasize the appeal of the penitent by adding to it his own. He prays to the goddess:

> His god and goddess being angry with him, he calls upon thee,
> Turn towards him thy countenance, take hold of his hand.

The penitent continues :

> Besides thee, there is no guiding deity.
> I implore thee to look upon me and hear my sighs.
> Proclaim pacification,[3] and may thy soul be appeased.
> How long, O my mistress, till thy countenance be turned towards me.
> Like doves, I lament, I satiate myself with sighs.

The priest once more sums up the penitent's prayer:

> With pain and ache, his soul is full of sighs;
> Tears he weeps, he pours forth lament (?).

A trait which appears in many of these psalms is the anonymity beneath which the offended deity is veiled. His or her name is often not mentioned, the deity being simply referred to as god or goddess, and at times it is left doubtful whether the sinner has 'sinned' against the demands of a god or a goddess, or against several deities. This feature is not without signifi-

---

[1] Zimmern, no. 1 ; IV R. 29, no. 5.
[2] Lit., 'accepts.'
[3] In the original appears a phrase which signifies literally 'when at last,'— an abbreviation for 'when will there be rest,' and which has become a kind of technical phrase to indicate, again, the hoped-for pacification of the deity.

cance. In some cases, no doubt, the name of the specific deity was to be added by the penitent,[1] but in others this does not appear to be indicated. The anonymity is the natural result of the conception of sin involved in these productions. The sinner, becoming conscious of his guilt only as a conclusion drawn from the fact of his suffering from some misfortune, could only surmise, but never be entirely certain, wherein his offence consisted or what deity he had offended. In the case of the recital of incantation formulas, the question as to the offended deity was a minor one, and may indeed, at an earlier stage of thought, not have entered into consideration at all. This anonymity, therefore, which characterized the penitential psalms was not due to any advance in thought, but one can easily see how it led to such an advance. What may be called the personal aspects of the gods were less accentuated. The very fact that no particular god could in many cases be specified entailed, as a consequence, that the views held of the gods gained in abstractness. The general thought of one's dependence upon these supernatural powers, without further specification, superinduced a grouping of the gods under a common aspect, as the directors of man's fate. In short, the notion of deity, not indeed as a unit, but as a collective idea, begins to dawn in Babylonia. At the same time we must beware of exaggerating the force that this notion acquired. There is not the slightest trace of any approach to real monotheism in Babylonia, nor can it even be said that the penitential psalms constitute a bridge leading to such an approach. The strong hold that astrology at all times, and up to the latest periods, had upon both the popular and the educated mind was in itself sufficient to prevent the Babylonians from passing, to any considerable degree, beyond the stage in which the powers of nature were personified and imbued with real life. The peni-

---

[1] The colophon to one of them (IV R. 10, Reverse 52) declares that the production in question is a "penitential psalm for any god whatsoever."

tential psalms presuppose this belief as much as any other branch of the religious literature; they merely illustrate this belief in the purest form of which, in the course of its development, it was capable.

A psalm in which this anonymity of the offended god is more strongly brought out begins as follows.[1] The penitent prays:

> O that the wrath of my lord's heart return to its former condition,[2]
> O that the god who is unknown be pacified,
> O that the goddess unknown be pacified,
> O that the god known or unknown[3] be pacified,
> O that the goddess known or unknown be pacified,
> O that the heart of my god be pacified,
> O that the god or goddess known or unknown be pacified!

The penitent, it will be seen, does not know whether it is a god or a goddess whom he has offended. He therefore appeals to both. He goes on to say that he is not even aware of the sin that he has committed:

> The sin that I have committed I know not.

And yet he must have sinned or he would not suffer as he does. In addition to his confession, he imposes the hardship of fasting upon himself by way of penance:

> Food I have not eaten;
> Clear water I have not drunk.

The reference to fasting occurs so frequently in these psalms that one is tempted to conclude that such a bodily castigation was demanded by the ritual of the Babylonians:[4]

---

[1] IVR. 10. Zimmern, no. 4.
[2] *I.e.*, be pacified.
[3] *I.e.*, 'whoever he may be,' as we would say.
[4] Among many nations fasting is resorted to as a means of atonement. It must have been common among the Hebrews during the period of the Babylonian exile — perhaps through Babylonian influence. See Isaiah, lviii. 3.

An offence have I unwittingly committed against my god,
A sin against my goddess unwittingly been guilty of,
O lord, my sins are many, great are my transgressions,
O my god, my sins are many, great are my transgressions,
O my goddess, my sins are many, great are my transgressions,
Known or unknown god, my sins are many, great are my transgressions.

Again the sinner protests his innocence of the wrong he has done. He only knows that

The lord has looked upon me in the rage of his heart,
A god has visited me in his wrath,
A goddess has become angry with me and brought me into pain,
A known or unknown god has oppressed me,
A known or unknown goddess has brought sorrow upon me.
I seek for help, but no one takes my hand.
I weep, but no one approaches me.
I call aloud, but no one hears me.
Full of woe, I grovel in the dust without looking up.
To my merciful god I turn, speaking with sighs.
The feet of my goddess I kiss imploringly (?).
To the known or unknown god do I speak with sighs,
To the known or unknown goddess do I speak with sighs.
O lord, look upon me, accept my lament,
O goddess, look upon me, accept my lament,
O known or unknown goddess, look upon me, accept my lament!

In this strain he proceeds for some time, until he is interrupted by the priest, who briefly adds:

> O lord, do not cast aside thy servant,
> Overflowing with tears,[1] take him by the hand!

The penitent closes the prayer by another and still more earnest appeal:

The sin I have committed change to mercy,
The wrong I have done, may the wind carry off.
Tear asunder my many transgressions as a garment.
My god, my sins are seven times seven,[2] forgive me my sins.

---

[1] Lit., rushing water. [2] I.e., very numerous.

My goddess, my sins are seven times seven, forgive me my sins.
Known or unknown god, my sins are seven times seven, forgive me my sins.
Known or unknown goddess, my sins are seven times seven, forgive me my sins.
Forgive me my sins and I will humble myself before thee.
May thy heart be glad[1] as the heart of the mother that has given birth,
May thy heart be glad as that of a mother who has given birth, as that of a father who has begotten a child.

The proportions between the parts taken by the priest and penitent vary considerably. In the one quoted, the priest is only incidentally introduced; in others,[2] it is the penitent who plays the minor part. The penitential ritual varied accordingly; but since we cannot discover here, as we could in the case of the incantation texts, the special occasions for the variations, except for those that contain historical references, one must suppose that they could be used indifferently at the choice of the penitent or the priest. It is probable that at one time a large collection of such psalms was made in Babylonia, and that those we have represent compositions made from the rituals of various temples. In one psalm we have a distinct statement from which we may conclude that it belonged to the E-sagila temple at Babylon. Only a portion of it is preserved.[3] It is interesting, also, because of a reference to a dream that it contains, and which the god of Babylon is called upon to convert into a favorable sign for the petitioner. Zimmern is of the opinion that the hymn may have been an evening prayer, but it seems more satisfactory to place it merely in the general category of penitential psalms, with a request for a sign that the deity has been appeased. The sinner, after describing his woeful state, —

> Instead of food, I eat bitter tears,
> Instead of date-wine, I drink the waters of misery,

---

[1] Be pacified.   [2] *E.g.*, IVR. 61.   [3] *Ib.* 59, no. 2.

> For my drink I have bitter waters,
> Instead of clothes, I am enveloped in sin,[1] —

proceeds to a fervent appeal:

> O my god who art angry with me, accept my prayer,
> O my goddess who art wroth with me, accept my appeal,
> Accept my appeal, may thy liver be at rest!
> My lord in mercy and compassion [look upon me?]
> Who guides the span of life against the encroachments (?) of death, accept my prayer!
> O my goddess, look upon me, accept my appeal;
> May my sins be forgiven,[2] my transgressions be wiped out.
> May the ban be loosened, the chain broken,
> May the seven winds carry off my sighs.
> Let me tear away my iniquity, let the birds carry it to heaven,
> Let the fish take off my misfortune, the stream carry it off.
> May the beasts of the field take it away from me,
> The flowing waters of the stream wash me clean.
> Let me be pure like the sheen of gold.
> As a ring (?) of precious stone, may I be precious before thee.
> Remove my iniquity, save my soul.
> Thy [temple] court I will watch, thy image (?) I will set up.[3]
> Grant to me that I may see a favorable dream,
> The dream that I see, let it be favorable,
> The dream that I see, let it be unfailing,
> The dream that I see, turn it to a favorable [issue].
> The god Makhir (?), the god of dreams stand at my head.
> Let me enter into E-sagila, the temple of the gods, the house of life.
> Commend me to Marduk, the merciful one, for favor,
> I will be subservient to thy greatness, I will exalt thy divinity.

There follows a line from which one may further conclude that the psalm is one composed for the royal chief of

---

[1] Delitzsch, *Assyr. Wörterbuch*, p. 378. In another psalm the penitent says similarly, "Food I have not eaten, weeping is my nourishment, water I have not drunk, tears are my drink."

[2] Lit., 'released.' The underlying metaphor represents the individual held fast by sin, just as the demons seize hold of a man.

[3] A somewhat puzzling line, but which appears to convey the promise on the part of the penitent that if forgiven he will observe the rites demanded by the deity.

Babylonia. It is evidently only a ruler who can assure the deity that

> The inhabitants of my city,[1] may they glorify thy power.

We know from the historical texts that previous to a military engagement the kings were particularly desirous of some sign from the deity that might serve to encourage the soldiery. Such a sign was ordinarily a dream. The circumstances, therefore, seem to point to our psalm being a royal prayer for forgiveness of transgressions, uttered before some impending national crisis, in the hope of securing, with the divine pardon, the protection of the deity who, up to this point in the campaign, must have manifested his displeasure rather than his favor. More distinct references to national events are found in another royal penitential psalm:[2]

> How long, O my mistress, will the mighty foe oppress thy land,
> In thy great city Erech famine has settled,
> In E-ulbar, the house of thy oracle, blood is poured out like water,
> Throughout thy districts he has kindled conflagrations, and poured [fire] over them in columns (?).[3]
> O my mistress, I am abundantly yoked to misfortune,
> O my mistress, thou hast encompassed me, thou hast brought me into pain,
> The mighty foe has trodden me down as a reed,
> I have no judgment, I have no wisdom,
> Like a 'dry field' I am desolate night and day,
> I thy servant beseech thee,
> May thy heart be at rest, thy liver be pacified.

At times specific requests are inserted into these hymns, such as release from physical ills. Sickness being, as any other evil, due to divine anger, the sick man combines with his prayer for forgiveness of the sin of which he is guilty, the hope that his disease, viewed as the result of his sin, may be removed.

---

[1] Babylon. [2] IV R 19, no. 3; Zimmern, no. 5.
[3] Like a column. The metaphor is the same as in the Biblical phrase, "column of smoke."

A hymn addressed to Ishtar of Nineveh by Ashurnasirbal, a king of Assyria,[1] is of this character. It begins by an adoration of the goddess, who is addressed as

The producer, the queen of heaven, the glorious lady,
To the one who dwells in E-babbara ... who hath spread my fame,
To the queen of the gods to whom has been entrusted the commands of the great gods,
To the lady of Nineveh ..
To the daughter of Sin, the twin-sister of Shamash, ruling over all kingdoms,
Who issues decrees, the goddess of the universe,
To the lady of heaven and earth, who receives prayer, who hearkens to the petition, who accepts beseeching,
To the merciful goddess who loves righteousness.

The king calls upon Ishtar to listen to his prayers:

Look upon me, O lady, so that through thy turning towards me the heart of thy servant may become strong.

Ashurnasirbal appeals to the goddess on the ground of what he has done to promote the glory of the goddess in his land. He has devoted himself to the service of the goddess. He has observed the festivals in her honor. He has repaired her shrines. No less than fourteen images of the goddess were set up by the king. Nay, more, he claims that before his days Ishtar was not properly worshipped.

I was without understanding, and did not pray to thy ladyship,
The people of Assyria also lacked judgment, and did not approach thy divinity;
But thou, O Ishtar, mighty weapon of the great gods,
By thy grace[2] thou didst instruct me, and didst desire me to rule.

The statement that the Ishtar cult was introduced or even reinstated by Ashurnasirbal can hardly be taken literally; but

---

[1] Published by Brünnow, *Zeits. f. Assyr.* v. 66 *seq.* The king mentions his father, Shamshi-Ramman, in the hymn. If this is Shamshi-Ramman III., the date of the hymn would be *c.* 1100 B.C.

[2] Lit., 'lifting up of thy eyes.'

it distinctly points to a movement in the days of the dynasty to which the king belonged, that brought the worship of the goddess into great prominence.

In return for all that he has done to the house of Ishtar, the king pleads:

> I, Ashurnasirbal, full of affliction, thy worshipper,
> Who takes hold of thy divine staff,
> Who prays to thy sovereignty,
> Look upon me and let me appeal to thy power!
> May thy liver be appeased for that which has aroused thy anger;
> Let thy whole heart be strong towards me.
> Make my disease come forth and remove my sin,
> Let thy mouth, O lady, proclaim forgiveness. .
> The priestly vassal who worships thee without change,
> Grant him mercy and cut off his affliction.

The historical references found in the penitential psalms are valuable indications, not only for determining the age of these compositions, but for ascertaining the occasions on which they were employed. Neither the Babylonian nor the Assyrian rulers ever reveal to us in their official annals or dispatches any check that they may have encountered in their careers or any misfortune that may have occurred to them or to the state. These psalms tell their own story. They point to seasons of distress, when recourse had to be taken to appeals to the gods, accompanied by the confession of wrongs committed. As against the incantations which are the outcome of the purely popular spirit, and which are the *natural* expression of popular beliefs, the penitential psalms seem to represent a more official method of appealing to the gods. The advance in religious thought which these productions signal may, therefore, be due, in part at least, to a growing importance attached to the relationship existing between the gods and the kingdom as a whole, as against the purely private pact between a god and his worshippers. The use of these psalms by Assyrian rulers, among whom the idea of the kingdom assumes a greater significance than among the Babylonians, points in this direction. It is significant, at all events, that such psalms were also produced in Assyria; and while they are entirely modeled upon the earlier Babylonian specimens, the contribution to the religious literature thus made in the north must be regarded, not as the outcome of the extension of the literary spirit prevailing in Babylonia, but as prompted by a special significance attached to the penitential ritual in removing the obstacles to the advancement of the affairs of state.

Despite, therefore, the elevated thought and diction found in these psalms, there is a close bond existing between them and the next branch of the religious literature to be taken up, — the oracles and omens, which similarly stand in close contact with affairs of state, and to which, likewise, additions, and indeed, considerable additions, to the stock received from Babylonia were made by the Assyrian *literati*.

CHAPTER XIX.

ORACLES AND OMENS.

A STRONG element of magic, we have seen, was always present in the hymns and prayers of the Babylonians, and even in such as contained religious sentiments of an elevated and pure character. The finest prayer has almost invariably tacked on to it an incantation, or constitutes in itself an incantation. Accompanying the prayer were offerings to the deity addressed, or certain symbolical rites, or both, and the efficacy of the prayer was supposed to reside partly in the accompanying acts and partly in the mystic power of the *words* of the prayer as such. In large measure this indissoluble association of prayer and incantation is due to the circumstance that both Babylonians and Assyrians addressed their deities only when something was desired of the latter, — the warding off of some evil or the expectation of some favor. Even in the penitential psalms, that merit the term 'sublime,' the penitent pours out his soul at the shrine of grace in order to be released from some misfortune that has come over him or that is impending. Mere praise of the gods without any ulterior motive finds no place in the Babylonian or Assyrian ritual. The closest approach to this religious attitude may perhaps be seen in the prayers attached by the kings to their commemorative or dedicatory inscriptions. One feels that the rulers are impelled to do this from a certain sense of love and devotion to their protecting deities. Nebuchadnezzar's prayers form a conspicuous example of the strength which pure love and attachment to the gods acquired in Babylonia; but even in these specimens, a request of some kind — usually for long life and prosperity — is made. The spiritualization of the Babylonian religion has in this way most definite limitations imposed upon it. There is a point beyond which it could not go without giving rise to a totally changed conception of the gods and their relationship to men. Prayer in its higher form, as the result of an irresistible prompting of the emotions, without any other purpose than the longing to come into closer communion with a superior Power, involves such a change in religious conceptions, and hence is conspicuous in the Babylonian ritual by its absence.

A request of some kind being thus the motive that lies behind the Babylonian prayers, it follows that the means taken to ascertain the will or intention of the gods with regard to that request formed an essential feature of the ritual. Indeed, to ascertain the will of a deity constituted one of the most important functions of the priest — perhaps *the* most important function. The prayer was of no use unless it was answered, and the priest alone could tell whether the answer was afforded. The efforts of the priest were accordingly directed towards this end — the prognostication of the future. What was the intention of the deity? Would the hoped-for deliverance from evil be realized? Would the demon of disease leave the body? Would the symbolical acts, burning of effigies, loosening of knots, and the like, have the desired effect? Upon the success of the priest in performing this function of prognostication everything depended, both for himself and for the petitioner.

The natural and indeed necessary complement to the priest as exorciser is the priest as the forecaster of the future. Since no one, not even the king, could approach a deity directly, the mediation of the priest was needed on every occasion of a religious import. The ordinary means at the disposal of the priest for ascertaining the divine will or caprice were twofold, — directly through oracles or indirectly by means of omens derived from an examination of the sacrifices offered. A complete Babylonian ritual therefore required, besides the appeal made by the petitioner through the priests or with their assistance, an incantation introduced in some form, an offering, certain symbolical acts and omens. The offerings and the symbolical acts, as a matter of fact, appear to have preceded[1] the prayer and the incantation, but in the prayers they are referred to again, and generally just before the interpretation of the omens. The omens constituted the ulterior end in view. Because of the looked-for omens the offering was brought, the symbolical acts performed, the incantations recited. All these rites formed the preparation for the grand *finale*. The worshipper waited anxiously for the decision of the priest. Attached, therefore, to the prayers we frequently find directions intended for the priests as to the signs to which his attention should be directed, certain peculiarities exhibited in parts of the animal sacrificed from which certain conclusions may be drawn. The observation of these signs grows to the dimensions of a science equal in extent to the observation of the heavenly bodies whose movements, as indeed the whole of the natural world, were supposed to exert an influence over the fate of mankind.

It does not of course follow that in the case of every prayer an elaborate ritual was observed. Many of the prayers to the gods in their present form do not embody omens, as indeed many contain no reference to offerings or symbolical acts. While no conclusion can be drawn from this circumstance, since the omission may be due to the point of view from which in a given case a collection of prayers was made by the priest, still we may well believe that for the exorcising of evil spirits the utterance of sacred formulas was often considered quite sufficient. In the earlier stages of the Babylonian religion the priest's function may have ended when he had exorcised the demons by means of magic words. The demons were forced to yield. If they nevertheless held out, so much the worse for them or — for the priest, who, it was concluded, must have lost

---

[1] See King, *Babylonian Magic*, p. xxx.

his power over the spirits through some error committed by him. The resort to omens has wider aspects, as will presently be shown, than the connection with prayers and offerings, and a most reasonable view is that omens were first introduced into prayers on occasions when a worshipper wished to ascertain the will of a deity for a certain purpose, and to regulate his own conduct accordingly. In petitioning the deity a sacrifice was naturally offered. Through the sacrifice, which was rendered acceptable to the deity by the mediation of the priest, the desired answer to a question was obtained. From being resorted to in such instances, omens would naturally come to form part of the ritual for almost any occasion when a deity was appealed to, both in connection with incantations and symbolical acts when the omens would form a supplement to the magic element in the ritual, as well as in cases where no specific incantations are introduced. In both cases the omens would constitute the means resorted to for ascertaining whether the petitioner might look for a favorable reply to a request proffered or, in a more general way, find out anything that it may be important for him to know. The occasions for consulting the deity would be of a public or private character. How far it became customary for the general public to secure the mediation of a priest for securing aid from the gods in matters appertaining to personal welfare we have no means of definitely determining. We find, for example, a son consulting an oracle on behalf of his father in order to ascertain what day would be favorable for undertaking some building operation,[1] and he receives the answer that the fourth of the month will be propitious; and so there are other occasions on which private individuals consult the priests, but in general it was only on occasions of real distress that an individual would come to the sanctuary, — to seek relief from bodily ills, to ward off blows of adversity, to pacify a deity who has manifested his

---

[1] Harper's *Assyrian Letters*, no. 219.

or her displeasure. The expense involved—for the worshipper was not to appear empty-handed—would of itself act as a deterrent against too frequent visits to a sanctuary.

The public welfare occupied a much larger share in the Babylonian worship. In order to ensure the safety of the state, occasions constantly arose when the deities had to be consulted. It is no accident that so many of the prayers — the hymns and psalms — contain references to kings and to events that transpired during their reigns. In these references the occasions for the prayers are to be sought. Remarkable as is the expression which the consciousness of individual guilt finds in the religious literature of Babylonia, the anger of the deity against his land is much more prominently dwelt upon than the manifestation of his wrath towards an individual. It could not be otherwise, since the welfare of the state conditioned to so large an extent the happiness of the individual. The startling phenomena of nature, such as an eclipse, a flood, a storm, while affecting individuals were not aimed directly at them, but at the country viewed as the domain of a certain god or of certain gods. Blighted crops, famine, and pestilence had likewise a public as well as a private aspect. On all such occasions the rulers would proceed to the sanctuaries in order, with the assistance of the priests, to pacify the angered god. It was not sufficient at such times to pronounce sacred formulas, to make fervent appeals, but some assurances had to be given that the words and the symbolical acts would have the desired effect. Omens were sought for from the animals offered. There were other occasions besides those stated, when for the sake of the public welfare oracles were sought at the sanctuaries. If a public improvement was to be undertaken, such as the building of a palace, or of a temple, of a canal, or a dam, it was of the utmost importance to know whether the enterprise was acceptable to the deity. A day had to be carefully chosen for laying the foundations, when the god would be favorably disposed towards his subjects,— the kings under whose auspices such work was carried on. Similar precautions had to be taken to select a favorable day for the dedication. This again was determined by means of omens either derived from offerings or in some other way. The Babylonians and Assyrians believed, as did the Jews upon their return from the Babylonian exile, that 'unless the lord assists, the builders work in vain.' When we come to military campaigns where the individual disappears altogether in the presence of the majestic figure of the state, the will and disposition of the gods had to be consulted at every step,— regarding the plans of the enemy, at the enemy's approach, before the battle, in the midst of the fray, and at its termination.

The frequency with which the gods were approached in the interests of the state and the public weal, plied with questions upon which the fate of the land depended, is shown by the stereotyped form which such official solicitations in the course of time acquired. Dating from the reigns of Esarhaddon and Ashurbanabal we have an elaborate series of prayers addressed to the sun-god, all dealing with questions of a political import. These prayers, so admirably edited and analyzed by Knudtzon,[1] are all arranged according to a single pattern. Each one opens with a question or series of questions which Shamash, the sun-god, is asked to answer. The god is then implored not to be angry, but to lend his aid against any errors unwittingly committed in the sacrificial rites. For a second time the same question is put in a somewhat varying form. Another appeal is made, and the various omens derived from the inspection of animals are interpreted as a guide to the priests. According to the application of these omens to the sacrifice before the priest, a decision is rendered. It will be sufficient for our purposes to present a single specimen of such a fixed ritual.[2]

---

[1] *Assyrische Gebete an den Sonnengott für Staat und Königliches Haus* (Leipzig, 1893, 2 vols.). [2] Knudtzon, no. 1.

Esarhaddon, being hard pressed by a group of nations to the northeast of Assyria, led by a certain Kashtariti, and among whose followers the Gimirrites, the Medes, and Manneans are the most prominent, asks for an oracle from Shamash as to the outcome of the situation. The priest, acting as mediator, addresses[1] the god:

O Shamash! great lord! As I ask thee, do thou in true mercy answer me.

From this day, the 3d day of this month of Iyar[2] to the 11th day of the month of Ab[3] of this year, a period of one hundred days and one hundred nights is the proscribed term for the priestly activity.[4]

Will within this period, Kashtariti, together with his soldiery, will the army of the Gimirrites, the army of the Medes, will the army of the Manneans, or will any enemy whatsoever succeed in carrying out their plan, whether by strategy (?) or by main force, whether by the force of weapons of war and fight or by the ax, whether by a breach made with machines of war and battering rams[5] or by hunger, whether by the power residing in the name of a god or goddess,[6] whether in a friendly way or by friendly grace,[7] or by any strategic device, will these aforementioned, as many as are required to take a city, actually capture the city Kishassu, penetrate into the interior of that same city Kishassu, will their hands lay hold of that same city Kishassu, so that it falls into their power? Thy great divine power knows it.[8]

The capture of that same city, Kishassu, through any enemy whatsoever, within the specified period, is it definitely ordained by thy great and divine will, O Shamash! Will it actually come to pass?[9]

[1] That the priest recites the prayer and not the king is shown by the frequent introduction of the king's name in the 3d person. See, e.g., Knudtzon, nos. 40–47.

[2] 2d month.

[3] 5th month.

[4] I.e., the priest is only asked for an oracle regarding the events of the next one hundred days.

[5] Various machines are mentioned. The precise meaning of the technical terms employed is not known.

[6] By invoking the assistance of the gods.

[7] Peacefully, by mutual agreement and the promise of favors.

[8] One is reminded of the Arabic phrase. "Allah alone knows it," so frequently introduced in Mohammedan writings.

[9] Lit., 'Seen will it be seen, heard will it be heard?' The emphatic construction is identical with the one frequently employed in Biblical Hebrew.

It will be observed that, much as in a legal document, all contingencies are enumerated. In other prayers, still more are mentioned. A definite answer is required, and care is taken not to leave any loophole open by means of which the deity may escape from the obligation imposed upon him to manifest his intention. Shamash might answer that the city will not be captured, with the mental reservation that it will surrender, or he might throw Esarhaddon off his guard by announcing that "not by might nor by strength" will the city be taken, and the king may be surprised some morning to learn that the catastrophe has been brought about through the power residing in the 'word.' These precautions were taken, not so much because it was supposed that the gods and priests were tricky, but because all conditions had to be carefully fulfilled in order to ensure an answer, and, if at all possible, of course a favorable answer. To the same end, great care had to be taken that in the preparation of the offering which accompanied the prayer no mistake should be made. The sacrificial animal — in the case before us a lamb — had to be guarded against all imperfections, impurities, and contaminations. The priest had to be careful to put on the proper dress, to speak the proper words, and to be himself free from any ritualistic impurity. Before proceeding to the inspection of the animal, in order to forecast the future, the priest had to take care that nothing might happen to interfere with the proper observation of the rites. This section of the prayer is characterized by the word "*ezib*" repeated at the beginning of every line, and which conveys the appeal that what follows may be precluded from happening.[1] The priest first prays to Shamash:

Preclude that after the specified period [the catastrophe may not come to pass].

---

[1] Knudtzon (p. 25) did not grasp the negative force of *ezib*. The word is a request that something might *not* happen.

Preclude whatever they [*i.e.*, the enemies] may plan may not be carried out (?).
Preclude them from making a slaughter and from plundering. . . .
Whether the decision of this day be good or bad, ward off a stormy day with pouring rain.

This last phrase, which is somewhat obscure, seems to be a request made in the contingency of an unfavorable omen being received. The sun-god is asked, at all events, not to hide his countenance under clouds and rain on the decisive day of battle. Coming after these preliminary requests to the sacrifice, the priest continues:

Prevent anything unclean from defiling the place of inspection,[1]
Prevent the lamb of thy divinity, which is to be inspected, from being imperfect and unfit.
Guard him who takes hold of the body of the lamb, who is clothed in the proper sacrificial dress, from having eaten, drunk, or handled anything unclean.
Make his hand firm (?), guard the seer, thy servant, from speaking a word hastily.[2]

The priest thereupon repeats his question to the sun-god:

I ask thee, O Shamash! great lord! whether from the 3d day of this month of Iyar, up to the 11th day of the month of Ab of this year, Kashtariti, with his soldiers, whether the Gimirrites, the Manneans, the Medes, or whether any enemy whatsoever will take the said city, Kishassu, enter that said city, Kishassu, seize said city, Kishassu, with their hands, obtain it in their power.

The various terms used in describing the taking of a city are once more specified, so as to fulfill all the demands of definiteness in the question.

---

[1] Where the animal is to be inspected, probably the altar itself.
[2] In the Jewish ritual and many others, stress is laid upon pronouncing the words of a prayer clearly and deliberately, especially such words as have a particularly sacred value.

The priest is now ready to proceed with an examination of the animal before him. A varying list of omens are introduced into the prayers under consideration. That they are so introduced is a proof of the official character of these texts. The omens were not, of course, intended to be recited. They are enumerated as a guide to the priests. The various signs that may be looked for are noted, and according to what the priest finds he renders his decision. Knudtzon has made the observation[1] that in the prayers published by him, the signs found on the animal are noted but not interpreted. This rather curious omission is again naturally accounted for on the assumption that these prayers in their present form are part of a ritual compiled solely for the benefit of priests attached to a Shamash sanctuary. Full directions were not required. All that the priest needed was to know what to look for. For the rest, he depended upon tradition or his own knowledge or judgment. The omens themselves, or rather the signs, refer to the condition in which certain parts of the animal are found or to peculiarities in the composition of the animal.

The priest is instructed to observe whether 'at the nape on the left side' there is a slit; whether 'at the bottom on the left side of the bladder' some peculiarity[2] is found or whether it is normal; whether 'the nape to the right side' is sunk and split or whether the viscera are sound. The proportions, too, in the size of the various parts of the body appear to have been of moment; and in this way, a large number of points are given to which the priest is to direct his attention. From a combination of all peculiarities and signs in a given instance, he divines the disposition of the god addressed, whether it is favorable or not. The whole ceremony is brought to a close by another appeal to the god to send an answer to the question put to him. The priest prays:

---

[1] *Assyrische Gebete*, p. 50.

[2] Exactly of what nature cannot be ascertained. The text (Knudtzon, no. 29, rev. 15) is defective at this point.

By virtue of this sacrificial lamb, arise and grant true mercy, favorable conditions of the parts of the animal, a declaration favorable and beneficial be ordained by thy great divinity. Grant that this may come to pass. To thy great divinity, O Shamash! great lord! may it[1] be pleasing,[2] and may an oracle be sent in answer!

In some of the prayers a second series of omen indications are given. What the oracle announced we are, of course, not told. The ritual is not concerned with results.

From the analysis just given it will be seen that the consultation of a deity was often entailed with much ceremony. No doubt the priests did all in their power to add to the solemnity of such an occasion. The kings on their side showed their lavishness in furnishing victims for the sacrifice. Again and again does Esarhaddon solicit Shamash to reveal the outcome of the military campaigns in which the king was engaged. The same individual, Kashtariti, and the Gimirrites, Medes, etc., are mentioned in many other prayers prepared in the course of the campaign; and elsewhere other campaigns are introduced. What Esarhaddon did, no doubt his successors also did, as he himself followed the example set by his predecessors. We are justified, then, in concluding that a regular 'oracle and omen ritual' was developed in Babylonia and Assyria — how early it is of course impossible to say. There is every reason to believe that in some form such a ritual existed in Babylonia before the rise of Assyria, but it is also evident that in a military empire like Assyria, there would be more frequent occasion for securing oracles than in Babylonia. The ritual may therefore have been carried to a greater degree of perfection in the north. The Assyrian conquerors, if we may judge from examples, were fond of asking for an oracle at every turn in the political situation. The king intends to send an official to a foreign land, but he is uncertain as to the wisdom of his decision. Accordingly, he

---

[1] The prayer or the lamb.
[2] Lit., 'proceed.'

puts the case before the god. If this decision is taken, he asks, Will the envoy carry out the orders of the king?

> Thy great divinity knows it.
> Is it commanded and ordained by thy great divinity,
> O Shamash? Is it to come to pass?[1]

In a similar way, questions are asked with reference to the course of a campaign. Will the Assyrian king encounter the king of Ethiopia, and will the latter give battle? Will the king return alive from the campaign? is a question frequently asked. Even for their quasi-private affairs, the kings sought for an oracle. Before giving his daughter in marriage to a foreign potentate, Esarhaddon desires to know whether the one seeking this favor, Bartatua, the king of Ishkuza,[2]

is to be trusted, will he fulfill his promises, will he observe the decrees of Esarhaddon, the king of Assyria, and execute them in good faith?

Again, when the king is about to associate his son with himself in the government, he first inquires whether this is agreeable to the deity.[3] The king fears lest his son may cause trouble, may provoke dissensions. Past experience prompts him to be careful before following his inclination.

Is the entrance of Siniddinabal, the son of Esarhaddon, the king of Assyria, whose name is written on this tablet, into the government in accord with the command of thy great divinity? Is it to come to pass?

The reference to the writing of the name is interesting. It would appear that the question is actually written by the priest and placed before the deity. The Greeks similarly put their questions to the Delphian oracle in writing. May it be that among the Babylonians the answer of the god was at times also

---

[1] Knudtzon, no. 66. Other examples are furnished in George Smith's *History of Ashurbanabal*, pp. 184, 185.

[2] A district to the northeast of Assyria; Knudtzon, no. 29.

[3] *Ib.* no. 107.

handed down on a tablet, as the Greek and Roman oracles were communicated in writing on the leaves of a tree?

If sickness entered the royal house, an oracle was likewise sought. The king is sick. Is it ordained that he will recover? We are told in one case that [1]

> Nikâ, the mother of Esarhaddon, the king of Assyria, is sick. She sees the hand of the goddess Nanâ of Uruk laid heavily upon her. . . . Is it ordained that this hand will be lifted off from the sufferer?

The occasions, it is evident, were exceedingly numerous when the Assyrian rulers appealed to the priests for oracles. Naturally, this appeal was not in all cases made with the elaborate formality illustrated by Esarhaddon's petitions to Shamash. At times the monarch, as the individual, would content himself with sending to the priest for an answer to a question, and the priest would reply in an equally simple and direct manner. Quite a number of such messages, sent by priests to their master, are included in the valuable publication of 'Assyrian Letters,' begun by Professor R. F. Harper.[2] The king's son wishes to set out on a journey. The father sends to the astrologers Balasi and Nabu-akheirba, and receives the reply:[3]

> As for Ashur-mukinpalea, about whom the king, our lord, has sent to us, may Ashur, Bel, Nabu, Sin, Shamash, and Ramman bless him. May the king, our lord, witness his welfare (?). Conditions are favorable for the journey. The second day is favorable, the fourth day very favorable.

Similarly, the astrologers send reports regarding the appearance and position of the moon and the stars, and of various phenomena that had to be taken into account in moments where decisive action had to be taken.

---

[1] *Ib.* no. 101.

[2] Four volumes comprising several hundred letters have already appeared under the title, *Assyrian Letters of the K. Collection* (London, 1896). For a good summary of the character of the Assyrian epistolary literature, see Johnston's article in the *Journal of the American Oriental Society*, xviii. 1, pp. 125–134.

[3] Harper, no. 77.

Before leaving the subject, it may be of interest to point out that among the literary remains of the Assyrian period there are "blank formulas" for oracles, the names in each instance to be filled out by the officiating priest. Such formulas were prepared, no doubt, for cases of common occurrence. Thus Esarhaddon, before appointing a person to a responsible position, took the precaution of ascertaining from some deity whether the appointment was a wise one. The name of the individual being written down, the priest asks the deity in a general way:[1]

> Will the man whose name appears on this tablet, and whom he [the king] is about to appoint to such and such a position, keep good faith, or will he manifest hostility towards the king, inciting to rebellion?

Esarhaddon may have had a special reason for using precautions against his officials, and even his sons. He came to the throne during a rebellion which involved the assassination of his father. Esarhaddon's own brothers were the murderers. We may well suppose that he trembled at every step he took, but his position is after all characteristic of the Assyrian rulers in general, many of whom came to the throne by violence and maintained themselves through force.

Other texts enable us to study the form of the oracles themselves. As yet, no oracle texts have been found belonging to the older Babylonian period, but we have again every reason to believe that what holds good for the days of Assyrian power applies to a much earlier period, though at the same time the greater frequency with which Assyrian rulers were wont to ply their gods with questions would increase the number of those whose special business it was to pronounce the oracles. The manifold duties of the priesthood would tend towards a differentiation of the priests into various classes. The priest, as exorciser, would become distinct from the priest as the inspector

---

[1] *E.g.*, Knudtzon, no. 124.

of omens, and the latter different again from the pronouncer of oracles. From the fact that Marduk was regarded as the special god of oracles by the Assyrians as well as the Babylonians,[1] we may conclude that this differentiation of the priestly classes took place already in the south, or at all events that oracle-giving as a distinct priestly function was recognized in Babylonia and carried over to the northern empire. If we may draw a general conclusion from the state of affairs in Esarhaddon's days, this function was largely in the hands of women. We know from other evidence that women were attached to the temple service from ancient times.[2] As sorceresses, too, they occupied a quasi-priestly position, since their help could be invoked in driving evil spirits into the person of one's enemy. The oracle-giver and the sorcerer or sorceress are correlated personages in religion. For various reasons — in part, perhaps, because of her physical differences from man — woman was invested with a certain mystery by ancient nations.[3] Hence the fact that among so many nations witchcraft is associated with woman, and similarly among many nations women perform the functions of the oracle. In a series of eight oracles addressed to Esarhaddon,[4] six are given forth by women. These oracles, it so happens, all issue from the goddess Ishtar of Arbela. The cult of this goddess at Arbela stood in high favor in the eighth century B.C. An influential body of priests congregated there, and the eight oracles in question appear to be a part of a more extensive collection made by the theologians of Arbela, of whose intellectual activity there are other traces. Arbela appears to have developed a special school of theology, marked by the attempt to accord a superior position to the great goddess Ishtar.

---

[1] Zimmern, *Busspsalmen*, p. 32. The popularity of the sun-cult in Assyria in connection with omens and oracles is probably due also in part to the influence of Marduk, who was, as we have seen, a solar deity.

[2] Lehman, *Samassumukin*, p. 42.

[3] See Ploss, *Das Weib*, pp. 594–606; also above, p. 267.

[4] IV R. pl. 61.

The one who pronounces the oracle speaks on behalf of Ishtar, and therefore employs the first person. The oracles all have reference to political events. They cannot, of course, be the answers to the questions asked in the prayers analyzed above, since these were addressed to the sun-god; but we may feel certain that the oracles of the Shamash priests or priestesses were much of the same order, varying only in minor particulars. The goddess invariably encourages the king. The priest, it would appear, hears the voice of the deity in the wind.

Fear not! The wind which speaks to thee —
Comes with speech from me, withholding nothing.[1]
Thine enemies, like the . . . of Siwan,[2]
At thy feet will be poured out.
The great mistress am I.
I am Ishtar of Arbela, who forces thine enemies to submission.
Is there any utterance of mine that I addressed to thee upon which thou couldst not rely?
I am Ishtar of Arbela.
Thine enemies, the Ukkites (?), I give to thee, even I, Ishtar of Arbela.
In front and behind thee I march.
Fear not!

This oracle, we are told in the subscript, was pronounced by a certain Ishtar-la-tashiat, a son [*i.e.*, a native] of Arbela. The dignity of the diction is very marked. The very frequent assurance 'fear not' and the solemn repetition of 'I am Ishtar' lend impressiveness to the message. The oracle, it will be seen, deals in general phrases. This indefiniteness characterizes most of them; and the more impressive the diction, the greater vagueness in the statements made. So an oracle, coming from Ishtar and Nabu and uttered by a woman Baya, a native of Arbela, announces:

---

[1] *I.e.*, Ishtar sends the wind with a clear message.
[2] 3d month.

> Fear not, Esarhaddon,
> I, the lord, to thee do I speak.
> The beams of thy heart I strengthen as thy mother,[1]
> Who gave thee life.
> Sixty great gods are with me[2]
> Drawn up to protect thee.
> The god Sin is on thy right, Shamash on thy left.
> Sixty great gods are round about thee
> Drawn up in battle array in the center of the citadel.
> On men do not rely.
> Lift up thine eyes to me. Look up to me!
> I am Ishtar of Arbela.
> Ashur is gracious to thee.
> Thy weakness I will change to strength (?).
> Fear not! glorify me!
> Is not the enemy subdued
> Who has been handed over to thee?
> I proclaim it aloud,
> What has been will be.[3]
> I am Nabu, the lord of the writing tablet,
> Glorify me.

A message of this kind could hardly have been satisfactory except as a general encouragement.

The popularity of the Nabu cult in Assyria, it will be recalled, is an offset against the supremacy of Marduk in the south. The Assyrian kings found it to their interest to incorporate as much of the Babylonian cult as was possible into their own religious ritual. To Shamash they assigned the rôle played by Marduk. There was no danger in paying homage to Nabu, the son of Marduk. Ishtar they regarded as their own goddess quite as much as Ashur. These four deities, therefore, Ishtar, Shamash, Nabu, and Ashur, are the special gods of oracles recognized by the Assyrian rulers. Marduk, who is the chief source of oracles

---

[1] Perhaps a proverbial phrase, having the force of 'I nurture thee as thy own mother did.'

[2] Constituting the host of Ishtar, which is elsewhere referred to, *e.g.*, IVR.² pl. 61, col. i. 27.

[3] Lit., 'the future or later things like the former.'

in the south, is more rarely appealed to in the north, though of course recognized as powerful. He could not be expected to regard with favor an empire that so seriously threatened his supremacy in the pantheon.

The occasion when an oracle was announced was often one of great solemnity. Just as the prayers in which the questions of the kings were embodied, were carefully written out, so that the priest in reciting them might not commit any mistakes, so the answer to the prayers were transmitted to the king in writing. Among the oracles of the days of Esarhaddon, there is one coming from Ashur in which the ceremonies accompanying the deliverance are instanced.[1] The oracle deals with the Gimirrites, the same people in regard to whom Esarhaddon so often consults the sun-god. It is marked by the more definite character of its announcements when compared with others. The text is in the form of a communication made to the king, and, like other official documents, it begins with a salutation. The gods give Esarhaddon greeting.[2]

> Ashur has given him the four ends of the earth.
> In the house where he shines and is great,[3] the king has no rival.
> Like the rising sun he shines.
> This is the greeting from Bel Tarbasi[4] and the assembled gods.

The god Ashur himself now addresses the king:

> As for those enemies that plot against thee, that force thee to march out,
> Thou didst open thy mouth [saying], "Verily I implore Ashur."
> I have heard thy cry.
> Out of the great gate of heaven I proclaim aloud,
> 'Surely I will hasten to let fire devour them.
> Thou shalt stand among them.

[1] Published by S. A. Strong, *Beiträge zur Assyriologie*, ii. 627-33.

[2] The opening lines, containing a reference to the Gimirrites, are imperfectly preserved.

[3] *I.e.*, he is the greatest scion of the reigning dynasty.

[4] 'Lord of the court'—a title of Ashur.

> In front of thee I shall rise up.[1]
> Up onto the mountain I bring them,
> There to rain down upon them destructive stones.
> Thine enemies I hew down,
> With their blood I fill the river.
> Let them behold and glorify me,
> For Ashur, the lord of gods, am I.'

This important and striking message, coming direct from Ashur we are told, is to be formally presented and read in the presence of the king. Instructions are added to the priests to pour out a libation of precious oil. Sacrifices of animals and waving of incense are to accompany the presentation.

The oracle, as the god's answer to the king's questions, thus gave rise to a ritual as elaborate as the rites connected with the preparations for the answer. The oracles were not always trustworthy, as we can well believe, and often they were not definite enough. If we may judge from an expression in one of the divine messages to Esarhaddon, the king appears to have entered a complaint against a former oracle, which was not to his liking. Ishtar accordingly sends the following message:[2]

> The former word which I spoke to thee,
> On it thou didst not rely.
> Now, then, in the later one you may have confidence.
> Glorify me!

Clearly, the Assyrian kings believed that the oracles existed to announce what they wanted to hear. They probably did not hesitate to follow their own judgment whenever they considered it superior to the advice given to them by the gods. There would, of course, be no difficulty in accounting for failures brought about through obedience to the oracles. The priests, hemmed in on every side by minute ceremonial observances, forfeited their power as mediators by the slightest failure in

---

[1] As a protection, just as Jahwe appears in a pillar of cloud to protect his people.
[2] IVR.² 61, col. vi. 47–52.

the observance of these rites. An error or a mishap would entail most serious consequences. A misleading oracle, therefore, and to a certain extent, unfavorable omens, would be the fault of the priests. The deity would send 'a lying message'[1] or bring about unfavorable omens as a sign of his or her displeasure. On the other hand, the priests in turn would not hesitate — speaking of course in the name of the gods — to accuse the kings of neglecting Ishtar or Nabu or Shamash, as the case may be. In an oracle addressed to Esarhaddon,[2] Ishtar of Arbela is represented as complaining that the king has done nothing for her, although she has done so much for him. Such a state of affairs cannot go on.

> Since they do nothing for me,
> I will not give anything to thee.

The king promptly responds by copious offerings, and the goddess appears to be pacified.

There is another feature connected with the oracles that must be touched upon before passing on. The oracles stand obviously in close relationship to the penitential psalms. It was, naturally, in times of political distress that the kings would be particularly zealous in maintaining themselves on good terms with the powerful gods. Without their aid success could not be expected to crown any efforts. Guiding their steps by frequent consultations of the priests, the appeals of the kings would increase in earnestness and fervor as the campaign progressed and assumed more serious aspects. When disaster stared them in the face, they would be forced to conclude that the gods were angered, and there was only one way left of averting the divine wrath — a free confession of sins, accompanied, of course, by offerings and magic rites. The Assyrian kings do not tell us in their annals of discomfitures that they

---

[1] See I Kings, xxii. 23.
[2] Strong, *Beiträge zur Assyriologie*, ii. 628, 629.

encountered. The penitential psalms supply this omission. We have such a psalm written in the days of Ashurbanabal,[1] in which that proud monarch humbles himself before the great god Nabu, and has the satisfaction in return of receiving a reassuring oracle. He prays:

I confess to thee, Nabu, in the presence of the great gods,
[Many ? (?)] are my sins beyond endurance?[3]
[Lord (?)] of Nineveh, I come before thee, the warrior among the gods, his brothers.
[Prolong (?)] the life of Ashurbanabal for a long period.
. . . At the feet of Nabu I prostrate myself.

The god reassures the king:

I will grant thee life, O Ashurbanabal, even I,
Nabu, to the end of days
Thy feet shall not grow weary, nor thy hands weak (?),
These lips of thine shall not cease to approach me,
Thy tongue shall not be removed from thy lips,
For I give thee a favorable message.
I will raise thy head, I will increase thy glory in the temple of E-babbara.[4]

The reference to the temple of Shamash at Sippar reveals the situation. Babylonia was the cause of much trouble to Ashurbanabal, owing chiefly to the intrigues of his treacherous brother Shamashshumukin.[5] Ashurbanabal at one time was not merely in danger of losing control over the south, but of losing his life in the rebellion organized by his 'faithless brother.' A successful rebellion is a clear sign of a god's displeasure. Marduk, as we have seen, was not often appealed to by the Assyrian kings, but Nabu seemed always ready to help them. Hence the king confesses his sins and makes an

---

[1] Published and translated by S. A. Strong, *Transactions of the Ninth International Oriental Congress* (1893), ii. 199-208.
[2] Supplied from the context, through comparison with similar compositions.
[3] Lit., 'my soul cannot overcome.'
[4] The composition continues in this strain, Ashurbanabal and Nabu speaking alternately. [5] See Tiele, *Babyl.-Assyr. Geschichte*, pp. 371 *seq.*

appeal to the great Babylonian god and not to Ashur. He is encouraged by the promise that his life will be spared, and that his supremacy will be recognized in Babylonia. The great sanctuary of Sippar is here employed figuratively for the temples of Babylonia in general. To be glorified in that famous temple was equivalent to a recognition of royal authority.

That these oracles served a practical purpose is definitely proved by the manner in which they are introduced by the kings in their annals. Ashurbanabal tells us that in the course of one of his campaigns against Elam, he addressed a fervent prayer to Ishtar of Arbela, and in reply the message comes, as in the texts we have been considering, "Fear not"; and she adds, "Thy hands raised towards me, and thy eyes filled with tears, I look upon with favor."[1]

Dreams.

It is, of course, not necessary to assume that the oracles of the gods were always delivered in the same formal manner, accompanied by elaborate ceremonies. The gods at times reveal themselves in a more direct manner to their favorites. In visions of the night they appear to encourage the Assyrian army by an oracle. On one occasion, when the army of Ashurbanabal approached a rushing stream which they were afraid to cross, Ishtar makes her appearance at night, and declares, "I walk in front of Ashurbanabal, the king who is the creation of my hands."[2] The army, thus reassured, crosses the river in safety. On another occasion, Ashurbanabal, when threatened by the king of Elam, receives a message from Ishtar revealed to a seer in a dream at night. The seer — no doubt a priest — reports to the king:[3] 'Ishtar, dwelling in Arbela, came with

---

[1] George Smith, *Annals of Ashurbanabal*, p. 121.
[2] Rassam Cylinder, V R. col. v. ll. 95–103.
[3] George Smith, *Annals of Ashurbanabal*, pp. 119–121.

quivers hung on her right and left side, with a bow in her hand, and girded (?) with a pointed, unsheathed sword. Before thee [*i.e.*, the king] she stood, and like the mother that bore thee.[1] Ishtar, supreme among the gods, addressed thee, commanding: "Be encouraged[2] for the fray. Wherever thou art, I am."'

In connection with the importance that the Babylonians and Assyrians, in common with all ancient nations, attached to dreams, divine messages thus revealed had a special significance fully on a par with the oracles that were formally delivered with an accompaniment of elaborate rites. A god appearing to one in a dream was a manifestation, the force of which could not be disputed. It mattered little to whom the dream was sent. Ashur, on one occasion, chose to reveal himself to an enemy of Ashurbanabal with a message. He appears in a dream before Gyges, the king of Lydia, and tells him,[3] "Pay homage to Ashurbanabal, the king of Assyria, and by the power of his name conquer thine enemies." Gyges obeys and sends a messenger to the Assyrian monarch to inform him of the dream. Occasionally in this way a deity might appear to a king, but in general it was to the professional 'dreamer' rather than to the laity to whom oracles were thus sent. The message was not necessarily delivered in person by the deity. Sin, the moon-god, on one occasion writes his message on the moon's disc:

> Against all who have evil designs
> And hostile sentiments towards
> Ashurbanabal, the king of Assyria,
> Will I send a miserable death.[4]

Every dream was of course sent by some god, but the dreams of others than those who acted as mediators between the gods and men were of a different character. They were omens. The gods would reveal themselves indirectly by means of pictures or symbols, and it would require the services of a priest

---

[1] With maternal kindness.
[2] Lit., 'look up.'
[3] Rassam Cylinder, col. II. ll. 98 *seq.*
[4] *Ib.* col. III. ll. 122-124.

again to interpret such symbols or omens. The gods were asked to send such dreams as might receive a favorable interpretation,[1] and when a dream came unsolicited, the gods were implored to convert the dream into a favorable omen.

In the case of dreams, it will be apparent, the dividing line between oracles proper and omens becomes exceedingly faint and it is very doubtful whether the Babylonians or Assyrians recognized any essential difference between the two. The suggestion has already been thrown out that there is a wider aspect to omens in the Babylonian religion than their employment in connection with sacrificial offerings. We have reached a point when it will be proper to take up this wider aspect.

[1] *E.g.*, IV R. 59, no. 2, 21b.

CHAPTER XX.

VARIOUS CLASSES OF OMENS.

There is a close connection between the various branches of the religious literature of Babylonia and Assyria that we have hitherto been considering. The magic incantations are, as we have seen, a form of prayer. On the other hand, prayers, whether hymns or confessions of sin with an appeal for relief from suffering or distress, or embodying the petition for a divine response to some question or questions, are never entirely dissociated from incantations, and are invariably based upon the same beliefs that give to the element of magic such a prominent place in the religion. The omens form part of this same order of beliefs. The connecting link between incantations and omens is the sense of mystery impressed upon man by two orders of phenomena — the phenomena of his own life and the phenomena of the things about him. In his own life, nothing was more mysterious to him than the power of speech. It is doubtful whether he recognized that the animals communicated with one another by means of the sounds that they emitted; but even if he did, the great gap separating such means of communication from the power residing in the combination of sounds, of which he could avail himself, must have been all the more impressive. In view of this, it is not difficult to understand that a magic force was attributed to words as such. Of course, a somewhat advanced degree of culture must have been reached before such a belief would be given a definite form of expression; but even in the simplest form of social organization the notion of *authority* necessarily exists, and authority is inseparable from words. The chief commands, and the conclusion is naturally drawn that the words he utters are imbued with the power to force obedience. These two factors — the mystery of speech and the practical demonstration of the power residing in words — are sufficient to account for the part played by incantations among all nations at a certain stage of their religious development; and once introduced, the conservatism attaching to religious rites would ensure their continuance even after the popular religious beliefs had passed far beyond the stage in question. The modifications introduced into the incantations would be nigh endless. There would develop a tendency to greater complications in the combination of words. At the same time their literary form would be improved. Prayers and hymns reflecting advanced religious sentiments would be produced, but the magic element connected with the words as such would not for that reason be lost sight of. The efficacy of such prayers would still depend upon their being uttered in the right manner and — what is equally to the point — by the right person. Corresponding to the chief in secular affairs — who alone can pronounce words that give evidence of their power by the results produced — is the priest in religious affairs to whom, as the mediator between the gods and men, the secret is entrusted of uttering the right words in the right way, so as to produce the desired results, to force, as it were, obedience from the gods, as a chief forces obedience from his subjects. In a more advanced stage of religious culture, the position of the priest is no less powerful and important. When incantations yield to prayers in the proper sense, or are combined with prayers, it is only the priests who can make the prayers effective by their interceding in some way with the gods, whether by adding their appeal to that of the supplicant, or by the performance of the rites accompanying prayer, or by their aid in leading the worshipper into the presence of the deity and standing with him before the throne of grace.

When man turns from a contemplation of self to the things around him, there is added to the sense of the mysterious which is aroused in him, the feeling of his own weakness which is borne in upon him with overpowering force. He cannot fail to realize how dependent he is upon the sun, the moon, the rain, and the storm. At every step, he takes dangers beset his path. The animal world is at times hostile, at times friendly; but whether the one or the other, it is essential for him to carefully *note* all that is going on around him. Every happening or sight of an unusual character arouses now his sense of fear, and again his hope. He learns to attach special importance to deviations from the normal course of things. There must be a reason for the exception from the rule. It betokens something, and, concerned as man primarily is for his own welfare, he naturally comes to connect both the regular phenomena of nature as well as the deviations, the normal traits and habits of the animal world as well as peculiar features occasionally occurring, with his own fate. To forestall the future was his only safeguard against the dangers in store for him. It was of the utmost importance to him to know what was coming or, at all events, to be on the lookout for *something*, in order to be in a proper frame to receive either the benefits or to meet the difficulties of the situation.

His powers of observation — upon which man in a primitive state depended almost entirely for his sustenance — were thus further strengthened by the necessity of protecting himself, so far as possible, against the uncertainties of the future. Nothing would escape him. The movement of the stars and planets, their position at different seasons and periods, the appearance of the clouds, an eclipse, the conditions of the streams, an earthquake, the direction of the winds, storms, the flight of birds, the barking of dogs, the movements of snakes and serpents, peculiar marks on the bodies of children, of adults and animals, monstrosities among mankind or the brute creation, the meeting with certain persons or animals, the rustling of leaves, the change of seasons, the lustre of precious stones, all attracted man's attention. Whatever he saw might portend something to him, in fact *did* portend something; hence the one great aim and ideal of his life was to *see* everything. Seeing meant foreseeing, and the man who could see everything—the *seer par excellence*, who could also understand what he saw—held in his hands the key that would unlock the secrets of the future. He possessed the means of forecasting events.

Apart, then, from the interpretation of omens in connection with sacrifices and incantations, the individual had to be on the outlook at all times for signs and portents. To neglect them would entail serious consequences.

This wider aspect of omens accounts for the extensive omen literature that arose in Babylonia and Assyria. Fully one-fourth of the portion of Ashurbanabal's library that has been discovered consists of omens,[1] tablets of various size in which explanations are afforded of all physical peculiarities to be observed in animals and men, of natural phenomena, of the position and movements of the planets and stars, of the incidents and accidents of public and private life,—in short, of all possible occurrences and situations.

As yet but a small proportion of this literature has been published, and a thorough understanding of it is impossible until systematic publications shall have been issued. Meanwhile it is safe to assert that, as in the case of incantations and prayers, the omens were generally combined into series by the Babylonian and Assyrian scribes.

[1] Illustrated by the four volumes of Bezold's *Catalogue of the Koujunjik*, Collection of the British Museum (London, 1889-96).

Omens from Planets and Stars.

Ihering observes[1] that the stars were observed by the Babylonians in the interest of navigation. While this is true, yet the chief motive in the development of astronomy in the Euphrates Valley was the belief that the movements of the heavenly bodies portended something that was important for man to know. That the stars served as guides to the mariner was only an additional reason for attaching great importance to the heavenly phenomena. Scientific observations were but means to an end; and the end was invariably the derivation of omens from the movements and position of the planets and stars. When, therefore, we find the astronomers sending reports to their royal masters apparently of a purely scientific character, we may be certain that although no omens are mentioned, both parties had omens in mind. The astronomical reports, of which quite a number have already been published,[2] may therefore be reckoned as part of the omen literature. The vernal equinox was a period of much significance. The astronomer royal accordingly reports:[3]

> On the sixth day of Nisan,[4]
> Day and night were balanced.
> There were six double hours of day,
> Six double hours of night.
> May Nabu and Marduk
> Be gracious to the king, my lord.

On another occasion the equinox took place on the 15th of Nisan,[5] and accordingly this is reported. Again, the appearance of the new moon was anxiously looked for each month, and the king is informed whether or not it was seen on the 29th or 30th day of the month.[6]

---

[1] *Vorgeschichte der Indo-Europaer*, pp. 221 *seq.*
[2] *E.g.*, IIIR. 51.
[3] *Ib.* no. 1.
[4] The 1st month of the year.
[5] IIIR. 51, no. 2.
[6] *Ib.* no. 3.

> A watch we kept
> On the twenty-ninth day,
> The moon we saw.
> May Nabu and Marduk
> Be gracious to the king, my lord.
> From Nabuâ of the city of Ashur.

An extraordinary event, such as an eclipse, is made the subject of a more elaborate report. The Babylonian astronomers had developed their scientific attainments to the point of calculating the time when an eclipse of the sun or the moon would take place. As this period approached, they watched for the eclipse. We have an interesting specimen of a report in which the astronomer announces that an expected eclipse for which a watch was kept for three days did not appear.[1] Another addressed to an official reads:[2]

> To the Agriculturist,[3] my lord,
> Thy servant Nabushumiddin,
> An officer of Nineveh,
> May Nabu and Marduk be gracious
> To the Agriculturist, my lord.
> The fourteenth day we kept a watch for the moon.
> The moon suffered an eclipse.

The reports pass over into indications of omens with an ease which shows that the observations of the astronomers were made with this ulterior motive in view. A report which forms a supplement to one above translated furnishes the interpretation given to the vernal equinox:[4]

> The moon and sun are balanced,
> The subjects will be faithful,[5]
> The king of the land will reign for a long time.

[1] IIIR. 51, no. 9.   [2] Ib. no. 7.
[3] What the station of this official was we are not told.
[4] IIIR. 58, no. 7.
[5] Lit., 'true speech in the mouth of the people,' i.e., there will be no sedition.

The complement, then, to the purely scientific observations is furnished by these official communications to the kings and others, setting forth in response, no doubt, to commands or inquiries, the meaning of any particular phenomenon, or of the position of the planets, or of any of the stars at any time, or of their movements. Of such communications we have a large number. They illustrate the great attention that was paid to details in the observation of the heavenly bodies. The moon as the basis of the calendrical system occupies the first place in these reports. Its movements were more varied than those of the sun. Through its phases, its appearance and disappearance at stated intervals, a safe point of departure was obtained for time calculations. While the sun through its daily course regulated the divisions of the day, the moon by its phases fixed the division of weeks and months. The moon never appeared quite the same on two successive nights nor in the same part of the heavens. The more variety, the more significance — was a principle of general application in the interpretation of omens. Whether the Babylonians also recognized an influence of the moon on the tides, we have no certain means of determining, but it is eminently likely that trained as their astronomers were in careful observation, this was the case. But apart from this, there were many events in public and private affairs that appeared to them to stand in close connection with the movements of the orb of night. Nothing that occurred being regarded as accidental, the conclusion was forced upon the Babylonians that the time when something was undertaken was of significance. The fact that certain undertakings succeeded, while others failed, was most easily explained upon the theory that there were periods favorable for the action involved and periods unfavorable. The gathering of past experience thus becomes a guiding principle in the interpretation of the movements of the moon; and what applies to the moon applies, of course, to the other planets and to the stars.

No doubt other factors are involved, such as association of ideas; but it is evident from a careful study of the omen literature that conclusions drawn from what appears to us as the accidental relation of past occurrences to the phenomena presented by the planets and stars constituted fully three-fourths of the wisdom of the Euphratean augurs. The same report, of which a portion has already been quoted,[1] continues after interpreting the meaning of the equinox with a diagnosis of other concurrent conditions:[2]

> Sun and moon are seen apart,[3]
> The king of the country will manifest wisdom.[4]
> On the fourteenth day sun and moon are seen together,
> There will be loyalty in the land,
> The gods of Babylonia are favorably inclined,
> The soldiery will be in accord with the king's desire,
> The cattle of Babylonia will pasture in safety.[5]
> From Ishtar-shumeresh.

The same conditions appearing on another day may portend precisely the reverse. So another report informs the king:[6]

> On the fifteenth day the sun and moon are seen together,
> A powerful enemy raises his weapons against the land,
> The enemy will smash the great gate of the city,
> The star Anu appears bright,
> The enemy will devastate.

It is quite evident that such reports must have been sent in response to royal orders asking for the meaning of existing conditions or of conditions that may be observed on certain days. At times the prognostications assume a remarkable degree of definiteness which forms a striking contrast to the general

---

[1] IIIR. 58, no. 7.
[2] Ib. no. 6.
[3] Are not seen at the same time.
[4] His decision will be wise.
[5] Safe from attacks.
[6] IIIR. 58, no. 13.

vagueness of the oracles. An official, Balasi, reports[1] on one occasion regarding the significance of the moon appearing unexpectedly:

> The moon is seen out of season,
> Crops will be small.
> On the twelfth day the moon is seen together with the sun.[2]
> Contrary to the calculated time,
> The moon and sun appear together,
> A strong enemy will devastate the land.
> The king of Babylonia will be forced to submit to his enemy.
> On the twelfth day, the moon with the sun is seen,
> On the twelfth day is seen.
> Evil is in store for Babylonia.
> It is a favorable sign for Elam and the west land,
> But surely unfavorable for Babylonia.

The reports were not always concerned with political affairs. Frequently there is a reference to lions and hyenas that might be expected to make their appearance because of certain natural phenomena. Often crops are referred to, and according as the conditions are favorable or not, fertility or famine is predicted in the official reports. On other occasions the astrologers venture the very safe prognostication that male children will be born or that there will be miscarriages, though it seems likely that in such cases the forecast is intended for the affairs of the palace alone.

We have seen[3] what great importance was attached by the Babylonians to eclipses. It will be appropriate, therefore, to give a specimen of an astrologer's report in reference to such a phenomenon:[4]

> The moon disappeared,[5] evil will settle in the land.
> The moon, contrary to calculation, disappeared.

---

[1] *Ib.* no. 12.
[2] This appears to be the unusual occurrence involved.
[3] See above, pp. 281, 332. [4] IIIR. 58, no. 14.
[5] *Ib.*, contrary to calculation.

An eclipse has taken place.
On the twenty-ninth day the moon disappeared
And the sun on the day of the eclipse entered the circle.[1]
It is an eclipse of Elam.[2]
If in the month of Kislev,[3] an eclipse is observed
That encircles (?) the sun and the moon disappears,
Upon the observation of the eclipse,
Then may the king be exalted.
May the heart of the king, my lord, rejoice.
From Khushi-ilu, the servant of the king, the eponym.

Another report reads:[4]

To the king, my lord,
Thy servant Ishtar-iddinabal,
The chief of the astronomers of Arbela.
May Nabu, Marduk, Ishtar of Arbela
Be gracious to the king, my lord,
On the twenty-ninth day a watch we kept.
At the observatory clouds,
The moon we did not see.

This report was sent on the second day of the month of Shebat.[5] From these specimens and others, it is evident that reports regarding the appearance or non-appearance of the new moon were regularly sent. But in addition to this, the kings sent to the observatory on numerous other occasions for information with reference to the significance of certain phenomena.

As in the case of the moon, so also for the sun and the stars, reports were transmitted that served as guides in directing the kings in their affairs. So on one occasion Nabu-mushesi forecasts that[6]

If the 'great lion' star is dark,
It is favorable for the country.

[1] The shadow.
[2] Favorable to Elam (so Oppert translates).
[3] 9th month.
[4] IIIR. 51, no. 5.
[5] 11th month.
[6] IIIR. 59, no. 13.

> If the 'king' star is dark,
> The chamberlain[1] (?) of the palace dies.

The official character of these reports is one of their significant features. Their great variety is an indication of the frequent occasions on which the kings consulted the astrologers. No important enterprise was undertaken without first ascertaining what phenomena might be looked for on the day fixed for any action, and what these phenomena portended. In the case of the Assyrian reports, it is natural to find many illusions to foreign nations, since war occupied so much of the time and energies of the Assyrian rulers. But we have seen that for private affairs the astrologers were also consulted, as well as for the internal affairs of the country. The reports illustrate the practical application of what became known in the ancient world as "Chaldaean wisdom." If, however, we would know the source whence the astrologers derived the knowledge which they furnished in their reports, we must turn to the long lists prepared by the priests, in which all possible phenomena connected with the planets and stars were noted and their meaning indicated. These compilations constitute the 'Priestly Codes' of the Babylonians, and, as already intimated, they were combined just as the incantations and prayers, into series. Many such series must have existed at one time in Babylonia. A great temple was incomplete without its observatory, and we are warranted in concluding that every great religious center of the Euphrates Valley had its collection of omen tablets. The natural ambition of the priests was to make such a series as complete as possible. The larger the number of observations it contained, the greater the possibility of finding an answer to the question put to them. To these lists additions would constantly be made, and, if we may judge from the manner of literary composition that prevailed among the ancient Hebrews and later among the Arabs, the work of the compilers

---

[1] Some palace official is mentioned.

of omen series consisted essentially in combining whatever material they could obtain, and adding such observations as they themselves had made. While, therefore, the omen code of one place might differ in details from that of another, not only would the underlying principles be the same in all, but each series would represent an aggregation of experiences and observations drawn from various quarters.

A large omen series of which as yet only fragments have been published[1] bears the title 'Illumination of Bel.' It is estimated that this astrological code embraced more than one hundred tablets. From the fragments published, the general method employed in the preparation of the series can be gathered. To the moon and to the sun, to each of the planets, and to the important stars a separate section was assigned. In this section the peculiarities, regular and irregular, connected with each of the bodies were noted, their appearance and disappearance, the conditions prevailing at rising and at setting, the relationship of the moon to the sun or to a star, of the stars to one another and to the ecliptic, were set forth. Since, however, the time when a phenomenon connected with a planet or star was as important as the phenomenon itself, observations were entered for the various months of the year and for various days in each month. The days were not arbitrarily chosen, but, as there is every reason to believe, selected on the basis of past experience. Similarly the interpretations of the phenomena were founded on the actual occurrence of certain events at certain times when the conditions indicated actually existed. A single occurrence might suffice for predicating a connection between the event and the phenomenon. The coincidence would constitute an observation, but the omen would naturally gain additional force if it was based on a repeated observation of the same phenomenon on the same day

---

[1] *E.g.*, IIIR. 52, no. 2; 60 and 61. Professor Craig of the University of Michigan is now preparing for publication all the fragments of this series. (See his *Assyrian and Babylonian Religious Texts*, ii. 7.)

of the same month. But such a case would be rare, and the effort of the astrologers would be directed simply towards gathering as many observations of phenomena as possible. They would rest content when they had found a single connection between the phenomenon and the event. Their success in giving an answer to a question put to them as to what might happen on a certain day, fixed for battle or for laying the foundations of an edifice, or for dedicating a temple, for setting out on an expedition, or for any undertaking whatsoever, would depend on the completeness of their lists, and correspondingly the interpretation of a phenomenon occurring on any day would entail no difficulties if in their consultation lists the phenomenon would be recorded.

The 22d tablet of the series 'Illumination of Bel' deals with the important subject of eclipses. It contains 88 lines, and furnishes us with a good specimen of the class of omens under consideration. It begins[1] with eclipses that may take place during the first month, and runs along through the twelve months of the year. The 14th, 15th, 16th, 20th, and 21st days of the month are those set down when eclipses have been observed. The official character of the omens is indicated by their repeated references to the nations with which Babylonia — and later Assyria — came into contact, and to the fate in store for the rulers of the country. For the third month, the tablet notes:

> In the month of Sivan, an eclipse happening on the 14th day, proceeding from east to west, beginning with the middle watch,[2] and ending with the morning watch, the shadow being seen in the east — the side of obscuration — furnishes an omen[3] for the king of Dilmun.[4] The king of Dilmun is slain.

---

[1] IIIR. 60. The first eleven lines are broken off.

[2] *Le.*, of the night. The night, it will be recalled, was divided into three watches of four hours each.   [3] Lit., a 'divine decision (or oracle) is given.'

[4] An island near the head of the Persian Gulf, often referred to in the historical texts. See Tiele, *Babyl.-Assyr. Gesch.* p. 88, etc.

An eclipse happening on the 15th day, the king of Dilmun is slain, and some one seizes the throne.

An eclipse happening on the 16th day, the king is deposed and slain, and a worthless person seizes the throne.

An eclipse happening on the 20th day, rains descend from heaven, and the canals are flooded.

An eclipse happening on the 21st day, sorrow and despair in the land. The land is full of corpses.

The eclipses for the fourth month furnish omens for the king of Guti — another district with which Babylonia and Assyria had frequent dealings.

An eclipse happening in the month of Tammuz on the 14th day, proceeding from the west to the south, beginning with the first watch and ending with the middle watch, the shadow being seen in the west — the side of obscuration — furnishes an omen for the king of Guti. Overthrow of Guti by force, followed by complete submission.

An eclipse happening on the 15th day,[1] rains descend from heaven, floods come upon the land, famine in the land.

An eclipse happening on the 16th day, women have miscarriages.

An eclipse happening on the 20th day, storms set in and famine; afterwards for a year storms destroy property.[2]

An eclipse happening on the 21st day, the armies of the king revolt and deliver him into the hands of enemies.

The eclipses of the following month deal with several countries.

An eclipse in the month of Ab[3] on the 14th day, proceeding from the south to the east, beginning with the first watch, or with the morning watch, and ending at sunrise, the shadow being seen in the south — the side of obscuration — furnishes an omen for the king of Umliash. The soldiery are engaged in severe conflicts for a year, and are slain by force of arms.

An eclipse happening on the 15th day,[4] the king dies, and rains descend from heaven, and floods fill the canals.

[1] Under the same circumstances.
[2] Lit., 'cattle'; but cattle appears to be used for 'property' in general, just as our English word 'chattel.'
[3] 5th month.
[4] Under the same circumstances.

An eclipse happening on the 16th day, the king of Babylonia dies. Pestilence[1] feeds upon the country.

An eclipse happening on the 20th day, the king of the Hittites[2] in person (?) seizes the throne.

An eclipse happening on the 21st day, a deity strikes (?) the king, and fire consumes king and land.

From these specimens, the general principle of the section is apparent. Since eclipses portend public and political disasters of some kind, the compiler has carefully gathered oracles given on previous occasions to some ruler, or observations of the events that occurred at the time of the recorded eclipses. The apparently restricted application of the omens was no hindrance to their practical use. In the event of an astrologer being consulted with regard to the significance of an eclipse on a certain day, his list would furnish a safe basis for further prognostications, suitable to the political conditions that prevailed. But in order to meet all contingencies, other lists furnishing further omens for eclipses were added. The 22d tablet of the 'Illumination of Bel' series is followed by one[3] which, while dealing with the same subject, approaches it somewhat differently, and is based on a different principle. It begins again with the first month, and in twelve paragraphs takes up in succession the months of the year. Choosing for comparison the same three months, the third, fourth, and fifth, which we selected in the case of the 22d tablet, it will be seen that, while the references are again to public affairs, the prognostications are of a more general character and of wider applicability.

If in the 3d month an eclipse takes place on the 14th day, rains will descend and flood the canals. Storms will cause inundations. The soldiery of Babylonia will destroy the country. An eclipse on the 15th day indicates that king against king will send troops.[4] The king of legions dies. An

---

[1] Lit., Nergal — the personification of pestilence and death.

[2] Repeated in the text by an error of the scribe.

[3] IIIR. 60, col. ii. 90 to col. iii. 24.

[4] *I.e.*, there will be war. One is reminded of the modern superstition which associates war with the 'northern light' in the heavens.

eclipse on the 16th day signifies that the king will be slain, and that some one will seize the throne.[1] An eclipse on the 20th day means that the king will hand his throne to his son. An eclipse happening on the 21st day portends rain,[2] and an invasion of the enemy's land.

For the 4th month an eclipse on the 14th day portends that rains will descend and the canals will be flooded. Rains will cause inundations. There will be famine. A large country will be reduced to a small one. An eclipse on the 15th day portends that rains will descend, canals will be flooded, and there will be famine in the land. An eclipse on the 16th day portends famine for a year. An eclipse on the 20th day portends destruction of the king and his army. An eclipse happening on the 21st day indicates that there will be a strong wind that will destroy the riches of the sea.[3]

For the 5th month an eclipse on the 14th day portends rains and flooding of canals. The crops will be good and king will send peace to king.[4] An eclipse on the 15th day portends destructive war. The land will be filled with corpses. An eclipse on the 16th day indicates that pregnant women will be happily delivered of their offspring. An eclipse on the 20th day portends that lions will cause terror and that reptiles will appear; an eclipse on the 21st day that destruction (?) will overtake the riches of the sea.[3]

The vagueness of many of the prognostications is in all probabilities intentional, just as we found to be the case in most of the oracles announced to the kings. To predict rains during the rainy months was comparatively safe. The storms which visited Babylonia annually brought with them destruction of cattle. They conditioned the fertility of the country, but pestilence was often caused by the evaporation of the waters. Again, military expeditions were usually undertaken in the spring of the year before the great heat set in, and in a country like Assyria, it was safe to hazard a vague prediction that hostilities would ensue, and that some district would be diminished.

What may be called the 'eclectic' character of the omen series under consideration thus becomes apparent. The lists

---

[1] *I.e.*, there will be sedition.
[2] So a variant text.
[3] *I.e.*, will play havoc with the inhabitants of the deep.
[4] *I.e.*, there will be peace.

consisted, on the one hand, of omens obtained on certain occasions and with reference to some specific circumstance, such as a campaign against some country, and, on the other hand, of prognostications of a more general character, based on the general climatic conditions of the country, and referring to events of frequent occurrence. All that the scribes in preparing the series were concerned with, was to collect as many omens as they could, and to arrange them in some convenient order. Just as they prepared lists referring to military events, so they put together others in which some other theme was treated. The reports and omen tablets thus complement one another. The latter are based on the former, and the former were obtained by the interpretation of phenomena, furnished by the tablets and applied to the particular case submitted to the priests. We need not, of course, suppose that *all* prognostications found in the series, especially in those parts of it which are of a more general character, were based upon reports actually made, any more than that the official reports to the kings even in later days were always based upon a consultation of some series of tablets. Individual judgment, both in compiling a series and in interpreting phenomena, must at all times have played some part. The reports and the series also embody to some extent the results of experience not previously put to writing; but these considerations do not alter the general proposition set forth in this chapter as to the practical purpose served by the omen series as well as by the reports, and the pragmatic origin of both.

The importance of eclipses gave to omens connected with such events a special significance. Eclipses, however, were after all rare events, and while because of their rarity they always portended something of great moment, still the ordinary phenomena were the ones that had to be studied by the astrologers with great care in order to obtain a rational view of the relationship between the phenomena of nature and the fate of the individual or of the state. Again, eclipses, as a general thing, pointed to a public disaster of some kind, and this recognized belief lightened the task of the priest considerably in this instance. In the case of ordinary phenomena it was much more difficult to find the connection between cause and effect; and in the vast majority of instances when kings and individuals sought the temples for omens, the heavens must have presented a normal and not an abnormal appearance.

What answers were the priests to give to the questions put to them? Was it a favorable period for undertaking a military campaign? On what day should the king set out? Was the day fixed on by the council of war favorable for a battle? On what day should the foundation for the temple or palace be laid? Will the sick person recover? Should one set out on a proposed journey? Is the day fixed for a marriage auspicious?

Recognizing by experience that the same thing undertaken at different times turned out differently, in the one case being brought to a successful issue, in the other followed by misfortune, the conclusion was forced upon the popular mind (as already set forth above) that the day on which something was done or was to be done was of great moment.

But how did one day differ from the other? That was the question for the priests to determine. During the hours that the sun was in control, the clouds produced constant changes in the appearance of the heavens, but because of their irregular character, these changes impressed the Babylonians less forcibly than the striking changes that the nights showed. The planets and stars never appeared alike on two successive nights. There was always some change in the position of some of the heavenly bodies. To these changes, then, the priests directed their attention. In the variations presented by the heavens at night they saw a potent reason for the varying results produced by the same act undertaken at different times.

If it made a difference at what moment something was done, that difference could only be determined by observing the variations that one night presented from the other. The astrologers observed that many of the stars were, or seemed to be, fixed in their orbits; others rose and set like the sun and moon, and appeared in different parts of the heavens at different seasons of the year. The regularity of these changes made it possible to study the course of these stars, and as knowledge progressed, to determine also in advance where a particular body would be seen at a certain time.

The planets accordingly were the bodies to which the astrologers especially directed their attention. It has been conjectured with some show of probability that one of the purposes served by the lofty seven-staged towers,[1] which were attached to many of the great temples, was for the better observation of the movements of the planets. The official standing of the astrologers is indicated by the references in texts to the 'court astrologer.'

However this may be, there is no doubt that at all the large temples and at many of the smaller ones, observations of the planets were recorded.

The collection of these observations formed the manuals for the priests in answering many of the questions put to them. Each of the great planets was identified (by a process of thought that we will have occasion to describe) with some deity, though this was not done until the attempt was also made to gather the astrological knowledge of the day into some kind of consistent system. Our own names of the planets, as handed down to us through the Greeks and Romans, are but the classical equivalents of the Babylonian deities.[2]

Jupiter is Marduk, the head of the Babylonian pantheon. Venus is the Babylonian Ishtar. Mars is Nergal, the god of

---

[1] See the chapter on "The Temples of Babylonia and Assyria."
[2] See Jensen, *Kosmologie der Babylonier*, pp. 134-139.

war and pestilence. Mercury is Nabu, the god of wisdom and the messenger of the gods, and Saturn is Ninib.

Among the astrological texts preserved, Ishtar-Venus figures more prominently than the other planets. The appearance of Ishtar during each month and for various days of the month was noted, and then interpreted, partly on the basis of past experience, but also by other factors that for the most part escape us. A tablet, furnishing omens derived from the position of the planet Venus and which may belong to the series 'Illumination of Bel,' deals with the periods of the disappearance of Venus as evening star, and her reappearance as morning star, and *vice versa*.[1]

In the month of Tammuz (4th month) Venus disappeared on the 25th day at sunset, for seven days was hidden,[2] and on the 2d day of Ab (5th month) was seen at sunrise. Rains in the land. Destruction of[3] . . .

In the month of Adar (12th month) Venus disappeared on the 25th day at sunrise. For a year (?) weapons are wielded[4] (?), gold[3] . . .

In the month of Marcheshwan (8th month), 10th day, Venus disappeared at sunrise, for two months and six days was hidden, and reappeared on the 16th day of Tebet (10th month). There will be abundant crops.

In the month of Elul (6th month), 26th day, Venus disappeared at sunset, for eleven days was hidden, and in the second[5] Elul, on the 7th day, reappeared at sunset. The heart of the land is good.[6]

In the month of Nisan (1st month), on the 9th day, Venus disappeared at sunset[8] (?), and for five months and sixteen days was hidden, and reappeared in the month of Elul (6th month), on the 25th day, at sunset. The heart of the land is good.

In the month of Ab (5th month), 10th day, Venus disappeared at sunset[7] (?), and for two[8] months and sixteen days was hidden, and reappeared on the 26th day of Marcheshwan (8th month). Rains in the land.

In the month of Nisan, 2d day, Venus appeared at sunrise. There will be distress in the land.

---

[1] IIIR. 63.
[2] Lit., "delayed in the heavens."
[3] Tablet defective.
[4] *I.e.*, there is war.
[5] Intercalated month.
[6] *I.e.*, it is a good sign.
[7] Tablet defective.
[8] Text erroneously 'one month.'

If Venus is stationary to the 6th day of Kislev (9th month) at sunrise, and then disappears on the 7th day of Kislev, and is hidden for three months to reappear on the 8th day of Adar (12th month) at sunset, it indicates that king against king will send hostility.

In the month of Kislev (9th month), 10th day, Venus appeared at sunrise. Lack of corn and hay in the land. If she remains in position up to the 14th day of Ab (5th month) at sunrise, and then on the 15th day disappears, and for three months is hidden, and on the 15th day of Marcheshwan (8th month) rises at sunset, the crops of the land will be good.

A colophon informs us that the tablet in question embodies a series of observations of the movements of Venus recorded by Babylonian scholars. It was evidently the purpose of the compilers to commit to writing as many variations in the appearance and disappearance of the planet as possible. The omens must either have been furnished at one time or they embody actual occurrences that were observed in connection with the observation recorded. In either case the omens served as guides for the priests in their replies to inquiries. An omen once furnished or an event once observed as having taken place under given conditions of a planet served for all times.

The omen lists for the other planets were arranged on the same principle as the Venus list. The motions of the planets were carefully observed. It was noted whether they rose brilliantly or with a pale color. Their position towards other stars was determined, and much more the like. Besides the planets, various stars that were distinguished by their brilliancy, as Sirius, Antares, Regulus, and also comets, were included in the sphere of astronomical calculations, and furnished omens to the priests.

These omens, so far as we may judge from the texts at present published, all hinge around the same series of events that are referred to in the illustrations given, — rain, crops, war, distress, the country's prosperity, the king's welfare or misfortune.

Another piece of evidence is thus furnished for the hypothesis that these lists are based upon reports made to royal masters, and that the reports again are obtained from the lists prepared for public and political needs. We must not, however, conclude from this fact that the observation of heavenly phenomena was of no significance at all for the private individual, but only that the position of the king and the general welfare of the country were regarded of larger moment.

Just as the gods were held responsible chiefly for the larger affairs of this world, the trifles being relegated to the spirits and demons,[1] so the planets and stars, as symbols of the gods, were regarded as auguries for the chief of the country rather than for the miscellaneous population, and more for the general welfare than for individual prosperity. The individual shared in the omen furnished, in so far as his well-being was dependent upon such important contingencies as whether there was to be war or peace, good crops or bad. A population so largely engaged in agriculture as the Babylonians were, would be satisfied if they could be reassured as to the outcome of their work in the fields. Ihering has properly emphasized the strong hold that the conception of communal interests obtained in Babylonia.[2] This conception is reflected in the prominence given to public and political affairs in the omen lists and 'omen' reports. Agriculture was the primal factor in producing this conception in the south; war which united the population, even though military service was forced upon the people, was the second factor; and in Assyria, where military expeditions occupied a much larger share of public attention than in Babylonia, war became the chief factor in keeping alive the thought of national solidarity.

Omen Calendars.

There was still another reason why the king and with him public affairs, received such prominence in the omen texts. As

---

[1] See above, p. 183.
[2] See Ihering, *Vorgeschichte der Indo-Europaer*, pp. 182 *seq.*

the nation's ruler he was not only an important personage by virtue of his power over his subjects, but also by virtue of his close relationship to the gods. The theory of the 'divine right of kings' was rigidly adhered to in Babylonia and Assyria. When the monarchs speak of themselves as nominated by this or that god to be the ruler of the country, this was not a mere phrase. The king was the vicar of the deity on earth, his representative who enjoyed divine favor and who was admitted into the confidence of the gods. In earlier days priestly functions were indissolubly associated with kingship. The oldest kings of Assyria call themselves 'the priests of Ashur,' and it is only as with the growth of political power a differentiation of functions takes place that the priest, as the mediator between the deity and his subjects, becomes distinct from the secular ruler.

The further development of this process led to the curious but perfectly natural anomaly that the king, from being originally identical with the priest, becomes in large measure dependent upon the latter in his relations to the gods. In the more advanced stages of the religious cult, the king requires the service of a priest to act as mediator between himself and the gods, precisely as all of his subjects need this mediatorship. The king cannot obtain an oracle directly. He must send to the temple and inquire of the priests. The priest must intercede for the king when he throws himself upon the mercy of an angered god or goddess. The royal sacrifice is not acceptable unless the priest stands by the side of the king.

Still there are traces left of the old direct relationship existing between the king and his gods. A god sometimes reveals himself directly to a ruler. Ishtar appears in a dream and gives him directions. Another and more significant trace of this older relationship is to be found in the importance assigned to the religious conduct of the king. If an individual offends a deity, the individual alone suffers, or at the most his family is involved in the punishment inflicted; but if the king sins, the whole country suffers, and correspondingly the king's atonement and reconciliation with the gods is essential for dispelling some national calamity. Frazer has shown by his admirable investigations[1] that this view of kingship is common to many nations of antiquity. While it did not lead among the Babylonians and Assyrians to that extreme which is best illustrated by Japan, where the Mikado, by virtue of his divine right, is hedged in with prescribed formalities that make him almost a prisoner, so closely is he watched by his attendants lest any mistake be made by him which is certain to entail serious consequences for the country, still the priests had to see to it that the rulers performed their duties towards the gods in the prescribed manner and with all possible accuracy.

The conduct of the king was of special significance at periods when for some reason or other, the gods were not favorably disposed. Partly on the basis of actual observation that eclipses (which were especially feared) had occurred on certain days of the month, partly as a consequence of the belief that the change in the moon's phase augured something good or evil for humanity, and in part perhaps through the coincidence that on a certain day of the month, mishaps of some kind had occurred several times, certain months and certain days of each month were regarded as favorable, while others were unfavorable. Some months and some days were suitable for dedicating a building, others were not. On some days an oracle might be sought, on others not. Some days were days of rejoicing, on others again mourning was appropriate. Advantage had to be taken of the favorable days to keep the deity in good humor, and it was equally important on the unfavorable ones to exercise great care not to do aught which might arouse the anger of a god, ready to be incensed. It is the king who can best accomplish the one thing and avoid the other. To him, as standing nearer the deity than any private individual, the country looked for

---

[1] See *The Golden Bough*, passim.

safety and protection. Calendars were prepared for each month of the year, in which the peculiar character of each day was noted and instructions added what was to be done on each day. These instructions all have reference to the king and to the king alone. A complete calendar for the intercalated month of Elul has been preserved.[1] It may serve as an example of the branch of the omen literature to which it belongs.

The thirty days of each month are taken up in succession. The deity to which each day is sacred is indicated, and various sacrifices or precautions prescribed.

A curious feature of this calendar was that, since it was the hope to make every day 'favorable,' each day was called so, even when it is evident that it was not.

For the 1st day of Elul the second,[2] sacred to Anu and Bel, a favorable day. When the moon makes its appearance in this month, the king of many peoples brings his gift, a gazelle together with fruit, . . . his gift to Shamash, lord of the countries, and to Sin, the great god, he gives. Sacrifices he offers, and his prayer to his god[3] is acceptable.

On the 2d day sacred to goddesses, a favorable day. The king brings his gift to Shamash, the lord[4] of countries. To Sin, the great god, he offers sacrifices. His prayer to the god is acceptable.

On the 3d day, a day of supplication to Marduk and Sarpanitum, a favorable day. At night, in the presence of Marduk and Ishtar,[5] the king brings his gift. Sacrifices he is to offer so that his prayer may be acceptable.

On the 6th day, sacred to Ramman and Belit,[6] a favorable day. The king, with prayer and supplication (?), at night in the presence of Ramman, offers his gift. Sacrifices he is to bring so that his prayer may be acceptable.

On the 7th day, supplication to Marduk and Sarpanitum, a favorable day

---

[1] IV Rawlinson, pls. 32, 33.

[2] *Ie.*, the intercalated Elul. After the 6th month (Elul) and after the 12th (Adar), a month was intercalated at certain intervals in order to bring the solar and lunar years into conjunction.

[3] Lit., 'raising of his hand to a god'—the attitude in prayer.

[4] Text erroneously 'mistress.'

[5] Here and elsewhere Ishtar is used in a generic sense for 'chief goddess'; in the present case Sarpanitum. See above, pp. 82, 151, 206.

[6] 'Belit,' as 'mistress' in general.

(*sc.* may it be). An evil day. ' The shepherd of many nations is not to eat meat roasted by the fire, or any food prepared by the fire. The clothes of his body he is not to change, fine dress (?) he is not to put on. Sacrifices he is not to bring, nor is the king to ride in his chariot. He is not to hold court nor is the priest to seek an oracle for him in the holy of holies.[1] The physician is not to be brought to the sick room.[2] The day is not suitable for invoking curses.[3] At night, in the presence of Marduk and Ishtar, the king is to bring his gift. Then he is to offer sacrifices so that his prayer may be acceptable.

This 7th day, it will be observed, is expressly called an evil day. It is evident, therefore, that the phrase 'favorable day' in the first line expresses a hope and not a fact, or is added to indicate the manner in which the day can be converted into a favorable one. Just as the 7th day, so the 14th, 21st, and 28th are called evil days, and the same ceremonies are prescribed for the king on these days. These days were evidently chosen as corresponding to the phases of the moon. But besides these four days, a fifth, namely, the 19th, is singled out in the same fashion. The comparison with the Biblical Sabbath naturally suggests itself. The choice of the 7th day and of the corresponding ones rests, of course, in both instances upon the lunar calendar, and there is also this similarity between the Sabbath of the Hebrews and the 'evil day' of the Babylonians, that the precautions prescribed in the Pentateuchal codes — against kindling fires, against leaving one's home, against any productive labor — point to the Hebrew Sabbath as having been at its origin an 'inauspicious day,' on which it was dangerous to show oneself or to call the deity's attention to one's existence. Despite the attempts made to change this day to one of 'joy,' as Isaiah would have it,[4] the Hebrew Sabbath continued to retain for a long time as a trace of its origin, a rather severe and sombre aspect.

---

[1] Lit., 'place of secrecy,' the reference being to that portion of the temple where the god sat enthroned.
[2] *I.e.*, of the palace.
[3] *I.e.*, upon one's enemies.
[4] Isaiah, lviii. 13.

A striking difference, however, between the Babylonian and the Hebrew rites is the absence in the latter of the theory that the atonement of a single individual suffices for the community. The precautions prescribed for the Sabbath are binding upon every one. Emphasis is laid in the Pentateuch upon the fact that the whole people is holy, whereas among the Babylonians the king alone is holy. He alone is to abstain from his ordinary acts, to conduct himself on the evil day with becoming humility, to put on no fineries, not to indulge in dainty food,[1] not to appear in royal state, neither to appeal to the gods (for they will not hear them), nor even to interfere with their workings by calling in human aid against the demon of disease, who may have been sent as the messenger of one of the gods. It is only at the close of the day that he can bring a sacrifice which will be acceptable. The king, by observing these precautions, insures the welfare of his people. The gods cared little for individual piety, but they kept a jealous eye on their earthly representative. His appeals were heard if properly presented and if presented at the right time, but woe to the people whose king has aroused the divine anger. Just as his acts of penitence have a representative character, so the gifts and sacrifices and supplications mentioned in the calendar are offered by the king on behalf of the whole people.

For the remaining days of Elul, the ordinances have much the same character as those instanced. The variation consists chiefly in the god or gods to whom the days are sacred. Now it is Nabu and his consort Tashmitum — on the 4th, 8th, and 17th days — to whom gifts and prayers are brought; again Ninib and his consort Gula, on the 9th,[2] — or Gula alone, on the 19th. To Marduk and Sarpanitum the 16th day is assigned, besides the 3d and 7th days as above set forth; to Ramman and his consort the 6th, to the old Bel and Belit the 5th, the 12th, the

---

[1] Meat, just as wine, was considered at all times a symbol of joy in the Orient.
[2] Perhaps also the 24th.

25th, and to Nergal and Bau the 27th. At times two male deities are in association. So Anu and Bel for the 1st and the 30th day, Ea and Nergal for the 28th, Sin and Shamash for the 18th, 20th, 21st, and 22d, or two goddesses, as Tashmitum and Sarpanitum, or a god alone, as Ea for the 26th, or Sin alone for the 13th, and once — the 29th day — Sin and Shamash are combined with the miscellaneous group of Igigi and Anunnaki. All the great gods are thus represented in the calendar. The basis on which the days are assigned still escapes us. It is hard to believe that any strict uniformity existed in this respect in the cults attached to the various Babylonian temples. Preference would be shown in each center to the chief god worshipped there, while to others would be assigned a position corresponding to some theological system devised by the priests. Uniformity and consistency are two elements that must not be looked for in the omen literature of any people. The very fact that omens have some rational basis, namely, observation and experience, is the very reason why the omen lists and omen calendars of one place should differ from those of another, and precisely to the same degree that observation and experience differ.

The intercalated months, by virtue of their extraordinary character, had perhaps a special significance, but every day of the year had an importance of some kind. This is shown by a Babylonian calendar, fortunately preserved in great part,[1] in which every day of the year is included, and either its character noted or some precautions prescribed. The indications in this calendar are marked by their brevity, and impress one as memoranda, intended as a guide to the priests.

The calendar consists of twelve columns. At the head of each column stands the name of one of the months. One or, at the most, two lines are devoted to each day of the month, the days being ranged in succession from one to thirty. For a series of days in the 2d month the indications are:

[1] V Rawlinson, pls. 48, 49.

21st day, hostility.
22d day, judgment favorable, invoking of curses.
23d day, heart not good.
24th day, gladness of heart.
25th day, wife not to be approached, heart not good.
26th day, secret.

Such indications it is evident are intelligible only to the initiated. With the help of the more complete calendars, such as the one above explained, we can in most cases determine what is meant by these memoranda. A note like 'hostility' is an omen that the gods are unfavorably inclined on that day. The 'judgment' referred to on the 22d day is the oracle. The day in question is suitable for obtaining a response to a question put to the deity, and a favorable occasion for invoking curses upon the enemy. It will be recalled that the 7th day of the second intercalated Elul is put down as one when it is not advisable to secure the ill will of the god against the enemy. An expression like 'heart not good' is explained by the contrast 'heart glad.' The 23d day of the month is a day of sorrow, the 24th one on which one may be cheerful without arousing the jealousy of the gods or demons. The 25th is again an unfavorable day in which, as a precaution, sexual intercourse is prohibited. Lastly, the word rendered 'secret'[1] is the same one that we came across in the precautions prescribed for the 7th day of the second Elul, where we are told that the priest is not to enter the 'secret' place. This term appears to describe the 'holy of holies' in the Babylonian temples where the oracles were obtained. The single word 'secret' was a sufficient indication for the priest that on the day in question he might enter the mysterious chamber of the temple without trepidation.

Many of the days of the year are simply set down as 'favorable' or 'unfavorable,' while others were noted as days

[1] The plural is used, but in a collective sense.

portending 'distress,' 'trouble,' 'tears,' 'injury,' 'everything favorable,' 'darkness,' 'moon obscured,' and the like. Of special interest are the prohibitions regarding food on certain days. On the 9th day of the 2d month "fish is not to be eaten or sickness will ensue." Swine's meat is forbidden on the 30th day of the 5th month, and in this case the particular kind of sickness — disease of the joints — is specified that will ensue in case of disobedience. On another day, the 25th of the 7th month, beef as well as pork is forbidden, while on the 10th day of the 8th month and the 27th day of the 6th month, dates are forbidden as a precaution against eye disease. One is not to cross a stream[1] on the 20th day of the 5th month; on certain days one is not to sell grain; other days are again noted as specially favorable for military movements.

Some of the precautions prescribed in this calendar may have been meant for the populace in general, such as the order not to cross a stream or to strike a bargain. The belief in lucky and unlucky days has a distinct popular flavor, but it is doubtful whether the ordinary public consulted the priests, as a general thing, in order to find out what days were lucky and what not. It is more plausible to assume that the priests embodied in their official calendars some of the notions that arose among the people, and gave to them an official sanction.

There are a considerable number of references to the king in the complete calendar under consideration, and we are permitted to assume, therefore, that the calendar served as a further guide for the priests in their instructions to the king. The allusion to oracles, curses, and weapons points in this same direction, and when, as in a number of instances, a day is described as one on which Shamash or some other god is 'angry,' it is in all probabilities against the ruler rather than against private individuals that the god's displeasure has been manifested. A similar official and public character is borne by

[1] The Euphrates or Tigris is no doubt meant.

another calendar, where months alone are indicated and their significance interpreted.[1] The twelve months are arranged in as many columns. Under each column the indications 'favorable' or 'not' are entered, while at the right end of the tablet the specifications are added for what undertakings the month is, or is not, favorable. One of these specifications is "the soldiery to make an attack upon a hostile city," and upon referring to the list of months, we learn that the 2d, 6th, 7th, 8th, and 12th months are favorable for such an undertaking, but the others are 'not.' Again, the 1st, 3d, 4th, 6th, 8th, 9th, 10th, and 11th are 'favorable' for "the entrance of any army upon foreign soil," but the remainder 'not.' The other specifications refer likewise to the movements of the armies. Such a calendar was evidently drawn up on the basis of omens, for a specific purpose, and, we may add, for some specific expedition to serve as a guide to the military commander. In the same way, calendars were drawn up devoted to indications regarding crops and for other purposes of public interest. To a more limited extent, private affairs are also touched upon.

To enter upon a further discussion of details is unnecessary at this point, and would carry us too far from the main purpose of this chapter, which is to point out the diverse ways in which the belief in omens is illustrated by the religious literature of the Babylonians.

It is sufficient to have made clear that the oracles and dreams, the lists of omens derived from eclipses, the works on the planets and stars and the calendars, all have the same origin due to observation of coincidences, to past experience, and to a variety of combinations, some logical and some fanciful, of supposed relationships between cause and effect; and not only the same origin, but the lists and calendars served also the same main purpose of guides for the priests in replying to the questions put to them by their royal masters and in forwarding

[1] IIIR. 52, no. 3, reverse.

instructions to the ruler for the regulation of his own conduct so that he and his people might enjoy the protection and good will of the gods. But the observation of the phenomena of the heavens, while playing perhaps the most prominent part in the derivation of omens, was not the only resource at the command of the priests for prognosticating the future. Almost daily, strange signs might be observed among men and animals, and whatever was strange was of necessity fraught with some meaning. It was the business of the priest to discover that meaning.

Omens from Terrestrial Phenomena.

Monstrosities, human and animal, and all species of malformations aroused attention. The rarer their occurrence, the greater the significance attached to them. In addition to this, the movements of animals, the flight of birds, the appearance of snakes at certain places, of locusts, lions, the actions of dogs, the direction of the winds, the state of rivers, and all possible accidents and experiences that men may encounter in their house, in the street, in crossing streams, and in sleep were observed. Everything in any way unusual was important, and even common occurrences were of some significance. The extensive omen literature that was produced in Babylonia is an indication of the extent to which men's lives were hedged in by the belief in portents. Several thousand tablets in the portion of Ashurbanabal's library that has been rescued from oblivion through modern excavations, deal with omens of this general class. Several distinct series, some embracing over one hundred tablets, have already been distinguished. One of these series deals with all kinds of peculiarities that occur in human infants and in the young of animals; another with the things that may happen to a man; a third with the movements of various animals, and more the like. As yet but a small portion of these tablets have been published,[1] but thanks to the indications given by Dr. Bezold in his great catalogue of the Kouyunjik Collection, a fair idea of the general character of the Babylonian omen literature may be formed. On what principle the omens were derived, it is again difficult to determine in detail, but that some logical principles controlled the interpretations cannot be doubted.

Jevons has shown[2] that in "sympathetic magic,"—of which the interpretation of omens is an offshoot,—the same logical methods are followed as in modern science. The famous 'Chaldean wisdom,' which is to be looked for in this widespread omen literature, would not have created so deep an impression on the ancient world, if the theologians of the Euphrates Valley, in incorporating primitive magic in the official religion, had not been successful in giving to their interpretations of occurrences in nature and in the animal world, the appearance, at least, of a consistent science.

Taking up as our first illustration the series devoted to birth portents, it is interesting to observe the system followed in presenting the various phases of the general subject. A broad distinction is drawn between significant phenomena in the case of human infants and in the case of the young of animals.

About a dozen tablets are taken up with an enumeration of omens connected with new-born children, and one gains the impression from the vast number of portents included in the lists that originally every birth portended something. The fact that births were of daily occurrence did not remove the sense of mystery aroused by this sudden appearance of a new life. Every part of the body was embraced in the omens: the ears, eyes, mouth, nose, lips, arms, hands, feet, fingers, toes, breast, generatory organs. Attention was directed to the shapes of

---

[1] The most extensive publication of omens is Boissier's *Documents Assyriens Relatifs aux Présages*, of which two volumes have appeared. Boissier's method of publication is not altogether satisfactory.

[2] *Introduction to the History of Religions*, pp. 28-35.

these various members and organs. The ears of a child might suggest the ears of a dog or of a lion or of a swine, and similarly the nose, mouth, lips, hands, or feet might present a peculiar appearance. A single member or the features in general might be small or abnormally large. All these peculiarities meant something; and since few if any children are born without presenting some peculiarities in some part of the body, it would seem as though the intention of the compilers of the series was to provide a complete handbook for the interpretation of signs connected with the birth of children. Naturally the total absence of some member of the body in case of the new-born or any malformation was a sign of especial significance. Hence we are told what was portended by a child born without hands or feet or ears or lips, or with only one of these members, or with only one eye, or with no mouth or no tongue, or with six fingers on one or on both hands, or six toes on one or on both feet, or without generatory organs.[1]

The rarer the phenomenon, the greater the significance is, as we have seen, a general principle in the science of augury. The birth of twins accordingly plays an important rôle in the series. In fact, the opening tablet is devoted in part to this phase of the subject. We are told, for example, that [2]

If a woman gives birth to twins, one male and one female, it is an unfavorable omen. The land is in favor,[3] but that house (wherein the child was born) will be reduced.

And again,

If a woman gives birth to twins, and both are brought out alive (?),[4] but the right hand of one is lacking, the ruler (?) will be killed by force, the land will be diminished. . . .

[1] A particularly bad omen. See IIIR. 65, 22, obverse.
[2] Boissier, *Documents Assyriens Relatifs aux Présages*, pp. 110 seq. Boissier has published portions of some twenty tablets of the series, ib. pp. 110-181.
[3] *I.e.*, will not suffer.
[4] The phrase used is obscure. My translation is offered as a conjecture.

If a woman gives birth to twins, and both are brought out alive (?), but neither of them have right hands, the produce of the country will be consumed by the enemy.

If a woman gives birth to twins, and both are brought out alive (?), but the right foot of one is missing, an enemy will for one year disturb the fixed order of the country.[1]

It will be observed that these omens bear on public as well as private affairs. The part played by public matters in them varies, but that the king and the country are so frequently introduced is an indication again of the official character given to these omen tablets. Only priests whose chief concern was with the court and the general welfare would have been impelled to mingle in this curious way the fate of the individual with that of the country at large. The birth of twins in itself is an omen for the house where the event occurs; but twins that are monstrosities, with a foot or a hand lacking, portend something of import to the general welfare.

The tablet proceeds, after finishing one phase of the subject, with omens to be derived from infants whose features resemble those of certain animals. In this case again we will see that the mind of the compiler is now directed towards the fate of the individual and again toward the ruler or the country. In the 2d tablet of the series we read that

If a woman gives birth to a child with a lion's head,[2] a strong king will rule in the land.

If a woman gives birth to a child with a dog's head, the city in his district[3] will be in distress, and evil will be in the country.

. . . .

If a woman gives birth to a child with a swine's head, offspring and possession (?) will increase in that house.

. . . .

If a woman gives birth to a child with a bird's head, that land will be destroyed.

---

[1] *I.e.*, an enemy will keep the land in turmoil.
[2] *I.e.*, like a lion. Elsewhere the preposition 'like' is used.
[3] Where the child is born.

If a woman gives birth to a child with a serpent's head, for thirty days (?) Nin-Gishzida[1] will bring a famine in the land, and Gilgamesh[2] will rule as king in the land.

In the same tablet[3] such monstrosities are taken up as children born with two heads, with a double pair of eyes, or with the eyes misplaced, with two mouths or more than two lips. The two heads, strange enough, generally portend good fortune, though not invariably. Thus an infant with two heads is an omen of strength for the country; and again

If a woman gives birth to a child with two heads, two mouths, but the regular number of eyes, hands, and feet,[4] it is an omen of vigorous life [for the country, but the son] will seize the king his father and kill him.

But

If a woman gives birth to a child with two heads and two mouths, and the two hands and two feet are between them,[5] disease will settle upon that city (where the monstrosity was born).

If the deformity consists in the misplacement of certain organs, the omen is invariably bad.

If a woman gives birth to a child with two eyes on the left side, it is a sign that the gods are angry against the land, and the land will be destroyed.

And again,

If a woman gives birth to a child with three eyes on the left side and one on the right, the gods will fill the land with corpses.

The third tablet proceeds with other parts of the body. It begins with a list of peculiarities observed in regard to the ears. The resemblance of certain features in children to the corre-

---

[1] A solar deity; see above, p. 99. Reference to minor deities are frequent in these omen texts.

[2] The reference appears to be to some misfortune that will be brought about through the solar deity Gilgamesh.

[3] Boissier, *Documents, etc.*, pp. 118–120.

[4] *I.e.*, only two.

[5] Between the two heads, *i.e.*, the hands and feet are misplaced.

sponding features of animals is an observation made by many nations. In modern times Lavater, it will be recalled, based his study of human physiognomy in part upon the resemblance of the nose, eyes, mouth, and ears, and general shape of the head to the features of such animals as the lion, jackass, dog, and swine. We may well believe, therefore, that when the Babylonians refer to a child with a lion's or a dog's ear, they had in mind merely a resemblance, but did not mean that the child actually had the ear of a lion or dog or the like.

At times the connection between the omen and its interpretation is quite obvious. In a portion of this same series we are told that [1]

If a woman gives birth to a child with a lion-like ear, a mighty king will arise in the land.

It will be recalled that a 'lion head' portends the same, and it is evident that in both cases the lion suggests strength. We are in the presence of the same order of ideas that controls the belief in 'sympathetic magic.' The corollary to 'like produces like' is 'like means like.' In other cases, the logic underlying the interpretation of the omen must be sought for in views connected with some accompanying feature.

If a woman gives birth to a child with the right ear missing, the days of the ruler will be long.

If a woman gives birth to a child with the left ear missing, distress will enter the land and weaken it.

While in general the absence of any part of the body is a sign of distress for the country and individual by a perfectly natural association of ideas, yet this general principle is modified by the further consideration that 'right' is a good omen and 'left' a bad one. But this consideration which makes the

[1] IIIR. 65, no. 1.

absence of the 'right' ear a good omen may again be offset by the entrance of a third factor. So we are told that

> If a woman gives birth to a child with a small[1] right ear, the house of the man[2] will be destroyed.

The omen of misfortune in this case is the deformity in the organ, and the fact that the more important right ear is deformed, so far from mitigating the force of the omen, accentuates its consequences.

If a deformed right ear is disastrous, we are prepared to learn that

> If a woman gives birth to a child with both ears short, the house of the man will be utterly rooted out.

No less than eleven varieties of deformed ears are enumerated. It must not be supposed, however, that the factors involved in this omen science are always or even generally so simple. In most cases the connection between the sign and the conclusion drawn, is not clear to us because of the multiplicity of factors involved. Further publication and study of omen texts will no doubt make some points clear which are now obscure, but we cannot expect ever to find out all the factors that were taken into account by the populace and the schoolmen, in proposing and accepting certain interpretations of certain omens, any more than we can fathom the reasons for the similar superstition found among other nations[3] of antiquity and modern times. Recognizing certain principles in some of the omens, we are justified in concluding that whatever else determined the interpretation of omens, caprice did not enter into consideration, but rather an association of ideas that escapes

---

[1] Abnormally small.

[2] *I.e.*, the father or master.

[3] The Egyptians carried the observation and interpretation of omens to quite as high a degree as the Babylonians and Assyrians. See, *e.g.*, Chabas, *Mélanges Égyptologiques*, 3ᵉ série, tome ii.; Wiedemann's *Religion of Ancient Egypt*, p. 263.

us, simply because our logic differs from the logic of primitive peoples in certain important particulars.

The list of peculiarities occurring in the case of babes continues as follows :

If a woman gives birth to a child whose mouth is shaped like a bird's, the country will be stirred up.

If a woman gives birth to a child without any mouth, the mistress of the house will die.

If a woman gives birth to a child with the right nostril lacking, misfortune is portending.

If a woman gives birth to a child with both nostrils lacking, the land will witness distress, and disease will destroy the house of the man.

If a woman gives birth to a child whose jaw is lacking, the days of the ruler will be long, but the house of the man will be destroyed.

If a woman gives birth to a child whose lower jaw is lacking, the ground will not bear fruit during the year.

It will be observed that, while most of the portents are evil, the ruler of the land is here generally vouchsafed immunity. The priests had to be somewhat on their guard lest by the very terror that they aroused, the hold of the rulers over the people might be loosened. Moreover, the rulers were sufficiently hedged in by their positions, as we have seen, and were in no danger of regarding themselves as safe from the anger of the gods.

Still quite frequently even the king is involved in the evil prophecy. The portion of the series dealing with portents derived from deformed hands and feet contains instances of this kind.

If a woman gives birth to a child with the right hand lacking, the land advances to destruction.

If a woman gives birth to a child with both hands lacking, the city will witness no more births, and the land will be utterly destroyed.

If a woman gives birth to a child with the fingers of the right hand lacking, the ruler will be captured by his enemy.

If a woman gives birth to a child with six toes on the right foot, through distress (?), the house of the man will perish.

If a woman gives birth to a child with six very small toes on the left foot, distress (?) will come to pass.

If a woman gives birth to a child with six toes on the right foot, some disaster is portending.

Altogether no less than ninety kinds of human deformities in the various parts of the body are enumerated and interpreted.

The significance of the portents is naturally increased if the woman who gives birth to a monstrosity happens to belong to the royal house. In such a case, the omen has direct bearings on national affairs. The good or evil sign affects the country exclusively. From a tablet of this nature,[1] belonging to a different series than the one we have been considering, we learn that six toes on the right foot or six on the left foot mean defeat, whereas six toes on both feet mean victory. Royal twins were a good omen, and so also a royal child born with teeth or with hair on its face or with unusually developed features.

The same desire to find some meaning in deviations from normal types led to the careful observation of deformities or peculiarities in the case of the young of domestic animals. In the fifth tablet of the series that we have chosen as an illustration, the compiler passes from babes to the offspring of domestic animals. From the opening line, which is all that has been published as yet,[2] and which reads:

If in the flock [3] a dog is born, weapons will destroy life and the king will not be triumphant

it would appear that the first subject taken up was the anomalous unions among animals, which naturally aroused attention when they occurred.

A number of tablets — at least seven — follow in which monstrosities occurring among the young of sheep are noted.

---

[1] Lenormant, *Choix des Textes Cunéiformes*, no. 87.

[2] Occurring at the end of the fourth tablet, as an aid for the correct arrangement of the series. IIIR. 65, no. 1, reverse, L. 28.

[3] Lit., 'stall,' which includes sheep, oxen, and swine.

The series passes on to signs to be observed among colts. From this point on, the series is too defective (so far as published) to warrant any further deductions; but it is safe to suppose that, as the young of ewes and mares were considered in special sections, so the young of swine and of cows were taken up in succession. The whole series would thus aim to cover that section of the animal kingdom that concerned man most, — his own offspring, and the young of those animals by which he was surrounded.

In these omens derived from the young of domestic animals, we are again overwhelmed at the mass of contingencies included by the priests in their compilations. Just as in the case of omens derived from infants, so here the parts of the body are taken up one after the other. All possible, and one is inclined to add various impossible, variations from the normal types are noted. The omen varies as the female throws off one, two, three, or whatever number of young ones up to ten. For example:[1]

> If among the sheep, five young ones are born, it is a sign of devastation in the land. The owner of the sheep dies, and his house is destroyed.

This is the omen in the case that the litter consists of five young ones, all normal. But if anomalies occur, as, *e.g.*,

> If five young ones are born, one with a bull's head, one with a lion's head, one with a dog's head, and one with a sheep's head, there will be a series of devastations in the land.

Again,

> If seven young are thrown off, three male and four female, that man[2] will perish.

And so if eight are born, it is a bad sign for the king who, we are told, "will be driven out of the country through sedition."

---

[1] Boissier, *Documents, etc.*, pp. 132, 133.
[2] *I.e.*, the owner of the stall. A variant reads 'king' instead of 'man.'

The variations are nigh endless.

If in the flock, young ones are thrown off with five legs, it is a sign of distress in the land. The house of the man will perish and his stalls will be swept away.

If the young ones have six legs, the population will decrease and devastation will settle over the country.

Having finished with litters, the series proceeds to peculiar marks found on single specimens; lambs that have a head and tail shaped like a lion or that have a lion's head, and a mane like that of an ass, or a head like a bird's, or like a swine, and so through a long and rather tiresome list.

Malformations in the shape or position of members of the animal, particularly the mouth, ears, tongue, tail, and eyes, or the absence of any one or of several of these parts were fraught with an importance corresponding to these symptoms among new-born babes.

If a young one has its ears on one side, and its head is twisted (?), and it has no mouth, the ruler will cut off the supply of water from his enemy.

In this instance the 'twisting' and the absence of the mouth appear to suggest the act of turning a canal into a different direction, so as to isolate a besieged city. When the text goes on to declare that

If the young one has its ears at its neck,[1] the ruler will be without judgment,

it is the association of ideas between 'ears' and 'judgment,'[2] that supplies the link. A misplaced ear is equivalent to misdirected judgment.

Consistent with this interpretation, the next line informs us that

If the young one has its ears below the neck,[3] the union of the country is weakened.

[1] *I.e.*, misplaced.
[2] In Babylonian, 'ear' is a synonym of 'understanding.'
[3] Still further misplaced.

Such glimpses into the peculiar thought controlling these omens are perhaps all that we will be able to obtain at least for a long time to come. For the rest, comparative studies with the omens of the other nations will alone serve to determine the multitudinous factors involved in the interpretations of the signs.

Before leaving the subject, however, a few more illustrations may be offered. Another portion of the same tablet — the eleventh — continues the omens derived from peculiarities in the ears of lambkins:

If the young one has no right ear, the rule of the king will come to an end, his palace will be uprooted, and the population of the city will be swept away, the king will lose judgment, . . . the produce of the country will be small, the enemy will cut off the supply of water.

If the left ear of the young one is missing, the deity will hear the prayer of the king, the king will capture his enemy's land, and the palace of the enemy will be destroyed, the enemy will lack judgment, the produce of the enemy's land will be taken away and everything will be plundered (?).

If the right ear of the young one falls off, the stall [1] will be destroyed.

If the left ear of the young one falls off, the stall will be increased, the stall [2] of the enemy will be destroyed.

If the right ear of the young one is split (?), that stall will be destroyed, the enemy (?) will advance against the city.

If the left ear of the young one is split (?), that stall will be increased, the king [3] will advance against the enemy's land.

In all these cases it will be observed that a defect in the right ear or an accident happening to it is an evil omen, whereas the same thing occurring in the case of the left is a favorable indication. The greater importance of the right side of anything evidently suggests in this case the interpretation offered, and yet this principle, as we have seen, is far from being of universal application. It depends upon *what* happens to the right ear. Above, we have seen that an unusually large

---

[1] Where the young one was born.
[2] *I.e.*, the flocks.
[3] Boissier's text has 'man,' — probably an error for 'king.'

ear betokens some good fortune, and in the tablet under consideration, illustrations are afforded of accidents to the right ear which furnish a good omen, while the same accident in the case of the left ear is regarded as a bad omen.

Our text continues:

> If the right ear of the young one is shrunk (?), the house of the owner will prosper.
> If the left ear is shrunk, the house of the owner will perish.
> If the right ear is torn off, the house of the owner will prosper.
> If the left ear is torn off, the house of the owner will perish.

But immediately following this we have again an evil omen for the right ear and a favorable one for the left. Three more tablets are taken up with omens associated with all manner of peculiarities in the formation of the ears, head, lips, mouth, and feet of lambkins, and it is not until the fifteenth tablet of the series is reached that another subject, the young of mares, is introduced.

The prognostications in the case of colts have about the same character as those in the case of lambkins. The same signs are singled out for mention, and the omens are not only, just as in the illustrations adduced, evenly divided between the fate of the country and its ruler, and of the owner of the colt or mare, but we can also observe a consistent application of the same principles, so far as these principles may be detected. A few illustrations will make this clear:[1]

> If a colt has no right legs, the house[2] will be destroyed.
> If a colt has no left legs, the days of the ruler will be long.
> If a colt has no legs, the country will be destroyed.
> If a colt has the right leg shortened,[3] . . . his stall[4] will be destroyed.
> If a colt has the left leg shortened, the stall[4] will be destroyed
> . . . .
> If a colt has no hoof on the right foreleg, the wife will cause trouble to her husband.

[1] IIIR. 65, no. 2, observe.
[2] Of the master.
[3] Lit., 'cut off.'
[4] Of the owner.

If a colt has no hoofs at all, there will be dissensions (?) within the country, and the enemy will enter the ruler's land.

In this way, twenty-one omens derived from as many varieties of strange formations in the legs of colts are enumerated. As in the case of lambkins, so for colts, the appearance of twins is endowed with a special significance.

If a mare gives birth to twins, male and female, and each has only one eye, the enemy triumphs and devastates Babylonia.
If the male or female colt has a mane like a lion, the country will be reduced.
If the male or female colt has a dog's hoof, the country will be reduced.
If the male or female colt has a lion's claw, the country will be enlarged.
If the male or female colt has a dog's head, the woman's[1] life will be bad. The country will be reduced.
If the male or female colt has a lion's head, the ruler will be strong.
If both colts, the male and female, resemble lions, the ruler over his enemies prevails (?).
If both colts, male and female, resemble dogs, the ruler over his enemy's country prevails (?).
If either a male or female colt is born resembling a lion, the king will be strong.
If either a male or female colt resembles a dog, herds of cattle will die, and there will be famine.
If a colt is born without a head, its master will be strong.
If a colt is born without eyes, the god Bel will bring about a change of dynasty.
If a colt is born without feet, the king increases his army and a slaughter will ensue.
If a colt is born without ears, for three years the gods will reduce the land.
If a colt is born without a tail, the ruler will die.

In conclusion it may be observed that, apart from the unusual character of these freaks which would suffice to attribute a special import to them, the notions current among the Babylonians, as among so many people of a period when creatures existed, the various parts of which were compounded

---

[1] The wife of the owner of the mare appears to be meant.

of different animals, may be regarded as an additional factor that served to add force to the class of omens we are considering. The monsters guarding the approaches to temples and palaces[1] were but one form which this popular belief assumed, and when a colt was observed to have a lion's or a dog's claw, an ocular demonstration was afforded which at once strengthened and served to maintain a belief that at bottom is naught but a crude and primitive form of a theory of evolution. In a dim way man always felt the unity of the animal world. Animals resembled one another, and man had some features in common with animals. What more natural than to conclude that at some period, the animals were composite creatures, and that even mankind and the animal world were once blended together.

The prevailing religious and semi-mythological ideas, accordingly, enter as factors in the significance that was attached to infants or to the young of animals, serving as illustrations of 'hybrid' formations.

Omens from the Actions of Animals.

The same order of ideas, only still further extended, may be detected in the sacredness attached to certain animals by so many nations of antiquity. It is now generally admitted that this 'sacredness' has two sides. A sacred animal may be 'taboo,' that is, so sacred that it must not be touched, much less killed or eaten; and, on the other hand, its original sanctity may lead people to regard it as "unclean," something again to be avoided, because of the power to do evil involved in the primitive conception of 'sacredness.'[2]

The swine and the dog are illustrations of this double nature of sanctity among the Semites. The former was sacred to some of the inhabitants of "Syria."[3] The Babylonians, as we have

---

[1] See above, p. 138.
[2] See Jevons, *Introduction to the History of Religion*, chapters vi.–ix.
[3] Robertson Smith, *Religion of the Semites*, pp. 143, 273.

seen, abstained from eating it on certain days of the year, while the Hebrews and Arabs regarded it as an absolute 'taboo.'

The dog to this day is in the Orient an "unclean" animal, and yet it is forbidden to do dogs any injury. If, then, we find the Babylonians attaching significance to the movements of this animal, it is obvious that by them, too, the dog was regarded as, in some way, sacred. It was an 'animal of omen,' sometimes good, at other times bad. A tablet informs us[1] that:

If a yellow dog enters a palace, it is a sign of a distressful fate for the palace.

If a speckled dog enters a palace, the palace[2] will give peace to the enemy.

If a dog enters a palace and some one kills him, the peace of the palace will be disturbed.

If a dog enters a palace and crouches on the couch, no one will enjoy that palace in peace.

If a dog enters a palace and crouches on the throne, that palace will suffer a distressful fate.

If a dog enters a palace and lies on a large bowl, the palace will secure peace from the enemy.

There follow omens in case dogs enter a sacred edifice:

If a dog enters a temple, the gods will not enlarge the land.

If a white dog enters a temple, the foundation of that temple will be firm.

If a black dog enters a temple, the foundation of that temple will not be firm.

If a brown[3] dog enters a temple, that temple will witness justice.

If a yellow dog enters a temple, that temple will[4] witness justice.

If a speckled dog enters a temple, the gods will show favor to that temple.

If dogs gather together and enter a temple, the city's peace will be disturbed.

---

[1] Lenormant, *Choix des Textes Cunéiformes*, no. 89; Boissier, *Documents, etc.*, p. 104.

[2] *I.e.*, the ruler of the palace.

[3] Lit., 'dark colored.'

[4] 'Not,' perhaps omitted.

The juxtaposition of palace and temple is an indication that a large measure of sanctity was attached to the former as the dwelling-place of one who stood near to the gods. The omens, accordingly, in the case of both palace and temple are again concerned with public affairs. But from the same tablet we learn that an equal degree of significance was attached to the actions of dogs when they entered private dwellings. Precautions must have been taken against the presence of dogs in that part of the house which was reserved for a man's family, for we are told:[1]

A dog entering a man's house was an omen that the ultimate fate of that house would be destruction by fire.

Care had to be taken lest dogs defiled a person or any part of the house. The omens varied again according to the color of the dog.

If a white dog defiles[2] a man, destruction will seize him.
If a black dog defiles a man, sickness will seize him.
If a brown dog defiles a man, that man will perish.
If a dog defiles a man's couch, a severe sickness will seize that man.
If a dog defiles a man's chair, the man will not survive the year.
If a dog defiles a man's bowl,[3] a deity will show anger towards the man.

On the other hand, dogs were not to be driven out of the streets. Their presence in the roads was essential to the welfare of the place. Hence an omen reads:

If dogs do not enter the highway,[4] destruction from an enemy will visit the city.

Through Diodorus, Jamblichus, and other ancient writers we know that the Babylonians and Assyrians attached importance to the movements of other animals, notably serpents, birds, and certain insects. The symbols on the boundary stones which

[1] Boissier, p. 103.
[2] By vomiting on him.
[3] Out of which one eats.
[4] *I.e.*, keep away from it.

have been referred to [1] are based on this belief. The serpent figures prominently among these symbols. In the Babylonian deluge story, the dove, raven, and swallow are introduced. Of these, the swallow appears to be the bird whose flight was most carefully observed. The sign which represents this bird in the cuneiform syllabary also signifies 'fate.'[2] The mischief wrought by swarms of insects, as grasshoppers and locusts, the danger lurking in the bites of scorpions sufficiently explain the importance attached to the actions of these animals. The mysterious appearance and disappearance of serpents and their strange twistings added an element in their case that increased the awe they inspired, while if Ihering be correct,[3] the omens derived from the flight of birds are a survival of the migratory period in the history of a nation, when birds served as a natural guide in choosing the easiest course to pass from one place to another. A large number of tablets in Ashurbanabal's library treat of the significance attached to the action of these various animals, and it is likely that these tablets form part of a large series, of which the illustrations above adduced regarding the movements of dogs form a part. In this series, the application of the omens to individuals is more strongly emphasized than in the series of birth portents. Naturally so, for it was the individual as a general thing who encountered the signs. In the case of the appearance of a serpent or snake, for example, the omen consisted in the fact that a certain person beheld it, and that person was involved in the consequences. Fine distinctions are again introduced that illustrate the intricacies of the system of interpretation perfected in Babylonia. If a snake passes from the right to the left side of a man, it means one thing; if from the left to the right, another; if the man who

---

[1] See p. 182.

[2] According to Hilprecht (*Old Babylonian Inscriptions*, I. part 2, p. 35), 'a goose or similar water-bird' was originally pictured by the sign, though he admits that the picture was 'later' used for swallow.

[3] *Vorgeschichte der Indo-Europaer*, pp. 451-55.

sees a snake does not tread upon it, the omen is different than in the case when he attempts to crush it. Again the omen varies according to the occupation of the man who encountered a snake. If he be a gardener, the appearance of the snake means something different than in the case of his being a sailor.

The place where the animal appears is also of import, whether in the street, the house, or the temple, and again, the time of its appearance, in what month or on what day. In the same way, an endless variety of omens are derived from the appearance of certain birds, the direction of their flight, their fluttering around the head of a man or entering a man's house. So, *e.g.*,

> If a raven[1] enters a man's house, that man will secure whatever he desires.

And again:

> If a bird throws a bit of meat or anything into a man's house, that man will secure a large fortune.

The omens from the appearance of flocks of birds in a town bore, as appears natural, upon public affairs rather than upon the fate of individuals, and similarly the appearance of birds in a temple was an omen for the whole country.

The public or private character of the omens was thus dependent in large measure upon the question whether the phenomena appeared to an individual directly or to the population of a place in general. Meeting a snake or scorpion in the course of a walk through the fields was an individual omen, and similarly the actions of sheep in a man's stall, whereas, a mad bull rushing through the city was a general omen. So we are told that

> If sheep in the stalls do not bleat (?), that stall will be destroyed.

---

[1] The term used is *Unagga*, Bezold's *Catalogue of the Koujunjik Collection*, p. 1841. See Jensen, *Kosmologie*, p. 153.

Whereas[1]

A bull crouching at the gate of a city is an omen that the enemy will capture that gate.

A bull goring an ox in the city is an unfavorable omen for the city, but if the bull enters the precincts of an individual, it is favorable for the individual.

A series of omens derived from the appearance of locusts again illustrates this principle. When the insects enter private precincts, the individual and his immediate surroundings are affected.[2]

If black and speckled locusts appear in a man's house, the master of the house will die.

If black and yellow locusts appear in a man's house, the supports of that house will fall.

If large white locusts appear in a man's house, that house will be destroyed and the owner will be in distress.

If white and brown locusts appear in a man's house, that house will be destroyed.

If small white and brown locusts appear in a man's house, the house will be destroyed and the owner will be in distress.

If yellow locusts appear in a man's house, the supports of that house will fall and the owner of the house will be unlucky.

If yellow-winged locusts appear in a man's house, the master of the house will die and that house will be overthrown.

OMENS FROM DREAMS.

It made little difference whether one encountered something while awake or saw it in one's dream. In fact, what one saw while asleep had as a general thing more importance. A special god of dreams, Makhir, is often referred to in the religious texts, and this is but another way of expressing the belief that the dreams were sent to a man as omens. An unusually wide scope was afforded to the compilers of omen

---

[1] Bezold, *Catalogue*, p. 1710.   [2] Boissier, *Documents, etc.*, pp. 3, 4.

series in their interpretations of dreams, for what might not a man see in visions of the night! If a lion [1] appears to a man, it means that the man will carry out his purpose; if a jackal, it signifies that he will secure favor in the eyes of the gods; a dog portends sorrow; a mountain goat, that the man's son will die of some disease; a stag, that his daughter will die; and so through a long list.

Again we are told [2] that

If (in a dream) a date appears on a man's head,[3] it means that that man will be in distress.
If a fish appears on a man's head, that man will be powerful.
If a mountain appears on a man's head, that man will be without a rival.
If salt appears on a man's head, his house will be well protected (?).

Similarly, interpretations are offered for the apparition of the dead or of demons, in dreams. The book of Daniel affords an illustration of the importance attached to dreams in Babylonia, and of the science developed out of the interpretations. The sarcastic touch introduced by the compiler of the book,[4] who represents Nebuchadnezzar as demanding of his priests not merely to interpret his dream, but to tell him what he dreamed, is intended to illustrate the limitations of the far-famed 'Chaldean wisdom.' It is also interesting to note in connection with the illustrations adduced, that the dreams of Nebuchadnezzar and Belshazzar [5] in the book of Daniel are so largely concerned with apparitions of animals.

The omens taken from dreams, together with the accidents that occurred to an individual, or the phenomena occuring in a man's house, afford us an insight into the purely popular phases of the science of augury. While eclipses and the movements of planets bear chiefly and almost exclusively on public affairs, and even birth portents frequently portend something to the ruler

---

[1] Bezold, *Catalogue*, pp. 1437, 1438.
[2] Bezold, *ib.* p. 918.
[3] *I.e.*, over him.
[4] Chapter II. 4–6.
[5] Chapter ii. 31–35, and vii. 2–12.

or to the country, it was through such omens as partook of a purely personal character that the intentions of the gods towards the individual were made manifest. By means of omens, the bond between the individual and the gods was not, indeed, established, but in large measure maintained. Here was a phase of the religion that touched each individual closely. What a person saw, what he dreamed, what happened to him, what appeared in his house or among the members of his household was of significance to him. To know what every phenomenon portended was essential to his welfare; and we may feel certain that the relations of the individual to the priests, so far as these existed, consisted largely in obtaining from the latter the interpretation of the omens that he encountered. On the other hand, the power of the priests over the populace was due to the popular belief in portents, and the attention given by the theologians to the collection of exhaustive omen series is a proof that the priests knew how to use their power.

These "Dream Books" must have been very numerous. The success of the priests here depended even more than in other branches of the omen literature upon exhausting, so far as possible, all contingencies. No doubt they were guided here also by two factors: association of ideas, and past experience through making of a single coincidence between a dream and some occurrence, a principle of general application. Some of the omens from dreams, however, appear to have themselves formed part of a larger series dealing in general with

Omens from Individual Experiences.

If one may judge from the specimens furnished by Dr. Bezold in his catalogue, this series was unusually extensive, embracing a large number of subjects connected with human activity, — a man's work in the field, his actions in commercial affairs, incidents of travel on sea or land, his relations to his kindred — the dead as well as the living — disease and death, down to such apparent trifles as the conditions of the walls of his house. Cracks in the wall were an omen; meeting a snake in the highway was an omen. A fall was an omen; dropping an instrument was an omen; in short, it is difficult to say what was not an omen. The character of the omens in this series does not differ in any essential particulars from those of other series. The important feature of the series is that it affords another and perhaps the most striking illustration of that phase of the omen literature which concerns the individual directly, and, it seems safe to add, exclusively.

Take, for example, omens connected with symptoms occurring in certain diseases. We are told that

> If the right breast is brown, it is a fatal (?) sign.
> If both breasts are brown, there will be no recovery.
> If the left breast is green, the sickness will be severe.

The symptoms affect the individual alone. Through this series we are thus enabled to determine more definitely the boundary line between omens involving the affairs of the country and king, and those involving the individual. A phenomenon affecting an individual, or appearing to him alone, or brought about through some action of his of a purely private character, carries in its train an omen of significance for himself or his immediate surroundings ; but the moment that these rather narrow limits are transcended, the fate of the individual becomes more or less closely bound up with the fortunes of the population and of the ruler of the country in general. The series also illustrates, perhaps better than any other, the control exercised by popular beliefs over the acts of the individual. For we may conclude, that if work on certain days or traveling at certain periods or the appearance of certain animals indicated something unfavorable to a man, he would studiously avoid bringing misfortune upon himself and observe the precautions involved in the interpretation of the vast mass of the accidents and incidents of existence. The task was a difficult one, indeed, impossible of being carried out to perfection, but this would not hinder him from making the attempt. He was satisfied if he warded off at least a fair number of unfavorable omens. Correspondingly, he would endeavor to so regulate his course as to encounter as large a number as possible of omens that were favorable to him. In this way his life would be spent with a constant thought of the gods and spirits, who controlled all things in this world. The popular belief in omens made it incumbent upon the individual not to lose sight at any time of his dependance upon powers over which he had but a limited control.

A certain phase of his religion thus entered largely into his life. That phase would occupy him by day and by night. It was a part of his religion which literally engaged him "upon lying down at night, and upon rising up, while sitting in the house, and while walking on the way." If, despite all his efforts, misfortune came, — and misfortunes, of course, came constantly, — there was no other recourse but to throw himself upon the mercy of some god or gods. The gods, especially Marduk, Ishtar, Shamash, and Ramman, by putting 'grace' into the omens, could at any time change them into favorable indications.

CHAPTER XXI.

THE COSMOLOGY OF THE BABYLONIANS.

VARIOUS traditions were current in Babylonia regarding the manner in which the universe came into existence. The labors of the theologians to systematize these traditions did not succeed in bringing about their unification. Somewhat like in the Book of Genesis, where two versions of the creation story have been combined by some editor,[1] so portions of what were clearly two independent versions have been found among the remains of Babylonian literature. But whereas in the Old Testament the two versions are presented in combination so as to form a harmonic whole, the two Babylonian versions continued to exist side by side. There is no reason to suppose that the versions were limited to two. In fact, a variant to an important episode in the creation story has been discovered which points to a third version.[2]

The suggestion has been thrown out that these various versions arose in the various religious centers of the Euphrates Valley. So far as the editing of the versions is concerned, the suggestion is worthy of consideration, for it is hardly reasonable to suppose that the theological schools of one and the same place should have developed more than one cosmological system. The traditions themselves, however, apart from the

---

[1] The so-called Elohistic version, Gen. i. 1–ii. 4; the Yahwistic version, Gen. ii. 5–24. Traces have been found in various portions of the Old Testament of other popular versions regarding creation. See Gunkel, *Schöpfung und Chaos*, pp. 29–114, 119–121.

[2] Gunkel, *ib.* pp. 28, 29. What Sayce (*e.g., Rec. of the Past*, N. S., i. 147, 148) calls the 'Cuthaean legend of the creation' contains, similarly, a variant description of Tiâmat and her brood.

literary form which they eventually assumed, need not have been limited to certain districts nor have been peculiar to the place where the systematization took place. Nothing is more common than the interchange of myths and popular traditions. They travel from one place to the other, and contradictory accounts of one and the same event may be circulated, and find credence in one and the same place.

The two distinct Babylonian versions of the creation of the world that have up to the present time been found, have come to us in a fragmentary form. Of the one, indeed, only some forty lines exist, and these are introduced incidentally in an incantation text;[1] of the other version, portions of six tablets[2] have been recovered; while of two fragments it is doubtful[3] whether they belong to this same version or represent a third version, as does certainly a fragment containing a variant account of the episode described in the fourth tablet of the larger group. The fragments of the longer version — in all 23 — enable us to form a tolerably complete picture of the Babylonian cosmology, and with the help of numerous allusions in historical, religious and astronomical texts and in classical writers, we can furthermore fill out some of the gaps.

Taking up the longer version, which must for the present serve as our chief source for the cosmology of the Babylonians, it is important to note at the outset that the series constitutes, in reality, a grand hymn in honor of Marduk. The account of the beginning of things and of the order of creation is but incidental to an episode which is intended to illustrate the greatness of Marduk, the head of the Babylonian pantheon. This episode is the conquest of a great monster known as

[1] Published by Pinches, *Journal Royal Asiat. Soc.*, 1891, pp. 393-408.

[2] Complete publication by Delitzsch, *Das Babylonische Weltschöpfungsepos* (Leipzig, 1896) with elaborate commentary.

[3] See Zimmern in Gunkel's *Schöpfung und Chaos*, pp. 415, 416, and on the other side, Delitzsch, *Babylonische Weltschöpfungsepos*, p. 20. Zimmern's doubts are justified.

Tiâmat,— a personification, as we shall see, of primaeval chaos. What follows upon this episode, likewise turns upon the overshadowing personality of Marduk. This prominence given to Marduk points of course to Babylon as the place where the early traditions received their literary form. Instead of designating the series as a 'Creation Epic' it would be quite as appropriate to call it 'The Epic of Marduk.'

The god of Babylon is the hero of the story. To him the creation of the heavenly bodies is ascribed. It is he who brings order and light into the world. He supplants the rôles originally belonging to other gods. Bel and Ea give way to him. Anu and the other great gods cheerfully acknowledge Marduk's power. The early traditions have all been colored by the endeavor to glorify Marduk; and since Marduk is one of the latest of the gods to come into prominence, we must descend some centuries below Hammurabi before reaching a period when Marduk's position was so generally recognized as to lead to a transformation of popular traditions at the hands of the theologians.

The evident purpose of the 'epic' to glorify Marduk also accounts for the imperfect manner in which the creation of the universe is recounted. Only the general points are touched upon. Many details are omitted which in a cosmological epic, composed for the specific purpose of setting forth the order of creation, would hardly have been wanting. In this respect, the Babylonian version again resembles the Biblical account of creation, which is similarly marked by its brevity, and is as significant for its omissions as for what it contains.

It but remains before passing on to an analysis of the 'epic' to note the great care bestowed upon its literary form. This is evidenced not only by the poetic diction, but by its metrical form,—a point to which Budge was the first to direct attention [1]

---

[1] *Proc. Soc. Bibl. Arch.* vi. 7.

and which Zimmern[1] clearly established. Each line consists of two divisions, and as a general thing four or eight lines constitute a stanza. The principle of parallelism, so characteristic of Biblical poetry, is also introduced, though not consistently carried out.

The epic was known from its opening words as the series 'when above.' Through this name we are certain of possessing a portion of the first tablet — but alas! only a portion. A fragment of fifteen lines and these imperfectly preserved is all that has as yet been found. So far as decipherable, it reads:

> There was a time when above the heaven was not named.[2]
> Below, the earth bore no name.
> Apsu was there, the original, their begettor,[3]
> Mummu [and] Tiâmat, the mother of them all.[3]
> But their waters[4] were gathered together in a mass.
> No field was marked off, no marsh[5] was seen.
> When none of the gods was as yet produced,
> No name mentioned, no fate determined,
> Then were created the gods in their totality.
> Lakhmu and Lakhamu, were created.
> Days went by[6] . . .
> Anshar and Kishar were created.
> Many days elapsed[6] . . .
> Anu [Bel and Ea were created].[7]
> Anshar, Anu (?) . . .

---

[1] *Zeits. f. Assyr.* viii. 121–124. Delitzsch, in his *Babylonische Weltschöpfungsepos*, pp. 61–68, has elaborately set forth the principles of the poetic composition. See also D. H. Mueller, *Die Propheten in ihrer ursprünglichen Form*, pp. 5–14.

[2] *I.e.*, did not exist. To be 'called' or to 'bear a name' meant to be called into existence.

[3] *I.e.*, of the waters.

[4] *I.e.*, of heaven and earth.

[5] The word used is obscure. Jensen and Zimmern render " reed." Delitzsch, I think, comes nearer the real meaning with " marsh." See Haupt's translation, *Proc. Amer. Oriental Soc.*, 1896, p. 161.

[6] Delitzsch supplies a parallel phrase like "periods elapsed."

[7] Supplied from Damascius' extract of the work of Berosus on Babylonia. See Cory, *Ancient Fragments*, p. 92; Delitzsch, *Babylonische Weltschöpfungsepos*, p. 94.

At this point the fragment breaks off.

Brief as it is, it affords a clear view of the manner in which the Babylonians regarded the beginning of things. Water was the primaeval element. 'Apsu' is the personified great 'ocean'—the 'Deep' that covers everything. With Apsu there is associated Tiâmat. Tiâmat is the equivalent of the Hebrew T'hôm,[1] which occurs in the second verse of the opening chapter of Genesis, and which is, like Apsu, the personification of the 'watery deep.' Apsu and Tiâmat are, accordingly, synonymous. The combination of the two may be regarded as due to the introduction of the theological doctrine which we have seen plays so prominent a part in the systematized pantheon, namely, the association of the male and female principle in everything connected with activity or with the life of the universe. Apsu represents the male and Tiâmat the female principle of the primaeval universe. It does not follow from this that the two conceptions are wholly dissociated from popular traditions. Theological systems, it will be found, are always attached at some point to popular and often to primitive beliefs.

Tiâmat was popularly pictured as a huge monster of a forbidding aspect. Traces of a similar conception connected with T'hôm are to be met with in the poetry of the Old and New Testament.[2] The 'Rahab' and 'Leviathan' and the 'Dragon' of the apocalypse belong to the same order of ideas that produced Tiâmat. All these monsters represent a popular attempt to picture the chaotic condition that prevailed before the great gods obtained control and established the order of heavenly and terrestrial phenomena. The belief that water

---

[1] The $\hat{o}$ is represented in Babylonian by $\hat{a}$, and the ending *at* in Tiâmat is an affix which stamps the Babylonian name as feminine. T'hôm in Hebrew is likewise a feminine noun, but it should be noted that at a certain stage in the development of the Semitic languages, the feminine is hardly distinguishable from the plural and collective.

[2] Gunkel, *Schöpfung und Chaos*, pp. 29–82, 379–398.

was the original element existing in the universe and the 'source' of everything, may also have had its rise in the popular mind. It was suggested in the Euphrates Valley, in part, by the long-continued rainy season, as a result of which the entire region was annually flooded. The dry land and vegetation appeared, only after the waters had receded. The yearly phenomenon brought home to the minds of the Babylonians, a picture of primaeval chaos.

In the schools of theology that arose with the advance of culture, these two notions — water as the first element and a general conception of chaos — were worked out with the result that Apsu and Tiâmat became mythical beings whose dominion preceded that of the gods. Further than this the questionings of the schoolmen did not go. They conceived of a time when neither the upper firmament nor the dry land existed and when the gods were not yet placed in control, but they could not conceive of a time when there was 'nothing' at all. This cosmological theory which we may deduce from the fragment of the first tablet of the creation series is confirmed by the accounts that have come down to us — chiefly through Damascius — of the treatment of the subject by Berosus.[1] Damascius explicitly places the Babylonians among those nations who fail to carry back the universe to an ultimate single source. There is nothing earlier than the two beings — Apsu and Tiâmat.[2]

The massing together of the primaeval waters completes the picture of chaos in the cuneiform account. From the popular side, the commingling corresponds to the *Tôhû wa Bôhû* of the Book of Genesis, but for the Babylonian theologians, this embrace of Apsu and Tiâmat becomes a symbol of 'sexual'

---

[1] For our purposes it is sufficient to refer for the relations existing between Damascius and the cuneiform records to Smith's *Chaldaeische Genesis*, pp. 63–66, to Lenormant's *Essai de Commentaire sur les fragments Cosmogoniques de Berose*, pp. 67 *seq.*, and to Jensen's *Kosmologie der Babylonier*, pp. 270–272.

[2] The names are given by Damascius as *Apasôn* and *Tauthe*.

union.[1] As the outcome of this union, the gods are produced. This dependence of the gods upon Apsu and Tiâmat is but vaguely indicated. Another theory appears to have existed according to which the gods were contemporaneous with primaeval chaos. The vagueness may therefore be the result of a compromise between conflicting schools of thought. However this may be, the moment that the gods appear, a conflict ensues between them and Apsu-Tiâmat. This conflict represents the evolution from chaos to order. But before taking up this phase of the epic, a few words must be said as to the names of the gods mentioned, and as to the order in which they occur.

There are three classes of deities enumerated. The first two classes consist, each, of a pair of deities while the third is the well-known triad of the old Babylonian theology. Between the creation of each class a long period elapses — a circumstance that may be regarded as an evidence of the originally independent character of each class. Now it has recently been shown [2] that Lakhamu is the feminine of Lakhmu. The first class of deities is, therefore, an illustration again of the conventional male and female principles introduced into the current theology. While there are references to Lakhmu and Lakhamu in the religious texts,[3] particularly in incantations, these two deities play no part whatsoever in the active pantheon, as revealed by the historical texts. In popular tradition,[4] Lakhmu survived as a name of a mythical monster.

Alexander Polyhistor[5] quotes Berosus as saying in his book on Babylonia that the first result of the mixture of water and

---

[1] Suggested by Professor Haupt (Schrader, *Cuneiform Inscriptions and the Old Testament*, p. 7).

[2] Hommel, *Proc. Soc. Bibl. Arch.* xviii. 19.

[3] See Jensen, *Kosmologie*, pp. 224, 225.

[4] Agumkakrimi Inscription (VR. 33, iv. 50); Nabonnedos (Cylinder, VR. 64, ii. 16, 17).   [5] Cory's *Ancient Fragments*, p. 58.

chaos — *i.e.*, of Apsu and Tiâmat — was the production of monsters partly human, partly bestial. The winged bulls and lions that guarded the approaches to temples and palaces are illustrations of this old notion, and it is to this class of mythical beings that Lakhmu belongs. The schools of theology, seizing hold of this popular tradition, add again to Lakhmu a female mate and convert the tradition into a symbol of the first step in the evolution of order out of the original chaos. Lakhmu and Lakhamu are made to stand for an entire class of beings that are the offspring of Apsu and Tiâmat. This class does not differ essentially from Apsu and Tiâmat, nor from the 'Leviathan,' the 'Dragon,' the winged serpents, and the winged bulls that are all emanations of the same order of ideas. Accordingly, we find Lakhmu and Lakhamu associated with Tiâmat when the conflict with the gods begins. They are products of chaos and yet at the same time contemporary with chaos, — monsters not so fierce as Tiâmat, but withal monsters who had to be subdued before the planets and the stars, vegetation and man could appear.

The introduction of Anshar and Kishar as intermediate between the monsters and the triad of gods appears to be due entirely to the attempt at theological systematization that clearly stamps the creation epic as the conscious work of schoolmen, though shaped, as must always be borne in mind, out of the material furnished by popular tradition. In connection with the etymology and original form of the chief of the Assyrian pantheon,[1] the suggestion was made that the introduction of Anshar into the creation epic is a concession made to the prominence that Ashur acquired in the north. We are now able to put this suggestion in a more definite form. The pantheon of the north, as we have seen, was derived from the south. Not that all the gods of the south are worshipped in the north, but those that are worshipped

[1] See above, pp. 198, 199.

in the north are also found in the south, and originate there. The distinctive features of Ashur are due to the political conditions that were developed in Assyria, but the unfolding of the conceptions connected with this god which make him the characteristic deity of Assyria, indeed, the only distinctive Assyrian figure in the Assyrian pantheon, does not preclude the possibility, of the southern origin of Ashur.

If, as has been made plausible by Hommel, Nineveh, the later capital of the Assyrian empire, represents a settlement made by inhabitants of a Nineveh situated in the south, there is no reason why a southern deity bearing the name Anshar should not have been transferred from the south to the north. The attempt has been made [1] to explain the change from Anshar to Ashur. The later name Ashur, because of its ominous character, effectually effaced the earlier one in popular thought. The introduction of the older form Anshar, not merely in the first tablet of the creation series, but, as we shall presently see, elsewhere, confirms the view of a southern origin for Ashur, and also points to the great antiquity of the Anshar-Ashur cult. It is not uncommon to find colonies more conservative in matters of religious thought and custom than the motherland, and there is nothing improbable in the interesting conclusion thus reached that Ashur, the head of an empire, so much later in point of time than Babylonia, should turn out to be an older deity than the chief personage in the Babylonian pantheon after the days of Hammurabi.

But while Anshar-Ashur under this view is a figure surviving from an ancient period, he is transformed by association with a complementary deity Kishar into a symbol, just as we have found to be the case with Lakhmu. By a play upon his name, resting upon an arbitrary division of Anshar into *An* and *Shar*, the deity becomes the 'one that embraces all that is above.' The element *An* is the same that we have in *Anu*, and is the

[1] See above, pp. 198, 199.

'ideographic'[1] form for 'high' and 'heaven.' *Shar* signifies 'totality' and has some connection with a well-known Babylonian word for 'king.' The natural consort to an all-embracing upper power is a power that 'embraces all that is below'; and since *Ki* is the ideographic form for 'earth,' it is evident that Ki-Shar is a creation of the theologians, introduced in order to supply Anshar with an appropriate associate. The two in combination represent a pair like Lakhmu and Lakhamu. As the latter pair embrace the world of monsters, so Anshar and Kishar stand in the theological system for the older order of gods, a class of deities antecedent to the series of which Anu, Bel, and Ea are the representatives. Besides the antiquity of Anshar and the factor involved in the play upon the name, the prominence of the Ashur cult in the north also entered into play (as already suggested) in securing for Anshar-Ashur, a place in the systematized cosmology. The Babylonian priests, while always emphasizing the predominance of Marduk, could not entirely resist the influences that came to them from the north. Ashur was not accorded a place in the Babylonian cult, but he could not be ignored altogether. Moreover, Assyria had her priests and schools, and we are permitted to see in the introduction of Anshar in the creation epic, a concession that reflects the influence, no doubt indirect, and in part perhaps unconscious, but for all that, the decided influence of the north over the south. The part played by Anshar in the most important episode of the creation epic will be found to further strengthen this view.[2]

Kishar, at all events, forms no part of either the Babylonian or of the active Assyrian pantheon. She does not occur in historical or religious texts. Her existence is purely theoretical — a creation of the schools without any warrant in popular tradi-

---

[1] I avoid the term "Sumerian" here, because I feel convinced that the play on Anshar is of an entirely artificial character and has no philological basis.

[2] See below, pp. 421–423.

tion, so far as we can see. A tablet is fortunately preserved[1] (though only in part) which enables us to come a step nearer towards determining the character of the series of powers regarded as antecedent to the well-known deities. In this tablet, no less than ten pairs of deities are enumerated that are expressly noted as 'Father-mother of Anu,' that is, as antecedent to Anu.[2] Among these we find Anshar and Kishar, and by their side, such pairs as Anshar-gal, *i.e.*, 'great totality of what is on high,' and Kishar-gal, *i.e.*, 'great totality of what is below,' Enshar and Ninshar, *i.e.*, 'lord' and 'mistress,' respectively, of 'all there is,' Du'ar and Da'ur, forms of a stem which may signify 'perpetuity,' Alala, *i.e.*, 'strength,' and a consort Belili. Lakhmu and Lakhamu are also found in the list. While some of the names are quite obscure, and the composition of the list is due to the scholastic spirit emanating from the schools of theology, the fact that some of the deities, as Alala, Belili, Lakhmu, and Lakhamu, occur in incantations shows that the theologians were guided in part by dimmed traditions of some deities that were worshipped prior to the ones whose cult became prominent in historic times. Anshar, Alala, Belili, Lakhmu, and Du'ar were such deities. To each of these an associate was given, in accord with the established doctrine of 'duality' that characterizes the more advanced of the ancient Semitic cults in general. Others, like Anshar-gal and Enshar, seem to be pure abstractions — perhaps only 'variants' of Anshar, and the number ten may have some mystical significance that escapes us. So much, at all events, seems certain that even the old Babylonian pantheon, as revealed by the oldest historical texts, represents a comparatively advanced stage of the religion when some still older gods had already yielded to others and a system was already in part produced which left out of consideration these older deities. This is

---

[1] IIR. 54, no. 3.

[2] For a different Interpretation of the phrase, see Jensen, *Kosmologie*, pp. 273, 274.

indicated by the occurrence of the triad Anu, Bel, and Ea as early as the days of Gudea,[1] and it is this triad which in the creation epic follows upon the older series symbolized by Anshar and Kishar. The later 'theology' found a solution of the problem by assuming four series of deities represented by Apsu and Tiâmat, by Lakhmu and Lakhamu, by Anshar and Kishar, and by the triad Anu, Bel, and Ea.

In a vague way, as we have seen, Apsu and Tiâmat are the progenitors of Lakhmu and Lakhamu. The priority, again, of Lakhmu and Lakhamu, as well as of Anshar and Kishar, is expressed by making them 'ancestors' of Anu, Bel and Ea. While in the list above referred to, Lakhmu and Lakhamu are put in a class with Anshar and Kishar, in the creation epic they form a separate class, and Delitzsch has justly recognized,[2] in this separation, the intention of the compilers to emphasize an advance in the evolution of chaos to order, which is the keynote of the Babylonian cosmology. Lakhmu and Lakhamu represent the 'monster' world where creatures are produced in strange confusion, whereas Anshar and Kishar indicate a division of the universe into two *distinct* and sharply defined parts. The splitting of 'chaos' is the first step towards its final disappearance.

The creation of Anshar and Kishar marks indeed the beginning of a severe conquest which ends in the overthrow of Tiâmat, and while in the present form of the epic, the contest is not decided before Anu, Bel, and Ea and the chief deities of the historic pantheon are created, one can see traces of an earlier form of the tradition in which Anshar — perhaps with some associates — is the chief figure in the strife.

Of the first tablet, we have two further fragments supplementing one another, in which the beginnings of this terrible conflict are described. With Apsu and Tiâmat there are associated a

---

[1] See p. 107.
[2] *Babylonische Weltschöpfungsepos*, p. 94.

variety of monsters who prepare themselves for the fray. The existence of these associates shows that the 'epic' does not aim to account for the real origin of things, but only for the origin of the *order* of the universe. At the beginning there was chaos, but 'chaos,' so far from representing emptiness (as came to be the case under a monotheistic conception of the universe) was on the contrary marked by a superabundant fullness.

Through Alexander Polyhistor,[1] as already mentioned, we obtain a satisfactory description of this period of chaos as furnished by Berosus. At the time when all was darkness and water, there flourished strange monsters, human beings with wings, beings with two heads, male and female, hybrid formations, half-man, half-animal, with horns of rams and horses' hoofs, bulls with human faces, dogs with fourfold bodies ending in fish tails, horses with heads of dogs, and various other monstrosities.

This account of Berosus is now confirmed by the cuneiform records. The associates of Tiâmat are described in a manner that leaves no doubt as to their being the monsters referred to. We are told that

> Ummu-Khubur,[2] the creator of everything, added
> Strong warriors, creating great serpents,
> Sharp of tooth, merciless in attack.
> With poison in place of blood, she filled their bodies.
> Furious vipers she clothed with terror,
> Fitted them out with awful splendor, made them high of stature (?)
> That their countenance might inspire terror and arouse horror,
> Their bodies inflated, their attack irresistible.

[1] Cory's *Ancient Fragments*, p. 58.
[2] An epithet descriptive of Tiâmat. "Ummu" is "mother" and "khubur" signifies "hollow"; "mother of the hollow" would be a poetic expression for "source of the deep," and an appropriate term to apply to Tiâmat. It has nothing to do with Omoroka. The latter, as Wright has shown, is a corruption of "O Marduk" (*Zeits. f. Assyr.* x. 71–74).

> She set up basilisks (?) great serpents and monsters[1]
> A great monster, a mad dog, a scorpion-man
> A raging monster, a fish-man, a great bull,
> Carrying merciless weapons, not dreading battle.

In all, eleven monstrous beings are created by Tiâmat for the great conquest. At their head she places a being Kingu, whom she raises to the dignity of a consort.

The formal installation of Kingu is described as follows:

> She raised Kingu among them to be their chief.
> To march at the head of the forces, to lead the assembly.
> To command the weapons to strike, to give the orders for the fray.
> To be the first in war, supreme in triumph.
> She ordained him and clothed him with authority (?).

Tiâmat then addresses Kingu directly:

> Through my word to thee, I have made thee the greatest among the gods.
> The rule over all the gods I have placed in thy hand.
> The greatest shalt thou be, thou, my consort, my only one.

Tiâmat thereupon

> Gives him the tablets of fate, hangs them on his breast, and dismisses him.
> 'Thy command be invincible, thy order authoritative.'[2]

The plan of procedure, it would appear, is the result of a council of war held by Apsu and Tiâmat, who feel themselves powerless to carry on the contest by themselves. The portion of the tablet[3] in which this council is recounted is in so bad a condition that but little can be made out of it. Associated with Apsu and Tiâmat in council, is a being Mummu, and since Damascius expressly notes on the direct authority of

---

[1] The word used is Lakhami, the plural of Lakhamu.

[2] This scene, the description of the monsters and the installation of Kingu, occurs four times in the 'Epic.' See p. 424.

[3] Delitzsch, *Babylonische Weltschöpfungsepos*, p. 25.

Berosus that Apsu and Tiâmat produced a son Moumis,[1] there is every reason to believe that Mummu represents this offspring. In the subsequent narrative, however, neither Apsu nor Mummu play any part. Tiâmat has transferred to Kingu and the eleven monsters all authority, and it is only after they are defeated that Tiâmat — but Tiâmat alone — enters the fray.

The rage of Tiâmat is directed against Anshar, Kishar, and their offspring. Anu, Bel, and Ea, while standing at the head of the latter, are not the only gods introduced. When the contest begins, all the great gods and also the minor ones are in existence.

The cause of Tiâmat's rage is indicated, though vaguely, in the portions preserved. In the opening lines of the epic there is a reference to the time 'when fates were not yet decided.' The decision of fates is in the Babylonian theology one of the chief functions of the gods. It constitutes the mainspring of their power. To decide fates is practically to control the arrangement of the universe — to establish order. It is this function which arouses the natural opposition of Tiâmat and her brood, for Tiâmat feels that once the gods in control, her sway must come to an end. On the part of the gods there is great terror. They are anxious to conciliate Tiâmat and are not actuated by any motives of rivalry. Order is not aggressive. It is chaos which manifests opposition to 'order.' In the second tablet of the series, Anshar sends his son Anu with a message to Tiâmat:

> Go and step before Tiâmat.
> May her liver be pacified, her heart softened.

Anu obeys, but at the sight of Tiâmat's awful visage takes flight. It is unfortunate that the second tablet is so badly preserved. We are dependent largely upon conjecture for what

[1] Cory, *ib.* p. 92.

follows the failure of Anu's mission. From references in subsequent tablets, it seems certain that Anshar sends out Ea as a second messenger and that Ea also fails. Tiâmat is determined upon destroying the gods, or at least upon keeping from them the 'decision of fates.' Anshar, it will be seen, stands at the head of the pantheon, and it seems natural that he, and not one of his offspring, should be the final victor. This indeed appears to have been the original form of the myth or at least one form of it. In a second form it was Bel to whom the victory was ascribed, and this Bel of the triad, we have seen, was En-lil, the chief god of Nippur; but both Anshar and Bel must give way to the patron deity of the city of Babylon — Marduk. Anshar-Ashur, the head of the Assyrian pantheon, could not be tolerated by the Babylonian priests as a power superior to Marduk. On the other hand, Anshar could not be set aside, for he survived in popular tradition. The result is a compromise. Marduk gains the victory over Tiâmat, but is commissioned to do so by the assembly of the gods, including Anshar. As for the older Bel, he voluntarily transfers to Marduk his name. In this way, the god Bel of the triad becomes one with Marduk.

Perhaps in one religious center and at a time when Ea was the chief god, still another version existed which assigned the triumph to Ea, for as will be pointed out, traditions waver between assigning to Ea or to Bel-Marduk so fundamental a function as the creation of mankind. In short, the present form of the creation epic is 'eclectic' and embodies what the Germans call a *tendenz*. To each of the great gods, Anshar, Anu, Bel, and Ea, some part in the contest is assigned, but the greatest rôle belongs to Marduk.

The second tablet closes with Anshar's decision to send his son Marduk against Tiâmat:

> Marduk heard the word of his father.
> His heart rejoiced and to his father he spoke.

THE COSMOLOGY OF THE BABYLONIANS.

With joyous heart he is ready to proceed to the contest, but he at once makes good his claim to supreme control in case he is victorious. He addresses the assembled gods:

> When I shall have become your avenger,
> Binding Tiâmat and saving your life,
> Then come in a body,
> In Ubshu-kenna,[1] let yourselves down joyfully,
> My authority instead of yours will assume control,
> Unchangeable shall be whatever I do,
> Irrevocable and irresistible, be the command of my lips.

The declaration foreshadows the result.

The third tablet is taken up with the preliminaries for the great contest, and is interesting chiefly because of the insight it affords us into Babylonian methods of literary composition. Anshar sends Gaga[2] to the hostile camp with the formal announcement of Marduk's readiness to take up the cause of the gods. Gaga does not face Tiâmat directly, but leaves the message with Lakhmu and Lakhamu:

> Go Gaga, messenger (?) joy of my liver,
> To Lakhmu and Lakhamu I will send thee.

The message proper begins as follows:

> Anshar your son has sent me,
> The desire of his heart he has entrusted to me.
> Tiâmat, our mother is full of hate towards us,
> With all her might she is bitterly enraged.

The eleven associates that Tiâmat has ranged on her side are again enumerated, together with the appointment of Kingu as chief of the terror-inspiring army. Gaga comes to Lakhmu

---

[1] "The chamber of fates" where Marduk sits on New Year's Day and decides the fate of mankind for the ensuing year. Jensen and Zimmern read *upshugina*, but see Delitzsch, *Babylonische Weltschöpfungsepos*, p. 135.

[2] The deity is mentioned by Sennacherib (Meissner-Rost, *Bauinschriften*, p. 108). See above, p. 238.

and Lakhamu and delivers the message verbatim, so that altogether this portion of the narrative is repeated no less than four times.[1] The same tendency towards repetition is met with in the Gilgamesh epic and in the best of the literary productions of Babylonia. It may be ascribed to the influence exerted by the religious hymns and incantations where repetition, as we have seen, is also common, though serving a good purpose.

The message concludes:

> I sent Anu, he could not endure her[2] presence.
> Ea[3] was afraid and took to flight.
> Marduk has stepped forward, the chief of the gods, your son,
> To proceed against Tiâmat, he has set his mind.

Marduk's declaration is then repeated.

Upon hearing the message Lakhmu and Lakhamu and "all the Igigi"[4] are distressed, but are powerless to avert the coming disaster. The formal declaration of war having been sent, the followers of Anshar assemble at a meal which is realistically described:

> They ate bread, they drank wine.
> The sweet wine took away their senses.
> They became drunk, and their bodies swelled up.

With this description the third tablet closes.

The meal symbolizes the solemn gathering of the gods. At its conclusion, so it would seem, Marduk is formally installed as the leader to proceed against Tiâmat. The gods vie with one another in showering honors upon Marduk. They encourage him for the fight by praising his unique powers:

[1] In the first tablet, in the second in connection with the mission of Anu, and twice in the third in connection with Marduk's visit.
[2] Tiâmat's presence.
[3] Called Nudimmud. Delitzsch, *Babylonische Weltschöpfungsepos*, p. 99, questions the identity with Ea, but his skepticism is unwarranted, though the title is also used of Bel.
[4] Here used to comprise the army of Tiâmat.

> Thou art honored among the great gods,
> Thy destiny is unique, thy command is Anu.[1]
> Marduk, thou art honored among the great gods,
> Thy destiny is unique, thy command is Anu,
> Henceforth thy order is absolute.
> To elevate and to lower is in thy hands,
> What issues from thee is fixed, thy order cannot be opposed,
> None among the gods may trespass upon thy dominion.
>
> . . . .
>
> Thy weapons will never be vanquished; they will shatter thy enemies.
> O lord! grant life to him who trusts in thee,
> But destroy the life of the god who plots evil.

As a proof of the power thus entrusted to Marduk, the gods give the latter a 'sign.' Marduk performs a miracle. A garment is placed in the midst of the gods.

> Command that the dress disappear!
> Then command that the dress return!

Marduk proceeds to the test.

> As he gave the command, the dress disappeared.
> He spoke again and the dress was there.

This 'sign,' which reminds one of Yahwe's signs to Moses as a proof of the latter's power,[2] is to be regarded as an indication that "destruction and creation" are in Marduk's hands. The gods rejoice at the exhibition of Marduk's power. In chorus they exclaim, "Marduk is king." The insignia of royalty, throne, sceptre, and authority are conferred upon him.

> Now go against Tiâmat, cut off her life,
> Let the winds carry her blood to hidden regions.[3]

Marduk thereupon fashions his weapons for the fray. Myth and realism are strangely intertwined in the description of these

---
[1] *I.e.*, thy power is equal to that of Anu.
[2] Exod. iv. 2–8; other parallels might be adduced.
[3] *I.e.*, far off.

weapons. Bow and quiver, the lance and club are mentioned, together with the storm and the lightning flash. In addition to this he

> Constructs a net wherewith to enclose the life of Tiâmat.
> The four winds he grasped so that she could not escape.[1]
> The south and north winds, the east and west winds
> He brought to the net, which was the gift of his father Anu.

His outfit is not yet complete.

> He creates a destructive wind, a storm, a hurricane,
> Making of the four winds, seven[2] destructive and fatal ones;
> Then he let loose the winds he created, the seven,
> To destroy the life[3] of Tiâmat, they followed after him.

Marduk, taking his most powerful weapon in his hand,[4] mounts his chariot, which is driven by fiery steeds. The picture thus furnished of the god, standing upright in his chariot, with his weapons hung about him and the seven winds following in his wake, is most impressive.

He makes straight for the hostile camp. The sight of the god inspires terror on all sides.

> The lord comes nearer with his eye fixed upon Tiâmat,
> Piercing with his glance (?) Kingu her consort.

Kingu starts back in alarm. He cannot endure the 'majestic halo' which surrounds Marduk. Kingu's associates — the monsters — are terrified at their leader's discomfiture. Tiâmat alone does not lose her courage.

Marduk, brandishing his great weapon, addresses Tiâmat:

> Why hast thou set thy mind upon stirring up destructive contest?

---

[1] *I.e.*, that a wind might not carry her off.

[2] Adding three to the ordinary winds from the four directions.

[3] For the explanation of the term used in the original — *kirbish* — see Delitzsch's excellent remarks, *Babylonische Weltschöpfungsepos*. pp. 132-134.

[4] Lit., 'storm,' — perhaps the thunderbolt, as Delitzsch suggests.

He reproaches her for the hatred she has shown towards the gods, and boldly calls her out to the contest:

> Stand up! I and thou, come let us fight.

Tiâmat's rage at this challenge is superbly pictured:

> When Tiâmat heard these words
> She acted as possessed, her senses left her;
> Tiâmat shrieked wild and loud,
> Trembling and shaking down to her foundations.
> She pronounced an incantation, uttered her sacred formula.

Marduk is undismayed:

> Then Tiâmat and Marduk, chief of the gods, advanced towards one another.
> They advanced to the contest, drew nigh for fight.

The fight and discomfiture of Tiâmat are next described:

> The lord spread out his net in order to enclose her.
> The destructive wind, which was behind him, he sent forth into her face.
> As Tiâmat opened her mouth full wide,
> He[1] drove in the destructive wind, so that she could not close her lips.
> The strong winds inflated her stomach.
> Her heart was beset,[2] she opened still wider her mouth,[3]
> He seized the spear and plunged it into her stomach,
> He pierced her entrails, he tore through her heart,
> He seized hold of her and put an end to her life,
> He threw down her carcass and stepped upon her.

The method employed by Marduk is so graphically described that no comment is necessary. After having vanquished Tiâmat, the valiant Marduk attacks her associates. They try to flee, but he captures them all — including Kingu — without much difficulty and puts them into his great net. Most important of

---

[1] Marduk.
[2] She lost her reason.
[3] Gasping, as it were, for breath.

all, he tears the tablets of fate from Kingu and places them on his breast. This act marks the final victory. Henceforth, the gods with Marduk — and no longer Tiâmat and her brood — decree the fate of the universe. There is great rejoicing among the gods, who heap presents and offerings upon Marduk. As the vanquisher of chaos, Marduk is naturally singled out to be the establisher of the fixed form and order of the universe. The close of the fourth tablet describes this work of the god, and the subject is continued in the following ones. Unfortunately, these tablets are badly preserved, so that we are far from having a complete view of the various acts of Marduk. He begins by taking the carcass of Tiâmat and cutting it in half.

> He cuts her like one does a flattened fish into two halves.

Previous to this he had trampled upon her and smashed her skull, as we are expressly told, so that the comparison of the monster, thus pressed out, to a flattened fish is appropriate.

He splits her lengthwise.

> The one half he fashioned as a covering for the heavens,
> Attaching a bolt and placing there a guardian,
> With orders not to permit the waters to come out.

It is evident that the canopy of heaven is meant. Such is the enormous size of Tiâmat that one-half of her body flattened out so as to serve as a curtain, is stretched across the heavens to keep the 'upper waters'—'the waters above the firmament' as the Book of Genesis puts it — from coming down. To ensure the execution of this design, a bolt is drawn in front of the canopy and a guardian placed there, like at a city wall, to prevent any one or anything from coming out.

This act corresponds closely to the creation of a "firmament" in the first chapter of Genesis. The interpretation is borne out by the statement of Alexander Polyhistor who, quoting from Berosus, states that out of one-half of Tiâmat the heavens were made.[1] The further statement that out of the other half the earth was fashioned is not definitely stated in our version of the creation. The narrative proceeds as follows:

He passed through the heavens, he inspected the expanse.[2]

To understand this phrase, we must consider the general character of the "epic," which is, as we have already seen, a composite production, formed of popular elements and of more advanced speculations. The popular element is the interpretation of the storms and rains that regularly visit the Euphrates Valley before the summer season sets in, as a conflict between a monster and the solar deity Marduk. After a struggle, winds at last drive the waters back; Tiâmat is vanquished by the entrance of the 'bad wind' into her body. The sun appears in the heavens and runs across the expanse, passing in his course over the entire vault. The conflict, which in the scholastic system of the theologians is placed at the beginning of things, is in reality a phenomenon of annual occurrence. The endeavor to make Marduk more than what he originally was — a solar deity — leads to the introduction of a variety of episodes that properly belong to a different class of deities. For all that, the orignal rôle of Marduk is not obscured. Marduk's passage across the heavens is a trace of the popular phases of the nature myth, and while in one sense, it is appropriately introduced after the fashioning of the expanse, it more properly follows immediately upon the conflict with Tiâmat. In short, we have reached a point in the narrative where the nature myth symbolizing the annual succession of the seasons blends with a cosmological system which is the product of comparatively advanced schools of thought, in such a manner as to render it difficult to draw the line where myth ends and cosmological system begins. For

[1] Cory's *Ancient Fragments*, p. 49.
[2] Lit., 'places,' here used as a synonym for 'heavens,' as an Assyrian commentator expressly states. See Delitzsch's remarks (*Babylonische Weltschöpfungsepos*, p. 147) against Jensen's and Zimmern's interpretation.

the moment, the nature myth controls the course of the narrative. The sun, upon running its course across the heavens, appears to drop into the great ocean, which the Babylonians, in common with many ancient nations, imagined to surround and to pass underneath the earth.

Hence the next act undertaken by Marduk is the regulation of the course of this subterranean sea. The name given to this sea was Apsu. Marduk however does not create the Apsu. It is in existence at the beginning of things, but he places it under the control of Ea.

> In front of Apsu, he prepared the dwelling of Nu-dimmud.[1]

This Apsu, as we learn from other sources,[2] flows on all sides of the earth, and since it also fills the hollow under the earth, the latter in reality rests upon the Apsu. Ea is frequently called "the lord of Apsu," but the creation epic, in assigning to Marduk the privilege of preparing the dwelling of Ea, reverses the true order of things, which may still be seen in the common belief that made Marduk the son of Ea. Marduk, the sun rising up out of the ocean, becomes the offspring of Ea, and even the political supremacy of Marduk could not set aside the prerogatives of Ea in the popular mind. In the cosmological system, however, as developed in the schools, such an attempt was made. While recognizing the 'deep' as the domain of Ea, the theologians saved Marduk's honor by having him take a part in fixing Ea's dwelling and in determining its limitations.

With the carcass of Tiâmat stretched across the upper firmament and safely guarded, and with the Apsu under control, the way is clear for the formation of the earth. This act in the drama of creation is referred to in the following lines, though in a manner, that is not free from obscurity. The earth is pictured as a great structure placed over the Apsu and corresponding in dimension with it — at least in one direction.

---

[1] *Ie.*, Ea. See above, p. 424, note 3.
[2] The complete proof is brought by Jensen, *Kosmologie*, pp. 246–253.

> The lord measured out the structure of Apsu.
> Corresponding to it, he fashioned a great structure [1] Esharra.

Esharra is a poetical designation of the earth and signifies, as Jensen has satisfactorily shown, "house of fullness" [2] or "house of fertility." The earth is regarded as a great structure, and placed as it is over the Apsu, its size is dependent upon the latter. Its measurement from one end to the other cannot exceed the width of the Apsu, nor can it be any narrower. The ends of the earth span the great Apsu. The following line specifies the shape given to Esharra:

> The great structure Esharra, which he made as a heavenly vault.

The earth is not a sphere according to Babylonian ideas, but a hollow hemisphere having an appearance exactly like the vault of heaven, but placed in position beneath the heavenly canopy. As a hemisphere it suggests the picture of a mountain, rising at one end, mounting to a culminating point, and descending at the other end. Hence by the side of Esharra, another name by which the earth was known was Ekur, that is, 'the mountain house.'

Diodorus Seculus, in speaking of the Babylonian cosmology, employs a happy illustration. He says that according to Babylonian notions the world is a "boat turned upside down." The kind of boat meant is, as Lenormant recognized,[3] the deep-bottomed round skiff with curved edges that is still used for carrying loads across and along the Euphrates and Tigris, the same kind of boat that the compilers of Genesis had in view when describing Noah's Ark. The appearance in outline thus presented by the three divisions of the universe — the heavens, the earth, and the waters — would be that of two heavy rain-

---

[1] To render the word used as "Palace" (so Delitzsch), while not incorrect, is somewhat misleading.
[2] *Kosmologie*, p. 199.
[3] *Magie und Wahrsagekunst der Chaldaer*, p. 163.

bows, one beneath the other at some distance apart, resting upon a large body of water that flows around the horizons of both rainbows, and also fills the hollow of the second one.[1] The upper 'rainbow' is formed by one-half of the carcass of Tiâmat stretched across in semi-circular shape; the lower one is the great structure Esharra made by Marduk, while the Apsu underneath is the dwelling of Ea. The creation epic, it may be noted once more, takes much for granted. Its chief aim being to glorify Marduk, but little emphasis is laid upon details of interest to us. The parcelling out of these three divisions among Anu, Bel, and Ea is therefore merely alluded to in the closing line of the fourth tablet:

> He established the districts[2] of Anu, Bel, and Ea.

The narrative assumes what we know from other sources, that the heavens constitute the domain of Anu, Esharra belongs to Bel, while Apsu belongs to Ea.

The mention of the triad takes us away from popular myth to the scholastic system as devised by the theologians. The establishment of the triad in full control marks the introduction of fixed order into the universe. All traces of Tiâmat have disappeared. Anu, Bel, and Ea symbolize the eternal laws of the universe.

There are, as we have seen, two factors involved in the rôle assigned to Marduk in the version of the creation epic under consideration,—one the original character of the god as a solar deity, the other the later position of the god as the head of the Babylonian pantheon. In the 'epic,' the fight of Marduk with Tiâmat belongs to Marduk as a solar deity. The myth is based, as was above suggested,[3] upon the annual phenomenon witnessed in Babylonia when the whole valley is flooded and

---

[1] See the illustration in Jensen's *Kosmologie*, pl. 3.
[2] The word used also means "cities." A Babylonian district is naught but an extended city.   [3] See p. 429.

storms sweep across the plains. The sun is obscured. A conflict is going on between the waters and storms, on the one hand, and the sun, on the other hand. The latter finally is victorious. Marduk subdues Tiâmat, fixes limitations to the 'upper and lower waters,' and triumphantly marches across the heavens from one end to the other, as general overseer.

This nature myth was admirably adapted to serve as the point of departure for the enlargement of the rôle of Marduk, rendered necessary by the advancement of the god to the head of the pantheon. Everything had to be ascribed to Marduk. Not merely humanity, but the gods also had to acknowledge, and acknowledge freely, the supremacy of Marduk.

The solar deity thus becomes a power at whose command the laws of the universe are established, the earth created and all that is on it. In thus making Marduk the single creator, the theologians were as much under the influence of Marduk's political supremacy, as they helped to confirm that supremacy by their system. With this object in view, the annual phenomenon was transformed into an account of what happened 'once upon a time.'

What impressed the thinkers most in the universe was the regular working of the laws of nature. Ascribing these laws to Marduk, they naturally pictured the beginnings of things as a lawless period. Into the old and popular Marduk-Tiâmat nature myth, certain touches were thus introduced that changed its entire character. This once done, it was a comparatively simple matter to follow up the conflict of Marduk and Tiâmat by a series of acts on Marduk's part, completing the work of general creation. The old nature myth ended with the conquest of the rains and storm and the establishment of the sun's regular course, precisely as the deluge story in Genesis, which contains echoes of the Marduk-Tiâmat myth, ends with the promulgation of the fixed laws of the universe.[1]

[1] Gen. viii. 22.

What follows upon this episode in the Babylonian epic is the elaboration of the central theme, worked out in the schools of Babylonian thought and intended, on the one hand, to illustrate Marduk's position as creator and, on the other, to formulate the details of the cosmological system.

With the fifth tablet, therefore, we leave the domain of popular myth completely and pass into the domain of cosmological speculation. Fragmentary as the fifth tablet is, enough is preserved to show that it assumes the perfection of the zodiacal system of the Babylonian schools and the complete regulation[1] of the calendar. In this zodiacal system, as has been intimated and as will be more fully set forth in a special chapter, the planets and stars are identified with the gods. The gods have their 'stations' and their 'pictures' in the starry sky. The stars are the 'drawings' or 'designs of heaven.' It is Marduk again who is represented as arranging these stations:

> He established the stations for the great gods.[2]
> The stars, their likeness,[3] he set up as constellations.[4]
> He fixed the year and marked the divisions.[5]
> The twelve months he divided among three stars.
> From the beginning of the year till the close (?)
> He established the station of Nibir[6] to indicate their boundary.
> So that there might be no deviation nor wandering away from the course
> He established with him,[7] the stations of Bel and Ea.

An epitome of the astronomical science of the Babylonians is comprised in these lines. The gods being identified with stars

---

[1] See above, p. 370, and chapter xxli.

[2] *Ie.*, for each of the great gods.   [3] *Ie.*, of the gods.

[4] A particular group of stars — the *mashi* stars — is mentioned, but the term seems to be used in a rather general sense. I cannot share Delitzsch's extreme skepticism with regard to the interpretation of the fifth tablet. Jensen seems to have solved the chief difficulties.

[5] Jensen and Zimmern interpret "he drew the pictures," referring the phrase to the contours of the stars; but the parallelism speaks in favor of connecting the words with the "year." The divisions of the year or seasons seem to be meant.

[6] *Ie.*, the planet Marduk, or Jupiter.   [7] *Ie.*, with Nibir.

and each of the latter having its place in the heavens 'to establish the stations for the great gods' is equivalent to putting the stars in position. The regulation of the year forms part of the astronomical science. The three stars that constitute 'divisions' to aid in marking off the months are Nibir, Bel, and Ea. That the Babylonians had such a system as is here outlined is confirmed by Diodorus Seculus.[1] The position of Nibir, or Jupiter, whose course keeps closer to the ecliptic than that of any other planet, served as an important guide in calendrical calculations. The stars are represented as clinging to their course through maintaining their relationship to Nibir, while at the side of Nibir and as additional guides, Bel is identified with the north pole of the equator and Ea with a star in the extreme southern heavens, to be sought for, perhaps, in the constellation Argo. The description concludes:

> He attached large gates to both sides,
> Made the bolt secure to the left and right.

The heavens are thus made firm by two gates, fastened with bolts and placed at either end. Through one of these gates the sun passes out in the morning, and at evening enters into the other. But the most important body in the heavens is the moon. Its functions are described in an interesting way:

> In the midst[2] he made the zenith[3] (?)
> Nannar[4] he caused to go forth and handed over to him[5] the night.
> He fixed him[5] as the luminary of night to mark off the days.

The passage is made clear by a reference to the Book of Genesis, i. 16, where we are told that the moon was created 'for the rule of night.' A distinction between the Biblical and the cuneiform cosmology at this point is no less significant. While

---

[1] See Jensen, *Kosmologie*, p. 354. George Smith already interpreted the passage in this way. [2] *I.e.*, of the heavens. Delitzsch renders "Schwerpunkt."
[3] Text *elâti*. Jensen, Zimmern, and Halevy translate "zenith," but Delitzsch questions this. [4] The moon-god. [5] *I.e.*, the moon.

according to Babylonian ideas, the moon alone, or at most the moon with the stars, regulates the days, the Hebrew version makes the moon and sun together the basis for the regulation of the 'days and years.' The sun according to Babylonian notions does not properly belong to the heavens, since it passes daily beyond the limits of the latter. The sun, therefore, plays an insignificant part in the calendrical system in comparison with the moon.

Marduk addresses the moon, specifying its duties, what position it is to occupy towards the sun at certain periods during the monthly course, and the like. The tablet at this point becomes defective, and before the address comes to an end, we are left entirely in the lurch. To speculate as to the further contents of the fifth tablet and of the sixth (of which nothing has as yet been found) seems idle. Zimmern supposes that after the heavenly phenomena had been disposed of, the formation of the dry land and of the seas was taken up, and Delitzsch is of the opinion that in the sixth tablet the creation of plants and trees and animals was also recounted. I venture to question whether the creation of the 'dry land and seas' was specifically mentioned. Esharra, the earth, is in existence and the Apsu appears to include all waters, but that the epic treated of the creation of plant and animal life and then of the creation of man is eminently likely. We have indeed a fragment of a tablet[1] in which the creation of the 'cattle of the field, beasts of the field, and creeping things of the field' is referred to; but since it is the 'gods who in unison' are there represented as having created the animal kingdom, it is hardly likely that the fragment forms part of our 'epic' in which all deeds are ascribed to Marduk. It belongs in all probability to a different cosmological version, but so much can be concluded from it, that the Babylonians ascribed the creation of animals to some divine power or powers; and that therefore our 'epic'

---

[1] Published by Delitzsch, *Assyrische Lesestücke* (3d edition), p. 94.

must have contained a section in which this act was assigned to Marduk.

A similar variation exists with reference to the tradition of the creation of mankind. There are distinct traces that the belief was current in parts of Babylonia which made Ea the creation of mankind.[1] Ea, it will be recalled, is the 'god of humanity' *par excellence*, and yet in the seventh (and probably closing) tablet of the series, Marduk is spoken of as the one "who created mankind."[2]

Variant traditions of this kind point to the existence of various centers of culture and thought in rivalry with one another. The great paean to Marduk would have been sadly incomplete had it not contained an account of the creation of mankind — the crowning work of the universe — by the head of the Babylonian pantheon. It is possible, therefore, that a tablet containing the address of a deity to mankind belongs to our series[3] and embodies orders and warnings given by Marduk after the creation of man, just as he addresses the moon after establishing it in the heavens. Purity of heart is enjoined as pleasing to the deity. Prayer and supplication and prostration are also commanded. It is said that

> Fear of god begets mercy,
> Sacrifice prolongs life,
> And prayer dissolves sin.

The tablet continues in this strain. It is perhaps not the kind of address that we would expect Marduk to make after the act of creation, but for the present we must content ourselves with this conjecture, as also with the supposition that the creation of mankind constituted the final act in the great drama in which Marduk is the hero.

When Marduk's work is finished, the Igigi gather around him in adoration. This scene is described in a tablet which for

---
[1] See the proof as put together by Jensen, *Kosmologie*, pp. 293, 294.
[2] Line 15.   [3] So Delitzsch, *Babylonische Weltschöpfungsepos*, pp. 19, 20.

the present we may regard[1] as the close of the series. No less than fifty names are bestowed upon him by the gods, the number fifty corresponding according to some traditions to the number of the Igigi. Marduk accordingly absorbs the qualities of all the gods. Such is the purpose of this tablet. The diction is at times exceedingly impressive.

God of pure life, they called [him] in the third place, the bearer of purification.
God of favorable wind,[2] lord of response[3] and of mercy,
Creator of abundance and fullness, granter of blessings,
Who increases the things that were small,
Whose favorable wind we experienced in sore distress.
Thus let them[4] speak and glorify and be obedient to him.

The gods recall with gratitude Marduk's service in vanquishing Tiâmat. Marduk is also praised for the mercy he showed towards the associates of Tiâmat, whom he merely captured without putting them to death.

As the god of the shining crown in the fourth place, let them [*i.e.*, mankind] exalt him.
The lord of cleansing incantation, the restorer of the dead to life,
Who showed mercy towards the captured gods,
Removed the yoke from the gods who were hostile to him.

A later fancy identified the 'captured gods' with eleven of the heavenly constellations.[5]

Mankind is enjoined not to forget Marduk

Who created mankind out of kindness towards them,
The merciful one, with whom is the power of giving life.
May his deeds remain and never be forgotten
By humanity, created by his hands.

[1] Following Delitzsch, *Babylonische Weltschöpfungsepos*, pp. 20, 21. I pass over two fragments which Delitzsch adds to our 'epic.' They are not sufficiently clear to be utilized for our purposes. Delitzsch may be right with regard to no. 20, but if so, it forms part or another version of the Marduk-Tiâmat episode. No. 19, treating of the bow of Marduk (?), does not seem to belong to our series.
[2] A standing phrase for "favor" in general.
[3] To prayer. [4] The gods or the Igigi.
[5] See p. 486 and Gunkel's note, *Schöpfung und Chaos*, p. 26.

Among other names assigned to him are 'the one who knows the heart of the gods,' 'who gathers the gods together,' 'who rules in truth and justice.' In allusion again to his contest with Tiâmat, he is called 'the destroyer of the enemy and of all wicked ones,' 'who frustrates their plans.'

With the help of a pun upon his having 'pierced' Tiâmat, he is called Nibir, *i.e.*, the planet Jupiter.[1]

> Nibir be his name, who took hold of the life of Tiâmat.
> The course of the stars of heaven may he direct.
> May he pasture all of the gods like sheep.[2]

But the climax is reached when, upon hearing what the Igigi have done, the great gods, father Bel and father Ea cheerfully bestow their own names upon Marduk.

> Because he created the heavens and formed the earth
> 'Lord of Lands'[3] father Bel called his name.
> When he heard of all the names that the Igigi bestowed
> Ea's liver rejoiced
> That they had bestowed exalted names upon his son.
> "He as I — Ea be his name.
> The control of my commands be entrusted to him.
> To him my orders shall be transmitted."

The historical background to this transference of the name of Bel has been dwelt upon in a previous chapter.[4] This "Marduk hymn" is to justify the transference of the rôle of the older Bel of Nippur to the younger god Marduk. Throughout the tablet describing the contest of Marduk with Tiâmat, Marduk is called Bel,[5] and while this name is used in the generic sense of "lord," the transference of the name of Bel to Marduk is evidently introduced to account for his assuming the prerog-

---

[1] See above, p. 434. The play is between Nibir (as though from the stem *ebêru*) and *itebbiru* ("he pierced"), a form of *ebêru*, and meaning 'to pass through.'

[2] This metaphor is carried over into astronomical science. The planets are known as "wandering sheep." See p. 459.   [3] *Bêl matâte*.   [4] See p. 118.

[5] Similarly in another version of the contest published by Delitzsch, *Assyr. Wörterbuch*, p. 390.

atives belonging to another god. The original 'lord' was En-lil of Nippur. The sacred significance of ancient Nippur made its patron deity the most important rival of Marduk. Bel could not be disposed of as Ea, who by virtue of his mythological relationships to Marduk — a solar deity — could be retained as the father of Marduk. There was nothing left but for Marduk to take the place of Bel. The constant introduction of the epithet 'Bel' into the Tiâmat story points to an older version in which Bel was the hero. In popular traditions, Bel continued to be pictured as armed with mighty weapons,[1] and, though ready to inflict severe punishment for disobedience to his commands, he engages in contests for the benefit of mankind. The earth being his special sphere of action, what more natural than that he should have had a prominent share in adapting it as a habitation for mankind. He would be directly interested in fighting the powers of darkness.

In the weapons that Marduk employs, particularly the lightning and the winds which belong to an atmospheric god rather than a solar deity, we may discern traces of the older narrative which has been combined with the Marduk-Tiâmat nature myth.[2] It may be that Kingu represents Bel's particular rival. In the narrative, it will be recalled, the contest with Tiâmat is sharply separated from that with Kingu and his associates. The division that thus suggests itself between Marduk and Tiâmat, on the one hand, Bel and the monsters with Kingu at their head, on the other, may certainly be termed a natural one. The solar deity Marduk disposed of the storms and rains of the winter, whereas, a god of "that which is below,"[3] *i.e.*, the earth and the atmosphere immediately above the earth, would appropriately be represented as ridding the earth of the monsters in order to

---

[1] See p. 54.

[2] Tiele (*Gesch. der Religion im Alterthum*, I. 176) assigns to Marduk a double character, making him both a god of light and a god of storms, but I venture to think that the latter attribute represents the transference of En-lil's power to Marduk.

[3] So Bel is called in contrast to Anu. See p. 53.

prepare it as a habitation for mankind. Ea was not such a serious rival to Marduk as the older Bel. Political rivalry between Nippur and Babylonia probably contributed towards the disposition to have Marduk completely absorb the rôle of Bel, whereas, this rivalry being absent in the case of Eridu (the original seat of Ea worship) and Babylon, the mythological relations between Ea and Marduk led, as already pointed out, in a perfectly natural way to making Marduk the son of Ea. Still, while cheerfully acknowledged by Ea as his equal, it is evident that in older traditions Ea was far superior to Marduk, and the latter replaces Ea as he does Bel. The real creator of mankind, according to certain traditions, is Ea, just as in all probabilities a third tradition existed which arose in Nippur giving to Bel that distinction. It is necessary, therefore, for Ea to declare that Marduk's name (*i.e.*, his power) is the same as Ea. The alteration of the traditions is thus justified by a harmonistic theology. Marduk has triumphed over Bel and Ea. The god of Babylon reigns supreme, his sway acknowledged by those whom he supplants. Marduk's declaration that in the event of his vanquishing Tiâmat he will assume authority over all the gods is thus formally confirmed. The epic closes grandiloquently:

> With fifty names, the great gods
> According to their fifty names, proclaimed the supremacy of his course.

The compiler has added to the epic what Delitzsch appropriately designates an 'epilogue,'—a declaration of affection for Marduk. The epilogue consists of three stanzas. All mankind—royalty and subjects—are called upon to bear in mind Marduk's glorious deeds, achieved for the benefit of the world.

> Let the wise and intelligent together ponder over it.
> Let the father relate it and teach it to his son.[1]

---

[1] One is reminded of the Biblical injunction with regard to the Laws of Yahwe, Deut. vi. 7: "Thou shalt teach them to thy sons and speak constantly of them."

> To leader and shepherd[1] be it told.
> Let all rejoice in the lord of gods, Marduk
> That he may cause his land to prosper and grant it peace.
> His word is firm, his order irrevocable.
> What issues from his mouth, no god can alter.

Marduk's anger, the poet says in closing, terrifies even the gods, but he is a god upon whose mercy one may rely, though he punishes the evil-doer.

Bearing in mind the general nature of the creation epic we have discussed, we must of course in our conclusions distinguish between those elements in it which reflect the intent of the compiler or compilers to glorify Marduk at the expense of other gods and such parts as bear the stamp of being generally accepted beliefs. Setting aside, therefore, the special rôle assigned to Marduk, we find that the Babylonians never developed a theory of real beginnings. The *creatio ex nihilo* was a thought beyond the grasp even of the schools. There was always *something*, and indeed there was always a *great deal* — as much perhaps at the beginning of things as at any other time. But there was no cosmic order. Instead of a doctrine of creation, we have a doctrine of evolution from chaos to the imposition of eternal laws. The manifestation of these laws was seen first of all in the movements of the heavenly bodies. There was a great expanse, presenting the appearance of a stretched-out curtain or a covering to which the stars and moon were attached. Along this expanse the wandering stars moved with a certain regularity. The moon, too, had its course mapped out and the sun appeared in this expanse daily, as an overseer, passing along the whole of it. This wonderful system was the first to be perfected, and to the solar deity,[2] which seemed to control everything, was ascribed the distinction of having introduced the heavenly order. This notion we may well believe was of

---
[1] *I.e.*, to the kings who are frequently called 'shepherds' in the historical texts.
[2] Or, according to the earlier view, to an atmospheric god.

popular origin, though elaborated in the schools to conform to a developed astrological science.

The stars and moon never passed beyond certain limits, and, accordingly, the view was developed which gave to the canopy of heaven fixed boundaries. At each end of the canopy was a great gate, properly guarded. Through one of these the sun passed in rising out of the ocean, through the other it passed out when it had run its course. Learned speculation could not improve upon this popular fancy. As the heavens had their limitations, so also the great bodies of water were kept in check by laws, which, though eternal, were yet not quite as inexorable as those controlling the heavenly bodies. The yearly overflow of the Euphrates and Tigris was too serious a matter to be overlooked, and we shall see in a following chapter[1] how this phenomenon was interpreted as a rivalry between Bel and Ea, deliberately caused by the former in anger toward mankind. Still, as a general thing, the 'deep,' presided over by Ea, kept within the limits assigned to it. The waters above the canopy were under rigid control, and the lower waters flowed around the earth and underneath it, and bordered the canopy of heaven at its two ends.

The earth itself was a vast hollow structure, erected as a "place of fertility" under the canopy of heaven and resting on the great 'deep.' Its vegetation was the gift of the gods. 'Fertility' summed up the law fixed for the earth. Much as in the Book of Genesis, "to multiply and increase" was the order proclaimed for the life with which the earth was filled.

The creation of mankind was the last act in the great drama. Assigned in some traditions to Ea, in others as it would seem to Bel, the transfer of the traditions to Marduk is the deliberate work of the schools of theological thought. The essential point for us is that mankind, according to all traditions, is the product of the gods. In some form or other, this belief was

[1] "The Gilgamesh Epic."

popularly held everywhere. Its original form, however, is obscured beyond recognition by the theory which it is made to serve.

A second version of the course of creation[1] agrees in the main with the first one, but adds some points of interest. In this version, likewise, Marduk is assigned the most important rôle — an evidence that it was produced under similar influences as the larger epic. So far as preserved, the second version differs from the first in its brevity and in the prominence given to such themes as the development of animal life and the growth of civilization. It fills out to a certain degree the gaps in the first version, due to the fragmentary condition of the fifth tablet and the loss of the sixth. The brevity of the second version is due in part to the fact that it is introduced into an incantation text, and, what is more, incidentally introduced.

It begins as does the larger epic with the statement regarding the period when the present phenomena of the universe were not yet in existence, but it specifies the period in a manner which gives a somewhat more definite character to the conception of this ancient time.

> The bright house of the gods was not yet built on the bright place,
> No reed grew and no tree was formed,
> No brick was laid nor any brick edifice[2] reared,
> No house erected, no city built,
> No city reared, no conglomeration[3] formed.
> Nippur was not reared, E-Kur[4] not erected.
> Erech was not reared, E-Anna[5] not erected.

[1] First published by Pinches, *Journal of the Royal Asiatic Society*, 1891, pp. 393-408.

[2] Clay, it will be recalled, was the building material in Babylonia.

[3] The word in the text is generally applied to "a mass" of animals, but also to human productions. See Delitzsch, *Assyr. Handwörterbuch*, p. 467.

[4] Bel's temple at Nippur.

[5] Temple of Ishtar at Erech or Uruk.

The deep¹ not formed, Eridu² not reared.
The bright house, the house of the gods not yet constructed as a dwelling.
The world³ was all a sea.

Again it will be observed that neither popular nor scholastic speculation can picture the beginning of things in any other way than as an absence of things characteristic of the *order* of the universe.

The bright⁴ house of the gods corresponds to Eshara and the canopy of heaven in the first version. The gods are again identified with the stars, and it is in the heavens — the bright place — that the gods dwell.⁵ The reference to the absence of vegetation agrees closely with the corresponding passage in the larger creation epic. The limitations of the cosmological speculations of the Babylonians find a striking illustration in the manner in which the beginnings of human culture are placed on a level with the beginnings of heavenly and terrestrial phenomena. Nippur, Erech, and Eridu, which are thus shown to be the oldest religious centers of the Euphrates Valley, were indissolubly associated in the minds of the people with the beginning of order in the universe. Such was the antiquity of those cities as seats of the great gods, Bel, Ishtar, and Ea, that the time when they did not exist was not differentiated from the creation of the heavens and of plant life. This conception is more clearly emphasized by the parallelism implied between Eridu and the 'deep.' The 'formation' of Apsu corresponds to the 'structure' made by Marduk according to the first version, as the seat of Ea. The waters were not created by Marduk, but

---

¹ *I.e.*, Apsu.

² City sacred to Ea at the mouth of the Persian Gulf.

³ Lit., 'totality of lands.'

⁴ Zimmern's rendering (Gunkel, *Schöpfung und Chaos*, p. 419) "sacred" (instead of 'bright') misses the point.

⁵ *Cf.* S. A. Smith, Miscellaneous, K. 2866, l. 8, "the great gods dwelling in the heaven of Anu." The reference, therefore, cannot be to "the gathering place of the gods," where the fates of mankind are decided.

they were confined by him within a certain space. In a vague way, the 'deep' itself rested in a vast tub. The waters flowed freely and yet not without limitation.

The contest with Tiâmat is not referred to in this second version, and this may be taken as an indication that the 'nature' myth was not an ingredient part of cosmological speculations, but only introduced into the first version because of its associations with Marduk.

The appearance of dry land is described somewhat vaguely as follows:

There was a channel[1] within the sea.
At that time Eridu was erected, E-Sagila[2] was built,
E-Sagila in the midst of the 'deep,' where the god of the glorious abode[3] dwells.

The mention of the channel appears to imply that the waters were permitted to flow off in a certain direction.

The conception would then be similar to the view expressed in Genesis, where the dry land appears in consequence of the waters being 'gathered' into one place.[4] The temple at Eridu is regarded as synonymous with the city, as the temples E-Kur and E-Anna are synonymous with Nippur and Erech respectively. Eridu at the head of the Persian Gulf, which for the Babylonians was the beginning of the great 'Okeanos' surrounding the world,[5] is the first dry land to appear and hence the

---

[1] The original has *ratum*. Delitzsch, *Assyr. Handwörterbuch*, p. 663, compares Hebrew *rahat*, "trough." Zimmern (Gunkel, *Schöpfung und Chaos*, p. 419) translates "Bewegung," but on what grounds I do not know. The passage is obscure; the text possibly defective.

[2] If the reading E-Sagila is original, it is here used as the name of Ea's temple in Eridu, but it is of course possible that E-Sagila has been deliberately introduced to enhance the glory of Marduk's temple in Babylon.

[3] Ea.   [4] Gen. i. 9.

[5] See Haupt, *Wo lag das Paradies*, p. 7 (*Ueber Land und Meer*, 1894-95, no. 15, Sonderabdruck), who furnishes numerous illustrations of the indefinite geographical notions of the ancients.

oldest place in the world. At this point in the narrative a line is interpolated which clearly betrays the lateness of the version. The mention of E-Sagila suggests to a Babylonian, naturally, the great temple of Marduk in the city of Babylon—'the lofty house.' Local pride and the desire to connect Babylon with the beginning of things leads to the insertion:

> Babylon was reared, E-Sagila built.

With this mention of Babylon, the connecting link is established which leads easily to the glorification of Babylon and Marduk. The thought once introduced is not abandoned. The rest of the narrative, so far as preserved, is concerned with Marduk. Eridu alone is beyond his jurisdiction. Everything else, vegetation, mankind, rivers, animals, and all cities, including even Nippur and Erech, are Marduk's work.

The Anunnaki[1] he[2] created together
And bestowed glorious epithets upon the glorious city, the seat dear to their heart.

The 'glorious city' is Eridu, though the compiler would have us apply it to Babylon.

With the founding of Eridu, a limit was fixed for the 'deep.' The rest of the dry land is formed according to the theory of the writer by the extension of this place.

> Marduk constructed an enclosure around the waters,
> He made dust and heaped it up within the enclosure.[3]

The *naiveté* of the conception justifies us in regarding it as of popular origin, incorporated by the theologians into their system.

But this land is created primarily for the benefit of the gods.

> That the gods might dwell in the place dear to their heart.

---

[1] The group of celestial beings.
[2] *I.e.*, Marduk.
[3] Read *u-ma-mi*.

Naturally not all of the gods are meant, — perhaps only the Anunnaki, — for the great gods dwell in heaven. The creation of mankind is next described, and is boldly ascribed to Marduk.

> Mankind he created.[1]

In the following line, however, we come across a trace again of an older tradition, which has been embodied in the narrative in a rather awkward manner. Associated with Marduk in the creation of mankind is a goddess Aruru.

> The goddess Aruru created the seed of men together with him.[2]

We encounter this goddess Aruru in the Gilgamesh epic,[3] where she is represented as creating a human being, — Eabani; and, curiously enough, she creates him in agreement with the Biblical tradition, out of a lump of clay. It has already been pointed out that according to one tradition Ea is the creator of mankind,[4] and the conjecture has also been advanced that at Nippur, Bel was so regarded. In Aruru we have evidently a figure to whom another tradition, that arose in some district, ascribed the honor of having created mankind. The Gilgamesh story is connected with the city of Erech, and it is probable that the tale — at least in part — originated there. It becomes plausible, therefore, to trace the tradition ascribing the creation of man to Aruru to the same place. A passage in the Deluge story, which forms an episode of the Gilgamesh epic, adds some force to this conjecture. After the dreadful deluge has come, Ishtar breaks out in wild lament that mankind, her offspring, has perished: "What I created, where is it?"[5] She is called 'the mistress of the gods,'[6] and if Jensen is correct in an ingenious restoration of a defective text,[7] Aruru is given

---

[1] Zimmern purposes to connect this line with the preceding, but the sense in that case is not at all clear.
[2] *Ie.*, with Marduk.
[3] Haupt's edition, p. 8, l. 34.
[4] See above, p. 437.
[5] Haupt, *ib.* p. 139, l. 116.
[6] *Ib.* L 111.
[7] *Kosmologie*, p. 294, note 1.

the same epithet in a lexicographical tablet. The Ishtar occurring in the Gilgamesh story is the old Ishtar of Erech. I venture to suggest, therefore, that Aruru and Ishtar of Erech are one and the same personage. Ishtar is, of course, as has been pointed out, merely a generic name [1] for the 'great goddess' worshipped under many forms. The more specific name by which Ishtar of Erech was known was Nanâ, but Nanâ again is nothing but an epithet, meaning, as the Babylonians themselves interpreted it, the 'lady' *par excellence*.[2] Have we perhaps in Aruru the real name of the old goddess of Erech? At all events, the occurrence of Aruru in this second 'creation' story points to her as belonging to the district of which Erech was the center. In this way, each one of the three most ancient sacred towns of Babylonia would have its 'creator,' — Bel in Nippur, Ea in Eridu, and Aruru in Erech. The chief deity of Erech, it will be recalled, was always a goddess, — a circumstance that supports the association of Aruru with that place. Aruru being a goddess, it was not so easy to have Marduk take up her rôle, as he supplanted Bel. Again, Erech and Babylon were not political rivals to the degree that Nippur and Babylon were. Accordingly a compromise was effected, as in the case of Marduk and Ea. Aruru is associated with Marduk. She creates mankind with Marduk, and it would seem to be a consequence of this association that the name of Marduk's real consort, Sarpanitum, is playfully but with intent interpreted by the Babylonian pedants as 'seed-producing.'[3]

Our second version thus turns out to be, like the first, an adaptation of old traditions to new conditions. Babylon and Marduk are designedly introduced. In the original form Nippur, Eridu, and Erech alone figured, and presumably, therefore, only the deities of these three places. Among them the work of creation was in some way parceled out. This distribution

---

[1] See p. 82.   [2] See p. 81.
[3] *Zerbanitum*, as though compounded of *zer* (seed), and *bani* (create). See p. 121.

may itself have been the result of a combination of independent traditions. In any early combination, however, we may feel certain that Marduk was not introduced.

After this incidental mention of Aruru, the narrative passes back undisturbed to Marduk.

> The animals of the field, the living creatures of the field he created,
> The Tigris and Euphrates he formed in their places, gave them good names,
> Soil (?), grass, the marsh, reed, and forest he created,
> The verdure of the field he produced,
> The lands, the marsh, and thicket,
> The wild cow with her young, the young wild ox,
> The ewe with her young, the sheep of the fold,
> Parks and forests,
> The goat and wild goat he brought forth.

The text at this point becomes defective, but we can still make out that the clay as building material is created by Marduk, and that he constructs houses and rears cities. Corresponding to the opening lines, we may supply several lines as follows:

> Houses he erected, cities he built,
> Cities he built, dwellings he prepared,
> Nippur he built, E-Kur he erected,
> Erech he built, E-Anna he erected.

Here the break in the tablet begins.

The new points derived from this second version are, (*a*) the details in the creation of the animal and plant world, (*b*) the mention of Aruru as the mother of mankind, and (*c*) the inclusion of human culture in the story of the 'beginnings.'

Before leaving the subject, a brief comparison of these two versions with the opening chapters of Genesis is called for. That the Hebrew and Babylonian traditions spring from a common source is so evident as to require no further proof. The agreements are too close to be accidental. At the same time, the variations in detail point to independent elaboration of the traditions on the part of the Hebrews and Babylonians.

A direct borrowing from the Babylonians has not taken place, and while the Babylonian records are in all probabilities much older than the Hebrew, the latter again contain elements, as Gunkel has shown, of a more primitive character than the Babylonian production. This relationship can only be satisfactorily explained on the assumption that the Hebrews possessed the traditions upon which the Genesis narrative rests long before the period of the Babylonian exile, when the story appears, indeed, to have received its final and present shape. The essential features of the Babylonian cosmology formed part of a stock of traditions that Hebrews and Babylonians (and probably others) received from some common source or, to put it more vaguely, held in common from a period, the limits of which can no longer be determined. While the two Babylonian versions agree in the main, embodying the same general traditions regarding the creation of the heavenly bodies and containing the same general conception of an evolution in the world from confusion and caprice to order, and the establishment of law, the variations in regard to the terrestrial phenomena must not be overlooked. According to the first version, mankind appears as the last episode of creation; in the second, mankind precedes vegetation and animal life.

If we now take up the two versions of creation found in Genesis, we will see that the same differences may be observed. According to the first, the so-called Elohistic version,[1] mankind is not created until the last day of creation; according to the second,[2] the so-called Yahwistic version, mankind is first created, then a garden is made and trees are planted. After that, the beasts of the field and the birds of heaven are called into existence.

---

[1] Gen. i. 1–ii. 4, embodied in the " Priestly Code."
[2] Gen. ii. 4 and extending in reality as far as iv. 25.

The resemblance of the second Babylonian version to the Yahwistic version extends even to certain phrases which they have in common. The opening words of the Yahwist —

And no plant of the field was yet in the earth, and no herb of the field had yet sprung up —

might serve almost as a translation of the second line of the Babylonian counterpart. The reference to the Tigris and Euphrates in the second Babylonian version reminds one of the four streams mentioned in the Yahwistic version, two of which are likewise the Tigris and Euphrates. Again, Tiâmat is mentioned only in the first Babylonian version, and T'hôm similarly only in the Elohistic version; while, on the other hand, the building of cities is included in the Yahwistic version,[1] as it forms part of the second Babylonian version. The points mentioned suffice to show that the Elohistic version is closely related to the larger creation epic of the Babylonians, while the Yahwistic version — more concise, too, than the Elohistic — agrees to an astonishing degree with the second and more concise Babylonian record.

The conclusion, therefore, is justified that the variations between the Babylonian versions rest upon varying traditions that must have arisen in different places. The attempt was made to combine these traditions by the Babylonians, and among the Hebrews we may see the result of a similar attempt in the first two or, more strictly speaking, in the first three chapters of Genesis. At the same time, the manner in which both traditions have been worked over by the Hebrew compilers of Genesis precludes, as has been pointed out, the theory of a direct borrowing from cuneiform documents. The climatic conditions involved in the Hebrew versions are those peculiar to Babylonia. It is in Babylonia that the thought would naturally arise of making the world begin with the close of the

---

[1] Gen. iii. 17.

storms and rains in the spring. The Terahites must therefore have brought these cosmological traditions with them upon migrating from the Euphrates Valley to the Jordan district.

The traditions retained their hold through all the vicissitudes that the people underwent. The intercourse, political and commercial, between Palestine and Mesopotamia was uninterrupted, as we now know, from at least the fifteenth century before our era down to the taking of Jerusalem by Nebuchadnezzar, and this constant intercourse was no doubt an important factor in maintaining the life of the old traditions that bound the two peoples together. The so-called Babylonian exile brought Hebrews and Babylonians once more side by side. Under the stimulus of this direct contact, the final shape was given by Hebrew writers to their cosmological speculations. Yahwe is assigned the rôle of Bel-Marduk, the division of the work of creation into six days is definitely made,[1] and some further modifications introduced. While, as emphasized, this final shape is due to the independent elaboration of the common traditions, and, what is even more to the point, shows an independent *interpretation* of the traditions, it is by no means impossible, but on the contrary quite probable, that the final compilers of the Hebrew versions had before them the cuneiform tablets, embodying the literary form given to the traditions by Babylonian writers.[2] Such a circumstance, while not implying direct borrowing, would account for the close parallels existing between the two Hebrew and the two Babylonian versions, and would also furnish a motive to the Hebrew writers for embodying *two* versions in their narrative.

[1] See Gunkel, *Schöpfung und Chaos*, p. 13.
[2] On the acquaintance of Hebrew writers of the Babylonian exile with cuneiform literature and on the influence exercised by the latter, see D. H. Mueller, *Ezechiel-studien*.

CHAPTER XXII.

THE ZODIACAL SYSTEM OF THE BABYLONIANS.

Planets, Stars, and Calendar.

It will be appropriate at this point, to give a brief account of the astronomical system as developed by the Babylonian scholars. The system forms a part of the Babylonian cosmology. The 'creation' narratives we have been considering are based upon the system, and the omen literature is full of allusions to it. Moreover, the understanding of some of the purely religious doctrines of the Babylonians is dependent upon a proper conception of the curious astrological speculations which from Babylonia made their way to the Greeks, and have left their traces in the astronomy of the present time.

The stars were regarded by the Babylonians as pictorial designs on the heavens. A conception of this kind is the outcome of popular fancy, and has its parallel among other nations of antiquity. We pass beyond the popular stage, however, when we find the stars described as the 'writing of heaven.'[1] Such a term is the product of the schools, and finds a ready explanation if we remember that the cuneiform script, like other scripts, was in its first stages pictorial. The Babylonian scholars not only knew this, but so well did they know it that writing continued to be regarded by them as picture drawing. The characters used by them were 'likenesses'[2] long after they had passed beyond the stage when they bore any resemblance to the pictures they originally represented. The expression 'writ-

---

[1] *E.g.*, IR. 52, no. 3, col. ii. l. 2; IIR. 38, 27b.
[2] The Greek name for the letters of the alphabet — *symbolon*, *i.e.*, a "likeness" — illustrates the same view of the pictorial origin of writing.

ing of heaven' was, therefore, equivalent to 'picture of heaven.'. The heavens themselves being regarded as a fixed vault, it followed that the movements observed there were caused by the stars changing their position; and the regular characters of these movements within certain periods led to speaking of the movements of the heavenly bodies as their 'courses.' It was furthermore apparent, even to a superficial observer, that some of the stars seemed fixed to their places, while others moved about. A distinction was thus drawn between wandering stars or planets and fixed stars. Groups of stars, the single members of which appeared in a constant relationship to one another, were distinguished partly by natural observation and partly as a convenient means of obtaining a general view of the starry canopy. It was such a group that more particularly justified the view which regarded the stars as pictorial designs. A line drawn so as to connect the stars of the group turned out to be a design of some sort. On omen tablets, geometrical figures are often found [1] and interpreted as omens, and it is plausible to suppose that the outlines presented by the stars of a group first suggested the idea of attaching significance to combinations of lines and curves. To connect these outlines with the pictures that formed the starting-point for the development of the script was again a perfectly natural procedure, although a scholastic one. The investigations of Delitzsch have shown that the more than four hundred cuneiform characters in use can be reduced to a comparatively small number of 'outlines' of pictures — to about forty-five. The subjects of these 'outlines' are all familiar ones, — sun, moon, stars, mountain, man, the parts of the human body, animals, plants, and utensils.[2] Association of ideas led to giving to the outlines presented by the groups of stars, a similar interpretation. The factor of imagina-

---

[1] For illustrations, see Lenormant, *Magie und Wahrsagekunst der Chaldaer*, pp. 520–523.

[2] See the summary on pp. 198, 199, of Delitzsch, *Ursprung der Keilschriftzeichen*.

tion, of course, entered into play, but it is also likely that the comparison of these heavenly figures with the pictures of the script was the controlling factor that led to identifying a certain group of stars with a bull, another with a scorpion, a third with a ram, a fourth with a fish, still another with a pig, and more the like. That animals were chosen was due to the influence of animistic theories, and the rather fantastic shape of the animals distinguished led to further speculations. So, eleven constellations, that is to say, the entire zodiac with the exception of the bull — the sign of Marduk — were identified with the eleven monsters forming the host of Tiâmat. The passage in the Marduk-Tiâmat myth[1] which speaks of the capture of these monsters through Marduk appears to have suggested this identification, which, fanciful though it is, has a scholastic rather than a popular aspect. Jensen (to whom, together with Epping and Strassmaier,[2] most of our knowledge of this subject is due) has shown[3] that of the twelve constellations in our modern zodiac, the greater number are identical with those distinguished by the Babylonians; and while it is probable that two or three of our constellations are of occidental origin, the zodiacal system as a whole is the product of the Babylonian schools of astronomy. From Babylonia the system made its way to the west and through western, more particularly through Greek, influence back again to India and the distant east. The number of constellations distinguished by the Babylonian astronomers has not yet been definitely ascertained. They certainly recognized more than twelve. Further investigations may show that they knew of most of the forty-eight constellations enumerated by Ptolemy.

The general regularity of the courses taken by the sun, moon, and planets made it a comparatively simple matter to map out

---

[1] See p. 438.
[2] Epping and Strassmaier, *Astronomisches aus Babylon* (Freiburg, 1889).
[3] *Kosmologie*, pp. 57-95. See especially the summary, pp. 82-84.

the limits within which these bodies moved. These limits impressed the Babylonians, as we have seen, with the thought of the eternal and unchangeable laws under which the planets stood. The laws regulating terrestrial phenomena, did not appear to be so rigid. There were symptoms of caprice, so that the order of the earth has the appearance of being an afterthought, suggested by the absolute order prevailing in the heavens. Comets, meteors, and eclipses alone seemed to interrupt this absolute order. As science advanced, it was found that even eclipses fell within the province of law. The course of astronomical science was thus clearly marked out — the determination of these laws.

The path taken by the sun served as a guide and as a means of comparison. Anu being both the chief god of heaven and the personification of heaven,[1] the sun's ecliptic became known as the 'way of Anu.' The division of this ecliptic into certain sections, determined by the constellations within the belt of the ecliptic, was the next step. The course of the moon and planets was determined with reference to the sun's ecliptic, and gradually a zodiacal system was evolved, the perfection of which is best exemplified by the fact that so much of the astronomical language of the present time is the same as that used by the ancient astronomers of the Euphrates Valley.

The sun and moon being regarded as deities, under the influence of primitive animistic ideas,[2] the stars would also come to be looked upon as divine. The ideograph designating a 'star' and which is prefixed as a determinative to the names of stars, consists of the sign for god repeated three times;[3] and in the case of those stars which are identified with particular deities, the simple determinative for god is employed. To regard the stars in general as gods is a consequence of ani-

[1] See p. 89.
[2] See p. 48.
[3] On this ideograph, see Jensen, *Kosmologie*, pp. 43, 44.

mistic notions; but the further steps in the process which led to connecting the planets and certain other stars with particular deities who originally had nothing to do with the stars, fall within the province of scholastic theory.

As the jurisdiction of gods originally worshipped in a limited district increased, a difficulty naturally arose among the more advanced minds as to the exact place where the deity dwelt. This difficulty would be accentuated in the case of a god like Marduk becoming the chief god of the whole Babylonian Empire. His ardent worshippers would certainly not content themselves with the notion that a single edifice, even though it be his great temple at Babylon, could contain him. Again, the development of a pantheon, systematized, and in which the various gods worshipped in Babylonia came to occupy fixed relationships to one another, would lead to the view of putting all the gods in one place. The sun and moon being in the heavens, the most natural place to assign to the gods as a dwelling-place was in the region where Shamash and Sin (as every one could see for himself) had their seats. The doctrine thus arose that the great gods dwell in the 'heaven of Anu.' A doctrine of this kind would be intelligible to the general populace, but it is doubtful whether a belief which involved the establishment of a direct connection between the most prominent stars — the planets with the chief gods — ever enjoyed popular favor in Babylonia. The association is marked by an artificiality and a certain arbitrariness that stamps it not only as the product of theological schools, but as a thought that would remain confined to a limited circle of the population. Jensen suggests [1] that the planets may at one time have been merely regarded as standing under the influence of the great gods, and that a planet from being regarded as the star *controlled* by Marduk, became identified with Marduk. It seems more plausible that the association should have been direct.

[1] *Kosmologie*, p. 134.

Even though the Babylonians may not have had any knowledge of the relative mass of the planets, in some way Jupiter must have appeared to them as the largest of the planets, and for this reason was identified with the head of the Babylonian pantheon, Marduk. In the creation epic, as we have seen, Jupiter-Marduk, under the name of Nibir, is represented as exercising a control over all the stars. Mythological associations appear to have played a part in identifying the planet Venus with the goddess Ishtar. A widely spread nature myth,[1] symbolizing the change of seasons, represents Ishtar, the personification of fertility, the great mother of all that manifests life, as proceeding to the region of darkness and remaining there for some time. The disappearance of the planet Venus at certain seasons, as morning star to reappear as evening star, suggested the identification of this planet with Ishtar. From these two examples we may conclude that the process which resulted in the identification of Saturn with Ninib, Mars with Nergal, Mercury with Nabu rested similarly on an association of ideas, derived from certain conceptions held of the gods involved. In regard to Ninib and Nergal it is of some importance to bear in mind that, like Marduk, they are at their origin solar deities, Ninib representing in the perfected theological system the morning sun, Marduk the sun of the early spring, and Nergal the mid-day sun and summer solstice.[2] The position of the planets Saturn and Mars, accordingly, with reference to the sun at certain periods of the year, may well have been a factor in the association of ideas involved.

The position of the sun, as the general overseer of the planets, led to the application of an interesting metaphor to express the relationship between the sun and the planets. Just as the human chiefs or kings were called 'shepherds,' — a

---

[1] See the following chapter on "The Gilgamesh Epic," and chapter xxv, "The Views of the Babylonians and Assyrians of the Life after Death."

[2] Jensen, *ib.* p. 140. See above, p. 67.

metaphor suggested, no doubt, by agricultural life,—so the planets were commonly known as 'sheep'[1] or, as Jensen suggests,[2] 'wandering sheep,' and it is rather curious that Mars-Nergal should have been designated as the 'sheep'[3] *par excellence*. The 'service' in which the planets stood to the sun is exemplified by another term applied to them, which designates them as the mediators carrying out the orders of their superior.

Lastly, it may be noted that each planet receives a variety of names and epithets in the astronomical texts,—a circumstance that points to the composite character of the developed planetary system of the Babylonians. Some of these names are of so distinctive a character as to justify the conclusion that they arose in the different centers where astronomical schools existed.

The process involved in the development of the system is thus complicated by factors introducing views originally confined to certain districts, and it becomes doubtful whether we will ever be able to trace all the steps involved in the process.

Corresponding to the unique position occupied by the superior triad Anu, Bel, and Ea in the theological system, a special place was assigned to them in the astronomical system. Anu is the pole star of the ecliptic, Bel the pole star of the equator, while Ea in the southern heavens was identified, according to Jensen,[4] with a star in the constellation Argo. Anu, Bel, and Ea represented the three most prominent fixed stars, but by the side of these a large number of other stars were distinguished and many of them identified with some deity. For some of these stars the modern equivalents have been ascertained through recent researches;[5] others still remain to be determined.

The astronomical science of the Babylonians thus resolves itself into these natural divisions:

---

[1] *bibbu*.   [2] *Ib.* p. 99.
[3] Perhaps because of the intensity of Mars' light.
[4] *Ib.* p. 27.   [5] See especially Jensen's *Kosmologie*, pp. 46-57 and 144-160.

(1) the constellations, especially those of the zodiac,
(2) the five great planets,
(3) the fixed stars, Anu, Bel, and Ea,
(4) miscellaneous stars, and
(5) the sun and moon.

The rivalry between the two great luminaries ends in a superior rank being accorded to the sun. Natural and indeed inevitable as this conclusion was, the scientific theory in the Euphrates Valley was presumably influenced to some extent by the circumstance that the head of the pantheon was a solar deity. We have seen that the tradition of this original character of Marduk survived in the popular mind.

Of the sun but little need be said here. As represented in the creation story, he was freer in his movements than any of the planets. He passed across the heavens daily as an overseer to see that everything was maintained in good order. As in Greek mythology, the sun was represented as riding in a chariot drawn by horses.[1] Scientific speculation advanced but little upon these popular fancies. The course that the sun took on the ecliptic was determined, and the ecliptic itself served as the guide for determining the position and movements of the stars. Under the growing influence of the Marduk cult and of such deities as Ninib, Nergal, and Nabu, associated with Marduk mythologically or politically, the old moon worship lost much of its prestige; but in astronomical science, the former independent rank of the moon is still in large measure preserved. In the enumeration of the planets the moon is mentioned first.[2] The moon is not a 'sheep' belonging to the flock of Shamash. The importance of the moon in the regulation of the calendar saved her from this fate. The beginning of the calendrical system, indeed, may

---

[1] Jensen, *ib.* pp. 108, 109.
[2] The constant order is moon, sun, Marduk, Ishtar, Ninib, Nergal, Nabu. *E.g.*, IIR. 48, 48–54a–b.

well have been of popular origin. Ihering[1] is of the opinion that agricultural occupations made the marking off of time a popular necessity, and this view is borne out by the early epithets of the months among the Babylonians,[2] which, as among the Hebrews, are connected with agriculture and the life of the agriculturist. The later names also bear traces of the same train of thoughts. Leaving aside details into which it is needless to enter here, the part of the calendar which touches upon the religion of the Babylonians is the sacred character given to the months by making each one devoted to some god or gods. In this association there may be observed the same curious mixture of several factors that controlled the identification of the planets with the gods. The theory underlying the pantheon and certain mythological conceptions are two of the factors that can be clearly seen at work. The triad Anu, Bel, and Ea are accorded the first rank.[3]

The first month, Nisan, is sacred to Anu and Bel.

The second, Iyar, is sacred to Ea as the "lord of humanity."

Then follows Sin to whom, as the first-born of Bel,[4] the third month, Siwan, is devoted.

The four succeeding months are parceled out among deities closely connected with one another, — Ninib, Nin-gishzida, Ishtar, and Shamash. Of these, Ninib and Nin-gishzida are solar deities. Ninib, as the morning sun, symbolizes the approach of the summer season, while Nin-gishzida, another solar deity,[5] represents an advance in this season. To them, therefore, the fourth and fifth months, Tammuz (or Du'zu) and Ab respectively, are sacred. Ishtar is the goddess of fertility, and the sixth month, which represents the culmination of the summer season, is accordingly devoted to her. As the last of the group comes

[1] *Vorgeschichte der Indo-Europaer*, pp. 151 seq.
[2] On the older and later names of the Babylonians, see Meissner, *Zeitschrift für die Kunde des Morgenlandes*, v. 180, 181, and on the general subject of the Babylonian months, Muss-Arnolt's valuable articles in the *Journal of Biblical Literature*, xi. 72-94 and 160-176.
[3] IVR.² pl. 33.   [4] En-lil.   [5] See above, p. 99.

Shamash himself, to whom the seventh month, Tishri (or Tashritum), is sacred. Marduk and Nergal come next, the eighth month, Marcheshwan,[1] being sacred to the former, the ninth Kislev to the great warrior Nergal. The factors here involved are not clear, nor do we know why the tenth month is sacred to Papsukal—perhaps here used as an epithet of Nabu—to Anu, and to Ishtar. The eleventh month, the height of the rainy season and known as the "month of the course of rainstorms," is appropriately made sacred to Ramman, 'the god of storms.' The last month, Adar, falling within the rainy season is presided over by the seven evil spirits. Lastly, an interesting trace of Assyrian influence is to be seen in devoting to Ashur, "the father of the gods," the intercalated month, the second Adar. This introduction of Ashur points to the late addition of this intercalated month, and makes it probable also that the intercalation is the work of astronomers standing under Assyrian authority. A second intercalated month is Elul the second. This month is sacred to Anu and Bel, just like Nisan, the first month. The list, therefore, begins anew with the intercalated month. Such a procedure is natural, and one is inclined to conclude that the intercalated Elul is of Babylonian origin and older than the intercalated Adar.

It does not appear that the female consorts of the gods shared in the honors thus bestowed upon the male deities. Variations from the list as given also occur. So Ashurbanabal calls the seventh month, Elul, the month of 'the king of gods Ashur,'[2] while Sargon[3] assigns the fourth month to the 'servant of Gibil,' the fire-god, by which Nin-gishzida is meant, and the third month he calls the month of "the god of brick structures."[4]

In fact, the assigning of the months to the gods appears to partake more or less of an arbitrary character. Absolute uniformity probably did not prevail throughout Babylonia until a

---

[1] Lit., 'Arakh-shamnu,' *i.e.*, month eight.
[2] Rassam, Cylinder, col. lii. l. 32.
[3] Cylinder, Inscription l. 61.
[4] *Ib.* l. 58,—a rather curious title of Sin.

comparatively late period. Nor does it appear that any popular significance was attached to the sacred character thus given to the months. It was the work of the schools, as are most of the features involved in the elaboration of the calendar.

In somewhat closer touch with popular notions and popular observances were the names of the months. Confining ourselves to the later names,— the forms in which they were transmitted during the period of the Babylonian exile to the Jews,[1]—we find that the first month which, as we shall see, was marked by sacred observances in the temples of Marduk and Nabu at Babylon and Borsippa was designated ideographically as 'the month of the sanctuary,' the third as the period of 'brick-making,' the fifth as the 'fiery' month, the sixth as the month of the 'mission of Ishtar'—a reference to the goddess' descent into the region of darkness. Designations like ' taking (*i.e.*, scattering) seed ' for the fourth month, ' copious fertility ' for the ninth month, 'grain-cutting' period for the twelfth, and 'opening of dams'[2] for the eighth contain distinct references to agriculture. The name ' destructive rain ' for the eleventh month is suggested by climatic conditions. Still obscure is the designation of the seventh month as the month of the 'resplendent mound,'[3] and so also is the designation of the second month.[4]

The calendar is thus shown to be the product of the same general order of religious ideas that we have detected in the zodiacal and planetary systems. Its growth must have been

[1] The Talmud preserves the tradition of the Babylonian origin of the Hebrew calendar (*Jerusalem Talmud Rosh-Hashshanā*, I. 1).

[2] For the irrigation of the fields.

[3] In some way indicative of its sacred character. It is to be noted that this month — Tishri — is the festival month among the Hebrews and originally also among the Arabs. The ' mound ' is a reference to the temples which were erected on natural or artificial eminences.

[4] The latter is described by a series of ideographs, " herd " and " to prosper." Is there perhaps a reference to cows giving birth to calves in this month, the early spring? For another, but improbable, explanation, see *Babylonian and Oriental Record*, iv. 37.

gradual, for its composite character is one of its most striking features. The task was no easy one to bring the lunar year into proper conjunction with the solar year, and there are grounds for believing that prior to the division of the year into twelve parts, there was a year of ten months corresponding to a simpler, perhaps a decimal, system, which appears to have preceded the elaborate sexagesimal system.[1]

However this may be, the point of importance for our purposes is to detect the extension of religious ideas into the domain of science, and, on the other hand, to note the reaction of scientific theories on the development of religious thought. The cosmology of the Babylonians results from the continued play of these two factors. Hence the strange mixture of popular notions and fancies with comparatively advanced theological speculations and still more advanced scientific theories that is found in the cosmological system. Even mysticism is given a scientific aspect in Babylonia. The identification of the gods with the stars arises, as we have seen, from a scientific impulse, and it is a scientific spirit again that leads to the introduction of the gods into the mathematics of the day.[2] A number is assigned to each of the chief gods. And, though such a procedure has its natural outcome in Cabbalistic tendencies, we can still discern in the ideas that lead to this association of numbers with gods, influences at work that emanated from the astronomical schools. Thus the moon-god Sin is identified with the number thirty, suggested by the days of the ordinary month. Ishtar, the daughter of Sin, is number fifteen, the half of thirty. The unit in the sexagesimal — the number sixty — is assigned to Anu, the chief of the triad, while the other two members, Bel and Ea, follow as fifty and forty respectively. The dependence of this species of identification upon the ca-

[1] Lehmann (*Actes du 8ème Congrès International des Orientalists*, Leiden, 1891, l. 169, note) admits the probability of an earlier and more natural system.
[2] Lotz, *Quaestiones de Historia Sabbati*, pp. 27–29.

lendrical system is made manifest by the inferior rank given to the sun, which receives the number twenty, the decimal next to that assigned to Sin, while Ramman, the third member of the second triad,[1] is identified with ten.[2] Absolute consistency in this process is, of course, as little to be expected as in other semi-mystical aspects of the science of the Babylonians; nor is it necessary for our purposes to enter upon the further consequences resulting from this combination of gods with numbers. The association of ideas involved in the combination furnishes another and rather striking illustration of the close contact between science and religion in the remarkable culture of the Euphrates Valley.

There was no conflict between science and religion in ancient Babylonia. Each reacted on the other, but the two factors were at all times closely united in perfect harmony, — a harmony so perfect, indeed, as to be impressive despite its *naïveté*.

[1] Sin, Shamash, and Ramman. See pp. 108, 163.
[2] See for other combinations Lotz *ib.*, and compare, *e.g.*, VR. 36, where the number ten is associated with a large number of gods, — Anu, Anatum, Bel, Ishtar, etc.

CHAPTER XXIII.

THE GILGAMESH EPIC.

We have seen [1] that the religion of Babylonia permeates all branches of literature, so that it is not always possible to draw a sharp dividing line between sacred and secular productions.

To account for this, it is but necessary to bear in mind what the previous chapters have aimed to make clear, that religion furnished the stimulus for the unfolding of intellectual life, and that the literary and scientific productions represent the work of men primarily interested in religion. The significance attached as omens to heavenly phenomena led by degrees to the elaborate astronomical system outlined in the previous chapter. But the astronomers of Babylonia were priests, and indeed the same priests who compiled the hymns and incantations. What is true of astronomy applies to medicine, so far as medicine had an existence independent of incantations, and also to law. The physician was a priest, as was the judge and likewise the scribe.

It is natural, therefore, to find that what may be called the great national epic of the Babylonians was of a religious character. The interpretation given to the traditions of the past was religious. The distant past blended with the phenomena of nature in such a way as to form a strange combination of poetry and realism. But thanks to this combination, which is essentially a process of the popular mind, the production that we are about to consider brings us much closer to the popular phases of the Babylonian religion than does the cosmology or the zodiacal system.

After all, a nation is much more interested in its heroes and

[1] See above, pp. 245-247.

in its own beginnings, than in the beginnings of things in general. Some speculation regarding the origin of the universe is perhaps inevitable the moment that the spirit of inquiry arises, but these speculations are soon entrusted into the hands of a minority, — the thinkers, the priests, the astronomers, — who elaborate a system that gradually separates itself from popular thought and exercises little influence upon the development of religious ideas among the masses.

The Book of Genesis passes rapidly over the creation of stars, plants, and animals, as though anxious to reach the history of man, and when it comes to the traditions regarding the ancestors of the Hebrews, the details are dwelt upon at length and pictured with a loving hand. Similarly among the Babylonians, there is a freshness about the story of the adventures of a great hero of the past that presents a contrast to the rather abstruse speculations embodied in the creation epic. In this story, in which a variety of ancient traditions have been combined, there is comparatively little trace of the scholastic spirit, and although, as we shall see, the story has been given its final shape under the same influences that determined the other branches of religious literature, the form has not obscured the popular character of the material out of which the story has been constructed.

The name of the hero of the story was for a long time a puzzle to scholars. Written invariably in ideographic fashion, the provisional reading Izdubar[1] was the only safe recourse until a few years ago, when Pinches discovered in a lexicographical tablet the equation

$$\text{Izdubar} = \text{Gilgamesh.}[2]$$

The equation proved that the Babylonians and Assyrians identified the hero with a legendary king, Gilgamos, who is

---

[1] Or Gishdubar or Gishtubar.

[2] *Babylonian and Oriental Record*, iv. 264. For previous readings of the name, see Jeremias' article on 'Izdubar' in Roscher's *Ausführliches Lexicon der Griechischen und Römischen Mythologie*, ii. col. 773, 774.

mentioned by Aelian.[1] To be sure, what Aelian tells of this hero is not found in the Izdubar epic, and appears to have originally been recounted of another legendary personage, Etana.[2] There is therefore a reasonable doubt whether the identification made by Babylonian scholars represents an old tradition or is merely a late conjecture arising at a time when the traditions of Izdubar were confused with those of Etana. Still, since Etana appears to be a phonetic reading and can be explained etymologically in a satisfactory manner, the presumption is in favor of connecting Gilgamesh with the hero of the great epic. For the present, therefore, we may accept the identification and assume that in Aelian, as well as in the sources whence he drew his information, Izdubar-Gilgamesh has been confused with Etana.[3]

The ideographic form of the name is preceded invariably by the determinative for deity, but the three elements composing the name, *iz*, *du*, and *bar*, are exceedingly obscure. The first element is a very common determinative, preceding objects made of wood or any hard substance. The word for weapon is always written with this determinative; and since Izdubar is essentially a warrior, one should expect *dubar* to represent some kind of a weapon that he carries. On seal cylinders Gilgamesh appears armed with a large lance.[4] However this may be, Jeremias' proposition to render the name as "divine judge of earthly affairs"[5] is untenable, and the same may be said of other conjectures.

---

[1] *Historia Animalium*, xii. 21. [2] See p. 524.

[3] In the Oriental legends of Alexander the Great, this confusion is further illustrated. To Alexander are attached stories belonging to both Izdubar and Etana. See Meissner's *Alexander and Gilgamos*, pp. 13–17 (Leipzig, 1894).

[4] See, *e.g.*, Perrot and Chipiez, *History of Art in Babylonia and Assyria*, I. 84.

[5] Article 'Izdubar,' col. 776; see Delitzsch, *Handwörterbuch*, p. 678. Hommel (*e.g.*, *Altisraelitische Ueberlieferung*, p. 39) regards Gilgamesh as a contraction from Gibil (the fire-god) and Gam (or Gab), together with *ish*, an 'Elamitic' ending. If the name is Elamitic, one should hardly expect a Babylonian deity entering as one of the elements.

The fact that the name is written with the determinative for deity must not lead us to a purely mythical interpretation of the epic. There was a strong tendency in Babylonia to regard the early kings as gods. Dungi and Gudea, who are far from being the earliest rulers in the Euphrates Valley, appear in tablets with the determinative for deity attached to their names,[1] and it would be natural, therefore, that a hero belonging to a remote period should likewise be deified. There can be no doubt that there is a historical background to the Gilgamesh epic, and there is equally no reason to question the existence of an ancient king or hero who bore the name Gilgamesh. The deification of the hero superinduced the introduction of mythical elements. It was an easy process also, that led to tales which arose as popular symbols of occurrences in nature, being likewise brought into connection with a hero, who was at the same time a god.

The Gilgamesh epic thus takes shape as a compound of faint historical tradition and of nature myths. The deified hero becomes more particularly a solar deity. The popularity of the hero-god is attested by the introduction of his name in incantations,[2] and by special hymns being composed in his honor. One of these hymns,[3] of a penitential character, is interesting as illustrating the survival of the recollection of his human origin. Gilgamesh is addressed by a penitent, who seeks healing from disease:

O Gilgamesh, great king, judge of the Anunnaki,
Prince, great oracle [4] of mankind,
Overseer of all regions, ruler of the world, lord of what is on earth,
Thou dost judge and, like a god, thou givest decisions,[5]

---

[1] See above, p. 167.
[2] See above, p. 284.
[3] Haupt's *Das Babylonische Nimrodepos*, p. 93.
[4] Lit., 'he who is applied to for giving a decision.'
[5] *Ta-ṭar-ra-as.*

> Thou art established on the earth, thou fulfillest judgment,
> Thy judgment is unchangeable, thy [command is not revoked],
> Thou dost inquire, thou commandest, thou judgest, thou seest, and thou directest.
> Shamash has entrusted into thy hand sceptre and decision.

It will be observed that Gilgamesh is appealed to as a 'king' and 'prince.' His dominion is the earth, and the emphasis placed upon this circumstance is significant. In accord with this peculiar province of the god, the hymn continues:

> Kings, chiefs, and princes bow before thee,
> Thou seest their laws, thou presidest over their decisions.

At the same time, his dependence upon Shamash is emphasized. As a minor solar deity, he receives his powers from the great judge Shamash. This double character of Gilgamesh furnishes the key to the interpretation of the epic in which he is the central figure.

The poem in its final shape comprised twelve tablets of about three thousand lines. Unfortunately only about half of the epic has been found up to the present time. The numerous fragments represent at least four distinct copies, all belonging to the library of Ashurbanabal. To Professor Paul Haupt we are indebted for a practically complete publication of the fragments of the epic;[1] and it is likewise owing, chiefly, to Professor Haupt that the sequence in the incidents of the epic as well as the general interpretation of the composition has been established.[2]

---

[1] *Das Babylonische Nimrodepos* (Leipzig, 1884-91). This edition includes all but the twelfth tablet, which was published by Haupt in the *Beiträge zur Assyriologie*, i. 48-79. For other publications of Haupt on the Gilgamesh epic, see the Bibliography, § 6. The identification with the Biblical Nimrod is now definitely abandoned by scholars, though the picture drawn of Nimrod is influenced by the traditions regarding Gilgamesh. See p. 515.

[2] The best general work on the epic (based on Haupt's edition) is A. Jeremias' *Izdubar-Nimrod* (Leipzig, 1891), a reprint with additions, of his article on 'Izdubar' in Roscher's *Ausführliches Lexicon der Griechischen und Römischen Mythologie*, ii.

The center of action in the first tablets of the series and in the oldest portions of the epic is the ancient city Uruk, or Erech, in southern Babylonia, invariably spoken of as *Uruk supûri*, that is, the 'walled' or fortified Uruk. A special significance attaches to this epithet. It was the characteristic of every ancient town, for reasons which Ihering has brilliantly set forth,[1] to be walled.[2] The designation of Uruk as 'walled,' therefore, stamps it as a city, but that the term was added, also points to the great antiquity of the place,—to a period when towns as distinguished from mere agricultural villages were sufficiently rare to warrant some special nomenclature. From other sources the great age of Uruk is confirmed, and Hilprecht[3] is of the opinion that it was the capitol of a kingdom contemporaneous with the earliest period of Babylonian history. A lexicographical tablet[4] informs us that Uruk was specially well fortified. It was known as the place of seven walls and, in view of the cosmic significance of the number seven among the Babylonians, Jensen supposes[5] that the city's walls are an imitation of the seven concentric zones into which the world was divided. However this may be, a city so ancient and so well fortified must have played a most important part in old Babylonian history, second only in importance, if not equal, to Nippur. The continued influence of the Ishtar or Nanâ cult of Erech also illustrates the significance of the place. It is natural, therefore, to find traditions surviving of the history of the place.

The first tablet of the Gilgamesh epic contains such a reminiscence. The city is hard pressed by an enemy. The misfortune appears to be sent as a punishment for some

---

[1] *Vorgeschichte der Indo-Europäer*, p. 112.
[2] The words for 'city' in the Semitic languages embody this idea.
[3] *Old Babylonian Inscription*, I. 2, p. 48.
[4] IIR. 50, 55–57; VR. 41, 17, 18. An interesting reference to the wall of Erech occurs Hilprecht, *ib.* I. 1, no. 26.
[5] *Kosmologie*, p. 172.

offence.[1] Everything is in a state of confusion. Asses and cows destroy their young. Men weep and women sigh. The gods and spirits of "walled Uruk" have become hostile forces. For three years the enemy lays siege to the place. The gates of the city remain closed. Who the enemy is we are not told, and such is the fragmentary condition of the tablet that we are left to conjecture the outcome of the city's distress.

In the second tablet, Gilgamesh is introduced as a hero of superior strength and in control of Uruk. Is he the savior of the city or its conqueror? One is inclined to assume the latter, for the inhabitants of Uruk are represented as complaining that Gilgamesh has taken away the sons and daughters of the place. From a passage in a subsequent tablet it appears that Uruk is not the native place of the hero, but Marada.[2] Moreover, the name Gilgamesh is not Babylonian, so that the present evidence speaks in favor of regarding the first episode in the epic as a reminiscence of the extension of Gilgamesh's dominion by the conquest of Uruk. When this event took place we have no means of determining with even a remote degree of probability. The representation of Gilgamesh on very ancient seal cylinders[3] warrants us in passing beyond the third millennium, but more than this can hardly be said.

Gilgamesh is a hero of irresistible power. The inhabitants of Uruk appeal for help to Aruru, who has created Gilgamesh:

> He has no rival. . . .
> Thy inhabitants [appeal for aid?].
> Gilgamesh does not leave a son to his father.
> Day and night, . . .

---

[1] Jeremias' *Izdubar-Nimrod*, p. 15, conjectures that the death of the king has evoked distress, but that is highly improbable. That the fragment under consideration belongs to the beginning of the epic is tolerably certain, though not absolutely so.

[2] Sixth tablet, L 192. He brings offerings to Lugal-Marada, *i.e.*, the king of Marada — a solar deity. See p. 486.

[3] Heuzey, *Sceaux inédits des Rois d'Agade* (*Revue d'Assyriologie*, iv. 3, p. 9).

> He, the ruler of walled Uruk, . . .
> He, their ruler, . . .
> The strong, the preëminent, the cunning, . . .
> Gilgamesh does not leave the virgin to [her mother],
> The daughter to her warrior, the wife to her husband.
> The gods [of heaven] hear their cry.
> They cry aloud to Aruru, "Thou hast created him,
> Now create a rival (?) to him, equal to taking up the fight against him (?)."

So much at least is clear from the badly mutilated lines that Gilgamesh has played sad havoc with the inhabitants of Uruk. In personal combat, as it would appear, he has triumphed over the warriors of the place. The son is taken away from his father, the virgins are taken captive, warriors and husbands are snatched from those dear to them. Aruru is here appealed to as the creator of mankind.[1] She who has created the hero is asked to produce some one who can successfully resist Gilgamesh. Aruru proceeds to do so.

> Aruru, upon hearing this, forms a man of Anu.[2]
> Aruru washes her hands, takes a bit of clay, and throws it on the ground.
> She creates Eabani, a hero, a lofty offspring, the possession of Ninib.[3]

This creature Eabani is described as having a body covered with hair. He has long flowing locks and lives with the animals about him.

> Eating herbs with gazelles,
> Drinking from a trough with cattle,
> Sporting with the creatures of the waters.

The description evidently recalls man living in a savage state, and, to judge from illustrations of Eabani on seal cylinders,

---

[1] See above, p. 448.

[2] *Anu* here used in the generic sense of 'lofty,' 'divine.' The phrase is equivalent to the Biblical 'image of God.'

[3] A phrase in some way again indicative of Eabani's likeness to a deity.

the mythological fancy of the period when strange monsters existed of hybrid formation, half-man, half-beast, has influenced the conception of this strange creature who is to combat the invincible Gilgamesh. But Gilgamesh frustrates the plan. He sends a messenger known as *Sâdu*, that is, 'the hunter,' and described as a "wicked man," to ensnare Eabani.[1] For three days in succession, the hunter sees Eabani drinking at the trough with the cattle, but is unable to catch him. The sight of this 'wild man of the woods' frightens the hunter. He returns to Gilgamesh for further instructions.

Gilgamesh spoke to the hunter:

> Go, hunter mine, and take with thee Ukhat.
> When the cattle comes to the trough,
> Let her tear off her dress and disclose her nakedness.
> He [2] will see her and approach her.
> His cattle, which grew up on his field, will forsake him.

Ukhatu is a name for a harlot devoted to the worship of Ishtar. Other names for such devotees are *Kharimtu*[3] and *Kizritu*.[4] Elsewhere the city Uruk is called "the dwelling of Anu and Ishtar, the city of the *Kizrêti*, *Ukhâti*, and *Kharimâti*,"[5] and in a subsequent tablet of the Gilgamesh epic [6] these three classes of harlots are introduced as the attendants of Ishtar, obedient to her call. The conclusion is therefore justified that Uruk was one of the centers — perhaps the center — of the obscene rites to which Herodotus [7] has several references. Several other incidental allusions in cuneiform literature to the sacred prosti-

---

[1] That Gilgamesh undertakes this, and not the gods acting in the interest of Uruk (as Jeremias and others assume), follows from a passage in Haupt's edition, pp. 10, 40.

[2] Eabani.

[3] Identical with our own word "harem."

[4] Perhaps "ensnarer."

[5] So in the "Dibbarra" legend. See p. 531 and Delitzsch, *Handwörterbuch*, p. 41.

[6] Sixth tablet, ll. 184, 185.

[7] Book I. §§ 181, 182, 199.

tution carried on at Babylonian temples confirm Herodotus' statement in general,[1] although the rite never assumed the large proportions that he reports.

On the other hand, Herodotus does not appear to have understood the religious significance of the custom that he designates as 'shameful.' The name given to the harlot among Babylonians and Hebrews,[2] *Kadishtu* or *K'deshâ*, that is, 'the sacred one,' is sufficient evidence that, at its origin, the rite was not the product of obscene tendencies, but due to naïve conceptions connected with the worship of Ishtar as the goddess of fertility.

The introduction of Ukhat, however, as an aid to carry out the designs of Gilgamesh is devoid of religious significance, and one is inclined to regard the Eabani episode, or at least certain portions of it, as having had at one time an existence quite independent of Gilgamesh's adventures. The description of Eabani is, as we have seen, based upon mythological ideas. The creation of Eabani recalls the Biblical tradition of the formation of the first man, and Ukhat appears to be the Babylonian equivalent to the Biblical Eve, who through her charms entices Eabani away from the gazelles and cattle,[3] and brings him to Uruk, the symbol of civilized existence.

It is significant that in the Biblical narrative, the sexual instinct and the beginnings of culture as symbolized by the tree

---

[1] See Jeremias' *Izdubar-Nimrod*, pp. 59, 60; Nikel, *Herodot und die Keilschriftforschung*, pp. 84–86.

[2] The protest of the Pentateuch (Deut. xxiii. 18) against the *K'deshâ*, as also against the 'male devotee' (*Kadesh*), shows the continued popularity of the rites.

[3] It is to be noted that in the Yahwistic narrative, Adam is in close communication with the animals about him (Gen. ii. 20). It is tempting also to connect the Hebrew form of Eve, *Khauwâ* (or *Khauwat*) in some way with Ukhat, not etymologically of course, but as suggestive of a dependence of one upon the other,—the Hebrew upon the Babylonian term. Professor Stade (*Zeits. f. Alttest. Wiss.*, 1897, p. 210) commenting upon Gen. ii. 20, points out that Yahwe's motive for asking Adam to name the animals was the hope that he would find a 'helpmate' among them. In the light of the Babylonian story of Eabani living with animals, Stade's suggestion receives a striking illustration.

of knowledge are closely associated. According to rabbinical traditions, the serpent is the symbol of the sexual passion.[1]

Eve obtains control of Adam with the aid of this passion. In the episode of Eabani, Ukhat, and the hunter — who, be it noted, plays the part of the tempter — we seem to have an ancient legend forming part of some tradition regarding the beginnings of man's history, and which has been brought into connection with the Gilgamesh epic, — when and how, it is impossible, of course, to say.

The hunter follows the instructions of Gilgamesh. Eabani falls a victim to Ukhat's attractions.

> Ukhat exposed her breast, revealed her nakedness, took off her clothing.
> Unabashed she enticed him.

The details of the meeting are described with a frank simplicity that points again to the antiquity of the legend.

> For six days and seven nights Eabani enjoyed the love of Ukhat.
> After he had satiated himself with her charms,
> He turned his countenance to his cattle.
> The reposing gazelles saw Eabani,
> The cattle of the field turned away from him.
> Eabani was startled and grew faint,
> His limbs grew stiff as his cattle ran off.

But Ukhat has gained control of him. He gives up the thought of gazelles and cattle, and returns to enjoy the love of Ukhat. His senses return,

> And he again turns in love, enthralled at the feet of the harlot,
> Looks up into her face and listens as the woman speaks to him.
> The woman[2] speaks to Eabani:
> " Lofty art thou, Eabani, like to a god.
> Why dost thou lie with the beasts?
> Come, I will bring thee to walled Uruk,

---

[1] See Trumbull, *The Threshold Covenant*, p. 239.
[2] *Kharimtu*. In Arabic the word is likewise used for ' woman ' in general.

> To the glorious house,[1] the dwelling of Anu and Ishtar,
> To the seat of Gilgamesh, perfect in power,
> Surpassing men in strength, like a mountain bull."

It would appear from these lines that previous to the coming of Ukhat, Eabani had satisfied his desire on the beasts. In Ukhat, however, he found a worthier mate, and he accordingly abandons his former associates to cling to her.

> He yields and obeys her command.
> n the wisdom of his heart he recognized a companion.[2]

In the continuation of the story Eabani becomes the companion of Gilgamesh, but I venture to think that the title was transferred in the development of the epic from Ukhat, to whom it originally belonged. It is she who awakens in Eabani a sense of dignity which made him superior to the animals. The word translated 'companion'[3] may be appropriately applied to Ukhat. Eabani clings to her, as Adam does to Eve after she 'is brought'[4] to him. Ukhat becomes Eabani's 'companion,' just as Eve becomes the 'helpmate' of Adam.

These considerations strengthen the supposition that the Eabani-Ukhat episode is quite distinct from the career of Gilgamesh. Had the epic originated in Babylon or Nippur, Eabani and Ukhat would have been brought to Babylon or Nippur. As it is, Eabani asks Ukhat to conduct him

---

[1] The temple at Uruk is meant.

[2] Jeremias translates 'seeks a friend,' and refers the words to Gilgamesh, but there is nothing in the narrative to justify us in assuming that Eabani was thinking of the hero.

[3] It is used as a synonym of *tappu*, 'associate,' Delitzsch, *Handwörterbuch*, p. 10. Ideographically, it is composed of two elements, 'strength' and 'acquire.' 'Companion in arms' is the fellowship originally meant.

[4] The Hebrew verb (Gen. ii. 22) expresses sexual union and precisely the same verb is used in the cuneiform narrative when Eabani comes to Ukhat (Haupt's edition, p. 11, l. 21).

> To the glorious dwelling, the sacred seat of Anu and Ishtar,
> To the seat of Gilgamesh, perfect in power,
> Surpassing men in strength like a mountain bull.

Unfortunately, the tablet at this point is defective,[1] and the following three tablets are represented by small fragments only, from which it is exceedingly difficult to determine more than the general course of the narrative.

Ukhat and Eabani proceed to Uruk. There is an interesting reference to 'a festival' and to festive garments,[2] but whether, as would appear, Ukhat and Eabani are the ones who clothe themselves[3] upon reaching Uruk or whether, as Jeremias believes, a festival was being celebrated at the place it is impossible to say. Eabani is warned in a dream not to undertake a test of strength with Gilgamesh,[4]

> Whose power is stronger than thine,
> Who rests not, . . . neither by day or night.
> O Eabani, change thy . . .
> Shamash loves Gilgamesh,
> Anu, Bel, and Ea have given him wisdom.
> Before thou comest from the mountain
> Gilgamesh in Uruk will see thy dream.[5]

Dreams play an important part in the epic. They constitute the regular means of communication between man and the gods, so regular that at times the compilers of the epic do not find it necessary to specify the fact, but take it for granted. To Gilgamesh, Eabani's coming is revealed and he asks his mother Aruru to interpret the dream.

The third and fourth tablets take us back to the history of Uruk. Gilgamesh, aided by his patron Shamash, succeeds in

---

[1] We can still distinguish (Haupt, 12, 47) 'I will fetch him.' Jeremias' rendering, "I will fight with him," is erroneous.

[2] Haupt, 13, 7-8.   [3] Cf. Gen. iii. 5 and 21.

[4] The text of the following lines restored by combining Haupt, p. 13, with a supplementary fragment published by Jeremias' *Izdubar-Nimrod*, pl. 3.

[5] *I.e.*, he will be told about thy dream through the wisdom given to him.

gaining Eabani as a 'companion' in a contest that is to be waged against Khumbaba, who threatens Uruk. The name of this enemy is Elamitic, and it has been customary to refer the campaign against him to the tradition recorded by Berosus of a native uprising against Elamitic rule, which took place about 2400 B.C.[1] It must be said, however, that there is no satisfactory evidence for this supposition. Elam, lying to the east of the Euphrates, was at all times a serious menace to Babylonia. Hostilities with Elam are frequent before and after the days of Hammurabi. If Gilgamesh, as seems certain, is a Cassite,[2] the conflict between him and Khumbaba would represent a rivalry among Cassitic or Elamitic hordes for the possession of Uruk and of the surrounding district. While the Cassites do not come to the front till the eighteenth century, at which time the center of their kingdom is Nippur, there is every reason to believe that they were settled in the Euphrates Valley long before that period. The course of conquest — as of civilization in Babylonia — being from the south to the north, we would be justified in looking for the Cassites in Uruk before they extended their dominion to Nippur. At all events, the conflict between Gilgamesh and Khumbaba must be referred to a much more ancient period than the rise of the city of Babylon as a political center.

Shamash and Gilgamesh promise Eabani royal honors if he will join friendship with them.

> Come, and on a great couch,
> On a fine couch he[3] will place thee.
> He will give thee a seat to the left.
> The rulers of the earth will kiss thy feet.
> All the people of Uruk will crouch before thee.

Eabani consents, and in company with Gilgamesh proceeds to the fortress of Khumbaba. It is a long and hard road that

---

[1] See, *e.g.*, Jeremias' *Izdubar-Nimrod*, p. 21.
[2] So, *e.g.*, Hommel (*Altisraelitische Ueberlieferung*, p. 35). He is certainly not a native of Babylonia.   [3] Gilgamesh.

they have to travel. The terror inspired by Khumbaba is compared to that aroused by a violent storm, but Gilgamesh receives assurances, in no less than three dreams, that he will come forth unharmed out of the ordeal.

The fortress of Khumbaba is situated in a grove of wonderful grandeur, in the midst of which there is a large cedar, affording shade and diffusing a sweet odor. The description reminds one forcibly of the garden of Eden, and the question suggests itself whether in this episode of the Gilgamesh epic, we have not again a composite production due to the combination of Gilgamesh's adventures with the traditions regarding Eabani. Unfortunately the description of the contest with Khumbaba is missing. There is a reference to the tyrant's death,[1] but that is all. In the sixth tablet, Gilgamesh is celebrated as the victor and not Eabani. We may conclude, therefore, that the episode belongs originally to Gilgamesh's career, and that Eabani has been introduced into it. On the other hand, for Eabani to be placed in a beautiful garden would be a natural consequence of his deserting the gazelles and cattle, — the reward, as it were, of his clinging to Ukhat. Separating the composite elements of the epic in this way, we have as distinct episodes in Gilgamesh's career, the conquest of Uruk and of other places,[2] and his successful campaign against Khumbaba. With this story there has been combined a popular tradition of man's early savage state, his departure from this condition through the sexual passion aroused by Ukhat, who becomes his 'companion,' and with whom or through whom he is led to a beautiful garden as a habitation.

The sixth tablet introduces a third element into the epic, — a mythological one. The goddess Ishtar pleads for the love of Gilgamesh. She is attracted to him by his achievements and his personality. The tablet begins with a description of the

[1] Haupt, p. 26.
[2] A city Ganganna is mentioned in the first tablet (Haupt, pp. 51, 6).

celebration of Gilgamesh's victory. The hero exchanges his blood-stained clothes for white garments, polishes his weapons, and places a crown on his head.

> To secure the grace of Gilgamesh, the exalted Ishtar raises her eyes.
> Come, Gilgamesh, be my husband,
> Thy love[1] grant me as a gift,
> Be thou my husband and I will be thy wife.
> I will place thee on a chariot of lapis lazuli and gold,
> With wheels of gold and horns of sapphire (?)
> Drawn by great . . . steeds (?).
> With sweet odor of cedars enter our house.
> Upon entering our house,
> . . . will kiss thy feet.
> Kings, lords, and princes will be submissive to thee,
> Products of mountain and land, they will bring as tribute to thee.

Ishtar appears here as the goddess of love and fertility. As such she promises Gilgamesh also abundance of herds. But Gilgamesh rejects the offer, giving as his reason the sad fate encountered by those who were victims of Ishtar's love:

> Tammuz, the consort of thy youth (?),
> Thou causest to weep every year.
> The bright-colored *allallu* bird thou didst love.
> Thou didst crush him and break his pinions.
> In the woods he stands and laments, "O my pinions!"
> Thou didst love a lion of perfect strength,
> Seven and seven times[2] thou didst bury him in the corners (?),
> Thou didst love a horse superior in the fray,
> With whip and spur[3] thou didst urge him on.
> Thou didst force him on for seven double hours,[4]
> Thou didst force him on when wearied and thirsty;
> His mother Silili thou madest weep.

In this way Gilgamesh proceeds to upbraid the goddess, instancing, in addition, her cruel treatment of a shepherd, and apparently also of a giant, whom she changed to a dwarf. The

---

[1] So Haupt, *Beiträge zur Assyriologie*, i. 112.
[2] *I.e.*, again and again.   [3] This is the general sense of the three terms used.
[4] *I.e.*, an army's march of fourteen hours. See pp. 490, 503, 521.

allusions, while obscure, are all of a mythological character. The weeping of Tammuz symbolizes the decay of vegetation after the summer season. The misfortunes that afflict the bird, lion, and horse similarly indicate the loss of beauty and strength, which is the universal fate of those who once enjoyed those attributes. Ishtar, as the great mother, produces life and strength, but she is unable to make life and strength permanent. Popular belief makes her responsible for decay and death, since life and fertility appear to be in her hand. Gilgamesh, as a popular hero, is brought into association by popular traditions with Ishtar, as he is brought into relationships with Eabani and Ukhat. A factor in this association was the necessity of accounting for Gilgamesh's death. As a hero, the favorite of the gods and invincible in battle, he ought to enjoy the privilege of the gods — immortality. The question had to be answered how he came to forego this distinction. The insult he offers to Ishtar is the answer to this question. Knowing that Ishtar, although the giver of life, does not grant a continuance of it, he who is produced by Aruru will have nothing to do with the great goddess. But his refusal leads to a dire punishment, more disastrous even than the alliance with Ishtar, which would have culminated in his being eventually shorn of his strength.

Ishtar, determined that Gilgamesh should not escape her, flies in rage to her father Anu, the god of heaven, and tells of the manner in which she has been treated. Anu comforts her. Yielding to Ishtar's request he creates a divine bull, known as Alû, *i.e.*, the strong or supreme one,[1] who is to destroy Gilgamesh. At this point in the narrative Eabani is again introduced. Gilgamesh and Eabani together proceed to the contest with the bull, as they formerly proceeded against Khumbaba. On seal cylinders this fight is frequently pictured.[2] In agreement with the description in the narrative, Eabani takes hold

---

[1] The same word appears in incantation texts as a term for a class of demons.
[2] See, *e.g.*, Jeremias' *Izdubar-Nimrod*, p. 26.

of the tail of the animal, while Gilgamesh despatches him by driving a spear into the bull's heart. Ishtar's plan is thus frustrated.

> Ishtar mounts the wall of walled Uruk.
> In violent rage she pronounces a curse:
> "Cursed be Gilgamesh, who has enraged me,
> Who has killed the divine bull."

Eabani adds insult to injury by challenging the goddess.

> Eabani, upon hearing these words of Ishtar,
> Takes the carcass (?) of the divine bull and throws it into her face.
> Woe to thee! I will subdue thee,
> I will do to thee as I have done to him.[1]

The mythological motives that prompted the introduction of Ishtar into this tablet now become apparent. The division of the epic into twelve parts is due to scholastic influences. It is certainly not accidental that the calendar also consists of twelve months. While it is by no means the case that each tablet corresponds to some month, still in the case of the sixth and, as we shall see, in the case of the seventh and eleventh tablets, this correspondence is certain. The sixth month is designated as the month of the "Mission of Ishtar." What this mission is we shall see in a subsequent chapter.[2] In this month was celebrated a festival to Tammuz, the young bridegroom of Ishtar, who is slain by the goddess. The prophet Ezekiel gives us a picture of the weeping for Tammuz,[3] which formed the chief ceremony of the day.

It is this character of the month that accounts not only for the introduction of the Ishtar episode in the sixth tablet, but which finds further illustrations in the mourning which Ishtar and her attendants indulge in after the death of the divine bull.

> Ishtar assembled the Kizrêti,
> Ukhâti and Kharimâti.
> Over the carcass of Alû they raised a lamentation.

[1] *I.e.*, to the bull. [2] Chapter xxv. [3] Ez. viii. 14.

These three classes of sacred prostitutes have already been dwelt upon.[1] With more material at our disposal regarding the cult of Ishtar or Nanâ of Erech, we would be in a position to specify the character of the rites performed at this temple. The statements of Herodotus and of other writers suffice, however, to show that the three terms represent classes of priestesses attached to the temple. In this respect the Ishtar cult of Erech was not unique, for we have references to priestesses elsewhere. However, the function of the priestess in religious history differs materially from that of the priest. She is not a mediator between the god and his subjects, nor is she a representative of the deity. It is as a 'witch,' that by virtue of the association of ideas above set forth,[2] she is able to determine the intentions of the gods. Her power to do harm is supplemented by her ability to furnish oracles. In this capacity we have already come across her,[3] and we may assume that giving oracles constituted a chief function of the priestess in Babylonia. It was furthermore natural to conclude that as a 'witch' and 'oracle-giver,' the priestess belonged to the deity from whom she derived her power. When we come to the cult of a goddess like Ishtar, who is the symbol of fertility, observances that illustrated this central notion would naturally form an ingredient part of that 'sympathetic magic,' — the imitation of an action in order to produce the reality — which dominates so large a proportion of early religious ceremonialism. Among many nations the mysterious aspects of woman's fertility lead to rites that by a perversion of their original import appear to be obscene.[4] In the reference to the three classes of sacred prostitutes, we have an evidence that the Babylonian worship formed no exception to the rule. But with this proposition that the prostitutes were priestesses attached to the Ishtar cult and who took part in ceremonies intended to symbolize fertility, we must for the present rest content.

[1] See above, p. 475. [2] See p. 267. [3] See above, p. 234.
[4] Trumbull, *The Threshold Covenant*, chapter vii.

Gilgamesh, secure in his victory, proceeds to offer the horns of the divine bull to his patron Lugal-Marada, the 'king' of Marad, and who appears to be identical with Shamash himself. The offering is accompanied by gifts to the sanctuary of precious stones and oil. There is general rejoicing.

The episode of Gilgamesh's contest with the bull also belongs to the mythological phases of the epic. The bull is in Babylonian mythology[1] as among other nations a symbol of the storm. It is in his rôle as a solar deity that Gilgamesh triumphs over the storm sent by Anu, that is, from on high. In the following chapter, we will come across another form of this same myth suggested evidently, as was the fight of Marduk with Tiâmat, by the annual storms raging in Babylonia. Gilgamesh triumphs as does Marduk, but when once the summer solstice, which represents the sun's triumph, is past, the decline of the sun's strength begins to set in. This is indicated by the subsequent course of the narrative.

The scene of rejoicing at Gilgamesh's triumph is changed to one of sadness. Eabani is snatched away from Gilgamesh. The few fragments of the seventh and eighth tablets do not suffice for determining exactly in what way this happened, but Ishtar is evidently the cause of the misfortune. A fatal illness, it would seem, seizes hold of Eabani, — whether as the result of a further contest or directly sent, it is impossible to say. For twelve days he lingers and then is taken away. As usual, the catastrophe is foreseen in dreams. For a third time[2] he sees a vision of fire and lightning, which forebodes the end.

The fragmentary condition of the epic at this point is particularly unfortunate. There is a reference to Nippur,[3] of which it would be important to know the purpose.

The relationship between Gilgamesh and Eabani would be

---

[1] See p. 536.
[2] Or as a third dream. It will be recalled that in a previous portion of the epic (p. 481), Gilgamesh has three dreams in succession.   [3] Haupt, pp. 45, 53.

much clearer if the seventh and eighth tablets were preserved in good condition. The disappearance of Eabani before the end of the epic confirms, however, the view here maintained, that the career of Eabani was originally quite independent of Gilgamesh's adventures. His death is as superfluous as is his association with Eabani. In all critical moments Gilgamesh appears to stand alone. He conquers Uruk, and it is he who celebrates the victory of the divine bull. The subsequent course of the narrative after Eabani's death, except for the frequent mention of Gilgamesh's lament for his companion, proceeds undisturbed. Moreover, Eabani's punishment appears to be identical with that meted out to Gilgamesh. The latter is also stricken with disease, but in his case, the disease has a meaning that fits in with the mythological phases of the epic. The seventh month — the one following the summer solstice — marks the beginning of a turning-point in the year. As the year advances, vegetation diminishes, and the conclusion was naturally drawn that the sun upon whom vegetation depended had lost some of his force. This loss of strength is pictured as a disease with which the sun is afflicted. In this way, the seventh tablet — and possibly also the eighth — continues the nature myth embodied in the sixth.

Haupt has ingeniously conjectured that the sickness which affects Gilgamesh is of a venereal character. The hero wanders about in search of healing. His suffering is increased by his deep sorrow over the loss of his 'companion.' The death of Eabani presages his own destruction, and he dreads the dreary fate in store for him. The ninth tablet introduces us to this situation.

> Gilgamesh weeps for his companion Eabani.
> In distress he is stretched out on the ground.[1]
> 'I will not die like Eabani.
> Sorrow has entered my body.
> Through fear of death, I lie stretched out on the ground.'

[1] Attitude of despair.

He determines to seek out a mysterious personage, whom he calls Parnapishtim,[1] the son of Kidin-Marduk.[2] This personage has in some way escaped the fate of mankind and enjoys immortal life. He is called the "distant one." His dwelling is far off, "at the confluence of the streams." The road to the place is full of dangers, but Gilgamesh, undaunted, undertakes the journey. The hero himself furnishes the description.

> I came to a glen at night,
> Lions I saw and was afraid.
> I raised my head and prayed to Sin.
> To the leader (?) of the gods my prayer came.
> [He heard my prayer (?)], and was gracious to me.

On many seal cylinders and on monuments, Gilgamesh is pictured in the act of fighting with or strangling a lion. In the preserved portions of the epic no reference to this contest has been found.[3] We should look for it at this point of the narrative. The following lines contain a reference to weapons, — ax and sword, — and in so far justify the supposition that some contest takes place. But the text is too mutilated to warrant further conjectures. After escaping from the danger occasioned by the lions, Gilgamesh comes to the mountain Mashu, which is described as a place of terrors, the entrance to which is guarded by 'scorpion-men.'

> He reached the mountain Mashu,
> Whose exit is daily guarded, . . .
> Whose back extends to the dam of heaven,

---

[1] *Ie.*, 'offspring of life.' I adopt Delitzsch's reading of the name. Zimmern and Jensen prefer *Sitnapishtim*, but see Haupt's remarks on the objections to this reading in Schrader, *Keilinschriften und das Alte Testament* (3d edition) *a. l.* At the recent Eleventh International Congress of Orientalists, Scheil presented a tablet dealing with the deluge narrative. If his reading is correct, the evidence would be final for the form Pirnapishtim, formerly proposed by Zimmern (*Babylonische Buss-psalmen*, p. 26). See p. 507, note 1.

[2] "Client of Marduk." The name Marduk appears here under the ideographic designation *Tutu*. The identification with Marduk may be due to later traditions.

[3] Jeremias' suggestion (*Izdubar-Nimrod*, p.18) that the fight with the lion belongs to the first tablet, where mention is made of a wild animal of some kind, is not acceptable.

And whose breast [1] reaches to Aralu; [2]
Scorpion-men guard its gate,
Of terror-inspiring aspect, whose appearance is deadly,
Of awful splendor, shattering mountains.
At sunrise and sunset they keep guard over the sun.

It will be recalled that the earth is pictured by the Babylonians as a mountain. The description of Mashu is dependent upon this conception. The mountain seems to be coextensive with the earth. The dam of heaven is the point near which the sun rises, and if the scorpion-men guard the sun at sunrise and sunset, the mountain must extend across to the gate through which the sun passes at night to dip into the great *Apsu*.[3]

Aralu is situated under the earth, and Mashu, reaching down to Aralu, must be again coextensive with the earth in this direction. The description of Mashu accordingly is a reflex of the cosmological conceptions developed in Babylonia. The scorpion-men pictured on seal cylinders[4] belong to the mythical monsters, half-man, half-beast, with which the world was peopled at the beginning of things. However, there is also an historical background to the description. The name Mashu appears in texts as the Arabian desert to the west and southwest of the Euphrates Valley.[5] It is called a land of dryness, where neither birds nor gazelles nor wild asses are found. Even the bold Assyrian armies hesitated before passing through this region. In the light of the early relationships between Babylonia and Arabia,[6] this reference to Mashu may embody a tradition of some expedition to Southern Arabia.[7] Beyond Mashu

---

[1] *I.e.*, inner side.

[2] The name of the cave underneath the earth where the dead dwell.

[3] See above, p. 443.

[4] See, *e.g.*, Jeremias' *Izdubar-Nimrod*, p. 28.

[5] See the passages in Delitzsch, *Wo Lag das Paradies*, pp. 242, 243.

[6] See above, p. 39, and Hommel's full discussion, *Altisraelitische Ueberlieferung*, chapter iii.

[7] Hommel (*Altisraelitische Ueberlieferung*, pp. 35, 37) suggests a migration of Cassites from Elam to Eastern Africa.

lay a great sea, — perhaps the Arabian Sea, — which Gilgamesh is obliged to cross ere he reaches his goal.

Gilgamesh is terrified at the sight of these scorpion-men but the latter have received notice of his coming and permit him to pass through the gate.

> A scorpion-man addresses his wife:
> "He who comes to us is of divine appearance."

The wife of the scorpion-man agrees that Gilgamesh is in part divine, but she adds that in part he is human. In further conversation, the scorpion-man announces that it is by express command of the gods that Gilgamesh has come to the mountain. Gilgamesh approaches and tells the scorpion-man of his purpose. The hero, recovering his courage, is not held back by the description that the scorpion-man gives him of the dangers that beset the one who ventures to enter the dreadful district. The gate is opened and the journey begins.

> He gropes his way for one double hour,
> With dense darkness enclosing him on all sides.
> He gropes his way for two double hours,
> With dense darkness enclosing him on all sides.

After traversing a distance of twenty-four hours' march, Gilgamesh beholds a tree of splendid appearance, decorated with precious stones and bearing beautiful fruit. Finally he reaches the sea, where the maiden Sabitum has her palace and throne. Upon seeing the hero, the maiden locks the gates of her palace and will not permit Gilgamesh to pass across the sea. Gilgamesh pleads with Sabitum, tells of the loss of his friend Eabani, 'who has become dust,'[1] and whose fate he does not wish to share.

> Gilgamesh speaks to Sabitum:
> "[Now] Sabitum, which is the way to Parnapishtim?
> If it is possible, let me cross the ocean.
> If it is not possible, let me stretch myself on the ground."[2]

---

[1] Haupt, pp. 12, 67.   [2] Attitude of despair.

Sabitum speaks to Gilgamesh:
" O Gilgamesh! there has never been a ferry,
And no one has ever crossed the ocean.
Shamash, the hero, has crossed it, but except Shamash, who can cross it?
Difficult is the passage, very difficult the path.
Impassible (?) the waters of death that are guarded by a bolt.
How canst thou, O Gilgamesh, traverse the ocean?
And after thou hast crossed the waters of death, what wilt thou do?"

Sabitum then tells Gilgamesh that there is one possibility of his accomplishing his task. If Ardi-Ea,[1] the ferryman[2] of Parnapishtim, will take Gilgamesh across, well and good; if not, he must abandon all hope.

The ocean, though not expressly called *Apsu*, is evidently identical with the great body of waters supposed to both surround the earth and to flow beneath it.[3] The reference to 'the waters of death' thus becomes clear. The gathering-place of the dead being under the earth, near to the *Apsu*, the great 'Okeanos' forms a means of approach to the nether world. It is into this ocean, forming part of the *Apsu*, that the sun dips at evening and through which it passes during the night. The scene between Gilgamesh and Sabitum accordingly is suggested, in part, by the same cosmological conceptions that condition the description of the mountain Mashu.

Sabitum herself is a figure that still awaits satisfactory explanation. She is called the goddess Siduri.[4] The name of this goddess is found as an element in proper names, but of her traits we know nothing. Sabitum appears originally to have been a term descriptive of her, and Hommel[5] may be right in explaining the name as 'the one from Sabu,'[6] and in taking the latter as the name of a district in Arabia. It is tempting to think of the famous Saba in Southern Arabia.

---

[1] *I.e.*, 'servant of Ea.' The reading Ardi-Ea is preferable to Arad-Ea.
[2] Lit., 'sailor.'   [3] See above, p. 443.
[4] Haupt, pp. 64, 36; 65, 1   [5] *Alttisraelitische Ueberlieferung*, p. 35.
[6] *Tum* is the feminine ending.

Obedient to the advice of Sabitum, Gilgamesh tells Ardi-Ea his story and also his desire.

> Now Ardi-Ea, which is the way to [Parnapishtim?].
> If it is possible, let me cross the ocean,
> And if not possible, let me lie outstretched on the ground.

Ardi-Ea consents, and tells Gilgamesh to take his ax, to go into the woods, and to cut down a large pole that may serve as a rudder.

> Gilgamesh, upon hearing this,
> Takes an ax in his hand, . . .
> Goes to the wood and makes a rudder five *gar*[1] long.
> Gilgamesh and Ardi-Ea mount the ship.
> . . . .
> The ship tosses from side to side.
> After a course of one month and fifteen days, on the third day[2]
> Ardi-Ea reaches the waters of death.

This appears to be the most dangerous part of the voyage. Ardi-Ea urges Gilgamesh to cling to the rudder, and counts the strokes he is to take.[3] The waters are not extensive, for only twelve strokes are enumerated; but the current is so strong that it is with the utmost difficulty that Gilgamesh succeeds in passing through them. At last, Gilgamesh is face to face with Parnapishtim. The latter is astonished to see a living person come across the waters. Gilgamesh addresses Parnapishtim from the ship, recounts his deeds, among which we distinguish[4] the killing of a panther, of Alû, of the divine bull, and of Khumbaba. The death of Eabani is also dwelt upon, and then Gilgamesh pleads with Parnapishtim, tells him of the long, difficult way that he has traveled, and of all that he has encountered on the road.

> Difficult lands I passed through,
> All seas I crossed.

---

[1] A large measure.

[2] Of the week? Hommel and others interpret that Gilgamesh accomplishes the 'forty-five days' journey' in three days.

[3] This I take to be the meaning of the numbers introduced at this point.

[4] The text is badly mutilated.

Parnapishtim expresses his sympathy:

> Gilgamesh has filled his heart with woe,
> But neither gods nor men [can help him (?)].

Parnapishtim thereupon addresses Gilgamesh, showing him how impossible it is for any mortal to escape death. The inexorable law will prevail as long as 'houses continue to be built,' as long as 'friendships' and 'hostilities' prevail, as long 'as the waters fill (?) the sea.' The Anunnaki, the great gods, and the goddess Mammitum, the creators of everything

> Determine death and life.
> No one knows the days of death.[1]

At this point Gilgamesh propounds a most natural question: How comes it, if what Parnapishtim says is true, that the latter is alive, while possessing all the traits of a human being? The eleventh tablet of the epic begins:

> Gilgamesh speaks to him, to Parnapishtim, the far-removed:
> "I gaze at thee in amazement, Parnapishtim.
> Thy appearance is normal. As I am, so art thou.
> Thy entire nature [2] is normal. As I am, so art thou.
> Thou art completely equipped for the fray.[3]
> Armor [4] (?) thou hast placed upon thee.
> Tell me how thou didst come to obtain eternal life among the gods."

In reply, Parnapishtim tells the story of his escape from the common fate of mankind. The story is a long one and has no connection with the career of Gilgamesh. It embodies a recollection of a rain-storm that once visited a city, causing a general destruction, but from which Parnapishtim and his family miraculously escaped. The main purport of the tale is not to emphasize this miracle, but the far greater one that, after having been saved from the catastrophe, Parnapishtim should also have been granted immortal life. The moral, however, is that the ex-

---

[1] There is no limit to the rule of death. Death alone is 'immortal.'
[2] As Haupt correctly interprets.
[3] This appears to be the sense of this rather obscure line.
[4] Read [sir-la]-am?

ception proves the rule. With this tradition of the destruction of a certain place, there has been combined a nature myth symbolizing the annual overflow of the Euphrates, and the temporary disappearance of all land that this inundation brought about, prior to the elaborate canal system that was developed in the valley. It is the same myth that we have come across in the creation epic and which, as we have seen, was instrumental in moulding the advanced cosmological conceptions of the Babylonians.

In Parnapishtim's tale, the myth is given a more popular form. There is no attempt made to impart a scholastic interpretation to it. In keeping with what we have seen to be the general character of the Gilgamesh epic, the episode introduced at this point embodies popular traditions and, on the whole, popular conceptions. The spirit of the whole epic is the same that we find in the Thousand and One Nights or in the Arabian romance of Antar.

The oriental love of story-telling has produced the Gilgamesh epic and, like a true story, it grows in length, the oftener it is told. Gilgamesh is merely a peg upon which various current traditions and myths are hung. Hence the combination of Gilgamesh's adventures with those of Eabani, and hence also the association of Gilgamesh with Parnapishtim. A trace, perhaps, of scholastic influence may be seen in the purport of Parnapishtim's narrative to prove the hopelessness of man's securing immortality; and yet, while the theology of the schools may thus have had some share in giving to the tale of Parnapishtim its present shape, the problem presented by Gilgamesh's adventures is a popular rather than a scholastic one. Even to the primitive mind, for whom life rather than death constitutes the great mystery to be solved, the question would suggest itself whether death is an absolutely necessary phase through which man must pass. The sun, moon, and stars do not die, the streams have perpetual life; and since all manifestations of life were looked at from one point of view, why should not man also remain alive? Beyond some touches in the narrative, we may, therefore, regard Parnapishtim's story, together with the 'lesson' it teaches, as an interesting trace of the early theology as it took shape in the popular mind. What adds interest to the story that Parnapishtim tells, is its close resemblance to the Biblical story of the Deluge. It also recalls the destruction of Sodom, and we shall have occasion[1] to show the significance of these points of contact. Bearing in mind the independent character of the Parnapishtim episode, and the motives that led to its being incorporated in the adventures of Gilgamesh, we may proceed with our analysis of this interesting eleventh tablet. Thanks to the labors of Haupt, the numerous fragments of it representing several copies, have been pieced together so as to form an almost complete text.[2] In reply to Gilgamesh's queries,

> Parnapishtim spoke to Gilgamesh:
> "I will tell thee, Gilgamesh, the secret story,
> And the secret of the gods I will tell thee.
> The city Shurippak, a city which, as thou knowest,
> Lies on the Euphrates,
> That city was old,[3] for the gods thereof,
> Decided to bring a rainstorm upon it.
> All of the great gods, Anu, their father,
> Their counsellor, the warrior Bel,
> The herald Ninib,
> Their leader En-nugi,
> The lord of unsearchable wisdom, Ea, was with them,
> To proclaim their resolve to the reed-huts.
> Reed-hut, reed-hut, wall, wall!
> Reed-hut, hear! Wall, give ear!"

The ordinary houses of Babylonia were constructed of reeds,

---

[1] See below, p. 507.

[2] The restored text in Haupt's edition of the *Nimrodepos*, pp. 134-149.

[3] Zimmern ingeniously suggests *la bir*, "not pure," instead of the rendering 'old.'

while the temples and palaces were built of hard-baked clay. "Reed-hut" and "clay structure," thus embracing the architecture of the country, are poetically used to designate the inhabitants of Shurippak. The address to the huts and structures has been appropriately compared by Professor Haupt to the opening words of Isaiah's prophecies.[1]

> Hear, Heavens! and give ear, Earth!

Ea's words are intended as a warning to the people of Shurippak. The warning comes appropriately from Ea as the god of humanity, who according to some traditions is also the creator of mankind, and who is the teacher and protector of mankind. Opposed to Ea is Bel, the old Bel of Nippur, who is represented as favoring the destruction of humanity. The story in this way reflects a rivalry between the Ea and Bel cults.

Of Shurippak, against which the anger of the gods is enkindled, we unfortunately know nothing,[2] but it is fair to assume that there was an ancient city of that name, and which was destroyed by an overflow of the Euphrates during the rainy season. The city need not necessarily have been one of much importance. Its sad fate would naturally have impressed itself upon the memory of the people, and given rise to legends precisely as the disappearance of Sodom[3] or of the destruction of the tribes of Ad and Thamud gave rise to fantastic stories among Hebrews and Arabs respectively.[4]

Ea, not content with the general warning, sends a special message to Parnapishtim, one of the inhabitants of Shurippak.

> O man of Shurippak, son of Kidin-Marduk![5]
> Erect a structure,[6] build a ship,

---

[1] Isaiah i. 1.
[2] See Jensen's remarks, *Kosmologie*, p. 387. There is no reference to Shurippak in IIR. 46, 1, as Haupt has shown (see his note in the 3d edition of Schrader's *Keilinschriften und das Alte Testament*). [3] Gen. xix.
[4] Hughes, *Dictionary of Islam*, sub "Ad" and "Salih."
[5] See above, p. 488, note 2.
[6] Lit., 'construct a house'; house is used for any kind of structure in general.

> Abandon your goods, look after the souls,[1]
> Throw aside your possessions, and save your life,
> Load the ship with all kinds of living things.

The god then tells Parnapishtim in what manner to build the ship. Its dimensions should be carefully measured. Its breadth and depth should be equal, and when it is finished, Parnapishtim is to float it. The warning from Ea comes to him in a dream, as we learn from a subsequent part of the story. Parnapishtim does not deem it necessary to dwell upon this, for it is only through dreams that the gods communicate with kings and heroes.

Parnapishtim declares his readiness to obey the orders of Ea, but like Moses upon receiving the command of Yahwe, he asks what he should say when people question him.

> What shall I answer the city, the people, and the elders?

Ea replies:

> Thus answer and speak to them:
> Bel has cast me out in his hatred,
> So that I can no longer dwell in your city.
> On Bel's territory I dare no longer show my face;
> Therefore, I go to the 'deep' to dwell with Ea my lord.

Bel's domain is the earth, while Ea controls the watery elements. Bel's hostility to mankind is limited to the inhabitants of the dry land. The moment that Parnapishtim enters Ea's domain he is safe. The answer thus not only furnishes the real motive for the building of the ship, but further illustrates the purport of the narrative in its present form. It is a glorification of Ea at the expense of Bel, and it is not difficult to detect the thought underlying the story that the evils afflicting mankind on earth are due to the hostility of the 'chief demon,'[2] who becomes the controller of the earth and of the atmosphere

---

[1] *I.e.*, let your property go and save your family.
[2] See above, p. 53.

immediately above the earth. Ea's answer is not intended to be equivocal, for he further orders Parnapishtim to announce to his fellow-citizens the coming destruction.

> Over you a rainstorm will come,
> Men, birds, and beasts will perish.

The following line[1] is defective, but it appears to except from the general destruction the fish as the inhabitants of the domain controlled by Ea. The time when the catastrophe is to take place is vaguely indicated.

> When Shamash will bring on the time, then the lord of the whirlstorm
> Will cause destruction to rain upon you in the evening.

The 'lord of the whirlstorm' is Ramman, and the reference to this deity specifies the manner in which the catastrophe will be brought about. As in the Biblical story, 'the windows of heaven are to be opened,' the rains will come down, driven by the winds that are to be let loose. It has been supposed that because the ship of Parnapishtim drifts to the north that the storm came from the south.[2] No stress, however, is laid upon the question of direction in the Babylonian narrative. The phenomenon of a whirlstorm with rain is of ordinary occurrence; its violence alone makes it an exceptional event, but — be it noted — not a miraculous one. Nor are we justified in attributing the deluge to the rush of waters from the Persian Gulf, for this sheet of water is particularly sacred to Ea as the beginning of the "great deep." It would be an insult to Ea's dignity to suppose that he is unable to govern his own territory. The catastrophe comes from above, from Ramman and his associates who act at the instigation of the belligerent Bel.

Parnapishtim begins at once to build the ship. He gathers his material, and on the fifth day is ready to construct the hull. The ship resembles the ordinary craft still used on the Eu-

---

[1] L. 45.
[2] Jensen, *Kosmologie*, p. 368; Jeremias, *Izdubar-Nimrod*, p. 37.

phrates. It is a flat-bottomed skiff with upturned edges. On this shell the real 'house'[1] of Parnapishtim is placed. The structure is accurately described. Its height is one hundred and twenty cubits, and its breadth is the same, in accordance with the express orders given by Ea. No less than six floors are erected, one above the other.

> Then I built six stories,[2]
> So that the whole consisted of seven apartments.
> The interior[3] I divided into nine parts.

The structure may properly be called a 'house boat,' and its elaborate character appears from the fact that it contains no less than sixty-three compartments. Parnapishtim carefully provides plugs to fill out all crevices, and furthermore smears a large quantity of bitumen without and within.

> I provided a pole,[4] and all that was necessary,
> Six *sar*[5] of bitumen[6] I smeared on the outside,[7]
> Three *sar* of pitch [I smeared] on the inside.

He also has a large quantity of oil placed on the boat, oxen, jars filled with mead[8] oil, and wine for a festival, which he institutes at the completion of the structure. The preparations are on a large scale, as for the great New Year's Day celebrated in Babylonia. The ship is launched, and, if Professor Haupt is correct in his interpretation, the ship took water to the extent of two-thirds of its height.

> The side of the ship dipped two-thirds into water.

---

[1] See above, p. 496, note 6.
[2] Or decks (so Haupt).
[3] Of each story or deck.
[4] Poles are used to this day to propel the crafts on the Euphrates.
[5] The largest measure.
[6] The same word (*kupru*) is used as in Gen. vi. 14.
[7] Some part of the outside of the structure is designated.
[8] Haupt translates "Sesammeth."

Parnapishtim now proceeds to take his family and chattels on board.

> All that I had, I loaded on the ship.
> With all the silver that I had, I loaded it,
> With all the gold that I had, I loaded it,
> With living creatures of all kinds I loaded it.
> I brought on board my whole family and household,
> Cattle of the field, beasts of the field, workmen, — all this I took on board.

Parnapishtim is ready to enter the ship, but he waits until the time fixed for the storm arrives.

> When the time came
> For the lord of the whirlstorm to rain down destruction,
> I gazed at the earth,
> I was terrified at its sight,
> I entered the ship, and closed the door.
> To the captain of the ship, to Puzur-Shadurabu,[1] the sailor,
> I entrusted the structure [2] with all its contents.

The description of the storm follows, in diction at once impressive and forcible.

> Upon the first appearance of dawn,
> There arose from the horizon dark clouds,
> Within which Ramman caused his thunder to resound.
> Nabu and Sharru [3] marched at the front,
> The destroyers passed across mountains and land,
> Dibbarra [4] lets loose the . . . .[5]
> Ninib advances in furious hostility.
> The Anunnaki raise torches,
> Whose sheen illumines the universe,
> As Ramman's whirlwind sweeps the heavens,
> And all light is changed to darkness.

[1] "Puzur" signifies 'hidden,' 'protected.' "Shadu rabu," *i.e.*, 'great mountain,' is a title of Bel and of other gods (see above, pp. 56 and 278). Here, probably, Shamash is meant.   [2] Lit., 'great house' or 'palace.'

[3] *I.e.*, 'king,' frequently found as a title of Marduk in astronomical texts (Jensen, *Kosmologie*, p. 145).

[4] The god of war and pestilence.

[5] "Tar-gul-le," some mischievous forces.

The destructive elements, thunder, lightning, storm, rain, are thus let loose. The dreadful storm lasts for seven days. The terror of men and gods is splendidly portrayed.

> Brother does not look after brother,
> Men care not for another. In the heavens,
> Even the gods are terrified at the storm.
> They take refuge in the heaven of Anu.[1]
> The gods cowered like dogs at the edge of the heavens.

With this description the climax in the narrative is reached. The reaction begins. Ishtar is the first to bewail the destruction that has been brought about, and her example is followed by others of the gods.

> Ishtar groans like a woman in throes,
> The lofty goddess cries with loud voice,
> The world of old has become a mass of clay.[2]

Ishtar appears here in the rôle of the mother of mankind. She feels that she has none but herself to blame for the catastrophe, for, as one of the great gods, she must have been present at the council when the storm was decided on, and must have countenanced it. She therefore reproaches herself:

> That I should have assented[3] to this evil among the gods!
> That when I assented to this evil,
> I was for the destruction of my own creatures![4]
> What I created, where is it?
> Like so many fish, it[5] fills the sea.

From the words of Ishtar it would appear that the storm had assumed larger dimensions than the gods, or at least than some of them, had anticipated. At the beginning of the episode, Shurippak alone is mentioned, and Ishtar apparently wishes to say that when she agreed to the bringing on of the storm, she

---

[1] The highest part of heaven.
[2] *I.e.*, has been destroyed.
[3] Lit., 'spoken' or 'ordered.'
[4] Lit., 'my mankind.'
[5] *I.e.*, Mankind.

was not aware that she was decreeing the destruction of all mankind. It is evident that two distinct traditions have been welded together in the present form of the Babylonian document, one recalling the destruction of a single city, the other embodying in mythological form the destructive rains of Babylonia that were wont to annually flood the entire country before the canal system was perfected.

Some particularly destructive season may have formed an additional factor in the combination of the traditions. At all events, the storm appears to have got beyond the control of the gods, and none but Bel approves of the widespread havoc that has been wrought. It is no unusual phenomenon in ancient religions to find the gods powerless to control occurrences that they themselves produced. The Anunnaki — even more directly implicated than Ishtar in bringing on the catastrophe — join the goddess in her lament at the complete destruction wrought.

> The gods, together with the Anunnaki, wept with her.
> The gods, in their depression, sat down to weep,
> Pressed their lips together, were overwhelmed with grief (?).
> The storm could no longer be quieted.
> For six days and nights
> Wind, rain-storm, hurricane swept along;
> When the seventh day arrived, the storm began to moderate,
> Which had waged a contest like a great host.
> The sea quieted down, wind and rain-storm ceased.

Parnapishtim then gazes at the destruction.

> Bitterly weeping I looked at the sea,
> For all mankind had been turned to clay.[1]
> In place of dams, everything had become a marsh.
> I opened a hole so as to let the light fall upon my face,
> And dumbfounded, I sat down and wept.
> Tears flowed down my face.
> I looked in all directions, — naught but sea.

[1] From which they were made. See pp. 448 and 511.

But soon the waters began to diminish.

> After twelve double hours [1] an island appeared,
> The ship approached the mountain Nisir.

The name given to the first promontory to appear is significant. *Nisir* signifies 'protection' or 'salvation.' The houseboat clings to this spot.

> At this mountain, the mountain Nisir, the boat stuck fast.

For six days the boat remains in the same position. At the beginning of the seventh day, Parnapishtim endeavors to ascertain whether the waters have abated sufficiently to permit him to leave the boat.

> When the seventh day approached
> I sent forth a dove.
> The dove flew about
> But, finding no resting place, returned;
> Then I sent forth a swallow.
> The swallow flew about
> But, finding no resting place, returned;
> Then I sent forth a raven.
> The raven flew off, and, seeing that the waters had decreased,
> Cautiously [2] (?) waded in the mud, but did not return.

Parnapishtim is satisfied, leaves the ship, and brings a sacrifice to the gods on the top of the mountain. In seven large bowls he places calamus, cedarwood, and incense.

> The gods inhaled the odor,
> The gods inhaled the sweet odor,
> The gods gathered like flies around the sacrificer.

A solemn scene ensues. Ishtar, the 'mistress of the gods,' swears by the necklace given to her by her father, Anu, that she will never forget these days.

---

[1] See p. 482, note 4.

[2] Haupt and Delitzsch render *ikkal*, 'ate,' as though from *akâlu*, but this is hardly in place. I take the stem of the word to be *nakâlu*.

> Let the gods come to the sacrifice,[1]
> But Bel must not come to the sacrifice;
> Since, without consultation,[2] he caused the rain-storm,
> And handed over my creation[3] to destruction.

Bel thus appears to be the one who alone knew of the extent which the destruction was destined to reach. The annihilation of all mankind was his work, undertaken without consulting his associates. The latter were aware only of the intended destruction of a single place, — Shurippak.

At this moment Bel approaches. He does not deny his deed, but is enraged that the planned destruction should not have been complete, since Parnapishtim and his household have escaped.

> As Bel approached
> And saw the ship, he was enraged,
> Filled with anger against the gods — the Igigi.
> 'What person has escaped (?)?
> No one was to survive the destruction.'

Ninib reveals the fact of Ea's interference:

> Ninib opened his mouth and spoke, spoke to the belligerent Bel :
> "Who but Ea could have done this?
> For is it not Ea who knows all arts?"

Ea appeals to Bel:

> Ea opened his mouth and spoke, spoke to the belligerent Bel:
> "Thou art the belligerent leader of the gods,
> But why didst thou, without consultation, bring on the rainstorm?
> Punish the sinner for his sins,
> Punish the evil-doer for his evil deeds,
> But be merciful so as not to root out completely,
> Be considerate not to destroy everything."

The terrors inspired by the deluge are well portrayed in the continuation of Ea's speech. He tells Bel that he should have brought on anything but a deluge.

---

[1] To have a share in it.
[2] Jensen and Haupt translate "inconsiderately," but this rendering misses the point.
[3] Lit., 'my humanity.'

> Instead of bringing on a deluge,
> Let lions come and diminish mankind.[1]
> Instead of bringing on a deluge,
> Let tigers come and diminish mankind.
> Instead of bringing on a deluge,
> Let famine come and smite the land.
> Instead of bringing on a deluge,
> Let pestilence [2] come and waste the land.

Ea then confesses that through his instigation Parnapishtim was saved.

> While I did not reveal the decision of the great gods,
> I sent Adra-Khasis [3] a dream which told him of the decision of the gods.

It is a misconception to regard this answer of the god as equivocal. Ea means to say that he did not interfere with the divine decree. He simply told Parnapishtim to build a ship, leaving to the latter to divine the reason. Ea, it is true, tells Parnapishtim of Bel's hatred, but he does not reveal the secret of the gods. After Ea's effective speech Bel is reconciled, and the scene closes dramatically, as follows:

> Bel came to his senses,
> Stepped on board of the ship,
> Took me by the hand and lifted me up,
> Brought up my wife, and caused her to kneel at my side,
> Turned towards us, stepped between us, and blessed us.
> ' Hitherto Parnapishtim was human,[4]
> But now Parnapishtim and his wife shall be gods like us.[5]
> Parnapishtim shall dwell in the distance, at the confluence of the streams.'
> Then they took me and placed me in the distance, at the confluence of the streams.

---

[1] Not destroy it altogether. [2] Lit., 'the god Dibbarra.'

[3] *I.e.*, the ' very clever' or ' very pious,' an epithet given to Parnapishtim. The inverted form, *Khasis-adra*, was distorted into *Xisusthros*, which appears in the writers dependent upon Berosus as the name of the hero of the Babylonian deluge. See, *e.g.*, Cory's *Ancient Fragments*, pp. 52, 54, 60, etc. The epithet appears also in the Legend of Etana (pp. 523, 524), where it is applied to a 'wise' young eagle.

[4] *I.e.*, mortal. [5] *I.e.*, immortal. *Cf.* Gen. iii. 22.

The streams are, according to Haupt,[1] the four rivers — Euphrates, Tigris, Karun, and Kercha, which at one time emptied their waters independently into the Persian Gulf. Parnapishtim's dwelling-place is identical with the traditional Paradise of the Babylonians and Hebrews.

It will be proper before leaving the subject, to dwell briefly upon the points of contact between this Babylonian tale and the Biblical narrative of the Deluge. The source of the tradition must be sought in the Euphrates Valley. The ark of Noah can only be understood in the light of methods of navigation prevailing in Babylonia; and it is in Babylonia, and not Palestine, that the phenomenon was annually seen of large portions of land disappearing from view.

The Babylonian tale is to be differentiated, as already suggested, into two parts, — the destruction of Shurippak and the annual phenomenon of the overflow of the Euphrates. The combination of these two elements results in the impression conveyed by Parnapishtim's narrative that the rain-storm took on larger dimensions than was originally anticipated by the gods. The Biblical narrative is based upon this combination, but discarding those portions of the tale which are of purely local interest makes the story of a deluge, a medium for illustrating the favor shown by Yahwe towards the righteous man, as represented by Noah. The Biblical narrative ends, as does the Babylonian counterpart, with the assurance that a deluge will not sweep over the earth again; but viewed from a monotheistic aspect, this promise is interpreted as signifying the establishment of eternal laws, — a thought that is wholly foreign to the purpose of the Babylonian narrative.

The slight variations between the Biblical and Babylonian narratives, and upon which it is needless to dwell, justify the conclusion that the Hebrew story is not directly borrowed from

---

[1] *Wo Lag das Paradies* (*Ueber Land und Meer*, 1894-95, no. 15).

the Babylonian version.[1] The divergences are just of the character that will arise through the independent development and the independent interpretation of a common tradition. The destruction of Shurippak has a Biblical parallel in the destruction of Sodom[2] and of the surrounding district. Sodom, like Shurippak, is a city full of wickedness. Lot and his household are saved through direct intervention, just as Parnapishtim and his family escape through the intervention of Ea. Moreover, there are traces in the Sodom narrative of a tradition which once gave a larger character to it, involving the destruction of all mankind,[3] much as the destruction of Shurippak is enlarged by Babylonian traditions into a general annihilation of mankind. It is to be noted, too, that no emphasis is laid upon Lot's piety, and in this respect, as in others, Parnapishtim bears more resemblance to Lot than to Noah.

The hostility between Bel and Ea, which we have seen plays a part in the Babylonian narrative, belongs to the larger mythological element in the episode, not to the specific Shurippak incident. Bel, as the god whose dominion includes the atmosphere above the earth, controls the 'upper waters.' At his

[1] The Hebrew account, it must be remembered, consists of two narratives dovetailed into one another. According to the one version — the Yahwistic — the rainstorm continued for forty days and forty nights; according to the other — the priestly narrative — one hundred and fifty days pass before the waters began to diminish and a year elapses before Noah leaves the ark. The Yahwistic narrative lays stress upon the ritualistic distinction of clean and unclean animals, but on the whole, the Yahwistic version approaches closer to the Babylonian tale. Evidence has now been furnished that among the Babylonians, too, more than one version of the tradition existed. At the Eleventh International Congress of Orientalists (September, 1897), Scheil presented a tablet, dating from the days of Hammurabi, in which the story of a deluge is narrated in a manner quite different from the Gilgamesh epic. The tablet also furnishes the phonetic reading *ŝi-ir*, and Scheil is of the opinion that these two syllables form the first element in the name of the hero. Unfortunately, the tablet is badly mutilated at this point, so that the question of the reading is not absolutely certain. See p. 488, note 2. [The reading Ut-napishtim is now generally adopted.]   [2] Gen. xix.

[3] Note the phrase in Gen. xix. 31, " there is no one on earth," and see Pietschman, *Geschichte der Phönizier*, p. 115.

instigation these waters descend and bring destruction with them. But Ea's dominion — the 'deep' and the streams — are beneficent powers. The descent of the upper waters is in the nature of an attack upon Ea's kingdom. It is through Ea that the mischief produced by Bel is again made good. Such a conception falls within the domain of popular mythology. An ancient rivalry between Nippur, the seat of Bel and Eridu (or some other seat of Ea worship), may also have entered as a factor, if not in giving rise to the story, at least in maintaining it. If this be so, the story would belong to a period earlier than Hammurabi,[1] since with the ascendancy of Babylon and of Marduk, the general tendency of religious thought is towards imbuing the gods with a kindly spirit towards one another, joining issues, as in the creation epic, for the glorification of Marduk. The absence of Marduk from the deluge story is another indication of the antiquity of the tradition.

Coming back now to the epic, Parnapishtim, whose sympathy has been aroused by the sight of Gilgamesh, makes an attempt to heal the hero of his illness.

> The life that thou seekest, thou wilt obtain. Now sleep!

Gilgamesh falls into a heavy stupor, and continues in this state for six days and seven nights. An interesting dialogue ensues between Parnapishtim and his wife.

> Parnapishtim says to his wife:
> "Look at the man whose desire is life.
> Sleep has fallen upon him like a storm."
> Says the wife to Parnapishtim:
> "Transform him, let the man eat of the charm-root,[2]
> Let him return, restored in health, on the road that he came.
> Through the gate let him pass out, back to his country."

---

[1] That the story was current as early as Hammurabi is now established by Schell's fragment (see note 2 on preceding page).

[2] The word used is *tû* which means a charm or incantation in general.

Parnapishtim says to his wife:
"The torture of the man pains thee.
Cook the food¹ for him and place it at his head."

It is interesting to note that the woman appears as the exorciser of the disease. The wife of Parnapishtim — whose name is not mentioned as little as is the wife of Noah or Lot — proceeds to prepare the magic food. A plant of some kind is taken and elaborately treated.

While he² slept on board of his ship,
She cooked the food and placed it at his head.
While he² slept on board of his vessel,
Firstly, his food . . . ;
Secondly, it was pealed;
Thirdly, moistened;
Fourthly, his bowl (?) was cleansed;
Fifthly, *Shibu*³ was added;
Sixthly, it was cooked;
Seventhly, of a sudden the man was transformed and ate the magic food.⁴

Gilgamesh awakes and asks what has been done to him. Parnapishtim tells him. But Gilgamesh is not completely healed. His body is still covered with sores. The magic potion must be followed by immersion into the fountain of life. Parnapishtim instructs Ardi-Ea to convey Gilgamesh to this fountain. He speaks to the ferryman.

The man whom thou hast brought is covered with sores.
The eruption on his skin has destroyed the beauty of his body.
Take him, O Ardi-Ea, to the place of purification,
To wash his sores in the water, that he may become white as snow.
Let the ocean carry off the eruption on his skin,
That his body may become pure.⁵
Let his turban be renewed and the garment that covers his nakedness.

Ardi-Ea carries out these instructions and Gilgamesh at last is healed. The hero is now ready to return to his land. But

---

¹ Made of the charm-root.
² Gilgamesh.
³ *Iz*, 'old age,' the name given to some plant of magic power.
⁴ *Tâ*.
⁵ Lit., 'good.'

though returning in restored health, he is not proof against death. Parnapishtim, at the suggestion of his wife, reveals the 'secret of life' to Gilgamesh just before the latter's departure. The ship is brought nearer to the shore, and Parnapishtim tells Gilgamesh of a plant that wounds as a thistle, but which possesses wonderful power. Gilgamesh departs on the ship, and with the help of Ardi-Ea finds this plant, which is called 'the restoration of old age to youth.' It is a long journey to the place. The plant grows at the side or at the bottom of a fountain. Gilgamesh secures it, but scarcely have his hands grasped the plant when it slips out of his hand and is snatched away by a demon that takes on the form of a serpent. All is lost! Gilgamesh sits down and weeps bitter tears. He pours out his woe to Ardi-Ea, but there is nothing left except to return to Uruk. He reaches the city in safety. His mission — the search for immortality — has failed. Though healed from his disease, the fate of mankind — old age and death — is in store for him. With the return to Uruk the eleventh tablet ends. It but remains, before passing on, to note that the narrative of the deluge in this tablet is connected with the character of the eleventh month, which is called the 'month of rain.' We may conclude from this that the mythological element in the story — the annual overflow — predominates the local incident of the destruction of Shurippak. Gilgamesh, we must bear in mind, has nothing to do with either the local tale or the myth, except to give to both an interpretation that was originally foreign to the composite narrative.

In the twelfth tablet — which is in large part obscure — we find Gilgamesh wandering from one temple to the other, from the temple of Bel to that of Ea, lamenting for Eabani, and asking, again and again, what has become of his companion. What has been his fate since he was taken away from the land of the living? The hero, now convinced, as it seems, that death will come to him, and reconciled in a measure to his fate, seeks to learn another secret, — the secret of existence after death. He appeals to the gods of the nether world to grant him at least a sight of Eabani. Nergal, the chief of this pantheon, consents.

> . . . he opened the earth,
> And the spirit [1] of Eabani
> He caused to rise up like a wind.

Gilgamesh puts his question to Eabani:

> Tell me, my companion, tell me, my companion,
> The nature of the land which thou hast experienced, oh! tell me.

Eabani replies:

> I cannot tell thee, my friend, I cannot tell thee!

He seems to feel that Gilgamesh could not endure the description. The life after death, as will be shown in a subsequent chapter, is not pictured by the Babylonians as joyous. Eabani reveals glimpses of the sad conditions that prevail there. It is the domain of the terrible Allatu, and Etana [2] is named among those who dwell in this region. Eabani bewails his fate.[3] He curses Ukhat, whom, together with Sadu, he holds responsible for having brought death upon him. In Genesis, it will be recalled, death likewise is viewed as the consequence of Adam's yielding to the allurements of Eve. Special significance, too, attaches to the further parallel to be drawn between Adam's punishment and Eabani's fate.

> Dust thou art, and unto dust shalt thou return

applies to Eabani as well as to Adam. He was formed of clay, as we have seen,[4] and when he dies he is 'turned to clay.'[5] Still the fortunes awaiting those who die are not alike. Those who

---

[1] *Utukku* — the name, it will be recalled, given to a class of demons. See p. 260.
[2] See p. 518.
[3] Haupt, *Beiträge sur Assyriologie*, l. 318, 319, has made it plausible that pp. 16–19 of his edition belong to the twelfth tablet of the epic, though perhaps to a different edition of the epic, as Jeremias suggests (*Izdubar-Nimrod*, p. 43).
[4] See above, p. 474. [5] Haupt's edition, pp. 67, 12.

die in battle seem to enjoy special privileges, provided, however, they are properly buried and there is some one to make them comfortable in their last hour and to look after them when dead. Such persons are happy in comparison with the fate in store for those who are neglected by the living. The one who is properly cared for, who

> On a soft couch rests,
> Drinking pure water,
> Who dies in battle, as you and I have seen,[1]
> His father and mother supporting his head,
> His wife [2] ... at his side, —

the spirit of such a one is at rest. The circumstances attending death presage in a measure the individual's life after death.

> But he whose corpse remains in the field,
> As you and I have seen,
> His spirit [3] has no rest in the earth.
> The one whose spirit is not cared for by any one,
> As you and I have seen,
> He is consumed by gnawing hunger, by a longing for food.
> What is left on the street he is obliged to eat.[4]

To be left unburied was the greatest misfortune that could happen to a dead person.

With this sentiment the epic closes. Gilgamesh must rest content with the unsatisfactory consolation that Eabani offers him. Man must die, and Gilgamesh cannot escape the universal fate. Let him hope for and, if possible, provide for proper burial when death does overtake him. He will then, at least, not suffer the pangs of hunger in the world of spirits to which he must go.

The twelfth tablet exhibits somewhat more traces of the

---

[1] Lit., 'thou hast seen it, I have seen it.'
[2] Text defective. Jeremias conjectures "kneeling."
[3] *Ekimmu*, another name for a class of demons. See p. 260.
[4] The correct translation of these lines we owe to Haupt (*Beiträge zur Assyriologie*, i. 69, 70).

theology of the schools than the others. Eabani's speech, while conveying sentiments that thoroughly represent the popular beliefs of Babylonia, is couched in terms that give to the address the character of a formal declaration of doctrines. The conjuring up of the spirit of Eabani is also a feature that appears to be due to theological influences, and the whole episode of Gilgamesh's wandering from place to place seeking for information appears to be a 'doublet' suggested by the hero's wanderings, as narrated in the ninth and tenth tablets.

The problem propounded in the earlier tablets — the search for immortality — is, as has been shown, a perfectly natural one and of popular origin, but the problem with which Gilgamesh wrestles in the twelfth tablet, — the secret of the life after death, — while suggested by the other, belongs rather to the domain of theological and mystic speculation. This aspect of the twelfth tablet is borne out also by the fact that the problem is not solved. The epic ends as unsatisfactorily as the Book of Job or Ecclesiastes. There is a tone of despair in the final speech of Eabani, which savors of the schools of advanced thought in Babylonia. For the problem of immortality, a definite solution at least is offered. Man can reach old age; he may be snatched for a time from the grasp of death, as Gilgamesh was through the efforts of Parnapishtim, but he only deludes himself by indulging in hopes of immortal life. 'Man must die' is the refrain that rings in our ears. The plant of 'eternal youth' slips out of one's hand at the very moment that one believes to have secured it.

The Gilgamesh epic, as we have it, thus turns out to be a composite production. Gilgamesh, a popular hero of antiquity, becomes a medium for the perpetuation of various popular traditions and myths. The adventures of his career are combined with the early history of man. Of actual deeds performed by Gilgamesh, and which belong to Gilgamesh's career as a hero, warrior, and ruler, we have only four, — the conquest of Erech, his victory over Khumbaba, the killing of the divine bull, and the strangling of the lion.[1] The story of Eabani, Ukhat, and Sadu is independent of Gilgamesh's career, and so also is the story of his wanderings to Mashu and his encounter with Parnapishtim. Gilgamesh is brought into association with Eabani by what may be called, a natural process of assimilation. The life of the hero is placed back at the beginning of things, and in this way Gilgamesh is brought into direct contact with legends of man's early fortunes, with ancient historical reminiscences, as well as with nature-myths that symbolize the change of seasons and the annual inundations.

Popular philosophy also enters into the life of the hero. Regarded as a god and yet of human origin, Gilgamesh becomes an appropriate illustration for determining the line that marks off man's career from the indefinite extension of activity that is a trait of the gods. Gilgamesh revolts against the universal law of decay and is punished. He is relieved from suffering, but cannot escape the doom of death. The sixth tablet marks an important division in the epic. The Ishtar and Sabitum episodes and the narrative of Parnapishtim — itself a compound of two independent tales, one semi-historical, the other a nature-myth — represent accretions that may refer to a time when Gilgamesh had become little more than a name, — a type of mankind in general. Finally, scholastic speculation takes hold of Gilgamesh, and makes him the medium for illustrating another and more advanced problem that is of intense interest to mankind, — the secret of death. Death is inevitable, but what does death mean? The problem is not solved. The

---

[1] The reference to the killing of a panther in the tenth tablet (Haupt, p. 71, 6) is too obscure to be taken into consideration. Gilgamesh's fight with a 'buffalo' (so Ward, "Babylonian Gods in Babylonian Art," *Proc. Amer. Or. Soc.*, May, 1890, p. xv) is pictured on seal cylinders. No doubt, various deeds of Gilgamesh were recounted in the missing portions of the epic, and it is also quite likely that besides the stories in the epic, others were current of Gilgamesh to which a literary form was never given.

close of the eleventh tablet suggests that Gilgamesh will die. The twelfth tablet adds nothing to the situation — except a moral. Proper burial is essential to the comparative well-being of the dead.

The fact that Gilgamesh is viewed as a type in the latter half of this remarkable specimen of Babylonian literature justifies us in speaking of it, under proper qualification, as a 'national epic.' But it must be remembered that Gilgamesh himself belongs to a section of Babylonia only, and not to the whole of it; and it is rather curious that one, of whom it can be said with certainty that he is not even a native of Babylonia, should become the personage to whom popular fancy was pleased to attach traditions and myths that are distinctively Babylonian in character and origin.

The story of Gilgamesh was carried beyond the confines of Babylonia.[1] Gilgamesh, to be sure, is not identical with the Biblical Nimrod,[2] but the Gilgamesh story has evidently influenced the description given in the tenth chapter of Genesis of Nimrod, who is viewed as the type of Babylonian power and of the extension of Babylonian culture to the north.

The Gilgamesh epic is not a solar myth, as was once supposed,[3] nor is the Biblical story of Samson a pure myth, but Gilgamesh becomes a solar deity, and it is hardly accidental that Samson, or to give the Hebrew form of the name, Shimshon, is a variant form of *Shamash*,[4] — the name of the sun in Babylonian and Hebrew. The Biblical Samson appears to be modelled upon the character of Gilgamesh. Both are heroes, both con-

---

[1] The Parnapishtim episode passed on to the Arabs, where the hero of the deluge appears under the name of Khadir — a corruption of Adra-Khasis. See Lidzbarski, "Wer ist Chadir?" *Zeits. f. Assyr.* vii. 109–112, who also suggests that Ahasverus, 'the Wandering Jew,' is a corruption of Adrakhasis.

[2] It will be recalled that Nimrod is termed a 'mighty hunter' (*ṣâid*). This suggests a comparison with Sadu, 'the hunter,' in the Gilgamesh epic. See above, p. 475.

[3] Originally suggested by H. C. Rawlinson.

[4] The ending *ôn* is an emphatic affix — frequent in proper names.

querors, both strangle a lion, and both are wooed by a woman, the one by Delila, the other by Ishtar, and both through a woman are shorn of their strength. The historical traits are of course different. As for the relationships of the Gilgamesh epic to the Hercules story, the authority of Wilamowitz-Möllendorf [1] is against an oriental origin of the Greek tale, and yet such parallels as Hercules' fight with a lion, his conquest of death, his journey and search for immortality (which in contrast to Gilgamesh he secures), certainly point to an influence exercised by the oriental tale upon the Greek story. It is not surprising that the elements contributed through this influence have been so modified in the process of adaptation to the purely Greek elements of the Hercules story, and, above all, to the Greek spirit, as to obscure their eastern origin.[2] Most curious as illustrating the continued popularity of the Gilgamesh story in the Orient is the incorporation of portions of the epic in the career of Alexander the Great.[3] In Greek, Syriac, and Rabbinical writings, Alexander is depicted as wandering through a region [4] of darkness and terror in search of the 'water of life.' He encounters strange beings, reaches the sea, but, like Gilgamesh, fails to secure immortality. Such were the profound changes wrought by Alexander's conquests that popular fancy, guided by a correct instinct of appreciation of his career, converted the historical Alexander into a legendary hero of vast dimensions.[5] The process that produced the Gilgamesh epic is

[1] *Euripides' Herakles*, Einleitung.

[2] On this subject see the Introduction to Berard's *De l'origine des cultes Arcadiens*, and for a further discussion of the relationships between Izdubar and Hercules, see Jeremias' *Izdubar-Nimrod*, pp. 70-73, or his article in Roscher's *Ausführliches Lexicon der Griechischen und Römischen Mythologie*, ii. 821-823.

[3] Meissner, *Alexander und Gilgamos* (Leipzig, 1894), pp. 13-17.

[4] In the Greek and other versions, the mountain Musas or Masis is mentioned,— that is, *Mashu*, as in the Gilgamesh epic. See p. 488.

[5] See especially Budge, *The Life and Exploits of Alexander the Great* (London, Introduction, 1896); Nöldeke, *Beiträge zur Geschichte des Alexander-Romans* (Vienna, 1890) and Gaster, *An Old Hebrew Romance of Alexander* (*Journal Royal Asiat. Soc.*, 1897, pp. 485-498).

repeated, only on a larger scale, in the case of Alexander. Not one country, but the entire ancient culture world, — Babylonia, Persia, Egypt, Arabia, Judea, and Syria, — combine to form the legendary Alexander. Each country contributes its share of popular legends, myths, and traditions. Babylonia offers as her tribute the exploits of Gilgamesh, which it transfers in part to Alexander. The national hero becomes the type of the 'great man,' and as with new conditions, a new favorite, representative of the new era, arises to take the place of an older one, the old is made to survive in the new. Gilgamesh lives again in Alexander, just as traits of the legendary Alexander pass down to subsequent heroes.

CHAPTER XXIV.

MYTHS AND LEGENDS.

NOT many years ago the impression appeared to be well founded that the Semites were poor in the production of myths and legends as compared, for example, to the Hindus or Greeks. The religious literature of the Babylonians, originating undoubtedly with the Semitic inhabitants of the Euphrates Valley, reverses the impression. The 'creation' and 'Gilgamesh' epics suffice, not merely for what they contain, but for what they imply, to accord to Babylonian mythology a high rank; but in addition to these epics we have a large number of tales of gods, demi-gods, demons, and spirits that illustrate the capacity of the Babylonians for the production of myths. Indeed, there is no longer any reason for doubting that the Babylonian mythology exercised considerable influence upon that of the Greeks. Further discoveries and researches may show that distant India also felt at an early period the intellectual stimulus emanating from the Euphrates Valley. At all events, many of the features found in Babylonian myths and legends bear so striking a resemblance to those occurring in lands lying to the east and west of Babylonia, that a study of Aryan mythology is sadly deficient which does not take into account the material furnished by cuneiform literature. How extensive the Babylonian mythology was must remain for the present a matter of conjecture, but it is easier to err on the side of underestimation than on the side of exaggeration. If it be remembered that by far the smaller portion only of Ashurbanabal's library has been recovered, and that of the various literary collections that were gathered in the religious centers of the south, scarcely anything has as yet been found, it is certainly remarkable that we should be in possession of an elaborate tale of a demi-god, Etana, of an extensive legend recounting the deeds of the war and plague-god Dibbarra, and of two genuine storm myths, while the indications in Dr. Bezold's catalogue of the Kouyunjik collection justify us in adding to the list several other myths and legends, among the still unpublished tablets of the British Museum.[1] These myths and legends have a twofold value for us, a direct value because of the popular religious ideas contained in them, and an indirect value by virtue of the interpretation given to these ideas by the compilers. In the literary form that the popular productions received, the influence of those who guided the religious thought into its proper channels is to be clearly seen.

THE ETANA LEGEND.

It will be recalled that we came across a hero Etana in the Gilgamesh epic.[2] The name of the hero is Semitic, and signifies 'strong.'[3] An identical name appears in the Old Testament,[4] and it is possible that the Babylonian Etana represents, like Gilgamesh, some ancient historical person of whom a dim tradition has survived among other nations besides the Babylonians. The deeds recounted of him, however, place the

---

[1] Some of these were already indicated (but only indicated) by George Smith in his *Chaldaeische Genesis* (German translation), pp. 136-142. It is the merit of Dr. E. J. Harper to have prepared an excellent publication of the material contained in Smith's work, pp. 103-120, under the title "Die Babylonischen Legenden von Etana, Zu, Adapa und Dibbarra" (Delitzsch and Haupt's *Beiträge zur Assyriologie*, ii. 390-521). Additional material is furnished by two publications of mine: (*a*) a monograph, "A Fragment of the Dibbarra Epic" (Boston, 1891), and (*b*) "A New Fragment of the Babylonian Etana Legend" (Delitzsch and Haupt's *Beiträge zur Assyriologie*, iii. 363-381). See also Friedrich Jeremias in Chantepie de la Saussaye's *Lehrbuch der Religionsgeschichte* (2d edition), i. 218-221.

[2] See above, p. 511.

[3] See my remarks in Delitzsch and Haupt's *Beiträge zur Assyriologie*, iii. 376.

[4] 1 Kings, v. 11.

hero entirely in the domain of myth. His patron is Shamash, the sun-god, and in popular tradition he becomes a member of the pantheon of the nether world.

In the portions of the Etana legend preserved,[1] two episodes are detailed in the hero's career, one regarding the birth of a son, the other a miraculous journey. The former episode justifies the assumption of a historical starting-point for the legend of Etana.[2] Among many nations the birth of a hero or of a hero's son is pictured as taking place under great difficulties. Etana's wife is in distress because she is unable to bring to the world a child which she has conceived. Etana appeals to Shamash. Through the mediation of the priests he has offered sacrifices, and he now prays to Shamash to show him the "plant of birth."

> The oracles[3] have completed my sacrifices,
> They have completed my free-will offerings to the gods.
> O Lord, let thy mouth command,
> And give me the plant of birth,
> Reveal to me the plant of birth,
> Bring forth the fruit, grant me an offspring.

Of Shamash's reply only one line is preserved intact, in which he tells Etana:

> Take the road, ascend the mountain.

It is presumably upon the mountain that the plant grows whose magical power will insure the happy delivery of the expected offspring. Harper calls attention to a remarkable parallel to this incident which is found in the Armenian and Mandaean legends of the birth of Rustem, the son of Sal. The latter's wife is unable to deliver her child because of its size. Sal, who was reared by an eagle, has in his possession a pinion

---

[1] Harper in Delitzsch and Haupt's *Beiträge zur Assyriologie*, ii. 391-408.
[2] *Ib.* pp. 405 *seq.*
[3] Lit., 'the Inquirers,' a designation of the priests in their capacity of oracle-seekers.

of the eagle, by means of which he can, when in distress, invoke the presence of the bird. The father throws the pinion into the fire, and the eagle appears. The latter gives the mother a medicinal potion, and the child is cut out of the womb. Etana, like Rustem, is accompanied by an eagle, and it would appear that the eagle aids Etana in obtaining the plant.[1] The eagle, in many mythologies, is a symbol of the sun, and it is plausible to conclude that the bird is sent to Etana at the instigation of Shamash. Who the son is that Etana expects we are not told, and naturally from a single episode like this — and one so fragmentarily preserved — no safe conclusions may be drawn. But the epic (if we may apply this term) must have recounted some achievements of Etana, and as the 'strong' one, his deeds must have borne some resemblance to those of Gilgamesh. The birth of the son, it is furthermore fair to presume, took place towards the end of Etana's career, when his own life was drawing to a close. If a fragment[2] of the tale were only better preserved, we would have an episode of Etana's earlier career. But such is the condition of this fragment that, at the most, it can be said that Etana is engaged in some conflict against a city, in which Ishtar, Bel, the Anunnaki, the Igigi, and some minor gods, as En-ninna, Sibittum, are involved. The Etana series, as we learn from the colophon to this fragment, was known by a designation in which a city[3] occurs, and it may be that this is the city against which Etana, aided by the gods, proceeds. Leaving this aside, it is fortunate that we have at least another episode in Etana's career which enables us to establish the connecting link between the hero as an historical personage and as a god or demi-god. As Gilgamesh offers an insult to Ishtar, so Etana encounters the ill-will of the great goddess, though through no direct offense.

[1] The matter is not certain because of the sad condition of the fragments.
[2] K. 2606, Harper, *ib.* pp. 399, 400.
[3] Only a part of the name, *I-si*, is preserved.

The eagle tempts Etana to mount with him into the upper regions. Etana is represented as giving, in part, an account of this adventure, in the first person. The gates of the upper regions are opened, and Etana is terrified at the majestic sight which greets him. He sees a throne, and throws himself on his countenance in terror. The gates are significantly designated as the gate of Anu, Bel, and Ea, and the gate of Sin, Shamash, Ramman, and Ishtar. The introduction of the two classes of the theological triads[1] reveals the influence of a scholastic elaboration of some popular myth. The eagle reassures Etana, and addresses him as follows:

> My friend lift up (?) [thy countenance],
> Come and let me carry thee to the heaven [of Anu].
> On my breast place thy breast,
> On my pinion place thy palms,
> On my side place thy side.

Etana obeys, and thus, securely attached to the eagle, begins the daring journey. They fly for the space of a double hour,[2] when

> The eagle addresses Etana:
> Look, my friend, how the earth appears;
> Look at the sea and at its side, the house of wisdom;[3]
> The earth appears as a mountain, the sea has become a pool (?).
> A second double hour he (*i.e.*, the eagle) carried him on high.
> The eagle spoke to Etana:
> Look, my friend, how the earth appears;
> The sea is a mere belt (?) around the earth.
> A third double hour he carried him on high.
> The eagle spoke to Etana:
> Look, my friend, how the earth appears;
> The sea is a mere gardener's ditch.[4]

---

[1] See pp. 108, 163.
[2] *I.e.*, an army's march of two hours.
[3] The dwelling of Ea. See Meissner, *Alexander and Gilgamos*, p. 17.
[4] *I.e.*, still smaller.

In this way they reach the gate of Anu, Bel, and Ea in safety, where they take a rest. The eagle is not yet satisfied, and urges Etana to follow him to the domain of Ishtar.

> Come, my friend [let me carry thee to Ishtar],
> With Ishtar, the mistress [of the gods, thou shalt dwell],
> In the glory of Ishtar, the mistress of the gods, [thou shalt sit?].
> On my side place thy side,
> On my pinion place thy palms.

The gods, it will be seen, dwell on high in accordance with the view developed by astronomical speculations.[1] Anu, Bel, and Ea are here evidently identified with the fixed stars bearing their names,[2] while under Ishtar the planet Ishtar-Venus is meant. Etana yields to the eagle's suggestion. They mount still higher. Earth and ocean grow still smaller, the former appearing only as large as 'a garden bed,' the latter like 'a courtyard.' For three double hours they fly. Etana appears to warn the eagle to desist from his rash intention, but the warning comes too late. Etana and the eagle are thrown down from the lofty regions. With lightning speed the descent takes place, until the two reach the ground. The further course of the narrative is obscure. Was Etana punished by being sent to the nether world, where we find him in the Gilgamesh epic?[3] There is a reference, unfortunately quite obscure, to the death of Etana, and perhaps to his shade,[4] in a portion of the tablet. One certainly expects both Etana and the eagle to be punished for their rash act, but until we can determine with certainty what became of both, and with what purport the tale is introduced into the career of Etana, the question must be left open, as also the possibility of a connection between this flight of Etana and the similar Greek myth of Ganymede. The introduction of the eagle points clearly to the mythological character of the tale, but flights of eagles occur so frequently

---

[1] See above, p. 458.
[2] See p. 460.
[3] See p. 511.
[4] Harper, *ib.* p. 404, note.

in the myths and legends of various nations that no great stress is to be laid upon further parallels that might be adduced.[1] The story found in Aelian and which has already been referred to[2] alone calls for mention here. According to this story, Gilgamesh, whose birth is feared by his cruel grandfather Sokkaros, king of Babylonia, is thrown from the tower where his mother was imprisoned and in which he was born, but in falling is caught by an eagle and taken to a gardener who rears the child. The eagle being the associate of Etana, the suspicion is justified that the child thus miraculously saved is in reality Etana and not Gilgamesh. At all events, there must be some connection between the story of Aelian and the Babylonian legend under consideration. The fate of the eagle is recounted in another tablet of the Etana series,[3] which again furnishes an episode paralleled in the mythologies of other nations.

The eagle has lost favor with Shamash. Enmity has arisen between the eagle and the serpent, and, curiously enough, the latter stands under the protection of the sun-god. What the cause of the enmity between eagle and serpent was, may have been recounted in a missing portion of the tablet. The eagle forms a plan of destroying the serpent's brood. He is warned against this act by a young eagle, who is designated as a 'very clever young one.'

Do not eat, O my father, the net of Shamash is laid (?);
The trap, the ban of Shamash, will fall upon thee and catch thee.
Who transgresses the law of Shamash, from him Shamash will exact revenge.

But the eagle, we are told, paid no heed to the warning.

He descended and ate of the young of the serpent.

The serpent appeals to Shamash. He tells the sun-god of the cruel deed of the eagle:

[1] See Harper, *ib.* pp. 406, 407.
[2] See above, p. 469. [3] Harper, pp. 392–394.

> See, O Shamash, the evil that he has done to me.
> Help (?), O Shamash, thy net is the broad earth.
> Thy trap is the distant heavens.
> Who can escape thy net?[1]
> Zu,[2] the worker of evil, the source of evil [did not escape?[3]].

Shamash responds to the appeal:

> Upon his hearing the lament of the serpent,
> Shamash opened his mouth and spoke to the serpent:
> Go and ascend the mountain;
> The carcass of a wild ox make thy hiding-place.
> Open him, tear open his belly.
> Make a dwelling place [of his belly].
> All the birds of heaven will come down;
> The eagle with them will come down.
> . . . .
> Upon penetrating to the meat he will hastily proceed,
> Making for the hidden parts.[4]
> As soon as he has reached the inside,[5] seize him by his wing,
> Tear out his wing, his feather (?), his pinion,
> Tear him to pieces, and throw him into a corner,
> To die a death of hunger and thirst.

This devilish plan is successfully carried out. With considerable skill the narrative describes how the eagle, suspecting some mischief, did not join the other birds, but when he saw that they escaped without harm felt reassured. He tells his brood:

> Come, let us go and let us also pounce down upon the carcass of the wild ox and eat, we too.

The eagle is again warned by his "very clever" offspring. The rest of his brood join in the appeal, but

> He did not hearken to them, and obeyed not the advice of his brood.
> He swooped down and stood upon the wild ox.

---

[1] *I.e.*, one cannot escape from Shamash, since he traverses all space.

[2] A personification of the storm. See below, pp. 537 *seq.* The line is very obscure owing to the break in the tablet.   [3] So Harper, but see pp. 541, 542.

[4] *I.e.*, he will dig his beak into the juicy part of the meat.

[5] Of the carcass.

Still, he is not entirely free from suspicion, and the narrative continues:

> The eagle inspected the carcass, looking carefully to the front and behind him.
> He again inspected the carcass, looking carefully to the front and behind him.

Detecting nothing to justify his suspicions, he digs his beak into the carcass, but scarcely has he done so when the serpent seizes hold of him. The eagle cries for mercy, and promises the serpent a present of whatever he desires. The serpent is relentless. To release the eagle would be to play false to Shamash.

> If I release thee ...
> Thy punishment will be transferred to me.

Thus the serpent justifies what he is about to do. In accordance with the instructions of the sun-god, the eagle is stripped of his wings and feathers, and left to die a miserable death. In its present form this tale of the eagle and serpent forms part of the Etana story.[1] Jeremias is right in questioning whether it originally had anything to do with Etana.[2] Two distinct stories have been combined, much as in the Gilgamesh epic several tales have been thrown together. The association of Etana with the eagle suggests the introduction of the episode of the eagle's discomfiture. If one may judge of the two episodes related of Etana, he is not a personage regarded with favor by the compilers. In both episodes we find him in distress. His flight with the eagle is regarded as a defiance of the gods, though more blame attaches to the eagle than to him. Shamash can hardly have regarded with favor the ambition of a human being to mount to the dwelling of the gods. Gilgamesh makes no such attempt, and Parnapishtim is not carried

---

[1] As shown by the colophon of K. 2606, and also by the fact that K. 1547, which contains on the obverse the tale, contains on the reverse Etana's prayer to Shamash.
[2] De la Saussaye's *Lehrbuch der Religionsgeschichte* (2d edition), I. 218.

on high, but to "the confluence of the streams." Gilgamesh, it will also be recalled, is unable to pass to the nether world where Eabani is placed, and in the following chapter we will come across a tale intended to illustrate the impossibility of any one ever returning from the hollow under the earth where the dead dwell. The story of Etana appears, therefore, to emphasize the equal impossibility for any mortal to ascend to the dwelling of the gods. Etana is deified, but he belongs permanently to the region where all mortals go after their career on earth is ended, — the nether world. One gains the impression, therefore, that Etana is a hero of antiquity who is not approved of by the Babylonian priests. Similarly, the conflict between the eagle and the serpent suggests an opposition to the view which makes the eagle the symbol and messenger of Shamash. The eagle recalls the winged disc, the symbol of Ashur,[1] and the eagle occurs also as a standard among the Hittites,[2] with whom, as we know, the Babylonians came into contact. The story of Shamash, himself, laying the trap for the eagle looks like a myth produced with some specific intent, an illustration of legitimate sun-worship against rival cults. As a matter of course, in the case of such a myth, it is difficult to say where its popular character ends and the speculative or scholastic theory begins. But whatever may have been the original purport of the tale, for our purposes its significance consists in the view unfolded of Shamash as the one who wreaks vengeance on the evil-doer. Shamash appears in the episode in the rôle of the just judge that characterizes him in the hymns and incantations. Etana's reliance upon the eagle leads to disgrace and defeat. In a representation of the hero's flight on a seal cylinder,[3] the disapproval of the act

---

[1] See above, p. 195.

[2] Perrot and Chiplez, *History of Art in Sardinia, Phœnicia, Judea, Syria, and Asia Minor*, ii. 176.

[3] Pinches, *Babylonian and Assyrian Cylinders, etc., of Sir Henry Peak*, no. 18. *Cf.* Harper, *ib.* p. 408.

is indicated by the addition of two dogs in a crouching position, their gaze directed towards the bird. The dogs are a symbol of the solar-god Marduk.[1]

THE LEGEND OF DIBBARRA.

Of more direct religious import is a story recounted in a series comprising five tablets of the deeds of the war and plague-god whose name is provisionally read Dibbarra.[2] He is a solar deity identified in the theological system of the Babylonians with Nergal, but originally distinct and in all probability one of the numerous local solar deities of Babylonia like Nin-girsu and Nin-gishzida, Ishum and others, whose rôles are absorbed by one or the other of the four great solar deities,— Shamash, Marduk, Ninib, and Nergal. Nergal representing the sun of midday and of the summer solstice, which brings in its wake destruction of various kinds, it was appropriate that a god who came to be specifically viewed as the god who causes disease should be regarded as an aspect of the terrible Nergal. In the legend that we are about to consider, Dibbarra appears as the god of war. He is designated as the 'warrior.' The name of the god is written ideographically with a sign that has the meaning of 'servant' and 'man.' To this sign the phonetic complement *ra* is added. In view of a passage in a lexicographical tablet, according to which the name of the god is designated as the equivalent of the god Gir-ra, Jensen concluded that the name was to be read Gira, and Delitzsch[3] is inclined to follow him. A difficulty, however, arises through the circumstance that the element *Gir* in the name Gir-ra is itself an ideograph. In any case, the designation of the god as a 'servant' shows that he is described here by an

---

[1] A lexicographical tablet, IIR. 56, col. iii. 22–25, mentions four dogs of Marduk.
[2] See p. 232.
[3] See Harper, *ib.* p. 426.

epithet,[1] and not by his real name, which is to be sought rather in the sense of 'strong,' that is one of the meanings of the ideograph *gir*. The epithet 'servant' belongs to the period when the god took his place in the theological system as one of the attendants of the great Nergal, just as the plague-god is himself accompanied by a god Ishum, who acts as a kind of messenger or attendant to him. It should be added that what little evidence there was for the conventional reading Dibbarra[2] has now been dispelled, so that but for the desire to avoid useless additions to the nomenclature of the Babylonian deities, the form Gir-ra would have been introduced here, as for the present preferable.

Where the cult of Dibbarra centered we do not know, but that he presided over a district that must have played a prominent part at some period of Babylonian history is shown by the elaborate legend of his deeds for which, as in the case of Gilgamesh and Etana, we are justified in assuming an historical background. In fact, the legend of Dibbarra is naught but a poetic and semi-mythical disguise for severe conflicts waged against certain Babylonian cities by some rival power that had its seat likewise in the Euphrates Valley.

Of the five tablets, but four fragments have as yet been found in such a condition as to be utilized. The longest of these contains an address to Dibbarra by his faithful attendant Ishum, in which the power of the war-god is praised and some of his deeds recounted.

> [The sons of] Babylon were (as) birds
> And thou their falconer.
> In a net thou didst catch them, enclose them, and destroy them,
> O! Warrior Dibbara,
> Leaving the city,[3] thou didst pass to the outside,
> Taking on the form of a lion, thou didst enter the palace.
> The people saw thee and drew (?) their weapons.

---

[1] The *ra* is either a phonetic complement to the Ideograph or is perhaps added to suggest to the reader the identification with Gir-ra.   [3] Babylon.

[2] Namely, the connection with Hebrew *deber*, 'pestilence.' *Cf.* Harper, *ib.* p. 426.

The reference in these lines is to an attack upon the city of Babylon. The war-god is pictured as striking out in all directions, imprisoning the inhabitants of Babylon within the city walls, working havoc outside of the city, and not stopping short at entering the palace. The metaphor of the war-god taking on the form of a lion confirms the identification of Dibbarra with Nergal, who is generally pictured as a lion.

In the following lines the enemy who makes this attack on Babylon is introduced. He is designated as a 'governor,' and Dibbarra is represented as giving him certain instructions to carry out. The title 'governor' given to this enemy may be taken as an indication that the epic deals with the rivalry existing among the states of Babylonia, each represented by its capitol. Ishum continues his address to Dibbarra:

The heart of the governor, intent upon taking vengeance on Babylon, was enraged,
For capturing the possessions of the enemy, he sends out his army,
Filled with enmity towards the people.

Dibbarra is represented as addressing this governor:

In the city whither I send thee,
Thou shalt fear no one, nor have compassion.
Kill the young and old alike,
The tender suckling likewise — spare no one.
The treasures of Babylon carry off as booty.

Ishum continues his narrative:

The royal host was gathered together and entered the city.
The bow was strung, the sword unsheathed.
Thou didst blunt[1] (?) the weapons of the soldiers,
The servitors of Anu and Dagan.
Their blood thou caused to flow like torrents of water through the city's highways.
Thou didst tear open their intestines, and cause the stream to carry them off.

[1] Text obscure. "Sharpen badly" seems to be the idiomatic phrase used.

Dagan is here used for Bel,[1] and the phrase 'servitors of Anu and Dagan' embraces the inhabitants of Babylon. Marduk, the lord of Babylon, is enraged at the sight, but apparently is powerless.

> The great lord Marduk saw it and cried "Alas!"
> His senses left him.
> A violent curse issued from his mouth.

At this point the tablet is defective, and when it again becomes intelligible we find Ishum describing an attack of Dibbarra upon another of the great centers of the Euphrates Valley — the city of Uruk. Uruk is called the 'dwelling of Anu and Ishtar,' the city of the *Kizrêti, Ukhâti*, and *Kharimâti*[2] — the sacred harlots. Uruk suffers the same fate as Babylon:

> A cruel and wicked governor thou didst place over them,
> Who brought misery upon them, broke down (?) their laws.
> Ishtar was enraged and filled with anger because of Uruk.

Her opposition, however, is as powerless to stem Dibbarra's attack as was Marduk's grief at the onslaught on Babylon.

Dibbarra's greed is insatiable. Ishum continues his address to him:

> O warrior Dibbarra, thou dost dispatch the just,
> Thou dost dispatch the unjust,
> Who sins against thee, thou dost dispatch,
> And the one who does not sin against thee thou dost dispatch.

The following lines reveal the purpose of Ishum's long speech. A war more terrible even than the conflicts recounted is planned by Ishum, one that is to involve all creation and extend to the higher regions. Ishum asks Dibbarra's consent to the fearful destruction held in view:

> The brightness of Shul-pauddu[8] I will destroy.
> The root of the tree I will tear out
> That it no longer blossom;

---

[1] See above, p. 154. [8] A solar deity. See p. 99.
[2] See p. 475.

Against the dwelling of the king of gods, I will proceed. . . .
The warrior Dibbarra heard him.[1]
The speech of Ishum was pleasant to him as fine oil,
And thus the warrior Dibbarra spoke:
Sea-coast [against] sea-coast, Subartu against Subartu, Assyrian against Assyrian,
Elamite against Elamite,
Cassite against Cassite,
Sutaean against Sutaean,
Kuthaean against Kuthaean,
Lullubite against Lullubite,
Country against country, house against house, man against man.
Brother is to show no mercy towards brother; they shall kill one another.

The lines remind one of the description in the Gilgamesh epic of the terror aroused by the deluge,[2] and one might be tempted to combine Dibbarra's speech with the preceding words of Ishum, and interpret this part of the Dibbarra legend as another phase of the same nature myth, which enters as a factor in the narrative of the Deluge. However, the continuation of Dibbarra's speech shows that a great military conflict is foretold. The countries named are those adjacent to Babylonia, and the intention of the writer is evidently to imply that the whole world is to be stirred up. This fearful state of hostility is to continue until

After a time the Akkadian will come,
Overthrow all and conquer all of them.

Akkad, it will be recalled, is a name for Babylonia. The triumph of Babylon is foretold in these lines. The Akkadian is, therefore, none other than Hammurabi, who succeeds in obtaining the supremacy over the entire Euphrates Valley, and whose successors for many centuries claimed control of the four quarters of the world.

It is evident from this 'prophecy' that the Dibbarra legend received its final shape under influences emanating from Babylon, precisely as we found to be the case in the 'creation' story

---

[1] Ishum. [2] See above, p. 501.

and in the Gilgamesh epic. The hostility that precedes the coming of Hammurabi points to the violence of the conflicts in which that warrior was engaged, while the exaggeration of this hostility shows how strong and permanent the impression of Hammurabi's achievements must have been. The designation of the conqueror as the Akkadian gives him to a certain extent the character of a Messiah, who is to inaugurate an era of peace, and whose coming will appease the grim Dibbarra. It is by no means impossible that Hebrew and Christian conceptions of a general warfare which is to precede the golden age of peace are influenced by the Babylonian legend under consideration.

Dibbarra gives his consent to Ishum's plan:

Go, Ishum, carry out the word thou hast spoken in accordance with thy desire.

Ishum proceeds to do so. The mountain Khi-khi is the first to be attacked.

> Ishum directed his countenance to the mountain Khi-khi.
> The god Sibi,[1] a warrior without rival,
> Stormed behind him.
> The warrior[2] arrived at the mountain Khi-khi.
> He raised his hand, destroyed the mountain.
> He levelled the mountain Khi-khi to the ground.
> The vineyards in the forest of Khashur he destroyed.

In a geographical list[3] a mountain Khi-khi, belonging to the Amoritic country, is mentioned, and a mountain Khashur described as a cedar district. There can be, therefore, no doubt that some military expedition to western lands is recounted in our tablet. The continuation of the narrative is lost, all but a small fragment,[4] which tells of the destruction of a city — otherwise unknown — called Inmarmaru. At the instigation

---

[1] *I.e.*, seven. A collective personification of the seven evil spirits.
[2] Ishum. [4] The one published by the writer.
[3] IIR. 51, 19c and 4a. Khashur is also used as a name for the cedar. See Delitzsch, *Assyr. Handwörterbuch*, p. 295a.

of Dibbarra, Ishum enters this city and destroys it. The outrages committed are described at some length. Ea, the god of humanity, hears of the havoc wrought. He is 'filled with wrath.' Unfortunately, the fragment is too mutilated to permit us to ascertain what steps Ea takes against Dibbarra. Marduk is also mentioned in this connection. Under the circumstances, one can only conjecture that in the missing portions of this tablet, and perhaps also in two others, the wars preceding the advent of the Akkadian[1] are recounted in poetic and semi-mythical form. If this conjecture is justified, the main purport at least of the Dibbarra legend becomes clear. It is a collection of war-songs recalling the Hebrew anthology, "Battles of Yahwe,"[2] in which the military exploits of the Hebrews were poetically set forth.

The closing tablet of the Dibbarra legend is preserved,[3] though only in part. It describes the appeasement of the dreadful war-god. All the gods, together with the Igigi and Anunnaki, are gathered around Dibbarra, who addresses them:

> Listen all of you to my words.
> Because of sin did I formerly plan evil,
> My heart was enraged and I swept peoples away.

He tells how he destroyed the flocks and devastated the fruits in the fields, how he swept over the lands, punishing the just and the wicked alike, and sparing no one. Ishum takes up the strain and urges Dibbarra to desist from his wrath:

> Do thou appease the gods of the land, who were angry,
> May fruits (?) and corn[4] flourish,
> May mountains and seas bring their produce.

---

[1] Hammurabi is the conqueror of Palestine mentioned in Gen. xlv. under the name Amraphel. See, *e.g.*, Hommel, *Altisraelitische Ueberlieferung*, p. 106.

[2] Num. xxi. 14. The 'song of Deborah' (Judges, v.) belongs to this collection. For further specimens of Babylonian war-songs, see Hommel, *ib.* pp. 180-190, — all dealing with the memorable Hammurabi period.

[3] K. 1282, Harper, *ib.* pp. 432 *seq.*, and King's fragment, *Zeitschrift für Assyriologie*, xl. 60, 61.   [4] The gods of vegetation are mentioned.

The era of peace and prosperity is thus inaugurated, and the legend closes with solemn assurances from Dibbarra that he will bless and protect those who properly honor him.

He who glorifies my name will rule the world.
Who proclaims the glory of my power
Will be without a rival.
The singer who sings [of my deeds] will not die through pestilence.
To kings and nobles his words will be pleasing.
The writer who preserves them will escape from the grasp of the enemy.
In the temple where the people proclaim my name
I will open his ear;[1]
In the house where this tablet is set up, though war[2] may rage,
And god Sibi work havoc,
Sword and pestilence will not touch him—he will dwell in safety.
Let this song resound forever and endure for eternity.
Let all lands hear it and proclaim my power.
Let the inhabitants of all places learn to glorify my name.

This closing address represents a late addition to the poem that somewhat modifies its original import. Wars did not cease with the establishment of Babylon's control. Many conflicts arose, but on the whole, Babylonia was an empire of peace. The people were inclined towards a life of ease, and the development of commerce served as a wholesome check against too frequent military disturbances. The war-songs, as a glorification of the nation's past, retained their popularity, but the lesson drawn from the songs was the great blessing that peace and freedom from turmoil brought with them. For the warlike Assyrians, Dibbarra enraged may have been a more popular figure, but to the peace-loving Babylonian, the appeased Dibbarra appealed with greater force. The story of Dibbarra's deeds became in this way in the course of time an object lesson, a kind of religious allegory handed down from one generation to the other as an illustration of the horrors of war and

---

[1] *I.e.*, give wisdom to the one who honors me.
[2] Text 'Dibbarra.'

of violence in general. With the tendency — so characteristic of the Babylonian religion [1] — for great gods to absorb the rôles of minor ones, Nergal became the god of war *par excellence*, while Dibbarra, Ishum, and Sibi were chiefly viewed as powers responsible for such forms of violence as pestilence and distress. To ensure the favor of a god of pestilence was of importance for every individual, and one of the safest means of obtaining this favor was to sing his praises, to recall his power, — to glorify him and thus to keep him, as it were, in good humor. What better means of accomplishing this than to have the record of his deeds constantly before one's eyes? The British Museum contains two specimens of tablets on which a portion of the Dibbarra legend is inscribed, and which are pierced with holes in a manner as to leave no doubt [2] that the tablets were intended to be hung up in houses with a view of securing protection from Dibbarra and his associates. The reference in the closing lines of the story:

> The house where this tablet is set up,

thus becomes clear. As the Hebrews were commanded, in order to secure the protection of Yahwe, to write his law

> On the doorposts of the house,[3]

so the Babylonians were instructed by their priests to hang tablets in their homes — probably at the entrance — on which Dibbarra was glorified. Naturally, it was impossible to inscribe the whole story on a little tablet, just as it was impossible to place the entire law of Yahwe on the doorposts. In both cases a significant extract served as a part, representative of the whole. In the case of the Dibbarra legend, the closing portion was selected, which emphasized the necessity of keeping the deeds of Dibbarra and the greatness of his power in mind. Like the Gilgamesh epic, so the Dibbarra legend was to be

---

[1] See above, p. 114.   [3] Deut. vi. 9.
[2] As Mr. King has shown (*Zeitschrift für Assyriologie*, xi. 53). See above, p. 269.

taught by the father to his son. The scribes were enjoined to teach the story to the people. The poets were to make it the subject of their songs, and kings and nobles were not exempt from the obligation to listen to the tale.

The Myth of the Storm-God Zu.

Birds and bulls were to the Babylonians the symbols of storms and clouds. In the Gilgamesh epic, it will be recalled, Anu sends a divine bull to engage in a contest with Gilgamesh.[1] The text of the epic being unfortunately defective, we have no definite indication of the character of the attack to be made upon the hero by the messenger from the god of heaven; but since storms and disease are the two chief weapons in the hands of the gods, and inasmuch as Gilgamesh in a later section of the epic is struck down by disease, it is more than likely that the bull represents a storm that is to sweep the hero and his companion off the earth. The winged bulls placed at the entrance of palaces embody the same idea, and in addition to the explanation for these fantastic figures above[2] suggested, it is noteworthy that the two types of animals chosen for this symbolical decoration of edifices, the bull and the lion, again illustrate the same two means at the disposal of the gods for the punishment of man, the bull representing the storms, and the lion being the symbol of Nergal, who is the god of pestilence, as well as of war and of violent destruction in general.

A storm-god symbolized under the form of a bird is Zu. The underlying stem of the word conveys the notion of strength and violence. How bulls came to be chosen as symbols of storms is not altogether clear. Possibly the element of 'strength' formed the connecting link in the chain of the association of ideas. In the case of birds, on the other hand, the association is to be sought in the appearance of the clouds during a storm

---

[1] See p. 483.   [2] See p. 263.

moving across the heavens like a flock of birds. In the Etana legend, a reference occurs to Zu, who, as it would appear, is unable to escape from the control of the supreme judge Shamash.[1] Zu is there called the chief worker of evil — a kind of arch satan. A story has been found which illustrates an attempt made by the bird Zu to break loose from the control of the sun. A storm was viewed as a conflict between the clouds and the sun, much as an eclipse symbolized a revolt in the heavens. The myth represents the conflict as taking place between Zu and En-lil, the Bel of Nippur. The latter holds in his possession the tablets of fate, by means of which he enjoys supreme authority over men and gods. Zu's jealousy is aroused, and he plans to tear these tablets from En-lil. The tablets of fate, it will be recalled, play an important part in the Marduk-Tiâmat episode.[2] Kingu — the symbol of chaos, like Tiâmat — wears them on his breast, but he is obliged to yield them to the conqueror of Tiâmat and of her brood, who replaces 'chaos' by 'order.' This conqueror was originally Bel of Nippur, and the Zu myth in representing En-lil as holding the tablets of fate confirms the view above set forth,[3] according to which the original Tiâmat tale has been modified by the substitution of Marduk for the old Bel. But the story, while thus admitting the legitimacy of En-lil's claim to supreme power, is yet so constructed as to contribute to the glory of Marduk. The attack of the Zu-bird was suggested — as the Tiâmat myth — by the annual storms that work such havoc in Babylonia. The forces of 'chaos' are let loose, and an attempt is made to overthrow the 'order' of the world, symbolized by the tablets of fate which En-lil holds in his possession. Whoever has these tablets is invincible. But En-lil is unable to resist the attack of Zu. The tablets are taken away from him, and it is left for Marduk to recapture them. The tablets once in Marduk's

---

[1] See p. 525. [2] See pp. 420, 428.
[3] See pp. 439 *seq*.

possession, En-lil's supremacy comes to an end, and the triumph of Marduk is complete. To substantiate this interpretation of the myth, an analysis of the text is necessary. The beginning of the story is unfortunately missing. It appears to have been devoted to a glorification of the god who controls the fate of the universe. The second column opens as follows:

> And the oracles of all the gods he determined.

From the context it is clear that Bel of Nippur is meant. Up to this point, the myth reflects the old view according to which it was En-lil who succeeded in overcoming Tiâmat or at any rate, in snatching the tablets of fate from the breast of Kingu. Nippur's god lays claim to being the one who established 'order' in the universe. His authority could only be threatened if he were robbed of the tablets which symbolize absolute control over the course of affairs. Zu boldly attempts this:

> His eyes saw the mark of rulership,
> The crown of his [1] sovereignty, the garment of his [1] divinity.
> Zu saw the divine tablets of fate.
> He looked at the father of the gods, the god of Dur-an-ki,[2]
> Desire for rulership seizes hold of his heart.[3]
> 'I will take the tablets of the gods
> And decree the decisions [of all the gods.']
> I will establish my throne, I will proclaim laws.
> I will give all orders to all the Igigi.'

Zu proceeds to the dwelling-place of En-lil and waits for a favorable moment to make an attack.

His heart was bent on the contest.
With his gaze directed toward the entrance of the dwelling,[4] he awaits for the beginning of day.

---

[1] *I.e.*, En-lil's.

[2] *I.e.*, 'the bond of heaven and earth,' the name probably of a temple-tower in Nippur, sacred to En-lil.

[3] Zu's heart. These two lines are repeated.

[4] The word *Kissu* applies more especially to the dwelling places of the gods. Delitzsch, *Assyr. Handwörterbuch*, p. 349b.

As En-lil poured forth the brilliant waters,
Took his seat on his throne and put on his crown,
He[1] snatched the tablets of fate out of his hands,
Seized the authority — the promulgation of laws.
Thereupon Zu flew off and hid himself in his mountain.

On seal cylinders a god is frequently pictured pouring forth streams of water from jars placed on his shoulders. This is generally the sun-god, but the symbol also seems to belong to other deities[2] and is appropriate to Bel of Nippur, who as the god of the atmosphere above the earth, controls the upper waters. As long as these are poured out by him, they are beneficent; but once beyond his control, the blessing of rain is turned into the curse of a deluge and storm, flooding the fields and sweeping away the habitations of men. This misfortune happens when Zu robs En-lil of the tablets by means of which law and order are established. En-lil is powerless. The bold act of Zu causes consternation among the gods. Anu calls upon some one to pursue Zu and capture him. The bird dwells in an inaccessible recess in the mountains, and the gods are afraid to approach his nest. The scene that ensues reminds us of the episode of the creation epic, where Anshar calls upon Anu, Bel, and Ea in turn to subdue Tiâmat.

Anu opens his mouth and speaks,
Addressing the gods his children:
'Who will force Zu to submit
And thus make his name great among the inhabitants of the whole world?'

Ramman the storm-god *par excellence* is first called upon by the assembled gods:

'Ramman the chief,' they cried, 'the son of Anu.'
Anu communicated to him[3] the order.[4]
'Go, my son Ramman, conqueror who yields to no one,

---
[1] Zu.
[2] See *e.g.*, Ward, *Seal Cylinders of the Metropolitan Museum of Art*, p. 12.
[3] Ramman.
[4] These two lines are repeated.

> Subdue Zu with thy weapon,[1]
> That thy name be glorified in the assembly of the great gods.
> Thou shalt be without a rival among the gods thy brothers.'

Anu furthermore promises Ramman that if he triumphs, lofty shrines will be erected in his honor in many cities.

> 'Temples will be built in thy honor,
> In all quarters of the world thy cities [2] will be situated,
> Thy cities [3] will reach up to Ekur.[4]
> Show thyself strong among the gods, so that thy name be powerful.'

Ramman, however, is afraid of the contest.

> Ramman answered the speech,
> Addressing his father Anu:
> 'My father, who can proceed to the inaccessible mountain?
> Who is there like Zu among the gods, thy children?'

He furthermore pleads that Zu, who has the tablets of fate in his hands, is invincible. He has the power to decree the fates of the gods, and all must bow to his will. At this point, unfortunately, the text becomes defective. Anu calls upon two other gods to take up the contest with Zu. The name of one of these is altogether lost; the second is called Bar,[5] and is designated as an offspring of Ishtar. Both these deities decline, answering Anu in precisely the same manner as Ramman. What finally happens we are left to conjecture. Harper[6] supposes that Shamash is finally called upon by Anu and accepts the challenge. He bases this opinion upon the passage in the Dibbarra legend[7] where the serpent, appealing to Shamash, extols the sun-god's power by declaring that even Zu could not escape the net of Shamash. There are, however, grave objections to this view. In the first place, the passage in ques-

---

[1] The thunderbolt.   [2] Cities sacred to thee.
[3] *I.e.*, the sacred edifices in these cities.
[4] The lofty dwelling of the gods is here meant. See chapter xxvii.
[5] Ideographic reading — the ideograph signifies 'shrine.' The verbal stem *barâru* means 'to shine.'   [6] See p. 414.   [7] See p. 525.

tion occurs in a defective part of the text, and Harper himself[1] is not certain of the restoration that he proposes.[2] Secondly, if Shamash conquers Zu, we should expect the sun-god to have the tablets of fate in his possession. Such, however, is not the case, and the only god besides En-lil who is represented in the religious literature of the Babylonians as holding the tablets is Marduk. Moreover, in a hymn to Marduk, which Harper himself quotes,[3] the bird Zu is referred to as among the evil forces captured by Marduk. In view of this, there seems no reason to question that, in the present form of the Zu myth, Marduk was introduced as the hero, precisely as, in the present form of the Tiâmat episode, Marduk successfully carries out a deed from which the other gods shrink in fear. The theological purport of the myth thus becomes clear. It is to account for the fact that Marduk holds the tablets which were originally in the hands of En-lil. Marduk supplants the old Bel. In the Tiâmat episode his name is substituted for that of En-lil, and the latter is represented as giving his consent to the transfer of his name to the god of Babylon. In the Zu myth, En-lil's claim to the supreme control of the laws and fate of the universe is freely acknowledged, but, En-lil being unable to resist the attack of Zu, it was left for Marduk to capture the bird and thus acquire by his own efforts what the old Bel had lost through lack of strength. Babylon replaces Nippur as the center of power in the Euphrates Valley, and the god of Babylon, naturally, was imbued by his worshippers with prerogatives that originally belonged to the rival god of Nippur.[4]

If this view is correct, Harper's interpretation must be aban-

[1] See p. 400. [3] See p. 417.

[2] It is quite possible that the line in question declares that Zu is in collusion with the eagle, against whom the serpent seeks the assistance of Shamash.

[4] It is hardly possible that the illustration on seal cylinders mentioned by Ward, ib. pp. 13, 14, represents the Zu bird brought before a deity for punishment; and certainly not before Shamash, who only enters into the story in so far as Marduk is a solar deity.

doned. The Zu myth does not represent, as he supposes, an attack upon Marduk as the symbol of the early morning sun, but upon En-lil, the Bel of Nippur, as the one who, by virtue of having the tablets of fate in his possession, controls the laws of the universe and fixes the fate of the gods and of mankind. The annual rain-storm passing apparently beyond the control of the gods is viewed as a revolt against En-lil's authority. It is left for Marduk to reëstablish order, and in return, he retains control of the precious tablets. That the conception of Marduk as a solar deity constitutes a factor in the myth is not, of course, to be denied, precisely as in the Tiâmat myth, the solar character of Marduk plays an important part. The sun triumphs over the storms. Rain and wind are obliged at last to yield their authority to the former. But for the theologians of Babylon, the position of Marduk as the head of the pantheon was a much more important factor. The myth served to show how Marduk came to supplant the rôle of the old Bel of Nippur.

Viewed in this light, the Zu myth appears in more senses than one as a pendant to the Marduk-Tiâmat episode. Not only do both symbolize the same natural phenomenon, but in both, Bel of Nippur was originally the central figure of the pantheon, and in both Marduk replaces Bel. The Zu myth is made to account in a somewhat more respectful, conciliatory manner for the position of Marduk as the head of the pantheon. Instead of setting aside En-lil altogether, as was done by the compilers of the Tiâmat myth, Marduk conquers for himself the supremacy that his followers claimed for him. The contradictions between the two myths need not disturb us. As variant versions of a tale intended to account for one and the same fact, — the supremacy of Marduk, — they may well have arisen even in the same place. Such inconsistencies as the assumption, in the Zu version of the nature myth, that En-lil is the original establisher of order in the world, as against the Tiâmat version where Marduk snatches the tablets of fate directly from Kingu, are inevitable when stories that arose among the people are taken in hand by theologians and modified and adapted to serve doctrines developed under scholastic influences.

THE ADAPA LEGEND.

The myths and legends that we have so far considered — including the creation and Gilgamesh epics — will have illustrated two important points: firstly, the manner in which historical occurrences were clothed in mythical form and interwoven with purely legendary tales, and, secondly, the way in which nature myths were treated to teach certain doctrines. The story of Gilgamesh is an illustration of the hopelessness of a mortal's attempt to secure the kind of immortal life which is the prerogative of the gods. Popular tales, illustrative of the climatic conditions of Babylonia, serve as a means of unfolding a doctrine of evolution and of impressing upon the people a theological system of beliefs regarding the relationship of the gods to one another. A collection of war-songs is given a semi-mythical form, and the original purport of the collection is modified to serve as a talisman against misfortunes. In the case of these legends it is necessary and, as we have seen, also possible to distinguish between their original and present form and to separate the story, as in the case of the Gilgamesh epic, into its component parts.

The legend that we are about to consider proves that this process of the adaptation of popular myths begins at a very early period. The text was found on the cuneiform tablets discovered at El-Amarna in Egypt.[1] Since the El-Amarna tablets date from the fifteenth century B.C., we have a proof of the compilation of the legend in question at this date. The legend is again suggested by the storms which visited Babylonia, but

---

[1] Published by Winckler and Abel, *Der Thontafelfund von El-Amarna*, iii. 166a, b; translated also by Harper, *ib.* pp. 420, 421.

instead of a pure nature-myth, we have a tale which concerns the relationship between the gods and mankind. In its present form, it is an object lesson dealing with the same problem that we came across in the Gilgamesh epic and that we will meet again in another form,—the problem of immortality.

The beginning of the story, as in the case of the Zu myth, is missing, but we are in a position to restore at least the general context. A fisherman, Adapa, is engaged in plying his trade when a storm arises. Adapa is designated as the son of Ea. The place where he is fishing is spoken of as 'the sea.' The Persian Gulf is meant, and this body of water (as the beginning of the great Okeanos) being sacred to Ea,[1] the description of Adapa as the son of Ea is a way of conveying the idea that, like Parnapishtim, he stands under the protection of Ea. The story, like most legends, assumes a period of close intercourse between gods and men, a time when the relationship involved in being 'a son of a god' had a literal force which was lost to a more advanced generation. Adapa, accordingly, is portrayed as fishing for the 'house of his lord,' *i.e.*, for Ea. When the storm breaks loose the fisherman, though a mortal, subdues the fierce element. The storm comes from the south, the direction from which the most destructive winds came to Babylonia. The south wind is pictured, as in the Zu myth, under the form of a bird. The wind sweeps Adapa into the waters, but, since this element is controlled by Adapa's father,—the god Ea,—Adapa succeeds in mastering the south wind, and, as we learn from the course of the narrative, in breaking the wings of the storm-bird. When the tablet becomes intelligible we find Adapa engaged in this contest with the south wind.[2]

The south wind blew and drove him[3] under the water. Into the dwelling-place[4] [of the fish] it engulfs him. 'O south wind, thou hast overwhelmed me with thy cruelty (?). Thy wings I will break.'

[1] See above, p. 63.
[2] My rendering is given in continuous lines. The legend is in narrative, not in poetic form.
[3] Adapa.
[4] Lit., 'house.'

Adapa's threat is carried out.

> Even as he spoke the wings of the south wind were broken. For seven days the south wind did not blow across the land.

Seven is to be interpreted as a round number, as in the Deluge story, and indicates a rather long, though indefinite, period. Anu, the god of heaven, is astonished at this long-continued disappearance of the south wind, and asks a messenger of his, who is called the god Ilabrat, for the cause. Anu inquires:

> "Why has the south wind not blown for seven days across the land?" His messenger Ilabrat answered him: "My lord! Adapa, the son of Ea, has broken the wings of the south wind."

Of this god Ilabrat nothing is known. The interpretation of his name is doubtful.[1] He probably is one of the numerous local gods who was absorbed by some more powerful one and who thus came to have a position of inferior rank in the pantheon.

Anu, upon hearing the news, is enraged, and cries for 'help' against an interference in his domain. He denounces Adapa in solemn assembly, and demands his presence of Ea, in whose domain Adapa has taken refuge. The text at this point is defective, but one can gather that Ea, who constitutes himself Adapa's protector, warns the latter, as he warned Parnapishtim. He advises him to present himself at the throne of Anu for trial, and to secure the intervention of two gods, Tammuz and Gishzida, who are stationed at the gate of heaven, Anu's dwelling-place. To accomplish this, Adapa is to clothe himself in garments of mourning, and when the doorkeepers ask him the reason for his mourning, he is to answer:

> .... Two gods have disappeared from our earth, therefore do I appear thus.

[1] Neither Delitzsch's suggestion 'god of dwellings' nor Harper's 'god thou art strong' is acceptable.

And when he is asked:

"Who are the two gods who have disappeared from the earth?"
Tammuz and Gishzida will look at one another; they will sigh and speak a favorable word before Anu, and the glorious countenance of Anu they will show thee.

Tammuz and Gishzida will know that they are meant. The mourning of Adapa will be regarded as a sign of reverence for the two gods, whose sympathy and good-will will thus be secured.

The introduction of Tammuz and Gishzida introduces a widely spread nature-myth into the story. Gishzida is identical with Nin-gishzida, a solar deity whom we came across in the old Babylonian pantheon.[1] Tammuz similarly is a solar deity. Both represent local solar cults. At a later period, Nin-gishzida is entirely absorbed by Ninib, but the Adapa legend affords us a glimpse of the god still occupying an independent, though already inferior, position. The Babylonian calendar[2] designates the fifth month as sacred to Gishzida, while the fourth month is named for Tammuz. The two deities, therefore, take their place in the systematized pantheon as symbolical of the phases of the sun peculiar to its approach to the summer solstice. The disappearance of the two gods signifies the decline of the year after the summer solstice. Of Tammuz, the popular myth related that it was Ishtar,[3] represented as his consort, who carried him off. Since the disappearance of Gishzida embodies precisely the same idea as that of Tammuz, it was natural that the story should in time have been told only of the one. The annual mourning for Tammuz was maintained in Babylonia to a very late period. The Adapa legend shows us that at one time the festival was celebrated in honor of the two related deities. The Tammuz festival was celebrated just before the summer solstice set in, so that the mourning was followed

---

[1] See p. 99.   [2] See p. 462.
[3] See the following chapter.

immediately by rejoicing at the reappearance of the god whose coming heralded the culmination of vegetation.

The destructive storms take place during the winter, when Tammuz and Gishzida have disappeared. Adapa's mourning is thus an indication of the season of the year when his encounter with the south wind took place. Since Adapa succeeds in overcoming the destructive wind, the wintry season has passed by. Summer is approaching. The time for celebrating both the fast and the festival of the two solar deities has arrived. Tammuz and Gishzida, the gods of spring, accordingly stand at Adapa's side, ready to plead his cause before Anu. So much being clear, we may advance a step further in the interpretation of the legend. By the side of Tammuz and Gishzida, there is still a third solar deity who belongs to the spring of the year, — Marduk, who, by virtue of his later position as the head of the pantheon, sets aside his two fellows and becomes the solar god of spring *par excellence*. Marduk, it will be recalled, is commonly designated as the son of Ea,[1] and we have seen that, apart from political considerations, the sun rising out of the ocean — the domain of Ea — was a factor in this association. Adapa dwells at the sea, and is forced into the ocean by the south wind, in the same way that the sun dips into the great 'Okeanos' every evening. The identification of Adapa with Marduk[2] thus becomes apparent, and as a matter of fact the Babylonian scribes of later times[3] accepted this identification.

The basis of the Adapa legend is, therefore, the nature-myth of the annual fight of the sun with the violent elements of nature. At the same time, other ideas have been introduced into it, and Adapa himself, while playing the rôle of Marduk, is yet not entirely confounded with this god. His name is never

---

[1] See pp. 139 *seq*.
[2] First suggested by Zimmern.
[3] Of the eighth century. See Harper, *ib*. p. 424.

written with the determinative for deity. Moreover, the nature-myth is soon lost sight of, in order to make room for an entirely different order of ideas. The real purport of the legend in its present form is foreshadowed by the further advice that Ea offers to Adapa:

When thou comest before Anu they will offer thee food of death. Do not eat. They will offer thee waters of death. Do not drink. They will offer thee a garment. Put it on. They will offer thee oil. Anoint thyself. The order that I give thee do not neglect. The word that I speak to thee take to heart. The messenger of Anu approached.[1] 'Adapa has broken the wings of the south wind. Deliver him into my hands. . . .'

Ea obeys the order, delivers up Adapa, and everything happens as was foretold.

Upon mounting to heaven and on his approach to the gate of Anu, Tammuz and Gishzida were stationed at the gate of Anu. They saw Adapa and cried 'Help,[2] Lord! Why art thou thus attired? For whom hast thou put on mourning?'[3]

Adapa replies:

'Two gods have disappeared from the earth, therefore do I wear a mourning garment.'
'Who are the two gods who have disappeared from the earth?'
Tammuz and Gishzida looked at one another, broke out in lament. 'O Adapa! Step before King Anu.' As he approached, Anu saw him and cried out to him:
'Come, Adapa, why hast thou broken the wings of the south wind?'
Adapa answered Anu: 'My lord! For the house of my lord[4] I was fishing in the midst of the sea. The waters lay still around me, when the south wind began to blow and forced me underneath. Into the dwelling of the fish it drove me. In the anger of my heart [I broke the wings of the south wind].'

Tammuz and Gishzida thereupon intercede with Anu on behalf of Adapa, and succeed in appeasing the god's wrath. If

---

[1] To Ea. [4] *I.e.*, Ea.
[2] Anu, it will be recalled, utters the same cry. See p. 546.
[3] Referring to his garments of mourning.

the story ended here, we would have a pure nature-myth — the same myth in a different form that we encountered in the Creation epic, in the Deluge story, and in the Zu legend. Adapa would be merely a designation of Marduk and nothing more. The sun triumphs over the storms, and the only objectionable feature in the tale — to a Babylonian — would be the degradation involved in obliging Marduk to secure the intercession of other gods. But this feature of itself suggests that the nature-myth has been embodied in the legend, but does not constitute the whole of it. A second element and one entirely independent in its character has been added to the myth.

Anu is appeased, but he is astonished at Ea's patronage of Adapa, as a result of which a mortal has actually appeared in a place set aside for the gods.

Why did Ea permit an impure mortal to see the interior of heaven and earth? He made him great and gave him fame.[1]

The privilege accorded to Adapa appears to alarm the gods. As among the Greeks and other nations, so also the Babylonian deities were not free from jealousy at the power and achievements of humanity. Adapa, having viewed the secrets of heaven and earth, there was nothing left for the gods but to admit him into their circle. The narrative accordingly continues:

'Now what shall we grant him? Offer him food of life, that he may eat of it.' They brought it to him, but he did not eat. Waters of life they brought him, but he did not drink. A garment they brought him. He put it on. Oil they brought him. He anointed himself.

Adapa follows the instructions of Ea, but the latter, it will be recalled, tells Adapa that food and water of *death* will be offered him. It is Ea, therefore, who, although the god of humanity, and who, moreover, according to the tradition involved in the Adapa legend, is the creator of mankind, who

[1] I follow Zimmern's rendition of the line.

prevents his creatures from gaining immortality. The situation is very much the same that we find in the third chapter of Genesis, when God, who creates man, takes precautions lest mortals eat of the tree of life and 'live forever.' The problem presented by the Hebrew and Babylonian stories is the same: why should not man, who is descended from the gods, who is created in the likeness of a god, who by virtue of his intellect can peer into the secrets of heaven and earth, who stands superior to the rest of creation, who, to use the psalmist's figure, is only 'a scale lower than god,' why should he not be like the gods and live forever? The Hebrew legend solves the problem in a franker way than does the Babylonian. God, while as anxious as Ea to keep man from eating of the tree of life, cautions Adam against the act, whereas Ea practises a deception in order to prevent man from eating. That in both tales eternal life is contained in food points again (as we have found to be the case with the Biblical narratives of Creation and of the Deluge) to a common source for the two traditions. Similarly the phrase 'waters of life' is a figure of speech of frequent occurrence in Biblical literature in both the Old and the New Testaments. It is no argument against a common source for the Hebrew and Babylonian stories explaining how man came to forego immortality, that the waters of life should be found in the one and not in the other. If we assume with Gunkel[1] that the stories embodied in the first chapters of Genesis were long current among the Hebrews before they were given a permanent form, the adaptation of old traditions to an entirely new order of beliefs involves a casting aside of features that could not be used and a discarding of such as seemed superfluous. The striking departures in the case of the Hebrew legends from their Babylonian counterparts are as full of significance as the striking agreements between the two. The departures and agreements must both be accounted for.

[1] *Schöpfung und Chaos*, pp. 168 *seq.*

For both there are reasons. So, to emphasize only one point, in a monotheistic solution of the problem under consideration, there was no place for any conflict among the gods. In Genesis God simply wills that man should not eat of the tree of life. In the Adapa legend the gods, including Anu, are willing to grant a mortal the food and water of life, simply because they believe that Ea, the creator of man, wishes him to have it. Accordingly, Anu and his associates are represented at the close of the legend as being grieved that Adapa should have foregone the privilege.

> Anu looked at him[1] and lamented over him. 'Come, Adapa, why didst thou not eat and not drink? Now thou canst not live.'

Adapa replies, unconscious of the deception practised on him:

> 'Ea, my lord, commanded me not to eat and not to drink.'

Adapa returns to the earth. What his subsequent fate is we do not know, for the tablet here comes to an end. It is possible that he learns what Ea has done, and that the god gives him the reason for the deception practised. A scene of this kind could not find a place in the Hebrew version that emphasizes the supreme authority of a power besides whom none other was recognized. God acts alone.

Adam, it will be recalled, after eating of the fruit of the tree of knowledge, makes a garment for himself. There can be no doubt that there is a close connection between this tradition and the feature in the Adapa legend, where Adapa, who has been shown the 'secrets of heaven and earth,' — that is, has acquired knowledge, — is commanded by Ea to put on the garment that is offered him. The anointing oneself with oil, though an essential part of the toilet in the ancient and modern Orient, was discarded in the Hebrew tale as a superfluous feature. The idea conveyed by the use of oil was the same as

---

[1] Adapa.

the one indicated in clothing one's nakedness. Both are symbols of civilization which man is permitted to attain, but his development stops there. He cannot secure eternal life.

On the other hand, in comparing the Hebrew and Babylonian versions of the problem of knowledge and immortality, one cannot help being struck by the pessimistic tone of the former as against the more consolatory spirit of the latter. God does not want man to attain even knowledge.[1] He secures it in disobedience to the divine will, whereas Ea willingly grants him the knowledge of all there is in heaven and earth. In this way the Hebrew and Babylonian mind, each developed the common tradition in its own way.

Leaving the comparison aside and coming back for a moment to the Adapa story, it is interesting to observe that as we have two tales, both intended to explain the position of Marduk at the head of the pantheon, the one by making him the conqueror of Tiâmat and forcing from Kingu the tablets of fate, the other by representing him as recovering from Zu the tablets which En-lil, who originally held them, could not protect against the storm-bird, so we have two solutions offered for the problem of immortality. The one in the Gilgamesh epic, where the hero is told of the plant of life, succeeds in finding it, but as he is about to eat the 'food' loses his grasp upon it. The exertions of man are in vain. True, there is Parnapishtim, a mortal who with his wife has obtained immortal life. He is the exception that proves the rule. Moreover, it is Bel, and not Ea, who places Parnapishtim 'at the confluence of streams,' there to live forever, and Bel does this as a proof of his pacification, a kind of indemnity offered to Ea for having destroyed the offspring of the god of humanity. The Adapa legend attacks the problem more seriously. Ea, the same god who has created man, endowed him with wisdom, bestowed all manner of benefits

---

[1] The phrase 'knowledge of good and evil' (Gen. ii. 17) is simply an expression equivalent to our 'everything,' or to the Babylonian 'secrets of heaven and earth.'

upon him, Ea, who protects humanity against Anu, against Bel, and other gods, Ea himself deceives man. Evidently the lesson that the Babylonian theologians intended to teach through the Adapa legend was, that it was not good for man to 'live forever.' Ea himself prevents it. That is the point of the story. Anu and the other gods are satisfied, but Ea does not desire it, and Ea's decision cannot be to the disadvantage of mankind, so dearly beloved by him. With this conclusion humanity must be content — and be resigned to the inevitable.

Of the various legends that we have been considering, the story of Adapa is perhaps the most significant, and none the less so for the manner in which a philosophical problem has been grafted on to a nature-myth. Adapa is made to play the rôle of Marduk, and it is nothing short of remarkable that at so early a period as the one to which the existence of the story can be traced back, a nature-myth should have been diverted from its original purpose and adapted to the end that the Adapa story serves in its present form. The process involved in this adaptation is a complicated one. The story serves as an evidence of the intellectual activity displayed in the schools of theological thought that must have flourished for many centuries before a story like that of Adapa could have been produced out of a nature-myth. Hardly less remarkable is it that the theologians and scribes of later times no longer understood the story, for otherwise they would not have identified Adapa with Marduk through the superficial circumstance that he is introduced into the story instead of Marduk, or some other solar deity allied to Marduk.

The Adapa legend takes us back to the beginning of man's career — to the time when, as in the early chapters of Genesis, man stood closer to the gods than at a later time, the time when there was a constant intercourse between man and the gods, and more especially between man and his protector, Ea. The story forms part of a stock of traditions of which we have another specimen in the Eabani-Ukhat episode, incorporated in the Gilgamesh epic.¹ No doubt when the treasures still existing in the British Museum shall have been thoroughly examined and as additional remains of the religious literature of the Babylonians will be brought to light, we will find further traces of these early traditions as well as of other myths. Those that we have discussed in this and in the preceding chapters illustrate the system adopted by the priests in elaborating these traditions and myths and in adapting them to serve as illustrations of certain doctrines and beliefs. We may also feel tolerably confident that the religious ideas conveyed through these various epics and legends and myths fairly represent both the popular and the advanced thought, as it unfolded itself in the course of time. By the aid of these specimens of the religious literature, we have been enabled to analyze the views of the Babylonians regarding the creation of the world, its structure, and government. We have obtained an insight into the problems of life and death which engaged the Babylonian thinkers, and we have noted some of the solutions offered for these problems. In a consideration of the views held by the Babylonians and Assyrians of the life after death, to which we now turn, it will again be a specimen of the religious literature that will serve as our main guide.

¹ See pp. 476 *seq*. Sayce has even gone so far as to suggest an identification of Adapa (by reading Adawa) with the Biblical Adam, but this conjecture is untenable.

CHAPTER XXV.

THE VIEWS OF LIFE AFTER DEATH.

The problem of immortality, we have seen, engaged the serious attention of the Babylonian theologians. While the solutions they had to offer could hardly have been satisfactory either to themselves or to the masses, it must not be supposed that the denial of immortality to man involved the total extinction of conscious vitality. Neither the people nor the leaders of religious thought ever faced the possibility of the total annihilation of what once was called into existence. Death was a passage to another kind of life, and the denial of immortality merely emphasized the impossibility of escaping the change in existence brought about by death. The gods alone do not pass from one phase of existence to the other. Death was mysterious, but not more mysterious than life. The Babylonian religion does not transcend the stage of belief, characteristic of primitive culture everywhere, which cannot conceive of the possibility of life coming to an absolute end. Life of some kind and in some form was always presupposed. So far as man was concerned, created by some god, — Bel, Ea, Aruru, or Ishtar, according to the various traditions that were current,[1] — no divine fiat could wipe out what was endowed with life and the power of reproduction.

No doubt, the impossibility for the individual to conceive of himself as forever deprived of consciousness, was at the bottom of the primitive theory of the perpetuity of existence in some form. Among ancient religions, Buddhism alone frees itself from this theory and unfolds a bold doctrine of the possibility

[1] See above, p. 448.

of a complete annihilation. The question, however, whether the continuity of existence was a blessing or a curse was raised by many ancient nations. The Babylonians are among these who are inclined to take a gloomy view of the passage from this world to the existence in store for humanity after death, and the religious leaders were either powerless or disinclined to controvert this view.

Location and Names of the Gathering Place of the Dead.

We have already had occasion[1] to refer to the great cave underneath the earth in which the dead were supposed to dwell, and since the earth itself was regarded as a mountain, the cave is pictured as a hollow within, or rather underneath, a mountain. A conception of this kind must have arisen among a people that was once familiar with a mountainous district. The settlers of the Euphrates Valley brought the belief with them from an earlier mountain home. The cave, moreover, points to cave-dwelling and to cave-burial as conditions that prevailed at one time among the populace, precisely as the imitation of the mountain with its caves in the case of the Egyptian pyramids, is due to similar influences. To this cave various names are assigned in the literature of the Babylonians, — some of popular origin, others reflecting scholastic views. The most common name is Aralû.[2] We also find the term 'house of Aralû.'[3] The etymology of the term is obscure. Aralû was pictured as a vast place, dark and gloomy. It is sometimes called a land, sometimes a great house. The approach to it was difficult. It lay in the lowest part of the mountain

---

[1] See pp. 487, 489, 511, 512.   [2] Or Arallu.

[3] IIR. 61, 18. Jensen, *Kosmologie*, p. 220, takes this as the name of a temple; but, since Aralû was pictured as a 'great house,' there is no reason why the designation should not refer to the nether world.

that represented the earth, not far from the hollow underneath the mountain into which the 'Apsu' flowed. Surrounded by seven walls and strongly guarded, it was a place to which no living person could go and from which no mortal could ever depart after once entering it. To Aralû all went whose existence in this world had come to an end. Another name which specifies the relationship of Aralû to the world is Ekur or 'mountain house' of the dead. Ekur is one of the names for the earth,[1] but is applied more particularly to that part of the mountain, also known as Kharsag[2]-kurkura, *i.e.*, 'the mountain of all lands' where the gods were born. Before the later speculative view was developed, according to which the gods, or most of them, have their seats in heaven,[3] it was on this mountain also that the gods were supposed to dwell. Hence Ekur became also one of the names for temple,[4] as the seat of a god. The dwelling of the dead was regarded as a part of the 'great mountain.' It belonged to Ekur, and the fact that it was designated simply as Ekur,[5] is a valuable indication that the dead were brought into close association with the gods. This association is also indicated by the later use of Aralû as the designation of the mountain within which the district of the dead, Aralû proper, lay[6] — synonymous, therefore, with Ekur. We shall see in the course of this chapter that the dead are placed even more than the living under the direct supervision of the gods.

A third name for the nether world which conveys an important addition to the views held regarding the dead, was Shuâlu. Jensen, it is true, following Bertin, questions the existence of

---

[1] See the admirable argument in Jensen, *Kosmologie*, pp. 185–193.
[2] Or, more fully, Kharsag-gal-kurkura, 'great mountain of all lands.'
[3] See above, p. 458.   [4] See the following chapter.
[5] See the passages in Jeremias' *Die Babylonisch-Assyrischen Vorstellungen vom Leben nach dem Tode*, p. 62.
[6] Sargon Annals, l. 156. Jensen's interpretation of the passage (*Kosmologie*, p. 231) is forced, as is also his explanation of IIR. 51, 11a, where a mountain Aralû is clearly designated.

this term in Babylonian,[1] but one does not see how the evidence of the passages in the lexicographical tablets can be set aside in the way that he proposes. Zimmern[2] does not appear to be convinced by Jensen's arguments and regards the question as an open one. Jensen's method of disposing of Shuâlu, besides being open to serious objections, fails to account for the fact that Shuâlu is brought into association with various Babylonian terms and ideographs for the grave.[3] This cannot be accidental. That the term has hitherto been found only in lexicographical tablets need not surprise us. Aralû, too, is of rare occurrence in the religious texts. The priests appear to avoid the names for the nether world, which were of ill omen, and preferred to describe the place by some epithet, as 'land without return,' or 'dark dwelling,' or 'great city,' and the like. Of such descriptive terms we have a large number.[4] The stem underlying Shuâlu signifies 'to ask.' Shuâlu is a place of inquiry,[5] and the inquiry meant is of the nature of a religious oracle. The name, accordingly, is an indication of the power accorded to the dead, to aid the living by furnishing them with answers to questions, just as the gods furnish oracles through the mediation of the priests.[6] The Old Testament supplies us with an admirable illustration of the method of obtaining oracles through the dead. Saul, when he desires to know what the outcome of a battle is to be, seeks out a sorceress, and through her calls up the dead Samuel[7] and puts

---

[1] *Kosmologie*, pp. 222-224.

[2] Gunkel's *Schöpfung und Chaos*, p. 154, note 5.

[3] In an article on 'Shuâlu' published in the *American Journal of Semitic Languages* (xiv.), I have set forth my reasons for accepting this word as a Babylonian term for the nether world.

[4] In the later portions of the Old Testament, the use of Sheol is also avoided. See the passages in Schwally, *Das Leben nach dem Tode nach den Vorstellungen des Alten Israels*, pp. 59, 60.

[5] Not 'Ort der Entscheidung,' as Jeremias, *ib.* p. 109, proposes.

[6] See above, p. 329.

[7] I Sam. xxviii. 11.

the question to him. Similarly, in the Gilgamesh epic, the hero, with the aid of Nergal, obtains a sight of Eabani[1] and plies him with questions. The belief, therefore, in this power of the dead was common to Babylonians and Hebrews, and, no doubt, was shared by other branches of the Semites. It is natural, therefore, to find the Babylonian term Shuâlu paralleled by the Hebrew Sheôl, which is the common designation in the Old Testament for the dwelling-place of the dead.[2] How widespread the custom was among Babylonians of inquiring 'through the living of the dead'[3] it is difficult, in default of satisfactory evidence, to say. The growing power of the priests as mediators between men and gods must have acted as a check to such practices. The priests, as the inquirers,[4] naturally proceeded direct to the particular god whose representative they claimed to be, and the development of an elaborate ceremonial in the temples in connection with the oracles[5] was a further factor that must have influenced the gradual abandonment of the custom, at least as an element of the *official* cult. Moreover, the belief itself belongs in the domain of ancestor worship, and in historical times we find but little trace of such worship among the Babylonians. We may, therefore, associate the custom with the earliest period of the Babylonian religion. This view carries with it the antiquity of the term Shuâlu. Like Aralû and the designation Ekur, it embodies the close association of the dead with the gods. The dead not only dwell near the gods, but, like the gods, they can direct the affairs of mankind. Their answers to questions put to them have divine justification. From this view of the dead to the

---

[1] See p. 511.

[2] See Schwally, *ib.* pp. 59–63.

[3] Isaiah, viii. 19.

[4] One of the names for the priest in Babylonia is Shâ'ilu, *i.e.*, 'inquirer,' and the corresponding Hebrew word Shô'êl is similarly used in a few passages of the Old Testament; *e.g.*, Deut. xviii. 11; Micah, vii. 3. See an article by the writer on "The Stem Shâ'al and the Name of Samuel," in a forthcoming number of the *Journal of the Society of Biblical Literature*.

[5] See above, pp. 333 *seq.*

deification of the latter is but a short step. It does not, of course, follow, from the fact that Shuâlu or Sheôl is the place of 'oracles,' that all the dead have the power to furnish oracles or can be invoked for this purpose. Correspondingly, if we find that the Babylonians did deify their dead, it does not mean that at one time all the dead were regarded as gods. Popular legends are concerned only with the heroes, with the popular favorites — not with the great masses. Eabani, who appears to Gilgamesh, is a hero, and so is Samuel. As a matter of fact, we have so far only found evidence that the ancient rulers whose memory lingered in the minds of the people were regarded by later generations as gods. So the names of Dungi and Gudea [1] are written on tablets that belong to the centuries immediately following their reign, with the determinative that is placed before the names of gods. Festivals were celebrated in honor of these kings, sacrifices were offered to them, and their images were placed in temples.[2] Again, Gimil-Sin (c. 2500 B.C.), of the second dynasty of Ur, appears to have been deified during his lifetime, and there was a temple in Lagash which was named after him.[3] No doubt other kings will be found who were similarly honored. We may expect to come across a god Hammurabi some day. Gilgamesh is, as we have seen, a historical personage whose career has been so thoroughly amalgamated with nature-myths that he ends by becoming a solar deity who is invoked in incantations.

The tendency to connect legendary and mythical incidents with ancient rulers is part and parcel of this process of deification. Of an ancient king, Sargon,[4] a story was related how he

---

[1] See p. 167.

[2] See above, p. 167, and Scheil, *Le Culte de Gudea*, etc. (*Recueil des Travaux*, xviii. 64 *seq.*)

[3] Thureau-Dangin, *Le Culte des Rois dans la période Prebabylonienne* (*Recueil des Travaux*, etc., xix. 486).

[4] See above, p. 36. The text is published IIIR. pl. 4, no. 7. Recently, Mr. Pinches has published a variant version of this story (*Proc. Soc. Bibl. Arch.* xviii. 257, 258).

was exposed in a boat, and, 'knowing neither father nor mother,' was found by a ferryman. The exploits of this king and of his successor, Naram-Sin, were incorporated in an omen text[1]— a circumstance that again illustrates how the popular fancy connected the heroes of the past with its religious interests. Still, there is no more reason to question the historical reality of Sargon[2] than to question the existence of Moses, because a story of his early youth is narrated in Exodus[3] which forms a curious parallel to the Sargon legend, or to question the existence of a personage by the name of Abraham, because an Abrahamitic cult arose that continues to the present day.[4]

This close association of the dead with the gods, upon which the deification of the dead rests, may be regarded as a legacy of the earliest period of the Babylonian religion, of the time when the intercourse between the gods and the living was also direct. The belief and rites connected with the dead constitute the most conservative elements in the religion of a people. The organized cult affects the living chiefly. So far as the latter are concerned, the rise of a priesthood to whom the religious needs of the people are entrusted, removes the living from that immediate contact with the gods which we note in the traditions of every people regarding the beginnings of mankind. The priests have no power over the dead. The dead require no 'mediator.' Hence, those who dwell in Aralû return to the early state of mankind when gods and mankind 'walked together.'

Another name that is of frequent occurrence in religious texts is Kigallu, which describes the nether world as a district

---

[1] IVR. 34.

[2] In view of recent discussions of the subject, it is important to note that Tiele already fifteen years ago recognized that Sargon was a historical personage. See his remarks, *Babyl. Assyr. Gesch.*, p. 112.

[3] Chapter ii.

[4] See Winterbotham, "The Cult of Father Abraham," in the *Expositor*, 1897, pp. 177-186.

of great extent, situated within the earth.[1] The chief goddess of the nether world is commonly known as the 'queen of Kigallu.' Furthermore, Irkalla, which was interpreted by the Babylonian theologians as 'great city' (or 'district'), is used both as a designation for the dwelling-place of the dead and for the consort of the queen of Aralû.[2]

Beside the names for the nether world above discussed, a large number of epithets and metaphors are found in the religious texts. The place to which the dead go is called the 'dark dwelling,' 'the land from which there is no return,' 'house of death,' 'the great city,' 'the deep land,' and, since Nergal, the ruler of the lower world, was the patron of the city Cuthah[3] (or Kutu), the name Cuthah was also used as a designation for Aralû. Lastly, it is interesting to note that in poetical usage the words for 'grave'[4] were also employed to describe the nether world. The question raised by this metaphor as to the relationship between the grave and the lower world can best be discussed when we come to consider the funeral rites.[5]

THE CONDITION OF THE DEAD AND THE IMPOSSIBILITY OF AN ESCAPE FROM ARALÛ.

Among the remains of Babylonian literature there is a remarkable production, which furnishes us with an admirable view of the fate in store for those who have left this world.[6] The composition is based upon a nature-myth, symbolizing the change of seasons. Ishtar, the great mother goddess, the goddess of fertility who produces vegetation, is, as we saw in the Gilga-

---

[1] See Jensen's *Kosmologie*, p. 215, and Meissner, *Altbabylonisches Privatrecht*, p. 21. The word is used for the foundation of a building, and is an indication, therefore, of the great depth at which the nether world was placed.
[2] See below, p. 567, and Jensen's *Kosmologie*, p. 259.
[3] See pp. 65, 66.   [4] *Kabru* and *Gigunu* ('dark place').
[5] See also below, pp. 566, 567.   [6] Published IV Rawlinson (2d edition), pl. 31.

mesh epic,[1] also the one who brings about the decline of vegetation. The change in nature that takes place after the summer solstice is passed and the crops have ripened was variously interpreted. According to one, and, as it would seem, the favorite, tradition, the goddess is represented as herself destroying the solar deity, Tammuz, whom she had chosen as a consort. Repentant and weeping, Ishtar passes to the lower world in search of her youthful husband,— the symbol of the sun on its approach to the summer solstice. While Ishtar is in the lower world, all fertility ceases, in the fields, as well as in the animal kingdom. At last Ishtar reappears, and nature is joyous once more. In the Semitic Orient there are only two seasons:[2] winter, or the rainy season, and summer, or the dry season. The myth was, therefore, a symbol of the great contrast that the two seasons presented to one another. Under various forms and numerous disguises, we find the myth among several branches of the Semites, as well as in Egypt and among Aryans who came into contact with Semitic ideas.[3] A festival celebrated in honor of Tammuz by the Babylonians is one expression of many that the myth received. The designation of the sixth month as "the mission of Ishtar"[4] is another. This myth was adapted by the theologians to illustrate the doctrines that were developed regarding the kind of existence led by the dead. The literary method adopted is the same that characterizes the elaboration of the Adapa myth and of the myths incorporated into the Gilgamesh epic. The story forms the point of departure, but its original purport is set aside to a greater or less degree, necessary modifications are introduced, and the moral or lesson is

---

[1] See p. 483.

[2] The Old Testament recognizes only two seasons, summer and winter. See, *e.g.*, Gen. viii. 22.

[3] See the discussion in Robertson Smith's *Religions of the Semites*, pp. 391-394; and also Farnall, *The Cults of the Greek States*, ii. 644-649.

[4] See above, p. 484.

distinctly indicated. In the case of the production that we are about to consider, the story of Ishtar's visit to the nether world is told — perhaps by a priest — to a person who seeks consolation. A dear relative has departed this life, and a survivor, — a brother, apparently, — is anxious to know whether the dead will ever come back again. The situation reminds one of Gilgamesh seeking out Eabani,[1] with this difference: that, whereas Gilgamesh, aided by Nergal, is accorded a sight of his friend, the ordinary mourner must content himself with the answer given to him. But what Gilgamesh is not permitted to hear,[2] the mourner is told. A description is given him of how the dead fare in Aralû.

The problem, however, is somewhat different in the story of the descent of Ishtar, from the one propounded in the twelfth tablet of the Gilgamesh epic. The question uppermost in the mind of the mourner is "Will the dead return?" The condition of the dead, which is most prominent in Gilgamesh's mind, is secondary. Both questions, however, are answered, and both answers are hopelessly sad. The nether world is joyless. Even the goddess Ishtar is badly treated upon entering it. The place is synonymous with inactivity and decay; and, though the goddess returns, the conclusion drawn is that the exception proves the inexorable rule. A goddess may escape, but mortals are doomed to everlasting sojourn, or rather imprisonment, in the realm presided over by Allatu and her consort Nergal. The tale begins with a description of the land to which Ishtar proceeds:

> To the land whence there is no return, the land of darkness (?)[3]
> Ishtar, the daughter of Sin, turned her mind,

[1] See above, p. 510.

[2] *I.e.*, according to one version (p. 511). Another version of this part of the Gilgamesh epic, which, however, is influenced by the tale of Ishtar's visit, is published in Haupt's *Nimrodepos*, pp. 16–19. In this version Eabani gives Gilgamesh a description of Aralû, which tallies with the one found in the Ishtar tale.

[3] Text defective. Jeremias' suggestion, "the land that thou knowest," misses the point. The person addressed does not know the land. 'Decay' is Schrader's conjecture (*Die Höllenfahrt der Istar*, p. 24). See Haupt's *Nimrodepos*, pp. 17, 40, and Delitzsch's *Assyr. Wörterbuch*, p. 321, note.

> The daughter of Sin turned her mind;
> To the house of darkness, the dwelling of Irkalla,
> To the house whence no one issues who has once entered it.
> To the road from which there is no return, when once it has been trodden.
> To the house whose inhabitants[1] are deprived of light.
> The place where dust is their[2] nourishment, their food clay.
> They[3] have no light, dwelling in dense darkness.
> And they are clothed like birds, in a garment of feathers;
> Where over gate and bolt, dust is scattered.

Ishtar, it will be observed, is here called the daughter of the moon-god, whereas in the Gilgamesh epic she appears as the daughter of Anu, the god of heaven. Both designations reflect the views developed in the schools, and prove that the story has been produced under scholastic influences. The goddess has her place in the heavens, in the planet bearing her name, and the designation of this planet as the daughter of Sin can only be understood in connection with the astronomical system, in which the moon plays so prominent a rôle[4] and becomes the father of all the great gods (except Shamash) who constitute the lesser luminaries of the night.

Irkalla is one of the names[5] for a god of the nether world, who is regarded as the associate of Allatu. The dwelling is elsewhere spoken of as a 'great palace' in which Allatu and her consort Nergal have their thrones. A gloomier place than the one described in these opening lines of the story cannot well be imagined. The picture reflects the popular views, and up to this point, the doctrines of the school are in agreement with the early beliefs. The description of the lower world is evidently suggested by the grave or the cave in which the dead were laid. The reference to dust and clay as the food of the dead shows that the doctrine taught in the Gilgamesh epic,[6] of man's being formed of clay and returning

---

[1] Lit., 'the one who has entered it.'
[2] *I.e.*, of the Inhabitants.
[3] The inhabitants.
[4] See p. 461.
[5] See below, p. 591.
[6] See pp. 502, 511.

to clay, was the common one. This view helps us to understand how the words for grave came to be used as synonyms for the nether world. The dead being placed below the earth, they were actually conveyed within the realm of which Aralû was a part, and since it became customary for the Babylonians to bury their dead together, the cities of the dead that thus arose could easily be imagined to constitute the kingdom presided over by Allatu and Nergal. At this point, however, the speculations of the schools begin to diverge from the popular notions. We may well question whether the Babylonian populace ever attempted to make clear to itself in what form the dead continued their existence. It may be that the argument from dreams, as the basis for the primitive belief in the continuation of life, in some form, after death has been too hard pressed,[1] but certainly the appearance of the dead in the dreams of the living must have produced a profound impression, and since the dead appeared in the same form that they had while alive, the conclusion was natural that, even though the body decayed, a vague outline remained that bore the same relation to the *corpus* as the shadow to the figure casting it. Two remarkable chapters in the Old Testament[2] illustrate this popular view prevailing in Babylonia, as to the condition of the dead in the nether world. The prophets Isaiah and Ezekiel both portray the dead as having the same form that they possessed while alive. The kings have their crowns on their heads; the warriors lie with their swords girded about them. The dead Eabani, it will be recalled, appears to Gilgamesh and is at once recognized by the latter. What distinguishes the dead from the living is their inactivity. They lie in Aralû without doing anything. Everything there is in a state of neglect and decay. The dead can speak, but the Babylonians probably believed, like the

---

[1] Particularly by Herbert Spencer and his followers.
[2] Isaiah, xlv. 9–20, and Ezekiel, xxxii. 18–31. In Isaiah, the Babylonian Aralû is specifically described, while Ezekiel writes under the influence of Babylonian ideas.

Hebrews, that the dead talk in whispers, or chirp like birds.[1] The dead are weak,[2] and, therefore, unless others attend to their needs, they suffer pangs of hunger, or must content themselves with 'dust and clay' as their food. Tender care during the last moments of life was essential to comparative well-being in Aralû.[3] The person who goes to Aralû in sorrow and neglect will continue sorrowful and neglected.

The theologians, while accepting these views in general, passed beyond them in an important particular. They could not reconcile the evident dissolution of the body with a continuation of even a shadowy outline. When a man died, the 'spirit,' which, according to the animistic theory, lodged somewhere within the body and produced the manifestations of life, sought for refuge in some other substance. The ease with which birds moved from one place to another suggested these beings as the ones in which the dislodged spirit found a home. The Babylonian thinkers were not alone in developing the view that the dead assumed the form of birds. Parallels to the pictures of the dead in the story of Ishtar's descent may be found in Egypt and elsewhere.[4] But what is important for our purposes is the consideration that, in Babylonia at least, the view in question is not the popular one, but the result of speculations about a problem that appeals only to those who make the attempt, at least, to clarify their ideas regarding the mystery of death. The next section of the story affords us a picture of the entrance to Aralû:

> When Ishtar arrived at the gate of the land without return,
> She spoke to the watchman of the gate:
> Ho! watchman — open thy gate.

---

[1] Isaiah, viii. 19.
[2] The Hebrew word for 'the dead,' *refâim*, conveys this idea.
[3] See p. 512.
[4] See Sara Y. Stevenson, "On Certain Symbols used in the Decoration of Some Potsherds from Daphne and Naukratis" (Philadelphia, 1892), p. 8.

> Open thy gate that I may enter.
> If thou dost not open the gate, if thou refusest me admission,
> I will smash the door, break the bolt.
> I will smash the threshold, force open the portals.
> I will raise up the dead to eat the living
> Until the dead outnumber the living.

The entrance to the nether world is strongly guarded. From other sources we learn that there was a 'spy'— perhaps identical with the watchman — stationed at the portal of the lower world, who reports all happenings to the queen Allatu through Namtar, the god (or spirit) of pestilence. The watchman is to prevent the living from entering, and also the dead from escaping.

The violence of Ishtar is an interesting touch in the narrative. As a goddess, she resents any opposition to her desires. Her anxiety to enter Aralû indicates that the original form of the myth, which must have represented the descent as forced and not voluntary, has been modified by the introduction of a new factor, — the search for her dead consort, Tammuz. The character of Ishtar as the goddess of war [1] may also have influenced this portrayal of her rage. In her violence, she threatens a conflict between the dead and the living. The former will destroy [2] the latter, as a victorious army butchers the hostile host. The watchman endeavors to pacify the enraged Ishtar:

> The watchman opened his mouth and spoke.
> Spoke to the great Ishtar:
> Hold, O mistress, do not destroy them.[3]
> I will go and mention thy name to the queen Allatu.

Allatu is grieved upon hearing the news of Ishtar's arrival, for Ishtar's disappearance from the world means death.

---

[1] See above, p. 83.
[2] 'Eating' appears to be a metaphor for destruction in general.
[3] The portals (?).

I must weep for the masters who forsake their consorts.
I must weep for the wives who are torn from their husbands' side.
For the children I must weep who are snatched away (?) before their time.
Go, watchman, open thy gate.
Deal with her according to the ancient laws.

The scene that follows embodies, again, views of the nether world as developed in the schools. Corresponding to the seven zones surrounding the earth,[1] the nether world is pictured as enclosed by seven gates. Through these Ishtar must pass, before she is ushered into the presence of Allatu.

The watchman went and opened his gate.
Enter, O mistress, welcome in Cuthah.[2]
The great house[3] of the land without return greets thee.[4]
Through the first gate he led her, and boldly removed the great crown from her head.
Why, O watchman, dost thou remove the great crown from my head?
Enter, O mistress, such are the laws of Allatu.

At the second gate, he removes the earrings of the goddess; at the third, her necklace is taken away, and, similarly, at each succeeding gate, a portion of her dress, the ornaments on her breast, her belt of precious stones, her bracelets, until, when the seventh gate is reached, the covering over her loins is removed, and she stands naked before Allatu. At each gate Ishtar asks the same question, why the watchman strips her, and the same answer is given.

The removal of one ornament after the other symbolizes, evidently, the gradual decay of vegetation, not, as has been supposed, that the dead enter Aralû naked.

Allatu calls upon her messenger, Namtar, to strike the goddess with disease in all parts of her body. The disease

---

[1] Jensen, *Kosmologie*, pp. 173 seq.

[2] Here used as an epithet of the nether world. See above, p. 563.

[3] Or 'palace.' The lower world, it will be recalled, is pictured as a house or a country. Here the two terms are combined. See Delitzsch, *Assyr. Wörterbuch*, p. 341.

[4] The phrases used are the ordinary terms of greeting. See, *e.g.*, VR. 65, 17b.

expresses the same idea as the removal of the ornaments,— decay of strength. There follows a description of the desolation on earth during Ishtar's sojourn with Allatu. Productivity comes to a standstill.

> The ox does not mount the cow, the ass does not bend over the she-ass.

Among mankind, likewise, fertility ceases. The gods lament the absence of Ishtar and the fate that overtook her. The astronomical conception of Ishtar as the planet Venus, at this point, is apparent. The gods complain.

> Ishtar has descended to the earth, and has not come up.

As a planet, Ishtar's seat is in the heavens. The disappearance of the planet has been combined with the nature-myth of the decay of vegetation. As the evening star, Venus dips down into the west, to reappear after a long interval in the east. The astral character of Ishtar dominates the latter half of the story in its present form. It is not the goddess of love and fertility nor the goddess of war who is rescued from her prison by Ea, but the planet Ishtar. Shamash is informed of the disaster by his servant, Pap-sukal.[1] The sun-god proceeds for aid to Sin and Ea. The latter furnishes relief. The sun enters Ea's domain every evening, and, since it is in the west that the planet sinks like the sun, the association of ideas becomes apparent which suggests Ea as the savior and the sun as the mediator.

> Ea created in his wisdom a male being.
> He formed Uddushu-namir, a divine servant.
> Go, Uddushu-namir, to the gate of the land without return, turn thy face.
> The seven gates of the land without return will be opened before thee.
> Allatu will see thee and welcome thee
> After her heart is pacified, her spirit[2] brightened.

---

[1] Gibil-Nusku may be meant. See the hymn, p. 278. Pap-sukal is a title of Nabu (p. 130), but also of other gods.

[2] Lit., 'liver.'

> Invoke against her the name of the great gods.
> Raise thy countenance, to Sukhal-ziku direct thy attention.
> Come, mistress, grant me Sukhal-ziku, that I may drink [1] therefrom.

Ea appears here again in the rôle of Creator.[2] The name of the mysterious being created by Ea signifies 'renewal of light.' The incident, it will be seen, is wholly symbolical. A touch of mysticism has also been introduced. Sukhal-ziku is a compound of a word meaning 'to sprinkle' and another which may mean 'grotto.'[3] Sukhal-ziku appears, therefore, to be the name for a mysterious fountain, the waters of which restore the dead to life.

Uddushu-namir having pronounced the name of the gods before Allatu, and having thus secured their aid, his request is in the nature of an order. But the request must not be interpreted literally, as though the waters were intended for him. It is for the sake of Ishtar that he desires to have the use of Sukhal-ziku. Allatu understands Uddushu-namir's speech in this sense, and is enraged at the order to yield up Ishtar.

> Allatu, upon hearing this,
> Smote her sides and bit her finger.[4]
> Thou hast demanded of me a request that should not be requested.
> Come, Uddushu-namir, I will curse thee with a terrible curse.
> Food from the gutters of the city be thy nourishment.
> The sewers (?) of the city be thy drink.
> The shadow of the wall be thy seat.
> The threshold be thy dwelling.
> Exile and banishment break thy strength.

The force of the curse lies in the closing words. Uddushu-namir is to be an outcast. He will not be permitted to enter

---

[1] For the translation of these lines see Jensen, *Kosmologie*, p. 233.

[2] See above, p. 441.

[3] So Jeremias' *Vorstellungen*, etc.; see p. 39. *Zikutu* from the same stem means a 'drinking bowl.'

[4] A biting of the lips is elsewhere introduced as a figure. See the author's monograph, "A Fragment of the Babylonian Dibbarra Epic," p. 14.

either city or house, but must remain at the wall or stop at the threshold. Properly prepared food and drink are to be denied him. He shall starve or perish miserably.

But the mission of Uddushu-namir has been accomplished. Allatu may curse as she pleases; the order of Ea must be obeyed.

> The goddess Allatu opened her mouth and spoke.
> To Namtar, her messenger, she addressed an order:
> Go, Namtar, smash the true palace.[1]
> Break down the threshold, destroy the door-posts (?) .
> Bring out the Anunnaki and place them on golden thrones.
> Besprinkle Ishtar with the waters of life and take her from me.

Namtar obeys the order. Ishtar is led through the seven gates. At each one, the articles taken from her on her entrance are returned: at the first, the loin cloth; at the second, the bracelets and ankle rings, and so on, until she emerges in her full beauty.

The close of the story thus brings to our gaze once more Ishtar as goddess of fertility, who gradually brings vegetation, strength, and productivity back again. This curious mixture in the story of the astral Ishtar, — the creation of the astronomers, — and the popular Ishtar, is a trait which shows how the old nature-myth has been elaborated in passing through the hands of the *literati*. The various steps in the process can still be seen. In the original form, the goddess must have been forced into an exile to the nether world, the exile symbolizing the wintry season when fertility and productivity[2] come to an end. Ishtar is stripped of her glory. She comes to Allatu, who grieves at her approach, but imprisons her in the 'great house,'

---

[1] See Delitzsch, *Assyr. Wörterbuch*, p. 341.

[2] So far as the domestic animals are concerned, it is true that they throw off their young in the spring. The reference to a similar interruption in the case of mankind (see above, p. 571) may embody the recollection of a period when a regular pairing season and breeding time existed among mankind. See Westermarck, *The History of Human Marriage*, pp. 27 seq.

and refuses to yield her up, until forced to do so by order of the gods. A similar story must have been told of Tammuz, the sun-god, who is also the god of vegetation. The two stories were combined. Ishtar marries Tammuz, and then destroys him. The goddess produces fertility, but cannot maintain it. Tammuz goes to the nether world. Ishtar repents, bewails her loss, and goes to seek for her consort and to rescue him. In rage she advances to Allatu, threatens to smash the door and break the lock unless admitted. The story in this form must have ended in the restoration of Tammuz. The identification of Ishtar with the planet Venus introduced a new factor. The disappearance of the planet fitted in well with the original nature-myth. The combination of the Ishtar-Tammuz story with this factor resulted in the tale as we have it now. The enraged Ishtar is the one who seeks for her consort. The Ishtar who is forced to give up her ornaments is the old goddess who falls into the hands of Allatu. During her absence, production comes to a standstill; decay sets in. The Ishtar who is rescued by Ea through the mediation of the 'Renewal of Light' is the astral Ishtar, as developed by the astronomers, and, finally, the Ishtar who receives her ornaments back again and comes to the upper world, is once more the goddess of vegetation, rescued from her exile to new glory. Up to this point, Tammuz has not been mentioned in the story. In the advice, however, that is given at the conclusion of the tale to mourners, the consort of Ishtar is introduced.

If she [1] will not grant her redemption,[2] turn to her [3] [thy countenance?]
To Tammuz, her youthful consort,
Pour out pure waters, costly oil [offer him?].

The mourners are furthermore instructed to institute a formal lamentation. The Ukhâti,[4] the priestesses of Ishtar, are to

---

[1] Allatu.
[2] *I.e.*, of the dead person.
[3] Ishtar.
[4] See p. 475.

sing dirges; flutes are to accompany the song. The thought intended, apparently, to be conveyed is that if Allatu will not give up the dead, the surviving relatives should endeavor to secure the good grace of Ishtar and Tammuz, who succeeded in subduing Allatu.

The closing lines are rendered obscure by a reference to the goddess Belili, who appears to be the sister of Tammuz. The reference assumes the knowledge of a tale in which the goddess was represented as breaking a costly vessel adorned with precious stones, in sign of her grief for the lost Tammuz. Suitable mourning for Tammuz, therefore, will secure the sympathy of Belili also. The story thus ends with a warning to all who mourn for their dead to remember Tammuz, to observe the rites set aside for the festival celebrated in his honor.

Bearing in mind the tentative character of any interpretation for the closing lines, we may mention Jeremias'[1] supposition that it is a deceased sister who addresses her sorrowing brother at the end of the story.

My only brother, let me not perish.
On the day of Tammuz, play for me on the flute of lapis lazuli, together
   with the lyre [2] of pearl play for me.
Together let the professional dirge singers, male and female, play for me,
That the dead may arise and inhale the incense of offerings.

The lines impress one as snatches from a dirge, sung or recited in memory of the dead, and introduced here as an appropriate illustration of the conclusion to be drawn from the tale. At all events, the consolation that the mourner receives lies in this thought,—the dead can hear the lamentation. The survivors are called upon not to forget the dead. When the festival of Tammuz comes, let them combine with the weeping for the god, a dirge in memory of the dead. Let them pray to Ishtar and Tammuz. If remembered by the

---

[1] *Vorstellungen*, pp. 6–8.   [2] Some instrument is mentioned.

living, the dead will at least enjoy the offerings made to them, regain, as it were, a temporary sense of life; but more cannot with certainty be hoped for.

The outlook for the dead, it will be seen, is not hopeful. Their condition is at best a tolerable one. What we may glean from other sources but confirms the general impression, conveyed by the opening and closing lines of the Ishtar story, or makes the picture a still gloomier one. The day of death is a day of sorrow, 'the day without mercy.' The word for corpse conveys the idea that things have 'come to an end.' Whenever death is referred to in the literature, it is described as an unmitigated evil. A dirge introduced into an impressive hymn to Nergal [1] laments the fate of him who

> . . . has descended to the breast of the earth,
> Satiated,[2] [he has gone] to the land of the dead.
> Full of lament on the day that he encountered sorrow,
> In the month which does not bring to completion the year,[3]
> On the road of destruction for mankind,
> To the wailing-place (?),
> The hero [has gone], to the distant invisible land.

We must not be misled by an epithet bestowed upon several gods, Marduk, Ninib, and Gula, of 'the restorer of the dead to life,' into the belief that the dead could be brought back from Aralû. These epithets appear chiefly in incantations and hymns addressed to the gods for some specific purpose, such as deliverance of a sufferer from disease. The gods are appealed to against the demons, whose grasp means death. Ninib and Gula are viewed as gods of healing.[4] To be cured through their aid was to be snatched from the jaws of death. Moreover, Ninib and Marduk, as solar deities, symbolize the sun of spring, which brings about the revivification of nature.

---

[1] IVR. 30, no. 2, obverse 23-35.
[2] The word is explained by a gloss, 'Shamash has made him great.'
[3] *I.e.*, the month in which one dies.   [4] See p. 175.

The return of vegetation suggests the thought that Ninib and Marduk have filled with new life what appeared to be dead. The trees that seemed entirely dead blossom forth; the bare earth is covered with verdure. Similarly, the suffering individual stricken with disease could be awakened to new life. It is this 'restoration' which lies in the power of the gods, but once a man has been carried off to Aralû, no god can bring him back to this earth.

An apparent exception to the rule, according to which all mankind eventually comes to Aralû, is formed by Parnapishtim and his wife, who dwell in a place vaguely described as 'distant,' situated at the 'confluence of the streams.' The place, as was pointed out in a previous chapter,[1] lies in the vicinity of the Persian Gulf, and, since it can only be reached by water, the natural conclusion is that it is an island. The temptation is strong to compare the dwelling of Parnapishtim with the belief found among the Greeks and other nations, of 'an island of the blessed.' This has been done by Jeremias[2] and others. However, we must bear in mind that the point in Parnapishtim's narrative is that he and his wife do *not die.* They are removed to the distant place by the gods and continue to live there. Again, we do not learn of any other person who inhabits this island. If to these considerations we add, that the name Parnapishtim signifies 'offspring of life,' that his wife's name is not mentioned, that we are not told what becomes of his family and servants, who are also saved from the deluge, it is evident that the incident of Parnapishtim's escape is an allegory, introduced into the story as a dramatic means of teaching the doctrine which we have seen dominates the tale, — that man, ordinarily, cannot secure immortal life.

If there is any connection between the island where Parnapishtim dwells and the Greek conception of 'an island of the blessed,' it is a trace of foreign influence in Babylonian mythol-

---

[1] See pp. 505, 506. [2] *Vorstellungen*, p. 81.

ogy. There is nothing to show that among the Babylonians, either among the populace or in the schools, a belief arose in a 'paradise' whither privileged persons were transported after death, nor is any distinction made by them between the good and the bad, so far as the future habitation is concerned. All mankind, kings and subjects, virtuous and wicked, go to Aralû. Those who have obtained the good will of the gods receive their reward in this world, by a life of happiness and of good health. The gods can ward off disease, or, rather, since disease (as all ills and misfortunes) is a punishment sent by some god or demon, forgiveness can be secured, the proof of which will consist in the restoration of the sick to health, but the moment that death ensues the control of the gods ends. To the Babylonians, the words of the Psalmist,[1] "who praises thee, O God, in Sheol?" came home with terrible force. They expressed, admirably, the Babylonian view of the limitations of divine power. The dead do not praise the gods, simply because it would be useless. The concern of the gods is with the living.

We are fortunate in possessing a pictorial representation of the nether world that confirms the view to be derived from a study of the religious literature. A number of years ago, Clermont-Ganneau directed attention to a remarkable bronze tablet which was purchased at Hamath in northern Syria.[2] The art was clearly Babylonian, and there was no reason to question the genuineness of the production. Quite recently a duplicate has been found at Zurghul, in Babylonia,[3] so that all suspicions are removed. The bronze tablet contains on the one side, the figure of a monster with a lion-like face and body, but provided with huge wings. Standing erect, his head rises above the tablet, his fore legs rest on the edge, and the demon is thus

---

[1] Psalms, vi. 6.

[2] *L'Enfer Assyrien* (*Revue Archaeologique*, 1879, pp. 337-349). See also Perrot and Chiplez, *History of Art in Chaldaea and Assyria*, I. 349 *seq.*

[3] Described by Scheil in the *Recueil de Travaux*, etc., xx. nos. 1 and 2. Scheil regards the Zurghul duplicate as older than the other.

represented in the attitude of looking over to the other side of the tablet. At the side of the monster, are two heads of hideous appearance.

The illustrations on the reverse are devoted to a portrayal of a funeral ceremony, and of the general aspects of the nether world. There are five distinct divisions,[1] marked off from one another by four heavy lines drawn across the tablet. In the first division appear the symbols of the chief gods of the Assyrian pantheon, Marduk, Nabu, Sin, Ishtar, Shamash, Ramman, etc.[2] These gods, as inhabiting the heaven, are placed at the head of the tablet. Next come seven evil spirits figured as various animals,[3] who, as inferior to the gods, and perhaps also as messengers of the latter, are assigned a place midway between heaven and earth. In the third section, there is pictured the funeral ceremony proper. A dead body lies on a couch. Two rather strange figures, but apparently priests, have taken up a position, one at each end of the funeral bier, performing some rite of purification. One of the priests has a robe of fish scales and is bearded; the other is smooth-faced and clothed in a long garment. Censers are placed near the priests. The latter appear at the same time to be protecting the body against two demons whose threatening gestures suggest that they are endeavoring to secure possession of the dead.[4] These demons may be the special messengers of the gods of the nether world, who have brought about the death of their victim. Below this scene, we come to a view of the nether world. The division is much larger than any of the others. Two hideous figures dominate the scene, both of fantastic

[1] Only four on the Zurghul duplicate.

[2] For the interpretation of these symbols, see Luschan, *Ausgrabungen in Sendschirli*, pp. 17-27, and Scheil's article. On the Zurghul tablet there are eight symbols, while the other contains nine.

[3] See pp. 263, 264. A text IV R. 5, col. I. compares each of the seven spirits to some animal. On the duplicate six demons are placed in the second division and the seventh in the third.

[4] On the duplicate these two demons do not occur.

shape, and evidently so portrayed as to suggest the horror of the nether world. One of these figures[1] stands erect in a menacing attitude; the other is resting in a kneeling position on a horse.[2] The second figure is a representation of the chief goddess of the nether world — Allatu. The demon at her side would then be the special messenger of this goddess, Namtar. The goddess has her two arms extended, in the act of strangling a serpent. The act symbolizes her strength. Her face is that of a lioness, and she is suckling two young lions at her breasts. If it be recalled that Nergal, the chief god of the lower world, is also pictured as a lion,[3] it seems but natural to conclude that the monster covering the one side of the tablet is none other than the consort of Allatu, the heads on either side of him representing his attendants. At the left side of Allatu are a series of objects, — a jar, bowl, an arrowhead (?), a trident, which, as being buried with the dead, are symbols of the grave. The goddess and the demon at her side direct their gaze towards these objects.

The nether world reaches down to the Apsu, — the 'deep' that flows underneath the earth. This is indicated in the design by placing the horse, on which the goddess rests, in a bark. The bark, again, is of fantastic shape, the one end terminating in the head of a serpent, the other in that of some other animal, — perhaps a bull. The bark reaches into the fifth division,[4] which is a picture of flowing water with fish swimming from the left to the right, as an indication of the direction in which the water flows. At the verge of the water stand two trees.[5] What these trees symbolize is not known, and there are other details in the third and fourth sections that still escape us. For our purposes, it is sufficient to note: (*a*) that the sections represent in a general way the divisions of the universe, the heavens, the

---

[1] Schell thinks that the face is that of a dog.
[2] On the Zurghul duplicate the horse is not pictured.   [3] See p. 529.
[4] This division is not marked in the duplicate from Zurghul.
[5] Not occurring on the duplicate.

atmosphere, the earth, the nether world, and the deep;[1] (*b*) that the nether world is in the interior of the earth, reaching down to Apsu; and (*c*) that this interior is pictured as a place full of horrors, and is presided over by gods and demons of great strength and fierceness.

Such being the view of the nether world, it is natural that the living should regard with dread, not only the place but also its inhabitants. The gloom that surrounded the latter reacted on their disposition. In general, the dead were not favorably disposed towards the living, and they were inclined to use what power they had to work evil rather than for good. In this respect they resembled the demons, and it is noticeable that an important class of demons was known by the name *ekimmu*, which is one of the common terms for the shades of the dead. This fear of the dead, which is the natural corollary to the reverence felt for them, enters as an important factor in the honors paid by the living to the memory of the deceased. To provide the dead with food and drink, to recall their virtues in dirges, to bring sacrifices in their honor, — such rites were practised, as much from a desire to secure the favor of the dead and to ward off their evil designs as from motives of piety, which, of course, were not absent. The dead who was not properly cared for by his surviving relatives would take his revenge upon the living by plaguing them as only a demon could. The demons that infested graveyards were in some way identified with the 'spirits,' or perhaps messengers, of the dead, who, in their anger towards the living, lay in wait for an attack upon those against whom they had a grudge.

[1] Scheil questions whether the divisions have this purpose. While perhaps not much stress is laid by the artist upon this symbolism, its existence can hardly be questioned. Note the five divisions of the universe in Smith's *Miscellaneous Texts*, p. 16. The water certainly represents the Apsu. Allatu rests upon the bark. We do not find among the Babylonians (as Scheil supposes) the view that the dead are conveyed across a sheet of water to the nether world. The dead are buried, and by virtue of this fact enter Aralû, which is in the earth. Egyptian influence is possible, but unlikely.

The Pantheon of Aralû.

We have seen how the mystery coupled with death led to the view which brought the dead into more direct relationship with the gods. Closely allied with this view is the power ascribed to the dead to work evil or good and, like the gods, to furnish oracles. This power once acknowledged, it was but a short step to the deification of the dead, or, rather, of such personalities who in life exercised authority, by virtue of their position or innate qualities. On the other hand, the gloominess of the nether world, the sad condition of its inhabitants, the impossibility of an escape or a return to this world, necessarily suggested to the Babylonians that the gods worshipped by the living had no control over the fate of the dead. The gods, to be sure, were at times wrathful, but, on the whole, they were well disposed towards mankind. When angry, they could be pacified, and it was impossible to believe that they should deliberately consign their creatures to such a sad lot as awaited those who went down to Aralû. The gods who ruled the dead must be different from those who directed the fate of the living. A special pantheon for the nether world was thus developed. Such deities as Marduk, Ea, Nabu, Shamash, or Ashur, who acted, each in his way, as protectors of mankind, could find no place in this pantheon; but a god like Nergal, who symbolized the midday sun, and the sun of the summer solstice that brought misery and fever to the inhabitants of the Euphrates Valley; Nergal, who became the god of violent destruction in general, and, more particularly, the god of war, the god whose emblem was the lion, who was cruel and of forbidding aspect,—such a god was admirably adapted to rule those who could only look forward to a miserable imprisonment in a region filled with horror. Nergal, therefore, became the chief god of the pantheon of the lower world.

In the religious texts, the cruel aspects of this god are almost exclusively emphasized. He is the one god towards whom no love is felt, for he is a god without mercy. The fierce aspects of the solar Nergal are accentuated in Nergal, the chief of the pantheon of Aralû. He becomes even more ferocious than he already was, as a god of war. His battle is with all mankind. He is greedy for victims to be forever enclosed in his great and gloomy domain. Destruction is his one and single object; nothing can withstand his attack. Armed with a sword, his favorite time for stalking about is at night, when he strikes his unerring blows. Horrible demons of pestilence and of all manner of disease constitute his train, who are sent out by him on missions of death. The favorite titles by which he is known appear in a hymn [1] addressed to him, as god of the lower world. He is invoked as the

> Warrior, strong whirlwind, sweeping the hostile land,[2]
> Warrior, ruler of Aralû.

Another hymn [3] describes him as a

> Great warrior who is firm as the earth.
> Superior as heaven and earth art thou,
>
> . . . .
>
> What is there in the deep that thou dost not secure?
> What is there in the deep that thou dost not clutch?

While references to the local character of the god as patron of Cuthah survive, the name Cuthah itself becomes synonymous with the nether world. The old solar deity is completely overshadowed by the terrible ruler of the lower world. It is due to this that the real consort of the local Nergal, the goddess Laz, is rarely mentioned in the religious literature. The priests, when they spoke of Nergal, had in mind always the companionship with Allatu. But the association of ideas which thus led to assign-

---

[1] IVR. 26, no. 1. [3] IVR. 30, no. 1; obverse 5, 14.
[2] *I.e.*, the nether world.

ing a god who was originally a solar deity, a place in the lower world bears the impress of the schools. The popular development of Nergal ceased, when he became the local god of Cuthah. It is only as an outgrowth of the systematized pantheon that we can understand the transformation involved in making of a local deity, the head of a pantheon that is itself an outcome of the later phases assumed by the religion.

The problem suggested by this transformation was recognized by the theologians. A curious tale was found among the El-Amarna tablets which endeavors to account for Nergal's presence in the world of the dead. Unfortunately, the tablet on which the story is inscribed is so badly mutilated that we can hardly gather more than the general outlines.[1] A conflict has arisen between the gods on high and a goddess who has her seat in the lower world. This goddess is none other than Allatu. She is described as Eresh-Kigal,[2] *i.e.*, queen of Kigal or of the nether world. The scene reminds us of the contest between the gods and Tiâmat, as embodied in the creation epic. The gods choose Nergal as their leader. Assisted by fourteen companions, whose names — 'fever,' 'fiery heart,' 'lightning sender ' — remind us again of the eleven monsters that constitute Tiâmat's assistants,[3] Nergal proceeds to the lower world, and knocks at the gate for admission. Namtar, the plague-demon, acts as the messenger. He announces the arrival of Nergal to Allatu. The latter is obliged to admit Nergal, just as in the story of Ishtar's descent, she is forced to receive Ishtar. Fourteen gates of the lower world are mentioned. At each one, Nergal stations one of his companions and passes on to the house of

---

[1] See Jensen's valuable articles, "The Queen in the Babylonian Hades and her Consort," in the *Sunday School Times*, March 13 and 20, 1897. The text is published, Winckler and Abel, *Der Thontafelfund von El-Amarna*, iii. 164, 165.

[2] Written phonetically *e-ri-ish*. The word is entered as a synonym of *sharratum*, 'queen,' VR. 28, no. 2; obverse 31. This phonetic writing furnishes the reading for *Nin* in Nin-Kigal.

[3] See pp. 418, 419.

Allatu. He seizes the goddess, drags her from her throne, and is about to kill her when she appeals for mercy. She breaks out in tears, offers herself in marriage if Nergal will spare her.

> You shall be my husband and I will be your wife.
> The tablets of wisdom I will lay in your hands.
> You shall be master and I mistress.

Nergal accepts the condition, kisses Allatu, and wipes away her tears.

One cannot resist the conclusion that the tale is, as already suggested, an imitation of the Marduk-Tiâmat episode. Allatu is a female like Tiâmat. Nergal acts for the gods just as Marduk does. The attendants of Nergal are suggested by the monsters accompanying Tiâmat; the tables of wisdom which Nergal receives, correspond to the tablets of fate which Marduk snatches from Kingu.[1] But while the conflict between Marduk and Tiâmat is an intelligible nature-myth, symbolizing the annual rainstorms that sweep over Babylonia, there is no such interpretation possible in the contest between Nergal and Allatu. The story is not even a glorification of a local deity, for Nergal appears solely in the rôle of a solar deity. The attendants given to him — heat, lightning, and disease — are the popular traits in the story; but with the chief characters in the old nature-myth changed, — Marduk or the original Bel replaced by Nergal, and Tiâmat by Allatu, — the story loses its popular aspect, and becomes a medium for illustrating a doctrine of the schools. If this view of the tale be correct, we would incidentally have a proof (for which there is other evidence) that as early as the fifteenth century, the Marduk-Tiâmat story had already received a definite shape. But the most valuable conclusion to be drawn from the Nergal-Allatu tale is that, according to the popular conceptions, the real and older head of the pantheon of the lower world was a goddess, and not a god.

[1] See p. 428.

Allatu takes precedence of Nergal. In the story of Ishtar's descent to the lower world, a trace of the earlier view survives. Allatu is introduced as the ruler of the lower world. Nergal plays no part. Viewed in this light, the design of the tale we have just discussed becomes still more evident. It was inconsistent with the prominence assigned to male deities in the systematized pantheon, that the chief deity of the lower world should be a female. Allatu could not be set aside, for the belief in her power was too strongly imbedded in the popular mind; but a male consort could be given her who might rule with her. Another factor that may have entered into play in the adaptation of the Marduk-Tiâmat story to Nergal and Allatu, and that gave to the adaptation more plausibility, was the disappearance of the summer sun after he had done his work. Nergal did not exert his power during the whole year, and even as the sun of midday, he was not in control all day. When he disappeared, there was only one place to which he could go.

As of Tammuz and of other solar deities,[1] it was probably related of Nergal, also, that he was carried to the lower world. This popular basis for the presence of Nergal in the lower world may have served as a point of departure for the scholastic development of Nergal. However, the tale of Nergal and Allatu goes far beyond the length of popular belief in making Nergal conquer Allatu, and force himself, in a measure, into her place. Before Nergal appears on the scene, a god, Ninazu, was regarded as the consort of Allatu.[2]

The conception which gives the Babylonian Hades a queen as ruler is of popular origin, in contrast to the scholastic aspect of Nergal as the later king of the lower region. Jensen is of the opinion that the feminine gender of the word for earth in Babylonian superinduced the belief that the ruler of the kingdom

---

[1] See below, p. 588 seq.
[2] See below, p. 590

situated within the earth was a woman. Allatu would, according to this view, be a personification of the 'earth.' But a factor that also enters into play is the notion of productivity and fertility which gave rise to the conception of the great mother-goddess, Ishtar.[1] Allatu is correlated to Ishtar. From the earth comes vegetation. The origin of mankind, too, is traced to the earth, and to the earth mankind ultimately returns.[2] Hence, the receiver of life is a goddess equally with the giver of life, and indeed, Ishtar and Allatu are but the two aspects of one and the same phenomenon.[3] Allatu signifies 'strength.' The name is related to the Arabic *Allah* and the Hebrew *Eloah* and *Elohim*. The same meaning — strength, power, rule — attaches to many of the names of the gods of the Semites: Adôn, Etana, Baal, El, and the like.[4] It is interesting to note that the chief goddess of Arabia is *Allat*,[5] — a name identical with our Allatu.

The bronze relief above described furnished us with a picture of this queen of the lower world. The gloom enveloping the region controls this picture. Allatu is of as forbidding an aspect as Tiâmat. She is warlike and ferocious. When enraged, her anger knows no bounds. Her chief attendants are the terrible Namtar and a scribe — also a female — known as Belit-seri. Of these two personages, Namtar, the personification of disease, is a popular conception, whereas the addition of a scribe points again to the influence of the schools. Marduk, the chief god of the living, has a scribe who writes down, at the god's dictation, the fate decreed for individuals. Corresponding to this, the ruler of the lower world has a scribe who writes down on the tablets of wisdom the decrees of the god-

---

[1] See above, p. 79.
[2] See pp. 448, 511.
[3] See Farnell, *The Cults of the Greek States*, ii. 627.
[4] See the reference in note 3 to p. 519.
[5] Wellhausen, *Reste Arabischen Heidenthums*, pp. 28, 29. That the Syro-Arabian *Allat* resembles Ishtar rather than Allatu, points again to the original identity of the two goddesses.

dess, and, at a later stage, the decrees of Nergal as well. Belit-seri, whose name signifies 'mistress of the field,' was originally a goddess of vegetation, some local deity who has been reduced to the rank of an attendant upon a greater one; and it is significant that almost all the members of the nether-world pantheon are in some way connected with vegetation.

Tammuz, of whose position in this pantheon we have already had occasion to speak, is the god of spring vegetation. Another solar deity, Nin-gishzida,[1] who is associated in the Adapa legend with Tammuz, is the deity who presides over the growth of trees. En-meshara, who also belongs to the court of Nergal and Allatu, appears to represent vegetation in general. To these may be added Girra (or Gira), who originally, as it would appear, a god of vegetation, is eventually identified with Dibbarra,[2] Gil, whom Jensen[3] regards as 'the god of foliage,' and Belili, the sister of Tammuz.[4] Of this group of deities, Tammuz and Nin-gishzida are the most important. In the Adapa legend, it will be recalled, they are stationed as guardians in heaven. As solar deities, they properly belong there. Like Nergal, they have been transferred to the nether world; and in the case of all three, the process that led to the change appears to have been the same. The trees blossom, bear fruit, and then decay; the fields are clothed in glory, and then shorn of their strength. The decay of vegetation was popularly figured as due to the weakness[5] of the god who produced the fertility. Tammuz has been deceived by Ishtar; Nin-gishzida has been carried off to the lower world. In the month of Tebet,—the tenth month,—there was celebrated a festival of mourning for the lost En-meshara. It is the time of the winter solstice. A similar fate must have overtaken Belit-

---

[1] See p. 546 *seq.*
[4] See p. 574.
[2] See below, p. 594, note 1, and Jensen's *Kosmologie*, pp. 145, 480, 483, 487.
[3] *Sunday School Times*, 1897, p. 139.
[5] See Frazer, *The Golden Bough*, i. 240 *seq.* and 274, 275.

seri, Girra, and Gil. For a time, at least, they are hidden in the realm of Allatu. Of all these deities, stories were no doubt current that formed so many variations of one and the same theme, symbolizing their disappearance and the hoped-for return, the same story that we encounter in the myth of Venus and Adonis, in the myth of Osiris, and, in some guise or other, among many other nations of the ancient world. Of Girra, it may be well to remember that he is viewed merely as a form of Nergal in the later texts. Belili, it will be recalled, is associated with Tammuz in the story of Ishtar's journey.[1] She is not, however, the consort of the god, but his sister. The antiquity of her cult follows from the occurrence of her name in the list of gods antecedent to Anu,[2] and where Alala is entered as her consort. Whatever else the relationship of 'sister' to Tammuz means, it certainly indicates that Belili belongs to the deities of vegetation, and it may be that she will turn out to be identical with Belit-seri, which is merely the designation of some goddess, and not a real name.[3] One is inclined also to suspect some, albeit remote, connection between Alala, the consort of Belili, and the Alallu bird who is spoken of in the Gilgamesh epic as having been deprived of her pinions by Ishtar.[4] In the tale, Tammuz, the Alallu bird, a lion, and a horse are successively introduced as those once loved and then deceived by Ishtar. The lion is, as has been several times indicated, the symbol of Nergal; the horse appears in the Hades relief above described as the animal upon which Allatu is seated, and it seems legitimate, therefore, to seek for Alallu also in the

---

[1] See p. 574.   [2] See p. 417.

[3] Cheyne (*Expository Times*, 1897, pp. 423, 424) ingeniously regards *Belili* as the source of the Hebrew word *Beliyaal* or *Belial*, which, by a species of popular etymology, is written by the ancient Hebrew scholars as though compounded of two Hebrew words signifying 'without return.' The popular etymology is valuable as confirming the proposition to place Belili in the pantheon of the lower world. From its original meaning, the word became a poetical term in Hebrew for 'worthless,' 'useless,' and the like, *e.g.*, in the well-known phrase "Sons of Belial."

[4] See p. 482.

nether world. While it may be that a long process intervened, before such a species of symbolization was brought about as the representation of an ancient deity in the guise of a bird, still, if it will be recalled that Zu is a deity, pictured as a bird,[1] there is every reason to interpret the bird Alallu merely as the symbol of some deity, just as the lion is certainly such a symbol.

Jensen would add Etana to the list of gods of vegetation who form part of Allatu's court. While the etymology he proposes for the name is not acceptable, there is no doubt that to Etana, like Gilgamesh, the character of a solar deity has been imparted. His presence in the nether world is due to the story of his flight with the eagle and the fall.[2] If he falls from heaven, he naturally enters the realm of Allatu, and it is possible that the story in its original form was suggested by a myth illustrating the change of seasons. The question, however, must for the present remain an open one.

A god associated with the nether world who again appears to be a solar deity is Nin-azu. His name points to his being 'the god of healing.' A text states[3] that Allatu is his consort. Such a relationship to the chief goddess of the nether world may be regarded as a survival of the period when Nergal had not yet been assigned to this place. The introduction of a distinctly beneficent god into the pantheon of the lower world, and as second in rank, shows also that the gloomy conception of the lower world was one that developed gradually. Tammuz, Nin-gishzida, and the like are held enthralled by Allatu, and remain in the nether world against their will; but if Allatu chooses as her consort a 'god of healing,' she must have been viewed as a goddess who could at times, at least, be actuated by kindly motives. The phase of the sun symbolized by Nin-azu is, as in the case of Tammuz and others, the sun of the springtime and of the morning. If it be recalled that

---

[1] See p. 537.
[2] See above, p. 523.
[3] IIR. 59; reverse 33-35.

Gula, the great goddess of healing, is the consort of Ninib,[1] it will be clear that Nin-azu must be closely related to Ninib — and is, indeed, identified with the latter.[2] With Nergal in control, Nin-azu had to yield his privilege to be the husband of Allatu. The substitute of the fierce sun of the summer solstice for the sun of spring is a most interesting symptom of the direction taken by the Babylonian beliefs, regarding the fate of the dead. It may be that in the earlier period, when more optimistic views of Aralû were current, Gula, who is called the one 'who restores the dead to life,' may have had a place in the pantheon of the lower world; not that the Babylonians at any time believed in the return of the dead, but because the living could be saved from the clutches of death. Ninib and Gula, as gods of spring, furnished the spectacle of such a miracle in the return of vegetation. In this sense, we have seen that Marduk, the god of spring, was also addressed as 'the restorer to life.' But while the revivification of nature controls the conception of gods of healing, like Nin-azu, Ninib, and Gula, the extension of the idea would lead, naturally, to the association of these gods with the ruler of the nether world, at a time when it was still believed that this ruler could be moved by appeals to loosen her hold upon those whom she was about to drag to her kingdom. But it is important always to bear in mind that beyond this apparent restoration of the dead to life, the Babylonians at no time went.

In the Ishtar story[3] a god Irkalla is introduced. Jeremias[4] takes this as one of the names of Allatu, but this is unlikely.[5] From other sources[6] we know that Irkalla is one of the names

---

[1] See above, p. 175.

[2] IIR. 57, 51a, a star, Nin-azu, is entered as one of the names of the planet Ninib.

[3] See above, p. 565. The name occurs also in Haupt's *Nimrodepos*, pp. 19, 29.

[4] *Vorstellungen*, p. 68.

[5] The name of the goddess is written throughout the story Nin-Kigal; *i.e.*, 'queen of the nether world.' Nin-Eresh. See p. 584, note 2.

[6] Smith, *Miscellaneous Texts*, p. 16.

of the nether world. It is in some way connected with Urugal,[1] *i.e.*, 'great city,' which is also a common designation for the dwelling-place of the dead. Hence, Irkalla is an epithet describing a deity as 'the god of the great city.' The Babylonian scholars, who were fond of plays upon words, brought the name Nergal, as though compounded of Ne-uru-gal (*i.e.*, 'ruler of the great city'), into connection with Uru-gal, and thus identified Irkalla with Nergal. But, originally, some other god must have been meant, since Allatu appears as the sole ruler of the lower world in the Ishtar story, unless, indeed, we are to assume that the name has been introduced at a late period as a concession to Nergal. It is more plausible that a god like Nin-azu was understood under 'the god of the great city.' Besides these gods, there is another series of beings who belong to Allatu's court, — the demons who are directly responsible for death in the world. Of this series, Namtar is the chief and the representative. As the one who gathers in the living to the dark abode, it is natural that he should be pictured as guardian at the gates of the great palace of Allatu. But by the side of Namtar stand a large number of demons, whose task is similar to that of their chief. A text[2] calls the entire group of demons, — the demon of wasting disease, the demon of fever, the demon of erysipelas,[3] and the like, — 'the offspring of Aralû,' 'the sons and messengers of Namtar, the bearers of destruction for Allatu.' These demons are sent out from Aralû to plague the living, but once they have brought their victims to Aralû, their task is done. They do not trouble the dead. The latter stand, as we have seen, under the direct control of the gods.[4]

The story of Ishtar's descent to the lower world[5] shows us that the group of spirits known as the Anunnaki, also, belong to

---

[1] Jensen, *Kosmologie*, p. 259, note.
[2] IVR. 1, col. i. 12; col. iii. 8–10.
[3] *Te'û*. See IVR. 22, 51a, and Bartels, *Zeitschrift für Assyriologie*, viii. 179–184.
[4] See above, pp. 183, 560.
[5] Obverse ll. 33, 37.

the court of Nergal and Allatu. Ramman-nirari I. already designates the Anunnaki as belonging to the earth,[1] though it is an indication of the vagueness of the notions connected with the group that in hymns, both the Anunnaki and the Igigi are designated as offspring of Anu, — the god of heaven.[2] They are not exclusively at the service of Nergal and Allatu. Bel, Ninib, Marduk, and Ishtar also send them out on missions. Evidently, the fact that their chief function was to injure mankind suggested the doctrine which gave them a place in the lower world with the demons. The distinction between Anunnaki and the Igigi is not sharply maintained in the religious literature. Though Ramman-nirari places the Igigi in heaven, it is not impossible that a later view transferred them, like the Anunnaki, to the lower world. There were, of course, some misfortunes that were sent against mankind from on high. Ramman was a god who required such messengers as the Igigi, and besides the Igigi, there were other spirits sent out from above. But, as in the course of time the general doctrine was developed which made the gods, on the whole, favorably inclined towards man, while the evil was ascribed to the demons[3] — as occupying the lower rank of divine beings — we note the tendency also to ascribe the ills that humanity is heir to, to the forces that dwell under the earth, — to Nergal and Allatu and to those who did their bidding. Probably, Lakhmu and Lakhamu were also regarded, at least by the theologians, as part of Allatu's court, just as Alala and Belili[4] were so regarded.

The confusion resulting from the double position of Nergal in the religious literature, as the deity of the summer solstice and as the chief of the nether-world pantheon, raises a doubt whether some gods who are closely associated with Nergal are to be placed on high with the gods or have their seats below with Nergal. Among these, three require mention here: Dibbarra, Gibil, and Ishum. Of these, the first two

[1] See above, p. 185. [2] See p. 186. [3] See p. 183. [4] See pp. 417, 598.

are directly identified with Nergal in the systematized pantheon,[1] while Ishum is closely associated with Nergal, or appears as the attendant of Dibbarra.[2] These gods, symbolizing violent destruction through war and fire, are evidently related to the Nergal of the upper world,—to Nergal, the solar deity; but in the later stages of the religion, the Nergal of the lower world almost completely sets aside the earlier conception. It is, therefore, likely that deities who stand so close to the terrible god as those under consideration, were also regarded as having a position near his throne in the lower world.

The pantheon of Aralû thus assumes considerable dimensions. At the same time, we observe the same tendency towards concentration of power in this pantheon as we have seen was the case in the pantheon of the upper world.[3] As in Babylonia there are practically only a few gods,—Marduk, Nabu, Ishtar, Shamash, and Sin,—who exercised considerable control; and, as in Assyria we find this tendency still more accentuated in the supreme rank accorded to Ashur, so in the lower world Nergal and Allatu are the real rulers. The other gods, and, naturally, also the demons, occupy inferior positions. As messengers, guardians, spies, or attendants, they group themselves around the throne of the two rulers. A noticeable feature, however, in the pantheon of the lower world consists in the high position held by the consort of the head of the pantheon. Allatu does not sink to the insignificant rank of being merely a pale reflection of Nergal, as do the consorts of Marduk, Shamash, Ashur, and the like.[4] As a trace of the earlier supreme control exercised by her, she con-

---

[1] Jensen's *Kosmologie*, pp. 483, 484. In the new fragment of the Deluge story discovered by Scheil (referred to above, p. 507, and now published in the *Recueil de Travaux*, xix. no. 3) the word *di-ib-ba-ra* occurs, and the context shows that it means 'destruction.' In view of this, the question is again opened as to the reading of the name of the god of war and pestilence. The identification of this god with Girra (pp. 528, 588) may belong to a late period. [3] See pp. 111, 171, 190.
[2] See p. 529.   [4] See chapter v.

tinues to reign with her husband. In the popular mind, indeed, despite the influence of theological doctrines, Allatu continues to be more prominent than Nergal. Nergal is obliged to abide by the compact he made with Allatu. He rules *with* her, but not over her. The theology of the schools did not venture to set Allatu aside altogether; and this limitation in the development of the doctrine that elsewhere gave the male principle the supremacy over the female, may be taken as a valuable indication of the counter-influence, exercised by deeply rooted popular beliefs, over the theoretical elaboration of the religion at the hands of the religious guides.

The Tombs and the Burial Customs.

Our knowledge of the customs observed by the Babylonians and Assyrians in disposing of their dead leaves much to be desired. Most of the graves discovered in the ruins of Babylonian cities belong to the Persian or to the Greek period. In some cases,[1] where we have reason to believe that older graves have been found, it is almost impossible to estimate their age. Recently, the expedition of the University of Pennsylvania to Nippur has unearthed remains that appear to belong to an older period, though nothing can be dated with any degree of certainty earlier than 2500 B.C.[2] Still, with proper caution, even the material belonging to a later period may be used for the older periods. Burial customs, as has already been emphasized, constitute the most conservative elements in a religion. Such rites are much less liable to change than the cult of the gods. Foreign invasion would not affect the funeral rites, even where other religious customs are altered. Even so violent a change as that produced by the introduction of Mohammedanism into Mesopotamia has not removed traces of the

---

[1] So at Zurghul (or Zerghul) and el-Hibba. See Koldewey in *Zeitschrift für Assyriologie*, ii. 403–430.

[2] See the valuable chapter in Peters' work on *Nippur*, ii. 214–234.

old Babylonian religion. Dr. Peters has shown that the district in the Euphrates Valley selected by the modern Arabs and Persians for the interment of their dead [1] derives its sanctity from the days of the old Babylonian kingdom, and many of the customs observed by the modern Moslems tally with the funeral rites of ancient Babylonia.[2] That the dead were always buried, and that cremation was practically unknown, may now be regarded as certain. The conception of Aralû, which, we have seen, belongs to the most ancient period of religion, is only intelligible upon the assumption that burial was the prevailing custom. On one of the oldest monuments of Babylonian art, — the stele of vultures, — earth-burial is represented.[3] A few years ago, some German scholars [4] claimed to have furnished the proof that the Babylonians cremated their dead. But, in the first place, the age of the tombs found by them was not clearly established; and, secondly, it was not certain whether the charred remains of human bodies were due to intentional burning or accidental destruction by fire, at the time that the city explored by the German scholars was destroyed. The fact that, as the explorers themselves observed, the bodies were not completely burned argues in favor of the latter supposition. The explanation offered by Koldewey [5] for this peculiar condition of the remains — that the burning was symbolical, and, therefore, not complete — is unsatisfactory in every particular. There can be no doubt that some, at least, of the tombs discovered at Warka by Loftus [6] belong to the period before the conquest of the country by Cyrus, and this is certainly the case with many of the tombs discovered at Nippur. Nowhere do we find traces of burning

[1] *Proceedings of the American Oriental Society*, 1896, p. 166. The dead are often conveyed hundreds of miles to be interred in Nejef and Kerbela.
[2] Peters' *Nippur*, ii. 325, 326.
[3] See below, p. 597.   [5] *Ib.*
[4] Koldewey, *Zeitschrift für Assyriologie*, ii. 406 *seq.*
[6] *Travels and Researches in Chaldaea and Susiana*, chapter xviii.

of bodies.[1] If it should turn out that cremation prevailed for a certain period, the fashion, we may feel certain, was due to foreign influences, but it is more than questionable whether it was ever introduced at all. Certainly, earth-burial is the characteristically Babylonian (and general Semitic) method of disposing of the dead.

The characteristic feature of the Babylonian tombs is their simplicity. The dead body, which was often covered with palm woods, was placed generally on the side — though occasionally on the back — on a board of wood, or wrapped in a mat of reeds or palm fibers, and covered with a tub-shaped clay dish. On the dish there was frequently an ornamental design, but beyond this, there was no attempt at decoration. The body was frequently pressed together in order to be brought within the compass of the dish. Sometimes, the knees were pulled up or the body placed in a semi-sitting posture, and there are indications that the bodies were often divided into two or three parts prior to burial. On the stele of vultures,[2] representing the triumph of Eannatum over his enemies, attendants are seen building a mound over the symmetrically arranged bodies of the king's soldiers slain in battle. The monument belongs to the most ancient period of Babylonian history, and we are justified, therefore, in regarding this method of earth-burial as the oldest in vogue. The dead, it would seem, are placed on the ground, or near the surface, and covered with a mound. This custom would account for the use of a dish to cover the body after it became customary to place the dead in small houses or vaults built for the purpose. The shape of the dish, or tub, recalls the earth-mound over the dead, and the tenacity of conventional methods is apparent in the modern custom, even among Western nations, of raising a

---

[1] Peters' *Nippur*, ii. 234. Other mounds examined by Peters between Warka and Nippur bear out the conclusion.
[2] De Sarzec, *Découvertes en Chaldée*, pl. 3.

mound over the grave, even though the body is placed at a depth of six feet and more below the surface. A modification of the form of coffin was the jar into which the body was forced. To do this, still greater violence had to be employed. Instead of one jar, two were also used, the body placed partly in one, partly in the other, and the two were then joined with bitumen. In the Persian period, a slipper-shaped coffin was used, into which the body was inserted through an aperture at one end; but there is no evidence that the Babylonians employed this method. With the bodies, various objects were interred, many of which had a special significance. Except, perhaps, at a very early period [1] the dead were not buried naked, but covered with a garment. The seal cylinder, which, as Herodotus tells us,[2] every person of position carried about his person, and which, when impressed on a clay tablet, served as his signature, was buried with the dead as an ornament that had a personal value. The staff which the man was in the habit of carrying is found in the grave, and also such weapons as arrow-heads and spears. Various ornaments of copper, iron, gold, and stone, rings, necklaces or bands of gold were probably placed with the dead as a sign of affection, not because of any belief that the deceased needed these objects. Toys, too, are found in the graves, and we may assume that these were placed in the tombs of children. The frequent presence of shells in the tombs is still unexplained. On the other hand, remains of food, dates, grain, poultry, and fish, that have been found in graves belonging to various periods, may be regarded as a proof for the existence of the belief that the dead could suffer pangs of hunger. The closing lines of the Gilgamesh epic,[3] where the fate of the neglected dead is portrayed, confirms this view. But such remains are more frequent in the early graves than in those of a later time. Animal sacrifices at

---

[1] On the stele of vultures, the dead are naked.
[2] Book I, § 195.   [3] See p. 512.

the grave appear to be very old.¹ Offerings of food and water were made to the dead, not only at the time of the burial, but afterwards by surviving relatives. The son performs the office of pouring out water to the memory of his father.² The close of the legend of Ishtar's journey suggests that the festival of Tammuz was selected as an 'All-Souls' day. The weeping for the lost Tammuz served as an appropriate link for combining with the mourning for the god the lament for the dead. The water jar is never absent in the old Babylonian tombs, and by the side of the jar the bowl of clay or bronze is found, and which probably served the same purpose as a drinking utensil for the dead. How early it became customary to bury the dead together we do not know. It may be that at one time they were buried beneath the dwellings that they occupied when alive, under the threshold or in the walls;³ but the conception of Aralû as a great gathering-place of the dead would hardly have arisen, unless the 'city of the dead' by the side of the 'city of the living' had become an established custom. We are, therefore, justified in assuming that as the villages grew into towns, the huddling together of the living suggested placing the dead together in a portion of the town set aside for the purpose. In comparison with the elaborate constructions in the Egyptian cities of the dead, the Babylonian necropolis was a shabby affair. Vaults, rarely more than five feet high, served as the place where the dead were deposited. These vaults were constructed of bricks, and an extended series of them gave to the necropolis the appearance of little houses, suggestive of primitive mud huts. This simplicity, due in the first instance to the lack of stone as building material in Babylonia, corresponded to the very simple character which the

---

[1] Such sacrifices are pictured on the stele of vultures.

[2] IIIR. 43, col. iv. L 20; Belser, *Beiträge sur Assyriologie*, ii. 175, 18; Pinches, *Babylonian Texts*, p. 18.

[3] For this custom see Trumbull, *The Threshold Covenant*, p. 25; Peters' *Nippur*, ii. 202, 203.

dwelling-house retained. The one-story type of dwelling, with simple partitions, prevailed to the latest period. It was only in the temples and palaces that architectural skill was developed. In Assyria, although soft stone was accessible, the example of Babylonia was slavishly followed. It is due to this that so few traces of private houses have been found in the Mesopotamian explorations,[1] and the almost primitive character of the graves — more primitive, by virtue of the strength of the conservative instinct in everything connected with the dead, than the dwellings of the living — readily accounts for their nearly complete destruction. Simple as the houses of the dead were, they were yet carefully guarded against the invasion of air and dust; and even after centuries of neglect the contents are found to be perfectly dry.

The explorations at Nippur show that the tub and bowl forms of the coffin continued to be used during the period extending from Hammurabi to Nabonnedos. In later times, it would appear, the custom of placing food and drink with the dead fell into disuse.[2] We may perhaps find that, as was the case in Egypt, symbolical representations of food — a clay plate with the food modeled in clay — took the place of the old custom. Fewer utensils, too, are found in the graves of the later period; but, on the other hand, ornaments increase, until, when we reach the Persian and Greek periods, mirrors are quite common, and golden veils are placed over the dead, while handsome earrings, breastpins, and necklaces indicate the growth of this luxurious display. The clay coffins, too, are beautifully glazed and ornamented with elaborate designs. A trace of foreign — perhaps Graeco-Egyptian — influence may be seen in the human head modeled on the coffin. Naturally, at all times the different ranks occupied by the dead involved more or less modifications of the prevailing customs. The rich were placed in more

---

[1] Recently, Scheil has discovered some private dwellings at Abu-Habba, which will be described in his forthcoming volume on his explorations at that place. See also Peters' *Nippur*, ii. 200, 201.   [2] Peters' *Nippur*, ii. 220.

carefully built vaults than the poor. The coverings and ornaments varied with the station of the deceased; but in general it may be said that, during the earlier periods of Babylonian-Assyrian history, simplicity was the rule, and the objects placed in the tombs were more carefully chosen with reference to the needs of the dead and the career that he led while living, while the tendency in later times was away from the religious beliefs that gave rise to the funeral customs, and in the direction of luxury and display. This development, however, is independent of *proper* burial, upon which, as we have already had occasion to see, great stress was at all times laid. The greatest misfortune that could happen to a dead person was for his body to remain overground, or to be removed from the tomb and exposed to the light of day. In the early monument of Babylonian art, — the 'stele of vultures,'[1] — already referred to, the dead foes are punished by being stripped of their clothing and exposed to the attack of vultures, who are seen carrying off human heads, legs, and arms. To emphasize the contrast, the king's soldiers are portrayed as being buried in symmetrical rows, the head of each body being covered by the feet of the body in the row above. When the Babylonian and Assyrian kings wish to curse the one who might venture to destroy the monuments set up by them, they know of nothing stronger than to express the hope

> That his body may be cast aside,
> No grave be his lot.[2]

The kings punished their enemies by leaving their bodies to rot in the sun, or they exposed them on poles as a warning to rebels. Ashurbanabal on one occasion speaks of having scattered the corpses of the enemy's host 'like thorns and thistles' over the battlefield.[3] The corpses of the Babylo-

---

[1] See p. 597. The date of the monument is prior to Sargon; *i.e.*, earlier than 3800 B.C.
[2] V R. 61, col. vi. ll. 54, 55.   [3] Rassam Cylinder, col. iii. l. 40.

nians who had aided in the rebellion against the king were given 'to dogs, swine, to the birds of heaven, to the fish of the sea' as food.[1] The same king takes pleasure in relating that he destroyed the graves of Elamitic kings and dragged the bodies from their resting-place[2] to Assyria. Their shades, he adds, were thus unprotected. No food could be tendered them and no sacrifices offered in their honor. Sennacherib, after he has crushed a rebellion that broke out in Babylonia, takes a terrible revenge upon the instigator of the opposition, Mardukbaliddin, by removing the bodies of the latter's ancestors from the vaults wherein they were deposited. The bones of an enemy are enumerated by Ashurbanabal among the spoil secured by him.[3] The mutilation of the dead body was also a terrible punishment to the dead,[4] and we are told that the person who disturbed a grave is not to be permitted to enter the temple. The desecration of the grave affected not only the individual whose rest was thus disturbed, and who, in consequence, suffered pangs of hunger and other miseries, but reached the survivors as well. The unburied or disentombed shade assumed the form of a demon,[5] and afflicted the living.

Of the ceremonies incidental to burial, the bronze tablet above described affords us at least a glimpse. The dead were placed on a bier and wrapped in some kind of a cover. Priests were called in to perform rites of purification. One of the priests, it will be recalled,[6] is clad in a fish costume. The fish is the symbol of Ea, the god of the deep, who becomes

---

[1] Rassam Cylinder, col. iv. ll. 74-76.

[2] *Ib.* col. vi. ll. 70-76.

[3] Rassam Cylinder, col. iii. l. 64. The favorite mutilation was the cutting off of the head. On one of the sculptured slabs from the palace of Ashurbanabal, a pyramid of heads is portrayed. The cutting off of the hands, the lips, the nose, and the male organ, as well as the flaying of the skin, were also practised. (See Sennacherib's account IR. 42, col. vi. ll. 1–6; Rassam Cylinder (Ashurbanabal), li. 4 and iv. 136.)

[4] Rassam Cylinder, col. vii. ll. 46-48.   [5] *Ekimmu.* See p. 580.   [6] See p. 578.

the chief deity appealed to in incantations involving the use of water. The priest assumes the rôle of Ea, as it were, by the symbolical dress that he puts on. The rites appear to consist of the burning of incense and the sprinkling of water. It does not of course follow that everywhere the same custom was observed, but we may at least be certain that the priest played an important part in the last honors paid to the dead. The purification was intended to protect the dead from the evil spirits that infest the grave. The demons of disease, it is true, could no longer trouble him. They had done their work as messengers of Allatu. But there were other demons who were greedy for the blood and flesh of the dead. Though the dead had passed out of the control of the gods, the latter had at least the power to restrain the demons from disturbing the peace of the grave.

In the earlier days, when the bodies were placed on the ground or only a short distance below it, the building of the grave-mound was a ceremony to which importance was attached. In the stele of vultures, attendants are portrayed — perhaps priests — with baskets on their heads, containing the earth to be placed over the fallen soldiers.[1] These attendants are bare to the waist. The removal of the garments is probably a sign of mourning, just as among the Hebrews and other Semites it was customary to put on the primitive loin-cloth[2] as a sign of grief. In somewhat later times, we find sorrowing relatives tearing their clothing[3] — originally tearing off their clothing — and cutting their hair as signs of mourning.

---

[1] Heuzey offers another explanation of the scene which is less plausible. (See De Sarzec, *Découvertes en Chaldée*, p. 98.)

[2] Hebrew word *Saḳ*. The other rite of mourning among the Hebrews, the putting of earth on the head (*e.g.*, I Sam. iv. 12; II Sam. i. 2 and xv. 32; Neh. ix. 1), is a survival of the method of burial as portrayed in the 'stele of vultures.' The earth was originally placed in a basket on the head and used to cover the dead body.

[3] The mourning garb mentioned in the Adapa legend (p. 546) is probably a 'torn' garment.

The formal lament for the dead was another ceremony upon which stress was laid. It lasted from three to seven days.[1] The professional wailers, male and female, can be traced back to the earliest days of Babylonian history. Gudea speaks of them.[2] It would appear that at this early period persons were engaged, as is the case to this day in the Orient, to sing dirges in memory of the dead.[3] The function is one that belongs naturally to priests and priestesses; and, while in the course of time, the connection with the temple of those who acted as wailers became less formal, it is doubtful whether that connection was ever entirely cut off. The 'dirge singers, male and female,' referred to in the story of Ishtar's journey[4] were in the service of some temple. The hymns to Nergal[5] may be taken as samples of the Babylonian dirges.

The praise of Nergal and Allatu was combined with the lament for the sad fate of the dead. Gilgamesh weeping for his friend Eabani[6] furnishes an illustration. Gilgamesh is described as stretched out on the ground. The same custom is referred to in the inscriptions of Cyrus,[7] and it is interesting to note that a similar mode of manifesting grief still prevails in the modern Orient. In the Babylonian dirges, it would seem, the references to the virtues of the deceased (which are prominently introduced into the dirges of the present day) were few. The refrain forms a regular feature of these dirges, — an indication that, as is still the case in the Orient, there was a leader who sang the dirge, while the chorus chimed in at the proper moment. The principle of the stanza of two lines, one long and one short, that, as Budde has shown,[8] controls the wailing songs in the Old Testament (including the

---

[1] Hagen, *Cyrus-Texte* (*Beiträge zur Assyriologie*, ii. 219, 223).
[2] Inscription B, col. v. ll. 3–5. [5] *Ib.*
[3] Lane, *Modern Egyptians*, II. 286. [6] See p. 487.
[4] See p. 575. [7] Hagen, *Cyrus-Texte, ib.* and p. 248.
[8] "The Folk-Song of Israel," *The New World*, ii. 35; also his article "Das Hebräische Klagelied," *Zeitschrift für Alttestamentliche Wissenschaft*, ii. 1–52.

Book of Lamentations, which is based upon this very custom of lamenting the dead), may be detected in the Babylonian compositions. The accompaniment of musical instruments to the dirges also appears to be a very old custom in Babylonia. In the story of Ishtar's journey the wailers are called upon to strike their instruments. What kind of instruments were used in ancient times we do not know. In the Assyrian period, the harp and flute appear to be the most common.[1]

At the time that food and drink were placed with the dead in the grave, some arrangements must have been made for renewing the nourishment. Entrances to tombs have been found,[2] and Koldewey[3] is of the opinion that the clay drains found in quantities in the tombs, served as wells to secure a supply of fresh water for the dead. The wailing for the dead took place not only immediately after death, but subsequently. Ashurbanabal speaks of visiting the graves of his ancestors. He appears at the tombs with rent garments, pours out a libation to the memory of the dead, and offers up a prayer addressed to them. We have every reason to believe that the graves were frequently visited by the survivors. The festival of Tammuz became an occasion[4] when the memory of those who had entered Aralû was recalled.

While there are many details connected with the ceremonies for the dead still to be determined, what has been ascertained illustrates how closely and consistently these ceremonies followed the views held by the Babylonians and Assyrians regarding the life after death. Everything connected with death is gloomy. The grave is as dark as Aralû; the funeral rites consist of dirges that lament not so much the loss sustained by the living as the sad fate in store for the dead. Not a ray of sunshine

---

[1] In Egypt at present the tambourine is used to accompany the dirges (Lane, *ib.* p. 278).

[2] Peters' *Nippur*, ii. 173, and elsewhere.

[3] *Zeitschrift für Assyriologie*, ii. 414.

[4] See above, p. 575.

illumines the darkness that surrounds these rites. All that is hoped for is to protect the dead against the attack of demons greedy for human flesh, to secure rest for the body, and to guard the dead against hunger and thirst.

It is almost startling to note, to what a degree the views embodied in Old Testament writings regarding the fate of the dead, coincide with Babylonian conceptions. The descriptions of Sheol found in Job, in the Psalms, in Isaiah, Ezekiel, and elsewhere are hardly to be distinguished from those that we have encountered in Babylonian literature. For Job,[1] Sheol is

> The land of darkness and deep shadows.
> The land of densest gloom and not of light.
> Even where there is a gleam, there it is as dark night.[2]

The description might serve as a paraphrase of the opening lines in the story of Ishtar's journey. The Hebrew Sheol is situated, like the Babylonian Aralû, deep down in the earth.[3] It is pictured as a cavern. The entrance to it is through gates that are provided with bolts. Sheol is described as a land filled with dust. Silence reigns supreme. It is the gathering-place of all the living, without exception. He who sinks into Sheol does not rise up again.

> He does not return to his house.
> His place knows him no more.[4]

It is, clearly, 'a land without return,' as the Babylonians conceived it. The condition of the dead in Sheol is sad, precisely as the Babylonians pictured the life in Aralû. The dead are designated by a name[5] that indicates their weak condition. They can only talk in whispers or they chirp like birds. Their

---

[1] Job, x. 21, 22.

[2] *I.e.*, the darkness is so dense that no light can remove it.

[3] See the references in Schwally, *Das Leben nach dem Tode nach den Vorstellungen des Alten Israels*, pp. 59–68, and Jeremias' *Vorstellungen*, pp. 106–116.

[4] Job, vii. 10.   [5] *Refā'īm*.

gait is unsteady. In general, they are pictured as lying quiet, doomed to inactivity. Death is lamented as an evil. The dead have passed out of the control of Yahwe, whose concern is with the living. Yahwe's blessings are meted out in this world, but not in Sheol. These blessings consist chiefly of long life and plenty of offspring. The dead need not praise Yahwe. Ecclesiastes — although a late composition — expresses the old popular view in the summary of the fate of the dead,[1] when it is said that the dead know nothing of what is going on. Their memory is gone; they neither love nor hate, and they are devoid of any ambition. There is no planning, no wisdom, no judgment in Sheol.

Like the Babylonians, the Hebrews also believed that the condition of the individual at the time of death was an index of the condition in store for him in Sheol. He who goes to Sheol in sorrow is pursued by sorrow after death. Jacob does not want to go down to Sheol in sorrow,[2] because he knows that in that case sorrow will be his fate after death. To die neglected by one's family was fatal to one's well-being in Sheol. Life in Sheol was a continuation, in a measure, of the earthly existence. Hence, the warrior is buried with his weapons; the prophet is recognized by his cloak; the kings wear their crowns; the people of various lands are known by their dress.[3] Even deformities, as lameness, follow the individual into the grave. On the other hand, while the dead were weak and generally inactive, although capable of suffering, they were also regarded by the Hebrews as possessing powers superior to those of the living. As among the Babylonians, the dead stand so close to the higher powers as to be themselves possessed of divine qualities. Schwally aptly characterizes this apparent contradiction by saying 'that the dead are *Refā'īm* (weak), but, at the same time, *Elohīm*, *i.e.*, divine

---

[1] Chapter ix. 5-10. [2] Gen. xlii. 38.
[3] Incidentally, a proof that the dead were not buried naked.

beings.'[1] Yahwe has no power over the dead, but they receive some of his qualities. They are invoked by the living. The dead can furnish oracles, precisely as Yahwe can. They not only appear to the living in dreams, but their shades can be raised up from Sheol. A certain amount of worship was certainly paid to the dead by the ancient Hebrews.

Naturally, these popular views were subjected to considerable modification with the development of the religion of the Hebrews. While many features remained, as is shown by the occurrence of the primitive conception of Sheol in comparatively late productions, in one important particular, more especially, did the spread of an advanced ethical monotheism lead to a complete departure from the Babylonian conceptions. While, in the popular mind, the belief that there was no escape from Sheol continued for a long time, this belief was inconsistent with the conception of a Divine Being, who, as creator and sole ruler of the universe, had control of the dead as well as the living. As long as Yahwe was merely one god among many, no exception was made of the rule that the concern of the gods was with the living; but Yahwe as the one and only god, could not be pictured as limited in his scope. He was a god for the dead, as well as for the living. The so-called song of Hannah[2] expresses the new view when it praises Yahwe as the one 'who kills and restores to life, who leads to Sheol, and who can lead out of it.' Such a description of Yahwe is totally different from the Babylonians' praise of Ninib, Gula, or Marduk as the 'restorer of the dead to life,' which simply meant that these gods could restrain Allatu. The power to snatch the individual from the grasp of Sheol was also ascribed to the national god, Yahwe. Elijah's restoration of the widow's child[3] to life is an instance of this power, and Jonah,[4] who praises Yahwe for

---

[1] *Das Leben nach dem Tode*, etc., p. 67.
[2] I Sam. ii. Recognized by the critics as an insertion. See Budde, *Die Bücher Richter und Samuel*, p. 197.   [3] I Kings, xvii. 21, 22.   [4] Chapter ii. 7.

having delivered him when the gates of Sheol already seemed bolted, may not have had anything more in mind than what the Babylonians meant; but when the Psalmist, to indicate the universal rule of Yahwe, exclaims

> If I mount to heaven, thou art there,
> If I make Sheol my couch, thou art there,[1]

the departure from the old Hebrew and Babylonian views of the limitation of divine power is clearly marked. The inconsistency between the view held of Yahwe and the limitation of his power was not, however, always recognized. Hence, even in late portions of the Old Testament, we find views of the life after death that are closely allied to the popular notions prevailing in the earlier productions. It is not, indeed, till we reach a period bordering close on our era that the conflict between the old and the new is brought to a decided issue in the disputes of the sects that arose in Palestine.[2] The doctrines of retribution and of the resurrection of the dead are the inevitable consequences of the later ethical faith and finally triumph; but the old views, which bring the ancient Hebrews into such close connection with the Babylonians, left their impress in the vagueness that for a long time characterized these doctrines, even after their promulgation. The persistency of the old beliefs is a proof of the strong hold that they acquired, as also of the close bond uniting, at one time and for a long period, Hebrews and Babylonians. What applies to the beliefs regarding the dead holds good also for the rites. Many a modern Jewish custom[3] still bears witness to the original identity of the Hebrew and Babylonian methods of disposing of and caring for the dead.

---

[1] Psalms, cxxxix. 8; a very late production.

[2] Schürer, *A History of the Jewish People in the Time of Jesus Christ*, vol. II. Division ii. pp. 38, 39, 179–181.

[3] *E.g.*, the custom still in vogue among Orthodox Jews of placing the body wrapped in a shroud upon a board, instead of in a coffin.

There is but one explanation for this close agreement,— the same explanation that was given for the identity of traditions regarding the creation of the world, and for the various other points of contact between the two peoples that we have met with. When the Hebrew clans left their homes in the Euphrates Valley, they carried with them the traditions, beliefs, and customs that were current in that district, and which they shared with the Babylonians. Under new surroundings, some new features were added to the traditions and beliefs, but the additions did not obscure the distinctive character impressed upon them by Babylonian contact. We now know that relations with Babylonia were never entirely broken off by the Hebrews. The old traditions survived all vicissitudes. They were adapted to totally changed phases of belief, but the kernel still remained Babylonian. Beliefs were modified, new doctrines arose; but, with a happy inconsistency, the old was embodied in the new. Hence it happens, that in order to understand the Hebrews, their religion, their customs, and even their manner of thought, we must turn to Babylonia.

Further discoveries beneath the mounds of Mesopotamia and further researches in Babylonian literature will add more evidence to the indebtedness of the Hebrews to Babylonia. It will be found that in the sacrificial ordinances of the Pentateuch, in the legal regulations, in methods of justice and punishment, Babylonian models were largely followed, or, what is an equal testimony to Babylonian influence, an opposition to Babylonian methods was dominant. It is not strange that when by a curious fate, the Hebrews were once more carried back to the 'great river of Babylon,'[1] the people felt so thoroughly at home there. It was only the poets and some ardent patriots

---

[1] Professor Haupt has recently shown (in a paper read before the American Oriental Society, April, 1897, and before the Eleventh International Congress of Orientalists, September, 1897) that such is the meaning of the phrase, Psalms, cxxxvii. 1, which is ordinarily translated 'rivers of Babylon.'

who hung their harps on the willows and sighed for a return to Zion. The Jewish population steadily increased in Babylonia, and soon also the intellectual activity of Babylonian Jews outstripped that of Palestine.[1] The finishing touches to the structure of Judaism were given in Babylonia — on the soil where the foundations were laid.

[1] The Talmud of Babylonia, and not the Talmud of Palestine, became the authoritative work in the Jewish Church.

CHAPTER XXVI.

THE TEMPLES AND THE CULT.

The religious architecture of Babylonia and Assyria is of interest chiefly as an expression of the religious earnestness of rulers and people, and only in a minor degree as a manifestation of artistic instincts. The lack of a picturesque building material in the Euphrates Valley was sufficient to check the development of such instincts. Important as the adaptation of the clay soil of Babylonia for simple construction was for the growth of Babylonian culture, the limitations to the employment of bricks as a building material are no less significant. Ihering has endeavored to show [1] by an argument that is certainly brilliant and almost convincing, that the settlement of Semites in a district, the soil of which could be so readily used to replace the primitive habitations of man by solid structures, made the Semites the teachers of the Aryans in almost everything that pertains to civilization. House-building produced the art of measuring, led to more elaborate furnishings of the habitation, created various trades, introduced social distinctions, necessitated divisions of time, and gave the stimulus to commercial intercourse. But, on the other hand, the artistic possibilities of brick structures were soon exhausted. The house could be indefinitely extended in length and even height, but such an extension only added to the monotonous effect. With clay as a building material, so readily moulded into any desired shape, and that could be baked, if need be, by the action of the sun without the use of fire, it was almost as easy to build a large house as a small one. But the addition of rooms and wings and stories which differentiated the house from the palace

[1] *Vorgeschichte der Indo-Europaer*, pp. 126–141.

and the palace from the temple, served to make hugeness the index of grandeur. The best specimens of the religious architecture of Babylonia and Assyria are characterized by such hugeness. A proportionate increase of external beauty could only be secured by a modification of architectural style; but the conservative instincts of the people discouraged any deviation from the conventional shapes of the temples, which appear indeed to have been firmly established long before the days of Hammurabi. The influence of conventionality finds a striking illustration in the manner in which the temples of Assyria follow Babylonian models. Soft and hard stone suitable for permanent structures was easily procured in the mountainous district adjacent to Assyria. The Assyrians used this material for statues, altars, and for the slabs with which they decorated the exterior and interior walls of their great edifices. Had they also employed it as a building material, we should have had the development of new architectural styles; but the Assyrians, so dependent in everything pertaining to culture upon the south, could not cut themselves loose from ancient traditions, and continued to erect huge piles of brick, as the homage most pleasing in the eyes of their gods. The Book of Genesis characterized the central idea of the Babylonian and Assyrian temples when it represented the people gathered in the valley of Shinar — that is, Babylonia — as saying: 'Come, let us build a city and a tower that shall reach up to heaven.'[1] The Babylonian and Assyrian kings pride themselves upon the height of their temples. Employing, indeed, almost the very same phrase that we find in the Old Testament, they boast of having made the tops of their sacred edifices as high as 'heaven.'[2] The temple was to be in the literal sense of the

---

[1] Gen. xi. 4.

[2] *E.g.*, Tiglathpileser I., col. vii. ll. 102, 103; Meissner, *Altbabylonisches Privatrecht*, no. 46; Nebopolassar Cylinder (Hilprecht, *Old Babylonian Inscriptions*, i. 1, pls. 32, 33), col. i. L 38. Or 'as high as mountains'; *e.g.*, Nebuchadnezzar II., IR. 58, col. viii. ll. 61–63; and so frequently the Neo-Babylonian kings.

word a 'high place.' But, apart from the factor of natural growth, there was a special reason why the Babylonians aimed to make their sacred edifices high. The oldest temple of Babylonia at the present time known to us, the temple of Bel at Nippur, bears the characteristic name of E-Kur, 'mountain house.' The name is more than a metaphor. The sacred edifices of Babylonia were intended as a matter of fact to be imitations of mountains. It is Jensen's merit to have suggested the explanation for this rather surprising ideal of the Babylonian temple.[1] According to Babylonian notions, it will be recalled, the earth is pictured as a huge mountain. Among other names, the earth is called E-Kur, 'mountain house.' The popular and early theology conceived the gods as sprung from the earth. They are born in Kharsag-kurkura,[2] 'the mountain of all lands,' which is again naught but a designation for the earth, though at a later period some particular part of the earth, some mountain peak, may have been pictured as the birthplace of the gods, much as among the Indians, Persians, and Greeks we find a particular mountain singled out as the one on which the gods dwell. The transfer of the gods or of some of them to places in the heavens was, as we saw,[3] a scholastic theory, and not a popular belief. It was a natural association of ideas, accordingly, that led the Babylonians to give to their temples the form of the dwelling which they ascribed to their gods. The temple, in so far as it was erected to serve as a habitation for the god and an homage to him, was to be the reproduction of the cosmic E-Kur,—'a mountain house' on a small scale, a miniature Kharsag-kurkura. In confirmation of this view, it is sufficient to point out that E-Kur is not merely the name of the temple to Bel at Nippur, but is frequently used as a designation for temple in general; and, moreover, a plural is formed

---

[1] *Kosmologie*, pp. 185-195.
[2] Or *Kharsag-gal-kurkura*; see p. 558.
[3] See p. 458.

of the word which is used for divinities.¹ In Assyria we find one of the oldest temples bearing the name E-kharsag-kurkura,² that stamps the edifice as the reproduction of the 'mountain of all lands'; and there are other temples that likewise bear names³ in which the idea of a mountain is introduced.

To produce the mountain effect, a mound of earth was piled up and on this mound a terrace was formed that served as the foundation plane for the temple proper, but it was perfectly natural also that instead of making the edifice consist of one story, a second was superimposed on the first so as to heighten the resemblance to a mountain. The outcome of this ideal was the so-called staged tower, known as the *zikkurat*. The name signifies simply a 'high' edifice, and embodies the same idea that led the Canaanites and Hebrews to call their temples 'high places.'⁴

The oldest zikkurat as yet found is the one excavated by Drs. Peters and Haynes at Nippur,⁵ the age of which can be traced back to the second dynasty of Ur — about 2700 B.C. This appears to have consisted of three stages, one superimposed on the other. There is a reference to a zikkurat in the inscriptions of Gudea that may be several centuries older; but since beneath the zikkurat at Nippur remains of an earlier building were found, it is a question whether the staged tower represents the oldest type of a Babylonian temple. At no time does any special stress appear to have been laid upon the number of stories of which the zikkurat was to consist. It is not until a comparatively late period that rivalry among the rulers and natural ambition led to the increase of the superimposed stages until the number seven was reached. The older zikkurats were

¹ *Ekurrâti;* Delitzsch, *Assyr. Handwörterbuch,* p. 718b.
² IR. 35, no. 3, 22.
³ See below.
⁴ Hebrew *Bamôth.* Through the opposition of the Hebrew prophets, the term acquires distasteful associations that were originally foreign to it.
⁵ See Peters' *Nippur,* ii. 124 *seq.*

imposing chiefly because of the elevation of the terrace on which they were erected, and inasmuch as the ideal of the temple is realized to all practical purposes by the erection of a high edifice on an elevated mound, the chief stress was laid upon the height of the terrace. The terrace, in a certain sense, is the original zikkurat — the real 'high place' — and the temple of one story naturally precedes the staged tower, and may have remained the type for some time before the more elaborate structure was evolved. However this may be, we are justified in associating the mountain *motif* with the beginnings of religious architecture in the Euphrates Valley, precisely as the underlying cosmic notions belong to the earliest period of which we have any knowledge. That the staged tower when once evolved was regarded as the most satisfactory expression of the religious ideas follows from the fact that all the large centers of Babylonia had a zikkurat of some kind dedicated to the patron deity, and probably many of the smaller places likewise. A list of zikkurats[1] furnishes the names of no less than twenty; and while all of the important places are included, there are others which do not appear to have played an important part in either the religious or political history of the country, and which nevertheless had their zikkurat. To judge from the fact that in this list several names of zikkurat are connected with one and the same place, more than one zikkurat, indeed, could be found in a large religious center.[2]

The Construction and Character of the Zikkurats.

The zikkurat was quadrangular in shape. The orientation of the four corners towards the four cardinal points was only approximate.[3] Inasmuch as the rulers of Babylonia from a

---

[1] IIR. 50, obverse.
[2] Perhaps, however, these several names all designate a single zikkurat.
[3] Peters' *Nippur*, I. 246; ii. 120.

very early period call themselves 'king of the four regions,'[1] it has been supposed that the quadrangular shape was chosen designedly; but there is no proof that any stress was laid upon symbolism of this kind, or upon the orientation of the corners of the sacred edifices. More attention was bestowed upon making the brick structure huge and massive.

The height of the zikkurats varied. Those at Nippur and Ur[2] appear to have been about 90 feet high, while the tower at Borsippa which Sir Henry Rawlinson carefully examined[3] attained a height of 140 feet. The base of this zikkurat, which may be regarded as a specimen of the tower in its most elaborate form, was a quadrangular mass 272 feet square and 26 feet high. The second and third stories were of equal height, but the square mass diminished with each story by 42 feet. The height of the four upper stories was 15 feet each. At the same time, the mass diminished steadily at the rate of 42 feet, so that the seventh story consisted of a mass of only 20 feet square. Sargon's zikkurat at Khorsabad (the suburb of Nineveh) was about the same height.

The average number of stages of the zikkurat appears to have been three, as at Nippur and Ur, or four, as at Larsa.[4] In the pictorial representations of the towers,[5] we similarly find either three or four. In these smaller zikkurats, the height of

---

[1] For the meaning of this phrase, see Winckler's *Altorientalische Forschungen*, iii. 208–222, and Jensen's *Kosmologie*, p. 167.

[2] From Heuzey's note in De Sarzec, *Découvertes en Chaldée*, p. 31, it would appear that at Lagash there was a zikkurat of modest proportions, but Dr. Peters informs me that from his observations at Telloh, he questions whether the building in question represents a zikkurat at all, though, as we know from other sources, a zikkurat existed there in the days of Gudea.

[3] *Journal of the Royal Asiatic Society*, xviii.

[4] Of Sargon's zikkurat at Khorsabad, also, only four stories have been found. Perrot and Chipiez (*History of Art in Chaldaea and Assyria*, I. 388) suppose that there may have been seven.

[5] *E.g.* Perrot and Chipiez, *ib.* p. 128. Hommel, *Geschichte Babyloniens und Assyriens*, p. 19.

each tower, as in the first three stories of the tower at Borsippa, appears to have been alike; but the mass diminished in proportion in order to secure a space for a staircase leading from one story to the other. This method of ascent was older than the winding balustrade, which was better adapted to the more elaborate structures of later times. No doubt, as the towers increased in height, other variations were introduced — as, *e.g.*, in the proportions of the stories — without interfering with the essential principle of the zikkurat.

The ungainly appearance presented by the huge towers was somewhat relieved by decorations of the friezes and by the judicious use of color. Enameled bricks of bright hues, such as yellow and blue,[1] became common, and in the case of some of the towers it would appear that a different color was chosen for each story. Whether all the bricks in each story were colored or only those at the edge, or, perhaps, some rows, it is impossible to say. From Herodotus' description of the seven concentric walls of Ecbatana,[2] in which each wall was distinguished by a certain color, the conclusion has been drawn that the same colors — white, black, scarlet, blue, orange, silver, and gold — were employed by the Babylonians for the stages of their towers; but there is no satisfactory evidence that this was the case. That these colors were brought into connection with the planets, as some scholars have supposed, is highly improbable.

As already pointed out, no special stress seems to have been laid upon the number of stories of which the zikkurat consisted, but the natural result of ambition and rivalry among builders tended towards an increase of the height, and this end could be most readily attained by adding to the number of stories. Still, there may have been some symbolism which led to the choice of three, four, or seven stories, inasmuch as these numbers

---

[1] Peters (*Nippur*, i. 214) found many yellow-colored bricks at Borsippa.
[2] Book I, § 98.

have a sacred import among so many nations.[1] For the number seven, the influence of cosmological associations is quite clear. The two most famous of the zikkurats of seven stages were those in Babylon and in Borsippa, opposite Babylon. The latter bears the significant name E-ur-imin-an-ki,[2] *i.e.*, 'the house of the seven directions of heaven and earth.' The 'seven directions' were interpreted by the Babylonian theologians as a reference to the seven great celestial bodies, — the sun and moon and the five planets Ishtar, Marduk, Ninib, Nergal, and Nabu.[3] To each of these gods one story was supposed to be dedicated, and the tower thus became a cosmological symbol, elaborating in theological fashion the fundamental idea of the zikkurat as a reproduction of the dwelling-place of the gods. The identification of the five gods with the planets is a proof of the scholastic character of the interpretation, and hence of its comparatively late origin. This interpretation of the number seven, however, was not the only one proposed in the Babylonian schools. Two much older towers than those of Babylon and Borsippa bear names in which 'seven' is introduced. One of these is the zikkurat to Nin-girsu at Lagash, which Gudea[4] describes as 'the house of seven divisions of the world'; the other, the tower at Uruk,[5] which bore the name 'house of seven zones.' The reference in both cases is, as Jensen has shown,[6] to the seven concentric zones into which the earth was divided by the Babylonians. It is a conception that we encounter in India and Persia, and that survives in the seven 'climates' into which the world was divided by Greek and Arabic geographers. It seems clear that this interpreta-

---

[1] See a paper by E. W. Hopkins on *The Holy Numbers of the Rig-Veda* (Oriental Studies, Boston, 1894, pp. 141–147).

[2] Written ideographically, as the names of the zikkurats and of all sacred edifices invariably are.

[3] See above, p. 459.

[4] Inscription G, col. i. l. 14 ; D, col. ii. l. 11.

[5] IIR. 50; obverse 20. See p. 472.

[6] *Kosmologie*, pp. 171–174.

tion of the number seven is older than the one which identified each story with one of the planets.¹ Both interpretations have a scholastic aspect, however, and the very fact that there are two interpretations, justifies the suspicion that neither furnishes the *real* explanation why the number seven was chosen.

It by no means follows from the names borne by the zikkurats at Lagash and Uruk that they actually consisted of seven stories. The 'seven divisions' and the 'seven zones' are merely terms equivalent to 'universe.' The names given to the towers would have been equally appropriate if they consisted — as they probably did — of fewer stories than seven. But, on the other hand, the introduction of the number seven into the names may be regarded as a factor which influenced ambitious builders to make the number of stories seven. Over and above this, however, seven was chosen, primarily, because it was a large number, and, secondly, because it was a sacred number, — sacred in part because large, since 'largeness' and 'sacredness' are correlated ideas in the popular phases of early religious thought. In the same way, it is because seven was popularly sacred that the world was divided into seven zones and that the planets were fixed at seven, not *vice versa*.

The opinion of some scholars² that the zikkurats were used for astronomical observations remains a pure conjecture, of which it cannot even be said that it has probability in its favor. It is certain that the astronomical observations, since they were conducted by the priests, were made in the temple precincts; but a small room at the top of a pyramid difficult of access seems hardly a spot adapted for the purpose. Moreover, the sacred character of the zikkurat speaks against the supposition

---

[1] The suggestion is worthy of consideration whether the name 'seven directions of heaven and earth' may not also point to a conception of seven zones dividing the *heavens* as well as the earth. One is reminded of the 'seven' heavens of Arabic theology.

[2] So *e.g.*, Kaulen, *Assyrien und Babylonien* (3d edition), p. 58; Vigouroux, *La Bible et les Découvertes Modernes* (4th edition), I. 358.

that it should have been put to such constant use, and for purposes not directly connected with the cult. In the numerous astronomical reports that we have, there is not a single reference from which one could conclude that the observations reported were made from the top of a zikkurat.

But, on the other hand, it would appear that as the zikkurat developed from a one-story edifice into a tower, and as the number of the stages increased, the zikkurat assumed more of an ornamental character. While the ascent of the tower continued to be regarded to the latest days as a sacred duty, pleasing in the eyes of the deity, for the ordinary and more practical purposes of the cult, other buildings were erected near the tower. Within the temple area and bordering on it there were smaller shrines, while in front of the zikkurat there was a large open place, where the pilgrims who flocked to the sacred city, congregated. The sacrifices which formed the essential feature of worship were brought, not at the top of the zikkurat, but on altars that were erected at the base.

The ideographic designation of the zikkurat as a 'conspicuous house,'[1] which accords admirably with the motive ascribed in the eleventh chapter of Genesis to the builders of a zikkurat to erect an edifice that "could be seen," supports the view here taken of the more decorative position which the staged tower came to occupy, — an homage to the gods rather than a place where they were to be worshipped, something that suggested the dwelling-place of a god, to be visited only occasionally by the worshipper — in short, a monument forming part of a religious sanctuary, but not coextensive with the sanctuary. The differentiation that thus arose between the dwelling-place of the god and the place where he was to be worshipped is a perfectly natural one. To emphasize the fact that the zikkurat was the temple for the god, a small room was built at the top

---

[1] Lit., 'house to be seen,' *Igi-e-nir*. See, *e.g.*, VR. 29, no. 4, 40, and Delitzsch, *Assyr. Handwörterbuch*, p. 262.

of the zikkurat,[1] and it was a direct consequence of this same distinction between a temple for the gods and a temple for actual worship that led to assigning to zikkurats special names, and such as differed from the designation of the sacred quarter of which the zikkurat formed the most conspicuous feature.

Thus the name E-Kur, 'mountain house,' though evidently an appropriate designation for the zikkurat, becomes the term for the sacred area which included in time a large series of buildings used for the cult, whereas the zikkurat itself receives the special name of 'house of oracle';[2] and similarly in the case of the various other religious centers of Babylonia, the name of the zikkurat is distinct from that of the sacred quarter — the temple in the broader sense.

The special position which the zikkurat thus came to occupy is, of course, merely an outcome of the growth of the religious centers of the country, and involves no departure from the religious ideals of earlier days. The distinction is much of the same order as we find in the case of the Hebrew temple at Jerusalem, where the court in which the worshippers gathered was distinct from the 'holy of holies,' which was originally regarded as the dwelling of Yahwe, and in later times was viewed as the spot where he manifested himself. The name 'house of oracle' given to the zikkurat at Nippur is a valuable indication of the special sanctity that continued to be attached to the staged tower.

THE TEMPLE AND THE SACRED QUARTER.

But the zikkurat, while the most characteristic expression of the religious spirit of Babylonia, was by no means the only kind of sacred edifice that prevailed.

---

[1] So at Babylon, at least, according to Herodotus. Traces of such a room were also found in connection with the zikkurat at Nippur (Peters, *Nippur*, ii. 122.

[2] *Bit pirishti*. IIR. 50, obverse, 6. Another name (or perhaps the name of a second zikkurat at Nippur; see p. 616, note 2) is *Im-kharsag, i.e.*, 'mountain of awe.' Peters' rendering (*Nippur*, ii. 122) of the names is inaccurate.

The excavations at Nippur have afforded us for the first time a general view of a sacred quarter in an ancient Babylonian city. The extent of the quarter was considerable. Dr. Peters' estimate is eight areas for the zikkurat and surrounding structures, and to this we may add several acres more, since beyond the limits of the great terrace there were buildings to the southeast and southwest, used for religious purposes. It is likely that the extent of E-Sagila at Babylon was even greater. Outside of the temple area at Nippur, Peters[1] and Haynes unearthed a court of considerable size, lined with brick columns. The court was open to the sky, but the columns supported a roof which was apparently of wood. Similar courts have been found elsewhere, so that we are justified in regarding the Nippur structure as characteristic of the architecture of Babylonia. The court was attached to an edifice of considerable size, which contained among other things rooms in which the temple records were kept. The entrance to the court was by a large gateway, supported on each side by a brick column, double the diameter of those that surrounded the court. While the nature of the building is not perfectly clear, still the presence of the temple archives and the gateway make it probable that the structure was used in connection with the cult of some deity worshipped at Nippur. Lending weight to this supposition are the points of resemblance between this structure and the sacred edifices of the ancient Hebrews and Arabs. A court of sixty columns — made of wood, quadrangular in shape, with the supports and tops of metal — was the characteristic feature of the tabernacle.[2] Within this court, open to the sky, the people gathered for worship. The altar and the basin for ablutions stood in the court, while the holy tent containing the ark was set up near the eastern end of the place. Similarly at Mecca,[3]

---

[1] Peters' *Nippur*, ii. chapter vi.

[2] Schick, *Die Stiftshütte, der Tempel, und der Tempelplatz der Jetztzeit*, pp. 8, 9.

[3] Snouck-Hurgronje *Mekka* (Atlas, pl. I). The present structure, though comparatively modern, is built after ancient models.

the Kaaba, the pulpit, and the sacred fountain are grouped within a space enclosed on all sides by colonnades. Again, surrounding the Solomonic temple on three sides was a spacious court. This court was enclosed with colonnades.[1] It may well be, therefore, that the edifice around or near the fine court of columns at Nippur was a sacred structure, erected in honor of some deity. The two large brick columns at the entrance to the Nippur court are paralleled in the case of the Solomonic temple by the two large columns, known as Yakhin and Boaz, that stood at the gateway. These names are as yet unexplained. Their symbolic character, apart from other evidence, may be concluded from the circumstance that, as Schick has shown,[2] the columns stood free, and did not serve as a support for any part of the gateway.[3] There is no need, therefore, for any hesitation in comparing these two columns, whose presence in the Solomonic structure is certainly due to foreign influence, to those found at Nippur.[4]

That the columns at Nippur were erected in accordance with recognized custom follows from De Sarzec's discovery of two enormous round columns within the sacred quarter of Lagash.[5] In the light of Peters' excavations, the significance of the columns at Lagash becomes clear. Unfortunately, De Sarzec's excavations at Lagash at the point of the mound in question were interrupted, but he gives reasons for believing that other columns existed near the two large ones found by

---

[1] Schick, *ib.* pp. 125–131.

[2] *Die Stiftshütte, der Tempel, und der Tempelplatz der Jetztzeit*, p. 82.

[3] On the significance of the gate in sacred edifices, see Trumbull, *The Threshold Covenant*, pp. 102–108.

[4] Dr. Peters is of the opinion that at the entrance to the temple area proper at Nippur there also stood two large columns.

[5] *Découvertes en Chaldée*, pp. 62–64. Heuzey, in a valuable note, already suggests the comparison with the two columns of Solomon's which is here maintained on the basis of the excavations at Nippur.

him.[1] There is, therefore, every reason to conclude that at Lagash, as at Nippur and no doubt elsewhere, the two columns belonged to a great gateway leading into a large court of columns. That these columns served a symbolic purpose in the Babylonian temple as they did at Jerusalem, cannot be maintained with certainty, but is eminently likely.

The court of columns was surrounded by a series of rooms. If the view taken of the building is correct, these rooms were used for the temple administration. However this may be, there can be no doubt that the structures of various size found around the zikkurat at Nippur served as dwellings for the priests and the temple attendants, as stalls for the temple cattle, as shops for the manufacture and sale of votive objects, and the like. Within the temple area proper were the schools where young priests were trained to be scribes, and received instructions in the doctrines and rites. The astronomical observatories, too, were situated near the temple. The schools served, as they still do in the orient, as the gathering-place of the mature scholars. The systematized pantheon, and the cosmological and astronomical systems represent the outcome of the intellectual activity that manifested itself within the sacred quarters of the cities of Babylonia. The execution of justice being in the hands of the priests, the sacred area also contained the rooms where the judges sat. It is interesting to note that Gudea mentions a hall of judgment in the temple to Nin-girsu at Lagash. The number of such buildings attached to the temple precinct varied, of course, according to the needs and growth of each place. In Nippur, the numbers appear to have been very large. We may assume, likewise, that at Sippar, Uruk, Ur, and Larsa the zikkurat was the center of a considerable group of buildings, while at Babylon in the days of her greatest power, the temple area of E-Sagila must have presented the appearance of a little city by itself, shut off from the rest of the

[1] *Ib.* p. 64.

town by a wall which invariably enclosed the sacred quarter.
Within this large wall there were smaller ones, marking the
several divisions of the temple buildings. The construction of
the smaller edifices does not appear to have varied from the
ordinary form chosen for the one-story dwelling-houses in the
city proper. The material used for all structures — the large
and the small ones — was brick. In earlier times the bricks were
merely dried in the sun. The buildings, as a consequence, suffered much from the influence of the heat and rain, and required
frequent repairs. Often the tower would crumble away, and an
entirely new edifice would have to be erected. The later custom of kiln-dried bricks was an improvement, and still more
solidity was insured when the exterior series of brick was
glazed. In the older buildings, the bricks were merely piled
together, without cement. Afterwards straw was mixed with
the clay, but as early as Gudea's days the bitumen, abounding
in the valley, became the common cement employed in all edifices of importance. Wood was used in the case of smaller
sanctuaries (as also in palaces) for the roof, and the kings often
refer with pride to the efforts they made to obtain the precious
cedars of the Lebanon forests for their building enterprises.
The decoration was confined largely to the façades, the doors,
and the floors. A pleasing effect also was produced by the
judicious distribution of glazed and enameled bricks in
the walls. Colors were used with still greater lavishness in the
decorations of the interior. The brilliancy was heightened
by the use of precious stones and gold and silver for the walls
and floors and ceilings. The aim of the builders was, as they
constantly tell us, to make the buildings as brilliant as the
sunlight. The decorations of the brick walls and floors suggest
textile patterns, and to account for this, some scholars have
supposed that prior to the use of colored bricks, it was customary to cover the walls and floors of temples and palaces
with draperies and rugs. The suggestion lacks proof, but has

much in its favor. In exterior architecture no profound changes were ever introduced, but within the prescribed limits, the builders did their utmost to make their edifices testimonials of their zeal and power. They imported gold, copper, and diorite from the Sinai peninsula and Arabia, precious stones from Armenia and the Upper Euphrates, wood from Bahrein and from various parts of the Amanus range, and so all quarters of the ancient world of culture were ransacked for contributions to add to the splendor of the Babylonian and Assyrian cities. Much care was bestowed in the course of time upon the portals. The wooden gates were covered with bronze, in which art of decoration great skill was developed.[1] The columns of stone appear only in Assyrian edifices as decorations in the front of palaces, supporting a portal or portico that projects from the temple proper.[2] The introduction appears to be due to foreign influence, perhaps Hittite.[3]

To determine the interior arrangement of a sacred structure, we have two small Assyrian temples, excavated by Layard at Nimrod, to serve as our guide.[4] A long hall constituted the chief feature. At the extreme end of this hall was a small room, in which stood a statue of the god to whom the temple was dedicated. This room, known as the *papakhu* or *parakku*, was the most sacred part of the temple, and it is doubtful whether any but the king or the highest officials had access to it. Certainly, no one could approach the presence of the deity without the mediation of a priest. Both terms for this room convey the idea of its being

---

[1] The best example for Assyria is furnished by the magnificent bronze gates of Balawat, now in the British Museum. See Birch and Pinches, *The Bronze Ornaments of the Palace Gates of Balawat* (London, 1881).

[2] See the illustrations in Perrot and Chipiez, *History of Art in Chaldea and Assyria*, i. 142, 143.

[3] So Puchstein and Friedrich, but see Meissner-Rost, *Noch einmal das Bithilâni und die Assyrische Säule* (Leipzig, 1893).

[4] *Discoveries among the Ruins of Nineveh and Babylon*, plan 2.

"shut off"[1] from the rest of the building, precisely as the holy of holies in the temple of Jerusalem containing the ark, was separated from the central hall. Gudea[2] describes the papakhu as the "dark" (or inner) chamber.

We are fortunate in having a pictorial representation of such a papakhu. A stone tablet found at Sippar[3] represents Shamash seated in the "holy of holies" of the temple E-Babbara. The god sits on a low throne. In front of him is an altar table on which rests a wheel with radiant spokes,—a symbol of the sun-god. Into this sanctuary the worshipper, who is none other than the king Nabubaliddin, is led by a priest. The king is at pains to tell us in the inscription attached to the design, that he was careful to restore the image of Shamash after an ancient model, and his motive in adding an illustration to this tablet is that future builders may have no excuse for not being equally careful. We may, therefore, take the illustration as a sample of the general character of the sacred chambers in the Babylonian and Assyrian temples in the great centers. The papakhu was decorated with great lavishness. The floors and walls and also the ceiling were studded with precious stones. We may believe Herodotus[4] when he tells us that the statue of Marduk in his temple at Babylon and the table in front of it was of gold. It was to the papakhu that the priests retired when they desired to obtain an oracle direct from the god; and as in the course of time the sanctity of the spot increased, we may well suppose that the occasions when the deity was directly approached in his papakhu became rarer. Through the influence of the schools attached to the Marduk cult at Babylon, the New Year's Festival

---

[1] Papakhu for Pakhpakhu, from the stem *pakhû*, "to close." Parakku, from *Paráku*, "to shut off, to lock."
[2] Inscription D, col. ii. l. 9.
[3] V Rawlinson, pl. 60.
[4] Book I. sec. 183.

— the character of which we will have occasion to explain later on — came to be regarded as the season most appropriate for approaching the oracular chamber. During this festival, Marduk was supposed to decide the fate of mankind for the whole year, and the intercession of the priests on the occasion was fraught with great importance.

A special significance, moreover, came to be attached to the sacred chamber in the Marduk temple. Complementing in a measure, the cosmological associations that have been noted in connection with the zikkurat, the papakhu of Marduk was regarded as an imitation of a cosmical 'sacred chamber.' As the zikkurat represented the mountain on which the gods were born and where they were once supposed to dwell, so the sacred room was regarded as the reproduction of a portion of the great mountain where the gods assembled in solemn council. This council chamber was situated at the eastern end of the great mountain, and was known as Du-azagga, that is, 'brilliant chamber.' The chamber itself constituted the innermost recess of the eastern limit of the mountain, and the special part of the mountain in which it lay was known as Ubshu-kenna, written with the ideographic equivalents to 'assembly room.' It will be apparent that such a view of the papakhu is the result of theological speculation, and is not due, as is the conception of the zikkurat, to popular beliefs.

The assembly of the gods presupposes a systematization of the pantheon, and the fact that it is only the papakhu in Marduk's temple which is known as Du-azagga[1] is a sufficient indication of the influences at work which produced this conception. In the creation epic, there is a reference to the Ubshu-kenna[2] which shows the main purpose of a divine

---

[1] See the chief passage, IR. 54, col. ii. ll. 54–65; another name is E-Kua, 'dwelling.'

[2] See p. 423.

assembly in the eyes of the priests of Babylon. The gods meet there in order to do homage to Marduk. They gather around the victorious vanquisher of Tiâmat, as the princes gather round the throne of the supreme ruler, — the king of Babylon and of Babylonia.

One can see, however, that, as is generally the case with theological doctrines, there is a popular starting-point from which these views were developed. The Du-azagga is older than the Ubshu-kenna. Situated in the extreme east, the 'brilliant chamber' is evidently the place whence the sun rises in the morning. A hymn to Shamash [1] expressly speaks of the sun rising out of the Du-azagga, and, since the sun also appears to rise up out of the ocean, the Du-azagga is placed at a point close to the great Apsu, which flows underneath the mountain. In confirmation of this view, a syllabary [2] identifies the Du-azagga with the Apsu. Marduk, by virtue of his original quality as a solar deity, would naturally be pictured as coming forth from Du-azagga. In this sense the title Mar-Du-azaga,[3] 'son of Du-azagga,' is applied to him, just as he is called Mar-Apsi, the son of Apsu. But the same conception would hold good of Shamash, of Ninib, and of some other solar deities, though not of all. That Du-azagga came to be especially associated with Marduk is due simply to the preëminent rank that he came to occupy. Whether there was also a popular basis for the conception of an Ubshu-kenna, an 'assembly room' of the gods, is a question more difficult to answer. Certainly, the view that the gods gathered together in one place belongs to an age which attempted to fix, at least in some measure, the relationship of the divine beings to one another. The popular phase of the conception of a general

---

[1] V R. 50, col. I. l. 5.
[2] V R. 41, No. 1, Rev. 18.
[3] IV R. 57, 24a. Jensen's suggestion (*Kosmologie*, p. 242) to read Mar-duku is out of the question.

assembly house could, in any case, hardly have proceeded further than the assumption of some particular part of the great mountain, where the gods were wont to come together. The connection of this assembly place with the Du-azagga is distinctly the work of the theologians of Babylon. In their desire to make Marduk the central figure of the pantheon, they bring all the gods to his side. The Ubshu-kenna is thus transferred to the region whence the sun issues on his daily journey. The 'chamber' of Marduk becomes the most sacred spot in this region, and the Ubshu-kenna the general name for the region itself. As Marduk in Babylon was surrounded by his court, so in Ubshu-kenna the gods assemble to pay homage to the one freely acknowledged by them as the greatest, and who is pictured as sitting on his throne in Du-azagga. The further speculation which brought the gods together yearly on the occasion of the great Marduk festival belongs likewise, and as a matter of course, to the period when Marduk's sway was undisputed.

The ideas that were thus attached to the papakhu in E-Sagila are a valuable indication of the sanctity attached to that part of the temple where the god sat enthroned. In a general way, what holds good of Marduk's papakhu applies to every sacred chamber in a temple, and no doubt views were once current of the papakhu of Bel at Nippur and of the 'holy of holies' in E-Babbara[1] and elsewhere that formed in some measure, a parallel to what the Marduk priests told of their favorite sanctuary.

Coming back now to the large hall which led into the papakhu, the absence of bas-reliefs in this hall in the case of the Assyrian temples excavated by Layard, suggests that the walls of this hall were not lined with sculptured slabs, as was the case in the large rooms of the palaces; and we may con-

---

[1] What Jensen says (*Kosmologie*, p. 10) of the temple at Sippar would apply to the papakhu in the temple, rather than to the whole structure.

clude that in Babylonian temples, likewise, the decoration of the walls was confined as a general thing to enameled bricks, interspersed, perhaps, with metallic panels, and that mythological scenes — such as the contest with Tiâmat or Gilgamesh's adventures — were only occasionally portrayed. An aim which, as the rulers themselves tell us in their inscriptions, they always kept in view was to make both the exterior and interior of the temples resplendent with brilliant coloring — "brilliant as the sun." At the entrances to the Assyrian temples stood lions, chiseled out of soft limestone or the harder alabaster. At Telloh various fragments of large lion heads were found,[1] so that there is every reason not only to trace this custom to Babylonia, but to carry it back to a very early period. Besides the lion, a favorite religious symbol, as we have seen,[2] was the bull, and, since Nebuchadnezzar speaks of retaining the "bull" statue of the old temple to Nanâ (or Ishtar) at Erech, we may suppose that the representation of colossal bulls at the entrances to the temples also belongs to the characteristic features of Babylonian religious architecture. The lion, it will be recalled, is more particularly the symbol of Nergal, but he appears originally, like the bull, to have been a symbol of other gods as well — perhaps, indeed, of the gods in general. Similarly, the eagle, which becomes the special symbol of Ashur, appears prominently on the monuments of Entemena[3] and other ancient rulers, centuries before the Ashur cult comes into prominence.

In the large court in front of the zikkurats there stood the jars used in connection with the cult, and the presence of these jars furthermore suggests that there was an altar in the great court, precisely as in the case of the Solomonic temple.[4]

---

[1] De Sarzec, *Découvertes en Chaldée*, pls. 24, 25 *bis*, etc.

[2] See p. 537.

[3] De Sarzec, *Découvertes en Chaldée*, pls. 4, 4 *bis* and 43 *bis*. On the latter, bulls, lions, and eagle in combination.

[4] See p. 653.

In the larger of the temples found by Layard, there was a smaller hall in front of the large one. We may assume that the same was the case with the larger temples of Babylonia, and this three-fold division of the interior, — the vestibule, or *pronaos*, the main hall, or *naos*, and the papakhu, — further warrants the comparison of a Babylonian sacred edifice with the Solomonic temple,[1] where likewise we have the vestibule, the hall known as the 'holy' part, and the 'holy of holies,' the one leading into the other. As to the further disposition of the rooms in the main temple, we must be content to wait for further excavations. What we know is sufficient to warrant the supposition that there was practical uniformity in the interior arrangement of the Babylonian and Assyrian temples. What variation there existed was probably confined to the decoration of the walls, doorways, and to the façades. Meanwhile, it is something to have reached general results. The zikkurat was surrounded by a varying number of shrines that were used as places of assembly for worshippers. The latter gathered also in the large court in front of the zikkurat, where the chief altar probably stood.[2] In the large halls of the shrines, there were in all probabilities likewise altars. It seems natural to suppose that the hall of judgment, mentioned already in Gudea's inscription,[3] was attached to some shrine. Besides the zikkurats and shrines, there were smaller structures used as dwellings for the priests and temple officials, for storehouses, for the archives, and as stalls for the animals to be used in the sacrifices. At Nippur a smithy was found near the tem-

---

[1] See the plan in Schick, *Die Stiftshütte*, pl. 5. Layard (*Discoveries among the Ruins of Nineveh and Babylon*, pp. 642–648) points out some analogies between the constructions at Nimrod and Solomon's buildings, but what he says applies chiefly to the palaces.

[2] Herodotus, book i. sec. 183, speaks of two altars outside of the temple of Marduk in Babylon. In the case of so important a structure, the number of altars was naturally more numerous.

[3] See Heuzey's note in De Sarzec's *Découvertes en Chaldée*, p. 65.

ple precinct. There were workshops near the temple where the furnishings for the temple, such as the curtains and the utensils, were made, and there were magazines where votive tablets and offerings were manufactured and sold. The number of these structures varied, naturally, in each religious center, and increased in proportion to the growth of the center. The zikkurat, the great court, the shrines, and the smaller structures formed a sacred precinct, and it was this precinct as a whole that constituted the temple in the larger sense, and received some appropriate name. Thus E-Kur at Nippur, E-Sagila at Babylon, E-Zida at Borsippa are used to denote the entire sacred precinct in these cities, and not merely the chief structure. The zikkurat always had a special name of its own.

A factor that contributed largely to the growth of the sacred precinct in the large centers was the circumstance that the political importance of such centers as Nippur, Lagash, Ur, Babylon, and Nineveh led the rulers to group around the worship of the chief deity, the cult of the minor ones who constituted the family or the court of the chief god. The kings measured their importance by the number of the gods upon whose assistance they could rely. The priests came to the assistance of the kings in connecting the gods of the royal pantheon in such a way, as to satisfy the pride of both their royal and divine masters.[1] The ambition of the kings, more especially of the Assyrian empire, led also to the addition of foreign deities to the pantheon. For these also shrines were built within or near the sacred precinct.

Gudea sets the example for his successors by parading a large pantheon at the close of his inscriptions,[2] and a list of temples in Lagash, recently published by Scheil,[3] shows that

---

[1] See pp. 109 *seq*.
[2] See p. 106.
[3] *Recueil des Travaux*, etc., xvii. 39.

most, if not all, of the gods invoked by the ruler had a sanctuary erected in his or her honor. There were, as we have seen, several quarters in Lagash, and therefore several sacred precincts, so that we cannot be certain that all of these sanctuaries stood in one and the same quarter. But, since the list in question furnishes the name of no less than thirteen sacred edifices, we are certain that as many as four or five smaller chapels surrounded the precinct in which stood the great temple E-Ninnu, sacred to Gudea's chief god Ningirsu-Ninib.

The list is headed by the sanctuary to Nin-girsu. There follow temples to Bau, to Nin-gishzida, Nin-mar, Ninâ, Dumuzi-zu-aba, Nin-si-a, Ga-tum-dug known to us from the inscriptions of Gudea, besides others, like Shabra (?), Nin-sun, Nin-tu, that appear here for the first time. In Nippur, we find traces of the worship of Belit (or Nin-lil), of Ninib, and of Nusku, though with the exception of the first named, the worship of these gods has not been traced back further than the days of the Cassite dynasty. Subsequent excavations may, of course, change the present aspect; but one gains the impression from the most ancient inscriptions found at Nippur that at an early period Bel was a god much like the Hebrew Yahwe, " jealous " of having others at his side. Such a conception would help to account for the title ' lord ' being applied to him above all others, and also aids us in understanding the lasting impression he made upon the people of Babylonia, — an impression so profound that when the time came for En-lil to yield his supremacy to Marduk, no better means could be found of emphasizing the latter's authority, than by transferring to him the names and titles of the older Bel.[1] In this respect, however, Nippur was an exception, and in later times the Bel cult was affected by the same influences that led Gudea to group around the sanctuary to Nin-girsu, edifices sacred to other gods

[1] See pp. 140 *seq.*

and goddesses. Lugalzaggisi[1] of Erech enumerates an extensive pantheon,[2] which contains most of the chief deities, and from which we may conclude that the temple of Nanâ was similarly the center of a large precinct in which the cult of other deities was carried on. When we come to the cult of Marduk at Babylon and of Nabu at Borsippa, the inscriptions, chiefly those of Nebuchadnezzar, come to our aid in showing us the arrangement of the various chapels that were comprised within the sacred precincts of E-Sagila and E-Zida, respectively. In the first place, the close relationship between Marduk and Nabu was emphasized by placing a papakhu to Nabu in the precinct of E-Sagila, which — built in imitation of E-Zida at Borsippa — was called by the same name.[8] This papakhu, it would seem, was independent of a special temple to Nabu known as E-Makh-tila, and which lay in Borsippa. The consort of Marduk, Sarpanitum, likewise had her temple in Babylon, and naturally close to the chief sanctuary of Marduk.[4] Ea, the father of Marduk, had a small sanctuary known as E-karzaginna in the sacred precinct.[5] It does not follow, of course, that all the temples in a center like Babylon or Borsippa were concentrated in one place. Indeed, when Nebuchadnezzar speaks of three temples to Gula being erected in Borsippa,[6] it is certain that they could not have been within the precinct of E-Zida, and so the temples to Shamash and Ramman, Sin and Ishtar, as well as to Nabu in Babylon, had an independent position; but we are at least warranted in concluding that they were not far removed from E-Sagila, and so, likewise, the numerous temples enumerated by Nebuchadnezzar

---

[1] The date of this king has recently been pushed down by Thureau-Dangin, considerably later than the date assigned to him by Hilprecht (*Revue Semitique*, v. 265-269). [2] See p. 110.

[8] Nebuchadnezzar, IR. 65, col. I. ll. 34, 35.

[4] This is to be concluded from Nebuchadnezzar, *ib.* l. 32.

[5] See Tiele's note, *Zeitschrift für Assyriologie*, ii. 184, note.

[6] IR. 55, col. iv. ll. 54-57.

as erected or improved by him in Borsippa were not far distant from Nabu's sanctuary,—the famous E-Zida. The palaces of the kings were also erected near the temples. In Babylon, we know that before Nebuchadnezzar's days, the palace stood so close to E-Sagila that an enlargement of it was impossible without encroaching on the sacred quarter.[1] The tendency to combine with the worship of the chief god, the cult of others is as characteristic of Assyrian rulers as of their Babylonian predecessors. We are fortunate in possessing an extensive list,[2] enumerating the various deities worshipped in the temples of Assyria, and the occasions on which they are to be invoked. The information to be gained from this list is all the more welcome since the Assyrian kings are chiefly interested in transmitting an account of their military expeditions, and tell us comparatively little of the religious edifices in their capitols. From this list we learn that in the old temple sacred to Anu and Ramman,[3] in the city of Ashur—the oldest Assyrian temple known to us,[4]—some twenty deities were worshipped. Images at least of these deities must have stood in the temple;[5] but, since there is a distinct reference to *zikkurats*[6] in the list, for some of them special sanctuaries of some kind must have been erected within the precinct. From the same list we learn that there was a temple to Marduk[7] in Ashur in which the cult of the Shamash, Sarpanitum, Ramman, Ninib, Anunit was also carried on; similarly, in the temples of Ashur, of Gula, and of Ninib, other gods were worshipped. Provisions of some kind for the cult of these deities must have

---

[1] See Tiele, *Zeitschrift für Assyriologie*, ii. 190.

[2] III Rawlinson, pl. 66. The list also contains objects in the temples used for the cult.

[3] IIIR. 66. obverse, col. ii. ll. 2-25.   [4] See p. 207.

[5] The sign for image occurs in connection with some of the gods.

[6] The term can hardly be used here in the strict sense of 'towers,' but appears to have become a general word for a sacred structure.

[7] *Ib.* col. iii. ll. 22-34.

been made, and one cannot escape the conclusion that in the Assyrian capitols, the sacred precincts likewise covered considerable territory, and that the tendency existed towards a steady increase of the structures erected in connection with the cult of the patron deity. Sennacherib proudly describes Nineveh as the city which contained the shrines of all gods and goddesses.[1]

The Names of the Zikkurats and Temples.

We have seen that every sacred edifice had a special name by which it was known. This custom belongs to the oldest period of Babylonian history, and continues to the latest. Through these names, to which, no doubt, considerable significance was attached, we obtain a valuable insight into the religious spirit of the Babylonians; but it is important to note that the custom does not appear to have been as general[2] in Assyria, where the temples are simply known as the house of this or that god or goddess. Of special interest are those names which were suggested by the original design of the temples. Such are E-Kur, 'the mountain house' at Nippur, E-kharsagkurkura, 'the house of the mountain of all lands,' the name of several temples.[3] The same idea finds expression also in such names as E-kharsag-ella, or 'house of the glorious mountain,' the name of a temple to Gula in Babylon; E-kharsag, 'the mountain house,' a temple in Ur;[4] E-kur-makh, 'the house of the great mountain,' which a text[5] declares to be equivalent to E-kharsag-kalama. Closely allied with these names are those indicating in one way or the other, the height or greatness of

---

[1] Meissner-Rost, *Bauinschriften Sanherib's*, p. 7.

[2] See, *e.g.*, the list IIIR. 66. An exception is formed by the temple to Ramman in the city of Asshur, which has a special name. See the following note.

[3] Including the one to Ramman in Asshur.

[4] IR. 2. nos. 11, 2.

[5] IIR. 50, obverse 13.

the buildings, as the general aim of the builders. Prominent among such names are E-Sagila, 'the lofty house,' the famous temple and temple area at Babylon; E-makh, 'the great house,' a chapel to Nin-kharsag, situated perhaps within E-Sagila; E-gal-makh, 'the great palace,' an old temple in Ur; E-anna, 'the heavenly house,' that is, the house reaching up to heaven, which is the name of the temple of Ishtar or Nanâ at Erech; E-Igi-e-nir-kidur-makh,[1] 'the tower of the great dwelling' sacred to Ninni at Kish. To the same class belong such designations as E-dur-an-ki, 'the link of heaven and earth,'[2] the name of a zikkurat at Larsa; E-an-dadia, 'the house reaching to heaven,' the zikkurat at Agade; E-pa, 'the summit house,' the zikkurat to Nin-girsu at Lagash; E-gubba-an-ki, 'the point of heaven and earth,' one of the names of the zikkurat in Dilbat; E-dim-anna, 'the house of heavenly construction,' the chapel to Sin within the precinct of E-Zida at Borsippa, — a name that again conveys the notion of an edifice reaching up to heaven. The names of the zikkurats at Erech and Borsippa, 'the house of seven zones' and 'the house of the seven divisions of heaven and earth,' respectively, while conveying, as we saw,[3] cosmological conceptions of a more specific character, may still be reckoned in the class of names that embody the leading purpose of the tower in Babylonia, as may also a name like E-temen-an-ki, 'the foundation stone of heaven and earth,' assigned to the zikkurat to Marduk in Babylonia.

The sacred edifice, as the dwelling of the god to whom it is dedicated, leads to such names as E-Zida, 'the true house or fixed house,'[4] the famous temple to Nabu in Borsippa; E-dur-gina,[5] 'the house of the established seat,' a temple of Bel-sarbi[6]

---

[1] Ige-e-nir = zikkurat; Kidur = shubtu (dwelling); Makh = rabu (great).

[2] The name approaches closely to the conception of a zikkurat in the Book of Genesis, as a 'ladder' connecting heaven and earth. Gen. xxviii. 12.

[3] See above, p. 619.

[4] The ideas 'true, fixed, established, eternal' are all expressed by the element *Zida*.

[5] I adopt this reading as the one generally used. [6] See above, p. 242.

in Baz; E-ki-dur[1]-garza, 'the sacred dwelling,' a temple to Nin-lil-anna in Babylon; E-kua, 'the dwelling-house,' the name of the papakhu of Marduk in E-Sagila; E-gi-umunna, 'the permanent dwelling'; E-esh[2]-gi, a shrine to Nin-girsu at Lagash with the same meaning, 'permanent house.'

Another class is formed by such names as are suggested by the attributes of the deity to whom the edifices are dedicated. Such are E-babbara, 'the brilliant house,' which, as the name of the temples to Shamash at Sippar and Larsa, recalls at once the character of the sun-god. Similarly, E-gish-shir-gal, 'the house of the great luminary,' was an appropriate name for the temple to the moon-god at Ur. The staff or sceptre being the symbol of the god Nabu, suggests as the name of a sanctuary to him in Babylonia, the name E-pad-kalama-suma, 'the house of him who gives the sceptre of the world,' while the character of Shamash as the god of justice finds an expression in the name E-ditar-kalama, 'the house of the universal judge,' given to his temple or chapel in Babylon. The association of the number fifty with Ningirsu-Ninib leads to the name E-ninnu, 'house of fifty,'[3] for his temple in Lagash. Again, the position of Anu in the pantheon accounts for the name E-adda, 'house of the father,' given to his temple, just as E-nin-makh, 'the house of the great lady,' the name of a chapel in Babylon, at once recalls a goddess like Ishtar. Other names that describe a temple by epithets of the gods to whom they are sacred, are E-nun-makh, 'the house of the great lord,' descriptive of Sin; E-me-te-ur-sagga, 'the house of the glory of the warrior,' a temple sacred to Zamama-Ninib; E-U-gal, 'the house of the great lord,' a temple to En-lil. A name like E-edinna, 'house of the field,' a temple to the consort of Shamash at Sippar, may also have been suggested by some attribute of the goddess.[4]

---

[1] Or *tush*. Cf. Brünnow, Sign List, no. 10523.
[2] Or *ab*. See Jensen, *Keils Bibl.* 3, 1, pp. 15, 173.   [3] See above, p. 57.
[4] Compare the name 'Belit-seri,' 'mistress of the fields,' as the name of a goddess who belongs to the pantheon of the lower world. See p. 588.

Lastly, we have a class of names that might be described as purely ornamental, or as embodying a pious wish. Of such we have a large number. Examples of this class are E-tila, 'house of life.' Names extolling the glory and splendor of the temples are common. In a list of temples[1] we find such designations as 'house of light,' 'house of the brilliant precinct,' 'great place,' 'lofty and brilliant wall,'[2] 'house of great splendor,' 'the splendor of heaven and earth,' 'house without a rival,' 'light of Shamash.' The seat of Sarpanitum in E-Sagila, is known as 'the gate of widespread splendor'; E-salgisa, 'the treasury,' as the name of a temple in Girsu, may belong here. A temple to Gula in Sippar was called E-ulla; that is, 'the beautiful house.' The old temple to Sin at Harran bore the significant name E-khulkhul, 'house of joys,' while the pious wish of the worshipper is again expressed in the name 'threshold of long life,' given to the zikkurat in Sippar.[3] Among a series of names,[4] illustrating the religious sentiments of the people are the following : 'the heart of Shamash,' 'the house of hearkening to prayers,'[5] 'the house full of joy,' 'the brilliant house,' 'the life of the world,' 'the place of fates,' and the like.

These various classes of names are a valuable index of the varied and often remarkable conceptions held of the gods. To call a temple, for example, 'court of the world'[6] may have been due originally to a haughty presumption on the part of some one deeply attached to some god; but such a name must also have led to regarding the god as not limited in his affections to a particular district. Whatever tendencies existed in Babylonia and Assyria towards universalistic conceptions of

---

[1] IIR. 61, nos. 1, 2, 6.

[2] Text, *Kar*, *i.e.*, 'dam,' 'wall,' or 'quay.'

[3] IIR. 50, l. 8.

[4] Bezold Catalogue, etc., p. 1776.

[5] One is reminded of Isaiah's sentiment (lvi. 7) regarding the temple of Yahwe, which is to be called 'a house of prayer for the world.'

[6] Lit., 'enclosure.'

the divine beings were brought out in the temple names, and in part may have been advanced by these names. The custom still surviving in the Jewish Church of giving names to synagogues may be traced back to a Babylonian prototype.[1]

The History of the Temples.

The history of the temples takes us back to the earliest period of Babylonian history, and the temples of Assyria likewise date from the small beginnings of the Assyrian power. The oldest inscriptions of Mesopotamian rulers commemorate their services as builders of temples. Naram-Sin and Sargon glory in the title 'builder of the temple of En-lil in Nippur.' Of the rulers of the first period of Babylonian history, it so happens that we know more of Gudea than of any other. We may feel certain that he but follows the example of his predecessors, in devoting so large a share of his energies to temple building. Hammurabi is an active builder of sanctuaries, and so on, through the period of Assyrian supremacy down to the closing days of the Babylonian monarchy, the thoughts of the rulers were directed towards honoring the gods by improving, restoring, rebuilding, or enlarging the sanctuaries, as well as by endowing them with rich gifts and votive offerings. The Assyrian kings, though perhaps more concerned with embellishing their palaces, do not neglect the seats of the gods. Anxious to maintain the connection between their kingdom and the old cities of the south, the Assyrian monarchs were fond of paying homage to the time-honored sanctuaries of Babylonia. This feeling, which is of course shared by the Babylonian rulers, results in bringing about the continuity of the Babylonian and

---

[1] The synagogue is called a 'house' just as the Babylonian temple is, and among names of synagogues (or of congregations) in modern times that form close parallels to the names of Babylonian temples may be instanced 'house of prayer,' 'glory of Israel,' 'tree of life.' The custom of naming Christian churches after the apostles represents a further development along the order of ideas current in Babylonia.

Assyrian religion. If, despite the changes that the religious doctrines underwent, despite the new interpretations given to old myths and legends, despite the profound changes introduced into the relationship of the gods to one another through the systematization of the pantheon, if, despite all this, the Babylonians and Assyrians — leaders and people — continued to feel that they were following the religion of their forefathers, it was due to the maintenance of the old sanctuaries. We can actually trace the history of some of these sanctuaries for a period of over 3000 years. In their restorations, the later builders were careful not to offend the memory of their predecessors. They sought out the old dedicatory inscriptions, and took steps to preserve them. They rejoiced when they came upon the old foundation stones. In their restorations they were careful to follow original designs; and likewise in the cult, so far from deviating from established custom, they strongly emphasized their desire to restore the cult to its original character, wherever an interruption for one reason or the other had taken place. In all this, the rulers were acting in accord with the popular instincts, for the masses clung tenaciously to the old sanctuaries, as affording an unfailing means of protection against the ills and accidents of life.

To enumerate all the temples of Babylonia and Assyria would be both an impossible and a useless task. Besides those mentioned in the historical texts and in the legal literature, we have long lists of temples prepared by the pedagogues. Some of these lists have been published;[1] others are to be found among the unpublished material in the British Museum collections.[2] It is doubtful whether even these catalogues were exhaustive, or aimed at being so; moreover, a large number of gods are known to us only from the lists of the pedagogues.[3]

---

[1] E.g., IIR. 50 (zikkurats); IIR. 61; IIIR. 66.
[2] See Bezold Catalogue, etc., p. 1776 and elsewhere.
[3] E.g., IIR. 54–60; IIIR. 67–69; VR. 43, 46.

So, to mention some, taken from a valuable list[1] which gives chiefly the names of foreign gods, together with the places where they were worshipped, we learn of such gods as Lagamal, Magarida, Lasimu, A-ishtu, Bulala, Katnu, Kannu, Kishshat, Kanishurra, Khiraitum. Knowing, as we do, that at various periods foreign deities were introduced into Babylonia and Assyria,[2] it was necessary to make some provision for their cult; and, while no doubt most of these minor deities and foreign gods were represented only by statues placed in some temple or temple precinct, it is equally certain that some had a shrine or sanctuary of some kind specially erected in their honor. In hymns, too, deities are mentioned that are otherwise unknown. So in a litany, published by Craig,[3] a long series of gods is introduced. Some are identical with those included in the list just referred to,[4] others appear here for the first time, as Mishiru, Kilili Ishi-milku. Epithets also occur in lists and hymns, that appear to belong to deities otherwise unknown. We are safe, therefore, in estimating the number of temples, zikkurats, and smaller shrines in Babylonia and Assyria to have reached high into the hundreds. Sanctuaries must have covered the Euphrates Valley like a network. By virtue of the older culture of the south and the greater importance that Babylonia always enjoyed from a religious point of view, the sanctuaries of the south were much more numerous than those of the north. For our purposes, it is sufficient to indicate some of the most important of the temples of the south and north. The oldest known to us at present is the frequently mentioned temple of E-Kur at Nippur, sacred to En-lil or the older Bel. Its history can be carried back to a period beyond 4000 B.C.; how far beyond cannot be determined until the early chronology

---

[1] IIR. 60, no. 1, obverse.
[2] See p. 172. Some of the gods invoked by Sennacherib (see p. 238), as Gaga, Sherua, and perhaps also Khani, are foreign deities.
[3] Assyrian and Babylonian Religious Texts, i. 56-59.
[4] As Lagamal, Kanishurra.

is better known than at present. We know, however, that from the time of Sargon [1] and probably even much earlier, the rulers who had control of Nippur devoted themselves to the embellishment of the temple area. Climatic conditions necessitated frequent repairs. The temple also suffered occasionally through political tumults, but with each century the religious importance of E-Kur was increased. Ur-Bau, we have seen, about 2700 B.C., erected a zikkurat in the temple area. Some centuries later we find Bur-Sin repairing the zikkurat and adding a shrine near the main structure. As the political fortunes of Nippur varied, so E-Kur had its ups and downs. Under the Cassitic rule, an attempt was made to recover for Nippur the position which it formerly occupied, but which had now passed over to Babylon. It was of little avail. Bel had to yield to Marduk, and yet, despite the means that the priests of Marduk took to transfer Bel's prerogatives to the new head of the pantheon, the rulers would not risk the anger of Bel by a neglect of E-Kur. Kurigalzu, a king of the Cassite dynasty (*c.* 1400 B.C.) brings back from Elam [2] a votive object which, originally deposited by Dungi in the Ishtar temple at Erech, was carried to Susa by an Elamitic conqueror about 900 years before Kurigalzu. The latter deposits this object not in Marduk's temple at Babylon, but in Bel's sanctuary at Nippur. During the entire Cassitic period, the kings continued to build or make repairs in the temple precinct, and almost every ruler is represented by more or less costly votive offerings made to Bel's sanctuary. In this way, we can follow the history of the temple down to the Assyrian period. In the twelfth century the religious supremacy of E-Kur yields permanently to E-Sagila. The temple is sacked, part of it is destroyed, and it was left to rulers of the north like Esarhaddon and Ashurbanabal to once more restore E-Kur

---

[1] See Peters' *Nippur*, II. chapter x, "The History of Nippur."
[2] *Ib.* II. 260. (Published in Hilprecht's *Old Babylonian Inscriptions*, i. 1. pl. 21, no. 43. See also pl. 8, no. 15.)

and its dependencies to its former proportions. These kings, especially the latter, devote much time and energy in rebuilding the zikkurat and in erecting various buildings connected with the temple administration. Under the new Babylonian dynasty, however, E-Kur was again destroyed, and this time by the ruthless hands of southern rulers. Nebuchadnezzar, so devoted to Marduk and Nabu, appears to have regarded E-Kur as a serious rival to E-Sagila and E-Zida. Some traces of building operations at E-Kur appear to date from the Persian period, but, practically, the history of E-Kur comes to an end at the close of the seventh century. The sanctity of the place, however, remained; a portion of the old city becomes a favorite burial site, while other parts continue to be inhabited till the twelfth century of our era. The city of Bel becomes the seat of a Christian bishop, and Jewish schools take the place once occupied by the "star-gazers of Chaldea."

The history of E-Kur, so intimately bound up with political events, may be taken as an index of the fortunes that befell the other prominent sanctuaries of Babylonia.

The foundation of the Shamash temple at Sippar, and known as E-Babbara, 'the brilliant house,' can likewise be traced as far back as the days of Naram-Sin. At that time there was already a sanctuary to Anunit within the precincts of E-Babbara. Members of the Cassite dynasty devote themselves to the restoration of this sanctuary. Through a subsequent invasion of the nomads, the cult was interrupted and the great statue of Shamash destroyed. Several attempts are made to reorganize the cult, but it was left for Nabubaliddin in the tenth century to restore E-Babbara to its former prestige. Esarhaddon and Ashurbanabal, who pay homage to the old Bel at Nippur, also devote themselves to Shamash at Sippar. They restore such portions of it as had suffered from the lapse of time and from other causes. Nebuchadnezzar is obliged to rebuild parts of E-Babbara, and the last king of Babylonia,

Nabonnedos, is so active in his building operations at Sippar, that he arouses the anger of the priests of Babylon, who feel that their ruler is neglecting the sanctuaries of Marduk and Nabu. It is through Nabonnedos[1] and Nabubaliddin,[2] chiefly, that we learn many of the details of the history of E-Babbara during this long period.

Of the other important temples that date from the early period of Babylonian history, we must content ourselves with brief indications.

The temple to Shamash at Larsa, while not quite as old as that of Sippar, was quite as famous. Its name was likewise E-Babbara. It is first mentioned in the inscriptions of Ur-Bau (*c*. 2700 B.C.), and it continues to enjoy the favor of the rulers till the Persian conquest.[3]

The two chief places for the moon-cult were Ur and Harran. The name of Sin's temple[4] at the former place was E-Gish-shir-gal, 'the house of the great light'; at the latter, E-khulklul, 'the house of joys.' Around both sanctuaries, but particularly around the former, cluster sacred traditions. We have seen that the moon-cult at an early period enjoyed greater importance than sun-worship. The temples of Sin were centers of intellectual activity. It is in these places that we may expect some day to find elaborate astronomical and astrological records. Harran, indeed, does not appear at any time to have played any political rôle[5] (though it was overrun occasionally by nomads), so that the significance of the place is due almost entirely to the presence of the great temple at

---

[1] VR. 63.   [2] VR. pls. 60, 61.

[3] So, *e.g.*, as late as the days of Nebopolassar (Scheil, *Recueil des Travaux*, xviii. 16).

[4] Besides this temple, there were two others, perhaps only chapels, dedicated to Sin at Ur: (*a*) E-te-im-ila (mentioned first by Ur-Bau, IR. pl. 1, no 4), and (*b*) E-Kharsag (mentioned first by Dungi, IR. 2, II. no. 2). The zikkurat at Ur had, of course, a special name (IIR. 50, obverse 18).

[5] See Nöldeke, *Zeitschrift für Assyriologie*, xi. 107–109. Hilprecht's theory (*Old Babylonian Inscriptions*, I. 2, 55) has not been accepted by scholars.

the place. It is Nabonnedos,[1] again, who endeavors to restore the ancient prestige of the sanctuary at Harran. E-anna, 'the lofty house,' was the name of Ishtar's famous temple at Erech. The mention of this temple in one of the creation narratives[2] and the part played by Ishtar of Erech in the Gilgamesh epic are sufficient indications of the significance of this structure. Historical inscriptions from the earliest period to the days of Ashurbanabal and Nebuchadnezzar come to our further aid in illustrating the continued popularity of the Ishtar cult in E-anna. The Ishtar who survives in Babylonia and Assyria is practically the Ishtar of Erech, — that is, Nanâ.[3]

Passing by such sanctuaries as E-shid-lam, sacred to Nergal at Cuthah, and coming to E-Sagila and E-Zida, the two great temples of Babylon and Borsippa, respectively, it is of course evident from the close connection between political development and religious supremacy, that Marduk's seat of worship occupies a unique position from the days of Hammurabi to the downfall of Babylonia. While the history of E-Sagila and E-Zida cannot be traced back further than the reign of Hammurabi, the temples themselves are considerably older. Previous to the rise of the city of Babylon as the political center, the Nabu cult in E-Zida must have been more prominent than the worship of Marduk in E-Sagila. Marduk was merely one solar deity among several, and a minor one at that, whereas the attributes of wisdom given to Nabu point to the intellectual importance that Borsippa had acquired. The Nabu cult was combined with the worship of Marduk simply because it could not be suppressed. At various times, as we have seen,[4] Nabu formed a serious rival to Marduk, and it will be recalled that up to a late period we find Nabu given the preference to Marduk in official documents.[5] The inseparable association of

---

[1] V R. 64, col. I. 3-9; col. II. 46.
[2] See p. 444.
[3] See p. 81.
[4] See pp. 126 *seq.*
[5] See p. 129.

E-Sagila and E-Zida is a tribute to Nabu which, we may feel
certain, the priests of Marduk did not offer willingly. But this
association becomes the leading feature in the history of the
two temples. To pay homage to Marduk and Nabu meant
something quite different from making a pilgrimage to the seat
of Bel or presenting a gift to the Shamash sanctuary at Sippar.
It was an acknowledgment of Babylonia's prestige. The
Assyrian rulers regarded it as both a privilege and a solemn
duty to come to Babylon and invoke the protection of Marduk
and Nabu. In E-Sagila the installation of the rulers over Babylonia took place, and a visit to Marduk's temple was incomplete without a pilgrimage across the river to E-Zida. The
influence exerted by these two temples upon the whole course
of Babylonian history from the third millennium on, can hardly
be overestimated. From the schools grouped around E-Sagila
and E-Zida, went forth the decrees that shaped the doctrinal
development of the religion of Babylonia and Assyria. In
these schools, the ancient wisdom was molded into the shape in
which we find it in the literary remains of the Euphrates Valley.
Here the past was interpreted and the intellectual future of the
country projected. The thought of E-Sagila and E-Zida must
have stored up emotions in the breast of a Babylonian and
Assyrian, that can only be compared to a pious Mohammedan's
enthusiasm for Mecca, or the longing of an ardent Hebrew for
Jerusalem. The hymns to Marduk and Nabu voice this emo-
tion. There is a fervency in the prayers of Nebuchadnezzar
which marks them off from the somewhat perfunctory invocations of the Assyrian kings to Ashur and Ishtar. An appreciation of the position of E-Sagila and E-Zida in Babylonian
history is an essential condition to an understanding of the
Babylonian-Assyrian religion. The priests of Marduk could
view with equanimity the rise and growth of Assyria's power.
The influence of E-Sagila and E-Zida was not affected by such
a shifting of the political kaleidoscope. Babylon remained the

religious center of the country. When one day, a Persian conqueror — Cyrus — entered the precincts of E-Sagila, his first step was to acknowledge Marduk and Nabu as the supreme powers in the world; and the successors of Alexander continue to glory in the title 'adorner of E-Sagila and E-Zida.'[1] With the same zeal that distinguishes a good Babylonian, Antiochus Soter hastens to connect his reign with the two temples by busying himself with their enlargement and beautification. There was no better way in which he could indicate, at the same time, his political control over the country.

One more factor contributing to the general influence of the Babylonian temples remains to be noted. In the course of time, all the great temples in the large centers became large financial establishments. The sources whence the temples derived their wealth were various. The kings both of Babylonia and Assyria took frequent occasions to endow the sanctuaries with lands or other gifts. At times, the endowment took the form of certain quantities of wine, corn, oil, fruits, and the like, for which annual provision is made; at times, the harvest derived from a piece of property is set aside for the benefit of the temple. In other ways, too, the temples acquired large holdings, through purchases of land made from the income accruing to it, and from the tithes which it became customary to collect. This property was either farmed through the authorities of the temple for the direct benefit of the sanctuary, or was rented out to private parties under favorable conditions. We learn of large bodies of laborers indentured to temples, as well as of slaves owned or controlled by the temples. These workmen were engaged for various purposes, — for building operations, for service in the fields, for working raw material, such as wool, into finished products, and much more the like. But, more than this, the temples engaged directly in commercial affairs, lending sums of money and receiving interest. In some

---

[1] So Antiochus Soter, V R. 66, col. i. l. 3.

sanctuaries, a thriving business of barter and exchange was carried on. Crops are sold, houses are rented by the temple agents, and there was scarcely an avenue of commerce into which the temples did not enter. An active business was also carried on in the manufacture and sale of idols, votive offerings, amulets, and the like. A very large number of the legal documents found in the Babylonian mounds deal with the business affairs of the temples.[1] Such a state of affairs naturally contributed towards making the temples important establishments and towards increasing the influence of the priests over the people.

The temples of Assyria play a minor part in the religious life of rulers and people. True, grand structures were reared in Ashur, Calah, Nineveh, and Arbela, and no important step was taken by the kings without consulting Ashur, Ishtar, or Ramman through the mediation of the priests. The great cities of Assyria also become intellectual centers. The priests of Arbela created a school of theological thought, but all these efforts were but weak imitations of the example furnished by the temples of the south. Even Ashurbanabal, whose ambition was to make Nineveh the center of religious and intellectual progress, failed of his purpose. His empire soon fell to decay, and with that decay Nineveh disappears from the stage of history. Babylon and Borsippa, however, remain, and continue to hand down to succeeding generations, the wisdom of the past.

The Sacred Objects in the Temples, — Altars, Vases, Images, Basins, Ships.

The earliest altars were made of the same material as the zikkurats and sanctuaries. One found at Nippur at an

---

[1] For a further account of the financial side of the temple establishments, see Peiser's excellent remarks in his *Babylonische Verträge des Berliner Museums*, pp. xvii–xxix.

exceedingly low level was of sun-dried bricks.[1] How early this material was replaced by stone, we are not in a position to say. Gudea, who imports diorite from the Sinai Peninsula to make statues[2] of himself, presumably uses a similar material for the sacred furnishings of his temples, though custom and conventionality may have maintained the use of the older clay material for some time. In Assyria, altars of limestone and alabaster became the prevailing types. The shape and size of the altars varied considerably. The oldest known to us, the one found at Nippur, was about twelve feet long and half as wide. The upper surface was surrounded by a rim of bitumen.[3] Assyrian altars now in the British museum are from two to three feet high. The ornamentation of the corners of the rim of the altar led to giving the altar the appearance of horns.[4] The base of the altar was either a solid piece with a circular or oblong plate resting on it, or the table rested on a tripod.[5] The latter species was well adapted for being transported from place to place by the Assyrian kings, who naturally were anxious to maintain the worship of Ashur and of other gods while on their military expeditions. Much care was spent upon the ornamentation of the altars, and, if we may believe Herodotus, the great altars at Babylon were made of gold.[6] In front of the altars stood large vases or jars of terra cotta, used for ablutions and other purposes in connection with the sacrifices. Two such jars, one behind the other, were found at Nippur. They were ornamented with rope patterns, and the depth at which they were found is an indication of the antiquity and

---

[1] Hilprecht, *Old Babylonian Inscriptions*, I. 2, p. 24.

[2] Nine magnificent diorite statues of Gudea were found by De Sarzec at Telloh.

[3] Ashes — the trace of sacrifices — were also found on the altar.

[4] See the illustrations in Perrot and Chipiez, *History of Art in Chaldea*, etc., I. 143, 255. Similar horns existed on the Hebrew and Phœnician altars.

[5] See the illustrations in Perrot and Chipiez, *ib.*, I. 194, 256, 257. On seal cylinders altar titles are frequently represented.

[6] Book I. sec. 183.

stability of the forms of worship in the Babylonian temples. It may be proper to recall that in the Solomonic temple, likewise, there were a series of jars that stood near the great altar in the large court.[1]

A piece of furniture to which great religious importance was attached was a great basin known as 'apsu,'—the name, it will be recalled, for 'the deep.' The name indicates that it was a symbolical representation of the domain of Ea. In Gudea's days the symbol is already known,[2] and it continues in use to the end of the Babylonian empire. The zikkurat itself being, as we saw, an attempt to reproduce the shape of the earth, the representation of the 'apsu' would suggest itself as a natural accessory to the temple. The zikkurat and the basin together would thus become living symbols of the current cosmological conceptions. Gudea already regards the zikkurat as a symbol. To make the ascent is a virtuous deed.[3] The thought of adding a symbol of the apsu belongs, accordingly, to the period when this view of the zikkurat was generally recognized. The shape of the 'sea' was oblong or round. It was cut of large blocks of stone and was elaborately decorated. One of the oldest[4] has a frieze of female figures on it, holding in their outstretched hands flagons from which they pour water. In Marduk's temple we learn that there were two basins,—a larger and a smaller one. The comparison with the great 'sea' that stood in the court of Solomon's temple naturally suggests itself, and there can be little doubt that the latter is an imitation of a Babylonian model.

Another sacred object in the construction of which much care was taken was the ship in which the deity was carried in

---

[1] See Schick, *Die Stiftshütte*, etc., pp. 119 *seq.*
[2] *Keils Bibl.* 3, 1, p. 13; see also p. 89.
[3] Inscription G, col. I. ll. 15–17. See p. 621.
[4] Described in De Sarzec's *Découvertes en Chaldée*, pp. 216, 217. For other specimens, see *ib.* pp. 106, 171; and see also Hilprecht, *Old Babylonian Inscriptions*, i. 2, p. 39, note.

solemn procession. It is again in the inscriptions of Gudea[1] that we come across the first mention of this ship. This ruler tells us that he built the 'beloved ship' for Nin-girsu, and gave it the name Kar-nuna-ta-uddua, the ship of 'the one that rises up out of the dam of the deep.' The ship of Nabu is of considerable size, and is fitted out with a captain and crew, has masts and compartments.[2] The ship resembled a moon's crescent, not differing much, therefore, from the ordinary flat-bottomed Babylonian boat with upturned edges. Through Nebuchadnezzar[3] we learn that these ships were brilliantly studded with precious stones, their compartments handsomely fitted out, and that in them the gods were carried in solemn procession on the festivals celebrated in their honor.[4] A long list[5] of such ships shows that it was a symbol that belonged to all the great gods. The ships of Nin-lil, Ea, Marduk, Sin, Shamash, Nabu, Ninib, Bau, Nin-gal, and of others are specially mentioned. A custom of this kind of carrying the gods in ships must have originated, of course, among a maritime people. We may trace it back, therefore, to the very early period when the sacred cities of Babylonia lay on the Persian Gulf. The use of the ships also suggests, that the solemn procession of the gods was originally on water and not on land, and it is likely that this excursion of the gods symbolized some homage to the chief water-deity, Ea. However this may be, the early significance became lost, but the custom survived in Babylonia of carrying the gods about in this way. In Assyria, less wedded to ancient tradition, we find statues of the gods seated on thrones or standing upright, carried directly on the shoulders of men.[6] In Egypt sacred ships are very common, and it is interesting to note as

---

[1] Inscription D, col. iii, 1-12.
[2] See Winckler's note, *Keils Bibl.* 3, 2, p. 16.
[3] IR. 54, col. iii. L 10.
[4] *Ib.* 55, col. iv. ll. 1, 2.
[5] IIR. 61. no. 2, obverse.
[6] See Perrot and Chipiez, *History of Art in Chaldea and Assyria*, I. 75, 76.

a survival of the old Babylonian and Egyptian custom that an annual gift sent by the khedive of Egypt to Mecca consists of a tabernacle, known as Mahmal, that presents the outlines of a ship.[1] The ark of the Hebrews appears, similarly, to have been originally a ship of some kind.

The ships of the Babylonian gods had names given to them, just as the towers and sanctuaries had their names. The name of Nin-girsu's ship has already been mentioned. Marduk's ship was appropriately known as Ma-ku-a, 'the ship of the dwelling.'[2] Similarly, a ship of the god Sin was called 'ship of light,' reminding one of the name of the great temple to the moon-god at Ur, 'the house of the great luminary.' The ship of Nin-gal, the consort of Sin, was called 'the lesser light.' Bau's ship was described by an epithet of the goddess as 'the ship of the brilliant offspring,' the reference being to the descent of the goddess from father Anu.[3] These illustrations will suffice to show the dependence of the names of the ships upon the names of the temples, with this important difference, however, that the names of the ships are chosen from a closer association with the gods to whom they belong. So a ship of En-lil was known simply as 'the ship of Bel,' and the ship of Naru,[4] the river-god, was called 'the ship of the Malku (or royal) canal'[5]—an indication, at the same time, of the place where the cult of Naru was carried on.

THE PRIESTS AND PRIESTESSES.

At a certain stage in the religious development of a people, the priesthood is closely linked to political leadership. The

---

[1] See the illustration in Snouck-Hurgronje *Mekka*, pl. V.
[2] *Ie.*, of the god, E-Kua being the name of the sacred chamber in Marduk's temple at Babylon. See p. 629, note 1.
[3] See p. 60.
[4] See p. 282.
[5] The largest canal in Babylonia.

earliest form of government in the Euphrates Valley is theocratic, and we can still discern some of the steps in the process that led to the differentiation of the priest from the secular ruler. To the latest times, the kings retain among their titles some[1] which have reference to the religious functions once exercised by them. The king who continued to be regarded as the representative of a god, nominated by some deity to a lofty position of trust and power, stood nearer to the gods than his subjects. In a certain sense, the king remained the priest *par excellence*. Hence the prominent part played by the ruler in the religious literature of the country. A large proportion of the hymns were composed for royalty. The most elaborate ritual dealt with the endeavor to secure oracles that might serve as a guide for the rulers. Astronomical reports were made and long series of omen tablets prepared for the use of the royal household. The calendars furnished regulations for the conduct of the kings. A ceremonial error, an offence against the gods on the part of the kings, was certain of being followed by disastrous consequences for the whole country.

But even the smallest sanctuaries required some service, and it was not long before the religious interests were entrusted into the hands of those who devoted themselves to administering the affairs of the temples. The guardians of the shrines became the priests in fact, long before the priesthood of the rulers became little more than a theory; and as the temples grew to larger proportions, the service was divided up among various classes of priests.

The general name for priests was *shangû*, which, by a plausible etymology suggested by Jensen,[2] indicates the function of the priest as the one who presides over the sacrifices. But this

---

[1] *E.g.*, *ishakku*.
[2] *Sha* and *nakû*, *i.e.*, 'the one over the sacrifice.' *Zeitschrift für Assyriologie*, vii. 174, note.

function represents only one phase of the priestly office in Babylonia, and not the most important one, by any means. For the people, the priest was primarily the one who could drive evil demons out of the body of the person smitten with disease, who could thwart the power of wizards and witches, who could ward off the attacks of mischievous spirits, or who could prognosticate the future and determine the intention or the will of the gods. The offering of sacrifices was one of the means to accomplish this end, but it is significant that many of the names used to designate the priestly classes have reference to the priest's position as the exorciser of evil spirts or his power to secure a divine oracle or to foretell the future, and not to his function as sacrificer. Such names are *mashmashu*, the general term for 'the charmer'; *kalû*, so called, perhaps, as the 'restrainer' of the demons, the one who keeps them in check; *lagaru*, a synonym of kalu; *makhkhû*, 'soothsayer'; *surrû*, a term which is still obscure; *shâilu*, the 'inquirer,' who obtains an oracle through the dead or through the gods; *mushêlu*, 'necromancer'; *âshipu* or *ishippu*, 'sorcerer.'[1] These names probably do not exhaust the various kinds of 'magicians' that were to be found among the Babylonian priests. In the eighteenth chapter of Deuteronomy, no less than eleven classes of magic workers are enumerated, and there can be little doubt but that the Pentateuchal opposition against the necromancers, sorcerers, soothsayers, and the like is aimed chiefly against Babylonish customs. We have seen in previous chapters how largely the element of magic enters into the religious rites and literature of the Babylonian-Assyrian religion and how persistent an element it is. For the masses, the priest remained essentially a *mashmashu*. But we have also names like *ramku* and *nisakku*, 'libation pourer,' which emphasize the sacrificial functions of

---

[1] That these terms represent classes of priests is indicated by the fact that the abstract derivatives shangûtu, kalûtu, ishippûtu, and also ramkûtu (see below) are used as general terms for priesthood.

the priest; and in an interesting list of temple servitors,[1] 'the dirge singers' are introduced as a special class, and appropriately designated as *munambû*, 'wailer,' and *lallaru*, 'howler.' Of some terms in this list, like *asinnu*, it is doubtful whether they indicate a special class of priests or are terms for servitors in general, attached to a temple; in the case of others, like *nâsh pilakki*, 'ax carrier,' we do not know exactly of what nature the service was.[2] Lastly, priests in their capacity as scribes[3] and as judges[4] formed another distinct class, though it should be noted that in Assyria we meet with scribes occasionally who are not priests.[5]

The range thus covered by the temple service, — magic, oracles, sacrifices, the lament for the dead, and the judiciary, — is exceedingly large. The subdivisions, no doubt, varied in each center. In the smaller sanctuaries, those who offered the sacrifices may also have served as soothsayers and dirge singers, and the judicial functions may likewise have been in the same hands as those who performed other services. On the other hand, in a temple like E-Sagila the classes and subclasses must have been very numerous. Of the details of the organization we as yet know very little. There was a high priest, known as the *shangam-makhû*,[6] and from the existence of a title like *sur-makhû*, — that is, the chief *surrû*,[7] — we may conclude that each class of priests had its chief likewise. With the natural tendency in ancient civilizations for professions to become vested in families, the priests in the course of time became a caste; but there is no reason to believe that entrance into this caste was only possible through the accident of birth. That instruction in the reading and writing of the cuneiform characters, and hence the introduction into the literature, was

---

[1] IIR. 32, no. 3.
[2] 'A spear carrier of Marduk' occurs in contract tablets.
[3] *Dupsharru*.
[4] *Daianu*.
[5] *E.g.*, IIIR. 48, no. 6, ll. 26, 27.
[6] *Shangu* = priest; *makhu* = great.
[7] See above, p. 657.

open to others than the scions of priests is shown by the presence in the legal literature of formal contracts for instruction between teachers and pupils who belong to the 'laity.' These pupils could become scribes and judges, and their standing as 'priests' represented merely the Babylonian equivalent to a modern university degree. For such service as the bewailing of the dead and as musicians, persons were initiated who were taken from various classes and likewise for the menial duties of the temples, and it is only when we come to the more distinctive priestly functions, like the exorcising of evil spirits, securing an oracle, or performing sacrifices, that the rules limiting these privileges to certain families were iron bound. As among the Hebrews and other nations, stress was laid also upon freedom from physical blemishes in the case of the priests. The leper, we learn, was not fit for the priesthood.[1] In the astronomical reports that were spoken of in a previous chapter,[2] there are references to the 'watches' kept by the astronomers. These watches, however, were probably not observed for astronomical purposes alone, but represent the time division, as among the Hebrews, for the temple service. There were three night watches among the Babylonians,[3] and, in all probability, therefore, three day watches likewise. Relays of priests were appointed in the large sanctuaries for service during the continuance of each watch, and we may some day find that the Hebrews obtained their number of twenty-four priests for each 'watch' from a custom prevailing in some Babylonian temple.

An interesting feature of the Babylonian priesthood is the position occupied by the woman. In the historical texts from the days of Hammurabi onward, the references to women

---

[1] Delitzsch, *Assyr. Handwörterbuch*, p. 149b.
[2] See pp. 356 *seq.*
[3] On these night watches, see Delitzsch's article in the *Zeitschrift für Keilschriftforschung*, ii. 284-294.

attached to the service of temples are not infrequent. Gudea expressly mentions the 'wailing women,' and there is every reason to believe that the female wailers, like the male ones, belong to some priestly class. Again, examples of women as exorcisers and as furnishing oracles[1] may be instanced in Babylonia as well as in Assyria, and we have also references to female musicians as late as the days of Ashurbanabal. A specially significant rôle was played by the priestesses in Ishtar's temple at Erech, and probably at other places where the cult of the great mother goddess was carried on. The Ishtar priestess was known by the general term of Kadishtu, — that is, 'the holy one,' — or Ishtaritum, 'devoted to Ishtar'; but, from the various other names for the sacred harlot that we come across,[2] it would appear that the priestesses were divided into various classes, precisely like the priests. That in the ceremonies of initiation at Erech, and perhaps elsewhere, some rites were observed that on the surface appeared obscene is eminently likely; but there is no evidence that obscene rites, as instanced by Herodotus, formed part of the *regular* cult of the goddess. Except in the case of the Ishtar worship, the general observation may be made that the position of the priestess is more prominent in the early period of Babylonian history than in the days when the culture and power of Babylonia and Assyria reached its zenith.

Sacrifices and Votive Offerings.

The researches of Robertson Smith[3] and of others have shown that the oldest Semitic view of sacrifice was that of a meal, shared by the worshipper with the deity to be honored or

---

[1] See above, pp. 267, 343.

[2] *Kharimtu, Kizritu, Ukhatu, Shamuktu.* See IIR. 32, no. 2, ll. 31-36, and above, pp. 475, 484.

[3] See his article on "Sacrifice" in the 9th edition of the *Encyclopaedia Britannica* and his *Religion of the Semites*, Lectures VI-XI.

propitiated. Dependent as we are in the case of the Babylonian-Assyrian religion for our knowledge of sacrifices upon incidental references in historical or religious texts, it is not possible to say how far the Semitic dwellers of the Euphrates Valley were influenced by the primitive conception of sacrifice. Historical and votive inscriptions and a religious literature belong to a comparatively advanced stage of culture, and earlier views of sacrifice that may have existed were necessarily modified in the process of adaptation to later conditions. The organization of an elaborate cult with priests and numerous temple servitors changes the sacrifices into a means of income for the temple. The deity's representatives receive the share originally intended for the deity himself; and, instead of sanctifying the offering to a god by contact with the sacred element fire, the temple accepts the offering for its own use. It is likely, however, that among the Babylonians, as among the Hebrews, certain parts of the animal which were not fit to eat [1] were burned as a symbolical homage to a god. No references have as yet been found pointing to any special sanctity that was attached to the blood; but it is eminently likely that the blood was regarded at all times as the special property of the gods, and was poured on the altar. The two kinds of sacrifice — animals and vegetable products — date from the earliest period of the Babylonian religion of which we have any knowledge. In a long list of offerings, Gudea [2] includes oxen, sheep, goats, lambs, fish, birds (as eagles, cranes,[3] etc.), and also such products as dates, milk, and greens. From other sources we may add gazelles, date wine, butter, cream, honey, garlic, corn, herbs, oil, spices, and incense. Stress is laid upon the quality of the sacrifice.[4] The animals must be

---

[1] So in the regulations of the priestly code (Lev. lii. 14–17).
[2] Inscription G, cols. iii–vi.
[3] Hardly 'roosters,' as Jensen (*Kosmologie*, p. 517) proposes.
[4] See, *e.g.*, Gudea, Inscription F, cols. iii, iv.

without blemish, and if well nurtured, they would be all the more pleasing in the sight of the gods. The omission of dogs and swine is not accidental. Under that double aspect of sanctity which we find among the Babylonians as among so many nations, certain animals were too sacred to be offered, and, on the other hand, they were regarded as unclean.[1] In treating of the omen texts we already had occasion to speak of the peculiar ideas attached to the dog by the Babylonians,[2] and there is sufficient evidence to show that the boar likewise was viewed as a sacred animal, at least in certain parts of Babylonia.[3] No certain traces of human sacrifices have been found, either in Babylonian literature or in artistic representations.[4] If the rite was ever practised among the Babylonians or Assyrians it must have been at a very early period — earlier than any of which we as yet have any knowledge. On the other hand, a trace of some primitive form of tree worship may be recognized in the representation, so frequent on seal cylinders and monuments, of curious figures, in part human, in part animal, standing in front of the palm tree.[5] The symbol belongs to Assyria as well as to Babylonia. In some of the designs the figures — human heads and bodies but furnished with large wings — appear to be in the act of artificially fertilizing the palm tree by scattering the male blossom over the female palm. This plausible interpretation first suggested by E. B. Tylor[6] carries with it the conclusion that the importance

---

[1] See on this general subject Marillier's admirable articles, "La Place du Totemisme dans l'évolution religieuse" (*Revue de l'Histoire des Religions*, xxxvi).

[2] See pp. 397, 398.

[3] See Peters' *Nippur*, II. 131, and Hilprecht, *Cuneiform Texts*, ix. pl. xiii.

[4] See Ward, "On Some Babylonian Cylinders supposed to represent Human Sacrifices" (*Proc. Amer. Oriental Soc.*, May, 1888, pp. xxviii-xxx).

[5] See, *e.g.*, Layard, *Monuments of Nineveh*, 1st series, pls. 7, 25; Place, *Ninève et l'Assyrie*, pl. 46, etc.

[6] "The Winged Figures of the Assyrian and Other Ancient Monuments," *Proc. Soc. Bibl. Arch.*, xii. 383-393; see also Bonavia, "The Sacred Trees of the Assyrian Monuments," *Babylonian and Oriental Record*, vols. iii, iv, whose conclusions, however, are not always acceptable.

of palm culture in the Euphrates Valley not only gave the palm the character of a sacred tree, but lent to the symbol a wider significance to a more advanced age, as illustrating fertility and blessings in general. The scene, reproduced in almost endless variations in which both trees and figures become conventionalized, came to be regarded as a symbol of adoration and worship in general. As such, it survived in religious art and continued to be pictured on seal cylinders to a late age.

The occasions on which sacrifices were brought were frequent. If the gods were to be consulted for the purpose of obtaining an oracle, elaborate offerings formed a necessary preliminary. In this case, the animals presented at the altar served a double purpose.[1] They constituted a means of propitiating the god in favor of the petitioner, and at the same time the inspection of certain parts of the animal served as an omen in determining what was the will of the god appealed to. When the foundations were to be laid for a temple or a palace, it was especially important to secure the favor of the gods by suitable offerings, and, similarly, when a canal was to be built or any other work of a public character undertaken. Again, upon the dedication of a sacred edifice or of a palace, or upon completing the work of restoration of a temple, sheep and oxen in abundance were offered to the gods, as well as various kinds of birds and the produce of the orchards and fields. The Babylonian rulers appear to have accompanied their sacrifices on such occasions with prayers, and in a previous chapter we had occasion to discuss some of these dedicatory invocations.[2] In the Assyrian inscriptions, prayers are specifically referred to only as being offered before setting out on an expedition, before a battle, or when the kings find themselves in distress,[3] so that if the Babylonian custom likewise prevailed

---

[1] See chapter xix, " Oracles and Omens."
[2] See pp. 295-299.
[3] See, *e.g.*, Sennacherib, IR. 47, col. v. ll. 50-54; Ashurbanabal, Rassam Cylinder, col. ii. l. 116, and col. iv. L 9.

in Assyria, it did not form a necessary part of the sacrificial ritual. The sacrifice as a pure homage is illustrated by the zeal which the Assyrian kings manifest towards honoring the great temples of the south. The northern rulers were anxious at all times to reconcile the southern population to Assyrian control, and it was no doubt gratifying to the south to find Tiglathpileser II.,[1] upon entering the ancient centers like Sippar, Nippur, Babylon, Borsippa, Cuthah, Kish, Dilbat, and Erech, proceeding to the temples in those places in order to offer his sacrifices. The example of Tiglathpileser is followed by his successors down through the time of Ashurbanabal. As often as the Assyrian monarchs may have had occasion to proceed to Babylonia — and the occasions were frequent, owing to the constant disposition of the south to throw off the hated yoke — they emphasized their devotion to Marduk, Nabu, En-lil, Shamash, and the other gods who had their seats in the south. Sargon[2] goes so far in this homage as to pose as the reorganizer of the cults of Sippar, Nippur, Borsippa, and Babylon, and of restoring the income to temples in other places.[3] But there was another side to this homage that must not be overlooked. By sacrificing in the Babylonian temples, the Assyrian rulers indicated their political control over the south. Such homage as they manifested was the exclusive privilege of legitimate rulers, and it was important for the Assyrians to legitimize their control over the south.

A phase of sacrifice is represented by the libations of oil and wine to which frequent references are found in the historical texts. It appears to have been customary to anoint the foundation stones of temples and palaces with oil and wine. Over the thresholds, too, and over the stones — bearing commemorative or votive inscriptions — libations of oil, honey, and wine were poured.

---

[1] IIR. 67, 11, 12.   [2] Cylinder, l. 4.
[3] Winckler, *Die Keilschrifttexte Sargon's Prunkinschrift*, ll. 134, 135.

Nebopolassar[1] speaks of placing sweet herbs under the walls, and Nabonnedos[2] pours oil over the bolts and doors, as well as on the thresholds of the Shamash temple at Sippar, and fills the temple with the aroma of frankincense. Much importance was attached to this rite, and the kings take frequent occasion to adjure their successors who may in the course of restoring edifices come across stones bearing the record of former builders, to anoint these stones with oil and offer sacrifices.[3] Thus, Nabonnedos,[4] when he finds the inscription of Ashurbanabal in the Shamash temple at Sippar, carefully obeys the injunction. The rite bears all the marks of great antiquity. The instances of its occurrence in the Old Testament — notably in the case of Jacob's act of pouring oil over the holy stone at Bethel[5] — confirm this view; and the interpretation for the rite suggested by Robertson Smith[6] that the oil was originally the fat of the sacrificed animal smeared over an object or a person, as a means of investing them with sanctity, accounts satisfactorily for the invariable juxtaposition in the cuneiform texts of sacrificial offerings with the anointing of the inscribed stones.

We have no evidence that the rulers of Babylonia and Assyria were anointed with oil on their installation, though it is not improbable that such was the case. The use of the oil in this case is but a modification of the same rite, which, it is to be noted, loses some of its ancient force by the spread of the custom in the Orient of unguents as a part of the toilet.[7] The use of odorous herbs, which, we have seen, were placed under the walls, and of honey and wine, which were poured over bolts,[8] is also directly connected with the sacrificial cult.

---

[1] Hilprecht, *Old Babylonian Inscriptions*, i. 1, pl. 33, col. ii. ll. 54-56.

[2] VR. 65, col. ii. l. 13.

[3] See, e.g., Tiglathpileser I., IR. 16, col. viii. ll. 56, 57; Sennacherib, IR. 47, col. vi. l. 67-71.

[4] VR. 64, col. ii. ll. 43-45.

[5] Gen. xxviii. 18.

[6] *Religion of the Semites*, p. 364.

[7] See Robertson Smith, *ib.* p. 215.

[8] VR. 61, col. iv. ll. 33, 34.

The libation in its purer form appears in the custom of the Assyrian kings of pouring wine over the animal slain by them in the hunt. The act is intended to secure divine favor towards a deed which involved the destruction of something that by all ancient nations was held sacred, namely, life. Even a despot of Assyria felt that to wantonly destroy life could not be safely undertaken without making sure of the consent of the gods. Significantly enough, Ashurbanabal offers his libations after the lion or bull hunts to Ishtar as the "goddess of battle."[1] The animal is sanctified by being devoted to a goddess, just as the victims in a battle constitute the conqueror's homage offered to the gods who came to his assistance.

Sacrifices with libations are so frequently represented on the seal cylinder that this testimony alone would suffice to vouch for the importance attached to this rite in the cult. One of the most archaic specimens of Babylonian art[2] represents a worshipper, entirely naked, pouring a libation into a large cup which stands on an altar. Behind the altar sits a goddess who is probably Â or Malkâtu, the consort of the sun-god. The naked worshipper is by no means an uncommon figure in the early Babylonian art,[3] and it would appear that at one time it was customary to remove one's garments preliminary to stepping into the god's presence, just as among the Arabs the cult of the Caaba in Mecca was conducted by the worshippers at an early period without their clothes.[4] The custom so frequently referred to in the Old Testament to remove one's shoes upon entering sacred territory, — a custom still observed by the modern Muslim, who leaves his shoes outside of the Mosque, — may be regarded as an indication that at an earlier period people removed their garments as well as the sandals. It may

---

[1] IR. 7, no. ix.

[2] Heuzey in De Sarzec's *Découvertes en Chaldée*, p. 209.

[3] Several examples occur in De Sarzec's *Découvertes en Chaldée*. See also Ward, *Proc. Amer. Oriental Soc.*, May, 1888, p. xxix, and Peters' *Nippur*, ii. pl. 2.

[4] Wellhausen, *Reste Arabischen Heidenthums*, p. 106.

be that the order to take off the sandal alone, as recorded in the Old Testament, is nothing but a euphemistic phrase (suggested by a more refined age) to strip oneself. Certainly, when we find that in the days of Saul, the seers went about naked, there can no longer be any doubt that there was a time when the Hebrews, too, like the Arabs and Babylonians, entered the holy presence naked.

The institution of daily sacrifices is vouched for in the case of the larger religious centers like Babylonia, Borsippa, Sippar, Cuthah, as well as Nineveh for the late periods. Nebuchadnezzar, for example, tells us[1] that he provided for a sacrifice of six lambs daily in the temple E-shidlam at Cuthah, sacred to Nergal and Laz; while for Nabu's temple at Borsippa, the daily sacrifices were arranged on a still larger scale, and included two fattened bulls of perfect form, sixteen smaller animals, besides offerings of fish, birds, leek, various kinds of wine, honey, cream, and the finest oil, — all intended, as the king tells us, for the table of Nabu and his consort. No doubt the daily official sacrifices at Marduk's temple were even more elaborate. The custom of regular sacrifices in the larger temples may be traced back to an early period. The technical terms for such sacrifices are *sattâku* and *ginû*. Both terms convey the idea of being "fixed," perpetual,[2] and suggest a comparison with the Pentateuchal institution of the *tamid*,[3] *i.e.*, the daily sacrifice. Whenever the kings in their inscriptions mention the regular sacrifices, it is in almost all cases with reference to their reinstitution of an old custom that had been allowed to fall into neglect (owing to political disturbances which always affected the temples), and not as an innovation. Innovations were limited to increasing the amounts of these

---

[1] Grotefend Cylinder, col. ii. ll. 36–39.

[2] They are also used in the sense of any permanent provision for a temple through an endowment.

[3] Lit., 'the steady' sacrifice. See the technical employment, Dan. viii. 11.

regular sacrifices. So, for example, Nabubaliddin restores and increases the *ginê* of the great temple E-babbara at Sippar.[1] But regular sacrifices do not necessarily involve daily offerings. The same terms, *ginû* and *sattûku*, are applied frequently to monthly offerings, and except in the large religious centers, regular sacrifices were in all probabilities brought on certain days of each month, and not daily. The days thus singled out, as will be shown further on, differed for various sanctuaries. It would be important if we could determine the share in these regular sacrifices taken by the people at large, but the material at hand does not suffice for settling the question. There are frequent references to tithes in the clay tablets forming part of the archives of temples, and monthly tributes are also mentioned. We certainly may conclude from these references that the people were taxed in some way for the support of the temples. Ashurbanabal in one place speaks of reimposing upon the population of the south the provision for the *sattûku* and *ginû* due to Ashur and Belit[2] and the gods of Assyria; but, for all that, it is not certain that the regular sacrifices at the temples partook of a popular character. One gains the impression that, except on the occasions when the people came to the sanctuaries for individual purposes, the masses as such had but comparatively little share in it. In this respect the cult of the Hebrews, which has so many points in common with the Babylonian ritual as to justify the hypothesis that the details of sacrificial regulations in the priestly code are largely derived from practices in Babylonian temples, was more democratic. Closely attached as the Babylonians were to their sanctuaries, the regular sacrifices do not appear to have been an active factor in maintaining this attachment. A more decidedly popular character is apparent in the votive offerings made to the temples. These offerings cover a wide

---

[1] V R. 61, col. iv. L 48–col. v. L 6; see also Ashurbanabal, Rassam Cylinder, col. iv. L 90. [2] Belit here used for Ashur's consort; see p. 226.

range. Rulers and people alike felt prompted to make gifts to the sanctuaries on special occasions, either as a direct homage to the gods or with the avowed purpose and hope of securing divine favor or divine intercession.

The statues of themselves which the rulers from the days of Gudea[1] on were fond of erecting were dedicated by them as offerings to the gods, and this avowed aim tempers, in a measure, the vanity which no doubt was the mainspring of their action. The statues were placed in the temples, and from Gudea[2] we learn of the elaborate ceremonies connected with the dedication of one of the king's colossal blocks of diorite. For seven days all manual labor was interrupted in Lagash. Masters and slaves shared in the festivities. The temple of Nin-girsu is sanctified anew by purification rites, and the statue is formally presented to the god amidst sacrifices and offerings of rich gifts. The account given in the Book of Daniel[3] of the dedication of Nebuchadnezzar's statue may be regarded as an equally authentic picture of a custom that survived to the closing days of the Babylonian monarchy, except that we have no proof that divine honors were paid to these statues.[4] The front, sides, and back of Gudea's images were covered with inscriptions, partly of a commemorative character, but in part, also, conveying a dedication to Nin-girsu. Similarly, the steles of the Assyrian kings, set up by them either in the temples or on the highways beyond the confines of Assyria, and which had images of the rulers sculptured on them in high relief, were covered with inscriptions, devoted primarily to celebrating the deeds of the kings; but, since the victories of the armies were ascribed to the assistance furnished by the gods, an homage to Ashur or some other deity was involved in the

---

[1] See p. 652.
[2] Inscription B, cols. vii–viii.
[3] Chapter iii. 1–7.
[4] This touch appears to have been added by the Hebrew writer. Nebuchadnezzar is but a disguise for Antiochus Epiphanes.

recital. That the gods were accorded a minor share of the glory was but in keeping with the pride of the Assyrian rulers, who were less affected than the rulers of the south by the votive character of the statues.

Both Babylonians and Assyrians, however, unite in making images of the gods as a distinct homage, and in giving elaborate presents of gold, silver, precious stones, costly woods, and garments to the sanctuaries as votive offerings to the gods. These presents were used in the decoration of temples and shrines, as well as of the statues of the gods or as direct contributions to the temple treasury. Celebrations of victories were chosen as particularly appropriate occasions for making such votive offerings. So Agumkakrimi, upon bringing back to E-Sagila the statues of Marduk and Sarpanitum that had been taken away by ruthless hands, bestows rich gifts upon the temples and describes[1] at great length the costly garments embroidered with gold and studded with precious stones that were hung on Marduk and his consort. Equally vivid is the description of the high, conical-shaped caps, made of lapis lazuli and gold, and decorated, furthermore, with various kinds of stones, that were placed on the heads of the deities. Garments for the statues of the gods appear to have been favorite votive offerings at all times. Nabubaliddin, in restoring the cult of Shamash at Sippar, makes provisions for an elaborate outfit of garments,[2] specifying different garments for various periods of the year. It would appear from this that for the various festive occasions of the year, the garments of the gods were changed, much as in other religions — including the Catholic Church — the officiating priests are robed in different garments on the various festive or solemn occasions.

Votive tablets or discs of lapis lazuli, agate, turquoise, gold, silver, copper, antimony, and other metals with dedicatory

---

[1] VR. 33, col. ii. l. 22-col. iii. l. 12.
[2] VR. 61, col. vi. ll. 1-13.

inscriptions were deposited in the temples. What particular purpose they served we do not know. As a specimen of the more common formula on these tablets, a lapis lazuli tablet of Nippur may be chosen. It is offered by a Cassite king, and reads [1] as follows:

> To Bel
> His lord
> Kadashman-Turgu
> For his life
> Presented.

A knob-shaped object [2] of fine limestone contains a dedication in similar phrases to Marduk. It is offered by Bel-epush, who is probably identical with a Babylonian ruler of this name in the seventh century, — a contemporary of Sennacherib: [3]

> To Marduk, his lord
> Bel-epush for the preservation of his life
> Made and presented.

Kings, however, do not appear to be the only ones for whom these votive offerings were prepared. A dedication to a personage otherwise unknown and to all appearances a layman reads: [4]

> To Ea,[5] his lord, Bel-zir,
> Son of Ea-bân,
> For the preservation of his life
> Made and presented.

The formulas are thus seen to be conventional ones, though occasionally the inscription is somewhat longer. So, for example, Nazi-Maruttash, another Cassite king, puts a little prayer on a votive offering:

---

[1] Hilprecht, *Old Babylonian Inscriptions*, i. 1, pl. 23, no. 62.

[2] In the museum at Copenhagen. Described by Knudtzon in the *Zeits. f. Assyr.*, xii. 255.

[3] Tiele, *Babylonisch-Assyrische Geschichte*, p. 287.

[4] In the Berlin Museum (Knudtzon, *ib.*). It is also on a knob which contains remains of an iron stick, to which, evidently, the knob was fastened.

[5] Written A-e.

[To Bel, his lord]
Nazi-Maruttash,
Son of Kurigalzu,
To hearken to his supplication,
To be favorable to his prayer,
To accept his entreaty,
To lengthen his days,
[He made and presented].

This inscription appears, as Dr. Hilprecht informs us,[1] on an ax made of imitation lapis lazuli.[2] Other votive inscriptions are found on rings and on knobs of ivory or magnesite.[3] These various designs no doubt all had some symbolical significance. The ring suggests some ultimate connection between votive offerings and amulets. The seal cylinders, we know, although put to practical use in impressing the design on a clay tablet as a substitute for a personal signature, were also regarded as amulets, and this accounts for the frequency with which scenes of religious worship were introduced as designs on the cylinders. The ring is distinctly an amulet in Babylonia as elsewhere, and hence it is by no means improbable that the custom of carrying little inscribed tablets, discs, or knobs about the person as a protection against mischances preceded the use of such tablets as votive offerings to be placed in a temple.

A very common votive object in Babylonia, especially in the earlier period, was the clay cone. Such cones were found in large numbers at Lagash, while at Nippur Peters came across what may be safely regarded as a magazine where such cones (and other votive objects) were manufactured in large numbers.[4] The cones of Gudea bear conventional inscriptions of a votive character addressed to Nin-girsu. In other temples,

---

[1] Hilprecht, *Old Babylonian Inscriptions*, i. 1, p. 58.
[2] In reality, glass colored with cobalt. On this production of false lapis lazuli, see Peters' *Nippur*, ii. 134.
[3] For examples, see Hilprecht, *ib.*, pl. 18, no. 34; pl. 23, nos. 56, 57; pl. 25, nos. 66, 69; pl. 26, no. 70.
[4] Peters' *Nippur*, ii. 77, 133.

other gods were similarly remembered. It has been customary to regard these cones as phallic symbols;[1] but it should be noted that not only is the evidence for this lacking, but that what we know of the popular practices of the Babylonians does not warrant us in assuming any widespread phallic symbolism. The point of the cones suggests rather that the objects were intended to be stuck into the ground or into walls. At Lagash De Sarzec found, besides cones, a large number of copper statuettes[2] of gods and goddesses and of animals, — chiefly bulls, — all terminating in a sharp point or attached to a cone-shaped object. Others again are clearly human figures, either male personages holding the cone in their hands,[3] or females holding baskets on their heads, — the customary attitude of making an offering. These curious statuettes frequently bear inscriptions of a votive character, and there can be no doubt that they were used to be stuck into some substance. At one place, De Sarzec found a series set up in concentric circles[4] in the corners of an edifice and under the floor. Heuzey is of the opinion that these statuettes thus arranged were to serve as a warning for the demons, but it is more in keeping with the general character of the Babylonian religion to look upon these objects simply as votive offerings placed at various parts of a building as a means of securing the favor of the gods. The cone, I venture to think, is merely the conventionalized shape of a votive object originally intended to be stuck into some part of a sacred building. The large quantity of cones that have been found at Lagash, Nippur, and elsewhere is an indication of their popular use. It is not improbable that at one time, and, at all events, in certain temples, the cones and statuettes represented the common votive offerings with which worshippers

---

[1] So, *e.g.*, Peters' *Nippur*, ii. 237, 238, 378, 379.
[2] De Sarzec, *Découvertes en Chaldée*, pls. 1 bis and 28.
[3] The opinion has been advanced that the personage who holds the cone-shaped object is the fire-god turning the fire drill, but this is highly improbable.
[4] *Découvertes en Chaldée*, p. 239.

provided themselves upon entering the sacred precinct. To facilitate the reproduction of the statuettes, moulds were used, — another indication of the widespread use of these objects. Clay figures of gods and goddesses were also made in moulds or modelled by hand and served as votive offerings. At Nippur, the images represent chiefly Bel and Belit,[1] either separately or in combination; but figurines of Ishtar have also been found.[2] In some the goddess is represented as suckling a child. Often she is pictured as naked, clasping her breasts or her womb. The attitude which was suggested by the character of the goddess as the promoter of fertility appears to have been too obscene to a more refined age, and, accordingly, we find in later times the sexual parts suppressed or the figure properly clothed. The character of these figurines varied naturally with each religious center, and even in the same center modifications were introduced.

Whether these clay figurines, cones, and metallic statuettes were also placed by individuals in their dwellings, like the "plague" tablets,[3] we cannot as yet definitely say, but it is more than likely that such was the case. The *teraphim* familiar to us from the references in the Old Testament,[4] and evidently used as talismans, belong to the class of votive offerings under consideration. The figurines and cones, and also (though to a smaller degree) the copper statuettes, thus introduce us to the popular phases of the cult. As symbols of homage they appear to have survived to a late period, and their use as talismans did not materially affect their character as offerings, made by the people upon seeking the sanctuaries. The more costly objects, as vases,[5] artistically worked weapons, handsome "seas" bowls, altars, and statues of the gods and

---

[1] Peters' *Nippur*, ii. 376, and Hilprecht, *Cuneiform Texts*, ix. pl. 12.
[2] Peters, *ib.* pp. 374, 375.
[3] See p. 536.
[4] *E.g.*, Gen. xxxi. 19.
[5] See the specimens and descriptions in *Découvertes en Chaldée*, pl. 44 and p. 234.

other furniture for the temples were left to the rulers. Such offerings were made with great pomp. They were formally dedicated by large processions of priests, with the accompaniment of hymns and music. The kings of Assyria presented the captured gods as votive gifts pleasing to their deity.[1] They bring back with them from their campaigns the beams of the edifices that they destroyed and offer them to Ishtar.[2] Upon coming to Babylonia, they do not fail to bring presents of gold, silver, precious stones, copper, iron, purple, precious garments, and scented woods to Marduk and Sarpanitum, to Nabu and Tashmitum, and the other great gods.[3] The first fruits of extensive groves are offered by Ashurnasirbal to Ashur and the temples of his land.[4] The rulers of Assyria vie with the kings of Babylonia in presenting gardens[5] and lands to the gods as votive offerings; but for all that, in ancient Babylonia and Assyria, as among other peoples of antiquity, the more fervent religious spirit was manifested in the small tokens of the masses, whose attachment to the temples was of a different order from that which prompted the rulers of the north and south to a display, in which vanity and the desire to manifest their power play a larger part as one generation succeeds the other.

FESTIVALS.

We have seen[6] that in the developed system of the Babylonian religion, every day of the year had some significance, and that certain days in each month — so, *e.g.*, the 7th, 14th, 19th, 21st, and 28th — had a special significance. It has also been pointed out that in different religious centers, the days singled out for special significance differed. In view of this, we must

---

[1] Tiglathpileser I. (IR. 12, col. iv. l. 23) presents twenty-five gods of the land of Sugi.   [5] V R. 60, col. ii. ll. 11–16.
[2] Ashurnasirbal, IR. 25, col. iii. ll. 91, 92.
[3] Winckler, *Die Keilschrifttexte Sargon's Prunkinschrift*, ll. 141–143.
[4] IR. 27, 8–10.   [6] See pp. 373–383.

be prepared to find that the festival days were not the same in all parts of Babylonia, nor necessarily identical in the various periods of Babylonian and Assyrian history.

The common name for festival was *isinnu*. If we may judge from the use of *assinnu* as a general name for priest,[1] — a servant of a deity, — the underlying stem appears to signify simply 'to serve.' Another name that reveals more as to the character of the Babylonian festivals is *tashiltu*, which is used as a synonym for 'joy, delight.' The festivals were indeed joyous occasions, marked by abundance of offerings and merry-making, though, as we shall see, the somber note in the rejoicings was not absent. The kings dedicate their temples and palaces amidst manifestation of rejoicing. They pray that the gods may occupy the dwellings prepared for them "in joy and jubilance,"[2] and the reference to festivals in the historical texts are all of such a character as to make us feel that the Babylonian could apppreciate the Biblical injunction to "rejoice"[3] in the divine presence, on the occasions set apart as, in a peculiar sense, sacred.

Defective as our knowledge of the ancient Babylonian festivals still is, the material at our disposal shows that at a comparatively early period, there was one day in the year on which a festival was celebrated in honor of a god or goddess that had a more important character than any other. In the developed zodiacal system of Babylonia each month is sacred to a deity.[4] This system was perfected under the direct influence of the theological schools of Babylonia, but so much of it, at all events, rests upon ancient traditions which assigns a month to each god; and since Marduk is not accorded the first place, but takes his position in a group of solar deities,

---

[1] See above, p. 658.

[2] This is a standing phrase in the inscriptions of Nebuchadnezzar, as well as of other kings. See Delitzsch, *Assyr. Handwörterbuch*, p. 270b.

[3] Deut. xii. 18; xvi. 14, etc.

[4] See pp. 462, 463.

and since, moreover, these solar deities have a position in the calendar which accords with their specific solar character,[1] we may proceed a step further and assume with some confidence that the Babylonian scholars were guided — in large part, at least — by ancient traditions in parceling out the months as they did. Anu, Bel, and Ea, it is true, may have been assigned to the first three months because of the preëminent position of these three gods as a special triad; but even here the antiquity of the triad furnishes a guarantee that the association of some month with some deity belongs to a very ancient period of Babylonian history. This being the case, it would be natural that the first day of the month sacred to a deity would be regarded as his or her festival *par excellence*, and in the case of the cult of a deity spreading beyond its original limits, this festival would assume a more general character. On this day the people would come from all parts of the district within which the cult was carried on, to pay their homage to the god or goddess. In the days of Gudea, we find Bau occupying this superior rank. Her festival had assumed such importance as to serve for reckoning the commencement of the year.

Hence it became known simply as the day of zag-muku,[2] that is, the New Year's Day.[3] Whether this festival of Bau was recognized as the New Year's Day throughout Babylonia, we do not know, but it must have been observed in a considerably extensive district, or Gudea would have made the attempt to give some festival connected with his favorite deity Nin-girsu this character. As it is, he can only combine Bau's festival with the cult of Nin-girsu, by making the New Year's Day the occasion of a symbolical marriage between the god and the goddess. Nin-girsu is represented as offering marriage

---

[1] See *ib*.   [3] *rêsh shatti*. See p. 681.

[2] Or zag-mu. Gudea, Inscription G, col. iii. In the later inscriptions we find zag-mu-ku. The *k* or *ku* appears to be an afformative. See Amiaud, *Zeits. f. Assyr*. lii. 41. The reading za-am-mu-ku is found, IR. 67, col. i. l. 34.

gifts to Bau,[1] on the Zagmuku. How early Bau came to occupy so significant a rank has not been ascertained. It is her quality as the 'great mother,' as the goddess of fertility and abundance,[2] rather than any political supremacy of the district in which she was worshipped, that constitutes the chief factor in giving Bau this preëminence, just as we have found in the case of the other great goddesses of Babylonia, — Ninâ, Nanâ, Ishtar, — specific traits and not political importance lending them the significance they acquired.

At one time we may well suppose that the festival of En-lil at Nippur, which brought worshippers from all parts of Babylonia, was recognized as a 'New Year's Day,' and we may some day find evidence that at a still earlier period the first day of a month sacred to some other god, — Sin or Shamash or Nanâ-Ishtar of Erech, — was recognized in some districts as the starting-point for the year; but to an agricultural community, the spring, when the seeds are sown, or the fall, after the harvest has been gathered, are the two most natural periods for reckoning the beginning of the year. Since we know that at the time when Babylon acquired her supremacy the year began in the spring, the conservatism attaching to religious observances makes it more than probable that Bau's festival also fell in the spring.

After the ancient religious and political centers of the south yielded their privileges to Babylon, it was natural for the priests of Marduk to covet the honor of the New Year's festival for the new head of the pantheon. Accordingly, we find the Zagmuku transformed into a Marduk festival. That it did not originally belong to Marduk follows from the fact that it was celebrated in the month of Nisan, — the first month, — whereas the month sacred to Marduk was Arakh-shamna (or Marcheshwan), — the eighth month. The deliberate transfer of the

---

[1] Inscription G, *Ib.*, and Inscription D, col. ii. ll. 1–9. See also p. 59.
[2] See above, *Ib.*

Zagmuku to Marduk is also indicated by the fact that the festival of Nisan has another name by which it is more commonly designated,—Akitu.[1] The name seems to have been originally a general term for a festival, and it is natural that Marduk's festival should have come to be known as *the* festival, just as among the Hebrews the annual fall pilgrimage to the sanctuary at Jerusalem became known as *the* Hag,—the pilgrimage *par excellence*. To distinguish it from other festivals, Marduk's festival is sometimes spoken of as the "great" or the "lofty" Akitu. The first day was properly the Zagmuku, whereas the Akitu itself extended at least over the first eleven days of Nisan[2] and may indeed have lasted the entire month; but Zagmuku was also used for the festival period. The New Year's Day was marked by a solemn procession. The union of Nabu and Marduk was symbolized by a visit which the former paid to his father, the chief of the Babylonian pantheon. In his ship, magnificently fitted out,[3] Nabu was carried along the street known as Ai-ibur-shabû,[4] leading from Borsippa across the Euphrates to Babylon.

The street was handsomely paved,[5] and everything was done to heighten the impressiveness of the ceremony. The visit of Nabu marked the homage of the gods to Marduk; and Nabu set the example for other gods, who were all supposed to assemble in E-Sagila during the great festival. We have already pointed out that the cult of Nabu at Borsippa at one time was regarded with greater sanctity than the Marduk worship in Babylon. As a concession to the former supremacy of Nabu, the priests of E-Sagila, carrying the statue of Marduk, escorted Nabu back to Borsippa. The return visit raises the suspicion that it was originally Marduk who was obliged to pay an annual homage to Nabu.

---

[1] See, *e.g.*, Pognon Wadi Brissa, col. ix. ll. 12–18.
[2] This follows from a passage in Nebuchadnezzar's Inscription, IR. 54, col. ii. L 57.
[3] See p. 654.   [4] Signifying 'may the enemy not wax strong.'
[5] See Nebuchadnezzar's Inscription, IR. 56, col. v. ll. 38–54.

However this may be, the double ceremony became to such an extent the noteworthy feature of the Zagmuku or Akitu that when the chroniclers wish to indicate that, because of political disturbances, the festival was not celebrated, they use the simple formula:

> Nabu did not come to Babylon.
> Bel [*i.e.*, Marduk] did not march out.[1]

The Akitu festival brought worshippers from all parts of Babylonia and Assyria to the capitol. Kings and subjects alike paid their devotions to Marduk. The former approached the divine presence directly, and, seizing hold of the hands of Marduk's statue, were admitted into a kind of covenant with the god. The ceremony became the formal rite of royal installation in Babylonia. "To seize the hands of Bel" was equivalent to legitimizing one's claim to the throne of Babylonia, and the chroniclers of the south consistently decline to recognize Assyrian rulers as kings of Babylonia until they have come to Babylon and "seized the hands of Bel."[2] That this ceremony was annually performed by the kings of Babylonia after the union of the southern states is quite certain. It marked a renewal of the pledge between the king and his god. The Assyrian kings, however, contented themselves with a single visit. Of Tiglathpileser II.[3] and Sargon,[4] we know that they came to Babylonia for the purpose of performing the old ceremony; and others did the same.

The eighth and eleventh days of the festival month were

---

[1] So, *e.g.*, during the closing years of Nabonnedos' reign. Winckler, *Untersuchungen zur Altorient. Gesch.* I. 154; obv. 6 (7th year); 11 (9th year); 20 (10th year); 24 (11th year).

[2] On the meaning and importance of the rite, see Winckler, *Zeits. f. Assyr.* II. 302-304, and Lehmann's *Shamash-shumukin*, pp. 44-53.

[3] Eponym List, IIR. 52, no. 1 obv. 45.

[4] Winckler, *Die Keilschrifttexte Sargon's*, pp. 52, 124; of Ashurbanabal, the chronicler tells us that he proceeded to Babylonia in the month of Iyyar, but, this not being the proper month, he did not "seize the hands of Bel." See also Winckler, *ib.* p. xxxvi, note.

invested with special sanctity. On these days all the gods were brought together in the "chamber of fates" of Marduk's temple. In symbolical imitation of the assembly of the gods in Ubshu-kenna,[1] Marduk sits on his throne and the gods are represented as standing in humble submission before him, while he decrees the fates of mankind for the coming year. The Zagmuku festival in its developed form has striking points of resemblance to the Jewish New Year's Day. On this day, according to the popular Jewish tradition, God sits in judgment with a book before Him in which He inscribes the fate of mankind. Nine days of probation are allowed, and on the tenth day — the Day of Atonement — the fates are sealed. The Jewish New Year is known as Rôsh-hash-shanâ,[2] which is an exact equivalent of the Babylonian *rêsh shatti* (or zag-muku). A difference, however, between the Babylonian and the Jewish festival is that the latter is celebrated in the seventh month. It is not correct, therefore, to assume that the Hebrews borrowed their Rôsh-hash-shanâ from the Babylonians. Even after they adopted the Babylonian calendar,[3] they continued to regard the seventh month — the harvest month — as the beginning of the year. That among the Babylonians the seventh month also had a sacred character may be concluded from the meaning of the ideographs with which the name is written.[4] The question may, therefore, be raised whether at an earlier period and in some religious center — Nippur, Sippar, or perhaps Ur — the seventh month may not have been celebrated as the Zagmuku. At all events, we must for the present assume that the Hebrews developed their New Year's Day, which they may have originally received from Babylonia, independently of Marduk's festival, though, since the Rôsh-hash-shanâ does not come into prominence among the Jews until the period of the

---

[1] See pp. 423 and 629 *seq.*
[2] *I.e.,* 'The beginning of the year.'
Semitique, ii. 146-151.
[3] See p. 464.
See on this subject Karppe's article, *Revue*
[4] See *ib.,* note 3.

so-called Babylonian exile, the possibility of a direct Babylonian influence in the *later* conceptions connected with the day cannot be denied.[1]

Of the other festivals of the Babylonians and Assyrians but few details are known. Several references have already been made to the Tammuz festival.[2] Originally a solar festival, celebrated in the fourth month at the approach of the summer solstice, it became through the association of ideas suggested by the mourning of Ishtar for her lost consort Tammuz a kind of 'All Souls' Day,' on which the people remembered their dead. Dirges were sung by the wailing women to the accompaniment of musical instruments; offerings were made to the dead, and it is plausible to assume that visits were paid to the graves. The mourning was followed by a festival of rejoicing, symbolizing the return of the solar-god. The Tammuz festival appears to have had a strong hold upon the masses, by reason of the popularity of the Tammuz myth; nor was it limited to the Babylonians. Among the Phoenicians the cult of Tammuz, known by his title Adôn (whence Adonis), was maintained to a late period, and the Hebrews, likewise, as late as the days of Ezekiel,[3] commemorated with rites of mourning the lost Tammuz. The calendar of the Jewish Church still marks the 17th day of Tammuz as a fast, and Houtsma has shown[4] that the association of the day with the capture of Jerusalem by the Romans represents merely the attempt to give an ancient festival a worthier interpretation. The day was originally connected with the Tammuz

---

[1] The opinion of many scholars that the Rôsh-hash-shanâ dates from the Babylonian exile because not referred to in the Book of Deuteronomy is open to serious objections. The festival has traces of antiquity (like the Day of Atonement), and appears to have been *revived* during the captivity, under Babylonian influence.

[2] See especially pp. 484 and 575.

[3] Ezekiel, viii. 14. There is probably a reference also to the Tammuz festival in Zech. xii. 10, 11. The interpretation offered by Robertson Smith (*Religion of the Semites*, p. 392, note) for the mourning rites appears strained.

[4] *Over de Israelietische Vastendagen* (Amsterdam, 1897, pp. 4-6; 12-17).

cult. Eerdmans[1] has recently endeavored to show that the festival of Hosein, celebrated by the Shiitic sect of Mohammedanism in memory of the tragic death of the son of Ali, is in reality a survival of the Babylonian-Phoenician Tammuz festival. The spread of the Tammuz-Adonis myth and cult to the Greeks[2] is but another indication of the popularity of this ancient Semitic festival.

The old Zagmuku festival in honor of Bau and the Tammuz festival, celebrated in spring and summer, respectively, are also closely associated with agricultural life. The spring as the seedtime is, as we have seen, a natural period for beginning the calculation of the New Year, while a first harvest of the wheat and barley is reaped in Babylonia at the time of the summer solstice. We should expect, therefore, to find a third festival in the fall, at the close of the harvest and just before the winter rains set in. The seventh month — Tishri — was a sacred month among the ancient Hebrews as well as among the Babylonians, but up to the present no distinct traces of a festival period in Tishri have been found in Babylonian texts. We must content ourselves, therefore, with the conjecture, above thrown out, that an Akitu was originally celebrated in this month at some ancient religious center of the Euphrates Valley. Further publications of cuneiform texts may throw light upon this point. The unpublished material in European and American museums harbors many surprises.

In Ashurbanabal's annals[3] there is an interesting reference to a festival celebrated in honor of the goddess Gula, the goddess of healing,[4] on the twelfth day of Iyyar, the second month. The festival is described ideographically as Si-gar,[5] but from

[1] *Zeits. f. Assyr.* ix. 290 *seq.*
[2] See Farnell, *The Cults of the Greek States*, ii. 648 *seq.*
[3] Rassam Cylinder, col. I. ll. 11, 12.
[4] See pp. 105 and 173 *seq.*
[5] The readings Sun-gar and Shum-gar (so Jensen, *Keils Bibl.* ii. 155) are also possible.

the fact that the same ideographs are used elsewhere to describe a day sacred to Sin and Shamash,[1] it would appear that Si-gar is not a specific appellation, but a general name again for festival. This month Iyyar and this particular day, as a "favorable one," is chosen by Ashurbanabal for his installation as king of Assyria. The same month is selected for a formal pilgrimage to Babylonia for the purpose of restoring to E-Sagila a statue of Marduk that a previous Assyrian king had taken from its place,[2] and Lehmann is probably correct in concluding[3] that this month of Iyyar was a particularly sacred one in Assyria, emphasized with intent perhaps by the kings, as an offset against the sacredness of Nisan in Babylonia.

Festivals in honor of Ninib were celebrated in Calah in the months of Elul — the sixth month — and Shabat — the eleventh month.[4] The sixth month, it will be recalled, is sacred to Ishtar.[5] Ninib being a solar deity, his festival in Elul was evidently of a solar character. From Ashurbanabal,[6] again, we learn that the 25th day of Siwan — the third month — was sacred to Belit of Babylon, and on that day a procession took place in her honor. The Belit meant is Sarpanitum in her original and independent rôle as a goddess of fertility. The statue of the goddess, carried about, presumably in her ship, formed the chief feature of the procession. Ashurbanabal chooses this "favorable" day as the one on which to

[1] IV R. 32, 49b, where the 20th day of the intercalated Elul is so designated. An official — 'the great Si-gar' — is mentioned in a list, — II R. 31, no. 5, 33a.

[2] See the discussion (and passages) in Lehmann's *Shamash-shumukin*, pp. 43 *seq*. One is tempted to conclude that Marduk's statue was removed to Nineveh, not in a spirit of vandalism, but in order to enable Assyrian kings to 'seize the hands of Bel' without proceeding to E-Sagila. The Babylonians, no doubt, were offended by such an act, and in order to conciliate them, Ashurbanabal, who pursues a mild policy towards the south, orders the statue to be restored at the time that he appoints his brother Shamash-shumukin as governor of the southern provinces.

[3] *Ib.* p. 53, note.

[4] Ashurnasirbal's Inscription, IR. 23, col. ii. l. 134.

[5] See above, p. 462.

[6] Rassam Cylinder, col. viii. ll. 96–100.

break up camp in the course of one of his military expeditions. We would naturally expect to find a festival month devoted to the god Ashur in Assyria. This month was Elul — the sixth month.[1] The choice of this month lends weight to the supposition that Ashur was originally a solar deity.[2] The honors once paid to Ninib in Calah in this month could thus easily be transferred to the head of the Assyrian pantheon. Although in the calendar the sixth month is sacred to Ishtar, her festival was celebrated in the fifth month, known as Ab.[3] This lack of correspondence between the calendar and the festivals is an indication of the greater antiquity of the latter.

In the great temple to Shamash at Sippar, there appear to have been several days that were marked by religious observances. Nabubaliddin[4] (ninth century) emphasizes that he presented rich garments to the temple for use on six days of the year, — the 7th day of Nisan (first month), 10th of Iyyar (second month), 3d of Elul (sixth month), 7th of Tishri (seventh month), 15th of Arakh-shamna (or Marcheshwan, eighth month), and the 15th of Adar (twelfth month). These garments are given to Shamash, to his consort Malkatu, and to Bunene.[5] Since from a passage in a Babylonian chronicle[6] it appears that it was customary for Shamash on his festival to leave his temple, we may conclude that the garments were put on Shamash and his associates, for the solemn procession on the six days in question.

The festivals in Nisan and Elul are distinctly of a solar character. The choice of two other months immediately fol-

---

[1] George Smith, *The History of Ashurbanipal*, p. 126 (Cylinder B, col. v. L 77). See also Rassam Cylinder, col. iii. L 32.

[2] See above, pp. 195, 196.

[3] See Ashurbanabal Cylinder B, col. v. L 16 (*Keils Bibl.* ii. 248; also Meissner, *Beiträge zum Altbabylonischen Privatrecht*, no. 14 (p. 23).

[4] VR. 61, col. v. L 51–vi. L 8.

[5] See above, pp. 74 and 176.

[6] Winckler, *Zeits. f. Assyr.* li. 155 (col. ii. L 41).

lowing Nisan and Elul cannot be accidental. The interval of thirty-three days between the Nisan and Iyyar festivals and thirty-four days between the Elul and Tishri festivals may represent a sacred period.¹ Tishri, moreover, as has been pointed out, is a sacred month in a peculiar sense. Marcheshwan, it may be well to bear in mind, is sacred to Marduk, — a solar deity, — while the 15th of Adar, curiously enough, is an old solar festival that, modified and connected with historical reminiscences, became popular among the Jews of Persia and Babylonia during the Persian supremacy in the Semitic Orient, and survives to this day under the name of the Purim festival.² At all events, the six days may be safely regarded as connected in some way, direct or indirect, with solar worships, and it is natural to find that in so prominent a center of sun-worship as Sippar, *all* the solar festivals were properly and solemnly observed.

¹ One is reminded of the sanctity attaching in the Jewish ritual to the "counting" of the seven weeks intervening between Passover (the old Nisan festival) and Pentecost (an old summer festival). See Deut. xvi. 9. The 33d day of this period has a special significance in the Jewish Church.

² The non-Jewish origin of the Purim festival is generally accepted by critical scholars. Lagarde (*Purim — Ein Beitrag zur Geschichte der Religions*) endeavors to trace it back to a Persian fire festival; Zimmern (*Zeits. f. Alt. Wiss.*, 1891, pp. 160 *seq.*) connects it with the Babylonian Zagmuku. Sayce's supposition (*Proc. Soc. Bibl. Arch.* xix. 280, 281) is not to be taken seriously. The origin of the Jewish feast and fast of Purim is still obscure. The fact that there is both a fast (14th Adar) and a festival (15th Adar) is a safe indication of antiquity. Zimmern's view of a possible relationship between Purim and Zagmuku is untenable, but that there is a connection between Purim and *some* Babylonian festival follows from the fact that the two chief personages in the Book of Esther — namely, Mordecai and Esther — bear names identical with the two Babylonian deities, Marduk and Ishtar. This cannot be an accident. On the other hand, Haman and Vashti, according to Jensen (*Wiener Zeits. f. d. Kunde des Morgenlandes*, vi. 70), are Elamitic names of deities corresponding to the Babylonian Marduk and Ishtar. The case for Vashti is not clearly made out by Jensen, but, for all that, it is certain that the Babylonian elements in the institution have been combined with some bits of Persian mythology. The historical setting is the work of the Jewish compiler of the tale, that has of course some historical basis. See now Toy, *Esther as a Babylonian Goddess* (*The New World*, vi. 130–145).

It is disappointing that up to the present so little has been ascertained of the details of the moon-cult — the great rival to Shamash worship — in the old cities of Ur and Harran. In the Babylonian calendar, the third month — Siwan — is sacred to Sin, but since, as we have found, the festivals in honor of the gods do not always correspond to the assignment of the months, we cannot be certain that in this month a special festival in honor of Sin was observed. Lastly, besides the regular and fixed festivals, the kings, and more especially the Assyrian rulers, did not hesitate to institute special festivals in memory of some event that contributed to their glory. Agumkakrimi[1] instituted a festival upon restoring the statues of Marduk and Sarpanitum to Babylon, and Sargon does the same upon restoring the palace at Calah.[2] Dedications of temples and palaces were in general marked by festivities, and so when the kings return in triumph from their wars, laden with spoils and captives, popular rejoicings were instituted. But such festivals were merely sporadic, and, while marked by religious ceremonies, were chiefly occasions of general jollification combined with homage to the rulers. Such a festival was not called an *isinnu*, but a *nigûtu*,[3] — a 'merrymaking.'[4] More directly connected with the cult was a ceremony observed in Assyria upon the installation of an official, known as the *limmu*, who during his year of service enjoyed the privilege of having official documents dated with his name.[5] The ceremony involved a running[6] of some kind, and reminds one of the running between the two hills Marwa and Safa in Mekka that forms part of the religious observances

---

[1] V R. 33, col. v. l. 40.
[2] Winckler, *Die Keilschrifttexte Sargon's*, p. 172 and p. xxvi, note.
[3] *E.g.*, Sargon's *Annals*, l. 179; Cylinder, l. 20, V R. 33, col. v. l. 40 (*nigatu*).
[4] Not necessarily 'music festival,' as Delitzsch proposes (*Assyr. Handw.*, p. 447²).
[5] For examples, see the Assyrian contract tablets translated by Peiser, *Keils Bibl.* iv. 98 and *passim*.
[6] See the passage Shalmanaser obelisk, ll. 174, 175, and Peiser's comment, *Keils Bibl.* iv. 106, note.

in connection with a visit to the Kaaba.[1] The name of the ceremony appears to have been puru (or buru). To connect this word with the Jewish festival of Purim, as Sayce proposes,[2] is wholly unwarranted. The character of the Puru ceremony points to its being an ancient custom, the real significance of which in the course of time became lost. Fast days instituted for periods of distress might also be added to the cult, but these, too, like the special festivals, were not permanent institutions. For such occasions many of the penitential psalms which were discussed in a previous chapter[3] were composed. To conciliate angered gods whose temples had been devastated in days of turmoil, atonement and purification rites were observed. So Ashurbanabal[4] upon his conquest of Babylonian cities tells us that he pacified the gods of the south with penitential psalms and purified the temples by magic rites; and Nabubaliddin,[5] incidental to his restoration of the Shamash cult at Sippar, refers to an interesting ceremony of purification, which consisted in his taking water and washing his mouth according to the purification ritual of Ea and Marduk,[6] preliminary to bringing sacrifices to Shamash in his shrine. Sippar had been overrun by nomads,[7] the temple had been defiled, and before sacrifices could again be offered, the sacred edifice and sacred quarter had to be purified. The king's action was a symbol of this purification. Many such customs must have been in vogue in Babylonia and Assyria. Some — and these were the oldest — were of popular origin. On the seal cylinders there is frequently represented a pole or a conventionalized

---

[1] Burton, *A Pilgrimage to Mecca and Medina*, iii. chapter vii.
[2] See above, p. 686.
[3] Chapter xviii.
[4] Rassam Cylinder, col. iv. ll. 86–89.
[5] VR. 61, col. II. ll. 22–27.
[6] Ea and Marduk, it will be recalled, are the chief gods invoked in magic rites involving purification. See pp. 275, 276.
[7] See p. 646.

form of a tree, generally in connection with a design illustrating the worship of a deity.[1] This symbol is clearly a survival of some tree worship[2] that was once popular. The comparison with the *ashera* or pole worship among Phoenicians and Hebrews[3] is fully justified, and is a proof of the great antiquity of the symbol, which, without becoming a formal part of the later cult, retained in some measure a hold upon the popular mind. Other symbols and customs were introduced under the influence of the doctrines unfolded in the schools of thought in the various intellectual centers, and as an expression of the teachings of the priests. The cult of Babylonia, even more so than the literature, is a compound of these two factors, — popular beliefs and the theological elaboration and systematization of these beliefs. In the course of this elaboration, many new ideas and new rites were introduced. The official cult passed in some important particulars far beyond popular practices.

[1] See numerous examples in Menant's *Collection de Clercq* (Paris, 1888).
[2] See above, p. 662.
[3] Stade, *Geschichte des Volkes Israel*, i. 458 *seq.*

CHAPTER XXVII.

CONCLUSION.

General Estimate and Influence.

In forming a general estimate of a religion, one's verdict will largely depend upon the point of view from which the religion in question is regarded. It is manifestly unjust and illogical to apply modern standards to an ancient religion, not that such a religion would necessarily suffer by the comparison involved, but because of the totally different conditions under which religion developed in antiquity from those prevailing in modern times. The close association, nay, the inseparable bond, between religion and the state is only one of several determining factors that might be adduced, while the small scope permitted to individualism in matters of religious belief and practice in a country like Babylonia or Assyria was fraught with such peculiar results that all comparisons, even with other religions of antiquity, could only obscure and not illumine our judgment.

There are manifestly three phases of the religion of Babylonia and Assyria that need to be considered in reaching some general conclusions as to the character and rank to be accorded to it, — the doctrines, the rites, and the ethics. So far as the pantheon is concerned, the limitations in the development of doctrines connected with it were reached when the union of the several Euphratean states was permanently effected under Hammurabi. Marduk, a solar deity, takes his place as the head of the pantheon by virtue of the preëminent place occupied by his patron city, — Babylon. The other great gods, each representing some religious center that at one time or the other rose to importance, grouped themselves around Marduk, as the princes and nobles gather around a supreme monarch. A certain measure of independence was reserved for the great mother goddess Ishtar, who, worshipped under various names as the symbol of fertility, plenty, and strength, is not so decidedly affected by the change as deities like En-lil, Shamash, Sin, and Ea, who could at any time become rivals of Marduk. As the position of Marduk, however, became more and more assured without danger of being shaken, the feeling of rivalry in his relations to the other gods began to disappear. Marduk's supremacy no longer being questioned, there was no necessity to curtail the homage paid to Shamash at Sippar or to En-lil at Nippur; hence the religious importance of the old centers is not diminished by the surpassing glory of Babylon. There was room for all. Marduk's toleration is the best evidence of his unquestioned headship.

The centralization of political power and of religious supremacy is concomitant with the focussing of intellectual life in Babylon. The priests of Marduk set the fashion in theological thought. So far as possible, the ancient traditions and myths were reshaped so as to contribute to the glory of Marduk. The chief part in the work of creation is assigned to him. The storm-god En-lil is set aside to make room for the solar deity Marduk. But, despite such efforts, the old tales, once committed to writing on the practically imperishable clay, survived, if not in the minds of the people, at least in the archives of the ancient temples.

The antiquity of literature in Babylonia was the factor that prevented the cult from acquiring a uniform character in the various parts of the empire. The priests of Nippur, of Sippar, of Eridu, of Erech, Cuthah, Ur, and other places began long before the period of Hammurabi to compile, on the basis of past experience and as a guide for future needs, omen lists, incantation formulas, and sacrificial rituals. These collections created orthodox standards, and these standards, once acknowledged, the natural conservatism attaching to religious customs was sufficient to maintain their continuance. The uniformity of doctrine was thus offset by variations in the cult; and the policy adopted by both Babylonian and Assyrian rulers, in permitting each center to remain undisturbed, and in freely recognizing the religious independence of each, prevented the Babylonian and Assyrian religion from falling into the state of stagnation which would otherwise have been its fate.

In the views taken of the relationship between the gods and men, no notable advances were made when once the ethical spirit was infused into the religious beliefs. The problem of good and evil was solved in a simple fashion. By the side of the great gods there existed a large, almost infinite number of spirits and demons, who were generally held responsible for the evils affecting mankind.[1] These demons and spirits were in many cases gods 'fallen from grace,'—minor local deities who, unable to maintain themselves in the face of the growing popularity of the great gods, sank to an inferior position as messengers, forced to do the will of their masters and who could be controlled by the latter. But the intercession of the priests was essential to obtaining divine help against the mischievous workings of the spirits. Even the kings, though originally standing very close to the gods, could not dispense with the services of the priests, and by virtue of their conspicuous position had to exercise greater precautions than the masses not to offend the gods, by errors of commission or omission in the cult. The priests held the secret that could secure freedom from ills and promote the comparative well-being of rulers and subjects. They alone knew what incantations to use for each case that was brought before them, in what way the sacrifices were to be brought, when the deity

---

[1] See above, pp. 183, 266.

should be approached, and why divine anger had manifested itself. The intellectual leadership thus acquired by the priests, in addition to their control of religious affairs, was an additional factor in maintaining orthodox standards of belief when once they had become fixed. In the doctrines of life after death, this influence of the priesthood is distinctly seen. The popular notions were systematized, but the priests, true to their rule as conservators, did not pass beyond primitive conceptions. Some weak attempts at a philosophical view of the problem of death are attempted in the Gilgamesh epic as finally put together under the influence of the Babylonian schools of thought,[1] but the leaders shared with the people the sense of hopelessness when picturing the life in the great hollow Aralû. It is in the hymns and prayers, rather than in the cosmology and eschatology, that the spiritual aspirations of the priests (and to a limited degree of the masses) manifest themselves. In these productions, whether existing independently or incorporated into incantation rituals, we see the religion of Babylonia at its best. A strong emphasis is placed upon the doctrine that misfortunes and ills come as a punishment for sins of commission or omission. It is true that no distinction is drawn between ceremonial errors and real misdeeds, but the sense of guilt is aroused by the priests in the minds of those who come to the temples, seeking relief from the attacks of the evil spirits, or the bewitchment of sorcerers.

It is in this doctrine of guilt, as revealed through the magical texts, that we must seek both for the starting-point of the development of an ethical system (so far as such a system existed among the Babylonians), and also for the limitations of this system. The aim of the priests to observe the right ceremonies, to pronounce the right words in order to accomplish their aim, reacted on rulers and subjects, and led them to make the pleasure of the gods the goal of life. With fear of

---

[1] See pp. 513 *seq.*

the gods, upon which stress is always laid,[1] there is thus associated an equally strong love[2] of the divine powers. Obedience to the gods is primarily inculcated as a means of securing their protection and blessing; but the fear of the gods, we are told, is the cause of joy;[3] and the Babylonians passed far beyond the stage of making the satisfaction of one's own desires the standard of right and wrong. A penitential psalm declares[4] that what is pleasing to oneself may be sinful in the eyes of a god.

The kings pride themselves upon being the promoters of justice. Even the Assyrian rulers, who impress one while conducting their wars as bereft of all softer emotions, declare that their highest aim is to spread plenty and happiness.[5] Sennacherib calls himself a king who 'loves righteousness,'[6] and he, as well as his predecessors and successors, busies himself with actually restoring the rights of those of his subjects who have been wrongfully deprived of their possessions.

The standard of private morality was high both in Babylonia and Assyria. The legal and commercial tablets reveal that proper consideration was given to the treatment of woman — a most satisfactory index of ethical conditions.[7] She could hold property and dispose of it. Before the courts, her status did not differ materially from that of the male population. The husband could not divorce his wife without sufficient cause, and children owed obedience to the mother as well as to the father.[8]

---

[1] Babylonian and Assyrian kings alike speak constantly of their fear of the gods. See the passages in Delitzsch's *Assyrisches Handwörterbuch*, pp. 526, 527, to which many more could be added.

[2] See, *e.g.*, Nebuchadnezzar, IR. 53, col. I, L 31.

[3] IVR. 60*, B obv. 25.   [4] IVR. 60*, C obv. 14.

[5] So Sargon cylinder, IL 34-42.

[6] IR. 37, col. I. l. 4.

[7] See the writer's remarks in *Oriental Studies of the Oriental Club of Philadelphia*, pp. 119-121.

[8] See the so-called family laws (as early as the days of Hammurabi) in Meissner's *Beiträge zum Altbabylonischen Privatrecht*, p. 15, where the punishment in the case of the son who casts aside his mother is specifically referred to.

Polygamy, as a matter of course, prevailed, but it is an error to suppose that polygamy is inconsistent with high ideals of family life, even though it does not lead to the highest ideals.

Hatred, lying, cheating, using false measures, removing boundaries, adultery, insincerity are denounced in the incantation texts,[1] and in accord with this standard, we see in the recordsuits of lawsuits and agreements between parties[2] clear indications of the stringent laws that prevailed in order to protect citizens against infringement of their rights. It comes as a surprise, but also as a welcome testimony to the efficacy of justice in Assyria, to find Ashurbanabal emphasizing the fact that he established ordinances so that the strong should do no harm to the weak.[3]

The institution of slavery flourished in Babylonia and Assyria throughout all periods of their history,[4] but there were various grades of slaves. Some classes differed but little from that of servants, indentured for a longer or shorter period for certain services. The temple slaves appear to have largely belonged to this class. Mild treatment of slaves is enjoined and was the rule. The slaves are often the confidential agents of their masters who attend to the business affairs of the latter. We find slaves holding property in their own right. Contracts entered into by them are legal and binding. Injuries inflicted upon them by their masters are punished, and they are protected against losses and mishaps encountered while in service. While we have no evidence to show that the laws of Assyria were on a lower ethical plane than those of Babylonia, still, as the pupils and imitators of the Babylonians in almost everything pertaining to culture and religion, the general tone of life in Assyria was hardly as high as in the south. The war-

---

[1] See, *e.g.*, p. 291.
[2] See the admirable discussions on Babylonian jurisprudence in Kohler and Pelser's *Aus dem Babylonischen Rechtsleben* (parts i.-iii., Leipzig, 1890-97).
[3] S. A. Strong in *Journal of the Royal Asiatic Society*, 1891, p. 460.
[4] See on this subject Meissner, *De Servitute Babylonico-Assyriaca*, pp. 3, 4, 40-49.

like spirit of the rulers is but a symptom of the fiercer character of the people.

The tendency towards monotheism in the religion of Babylonia and Assyria has been referred to. We must remember that it was only a tendency. No decided steps in this direction were ever taken. Both in the south and in the north, this tendency is but the expression of the preëminent rank accorded to Marduk and Ashur, respectively. The independent existence of two heads in the combined pantheon was sufficient to prevent the infusion of an ethical spirit into this monotheistic tendency; and unless a monotheistic conception of the universe is interpreted in an ethical sense, monotheism (or monolatry) has no great superiority, either religiously or philosophically, over polytheism.

From the standpoint of religious doctrine, accordingly, the religion of Babylonia and Assyria does not occupy a unique position. In this respect, the Egyptian religion reaches a higher level. For all that, the influence exerted by the religion that developed in the Euphrates Valley was profound and lasting. We have had occasion in various chapters of this work to point out the close analogies existing between the thoughts, tradition, and practices of the Hebrews and the Babylonians.[1] A proper study of the Hebrew religion is closely bound up with an investigation of the religious antiquities of Babylonia; and as our knowledge of these antiquities increases, it will be found that not only are Hebrews and Babylonians equipped with many common possessions when starting out upon their intellectual careers, but that, at different times and in diverse ways, the stimulus to religious advance came to the Hebrews from the ancient centers of thought and worship in the Euphrates Valley. This influence was particularly strong during the period of Jewish history known as Babylonian exile. The finishing touches to the structure of Judaism

---

[1] See especially chapters xxi., xxv., and xxvi.

—given on Babylonian soil[1]—reveal the Babylonian trademark. Ezekiel, in many respects the most characteristic Jewish figure of the exile, is steeped in Babylonian theology and mysticism; and the profound influence of Ezekiel is recognized by modern scholarship in the religious spirit that characterizes the Jews upon the reorganization of their commonwealth.

It would be a mistake, however, to suppose that what Babylonia gave to others was always the best she had to offer. Degrading tendencies, too, found an entrance into post-exilic Judaism through Babylonian influence. Close contact of Jews with Babylonians served to make the former more accessible to the popular beliefs in incantations and in the power of demons than they would otherwise have been. Not that the Jews (as little as any other people) were ever entirely free from superstitious practices; but, living in an atmosphere charged, so to speak, with magic and astrology, it was inevitable that even the best among them should be infected by customs that they daily witnessed. In the Babylonian Talmud, the references to evil spirits are numerous. Specific incantations are introduced, and an elaborate system of angelology and demonology forms a feature of Talmudical Judaism in which, by the side of Persian influences,[2] we may detect equally strong traces of Babylonian ideas. In the upper strata of the ruins of Nippur, hundreds of clay bowls were found, inscribed with Jewish inscriptions, in the Aramaic dialect that was spoken by the Babylonian Jews.[3] Similar bowls were found elsewhere in the mounds of the Euphrates Valley.[4] These bowls indicate the presence of Jews in various parts of the country.[5] Placed

---

[1] See p. 611.
[2] See Kohut, *Die Jüdische Angelologie und Dämonologie in ihrer Abhängigkeit vom Parsismus* (Leipzig, 1866).
[3] Peters' *Nippur*, pp. 182, 395.
[4] See, e.g., Layard, *Nineveh and Babylon* (New York edition, 1853), p. 509.
[5] On the extent of the settlements of Jews in Nippur, see Hilprecht, *Cuneiform Texts*, ix. 27, 28.

in the graves as a protection for the dead against evil spirits, the inscriptions contain formulas of denunciation against the demons that constitute a striking parallel to the incantation texts of ancient Babylonia. Some of the demons are identical with those occurring in these texts, and by the side of the inscriptions, there are illustrations[1] and magical designs to which parallels exist on the Babylonian tablets.

This custom of endeavoring to secure protection for the dead through the power of the curses and propitiatory phrases inscribed on bowls continued in vogue as late as the ninth century at the least, and perhaps considerably later. There are indications also that Babylonian ideas found an entrance into the Jewish Kabbala, — the strange mystic system of the middle ages, the sources of which are to be sought in the apocalyptic chapters of Ezekiel and Daniel.

Christianity as well as Judaism felt the fascination of the mystic lore of Babylonia. Gunkel[2] has demonstrated the Babylonian origin of the myth embodied in the twelfth chapter of Revelations. This myth is but another form of the Marduk-Tiâmat contest, which, it will be recalled, is the chief episode in the Babylonian creation 'epic.'[3] More significant is the influence exerted by the religious ideas of Babylonia upon the various Gnostic sects that arose within the Christian Church. That the source of Gnosticism was to be sought in Mesopotamia was always recognized by scholars, but until the discovery of Babylonian literature, it was customary to seek for Jewish influences in the formation of the various Gnostic sects. Kessler[4] was the first to demonstrate clearly the dependence of the leading ideas of Gnosticism upon

---

[1] So, *e.g.*, on some of the bowls in the University of Pennsylvania collection, crude pictures of Bel-Marduk and Ishtar are portrayed.

[2] *Schöpfung und Chaos*, pp. 381–397.

[3] See pp. 432 *seq.*

[4] "Ueber Gnosis und die Altbabylonische Religion," *Verhandlungen des fünften Orientalisten Congress*, 1881, ii. 288–305.

the Babylonian cosmology and the conceptions deveolped with reference to the gods. More recently, Anz[1] has undertaken a renewed investigation of the subject, and, approaching the theme from various points of view, reaches conclusions confirmatory of Kessler's thesis. All of the Gnostic sects have certain fundamental doctrines in common, such as the dwelling of God in the abyss,[2] the migration of the soul after death through seven zones, the emanation of aeons from a supreme aeon.[3] All these doctrines exhibit such close affinities with Babylonian ideas as to warrant the assertion that the religion of Babylonia survives in Gnosticism; and since, as we know, Babylonian culture and customs maintained an undisturbed existence almost to the threshold of our era, there is no need to go back to the older periods of the Babylonian religion to find the connecting link, uniting Gnosticism with the Babylonian religion. The spread and influence of the Gnostic sects was notoriously wide. It is sufficient to recall the chief centers of Gnostic schools of thought in Antioch, Edessa, and Alexandria and the various branches of the powerful sect of the Ophites. The influence of these schools extended into Greece and Rome. While the Gnostic sects disappear in the sixth century, the influence of Gnosticism can be followed down to the twelfth century,—a significant testimony to the enduring qualities of Babylonian doctrines.

In the ancient world, prior to the rise of Christianity, Egypt, Persia, and Greece felt the influence of the Babylonian religion. Budge[4] is of the opinion that many of the magic practices carried on in the Egyptian temples are to be traced back to the incantation rituals perfected by the Babylonian priests. In view of the early contact between

---

[1] *Zur Frage nach dem Ursprung des Gnostisismus* (Leipzig, 1897).
[2] *I.e.*, Ea dwelling in the Apsu. See p. 430.
[3] Anu, the source of all gods. See p. 417.
[4] *The Life and Exploits of Alexander the Great*, pp. xii. *seq.*

Egypt and Babylonia, as revealed by the El-Amarna tablets, there were certainly abundant opportunities for the infusion of Babylonian views and customs into Egyptian cults. In Persia, the Mithra cult reveals the unmistakable influence of Babylonian conceptions;[1] and if it be recalled what a degree of importance the mysteries connected with this cult acquired among the Romans, another link will be added connecting the ramifications of ancient culture with the civilization of the Euphrates Valley. The strong admixture of Semitic elements both in early Greek mythology and in Grecian cults is now so generally admitted by scholars as to require no further comment.[2] These Semitic elements are to a large extent more specifically Babylonian. The spread of the Gilgamesh epic and of the Ishtar cult into Asia Minor and Greece may be instanced as illustrations of Babylonian influence; and granting that the Phoenicians acted largely as the mediators in carrying these ideas to the Greek settlements, still there must have been influences at work long before this direct contact with Semitic culture that prepared the way for the ready acceptance which Semitic conceptions and Semitic practices found. The time has not yet come for pronouncing an opinion as to the influence exerted by Babylonia upon lands in the distant East. The theory of DeLacouperie[3] and Ball, which proposes to trace the Chinese script to the hieroglyphic system of Babylonia, is still to be tested. Early commercial contact between the Euphrates Valley and India is maintained as a probable theory by several scholars,[4] and the possibility, therefore, of the spread of the religious ideas of Babylonia to the distant East is not to be rejected. Patient research and the additional

---

[1] See Anz, as above, pp. 78-85.

[2] R. Brown, *Semitic Influence in Hellenic Mythology* (London, 1898).

[3] *Western Origin of the Early Chinese Civilisation* (London, 1894).

[4] A paper on this subject was announced by Jas. Kennedy at the Eleventh International Congress of Orientalists.

discoveries (which are constantly being made) will alone place us in a position some day to give a definite answer to the question. Whatever that answer may be, the verdict as to the high quality and profound influence of the religion that arose in the valley of the Euphrates and that flourished for several millenniums will not be altered.

To show the general indebtedness of Grecian, Roman, mediaeval, and even modern civilization to Babylonian culture lies beyond the range of this work, but the profound impression made upon the ancient world by the remarkable manifestations of religious thought in Babylonia and by the religious activity that prevailed in that region is but an index of the influence that must have been exerted in other directions by the varied intellectual activity that converted a district, exposed to the by no means tender mercies of the elements, into one of the most notable illustrations of the power and achievements of man.

BIBLIOGRAPHY.

NOTE.

The bibliography is arranged in nine sections, the order adopted corresponding to the broad subdivisions of the book. The beginning is therefore made:

(1) With references to the most important or most useful publications, dealing with the excavations conducted in Babylonia and Assyria, the method of decipherment of the cuneiform inscriptions, the general history of Babylonia and Assyria, and the general aspects of the Babylonian-Assyrian culture. This section corresponds to the first two chapters of the book.

(2) The second section is devoted to books, monographs, articles, and chapters in books, dealing with the general subject of the Babylonian-Assyrian religion.

In neither of these two sections have I aimed at being exhaustive, though the second will be found, I think, to include almost everything of any value.

The detailed bibliography begins with the following section. Corresponding again to the treatment of the subject in the book, I take up in succession :

(3) The Pantheon.
(4) Religious Texts.
(5) Cosmology.
(6) Gilgamesh Epic (including the Deluge episode).
(7) Beliefs and Customs (Views of Life after Death, Funeral Rites, Legends, Ethics, *etc.*).
(8) Temples and Cult.
(9) Bearings of the Babylonian-Assyrian Religion on the Old Testament, and General Influence Exerted by the Religion.

Of these seven sections, all but the last aim at being exhaustive. It was not always easy to decide into what division a particular reference belonged, but I have been generally guided by the needs of students for whom this portion of the bibliography is particularly intended.

The fifth and sixth sections should be taken together; and similarly the seventh and eighth, while the fourth section should of course be consulted in connection with the third, fifth, sixth, seventh, and eighth.

Under each section the authors named are arranged in alphabetical order. Occasionally, I have added some comments to the reference given, as a guide or a warning to students. In a subject like Assyriology, where new discoveries are constantly being made and progress in the interpretation of texts is steadily going on, it is inevitable that views and translations should be subject to modification — sometimes slight, but frequently significant. I have endeavored to avoid repetition of references. In a few cases this was unavoidable. In the second section portions of books are referred to, which by virtue of their character as very general works had to be assigned a place also in the first section. Two or three of the references in the fourth section had to be repeated elsewhere; and I should also add that there are a few references which I have been unable to verify.

BIBLIOGRAPHY.

The following abbreviations are employed:

AB = Assyriologische Bibliothek, ed. by Friedrich Delitzsch and Paul Haupt.
AD = Andover Review.
AI = Académie des Inscriptions et Belles Lettres.
AJP = American Journal of Philology.
AJT = American Journal of Theology.
AJSL = American Journal of Semitic Languages and Literatures.
AL = Delitzsch's Assyrische Lesestücke. (3d ed.)
APC = Annales de Philosophie Chrétienne.
BA = Beiträge zur Assyriologie.
BAZ = Beilage zur Allgemeinen Zeitung (Munich).
BOR = Babylonian and Oriental Record.
BW = Biblical World.
CR = Comptes Rendus de l'Académie des Inscriptions et Belles Lettres.
DR = Deutsche Rundschau.
DRe = Deutsche Revue.
ET = Expository Times.
FLJ = Folk Lore Journal.
H = Hebraica.
IAQR = Imperial and Asiatic Quarterly Review.
ICO = International Congress of Orientalists.
JA = Journal Asiatique.
JAOS = Journal of the American Oriental Society.
JHUC = Johns Hopkins University Circulars.
JRAS = Journal of the Royal Asiatic Society.
JTVI = Journal of the Transactions of the Victoria Institute.
KAA = Koninklijke Akademie van Wetenschappen (Amsterdam).
KAW = Königliche Akademie der Wissenschaften zu Berlin.
M = Museon.
MVG = Mittheilungen der Vorderasiatischen Gesellschaft.
OTS = Old Testament Student.
PAOS = Proceedings of the American Oriental Society.

PR = Presbyterian Review.
PSBA = Proceedings of the Society of Biblical Archaeology.
R = Rawlinson's ' Selection from the miscellaneous Inscriptions of Western Asia.' (London 1861–1891.) 5 vols.
RA = Revue d'Assyriologie et d'Archéologie Orientale.
RAr = Revue Archéologique.
RB = Revue Biblique.
RC = Revue Critique.
RHR = Revue de l'Histoire des Religions.
RIA = Royal Irish Academy.
RP = Records of the Past.
RR = Revue des Religions.
RS = Revue Sémitique.
RT = Recueil de Travaux relatifs à la Philologie et à l'Archéologie Egyptiennes et Assyriennes.
SST = Sunday School Times.
TSBA = Transactions of the Society of Biblical Archaeology.
TZ = Theologische Zeitblätter.
WZKM = Wiener Zeitschrift für die Kunde des Morgenlandes.
ZA = Zeitschrift für Assyriologie.
ZATW = Zeitschrift für die Alttestamentliche Wissenschaft.
ZDMG = Zeitschrift der Deutsch-Morgenländischen Gesellschaft.
ZK = Zeitschrift für Keilschriftforschung.

Periodicals, the volumes of which correspond to years, are quoted by the years; others, by the volumes, or by series, or by series and volumes.

Roman numerals indicate volumes, except in the case of PAOS, where they indicate pages; Arabic numerals indicate pages or plates.

I.

EXCAVATIONS. — METHOD OF DECIPHERMENT. — HISTORY OF BABYLONIA AND ASSYRIA. — ORIGIN AND GENERAL ASPECTS OF BABYLONIAN AND ASSYRIAN CULTURE. — GENERAL BIBLIOGRAPHY.

(a) *Excavations and Decipherment.*

KAULEN, FR. — Assyrien und Babylonien nach den neuesten Entdeckungen. (4th ed. Freiburg 1891.)

[Popular account of excavations, method of decipherment, Babylonian literature and architecture. A work in English of this character is much to be desired. See also HOMMEL, F. — Geschichte Babyloniens und Assyriens. Berlin 1885. pp. 30–134; EVETTS, B. A. — New Light on the Holy Land. London 1891. pp. 79–129.]

(b) *History.*

DUNCKER, MAX. — Geschichte des Alterthums. Vols. I. and II, (5th ed. Berlin 1878.)
  [Also English translation of earlier edition.]

HOMMEL, F. — Geschichte Babyloniens und Assyriens. (Berlin 1885.)
—— Geschichte des alten Morgenlandes. (Stuttgart 1895.)
  [Chapters I., IV.-VIII.]

LENORMANT, FRANÇOIS [and ERNEST BABELON]. — Histoire ancienne de l'Orient. Vol. IV. (9th ed. Paris 1885.)

MASPERO, G. — The Dawn of Civilization: Egypt and Chaldaea. (London 1894.)
—— The Struggle of the Nations: Egypt, Syria, and Assyria. (London 1896.)
  [Replacing earlier historical works of this author.]

MEYER, ED. — Geschichte des Alterthums. Vol. I. (Stuttgart 1884.)

MUERDTER und DELITZSCH. — Kurzgefasste Geschichte Babyloniens und Assyriens. (2d ed. Stuttgart 1891.)

RAGOZIN, Z. — (1) The Story of Chaldea. (2) The Story of Assyria. (New York 1886-1887.)

RAWLINSON, GEORGE. — The Five Great Monarchies of the Ancient Eastern World. Vols. I.-III. (4th ed. London 1879.)
  [Antiquated, but still of some use.]

ROGERS, R. W. — Outlines of the History of Early Babylonia. (Leipzig 1895.)

SCHMIDT, VALDEMAR. — Assyriens og Aegyptens gamle Historie. (Copenhagen 1872-1877.)
  [pp. 347-461.]

TIELE, C. P. — Babylonisch-Assyrische Geschichte. (Gotha 1886.)
  [The best history that has as yet been published.]

WACHSMUTH, CURT. — Einleitung in das Studium der alten Geschichte. (Leipzig 1895.)
  [pp. 365-403 "Babylonier und Assyrier," — indication of ancient and modern sources for the study.]

WINCKLER, HUGO. — Geschichte Babyloniens und Assyriens. (Leipzig 1892.)

(c) Origin and General Aspects of Babylonian-Assyrian Culture.

BAUMSTARK, A. — Babylon and Babylonia.
   [In Pauly-Wissowa's Real Encyclopaedie, II. cols. 2667-2718.]

BEZOLD, C. — Assyria.
   [*Ib.* II. cols. 1751-1771.]

HOMMEL, F. — Der Babylonische Ursprung der Aegyptischen Kultur. (Munich 1892.)

IHERING, RUDOLPH VON. — Vorgeschichte der Indo-Europäer. (Leipzig 1894.) 2tes Buch, 'Arier und Semiten,' pp. 93-305.
   [A most suggestive sketch of the development and influence of Babylonian culture; also in English translation, 'The Evolution of the Aryan.' New York 1897.]

NIKEL, JOHANNES. — Herodot und die Keilschriftforschung. (Paderborn 1896.)

PEISER, F. E. — Skizze der Babylonischen Gesellschaft. (Berlin 1896.)
   [Brief but capital sketch of Babylonian culture and social life.]

(d) Bibliography.

BEZOLD, C. — Kurzgefasster Ueberblick über die Babylonisch-Assyrische Literatur. (Leipzig 1886.)
   [A new edition is needed of this most valuable work.]

DELITZSCH, FRIEDRICH. — 'Litteratura' in the appendix to his 'Assyrian Grammar.' (London 1889.) pp. 55-78.

KAULEN, FR. — Assyrien und Babylonien (as above). pp. 248-266.

LINCKE, A. — Bericht über die Fortschritte der Assyriologie in den Jahren 1886-1893. (Leipzig 1894.)

Full bibliographical reports are given in :

(1) The American Journal of Semitic Languages and Literatures (University of Chicago ; quarterly).
(2) Jahrbücher für Geschichte, ed. by I. Jastrow and E. Berner (Berlin ; annual).
(3) Orientalische Bibliographie, ed. by Lucian Scherman (Berlin ; semi-annual).

(4) Zeitschrift für Assyriologie, ed. by C. Bezold (Munich ; quarterly).
(5) Revue d'Assyriologie et d'Archéologie Orientale, ed. by J. Oppert and E. Ledrain (Paris ; published at irregular intervals).

II.

GENERAL WORKS AND ARTICLES ON THE RELIGION OF BABYLONIA AND ASSYRIA.

BERGER, P. — 'Assyrie' in Lichtenberger's 'Encyclopedie des Sciences Religieuses.'

BOSCAWEN, W. ST. CHAD. — Lectures on the Religion of Babylonia [abstract] BOR III. 118–120, 150–163.

—— The Religion of Babylonia in 'Religious Systems of the World.' (Swan Sonnenschein & Co. 1896. pp. 15–25.)

DELITZSCH, FRIEDRICH. — The Religion of the Kassites. H 1885. 189–191.

> [From Delitzsch's 'Sprache der Kossaer.' Leipzig 1884. pp. 51–54.]

EERDMANS, B. D. — Babylonian-Assyrian Religion.

> [In 'Progress,' a publication issued by the University Association, Chicago, Ill. 3d series, No. 6 (1897), pp. 403–415.]

FINZI, FELICE. — Ricerche per lo Studio dell' Antichita Assira. (Rome 1872.) Libro Secondo. Mitologia, pp. 433–554.

> [General sketch of the religion, more particularly of the pantheon and legends of Babylonia and Assyria.]

GUYARD, S. — Bulletin de la Religion Assyro-Babylonienne. RHR I. 327–345; V. 253–278.

HALEVY, JOSEPH. — La Religion des Anciens Babyloniens et son plus recent historien M. Sayce. RHR XVII. 169–218.

> [Elaborate review of Sayce's work on the 'Religion of the Babylonians, with summary of Halevy's own views.]

HEUZEY, LEON. — Description of Monuments in De Sarzec's 'Découvertes en Chaldée.' (Paris 1889–1891.) pp. 77–240.

> [Contains much valuable information on religious art, votive objects, representations of religious ceremonies. The publication is not yet complete.]

HEWITT, J. F. — Early History of Northern India, Part III. JRAS, 1889, 527–583.

> [An attempt to trace the origin of Indian civilization to emigrants from southern Babylonia. The investigation has little value.]

HINCKS, EDWARD. — On the Assyrian Mythology. RIA Transactions XXII. Polite Literature, 1854, 405–422.

HOMMEL, F. — Die Semitischen Völker und Sprachen. (Leipzig 1883.) pp. 356–396. Die Religion der alten Babylonier, pp. 266–356. Sprache und Literatur der Sumero-Akkadier.

[Specimens of hymns and incantations.]

JEREMIAS, FRIEDRICH. — 'Die Babylonier und Assyrier' in Chantepie de la Saussaye's 'Lehrbuch der Religionsgeschichte.' (2d ed. Freiburg 1897.) I. 163–221.

[An excellent sketch of the Babylonian-Assyrian religion.]

LENORMANT, FRANÇOIS. — Les Sciences Occultes en Asie. I. La Magie chez les Chaldéens et les Origines Accadiennes. II. La Divination et la Science des Présages chez les Chaldéens. (Paris 1874–1875.)

[Also in English translation (in part) under the title 'Chaldaean Magic.' London 1877.]

LOISY, A. — Études sur la Religion Chaldéo-Assyrienne. (RR, 1890–1892.)

[Seven articles.]

MEYER, ED. — Geschichte des Alterthums. I. 174–183. (Stuttgart 1884.)

MÜRDTER und DELITZSCH. — Kurzgefasste Geschichte Babyloniens und Assyriens. (2d ed. Stuttgart 1891.) pp. 23–53.

OPPERT, J. — 'Babylone et Chaldée' in Lichtenberger's 'Encyclopedie des Sciences Religieuses.'

PINCHES, T. G. — The Religious Ideas of the Babylonians. JTVI XXVIII. 1–22.

PRESSENSÉ, E. DE. — La Religion Chaldéo-Assyrienne. RHR XIV. 73–94.

RAWLINSON, GEORGE. — The Religions of the Ancient World. (New York 1883.)

[Chapter II. — The Religion of the Assyrians and Babylonians.]

—— The Religion of Assyria in 'Religious Systems of the World.' (Swan Sonnenschein & Co. London 1896.) pp. 26–41.

RAWLINSON, H. C. — The Religion of the Babylonians and Assyrians.

[In George Rawlinson's 'The History of Herodotus.' London 1859. Vol. I. Essay X.]

SAYCE, A. H. — The Origin and Growth of Religion as Illustrated by the Religion of the Ancient Babylonians. (London 1887.)

[Brilliant and suggestive, but unreliable in details. The translations attached to the volume are to be accepted with caution. See Halevy's elaborate review, RHR XVII. 169-218.]

STRONG, S. A. — Die Religion der Babylonier.

[Announced to appear.]

SCHWALLY, F. — 'Die Religion der Babylonier und Assyrier,' in Friedrich von Hellwald's 'Kulturgeschichte in ihrer natürlichen Entwicklung bis zur Gegenwart.' (4th ed. Leipzig 1896.) I. 423-433.

TIELE, C. P. — Babylonisch-Assyrische Geschichte. (1886.) pp. 515-557. Religion: Die Mythologie und Glaubenslehre.

—— Vergelijkende Geschiedenis der Aegyptische en Mesopotamische Godsdiensten. (Amsterdam 1869.) pp. 282-413. De Godsdienst van Babel en Assur.

[French translation (abridged) by G. Collins, 'Histoire Comparée des Anciennes Religions de l'Egypte et des Peuples Semitiques.' Paris 1882. pp. 145-255. La Religion de Babylonie et de l'Assyrie. Also English translation by J. Ballingue. 1882.]

—— Geschichte der Religion im Alterthum bis auf Alexander den Grossen. (Gotha 1895.) I. 127-216. Die Religion in Babylonien und Assyrien.

[Also in Dutch. Amsterdam 1893.]

III.

PANTHEON, GODS, SPIRITS, HEROES.

BALL, C. J. — Tammuz, the Swine-god. PSBA XVI. 195-200.

BARTON, G. A. — The Semitic Ishtar Cult. H IX. 131-165; X. 1-73.

—— Was Ilu Ever a Distinct Deity in Babylonia? H X. 206, 207.

BEZOLD, C. — A Cuneiform List of Gods. PSBA XI. 173, 174; see also IX. 377.

—— Note on the god Addu or Daddu. Ib. p. 377.

—— Ueber Keilinschriftliche Babylonisch-Assyrische Göttertypen. ZA IX. 114-125, 405-409.

CHWOLSON, D. A. — Ueber Tammûz und die Menschenverehrung bei den alten Babyloniern. (St. Petersburg 1860.)

DE CARA, CAESARE. — Identificazione d' Iside e d' Osiride con Ishtar ed Ashur. 8th ICO, Section Semitique 2me Fasc, 275-278.

DELITZSCH, FRIEDRICH. — Article on 'Thammuz' in 'Calwer, Bibellexikon.' (Calw und Stuttgart 1885.)

—— Articles on Dagon, Merodach, Nebo, Nergal, Nisroch, Rimmon. *Ib.*

EERDMANS, B. — Goddess Â (or Malkatu) in 'Melekdienst en Vereering von Hemellichamen in Israel's Assyrische Periode.' (Leiden 1891.) pp. 73-82.

GUYARD, S. — Le Dieu Assyrien Ninib. RC, 1879, 1er Mars.

HOFFMANN, G. — Neue und Alte Götter (Nin-gal, Nusku, Ea, Nabu, Gibil, Ninib, Nergal, Sin). ZA XI. 258-292.

[Chiefly discussions of symbols of these deities found upon seal cylinders.]

HOMMEL, FRITZ. — Die Identität der ältesten Babylonischen und Aegyptischen Göttergenealogie und der Babylonische Ursprung der Aegyptischen Kultur. 9th ICO II. 218-244.

—— Note on Ninib. PSBA XIX. 312-314.

JASTROW, MORRIS, Jr. — On the Assyrian Kuduru and the Ring of the Sun-god in the Abu-Habba Tablet. PAOS, Oct. 1888. XCV.-XCVIII.

JENSEN, P. — Ueber einige Sumero-Akkadische und Babylonisch-Assyrische Götternamen. ZA, 1886. I. 1-24.

[Anshar, Ashur, Igigi, Dûzu, or Tammuz. *Cf.* Schrader's remarks, *ib.* pp. 209-217.]

—— Die Götter Amurru (û) und Ashratu. ZA XI. 302-305.

—— Nik(k)al-Sharratu; Sharratu in Harran. ZA XI. 293-301.

JEREMIAS, A. — Articles on Ashur, Marduk, Nebo, Nergal, Shamash, Sin, Tammuz in Roscher's 'Ausführliches Lexikon der Griechischen und Römischen Mythologie.'

[Articles on Adar, Anu, Anunnaki, Ea, Etana announced to appear in the supplement to Roscher's 'Ausführliches Lexikon,' *etc.*]

LENORMANT, FRANÇOIS. — Il mito di Adone-Tammuz nei documenti cuneiformi. 4th ICO, 1878. I. 143-173.

—— Sur le nom de Tammuz. 1st ICO II. 149-165.

—— Les Dieux de Babylone et de l'Assyrie. (Paris 1877.)

Luzzato, P. — L'Existence d'un Dieu Assyrien nommé Semiramis. JA, 4th Series, XVII. 465-480.

Lyon, D. G. — Was there at the Head of the Babylonian Pantheon a Deity Bearing the Name El? PAOS, May 1883, clxiv.-clxviii.

—— The Pantheon of Assurbanipal. PAOS, Oct. 1888, xciv., xcv.

Menant, J. — Le Mythe de Dagon. RHR XI. 295-301.

[Also in 'Les Pierres Gravées de la Haute Asie. Recherches de la Glyptique Orientale.' Paris 1883.]

—— Le Panthéon Assyro-Chaldéen. Les Beltis. RHR VIII. 489-519.

[The representation of goddesses engraved on seal cylinders. See also 'Les Pierres Gravées de la Haute Asie,' etc., as above.]

Meyer, Eduard. — Articles Baal and Astarte (with references to Bel and Ishtar) in Roscher's 'Ausführliches Lexikon der Griechischen und Römischen Mythologie.'

Nicolsky, M. V. — La Déesse des Cylindres et des Statuettes Babyloniennes. RAr, 3me série, XX. 36-43.

Offord, J. — The Nude Goddess in Assyro-Babylonian Art. PSPA XVIII. 156, 157.

Oppert, Jules. — La Vraie Assimilation de la Divinité de Tello. CR, 1884, 231-233.

—— Le Dieu de Sirtella [*i.e.*, Lagash]. ZK II. 261, 262.

[M. Oppert accepts the reading Nin-girsu first proposed by Arthur Amiaud. *Ib.* pp. 151, 152.]

—— Adad. ZA IX. 310-314.

[Discussion of pronunciation. See also Hilprecht, 'Assyriaca,' pp. 76-78, and Jastrow, AJSL XII. 143.]

Pinches, Theo. G. — Note upon the divine name Â. PSBA XIII. 25-27, 42-56.

—— Was Ninib the Most High God of Salem? *Ib.* XVI. 225-229.

—— The Pronunciation of the Name of the Plague-god, Urra not Dibbarra. BOR I. 207, 208.

[See Scheil, RT. XX. 57.]

—— A Bilingual List of Assyrian Gods. Academy, 1887, No. 816.

[See Evetts, *ib.* No. 819.]

Rawlinson, H. C. — Notes on Captain Durand's Report upon the Islands of Bahrein. JRAS, 1880, 201-227.

[Contains important remarks on the origin of Ea worship at the Persian Gulf, pp. 202-208.]

Reisner, George. — The Different Classes of Babylonian Spirits. PAOS, April 1892, cxcv.; cxcvi.

Revillout, E. and V. — Istar Taribi. BOR II. 57-59.

Robiou, F. A. — A Study on Egyptian and Babylonian Triads. IAQR, 1894.

Sayce, A. H. — Who was Dagon? SST, 1893, No. 21.

—— The God Ramman. ZA II. 331, 332.

Scheil, Fr. V. — Le Dieu-roi Bur-Sin Planète. ZA XII. 265, 266.

—— Ishtar sous la symbole de la vache. RT XX. 62.

—— Le Culte de Gudea. RT XVIII. 64-74.

Schrader, E. — Die Göttin Ishtar als Malkatu und Sharratu. ZA III. 353-364; IV. 74, 75.

—— Die Malkat hash-Shamayim und ihr Aramäisch-Assyrisches Aequivalent. KAW Sitzungsberichte, 1886, 477-491.

[See also Stade in ZATW VI. 123-132; 289-339; and Kuenen KAA Afdeeling ' Letterkunde,' 1888, 157-189.]

Talbot, H. Fox. — The Legend of Ishtar Descending to Hades. TSBA II. 179-212. See also RPI, 141-149.

Thureau-Daugin, Fr. — La Lecture de l'Idéogramme AN-IM (Ramman). JA, 9th Series, II. 385-393.

[See also Oppert, ib. pp. 393-396.]

Tiele, C. P. — La Déesse Ishtar surtout dans le mythe Babylonien. 6th ICO, Part II. Section I. 493-506.

[See also discussion in the Comptes Rendus of the Congress, pp. 87-91.]

—— Die Beteekenis van Ea en zijn verkouding tot Marduk en Nabû. KAA Verslagen en Mededeelingen 'Letterkunde,' 1887, 67-81.

Ward, W. H. — The Babylonian Gods in Babylonian Art. PAOS, May 1890, xv.-xviii.

—— Was there a Babylonian Gate-god? Academy, 1888, No. 847.

Winckler, H.— Die Istar von Nineve in Egypten. MVG I. 286-289.

Witte, J. de. — Sur le nom de Thamouz attribué à Adonis. M, 1887, 81 *seq.*

Zehnpfund, R. — Altbabylonische Götter und Heldensagen. BAZ, 1891, Nos. 39, 40, 52, 56, 63.

IV.

Religious Texts.

Hymns, Incantations, Omens, Oracles, Prayers, Legends, Myths, Votive Texts.

Ball, C. J. — A Bilingual Hymn (IVR 46, 5-19) PSBA XV. 51-54.

—— A Babylonian Ritual Text. JRAS, 1892, 841-853.

Banks, E. J. — Sumerisch-Babylonische Hymnen der von George Reisner herausgegebenen Sammlung, umschrieben, übersetzt und erklärt. (Breslau 1897.)

Barton, G. A. — Esarhaddon's Account of the Restoration of Ishtar's Temple at Erech. PAOS, May 1891, cxxx.-cxxxii.

Bertin, G. — Akkadian Hymn to the Setting Sun. RP, new series, II. 190-193.

Bezold, C. — Remarks on Some Unpublished Cuneiform Syllabaries with Respect to Prayers and Incantations written in Interlinear Form. PSBA X. 418-423.

—— Translation and Analysis of a Hymn to the Sun-god (Sp III.). RA I. 157-161.

Boissier, Alfred. — Deux Documents Assyriens relatifs aux Présages. RS I. 63-70, 168-172.

—— Documents Assyriens relatifs aux Présages.

[Vols. I. and II., Paris 1894-1897. Vol. III. announced.]

—— Notes d'Assyriologie. RS VI. 143-151.

[Two texts — a Prayer and an Incantation.]

Boscawen, W. St. Chad. — The Babylonian Legend of the Serpent Tempter. BOR IV. 251-255.

—— Babylonian Teraphim. BOR I. 39, 40.

—— The Legend of the Tower of Babel. RP III. 129-132; also in the TSBA V. 303-312.

[The interpretation is erroneous.]

Brünnow, R. — Assyrian Hymns. ZA IV. 1-40, 225-258; V. 55-80.

[Hymns to Shamash, Marduk, and Ishtar.]

Budge, Ernest A. — Assyrian Incantations to Fire and Water. RP XI. 133-138; also in TSBA VI. 420-435.

CRAIG, JAS. A. — Prayer of the Assyrian King Ashurbanipal. H X. 75-87.

—— Assyrian and Babylonian Religious Texts, Vols. I. and II. (Leipzig 1895-1897.) AB XIII.

[Announces also volumes of texts (1) Prayers to Shamash and Ramman, and (2) Series 'Illumination of Bel.']

—— K 69 (a hymn). ZA XI. 276.

—— An Assyrian Incantation to the God Sin, cir. 650 B.C. H XI. 101-109.

DELATTRE, A. J. — The Oracles Given in Favor of Esarhaddon. RP, new series, III. 25-31; see also BOR III. 25-31.

DELITZSCH, FRIEDRICH. — Babylonisch-Assyrisches Psalmbuch.

[Announced to appear in the 'Abhandlungen der königlichen Gesellschaft der Wissenschaften zu Leipzig.']

—— Assyrische Lesestücke. (Leipzig 1885. 3d ed.)

[Contains a selection of religious texts as follows: pp. 93-99, Creation tablets; 99-121, Deluge episode; 117, 118, Oracle to Esarhaddon; 130-132, Incantations; 134-136, Hymn to Ishtar.]

EVETTS, B. T. A. — An Assyrian Religious Text. PSBA X. 478, 479 and two plates.

[Apparently a royal prayer.]

HALÉVY, J. — Assyrian Fragments. RP XI. 157-162.

[Part of a hymn, of a penitential psalm, etc.]

—— Documents religieux de l'Assyrie et de la Babylonie. (Paris 1882.)

—— Textes religieux Babyloniens en double Redaction. RS IV. 150-160, 245-251, 344-348.

—— 'Les Inscriptions peints de Citium' in 'Mélanges de Critique et d'Histoire,' pp. 165-196.

[Translation in large part and discussion of Ishtar's descent into the nether world.]

HARPER, EDWARD T. — Die Babylonischen Legenden von Etana, Zu, Adapa und Dibbarra. BA II. 390-521.

[See also Academy 1891, No. 976.]

HAUPT, PAUL. — Akkadische und Sumerische Keilschrifttexte. (Leipzig 1881-1882.)

[Contains pp. 75-79, 82-106 Incantations; 79, 115-131 Hymns and Psalms.]

Jastrow, Morris, Jr. — A fragment of the Babylonian "Dibbarra" Epic. Publications of the University of Pennsylvania. Series in Philology, Literature, and Archaeology, Vol. I., No. 2. (Boston 1891.)

—— A new Fragment of the Babylonian Etana Legend. BA III. 363-384.

Jensen, P. — De Incantamentorum Sumerico-Assyrorum seriei quae dicitur "šurbu" Tabula VI. ZK I. 279-322; II. 15-61; also 306-311, 416-425.

[Appeared as a revised and separate publication under same title with the addition of the words "commentatio Philologica." Munich, Straub, 1885.]

—— Hymnen auf das Wiedererscheinen der drei grossen Lichtgötter. ZA II. 76-94, 191-204.

[Hymns to Sin, Shamash, and Ishtar. A volume by Jensen, embodying translation of religious texts is in course of preparation for Schrader's 'Keilschriftliche Bibliothek.']

Jeremias, A. — Die Höllenfahrt der Ishtar. Eine altbabylonische Beschwörungslegende. (Munich 1886.)

King, L. W. — Babylonian Magic and Sorcery, being 'the Prayers of the Lifting of the Hand.' (London 1896.)

—— New Fragments of the Dibbarra Legend. ZA XI. 50-62.

Knudtzon, J. A. — Assyrische Gebete an den Sonnengott für Staat und königliches Haus aus der Zeit Asarhaddons und Assurbanipals. Band I. Autographierte Texte; Band II. Einleitung, Umschrift und Erklärung Verzeichnisse. (Leipzig 1893.)

Lenormant, François. — Chaldaean Hymns to the Sun. RP X. 119-128.

—— Hymne au Soleil. Texte primitif Accadien. JA, 7th Series, XII. 378; XIII. 1-98; postscriptum *ib.* XIV. 264, 265.

—— Une Incantation Magique Chaldéenne. RAr, 2d Series, XXXIV. 254-262.

—— Lettres Assyriologiques. 2me Série Études Accadiennes, Vols. II. and III. (Paris 1874-1879.)

[Contains numerous hymns and incantations accompanied by a French translation.]

—— Translations of religious texts in 'Les Origines de l'Histoire d'après la Bible et les Traditions des Peuples orientaux.' (Paris 1880-1882.) 2 vols.

Lyon, D. G. — Assyrian and Babylonian Royal Prayers. PAOS, October 1888. XCIII., XCIV.

—— On a Sacrificial Tablet from Sippar. PAOS, May 1886, xxx.

Messerschmidt, L. — Tabula VA. Th. 246, Babylonica Musei Berolinensis primum editur commentarioque instruitur. (Kirchhain 1896.)

[A hymn.]

Oppert, J. — 'Chants et Invocations' in Eichoff and David 'Chef d'œuvres litteraires de l'Inde, de la Perse, de l'Egypte et de la Chine.' (Paris.) II. 211–219.

[Translations of selected prayers, hymns, and incantations.]

—— Fragments Mythologiques. (Paris 1882.)

[Reprints of several articles.]

—— Translation of III. Rawlinson, pl. 65, in JA, 6th Series, XVIII. 449–453.

—— Hymnes en Sumerien et en Accadien ou Assyrien. 1st ICO. II. 217–224.

[A hymn to Ishtar in dialogue form.]

—— Le Champ Sacré de la Déesse Ninâ. CR, 1893, 326–344. See also ZA VII. 360–374.

[Contains important remarks about the goddess Ninâ in connection with the text published by Hilprecht, 'Old Babylonian Inscriptions,' I. 1, pls. 30, 31.]

—— Traduction de Quelques Textes Assyriens. . . . Louange du Dieu Nibir et de ses sept Attributions. 4th ICO I. 233–235.

—— L'Immortalité de l'âme chez les Chaldéens. (Paris 1875.)

[Legend of Ishtar's descent to the lower world.]

—— Chant en Sumerien et en Assyrien sur une épidémie. JA, 7th Series, I. 289–293.

[Translation of tablet K 1284 (incantation against Namtar) and of IIR 19.]

—— Notice sur d'anciennes formules d'Incantation et autres dans une langue antérieure au Babylonien. JA, 7th Series, I. 113–122.

[Translation of II Rawl. 17, 18.]

—— Babylonian legends found at Khorsabad. RP XI. 41–44.

[See also translations of various religious texts in 'Expedition Scientifique en Mesopotamie,' pp. 328–350.]

Peiser, F. E. — Ein Satz in den Beschwörungsformeln. ZA II. 102, 103.

PINCHES, T. G. — An Erechite's Lament. RP, new series, I. 84, 85.

[A penitential psalm with historical references; see also BOR I, 21–23.]

—— The Oracle of Ishtar of Arbela. RP XI. 59–72 ; also RP, new series, V. 129–140.

—— Sin-Gashid's Gift to the Temple É-Ana. BOR I. 8–11. See also RP, new series, I. 78–83.

—— and E. A. W. BUDGE. — Some New Texts in the Babylonian Character, relating Principally to the Restoration of Temples. PSBA, 1884. pp. 179–182.

RAWLINSON, H. C. — A Selection from the Miscellaneous Inscriptions of Western Asia. Vol. IV. 2d ed. revised (and with additions) by T. G. Pinches. (London 1891.)

[This fourth volume of the publications of tablets in the British Museum is almost exclusively devoted to religious texts. In the other volumes some texts of this character will be found as follows: Vol. II. pls. 17–19, incantations; 51–61, names and titles of gods and temples; miscellaneous. Vol. III. pls. 61–65, astronomical and astrological reports, omen tablets and portents; 66–69, lists and titles of gods and temples; miscellaneous. Vol. V. pl. 31, omen tablets (with explanations); 43, titles of Nebo, *etc.*; 46, No. 2, lists of gods and their epithets; 47, prayer (with commentary); 48, 49, religious calendar; 50, 51, hymn to Shamash. Note also that many of the historical texts in Vols. I.–V. contain invocations to gods.]

REISNER, GEORGE. — Sumerisch-Babylonische Hymnen nach Thontafeln Griechischer Zeit. (Berlin 1896.) Königliche Museen zu Berlin. Mittheilungen aus den Orientalischen Sammlungen No. X.

SAYCE, A. H. — Accadian Hymn to Istar. RP I. 155–160.

—— Accadian Poem on the Seven Evil Spirits. *Ib.* IX. 144–148.

—— An Accadian Liturgy. *Ib.* III. 125–130.

—— An Accadian Penitential Hymn. *Ib.* VII. 151–156.

—— Ancient Babylonian Charms. *Ib.* III. 145–154.

[Shurpu Series, 6th Tablet.]

—— An Assyrian Talismanic Tablet. BOR III. 17, 18.

—— Babylonian Augury by means of Geometrical Figures. TSBA IV. 302–314.

—— Fragment of an Assyrian Prayer after a Bad Dream. RP IX. 149–152.

SAYCE, A. H. — Babylonian Exorcisms. *Ib.* I. 131-135.

—— Tables of Omens Furnished by Dogs and Births. *Ib.* V. 167-176.

—— The Dedication of three Babylonians to the service of the Sun-god at Sippara. RP, new series, IV. 109-113.

[Interpretation false.]

—— The Overthrow of Sodom and Gomorrah (Accadian Account). RP XI. 115-118.

[Title, translation, and Interpretation alike fanciful.]

—— Two Accadian Hymns. *Ib.* XI. 129-132.

—— Two Hymns to the Sun-god [in preface, pp. ix.-x., to RP, new series, IV., 1890].

[Copious translations of magical texts, hymns, legends, *etc.*, by Sayce in Hibbert Lectures on 'The Religion of the Ancient Babylonians.' London 1887. See especially pp. 441-540.]

SCHEIL, F. V. — Psaume de Pénitence Chaldéen inedit. RB, 1896, 75-78.

—— Legende Chaldéenne trouvée à El-Amarna [Adapa]. RR Mars-Avril 1891.

—— Choix des Textes Religieux Assyriens. RHR XXXVI. 197-207.

—— Fragments de Poésie lyrique Babylonienne. RB VI. 28-30.

—— Fragment mythologique avec mention de Uddushu-namir patesi. RT XX. 62, 63.

—— Hymne Babylonien avec metre appartent. ZA XI. 291-298.

SCHRADER, E. — Die Höllenfahrt der Ishtar. Ein Altbabylonisches Epos. (Giessen 1874.)

SMITH, S. A. — Miscellaneous Texts. (Leipzig 1887.) pp. 1-5, 8-10.

[Portions of the Creation Series.]

STRONG, S. ARTHUR. — A Prayer of Assurbanipal. RP, new series, VI. 102-106; also 9th ICO II. 199-208.

—— Note on a Fragment of the Adapa Legend. PSBA XX. 274-279.

—— On Some Oracles to Esarhaddon and Assurbanipal. BA II. 627-645.

—— Votive Inscriptions. RP, new series, IV. 90-95.

—— A Hymn to Nebuchadnezzar. PSBA XX. 154-162.

TALBOT, H. Fox. — A Prayer and a Vision. TSBA I. 346-348 and RP VII. 65-68.

[Ashurbanabal's prayer to Ishtar and dream sent by the goddess.]

—— Assyrian Sacred Poetry. RP III. 131-138.

[Prayers and incantations.]

—— Assyrian Talismans and Exorcisms. *Ib*. III. 139-144.

—— War of the Seven Evil Spirits Against Heaven. *Ib*. V. 161-166.

[Incantation text.]

TALLQUIST, K. L. — Die Assyrische Beschwörungsserie Maqlû. (Leipzig 1894.)

WEISSBACH, F. H. — Ueber die ersten Tafeln im IV. Bande Rawlinsons.

[Announced.]

—— Eine Sumerisch-Assyrische Beschwörungsformel IV. Rawl. 16, No. 1 in 'Melanges Charles de Harlez.' (Leiden 1896.) pp. 360-371.

WINCKLER, H. and ABEL LUDWIG. — Thontafelfund von El-Amarna. (Berlin 1891.)

[Vol. III. pp. 166, *a* and *b*, Legend of Adapa; see Erman in KAW Sitzungsberichte XXIII. 585; Lehmann, ZA III. 380; other mythological fragments, pp. 164-165.]

ZIMMERN, HEINRICH. — Babylonische Busspsalmen, umschrieben, übersetzt und erklärt. (Leipzig 1885.) BA VI.

[Also published in part as a thesis.]

—— Beiträge zur Kenntniss der Babylonischen Religion. Erste Lieferung. Die Beschwörungstafeln Shurpu. (Leipzig 1896.) AB XII.

—— Zusatzbemerkungen zur Legende von Adapa. BA II. 437, 438.

—— Hexenbeschwörungen bei den Babyloniern. BAZ, 1891, No. 337.

—— An Old Babylonian Legend from Egypt [Adapa]. SST, 1892, No. 25.

V.

COSMOLOGY.

BARTON, G. A. — Tiâmat. JAOS XV. 1–28; also PAOS, May 1890, xiii.–xv.

BRUNENGO, GIUSEPPE. — L'Impero di Babilonia e di Ninive. (2 vols. Prato 1885.) Capo I. La Cosmogonia de Caldei comparata alla Mosaica, pp. 67–85. Capo II. La Ribellione degli Angeli e la Caduta del Uomo, (*i.e.*, Marduk and Tiâmat story), pp. 86–108. Capo IV. La Storia del Diluvio, pp. 124–140.

BUDGE, E. A. W. — The Fourth Tablet of the Creation Series, relating to the fight between Marduk and Tiâmat. PSBA VI. 5–11.

—— Fourth Tablet of the Creation Series. PSBA X. 86 and six pls.

DELITZSCH, FRIEDRICH. — Texte zur Weltschöpfung und zur Auflehnung und Bekämpfung der Schlange Tiâmat. AL, 3d ed., 1885. pp. 93–99.

—— Das Babylonische Weltschöpfungsepos. (Leipzig 1896.)

ENGEL, MORITZ. — Die Lösung der Paradiesfrage. (Leipzig 1885.)

HALEVY, J. — La Cosmologie Babylonienne d'après M. Jensen. RHR XXII. 180–208.

[Summary and critique of Jensen's 'Kosmologie der Babylonier.']

—— Recherches Bibliques — L'Histoire des Origines d'après la Genèse. Texte, Traduction et Commentaire. Tome I. Genèse I.–XXV. (Paris 1895.)

[Contains translations of the Babylonian Cosmological Texts, and discusses their bearings on the O. T. narrative. A most suggestive work.]

—— Recherches Bibliques — Chapter 28, La Création et les Vicissitudes du Premier Homme. RS I. 101–117, 193–202.

[Transliteration, translation, and discussion of the Babylonian Creation Tablets.]

HOMMEL, F. — Eine Neugefundene Weltschöpfungslegende. DR, 1892, 105–114; see also Neue Kirchliche Zeitung, I. 393 *seq.*, II. 89 *seq.*

—— The Oldest Cosmogony. SST, 1894, No. 7.

JENSEN, P. — Die Kosmologie der Babylonier. Studien und Materialien. (Strassburg 1890.)

JENSEN, P. — Ursprung und Geschichte des Tierkreises. DR, 1890, 112–116.

LAJARD, F. — Fragments d'un Mémoire sur le Système théogonique et cosmogonique des Assyriens ou des Chaldéens d'Assyrie. JA, 2d Series, XIV. 114–143.

LAURIE, THOMAS. — Cuneiform Inscriptions and the Deluge. Bibliotheca Sacra, XLII. 165–168.

LENORMANT, F. — Essai de Commentaire sur les Fragments cosmogoniques de Berose. (Paris 1871.)

[An elaborate treatise on the traditions of Berosus in connection with the cuneiform account of creation.]

LOISY, A. — Les Mythes Chaldéens de la Création et du Déluge. (Amiens 1892.) RR, 1896.

[From RR, 1890-1891. See § I.]

LUKAS, FR. — Die Grundbegriffe in den Kosmogonieen der Alten Völker. 1893. pp. 1–46.

[Translations by Jensen, pp. 1-14. Die Kosmogonie der Babylonier und der Genesis.]

MÜLLER, D. H. — Die Propheten in ihrer Ursprünglichen Form. (Wien 1895.) pp. 6–13.

[Translation of considerable portions of the Babylonian creation narratives. Follows Zimmern.]

MUSS-ARNOLT, W. — The Cuneiform Account of the Creation. Revised translation. BW III. 17–27.

—— A Comparative Study of the Translations of the Babylonian Creation Tablets, with special reference to Jensen's 'Kosmologie' and Barton's 'Tiâmat.' H IX. 6–23.

OPPERT, J. — Fragments Cosmogoniques in Ledrain's 'Histoire d'Israel.' (Paris 1882.) pp. 411–422.

[Translation of Creation Series of tablets of deluge.]

—— Le Poème Chaldéen du Déluge. (Paris 1885.)

—— Die Fragmente der Epopöen welche die Schöpfung und Sintfluth nach babylonischer Auffassung betreffen. Verhandlungen Deutscher Philologen und Schulmänner, XXXIV. 128, 129.

—— Traductions de quelques textes Assyriens. — Fragments des Récits de la Création. — Guerre de Merodach et Tiâmat. 4th ICO, 229-238.

Pinches, T. G. — A Babylonian Duplicate of Tablets I. and II. of the Creation Series. BOR IV. 25–33.
—— The New Version of the Creation Story. 9th ICO, 1892. II. 190–198; also JRAS, 1891, 393–408; and Academy, 1890, Nos. 968, 974, and the Times, 1889, Dec. 16.
—— The Non-Semitic Version of the Creation Story. RP, new series, VI. 107–114.
Sayce, H. — The Assyrian Story of the Creation. RP, new series, I. 122–146.
—— Babylonian Legend of the Creation RP XI. 109–114.
—— The Babylonian Story of the Creation according to the Tradition of Cutha. RP, new series, I. 147–153.
Schrader, E. — Cuneiform Inscriptions and the Old Testament. (London 1885.) I. 1–22.

[Translation of portions of the Creation Series with comments; third German edition announced.]

Smith, George. — The Chaldaean Account of Genesis. (2d ed. London 1881.) German trans. ed. by Friedrich Delitzsch (Leipzig 1876), under the title 'Chaldaeische Genesis.'
—— On Some Fragments of the Chaldaean Account of the Creation. TSBA IV. 363, 364.
Stucken, Ed. — Astralmythen der Hebraer, Babylonier und Aegypter. I. und II. Theil. (Leipzig 1896–1897.)

[Rather fanciful.]

Talbot, H. Fox. — The Fight between Bel and the Dragon. RP IX. 135–140.

[Portion of the Creation Series.]

—— The Fight between Bel and the Dragon and the Flaming Sword which turned every way. TSBA V. 1–21.
—— The Chaldaean Account of the Creation. RP IX. 115–118; also TSBA V. 426–440.
—— The Revolt in Heaven, from a Chaldaean Tablet. TSBA IV. 349–362.

[Portions of the Creation Series.]

WARREN, W. F.—Paradise Found. 10 ed. (Boston 1893.) Part IV. chapter 6. The Cradle of the Race in Akkadian, Assyrian, and Babylonian Thought.

[Discussion in connection with a general theory of the site of paradise.]

WARD, W. HAYES.—Contest between Bel-Merodach and the Dragon. PAOS, May 1879. X.

—— Dragon and Serpent in Chaldaean Mythology. PAOS, Oct. 1879, xvii.

—— Bel and the Dragon. AJSL XIV. 94–105.

—— The Dragon Tiâmat in Babylonian and Assyrian Art. PAOS, Oct. 1889, clxviii–clxix.

ZIMMERN, H.—Translations of the Babylonian Creation and Deluge Stories in Gunkel's 'Schöpfung und Chaos,' pp. 401–428.

—— 'König Tukulti bēl niši und die Kuthaische Schöpfungslegende.' ZA XII. 317–330.

[Translation of the Cuthaean Version of the Creation Story.]

VI.

THE GILGAMESH EPIC

(including the Deluge Story).

ADLER, C.—The Legends of Semiramis and the Nimrod Epic. JHUC, No. 55.

BOSCAWEN, W. ST. CHAD.—Hymn to Gilgames. BOR VII. 121–125.

—— The Twelfth Izdubar Legend. RP IX. 131–134.

CASANOWICZ, I. M.—Professor Haupt's Nimrod Epic. JHUC, No. 98.

CHEYNE, T. K.—Nimrod, a Kassite King. Academy, 1895, No. 47.

DE LACOUPERIE, TERRIEN.—The Deluge Tradition and its Remains in Ancient Chaldaea. BOR pp. 15–24, 49–55, 79–88, 102–111.

DELITZSCH, FRIEDRICH.—Article 'Nimrod' in 'Calwer Bibellexikon.'

—— Die Sintflutherzählung oder die elfte Tafel des Nimrod Epos. AL. (3d ed. Leipzig 1885.) 99–109.

DRYOFF, K.—Wer ist Chadir? ZA XII. 319–327.

GRIVEL, JOSEF. — Nimrod et les Ecritures Cunéiformes. TSBA III, 136-144.
  [Proposed identification of Nimrod and Marduk. See also Sayce, below.]

HAMILTON, L. LE CENCI. — Ishtar and Izdubar, the Epic of Babylon. Restored in modern verse. Vol. I. Illustrated. (London 1884.)

HARPER, E. T. — The Legend of Etana, Gilgamos and his Kindred in Folklore. Academy, 1891, No. 995; see also Nos. 985, 987, 988.

HAUPT, PAUL. — The Cuneiform Account of the Deluge. OTS, 1883, 77-85.

—— Das babylonische Nimrodepos. Keilschrifttext der sogenannten Izdubarlegenden mit dem Keilinschriftlichen Sintfluthberichte, nach den Originalen im Britischen Museum copiert und herausgegeben. (Leipzig 1884-1891.) 2 vols. AB III.

—— Die zwölfte Tafel des Babylonischen Nimrodepos. BA I. 48-79.

—— On Two Passages in the Chaldaean Flood Tablet. PAOS, March 1894, CV.-CXI.

—— On Some Passages in the Cuneiform Account of the Deluge, with special reference to the first column of the tablet. JHUC, No. 69.

—— Ergebnisse einer neuen Collation der Izubar Legenden. BA I. 94-152. See Halevy ZA IV. 61.

—— On the Dimensions of the Babylonian Ark. PAOS, Oct. 1888, lxxxix.-xc.; see also AJP IX. 419-424.

—— Der Keilinschriftliche Sintfluthbericht. Eine Episode des babylonischen Nimrodepos. (Leipzig 1881.)

—— Der Keilschriftliche Sintfluthbericht. Umschrift, Uebersetzung, und Erläuterungen in Schrader's 'Die Keilinschriften und das Alte Testament,' 3d ed., 1898.
  [Latest and most satisfactory translation.]

HOFFMANN, G. — Die Dubar-Sage und der Keilinschriftliche Sintfluthbericht. Die Grenzboten, Jahrgang 47.

HOMMEL, F. — Gis-dubarra, Gibilgamish, Nimrod. PSBA XV. 291-300; XVI. 13-15.

Heuzey, L. — La Lance Colossale d'Izbubar et les Nouvelles Formeles de M. de Sarzec. AI. Bulletin 1893, 305.

Jastrow, Morris, Jr. — The New Version of the Babylonian Account of the Deluge. The Independent, Feb. 10, 17, 1898.

Jensen, P. — Gishgimash (= Gilgamish) ein Kossaer? ZA VI. 340-342.

Jeremias, A. — Article 'Izdubar' in Roscher's 'Ausführliches Lexikon der Griechischen und Römischen Mythologie.' Vol. II. cols. 773-823.

—— Izdubar-Nimrod. Eine Altbabylonische Heldensage nach den Keilschriftfragmenten dargestellt. (Leipzig 1891.) See also article by Quentin in RHR XXXI. 162-177.

Lenormant, F. — Le Déluge et l'Épopée Babylonienne. (Paris 1873.)

Lidzbarski. — Zu den Arabischen Alexandergeschichten. ZA VIII. 263-312. See also *ib.*, 317-319.

—— Wer ist Chadhir? ZA VII. 104-116.

Meissner, Bruno. — Alexander und Gilgamos. (Leipzig 1894.)

—— Einige Bemerkungen zur Erklärung des Sintfluthberichtes. ZA III. 417-421.

Menant, J. — Le Déluge. Noé dans l'arche. (Paris 1880.)

Moor, Fl. — De la Geste de Gilgames confrontée avec la Bible et avec les Documents Historiques indigènes. M, June 1897.

Muss-Arnolt, W. — The Chaldaean Account of the Deluge. A revised translation. BW III. 109-118.

—— Remarks Introductory to a Comparative Study on the Translations of the Deluge Tablets. PAOS, April 1892, cxc.-cxcv.; also JHUC, No. 98.

Offord, J. — A New Fragment of the Babylonian Deluge Story. PSBA XX. 53, 54.

[Scheil's tablet from Sippara.]

Oppert, J. — The Chaldaean Perseus. BOR V. 1, 2; also CR, 1890, 464, 465.

[Identification of Izdubar-Gilgamesh with Gilgamos in Aelian's zoölogical work 'De Natura Animalium,' XII. 21. See also Sayce in the Academy, 1890, No. 966; Ward, *ib.*, No. 971; and Kohler, *ib.*, 1891, No. 985.]

—— Nimrod. Bulletin de l'Athenée Orientale, 1873, Jan.-Feb.

OPPERT, J. — Le Poème Chaldéen du Déluge. Traduit de l'Assyrien. (Paris 1885.)

PINCHES, T. G. — Exit Gishtubar. BOR IV, 264.
[Proposal to read the name of the Babylonian hero Gilgamesh. *Cf.* Sayce in Academy, 1890, No. 966, and Ward, *ib.*, No. 971.]

RAWLINSON, H. C. — The Izdubar Legends. Athenaeum, 1872, No. 2354.

ROCHETTE, RAOUL. — Mémoire sur l'Hercule Assyrien et Phenicien. AI Mémoires, 2me Partie, XVII. 9–374.

SAUVEPLANE, F. — Une Épopée Babylonienne. Ishtubar-Gilgames. (Paris 1894.)

SAYCE, A. H. — On Nimrod and the Assyrian Inscription. TSBA II. 248, 249; see also Academy, 1893, No. 1054.
[Proposed Identification of Nimrod with Amar-ud = Marduk, the head of the Babylonian Pantheon.]

—— The Higher Criticism and the Verdict of the Monuments. (London 1894.) pp. 97–119.

SCHEIL, F. V. — Notes d'Epigraphie et d'Archéologie Assyrienne. XXX. Un Fragment d'un Nouveau Récit du Déluge de l'Époque du Roi Ammizaduga. RT XX. 55–59; see also RB, 1898, 5–9.

—— The New Babylonian Account of the Deluge. The Independent, Jan. 20, 1898.

SMITH, GEORGE. — The Chaldaean Account of the Deluge. TSBA II. 203–234.

—— The Eleventh Tablet of the Izdubar Legends. The Chaldaean Account of the Deluge. TSBA III. 530–596; also RP VII. 133.

SUESS, ED. — Die Sintfluth in 'Das Antlitz der Erde.' (Leipzig 1883.) pp. 25–98.
[Discussion of the Babylonian tale with notes by Prof. Paul Haupt.]

TALBOT, H. FOX. — Ishtar and Izdubar, being the 6th Tablet of the Izdubar Series. Translated from the Cuneiform. TSBA V. 97–121; also RP IX. 119–128.

—— Commentary on the Deluge Tablet. TSBA IV. 49–83.

—— Tablet in the British Museum Relating Apparently to the Deluge. TSBA IV. 129–131.
[Talbot's supposition is erroneous.]

VII.

BELIEFS, LEGENDS, ETHICS, AND SPECIAL PHRASES OF THE RELIGION.

ADER, CYRUS. — The Views of the Babylonians Concerning Life after Death. AR, 1888, 92–101 ; see also PAOS, Oct. 1887, ccxxxviii.–ccxliii.

BALL, C. J. — Glimpses of Babylonian Religion. I. Human Sacrifices. II. The Gods and Their Images. PSBA XIV. 149–162.

BONAVIA, E. — The Sacred Trees of the Assyrian Monuments. BOR III. 7–12, 35–40, 56–61 ; see also IV. 95, 96.

—— The Sacred Trees of Assyria. 9th ICO, pp. 245–257.

[Arguments not conclusive.]

BOSCAWEN, W. ST. CHAD. — Notes on the Religion and Mythology of the Assyrians. TSBA IV. 267–301.

—— Texts Bearing on the Belief in Immortality. (1) 12th Izdubar Tablet. (2) Descent of Ishtar. (3) 7th Izdubar Tablet. (4) Hymn to Marduk. BOR IV. 251–254.

—— Babylonian Witchcraft. ET, 1898, 228–230.

—— Notes on Assyrian Religion and Mythology. TSBA VI. 535–542.

[Translations of some religious texts. General remarks.]

—— Babylonian Teraphim. BOR I. 39, 40.

—— The Babylonian Legend of the Serpent Tempter. BOR IV. 251–255.

—— Oriental Eschatology (Egypt and Chaldaea). BOR VI. 38–42.

—— The Plague Legends of Chaldaea. BOR I. 11–14.

CLERMONT-GANNEAU. — L'Enfer Assyrien. RAr, 2d Series, XXXVIII. 337–349.

CRAIG, JAMES A. — The Babylonian Ishtar Epic. OTS VIII. 249–256.

GOESSLING, E. — Die Hölle nach Babylonisch-Assyrischer Anschauung. TZ, 1895, No. 3.

HALEVY, J. — L'Immortalité de l'Âme chez les Peuples Semitiques. RAr, 2d Series, XLIV. 44–53.

[Translation and discussion of Ishtar's descent into the nether world.]

HALEVY, J. — Le Rapt de Perséphoné ou Proserpine par Pluton chez les Babyloniens. RS I. 372-376.

HAUG, M. — Die Unsterblichkeit der Seele bei den Chaldäern. BAZ, 1875, Nos. 70, 71.

HEUZEY, L. — Mythes Chaldéens. RA, 3d Series, XXVI. 295-308.

HILPRECHT, H. V. — Serpent and Tree in Babylonian Records. SST, 1893, No. 52.

HINCKS, EDWARD. — On the Assyrian Mythology. RIA Memoirs, 1854, 405-422.

HOMMEL, F. — Hexenverbrennungen im alten Babylonien. Münchener Neueste Nachrichten, 1896, No. 415.

JASTROW, MORRIS, JR. — The Ethics of the Babylonians and Assyrians. ER III. 65-77.

—— The Babylonian Term Shu'âlu. AJSL XIV. 165-170.

JENSEN, PETER. — The Queen in the Babylonian Hades and Her Consort. SST, 1897, Nos. 11, 12.

—— The Supposed Babylonian Origin of the Week and the Sabbath. SST, 1892, No. 3.

JEREMIAS, A. — Die Babylonisch-Assyrischen Vorstellungen vom Leben nach dem Tode. (Leipzig 1897.)

—— Articles 'Arallu' and 'Etana.'

[Announced to appear in the supplement to Roscher's 'Ausführliches Lexikon der Griechischen und Römischen Mythologie.']

KIESEWETTER, CARL. — Der Occultismus des Alterthums. (Leipzig 1896.) Book I. 364 *seq.*, 'Der Occultismus bei den Akkadern, Babyloniern, Chaldäern und Assyriern.'

[Based largely upon Lenormant's 'Chaldaean Magic.']

LAURENT, A. — La Magie et la Divination chez les Chaldéo-Assyriens. (Paris 1894.)

LENORMANT, F. — La Legende de Semiramis. (Paris 1872.)

[A transformed Ishtar legend.]

OPPERT, J. — L'Immortalité de l'Âme chez les Chaldéens. (Paris 1875.)

[Translation of Ishtar's descent into the nether world.]

PINCHES, T. G. — The Messianic Idea among the Early Babylonians and Assyrians. Academy, 1887, Nos. 816, 818, 820.

RAVENSHAW, E. C. — On the Winged Bulls, Lions, and Other Symbolical Figures from Nineveh. JRAS, 1854, 93-117.

 [Contains some interesting suggestions on Babylonian mythology, but the paper as a whole is antiquated.]

SAYCE, A. H. — Ancient Babylonian Moral and Political Precepts. RP VII. 119-122.

—— The Babylonian Legend of the Creation of Man. Academy, 1893, No. 1055.

—— Babylonian Folk-Lore. FLJ I. 16-22.

SCHEIL, FR. V. — Relief Ciselé représentant une Scène Funéraire Babylonienne. RT XX. 59-62.

—— Le Culte de Gudéa. RT XVIII. 64-74.

TALBOT, H. Fox. — On the Religious Belief of the Assyrians. Nos. I., II., III., IV. TSBA I. 106-115; II. 29-79, 346-352.

 [No. I. contains text and translation of two prayers; Nos. II. and III., Incantation Texts; No. IV., Future Punishment of the Wicked.]

—— Legend of the Descent of Ishtar. RP I. 141-149.

—— Revised Translation of the Descent of Ishtar with a Further Commentary. TSBA III. 118-135. Addenda pp. 357-360.

THUREAU-DAUGIN, F. — Le Culte des Rois dans la Période Prébabylonienne. RT XIX. 185-187.

TIELE, C. P. — Cyrus de Groote en de Godsdienst van Babel in 'Melanges, Charles de Harlez' (Leiden 1896), 307-312.

TYLER, THOMAS. — The Babylonian Idea of a Disembodied Soul. BOR I. 55-57.

TYLOR, EDWARD B. — The Winged Figures of the Assyrians and Other Ancient Monuments. PSBA XII. 383-393; see also RHR XXII. 209-220.

 [Explanation of the symbols on Assyrian sculptures.]

WARD, W. H. — On the Representation of the Solar Disk. AJT II. 115-118.

WARREN, W. F. — Gates of Sunrise in Ancient Babylonian Art. BOR III. 241-244.

ZIMMERN, H. — Vater, Sohn und Fürsprecher in der Babylonischen Gottesvorstellung. (Leipzig 1896.)

 [See review by Jastrow, AJT I. 468-474.]

VIII.

Temples and Cult.

BALL, C. J. — Glimpses of Babylonian Religion. I. Human Sacrifices. II. The Gods and Their Images. PSBA XIV. 149-162.

BOSCAWEN, W. ST. CHAD. — The Babylonian and Jewish Festivals. BOR IV. 34-38.

D'ALVIELLA, GOBLET. — Des Symboles qui ont influencé la Représentation figurée des Pierres Coniques chez les Semites. RHR XX. 135-150.

JEREMIAS, JOHANN. — Die Cultustafel von Sippar. BA I. 267-92.

[An important archive of the Shamash temple at Sippar, illustrative of the cult.]

KARPPE, S. — Mélanges de Critique Biblique et d'Assyriologie. RS II. 146-151.

[The Babylonian festival Zagmuk and the Biblical New Year.]

KOLDEWEY, ROBERT. — Die altbabylonischen Gräber in Surghul und El Hibba. ZA II. 403-430.

[Funeral customs.]

KOHUT, A. — The Talmudic Records of the Persian and Babylonian Festivals critically illustrated. AJSL XIV. 182-194. See also REJ XXIV. 256-271.

[Insufficient discussion.]

MENANT. — Les Sacrifices sur les Cylindres Chaldéens. Gazette Archeologique, 1883, Nos. 7-9.

PERROT & CHIPIEZ. — A History of Art in Chaldaea and Assyria. (London 1884.) Eng. trans. Vol. I. chapters III., IV.

[Temples and Tombs.]

PETERS, J. P. — Nippur. Explorations and Adventures on the Euphrates. Vol. II. chapter V., The Oldest Temple in the World. Chapter VIII., Coffins and Burial Customs.

PINCHES, T. G. — Sin-Gashid's Endowment of the Temple Ê-ana. RP, new series, I. 78-83. See also BOR I. 8-11.

—— A Fragment of a Babylonian Tithe List. Ib. I. 76-78.

—— Gifts to a Babylonian Bitili or Bethel. Ib. II. 142-145.

Rawlinson, H. C. — On the Birs Nimrud, or the Great Temple of Borsippa. JRAS, 1861, 1-24.

Reber, F. — Ueber altchaldäische Kunst. . . . Der Tempelbau. ZA I. 149-164.

Sayce, A. H. — A Babylonian Saint's Cylinder. RP VII. 157-170.
[Days sacred, and otherwise, of the month of Elul, with directions for religious ceremonies to be observed.]

—— On Human Sacrifice among the Babylonians. TSBA IV. 25-31.

Tiele, C. P. — De Hoofdtempel van Babel en die van Borsippa. KAW Afdeeling 'Letterkunde' (1886) 3de Reeks Deel III; also in German ZA II. 179-190.

Tristram, H. B. — Sacrifices in Babylonia and Phoenicia. SST, 1894, No. 1.

Ward, W. H. — On Some Babylonian Cylinders, supposed to Represent Human Sacrifices. PAOS, May 1888, xxviii.-xxx.

IX.

Bearings on the Old Testament; General Influence.

Anz, Wilhelm. — Zur Frage nach dem Ursprung des Gnostizismus. (Leipzig 1897.) pp. 58-112, Die Herkunft . . . aus Babylonien.

Ball, C. J. — The First Chapter of Genesis and the Babylonian Cosmogonies. PSBA XVIII.

Bonnett, E. — Les Découvertes Assyriennes et le Livre de la Genèse. (Paris 1884.)

Boscawen, W. St. Chad. — The Bible and the Monuments. (London 1895.)

Brandt, W. — Die Assyrisch-Babylonische Keilschriftliteratur und das Alte Testament. Deutsch-evang. Blätter, 1884. Heft 3. pp. 164-187.

Brown, Francis. — Critical review with valuable comments of E. Schrader's 'Die Keilinschriften und das Alte Testament.' AJP IV. 338-343.

—— The Sabbath in the Cuneiform Records. PR, 1882, 688-700.

—— Assyriology: Its Use and Abuse in Old Testament Study. (New York 1885.)

BROWN, ROBERT, JR. — Semitic Influence in Hellenic Mythology. (London 1898.)
  [Part III. discusses Babylonian Influence.]

BUDDENSIEG, R. — Die Assyrischen Ausgrabungen und das Alte Testament. (Heilbronn 1880.)

DELITZSCH, FRIEDRICH. — Wo Lag das Paradies? Eine Biblisch-Assyriologische Studie. (Leipzig 1881.)
  (See Francis Brown. OTS IV. 1-12.]

EVETTS, B. A. — New Light on the Bible and the Holy Land. (London 1892.)

GRUPPE, O. — Die Griechischen Kulte und Mythen in ihren Beziehungen zu den Orientalischen Religionen. (Leipzig 1887.)

GUNKEL, H. — Schöpfung und Chaos in Urzeit und Endzeit. (Göttingen 1895.)
  [A most important discussion of the relationship of the Biblical creation narratives to the Babylonian cosmology.]

HALEVY, J. — Recherches Bibliques. (Paris 1896.)

HAUPT, PAUL. — Wo Lag das Paradies? Ueber Land und Meer, 1894-1895, No. 15.
  [Also syllabus of lectures before the Gratz College of Philadelphia, Dec. 10, 1895, on 'The Site of Paradise and the Nimrod Epic.']

JASTROW, MORRIS, JR. — The Bible and the Assyrian Monuments. The Century Magazine, XLVII. 395-411.
  [Translated into French by E. Lacordaire in Revue des Revues, 1894 227-235.]

—— The Original Character of the Hebrew Sabbath. AJT II. 312-352.
  [Relationship between Hebrew and Babylonian Sabbath.]

—— Adam and Eve in Babylonian Literature.
  [Announced.]

JENSEN, P. — The Cult of Ashera and the Cult of Mary.
  [Announced to appear in the Sunday School Times, 1898.]

KESSLER, K. — Ueber Gnosis und Altbabylonische Religion. 5th ICO, II. Part I. 288-305.

KELLNER, M. L. — The Deluge in the Izdubar Epic and the Old Testament.
  [Reprinted from the Church Review, November, 1888.]

LACOUPERIE, T. DE. — Origin from Babylonia and Elam of the Early Chinese Civilization. Series of articles in the BOR III.–VIII.

> [Also in book form under the title, 'Origin of Early Chinese Civilization and its Western Sources.' (London 1894.) Lacouperie's method is unsatisfactory. The theory, however, merits further investigation.]

LOTZ, W. — Quaestiones de Historia Sabbati. (Leipzig 1883.)

LYON, D. G. — Assyrian Study : Its Bearing on the Old Testament. The Christian Register, 1885, Nos. 15, 16.

MENANT, J. — Remarques sur un Cylindre du Musée Britannique. La Bible et les Cylindres Chaldéens. CR, 1879, 270–286.

> [Discussion of a scene on a cylinder supposed to represent the first human pair and the serpent.]

MEYER, Ed. — Der Babylonische Einfluss auf Judenthum und Christenthum. BAZ, 1894, No. 344.

OPPERT, J. — Origines Communes de la Chronologie Cosmogonique des Chaldéens et des Dates de la Genèse. APC, 6th series, XIII. 237–240.

PALMER, A. S. — Babylonian Influence on the Bible and Popular Beliefs. Téhôm and Tiâmat, Hades and Satan : a Comparative Study of Genesis, i., ii. (London 1897.)

ROBIOU, F. — L'État Religieux de la Grèce et de l'Orient au Siècle d'Alexandre ... II. Les Regions Syro-Babyloniens et l'Eran. (Paris 1896.)

> [Unsatisfactory, and not based on independent researches.]

SAYCE, A. H. — The Higher Criticism and the Verdict of the Monuments. (London 1894.)

> [Suggestive, but unreliable. Full of inaccuracies.]

—— Fresh Light from the Ancient Monuments. (2d ed. London 1886.)

SCHLEUSSNER. — Die Bedeutung der Ausgrabungen in dem Euphrat- und Tigris-Gebiet für das Alte Testament. (Wittenberg 1892.)

SCHRADER, E. — Die Keilinschriften und das Alte Testament. 3d ed. (Announced for 1898.)

> [English translation of the 2d German ed., 'The Cuneiform Inscriptions and the Old Testament.' London 1885–1889.]

SILLEM, C. H. W. — Das Alte Testament im Lichte der Assyrischen Forschungen und ihrer Ergebnisse. (Hamburg 1877.)

SIMPSON, WILLIAM. — The Tower of Babel and the Birs Nimroud. TSBA IX. 307–332.

STUCKEN, EDWARD. — Astralmythen der Hebraer, Babylonier und Aegypter. Religionsgeschichtliche Untersuchungen, Parts I., II. (Leipzig 1896–1897.)

[Rather fanciful.]

TALLQUIST, K. L. — Altbabylonischer Aberglauben in den Abendländern. [In Norwegian]; Valvoja, Helsingfors, 1896, 498–520.

——— Fornbabyloniska och hebräiska psalmer. Finisk Tidskrift, Mars 1892.

TIELE, C. P. — Die Assyriologie und ihre Ergebnisse für die Religionsgeschichte.

[German translation by Friederici. Leipzig 1878.]

TOY, C. H. — Esther as a Babylonian Goddess. The New World, VI. 130–145.

VIGOUROUX, F. — Le Bible et les Découvertes Modernes en Palestine, en Egypte et en Assyrie. 4 vols. (Paris 1884–1885.)

[Written from a Catholic standpoint, but comprehensive and accurate.]

WAHRMUND. — Babylonierthum, Judenthum und Christenthum. (Leipzig 1882.)

WARD, W. H. — Light on Scriptural Texts from Recent Discoveries, Hebrew and Babylonian Poetry. The Homiletic Review, 1895, 408.

ZEHNPFUND, R. — Einige zeitgemässe Bemerkungen über den Wert der Assyriologie für die alttestamentliche Litteraturkritik. (Ernste Allotria. Dessau 1896.)

ZIMMERN, H. — Die Assyriologie als Hülfswissenschaft für das Studium des Alten Testaments und des Klassischen Alterthums. (Königsberg 1889.)

——— Zur Frage nach dem Ursprung des Purimfestes. (Zeits. f. alttest. Wiss., XI. 157–169.)

ZSCHOKKE, HERMANN. — Ueber die Wichtigkeit der Assyriologischen Forschungen, insbesondere für das Alttestamentliche Bibelstudium. (Vienna 1884.)

INDEX.

Â, or *Malkatu*, her names and their explanation, 74; position and relationship to Shamash, 74–5, 176, 685; temples of Â and Shamash in Larsa and Borsippa, 70, 241; temple E-edinna in Sippar, 640.

Ab, 5th month, sacred to Nin-gish-zida, 462, 547; "the mission of Ishtar," 564; festival of Ishtar, 685.

Abram and *Abraham*, followers of, in fight with Babylon, 2; cult of Father Abraham, 562.

Abu-Habba, excavations, 10; see also *Sippar*; temple records and legal documents, 165.

Abu-Shahrein = Eridu.

Abydenus, source for B.-A. religion, 1, 5.

Achaemenian inscriptions, 16.

Ad, Arabic tribe, 496.

Adad = Ramman, 157; solar deity of Syria, 156.

Adam, parallelism betw. A. and Eabani, 511; parallelism betw. A. and Adapa, 552.

Adapa Legend, a nature myth, 548, 544 ff.; found on El-Amarna tablets, 544; Adapa, son of Ea, 545; A. fighting the south wind, 545 ff.; seconded by Tammuz and Gish-zida, 548–9; identified with Marduk, 548; Adapa myth compared with 3d chapter of Genesis, 551.

Adar, 12th month, sacred to the Seven Evil Spirits, 463; 15th day, sacred to Shamash, Malkatu, and Bunene, 685; compared with Purim, 686.

Adar, 2d (intercalated), sacred to Ashur, 463.

Addu, equivalent of Ramman, 156.

Adôn, Phoenician equivalent for Tammuz; see *Tammuz*.

Adra-Khasis, epithet of Parnapishtim, 505.

Aelian, historian, mentions Gilgamesh, 469, 524.

Agade, ancient center, 35, 245; rulers, 36; temple E-ul-mash of Nanâ, 82; temple of Anunit-Ishtar, 117, 242; zikkurat E-an-dadia, 639.

Agriculture, A. and calendar, 462.

Agum, see *Agumkakrimi*.

Agumkakrimi, king of Babylon, recovers the statues of Marduk and Sarpanitum, 122, 152, 670, 687; cult of Shamash, 144; cult of Shukamuna, 162; institutes special festival for Marduk and Sarpanitum, 687.

Ahasverus, the wandering Jew, = Parnapishtim, 515.
Ai-ibur-shabû, name of street in Babylon, 679.
Airu, 2d month, sacred to Ea, 462, 677; 12th day of A., sacred to Gula, 683; installation of king Ashurbanabal, 684; sacred in Assyria, 684; 10th day of A., sacred to Shamash, Malkatu, and Bunene, 685.
A-ishtu, a foreign god, 644.
Akitu, see *Zag-muk*; festival, 679.
Akkad, see also *Sumer* and *Akkad*; = Babylonia, 176, 532.
Akkadian = Sumerian.
Alala, deity, 417; in incantations, 417; in Allatu's court, 593; consort of Belili, 589; connection with Alallu, 589.
Alallu, a bird; relations to Ishtar, 482, 589; connection with deity Alala, 589.
Alamu, phase of Nergal, 280.
Alexander Polyhistor, source for B.-A. religion, 1, 5, 413.
Alexander the Great, probably contemporary of Berosus, 1; A. and Gilgamos, 469, 516.
Alexandria, gnostic center, 699.
Allatu, goddess, 1st Bab. period, originally associated with Bel, 104; associated with Nin-azu, 586, 590; associated with Nergal, 104, 183, 565, 580, 583, 593; goddess of subterranean cave, 104, 282, 511, 565, 580; in incantations, 282; = Nin-ki-gal, 282, cf. 584; Namtar, her messenger, 570, 580, 587, 592; Bêlit-seri, her scribe, 587; pictured as a lion, 580; Allatu's court, 587, 592; authoress of evil and disease, 593; called Eresh-kigal, 584 (*cf.* 282); vanquished by Nergal, 584-5; imitation of Tiâmat-Marduk episode, 585; correlated to Ishtar, goddess of fertility, 587; explanation of name, 587.
All-Souls' Day, see under *Tammuz* and *Dead*, 599, 605, 682.
Altar, description of, 651; the "horns" of the altar compared with those of Hebrew and Phoenician altars, 652.
Alu-usharshid, king of Kish, 54.
Amalgamation of divinities, cause, features, and results, 74-5, 94-5.
Amanus, district famous for its wood, 627.
Amiaud, his attempt at a genealogical arrangement of Old Bab. pantheon, 108.
Am-na-na, in proper names of the 2d Bab. period, 169.
Amraphel = Hammurabi, 534.
Amulets, see *Talisman*, *Teraphim*, 672, 674.
Anatum, goddess, consort of Anu, 153.
Animism, starting-point of religious belief, 48; survivals of, 180 ff., 457; popular rather than theological, 187.
Anshar, god, in the cosmology, 197, 410, 417; = Ashur, 197, 414-5; A. and Kishar created, 197, 410; builds Esharra, 198; A. and Kishar intermediate betw. the monsters and the gods in cosmology, 414, 416; Anshar and Kishar in the creation epic and

their meaning, 418; conquers Tiâmat (one version), 422.
Anshar-gal, cosmological deity, 417.
Antar, Arabian romance of A., 494.
Antares, observations of, 372.
Antioch, gnostic center, 699.
Antiochus Soter, cult of Marduk and Nabu, 650.
Anu, god, 51; relationship to Ishtar, 84-5; Dêr, city of Anu, 88, 155, 162; god of heavenly expanse, 89, 147, 207, 432; abstract conception, 89; priest of Anu, 90; Anu as term for 'lofty,' 90; member of the great triad, 107, 152, 155, 207, 677; in Lugalzaggisi's pantheon, 110; artificial character in Hammurabi's pantheon, 152; position in Agum's pantheon, 152; dwells in Uruk, 53; Anatum, his consort, 153; in Ass. pantheon, 153-5, 201, 207; associated with Ramman, 154, 207, 212; associated with Dagan, 154, 209; disappears after Sargon, 155; in religious texts, 156; in Nebuchadnezzar's I. pantheon, 162; father of Anunnaki and Igigi, 186, 207, 593; fighting Tiâmat, 197; temple in Lagash, 53, 640; temple at Ashur, 207; succeeded by Ashur, 207; associated with Ishtar, 207; blesses handiwork, 208, 237; associated with Bel and Belit, 226-7; Anu and Ishtar, names of the west gates of Sargon's II. palace, 237; associated with Nusku, 277, 286; made god of heavenly expanse, 432; "Way of Anu" = ecliptic of sun, 457; pole star of the ecliptic, 460; Nisan, sacred to A. and Bel, 462, 677; Tebet, sacred to A., Papsukal, and Ishtar, 463; 2d Ululu, sacred to Anu and Bel, 463; in the Adapa myth, 546 ff.

Anunit, goddess, 51; a variant of Ishtar, 82, 85, 242; in proper names of 2d Bab. period, 169; worshipped at Agade, 117, 242; shrine in E-babbara at Sippar, 646.

Anunnaki, explanation of name, 184; number of, and its explanation, 185; spirits of earth, 185, 593; gods in whose service the A. are, 186; their character, 186; associated with Igigi, 186, 593; altar of A. and Igigi, 186; shining chiefs of Eridu, 186; ruled by Ishtar, 204 (*cf.* 502); Anu, their chief, 186, 207, 593; Bel, king of all the A., 222; associated with the great triad, 236; created by Marduk, 447; offspring of Anu, 593; A. and Mammitum determine death and life, 493; in the deluge story, 500, 502 (*cf.* 204); in Allatu's court, 593.

Apollodorus, source for B.-A. religion, 1, 5.

Apotheosis, see *Deification*.

Apsu, the deep, personified ocean, 411, 443, 489, 580; synonymous with Tiâmat, 411; male principle, 411; dominion of A. and Tiâmat precedes that of the gods, 412; gods, product of the union of A. and Tiâmat, 413; mythical monsters, product of the union of A. and Tiâmat, 414; basin, a sacred object and symbol, 653; comparison with the "sea" in Solomon's temple, 653.

Arabia, metals and stone exported, 627.

Arabians invade Mesopotamia, 34, 39.

Arakh-shamnu, 8th month, sacred to Marduk, 463, 678, 686; 15th day, sacred to Shamash, Malkatu, and Bunene, 685.

Aralû, the nether-world, 489, 557; called E-kur or mountain house, 558; distinction betw. Aralû, the mountain (=earth), and Aralû, the district of the dead proper, 558; names and epithets of A., 563, 592; pictorial representation of, 579 ff.; pantheon of, 582 ff.

Arbela, temple of Ishtar, 202-3, 205, 651; meaning of name, 203; theological center, 342, 651.

Archaeological religious monuments, 14.

Architecture, reed and clay materials for building, 495-6; see Temple.

Ardi-Ea, ferryman of Parnapishtim, 491; takes Gilgamesh to the fountain of life, 509.

Ark, see Ship.

Ark of the covenant compared with the Babylonian ship for the gods, 655.

Armenia, legend of Rustem parallel to Etana legend, 520 ff.; exports precious stones, 627.

Arts, patron gods, 177-8.

Aruru, goddess, creates mankind, together with Marduk, 448, 474; creates Eabani, 448, 474; = Ishtar, 448-9; creates Gilgamesh, 473-4.

Ashera compared with tree worship in Babylonia, 689.

Ashur, capital of Assyria, 42, 193, 651; modern name Kalah-Shergat, 198; temple to Ashur, 198, 651; temple to Ishtar, 205; temple to Anu, 207; temple to Shamash, 209; temple to Bel, 225; temple to Ea, 230; intellectual center, 651.

Ashur, god, consort of Belit, 150, 226, 668; rivaled by Ramman, 161; in Ass. pantheon, 189; head of Ass. pantheon, 191, 200; his unique position, 191-2, 215; local deity, 193; symbol, 194, 632; interpretation of symbol, 195-6, 685; general character of Ashur, 195; etymology of name, 196; Anshar another form of A., 197, 414; god of battle, 195, 199, 201; chief of pantheon and epithets, 200-2; king of the Igigi, 200; associated with Ninib, 214; his temples few, 215; associated with Ninib and Nergal, 216, 218; associated with Marduk, 224; associated with the great triad, 236; name of inner wall of Sargon's II. palace, 237; permits the king to grow old and protects the troop, 237; superiority to Marduk, 239; god of oracles, 344; Bel Tarbasi or lord of the court, 345; 2d Adar, sacred to A., 463; Ululu, sacred to A., 463, 685.

Ashurbanabal, library, 13; patron of science and art, 43, 229; rule, 44; recaptures Nanâ's statue, 85, 206; gives prominence to Nabu cult, 129; celebrates festival in honor of Gula, 218, 683; embellishes temple of Nergal at Tarbisu, 219; his pantheon, 238; sacrifices in Babylonia, 664; restores temple E-kur at Nippur, 645; Shamash cult in Sippar, 646; Ishtar cult in Uruk, 648.

Ashuretililani, king of Assyria, improves Nabu's temple at Calah, 229.

Ashurnasirbal, king of Assyria, 205; gives prominence to Ninib cult, 214; Calah, his capital, 215; builds sanctuaries to Ishtar, Sin, Gula, Ea, Ramman, 215; as a hunter, 216; builds sanctuary to Gula, 218; builds sanctuary to Sin at Calah, 219; his pantheon, 237; gives prominence to Ishtar cult, 325.

Ashur-rish-ishi, king of Assyria, 149, 204, 213.

Assyria, military superiority, 2; history by Herodotus, 3; art and antiquities, 7; character of country and culture, 30-1; character of people, 31; comparison with Babylonia, 31; architecture, 42; history, 41-4; conquest of, 44; sun worship, 78; Assyrian Ishtar cult as distinguished from Bab., 83, 85; Ass. Nabu cult as against Bab. Marduk cult, 128; religious beliefs more popular than Bab., 153; influence upon Bab. culture and religion, 179; pantheon, 188; divisions of Ass. pantheon, 188-9; comparison of Ass. and Bab. pantheons, 189, 201; attacked by Cassites, 199; A. god of oracles, 344; continuity of Ass. and Bab. religion owing to Ass. worship of Bab. deities, 642; Airu, sacred month in Ass., 684.

Assyrians, see *Assyria*.

Astrology, lunar worship influenced by A., 219-20; bar to monotheistic development, 319; observation of the planets, 370; questions put to the astrologer, 369.

Astronomy, factor in spreading lunar worship, 220, 245; mixture of astronomy and astrology in the observation of eclipses, 357; in the observation of the planets, 370; forms part of cosmology, 454; the determination of the laws under which the stars stood, 457; composite character of A. science, 460; divisions of, 460-1; moon and sun in, 461.

Azag-sir, minor deity in Ass. pantheon, 234.

Babbar, surname of Shamash, 72; etymology, 72.

Babylon, founded, 2; supremacy, 2; capture of, 4, 45; ancient center, 35; capital of Babylonia, 39, 116; Marduk, deity of, 54, 117-8, 531; E-sagila, temple of Marduk, 121, 241, 639; temple of Shamash, 242, 640; temple of Sin, 242; temple of Nin-makh, 242, 640; temple of Nin-khar-sag, 242; temple of Gula, 242, 638; attacked by Dibbarra, 531; zikkurat at Bab., 619, 639; temple to Nin-lil-anna (242), 640; religious center of the country, 649-50.

Babylonia, conceptions of netherworld, 2; notices in rabbinical literature, 3; extent, 26; character of country, 30; character of people, 31; character of culture, 34; Babylonian states and their history, 35 ff.; dynasties of, 39–41, 44–5, 489; united under Hammurabi, 116; Bab. and Ass. Ishtar cult, 83, 85; Bab. and Ass. Marduk cult, 128; Bab. beliefs less popular than Ass., 153; periods of Bab. religion, 162; gods common to all three periods of Bab. religion, 163; Bab. culture and beliefs influenced by Assyria, 179; comparison of Bab. and Ass. pantheons, 189, 201; country of Bel, 222; under Ass. rule, 223; source of Ass. culture, 222; independent of Assyria, 239; political and religious centers, 245; replaces Nippur, 542; sanctuary of Nabu, 640; sacrificial acts in Bab. and their meaning, 664; Nisan, the sacred month in Bab., 684; continuity of Bab. and Ass. belief owing to Ass. worship of Bab. gods, 642.

Babylonians, see also Babylonia; subjects of Bel, 222; humanity of Bel, 222.

Babylonian-Assyrian religion, 1; phases of, 46–7; age of essentials of religion, 114; gods of the B.-A. pantheon, 189; continuity of B.-A. religion, 642; see Assyria and Babylonia.

Bahrein, exports wood, 627.

Ba-kad, in the Cassite pantheon, 162, 172.

Balasi, astrologer, 340.

Balawat, explorations, 9; portals of palace at B., 627.

Bar, offspring of Ishtar declines to fight Zu, 541.

Bashtum, goddess in proper names of the 2d Bab. period, 169.

Battles of Yahwe, recalls Dibbarra epic, 534.

Bau, goddess, 51; her attributes, 59–60, 90, 678; temple in Uruazagga, 59, 103; Zag-muk, her festival, 59, 677; consort of Ningirsu, 59, 677; identification with Gula, 60; her sphere, 60; daughter of Anu, 59–60; mother of Ea and water-deity, 61; common features with Ga-sig (?)-dug, 61; Bau not Hebr. bohu, 60; her sons (Amiaud), 103; in Gudea's pantheon, 106; in incantations, 273; Bau's ship, 655.

Ba'u-ukin = Dungi (Winckler), 65.

Baz, city in Babylonia, temple of Belsarbi, 242, 639.

Bel, see also Marduk and Bel-Marduk; god, temple of, 4; temple at Nippur, 11, 37, 69, 51, 54, 151, 642, 644; position in the Babylonian theology, 52; oldest spelling and meaning of name, 52; temple in Lagash, 53; growth of his cult, 53; blending with Marduk, 54, 145, 146, 148, 222; phases of cult, 55; associations and relations with Ea, 62; associated with Allat, 104; in Lugalzaggisi's and Gudea's pantheon, 110; subordination to Marduk, 118; transfers his name to Marduk, 140, 222, 439, 635; god of earth *par excellence*, 140, 147, 432, 440, 497; creator of mankind, 141, 441; in the deluge story,

142, 497, 502, 504; Bel and the triad, 107, 145-9, 207, 677; Bel in Hammurabi's pantheon, 145-6, 162; in Cassite period, 146; temple at Dur-Kurigalzu, 146; in the Assyrian pantheon, 146-7, 225-6; in the neo-Bab. pantheon, 147; epithets, 146, 222, 225, 227, 274; relationship to the other members of the triad, 147, 226; Bel (and Belit) decree fates, 150, 153, 538; Dagan = Bel, 151, 154, 209, 225; relationship to Zakar, 172; lord of Annunaki and Igigi, 186; husband of Ishtar, 205; confused with Dagan, 151, 154, 209; Ninib, first-born of Bel, 217; Sin, first-born of Bel, 219, 462; Nusku, messenger of, 221; temple at Ashur, 225; dwells in E-khar-sag-kurkura, 225; associated with Anu and Belit, 226-8; consort of Ishtar, 205; of Belit, 226; B. and Belit, names of the northern gates of Sargon's II. palace, 237; lays foundations, 237 (*cf.* *Ninib*); associated with fire-god, 279, 286; Bel made lord of the earth by Marduk, 432; in the zodiacal system in conjunction with Nibir and Ea marks the three divisions of the year, 434-5; identified with north polar-star, 435, 460; Nisan, sacred to Anu and B., 462, 677; 2d Elul, sacred to Anu and B., 463; Bel in 11th tablet of Gilgamesh epic, 496; rivalry with Ea, 497, 507 ff.; god of Dur-an-ki, 539; on seal cylinders, 540; robbed of tablets of fate by Zu, 540; temple E-U-gal, 640; figurines of Bel, 674; Zagmuk, festival of, 678.

Bêl-epush, Babylonian prince, votive object, 671.

Bel-Marduk, see *Bel* and *Marduk*.

Belili, deity, 417; in incantations, 417; sister of Tammuz, 575, 588; in Allatu's court, 588, 593; consort of Alallu, 589.

Belit, goddess, 51; place of cult, 55, 635; titles and their meanings, 55-6, 227; sanctuaries, 56; in Lugalzaggisi's pantheon, 110; consort of En-lil, 111, 150, 151; consort of Ashur, 150, 226, 668; uses of "Belit," 151; Bel and Belit decree the fate, 150, 153; relationship to Zakar, 172; associated with Anu and Bel, 226-8; confusion in Ass. pantheon, 226-7; consort of Bel, 226; consort of Ea, 226-7, 231, 237; = Ishtar, 226-7; = Sarpanitum, wife of Bel-Marduk, 226, 684; Emashmash, her temple at Nineveh, 227; B. and Bel, names of the northern gates of Sargon's II. palace, 237; brings fertility, 237; temple at Babylon (see *Nin-khar-sag*), 242; = Nin-lil, 635; figurines of, 674.

Belit of Akkad = Belit, 162, 176.

Belit-ekalli, in the Cassite pantheon, 162; consort of Ninib, 173; = Gula, 173, 176; meaning, 173.

Belit-ilâni, consort of Ea, 226, 231, 237; B. and Ea, names of southern gates of Sargon's II. palace, 237; increases offspring, 237.

Belit mati = Belit of the land =

Ishtar, 151, 206, 215; perhaps = Belit, 227.

Bêlit-seri, scribe of Allatu, 587.

Bel-sarbi, god, his temple at Uaz, 242, 639; perhaps = Nergal, 242.

Bel-zir, a layman, offers a votive object, 671.

Berosus, source B.-A. religion, 1, 4, 412.

Birs Nimrud, explored, 9.

Bit-Khabban, town in Babylonia; its patron-gods, 176.

Bit-Khabban, district of Babylonia, sacred to Sin, 163.

Blood, sanctity of, 661.

Boaz, name of column in Solomon's temple, 624.

Borsippa, explorations, 9; temple of Nabu, 121, 229, 241, 639; its situation, 124, 125; beloved city of Marduk, 126; temple of Ramman, 242; 3 sanctuaries of Gula, 242, 636 (E-ul-la), 641; zikkurat at B., 617, 619, 639; E-makhtila shrine in E-zida to Nabu at Borsippa, 307, 606, 636.

Botta, P. E., excavations, 6.

Buddhism, doctrine of annihilation, 556-7.

Bulala, a foreign god, 644.

Bunene, in Nabubaliddin's pantheon, 162; in proper names of the 2d Bab. period, 169, 176; associated with Shamash and Malik, 176.

Bunene and *Malik*, attendants of Shamash, 177; consort of Malik, 177; associated with Shamash and Malkatu, 685.

Burial, see *Dead*.

Bur-Sin, repairs zikkurat and builds shrine in Nippur, 645.

Calah, capital of Assyria, 42, 193, 651; temple of Nabu, 128, 228; temple of Belit mâti, 151; temple of Ninib, 214; capital of Ashurnasirbal, 215; sanctuary of Sin, 219; intellectual center, 651; worship of Ninib, 215, 684; palace of Sargon II., 687.

Calendar, fixed by Marduk, 434; importance of moon for c., 436, 461; agriculture and c., 462; growth and character, 465; adopted by Hebrews, 464, 681.

Cappadocian wedge writings, 20.

Cassites, dynasty, 40-1, 480; cult of Bel of Nippur, 146, 645; cult of Shamash, 144, 646; cult of Ramman, 158; cult of Shukamuna, 152, 162; cult of Nin-dim-su, Bakad, Pap-u, Belit-ekalli, Shumalia, 162, 172; attack upon Assyria, 199.

Chaldaean Wisdom, 362, 384, 403.

Chaos, attempts at picturing c., 411, 419; gods contemporaneous with the primeval c., 413.

Christianity, influenced by Ass.-Bab. religion, 698.

Claudius Ptolemaeus' astronomy, 5.

Commercial literature in syllabaries, 135.

Cosmology, 247, 407 ff.; the Tiâmat episode, 140; two or more versions of creation, 141-2, 407-8; literary-religious character of, 247; rise and development of cosmological speculations, 249; distinction between popular and scholastic c., 249-50, 442-3; distinction as to contents and form, 250; historical kernel, 250; c. deities antecedent to the known gods of the B.-A. pantheon, 417; not *creatio ex nihilo*, but evolution of chaos to order, the keynote of c., 418, 442; similarities with Biblical account, 409, 433, 435, 451; creation of heaven, 435, 443; of sun, 435; of moon, 436; of earth, 443; of mankind, 443; second version, its similarities with and dissimilarities from the first version, 444 ff.; the gods of Nippur, Erech, Eridu, the original creators of the universe, Marduk a later introduction, 449–50; the mountain Mashu and the cosmological conceptions, 489; see *Creation epic*.

Court of the World, name of temple, 641.

Creation epic, purpose of, 409; similarity with the Biblical account, 409, 433; literary form, 409 ff.; a nature myth, 432-3; representation of sun, 461; see *Cosmology*.

Ctesias, source for B.-A. religion, 1, 4.

Cult and worship, cf. *Festivals* and *Rituals*; organization, 115, 133, 234; gods in cult and in invocations, 238; revival of old c. in Neo-Bab. period, 242-3; tree-worship, 688-9; compounded of popular belief and theology, 689.

Cuneiform, see *Wedge writing*.

Cuthah, ancient center, 35; = Tell-Ibrahim, 65; cult and temple Nergal (see *Luz*), 65, 164, 218, 563, 583, 648, 667; a designation for the nether-world, 563, 570; synonymous with nether-world, 583.

Cuthaeans, 532.

Cyrus, captures Babylon, 4, 45; adopts Babylonian religion, 45, 650.

Dagan, god, 51; confusion with Bel, 151, 154, 209, 225; associated with Anu, 154, 209; chiefly in Assyria, 208; comparison with Dagon, 208; probably Aramaic origin, 208; god of earth, 209.

Damascius (or Damascenus), see *Nicolas of Damascus*.

Damascus, in Syria, cult of Ramman, 159.

Damkina, consort of Ea, 64, 143, 231; meaning of name, 143; relationship to Ea and Marduk, 143; in magical texts, 143; Ea and Damkina grant long life, 153; title Belit-ilâni, 231; occasionally invoked in incantations, 276.

Damku, god, associated with Sharru-ilu and Sha-nit(?)-ka, 232; meaning of name, 232; evidently a title, 232; perhaps foreign deity, 232; worshipped at Magganubba, 232.

Damu and *Damu-gal*, epithets of Gula, 166, 175.

Daniel, book of; bearing upon B.-A. religion, 2, 3; Daniel and Bab. religion, 3 (*cf.* 668); illustrative of Babylonian dream lore, 403; authentic description of dedication of statue, 669.

Dead, universal, 556; location and names of the gathering place of the dead, 557 ff. (*cf. Nether-world*); All-Souls' Day, 599, 605, 682; under the special protection of the gods, 183, 558, 582, 592; furnish oracles to the living, 559, 560, 582, 657; deification of dead, 561, 582; condition of dead, 563 ff.; purified, 578, 602; can hear lamentations, 575, 577; cannot be brought back from Aralû, 576, 582; suffer hunger, 598-9; tombs and burial, 595 ff.

Death and burial, life after death, 512, 514, 556 ff.; cave burial, 557; pyramid burial, 557.

Deborah, song of, among the "Battles of Yahwe," 534.

Deification (Parnapishtim and Etana), 470, 527; of dead, 561, 582; of Gudea and Dungi, 167, 470, 561; of Gimil-Sin, 561; of Gilgamesh, 282, 284, 470, 561.

Delila, parallelism with Ishtar, 516.

Delitzsch, Friedrich, Sumerian question, 22; see Preface.

della Valle, Pietro, traveler, 15.

Deluge, in Gilgamesh epic and O. T., 495; place of origin of deluge, 498; embodying two distinct traditions, 502, 506; points of contact with Biblical narrative, 506 ff.; antiquity of the tradition, 508.

Demons, see also *Animism* and *Spirits;* chief demon, 57, 497; in incantations, 287; how exorcised, 330; when not to be exorcised, 378; messenger of god, 378; *Tar-gul-le*, in the deluge story let loose by Dibbarra, 500; the Utukku, 260 (*cf.* 511); the Ekimmu, 260 (*cf.* 512); authors of evil and disease, 183, 593, 306, 692.

Dêr, center of worship of Ninâ, 88; city of Anu, 88, 155.

de Sacy, Silvestre, decipherment of wedge writing, 15.

de Sarzec, Ernest, explorer, 11.

Dibbarra, in Ass. pantheon, 189; plague-god, 232, 505, 528; a spirit, 232; identified with Nergal, 232, 528-9, 594; minor god, 234; in the deluge story, 500 (*cf.* 505); solar deity, 528; god of war, "the warrior," 528-9; attendant of Nergal, 529, 588; attended by Ishum, 529; D.'s attack upon Babylon, 530-1; D.'s attack upon Uruk, 531; general war among mankind, 531 ff.; Dibbarra enraged and appeased, 535; identified with Girra, 588.

Dibbarra epic, see *Dibbarra*, 232, 528 ff.; recalls the "Battles of Yahwe," 534.

Dilbat, city in Babylonia; temple of Ninib, 242; zikkurat E-gubba-an-ki, 639.

Dilmun, island, 125.

Diodorus, source for B.-A. religion, 1, 4, 399, 435.

Dirges, sung by priests and priestesses, 604, 658; by priestesses, 660.

Divine names, variety of names of individual divinities and local uses thereof, 73; transference of name and its meaning, 118, 140-1; in proper names, 165-6, 169; obscurity of, 233.

Djumdjuma, 10.

Dogma, establishment of, 115, 133, 247, 690 ff.

Dreams, importance of, 322-3; on par with oracles, 350, 479; treated as omens, 350, 403 ff.; in the Gilgamesh epic, 481, 486, 497.

Du'ar, Da'ur, cosmological deity, 417.

Du-azagga, council chamber of the gods, 629; = Apsu, 630; place where the sun rises, 630.

Dumu-zi, god; his double aspect, 96–7; worship at Lagash, 635.

Dumuzi-zu-aba, god, 51; interpretation of name, 96; functions and character, 96; places of worship, 96; in Gudea's pantheon, 106.

Dungi, of Ur, builds temple of Nergal at Cuthah, 65; builds temple of Nanâ in Uruk, 81; builds temple to Nin-Mar, 100; deified, 167, 470, 561.

Dun-shagga, 51; son of Nin-girsu, 91; meaning of name, 94; in Gudea's pantheon, 106.

Dur-an-ki, name of a temple tower in Nippur, 539.

Dur-ilu, Ass. city near Elamitic frontier; cult of Kadi, 232.

Dur-Kurigalzu, temple of Bel, 146.

Dur-padda, a fort sacred to Ramman, 158.

Dur-zakar, sanctuary of Belit, 56.

Du'zu, see *Tammuz*.

Ea, god, 51; functions, 62, 78, 230; epithets, 62, 142, 173, 230; associations and relations with Bel, 62; king of Eridu, 62–3, 275; sanctuary in Girsu, 61; god of the water, 63, 147, 237, 275, 430, 699; explanation of name, 64; identification with Ninagal and other deities, 64; member of the great triad, 107, 148, 207, 230, 677; in Lugalzaggisi's and Gudea's pantheon, 111; survival of his cult, 123–4, 136; change of position since Hammurabi, 136; non-mention in historical texts, 136; prominence in religious texts, 136; Ea and Marduk in incantation texts, 139–40; transfers his name to Marduk, 118, 141, 439; god of humanity *par excellence*, 141 (*cf.* 264, 275, 297, 437, 441, 462, 497); formed of clay, 142; Ea in the deluge story, 142, 497, 504; Ea and Damkina grant long life, 153; god of fine arts, 177; fighting Tiâmat, 197, 422; Ninib, first-born of Ea, 217; shrine in E-Sagila, 220, 241; Belit, consort of, 226, 231, 237; Nabu, son of, 229; in the Ass. pantheon, 230; sanctuary at Ashur, 230; titles emphasizing his skill, 230; house of wisdom, 522; similarity and difference between Ea and Nabu, 230–1; Ea and Belitilâni, names of southern gates of Sargon's palace, 237; unlocks fountains, 237; shrine in E-Zida, 241; prominent in incantations, 137, 256, 275; the spirits hostile to, 264 (*cf.* 141); as a healer, 275; overcomes eclipse of moon, 276; associated with fire-god, 279, 286; in the Shurpu series, 288; conquers Tiâmat, 422; in the zodiac in conjunction with Nibir and Bel, 434–5; identified with some star in southern heaven, 435, 460; Iyar, his sacred month, 462, 677; Ea in the 11th tablet of the Gilgamesh epic, 496; rivalry with Bel, 497, 507 ff.; Persian Gulf, sacred to Ea, 498, 545; father of Adapa,

545; Ea in Ishtar's descent, 571; Ea's sanctuary E-karzaginna, 636.

Eabani, created by Aruru, 448, 474; E. and Ishtar, 484, 486; parallelism betw. Adam and E., 511; E.'s spirit conjured up by Nergal, 511 ff., 560, 565.

E-adda, temple of Anu, 53, 640; meaning of name, 640.

E-an-dadia, name of zikkurat at Agade, 639; meaning of name, 639.

E-anna, temple of Ninni in Girsu, 80; temple of Nanâ or Ishtar in Uruk, 81, 242, 311, 331, 639, 648; meaning of name, 639.

Eannatum, burial costumes, 597.

E-babbara, name of the temples of Shamash in Larsa and Sippar, 70, 628, 640; worship of Shamash, Malik, Bunene in E. at Sippar, 176, 628; meaning of name, 640; history of Ebabbara in Sippar, 646 ff.; with shrine of Anunit, 646; history of Ebabbara in Larsa, 647.

Ecbatana, concentric walls, 618.

Ecclesiastes, unsatisfactory ending like 12th tablet of Gilgamesh epic, 513.

Eclipses, e. of moon removed by Ea, 276; cause of e., 264, 276, 280; calculation of time of occurrence of e., 357; indication of omens the ulterior motive of observations of, 357, 368; omens gathered from observation of e. in the "Illumination of Bel" series, 364 ff.; eclipses portend public disaster, 366, 369; importance of omens deduced from observations of e., 368; e. of sun called the "way of Anu," 457.

Eden, Garden of, legendary, 2; identical with the confluence of streams, 506.

Edessa, gnostic center, 699.

E-dim-anna, chapel of Sin in E-Zida, 639; meaning of name, 639.

E-dingiranagin, see *E-anna-tuma*.

E-ditar-kalama, sanctuary of Shamash in Babylon, 242, 640; meaning of name, 640.

E-dur-an-ki, zikkurat at Larsa, 639; meaning of name, 639.

E-dur-gi-na, temple of Belsarbi, 242, 639; meaning of name, 639.

E-edinna, temple of Shamash's consort, 640; meaning of name, 640.

E-esh-gi, shrine of Nin-girsu at Lagash, 640.

E-gal-makh, temple in Ur, 639.

E-gish-shir-gal, temple of Sin at Ur, 76, 241, 295, 640, 647; meaning of name, 640.

E-gi-umunna, a sanctuary, 640; meaning of name, 640.

E-gubba-an-ki, zikkurat at Dilbat, 639; meaning of name, 639.

E-igi-e-nir-kidur-makh, temple to Ninni at Kish, 639; meaning of name, 639.

Ekallâte, name of city in Assyria, cult of Ramman and Shala, 212.

E-karzaginna, sanctuary of Ea in E-Sagila, 636.

E-kharsag, temple in Ur, 638.

E-kharsag-ella, temple of Gula in Babylon, meaning of name, 638.

E-kharsag-kalama, name of temple, 638; E-kur-makh, 638.

E-kharsag-kurkura, dwelling of Bel,

225; temple in Assyria, 615; meaning of name, 638.

E-khulkhul, temple of Sin in Harran, 76, 241, 641, 647; meaning of name, 641.

E-ki-dur-garza, temple to Nin-lil-anna in Babylon, 640; meaning of name, 640.

Ekimmu, a class of spirits, 260 (*cf.* 512, 581, 602).

E-kua, papakhu of Marduk in E-Sagila, 640; meaning of name, 640.

E-kur, temple of Bel, 11, 37, 51, 54, 69, 151, 642, 644; meaning of E-kur, 173, 217, 614, 638; = Eshara, 217; history of the temple, 644 ff.; = Kharsag(-gal)-kurkura, 558; lofty dwelling of gods, 541; designation for the nether-world, 558; = temple, 558, 614 (*cf.* 622); = earth, 614; in plural = divinities, 615.

E-kur-makh, name of temple, 638; = E-kharsag-kalama, 638.

Elali, in proper names of the 2d Bab. period, 170; epithet of Gibil, 170.

Elam, 35; Elamites invade Babylonia, 38, 480; capture Nanâ's statue, 85; Elamitic deities: Eria, 122, 162; Kadi, 188, 232, 234.

El-Amarna, tablets of, containing the Adapa legend, 544; contains legend of Nergal conquering and wedding Allatu, 584-5.

Elul, see *Ululu*.

E-makh, chapel to Nin-kharsag, 639.

E-makh-tila, shrine to Nabu at Borsippa, 307, 606, 636.

E-mash-mash, temple of Ishtar, 152; of Belit, 227.

E-me-te-ur-sagga, temple of Zamama-Ninib, 640; meaning of name, 640.

En-anna-tuma, patesi of Lagash, constructs storehouse to Nin-girsu, 58.

En-anna-tuma II., 2d dynasty of Ur, devotee of Nin-gal, 98.

E-nin-makh, chapel of Ishtar in Babylon, 242, 640; meaning of name, 640.

E-ninnu, temple of Nin-girsu, 57, 87, 635, 640.

En-ki, see *Ea*.

En-lil, see *Bel*.

En-meshara, attendant of Allatu, god of vegetation, 588; festival of E. in the 10th month, 588.

Ennanna = Ninni, 51.

En-ninna, a minor deity in the Etana legend, 521.

En-nugi, leader of the gods, 495.

En-temena, patesi of Lagash, 56; constructs storehouse to Nin-girsu, 58.

En-tena, see *En-temena* (better reading).

E-nun-makh, temple of Sin at Ur, 295, 640; meaning of name, 640.

Enshar, cosmological deity, 417.

En-zu, see *Sin*.

E-pa, zikkurat at Lagash, 639; meaning of name, 639.

E-pad-kalama-suma, sanctuary of Nabu in Babylonia, 640; meaning of name, 640.

Epics and legends, literary-religious character of, 247; historical spirit of, 250; nature myths, 250.

Erech = Warka = Uruk; see *Uruk*.

Eresh-Kigal = Allatu, 584.

Eria, Elamitic goddess, possibly identical with Erua, 122, 162.

Eridu, ancient center, 35, 245, 445; sanctuary of Ea, 62, 124, 445; lost her political prestige, 136; cult of Anunnaki and Igigi, 186; prominent in incantations, 256.

Erua, the " begetting " goddess, 123; amalgamation with Sarpanitum, 122-3, 130; dwelling in E-Zida, 123; consort of Nabu, 123; possibly identical with Eria, 122; water deity, 123; cult suppressed by Hammurabi, 130; place of worship, 130.

E-Sagila, temple of Marduk in Babylon, 121, 636; with a shrine of Sarpanitum, 121, 241, 636, 641; with shrine of Nusku, 220, 241; with shrine of Nabu, 127, 220, 636; with shrine of Ea, 220, 241; with shrine of Tashmitum, 220, 241; with shrine of Nin-kharsag, 639; sanctuary E-karzaginna of Ea, 636; meaning of name, 639; with papakhu of Marduk, 640; takes the place of E-kur, 645; history of E-Sagila, 648 ff.; place of installation of rulers, 649; influence of E-Sagila and E-Zida, 649.

E-Sagila, temple of Ea, 446.

E-salgisa, temple in Girsu, 641; meaning of name, 641.

Esarhaddon, king of Assyria, 200; restores temple of Nanâ-Ishtar at Erech, 85, 206; his pantheon, 238; restores Ekur, 645; Shamash cult in Sippar, 646.

Eschatological literature, gods and demons in e., 183.

E-shara, meaning, 173, 175, 198; offsprings of, 174; bride of E., 173, 175; built by Anshar, 198; built by Marduk, 198, 431; == Ekur, 217; placed by Marduk under control of Bel, 432.

E-shid-lam, temple of Nergal and Laz at Cuthah, 65, 648, 667.

Etana, legendary personage, 468, 505, 519 ff.; dwells in the netherworld, 511, 520, 523, 527, 590; E.'s patron, Shamash, 520; name occurs in O. T., 519; traditions among other nations, 519-21; E. and Ganymede, 523; deified, 527, 590; god of vegetation, 590.

E-temen-an-ki, zikkurat to Marduk at Babylon, 619, 639; meaning of name, 639.

Ethics, B.-A. religion, 291, 312, 692; belong to advanced period, 292, 304-5; in prayers, 298-9; gods whose nature create e. notions, 306, 692; in penitential psalms, 312 ff.; private morality, 694 ff.

E-tila, name of a temple, and meaning of name, 641.

E-tur-kalama, temple of Ishtar, 311.

E-U-gal, temple to En-lil, 640; meaning of name, 640.

E-ulla, temple to Gula in Sippar, 641; meaning of name, 641.

E-ul-mash, temple of Nanâ in Agade, 82.

Euphrates, stream of Garden of Eden, 2 (*cf.* 506); E. valley, central habitation of mankind, 2; old settlements of Hebrews, 2; course of, 27; comparison with Tigris, 30; one of the four streams forming the confluence of streams, 506 (*cf.* 2).

E-ur-imin-an-ki, zikkurat at Babylon, 619.
Eusebius, source for B.-A. religion, 1, 4, 5.
Eve, parallelism with Ukhat, 511.
Excavations, 6-15.
Exorcism, see *Incantations*.
E-Zida, temple of Nabu at Borsippa, 121, 229, 241, 639; with shrine of Erua, 123; with shrine of Sarpanitum, 241; with shrine of Tashmitum, 241; with shrine of Nusku, 241; with shrine of Ea, 241; with shrine of Sin, 639; history of E-Zida, 648 ff.; influence of E-Zida and E-Sagila, 649.
E-Zida, shrine of Nabu in E-Sagila, 127, 220, 229, 636.

Family, systematization of O. B. pantheon according to Davis, 109.
Fast days, special occasions, 688.
Fate tablets, tablets of fate in the hands of Bel, 538 (*cf.* 150, 153); in the Tiâmat story, 420, 428, 538; robbed by Zu, 540; compared with the tablets of wisdom, 585.
Festivals, zag-muk, 59, 127, 631, 677, 678; significance of every day, 675; special significance of special days, 675, 677, 680-1, 683-5; words for f. in Assyrian, 676, 687; each month sacred to a deity, 462-3, 676, 683-4; festivals and months sacred to divinities not always corresponding, 687; special festivals, 687-8; the puru ceremony, 688; fast days and rites, 688.
Fire, see *Water* (*cf.* Gibil-Nusku in incantations, 277); means of purification, 276, 279; belongs to all three divisions of the universe, 286.
Foreign gods in B.-A. religion (see also *Cassites*), 142, 644; Adad = Ramman, 156; Kadi, 188, 232, 234; Damku, 232; Eria, 122, 162 (Elamitic).
Fresnel, *Fulgence*, expedition, 8.

Gaga, Assyrian pantheon, 188; minor god, 234; Anshar's messenger to Tiâmat, 423; a foreign deity, 238, 644.
Gal-alim, 51; center of worship, 91; son of Nin-girsu, 91; in Gudea's pantheon, 106.
Gamlat, in Ass. pantheon, 188.
Ganymede and Etana, 523.
Ga-tum-dug, goddess, 51; similar to Bau, 61; worship at Lagash, 61, 635; in Gudea's pantheon, 106, 635.
Gate of Widespread Splendor, seat of Sarpanitum in E-Sagila, 121, 241, 636, 641.
Gegunu, epithet of Aralû, 563.
Genealogical systematization of Old Bab. pantheon according to Amiaud, 109.
Genesis, see *Cosmology*.
Gibil, fire-god, E-la-li, perhaps an epithet, 170; in Ass. pantheon, 189; amalgamated with Nusku, 220, 227; in incantations, 273, 277; older than Nusku, 277; epithets, 277, 280; a mythological conception, 277, 279; G.-Nusku, god of civilization, 278; medium betw. worshipper and deity, 279; associated with Anu, 277; asso-

ciated with Bel and Ea, 279; associated with Nin-gish-zida, 463; identified with Nergal, 594.

Gil, attendant of Nergal and Allatu, 588; god of foliage, 588.

Gilgamesh, hero of the Bab. epic, 83, 468 ff.; in incantations, 282, 284, 470; mythological explanation of, 282, 486–7; with omens, 387; solar deity, 470–1, 515; king of the earth, 471; born in Marada, 473; conquers Uruk, 473, 513; created by Aruru, 473–4; Shamash (see Lugal-Marada), his patron, 471, 479; love affair with Ishtar, 481 ff.; Lugal-Marada, his patron (see Shamash), 486; conquers Khumbaba, 480, 514; G.'s contest with the bull, 486, 514, 537; contest with lion, 488, 514; Gilgamesh half divine, half human, 490, 514; G. and Sabitum, 490–1; G. and Parnapishtim, 492 ff.; points of contact with O. T., 495, 515–6; G. and Eabani, 510, 565; seeking immortality and the secret of life after death, 513; parallelism with Samson, 516; parallelism with Hercules, 516; Gilgamesh and Alexander the Great, 469, 516; G. in Aelian, 469, 524; G.'s grandfather Sokkaros, 524.

Gimil-Sin, deified, 561; temple at Lagash, 561.

Gim-nun-ta-ud-du-a, son of Bau, 103; explanation of name, 103; probable functions, 103.

Gin-shul-pa-uddu, wife of Gudea, 99.

Girra, attendant of Nergal and Allatu, 588; identified with Dibbarra, 588; a form of Nergal in later texts, 589.

Girsu, see Lagash.

Gish-galla (?), quarter of Lagash, 57; temple of Ninni, 80.

Gish-zida, identical with solar deity Nin-gish-zida, 547; G. and Tammuz, doorkeepers of heaven, 546; 5th month sacred to G., 547; intercedes for Adapa with Anu, 548–9.

Gnosticism, influenced by B.-A. religion, 698.

Great Place, name of temple, 641.

Grotefend, Georg Friedrich, decipherment of wedge writing, 16.

Gudea, statues, 57, 652; his pantheon, 106 ff., 635; number of deities indicative of the extent of his sovereignty, 106; principle of order, 107; gods common to Gudea's and Lugalzaggisi's pantheon, 110; deified, 167, 470, 561; his zikkurat, 615, 619; builder of temples, 642; imports diorite from Sinai peninsula, 627, 651; Gudea's apsu, 653; Gudea's ship for Nin-girsu, 654; G.'s votive objects and inscription, 57, 668–9, 672.

Gula, identified with Bau, 60; associated with Ninib, 105 (cf. 576); goddess of healing, 105, 166, 175, 282 (cf. 576, 683); in Nebuchadnezzar's I. pantheon, 162, 175; epithets, 166, 173, 175, 576; goddess of nether-world, 174–5; position intermediate betw. gods of the living and gods of the dead, 175 (cf. 576); creator of mankind, 175; her sanctuary erected by Ashurnasirbal, 218; her festival celebrated by Ashurbanabal, 218, 683; = Nin-Karrak, 242; temple at Babylon (see *Nin-Karrak*), 242, 638; three sanctuaries at Borsippa, 242, 636 (E-ulla), 641; in incantations, 273, 282; 12th day of Iyar sacred to G., 683.

Gurmu, son of Bau, 103.

Gushgin-banda, 171; "brilliant chief," patron of metal-workers, 178.

Halévy, J., Sumerian question, 22–4.

Hallabi, city near Sippar, temple of Ninni, 117, 144.

Hamath, city in N. Syria, 578.

Hammurabi, king of Babylon, secures the hegemony in Babylonia, 116, 532; Marduk, the chief of his pantheon, 117; builds temples, 642; builds temple to Ninni at Hallabi, 117; builds E-Zida, 121; ignores cult of Nabu, 128; suppresses cult of Erua, 130; care of temple of Shamash at Larsa, 143–4; Shamash cult, 117, 143–4; at Sippar, 117, 143; at Larsa, 143; Ninni cult at Hallabi, 144–5; "proclaimer of Anu and Bel," 146–7; beloved shepherd of Belit, 150; list of names of gods in H.'s pantheon, 161–2; "The Akkadian," 532; H.'s character as a Messiah, 533; = Amraphel, 534.

Harran, city in Mesopotamia, sacred to Sin, 76, 241, 641, 647; its importance and political decline, 77; meaning of its name, 78; associations with Ur, 77; enjoys the patronage of Sargon II., 77; temple of Sin, 76, 241, 641; patronized by Nabonnedos, 77, 242.

Haynes, John H., excavations, 11.

Heart of Shamash, name of a temple, 641.

Hebrews, see *Old Testament*.

Hercules, parallelism with Gilgamesh, 516.

Herodotus, source for B.-A. religion, 1; history of Assyria, 3; history of Persia, 4; notices on B.-A. religion, 4; notices on Ishtar cult in Erech, 485.

Hillah, village, site of, 8.

Historical texts, value as source for religion, 51, 166, 246, 661; pantheon in h. t. compared with that in incantation texts, 297; source for knowledge of sacrifices, 661.

Hittites, eagle standard among the H., 527; influence on Assyrian architecture, 627.

Hommel, Fritz, Sumerian question, 21.

Homoroka = Marduk, 5.

House Full of Joy, name of temple, 641.

House of Fifty, see *E-ninnu*.

House of Great Splendor, name of temple, 641.

House of Hearkening to Prayers, name of temple, 641.

House of Light, name of temple, 641.

House of the Brilliant Precinct, name of temple, 641.

House of the Seven Divisions of Heaven and Earth, name of zikkurat at Borsippa, 639.

House of the Seven Zones, name of zikkurat at Uruk, 639.

House Without Rival, name of temple, 641.

Hymns and prayers, division of religious literature, 247, 293; where composed, 248; in connection with incantations, 293, 301; h. to Shamash, 300 ff.; to Sin, 303-4; dialogue style of composition 305; to Nebo, 306; no difference in thought betw. h. and incantation, 301, 307; illustrating relationship betw. man and gods, 309; deity as person of dialogue in, 310; see also *Prayers*.

Iamblichus, source of B.-A. religion, 399.

Idiklat = Tigris, 28.

Igi-dug-ga, title of Ea, 230.

Igigi, explanation of name, 185; number of, and explanation, 185; spirits of heaven, 185, 200; gods in whose service the I. are, 186; their character, 186; associated with Anunnaki, 186, 593; altar of I. and Anunnaki, 186; chiefs of Eridu, 186; Ashur, king of, 200; Anu, their chief, 186, 207, 593; associated with the great triad, 236.

Ilabrat, minor god, in the Adapa legend, 546.

Illumination of Bel, name of an omen series, 363.

Im = Ramman, 156.

Immeru = Ramman, 157.

Immortality, see *Dead*.

Im-pa-ud-du, son of Bau, 103; explanation of name, 103; function, 103.

Incantations, see also *Magical Texts*; in therapeutics, 246; means and methods of, 270-3; gods invoked in, 273; sacred objects invoked, 274; gods in incantations *par excellence*, 275; the fire-god in, 277; favorite time of, 280-1; i. services, 281, 283 ff.; principle of sympathetic magic, 284; mixed with ethical conceptions, 292; in connection with prayers, 293, 301; the oldest fixed ritual, 294; no line of demarcation betw. prayers and i., 297, 307; points in common with and differences from penitential psalms, 312; the natural expression of popular beliefs, 326; demons exorcised by i., 330; connecting link betw. omens and i., 352.

Inmarmaru, city in Dibbarra epic, 533.

Invocations, 165; In records of the 2d Bab. period, 167; combined invocations, 235; where found; 235, 245; motive and manner of, 236 ff.; Tiglathpileser I., 236; Rammanirari I., 237; Ashurnasirbal, 237; Shalmaneser II., 237; Sargon II., 237; Sennacherib, 238; Esarhaddon, 238; Ashurbanabal, 238; gods in invocation and in actual worship, 238.

Irkalla, a designation of the netherworld, 563, 566; name of the consort of the queen of Aralû, 563, 591; identified with Nergal, 592.

Isaiah, prophet, 2.

Ish-gu-tur, temple of Nin-Mar in Mar, 100.

Ishi-milku, a foreign deity, 644.

Ishme-Dagan, king of Assyria, evidence of age of Dagan cult, 208.

Ishtar, goddess Nanâ, 82, 85, 202, 311, 643; absorbs other deities, 82; epithets, 83, 151-2, 204, 237; functions in B.-A., 83, 459; functions in A., 83-5; in Gilgamesh epic, 84-5, 482, 501, 563-4; zodiacal interpr., 82-4, 310-1; relationship to Sin, 79, 84, 163, 565, 571; relationship to Anu, 84-5, 566; significance of these relationships, 85; variants, 82, 85, 202, 242; temple at Agade, 117, 242; temple at Calah, 151; temple E-mashmash, 152, 205, 227; relationship to Sin and Shamash, 163, 571; goddess of war, 83, 164, 204; during Cassite and Nebuchadnezzar's I. reign, 164, 645; variants of Assyrian Ishtar, 202; mighty over the Anunnaki, 204; milder nature in religious texts, 205; mother of mankind, 204-5, v. 237; relationship to her devotees, 205; temple Kidmuru, 202; temples at Arbela, Nineveh, and Ashur, 205; I. of Nineveh and I. of Arbela distinguished, 205; Ab her sacred month, 205, 462, 685; wife of Bel, 205; Belit of the land (151, 206), 215, = Belit, 226; temple in Uruk, 81, 242, 311, 531, 639; worship in Uruk, 103, 242, 472, 475, 531 (see *Nanâ*); wife of Ashur, 227; associated with the great triad, 236; Ishtar and Anu, names of west. gates of Sargon's II. palace, 237; causes the inhabitants to flourish, 237 (*cf.* 204); temple at Babylon, 242 (*cf. Ninmakh*), 640; in incantations, 273; in hymns, 310; temple E-tur-kalama, 311; in a penitential psalm, 318; prominence of cult of I. under Ashurnasirbal and before, 325, 342; in oracles and omens, 343-4; = Venus as name of planet, 370, 458-9, 571; importance of Ishtar-Venus in omen literature, 371-2; I. appears in a dream to the king, 374; personification of fertility, 459, 462, 482, 563, 587; causes decline, 483, 563; 10th month sacred to I., Papsukal, and Anu, 463; the Kizrêti, Ukhâti, and Kharimâti of I. in Uruk, 475, 485, 660; relationship to Tammuz, 84, 482, 484, 547, 564, 574; Ishtar's love fatal to her lovers, 482, 516; I. and Eabani, 484, 486; in the deluge, 501, 503-4; parallelism with Delila, 516; I. in the lower world, 564; the 6th month "the mission of Ishtar," 564, 684; festival celebrated in Ab, 685; correlated to Allatu, 587; I. cult under Ashurbanabal, 85, 206, 238, 648; cult under Nebuchadnezzar II., 648; figurines of, 674.

Ishtaritu, general designation of Ishtar priestess, 660.

Ishum, god, 51; identity with Pa-sag, 101; in proper names of, 2d Bab. period, 169; messenger of Nusku, 280; solar deity, 528; local deity, 528; attendant of Dibbarra, 529, 594; describes Dibbarra's deeds, 530 ff.; his wars, 533 ff.; associated with Sibi, 533; "the warrior," 533; associated with Nergal, 594.

Isin, ancient center, 35; kings, 37; Isin dynasty as "builders" of temple of Nanâ in Ur, 81.

Iskenderun, bay of, 122.
Iyar, see *Airu*.
Izdubar = Gilgamesh.

Jezreel plain, cult of Ramman, 159.
Job, book of, unsatisfactory ending like 12th tablet of Gilgamesh epic, 513.
Josephus, historical references to B.-A., 5.
Judges = priests, 625, 658.
Judith, book of, bearing upon B.-A. religion, 3.
Jupiter = Marduk, name of planet, 370, 434, 458-9, 676-7; see *Marduk*.

Kaaba, at Mecca, 624.
Kabru, epithet for Aralû, 563.
Kadashman-Turgu, Cassite king, votive tablet, 671.
Kadi, in Ass. pantheon, 188; Elamitic god, 232; worshipped in Dur-ilu, 232; minor god, 234.
Kadishtu, general designation of Ishtar priestess, 660.
Kalah-Shergat, excavations, 10; site of city of Ashur, 198.
Kallat-Eshara, epithet of Gula, 173.
Kanishurra, a foreign god, 644.
Kara-indash, king of Babylon, restores Shamash temple at Larsa, 144.
Kar-nuna-ta-uddua, ship of Ningirsu, 654; meaning of name, 654.
Karun, one of the four streams forming the confluence of streams, 506.
Katnu, a foreign god, 644.
Kercha, one of the four streams forming the confluence of streams, 506.

K'hadir = Parnapishtim, 515.
K'hani, tribe hostile to Babylon, 152.
K'hani, god, in Ass. pantheon, 188; a form of Nebo, 188; minor god, 234; a foreign deity, 644.
K'harimâti, sacred harlots of Uruk, 475, 531, 660.
K'harsag(-gal)-kurkura, "the (great) mountain of the earth," 558; native place of the gods, 558, 614; = Ekur, 558.
K'hashur, mountain destroyed by Ishum, 533.
K'hasis-Adra, see *Adra-khasis*, 505.
K'hi-gir-nun-na, son of Bau, 103.
K'hi-khi, mountain attacked by Ishum, 533.
K'hiraitum, a foreign deity, 644.
K'hi-shaga, a son of Bau, 103.
K'horsabad, unearthed, 6, 8; capital of Assyria, 193; sanctuary of Sin, 219; palace of Sargon, 225; names of its gates and walls, 237; sanctuary of Nin-Gal, 231; zikkurat at K., 617.
K'humbaba attacks Uruk, 480; conquered by Gilgamesh, 514.
K'husha, god of the 2d Bab. period, 168.
Kidin-Marduk, father of Parnapishtim, 488, 496.
Kidmuru, temple of Ishtar in Nineveh, 202.
Kigallu, a designation of the netherworld, 562.
Kilili, a foreign deity, 644.
Kingship, differentiation of kingly and priestly functions late, 374; traces of direct relationship betw. gods and king, 374-5.
Kingu, consort of Tiâmat, 420;

symbol of chaos, 538; deprived of the tablets of fate by Marduk, 428.

Kimmira, city on the Euphrates (?), sanctuary of Dumuzi-zu-aba, 96.

Kish, city in Babylonia, 54; temple of Zamama, 169; temple of Ninni, 639.

Kishar, god, K. and Anshar created, 197, 410; K. and Anshar intermediate betw. the monsters and the gods in creation, 414, 416–7; creation of theologians, 416; Anshar and Kishar in the creation epic and their meaning, 418.

Kishar-gal, cosmological deity, 417.

Kishshat, a foreign god, 644.

Kislev, 9th month, sacred to Nergal, 463.

Kizréti, Ukhâti, and Kharimâti, the harlots of Uruk, 475, 531, 660.

Koyunjik, mound, unearthed, 7, 9.

Ku(?)-anna, 51; place of worship, 102; functions, 102; consort of Ramman (?), 102.

Kudur-mabuk, 2d dynasty of Ur, "builder" of temple of Sin in Ur, 76, 295; of temple of Nanâ in Ur, 81.

Kumari, city in Babylonia, temple of Ramman, 242.

Kurigalzu, Cassite, king of Babylon, cult of Bel of Nippur, 147, 645.

Kutu, see Cuthah.

Lagamal, a foreign god, 644.

Lagash, governors, 36; temple of Anu, 53, 640; temple of Belit, 56; temple of Bau, 635; quarters of, 56–7; temple of Ningirsu-Ninib, 57, 87, 635, 640; center of worship of Ninni, 80; ancient center, 35, 245; temple of Dumuzi-zu-aba, 96; Dumuzi, temple of Ninmar, 635; temple of Nin-gish-zida, 99, 635; temple of Ninâ, 635; temple of Ku(?)-an-na, 152; temple of Gimil-Sin, 561; shrine of Ningirsu, 640; zikkurat of Nin-girsu, 619, 635, 639; temple of E-salgisa, 641; temple of Nin-si-a, 635; temple of Shabra, 635; temple of Nin-sun, 635; temple of Nintu, 635; votive objects, 673.

Lakhamu, L. and Lakhmu cosmological, 197, 410, 417; a monster, 414, 418; in incantations, 417; in Allatu's court, 593.

Larsa, ancient center, 35; rulers, 37–8; dynasty, 39; center of worship of Shamash, 69, 143–4, 241, 628, 640, 646; zikkurats at L., 617, 639.

Lasimu, a foreign god, 644.

Layard, Austen Henry, excavations, 7.

Laz, consort of Nergal, 219, 243; not mentioned in Ass. texts, 219; not mentioned in religious texts, 583.

Lebanon, cedar forests, 626.

Legal literature, see also Literature; source for study of religion, 166; religious character of, 245.

Libations, 664, 666; in Old Testament and in A.-B., 665.

Libit-Ishtar, 2d dynasty of Ur, builds temple of Nanâ in Ur, 81.

Life of the World, name of temple, 641.

Light of Shamash, name of temple, 641.

Lists of gods, 213, 216; character of, 233; prepared on the basis of religious texts, 233.

Literature, Ashurbanabal's library, 132; syllabaries, 135; religious l., 12, 13, 213, 216, 233, 245, 247, 690–1; temple records, 165; legal documents, 165–6; connection betw. religion and literature, 245, 691; historical texts, 246; uncertain demarcation betw. religious and secular l., 247; epics, see *Gilgamesh, Eabani, Adapa*; compound of popular belief and of theology, 689.

Local cults, origin of, 49; confusion with nature cult, 49–50; growth of, 49; policy of preservation of local cults by foreign conquerors, 69–70, 106, 111; confusion of (female) local cults, 80; prominence given to local gods as compared with others, 111; local cult features and general cult features compared, 110; survival of local cults, 113; factors obscuring local cults, 113–5; political factors, 113; popular factors, 114; theological factors, 114; absorption, 114, 168, 171; number of, 170, 234, 274; in lists, 233; of the Ass. pantheon, 234; importance diminishes, 235.

Loftus, William K., excavations, 9.

Lofty and Brilliant Wall, name of temple, 641.

Lot, bears more resemblance to Parnapishtim than Noah, 507.

Lugal-banda, god, 51; temple at Uruk, 95; local character, 95; identification with Nergal, 95; signification of name, 95.

Lugal-edinna, epithet of Nergal, 172, 280.

Lugal-erima (?), god, 51; his local character, 97; interpretation of name, 97.

Lugal-gira, epithet of Nergal, 172, 280.

Lugal-ki-mu-na, in proper names of the 2d Bab. period, 169.

Lugal-Marada, god, temple at Marad, 242, a solar deity, 473; patron of Gilgamesh, identical with Shamash, 486.

Lugal-mit-tu, in Samsuiluna's pantheon, 162; wall of L., 172; meaning of name, 172.

Lugal-zaggisi, old Babylonian king of Uruk, 101; his pantheon and its age, 110, 636; gods common to Lugal-zaggisi's and Gudea's pantheon, 110; priest of Anu, 110.

Lulubite, name of people, 532.

Lunar cycle and sun calendar, 78.

Ma-an-ish-tu-su, servitor of Â, 74.

Magarida, a foreign god, 644.

Magganubbi, city in n.-e. Assyria, sanctuary of Sin, 219; restored by Sargon II., 232; cult of Damku, Sharru-ilu, Sha-nit(?)-ka, 232.

Magical texts, subdivision of religious literature, 247; practical purposes, 246, 255; beginning of rituals, 247, 253–4, 269; number of, 247; comparative age of, 253, 256; primitive popular thought, 254, 292; method of composition, 254; titles of, 254–5; incantation rituals and their growth, 255, 283 ff.; Ea and Eridu prominent in, 256; compiled character, 256-7; date of composition, 257; bilingual redaction, 258; metrical traits, 259; source of study of popular beliefs, 259; occurrence of Gibil evidence of ancient age of, 277; pantheon in m. t. compared with that in historical texts, 297.

Mahmal, tabernacle, compared with the Bab. ship for the gods, 655.

Makhir, god of dreams, 323, 402.

Maklu series, 286 ff., 302.

Ma-ku-a, name of Marduk's ship, 655.

Malik, god, in Nabubaliddin's pantheon, 162, 176; associated with Shamash and Bunene, 176; in proper names of the time of Hammurabi, 176; often used as epithet of Shamash, 176; meaning of name, 176; Malik and Bunene, attendants of Shamash, 177; consort of Bunene, 177.

Malkatu = Â.

Malku, name of canal, 655; name of Naru's ship, 655.

Ma-ma, variant for Gula, 105.

Mammitu, goddess; M. and Anunnaki determine death and life, 493.

Mamu, a form of Gula in proper names of the 2d Bab. period, 169.

Mandaean, legend of Rustem parallel to Etana legend, 520 ff.

Mar, district in southern Babylonia, sacred to Nin-Mar, 100; temple Ish-gu-tur of Nin-Mar, 100.

Marad, city in Babylonia, temple of Lugal-Marada, 242; native place of Gilgamesh, 473.

Marcheshwan, see *Arakh-shamnu*.

Marduk, 2d Bab. period, deity of Babylon, 54, 96; child *par excellence* of Ea, 96, 548; prominence of his cult since Hammurabi, 116, 134-5, 690-1; his titles, 118, 126, 239, 240, 276, 500, 576, 630; identification with Bel and Ea, 118; solar deity, 118, 119, 528, 576, 690; his warlike traits, 119; in religious texts, 120; temples in Babylon (E-Sagila) and Borsippa, 121, 241, 636, 639; his papakhu, 640; his consort, 121-4, 228; statue brought from Nineveh to E-Sagila, 684; his statue recovered by Agum, 122, 152, 670, 687; lord of E-Sagila and E-Zida, 126; New Year's Day his festival, 127, 631, 678, 681; mediator betw. Ea and mankind, 139, 276; Marduk and Ea in incantation texts, 139-40; conquers Tiâmat, 140, 197, 408, 422; rivaled by Ramman, 158; during the Cassite period, 162; called Sag-ila, 169; lord of Anunnaki and Igigi, 186, 239; absorbs the rôle of other gods, 190, 409; builds Eshara, 198; blended with Bel, 54, 145-6, 148, 222, 542; Bel's titles applied to, 222, 409, 542, 635; position in the Assyrian pantheon, 224-5, 239; associated with Ashur, 224; associated with Ashur, Shamash, and Ramman, 224; second to Ashur, 239; prominence of his cult in the neo-B. period, 239-40; rivaled by Nabu in the pantheon of Nebopolassar, 240, 679; also in old Bab. period, 648; in incantations, 272–3, 276; in the Shurpu series, 288; in hymns, 307 ff.; lord of rest, 309; god of oracles, esp. in the south, 342, 345; zodiacal interpretation, 370, 434, 458–9, 676–7; his double aspect in the creation epic, 409, 432, 450; takes the tablets of fate from Kingu, 428 (cf. 542, 681); creates the universe, 428 ff., 447; establishes the districts of Anu, Bel, and Ea, 432; arranges the stations of the gods in the zodiacal system, 434; creates man, 437 (cf. Ea, Bel, 443, 448); the fifty names (of the Igigi) are bestowed upon M., 438; creates the Anunnaki, 447; = Nibir, i.e., Jupiter, exercises control over all the stars, 434, 458–9; 8th month sacred to M., 463, 678, 686; Marduk as Sharru in the deluge story, 500; absent in the deluge story, 508; dogs symbol of the solar god Marduk, 528; conquers Zu, 542; identified with Adapa, 548; temple at Ashur, 637; zikkurat at Babylon, 639; ship of Marduk, 655; procession on New Year, 679; spec. festival instituted by Agum, 687.

Marduk-baladan, of Babylon, 129.

Marduk-nadin-akhe, king of Babylon, carried statues of Ramman and Shala to Babylon, 212.

Marriage offerings, time of, 59; to Bau, 59.

Mars = Nergal, name of planet, 370, 459; the "sheep" *par excellence*, 459.

Mar-tu = Ramman, 166, 212.

Marwa, hill in Mecca, 687.

Mashu, mythical mountain, 488–9; = Musas or Masis, 516.

Masis, or Musas, = Mashu, 515.

Mecca, 623.

Medes, 44–5.

Median wedge writing, 19.

Meme, variant of Gula, 175.

Mer = Ramman, 157.

Mercury = Nabu, planet, 371, 459.

Mesopotamia, religious ideas and customs, 1, 3; seat of Terahites, 2; empire of Nimrod, 2; geography, 26, 27; character of, 28 ff.

Messiah, Hammurabi and the Hebr.-Christian notion of Messianic time, 533.

Mili-shikhu, king of Babylon, his cult of Shamash, 144; minor gods worshipped, 172.

Minor gods, 2d Bab. period, 171–2; by Mili-shikhu, 172; some Cassite deities, 172; in Ass. texts, 171; in neo-B. period, 171, 242–3; absorbed by greater gods, 111, 147, 171, 177, 190, 233; patron-gods of arts, 178; as personifications, 179; dividing line betw. spirits and m. g., 183, 233.

Mishiru, a foreign deity, 644.

Mitanni wedge writings, 20.

Months, connected with gods, 462 ff., 676; names of the months, 464; m. sacred to gods and their festivals not always corresponding, 687.

Monumental finds, 7.

Moon, importance of m. as omen giver, 358; manifold relations between man and m., 358; importance of m. for calendar, 436, 461; moon and sun in religion and astronomy, 461.

Moon-god, see *Sin*.

Moses, 130; parallelism with Sargon I., 562.

Mosul, excavations near, 5.

Mugheir, mound, excavated, 9; see also *Ur*.

Mummu, associated with Apsu and Tiâmat, 420–1.

Münter, Frederick, decipherment of wedge writing, 15.

Musas, or *Masis*, = Mashu, 516.

Mythology, see also *Nature;* extent and influence of Bab. m., 518 ff.

Nabonnedos, of Babylon, restores temple of Shamash in Sippar, 70, 647; last king of Babylonia, 45; restores temple of Sin in Harran, 77, 646; gives prominence to Shamash cult, 240–1.

Nabu, god, 2d B. period, 127; most prominent trait, 124; probable aqueous origin, 124–5, 220; rank as compared with that of Ea and Marduk, 125, 648; agricultural deity, 125; suppression of cult by Hammurabi and his successors, 126; becomes son of Marduk, 127, 240 (*cf.* 648–9); his shrine in E-Sagila, 127, 220–9, 636; prominence during the Assyrian period, 128–9, 228; his symbol, 128; temple at Calah, 128, 228–9; prominence during the neo-Bab. period, 129, 240; his epithets, 129–31, 229; meaning of name, 130; his functions, 130, 240; his cult with other Semites, 130; identified with Nusku, 220; his consort Tashmitum, 130, 228–9; his consort Nanâ, 224; favorite of Rammanniran III., 128, 228; temple E-Zida in Borsippa, 121, 229, 241, 639, 648; god of wisdom, 129, 229; son of Ea, 229; in the subscript to Ashurbanabal's tablets, 229–30; similarity and difference betw. N. and Ea, 230–1; in hymn, 306; shrine E-makh-tila in Borsippa, 307, 636; god of oracles in Assyria, 344, 348; = Mercury, name of planet, 371, 459; in the deluge, 500; sanctuary E-pad-kalamasuma, 640; Nabu's ship and procession, 654, 679.

Nabu-akhe-irba, astrologer, 340.

Nabu-bil-iddin, king of Babylon, 162, 685; restores cult of Sippar, 176, 628, 645, 670; votive offerings, 670.

Nabupolassar, see *Nebopolassar*.

Namar, district in Babylonia, sacred to Ramman, Nergal, and Nanâ, 159, 164.

Names, transference of name and interpretation of this act, 118, 140–1; composition of proper names, 165; Bab. etymologies of names, 173.

Namtar, god of pestilence, 569; strikes Ishtar with disease, 570; messenger of Allatu, 570, 580.

Nanâ, goddess, 51; titles, 81; center of worship, 81; position in the pantheon proper and in the cosmology, 81; her temples, E-anna in Uruk, 81, 242, 311, 531, 639; E-ul-mash in Agade, 82; in Ur,

81–2, 85, 202, 311, 639, 678; statue captured by Elamites and recaptured by Ashurbanabal, 85, 206; absorbs inferior local deities, 103; associated with Nergal and Ramman, 159, 164; worshipped by Assyr. kings, 206; consort of Nabu, 224; Zag-muk of Nanâ, 678.

Nannar = Sin, etymology of N., 75; N. attached to Ur, 75; Sin to Harran, 76; his position, 76; his representation, 76; his functions, 76, 78; his epithets, 76, 79, 89; relationship to Ningal, 97.

Naram-Sin, founds temple of Shamash in Sippar, 70, 646; his exploits incorporated in omen text, 562; builder of the temple of En-lil in Nippur, 642.

Nâru, river god in incantations, 282; ship of Nâru, 655; place of worship, 655.

Nature, worship, 48; confusion with local cults, 49–50; nature myth, 432–3, 487, 494.

Nazi-Maruttash, Cassite king, votive objects, 671–2.

Nebo, mount in Moab, place of death of Moses, 130.

Nebopolassar, king of Babylon, 129; makes Babylon independent, 239; makes cult of Marduk prominent, 239; makes cult of Nabu prominent, 240; Shamash cult at Larsa, 647, note 3.

Nebuchadnezzar I., expels the Cassites, 88, 158; cult of Marduk and Ramman, 158, 162; his pantheon, 162.

Nebuchadnezzar II., religion of N. and Daniel, 3; builder of Birs Nimrud, 9; rule, 44; worships Sarpanitum as the begetting deity, 122; makes cult of Marduk prominent, 240, 646; revives ancient cults, 242–3; restores temple of Nin-karrak at Sippar, 294; his prayers exemplification of ethical tendencies, 299; opposed to Bel cult in Nippur, 646; restores Shamash temple in Sippar, 646; Ishtar cult in Uruk, 648.

Nergal, god, 51; local cult and temple in Cuthah, 65, 164, 218, 563, 583, 648; worship in Palestine, 65; in Uruk, 66; his names and their meanings, 66; functions, 66–7, 537; development of his attributes, 67–8, 582, 593; identification with Lugal-banda, 95; with Irkalla, 592; associated with Allat, 104, 183, 565, 580, 593; associated with Ramman and Nanâ, 159, 164; Nergal in Samsuiluna's pantheon, 162; in Nebuchadnezzar's I. pantheon, 162; epithets, 172; chief of nether-world and subterranean demons, 183 (*cf.* 260), 511, 563, 582; associated with Ninib as god of the chase, 216, 218, 237; with Ninib and Ashur, 216, 218; god of war, 218, 582; Cuthah his sacred city, 164, 218, 563, 583; Kar-Nergal named in his honor, 219; temple at Tarbisu, 219; Laz his consort, 219, 243, 583; identified with Dibbarra, 232, 528–9, 594; perhaps = Bel-sarbi, 242; in incantations, 273, 280; phases of, 280, 459; = Mars as name of planet, 370, 459; 9th month sacred to N., 463; sun of midday and summer solstice, 528, 582; pictured as a lion, 530; the lion a symbol of Nergal, 537, 580, 582; identified with Gibil, 594; associated with Allatu, 104, 183, 565, 580, 583, 593; Nergal conquers and weds Allatu, 584-5; imitation of Tiâmat-Marduk fight, 585.

Nether-world, names of: Aralû, 557; Ekur, 558; Shuâlu, 558; Kigallu, 562; Irkalla, 563; Kutu or Cuthah, 563; epithets for n., 559, 563; Nergal, lord of the n., 563; the older head of the lower world a goddess, Allatu, not a god, 585.

New Year's Festival, see Zag-muk.

Nibir = planet Marduk or Jupiter, in the zodiac in conjunction with Bel and Ea, 434-5; exercises control over all the stars, 458.

Nicolas of Damascus, source B.-A. religion, 1, 412.

Niebuhr, Carsten, 15.

Niffer, excavations, 11; see *Nippur*.

Nika, mother of Esarhaddon, 340.

Nimrod, incidental biblical reference to, 2; not = Gilgamesh, 514.

Nimrud (mound), unearthed, 7; temple, 9, 627.

Ninâ, quarter in Lagash, 57, 86; explanation of name, 86.

Ninâ, goddess, 51; explanation of name, 86; centers of worship, 86-8, 635; associations with Nin-girsu, 87, 635; relations to Ea, 87-8; fusion with Ishtar of Nineveh, 88; interprets a dream, 101; a daughter of Nin-si-a, 102; in Gudea's pantheon, 106, 635.

Nin-a-gal, god, 51; meaning of name,

64; function, 64; identification with Ea, 64.

Nin-akha-kuddu, goddess, 51; her titles in incantation texts, 103, 282; in Lugalzaggisi's pantheon, 110; goddess of purification, 282; mistress of Uruk, 103, 282; water deity, 282; lady of spells, 282.

Nin-azu, "god of the great city," 592; associated with Allatu, 586, 590; god of healing, 590; identified with Ninib, 591.

Nin-dara, see *Nin-si-a*.

Nin-dim-su, god, in the Cassite pantheon, 162, 172; epithet of Ea, 173.

Nin-din-dug, name of Bau. (See Corrections.)

Nin-e-gal, variant of Nin-gal, 98.

Nineveh, center of action in book of Judith, 3; site of, 6; capital of Assyria, 46, 193, 651; cult of Ishtar, 152, 202-3; temple Emashmash of Ishtar, 152; resp. of Belit, 227; Sha-nit(?)-ka, mistress of, 233; worship of all gods and goddesses, 638; intellectual center, 651.

Nin-gal, god, 51; center of worship, 97; relationship to Nannar, 97; sanctuary at Khorsabad, 231; Nin-gal's ship, 655.

Nin-gir-su, solar deity, 51; subordinate to Bel, 53, 57; identity with Ninib, 57, 217 (*cf.* 528); temple E-Ninnu in Girsu, 57, 87, 634-5, 640; votive offerings, 57; agricultural deity = Shulgur, 58; identity with Tammuz, 58; relations to Nin-shakh, 93; in Gudea's pantheon, 106; in incantations,

273; zikkurat in Lagash or Girsu, 619, 635, 639; shrine in Lagash, 640; his ship, 654; consort of Bau, 59, 677.

Nin-gish-zida, solar deity, 51; a form of Nin-girsu, 92; meaning of name, 92; identified with Ninib, Nin-girsu, Nin-shakh, 99, 217, 528, 547; local character, 99, 528; temple in Girsu, 99, 635; in Gudea's inscriptions and incantation texts, 99, 106, 280; consort of Nusku, 280; brings famine in the land, 387; 5th month sacred to N., 462, 547; servant of Gibil, 463; 4th month sacred to, 463; identical with Gish-zida, 547; associated with Tammuz, 546, 588; presides over the growth of trees, 588.

Nin-gul, 51; consort of Lugal-banda, 95; interpretation of name, 95; place of worship, 96.

Ninib, see Nin-girsu, solar deity, 57, 217, 459, 462, 576, 684; consort of Gula, 105 (cf. 576, 591); of Belit-ekalli, 173; in Hammurabi's pantheon, 162; in Nebuchadnezzar's I. pantheon, 162, 164; god of war, 164, 214, 218; = Ud-zal, 166; associated with Ashur, 214; epithets, 213-4, 217; temple in Calah, 214-5 (cf. 684); favorite of Ashurnasirbal and Shamshi-Ramman, 214; god of the chase in association with Nergal, 216, 218, 237; hero of the heavenly and earthly spirits, 214; in association with Nergal and Ashur, 216; identical with Nin-girsu, 57, 217; with Nin-azu, 591; absorbs Nin-gish-zida and Nin-shakh, 217 (cf. 547); represents east sun and morning sun, 217; first-born of Ea, 217; offspring of Ekur, 217; first-born of Bel, 217; god of destructive cloud storm, 217, 500; other qualities in religious literature, 218, 576; name of outer wall of Sargon's II. palace, 237; lays the foundations of cities, 237; three forms, 238; temple in Dilbat, 242; in incantations, 273, 280; = Saturn, name of planet, 371, 459; 6th and 11th months sacred, 215, 684; 4th month sacred to N., 462; in the deluge story, 500 (cf. 217), 504; worshipped at Nippur, 635; temple of Zamama-Ninib, 640.

Nin-igi-azag, title of Ea, 230.

Nin-igi-nangar-bu, 171; presides over metal workers, 178.

Nin-Karrak = goddess Gula, 242; temple at Babylon (see Gula), 242; in incantations, 273; temple at Sippar, 294; in a prayer of Nebuchadnezzar, 294.

Nin-khar-sag = goddess Belit, 164; in Samsuiluna's pantheon, 162, 164; sanctuary at Babylon (see Belit), 242, 639.

Nin-kigal = Allatu, 282.

Nin-kurra, 171; lord of mountain, patron of stone workers, 178.

Nin-lil, see Belit.

Nin-lil-anna, in Nebuchadnezzar's II. pantheon, 242; temple in Babylon, 640.

Nin-makh = Ishtar, 242; temple at Babylon, 242.

Nin-mar, goddess, 51; center of worship, 100; her temples in Mar, 100; daughter of Ninâ, 100; popularity of cult, 100; in Gudea's pantheon, 106, 635; daughter of Marduk, 168; temple at Lagash, 635.

Ninni, goddess, = Enanna, 51; titles, 80; center of worship, 80; variant of Ishtar, 82; in Lugalzaggisi's and Gudea's panthea, 110; identical with Nanâ of Uruk, 111; temple at Hallabi, 117; her cult by Hammurabi, 144-5; "Ninni," consort of Zamama, 169; temple in Kish, 639.

Nin-shakh, god, 51; his character and functions, 93; identified with Ninib, 93, 217; relations to Nin-girsu and Nin-gishzida, 92-3; temple at Uruk, 93.

Ninshar, cosmological deity, 417.

Nin-si-a, god, 51; or Nin-dar-a, 90; center of worship, 91, 635; absorbed by Nin-girsu, 91; in Gudea's pantheon, 106, 635.

Nin-sun, god, temple of N. at Lagash, 635.

Nin-tu, god, temple of N. at Lagash, 635.

Nin-zadim, god, 171; patron of sculpture, 178.

Nippur, rulers, 37; temple of Bel, 11, 37, 69, 51, 54, 151, 642, 644; temple of Belit, 55, 635; inscriptions from Nippur, 103; prominence during Cassite period, 40, 146, 480; wall of Zakar, 172; wall of Lugal-mittu, 172; ancient center, 245, 445; chief god Bel, or En-lil, 445, 542; reference to N. in Gilgamesh epic, 486; rivalry betw. Nippur and Eridu, 508; replaced by Babylon, 542; zikkurat

at N., 617; worship of Ninib, 635; worship of Nusku, 635; votive objects, 671-3.

Nisaba, goddess, 51; agricultural deity, 101; traits in common with Ea, 101; sister of Ninâ, 101; centers of cult, 102; in Gudea's pantheon, 111; probably local in Uruk, 111.

Nisan, sacred to Anu and Bel, 462, 677; sacred in Babylonia, 684; 7th day sacred to Shamash, Malkatu, and Bunene, 685.

Nisir, mount on which the ship alights, 503.

Nisroch, Assyrian deity, 2.

Noah, resemblance to Parnapishtim less than is the case with Lot, 507.

Nu-gim-mud, title of Ea, 230.

Nun-gal, god of the 2d Bab. period, 168; temple in Sippar, 168; meaning of name, 168; solar deity, 168; becomes a demon, 168.

Nur-Ramman, of Ur, builder of Sin's temple in Ur, 76; builder of temples to Nin-gal and Nannar at Ur, 97.

Nusku, fire-god, in Ass. pantheon, 188, 220-1; in Bab. pantheon, 220; amalgamated with Gibil, 220, 277; identified with Nabu, 220-1; ideographic writing of name and its explanation, 220; solar deity, 220-1, 279; shrine in E-Sagila, 220, 241; epithets, 221, 277, 280; functions, 221; shrine in E-Zida, 241; in incantations, 271-3, 277, 286; younger than Gibil, 277; a mythological conception, 277, 279; Gibil-N, god of civilization, 278; medium betw. worshipper and deity, 279; associated with Anu, 277, 286; associated with Bel and Ea, 279, 286; Ishum, messenger of, 280; worship at Nippur, 635; see *Gibil*.

Okeanos, see under *Ea*, 63.

Old Testament, source for B.-A. religion, 1, 669 (*cf.* 696); relations betw. the Hebrews and B.-A., 2, 611, 697-8; contrast betw. Hebr. and B.-A. religion, 3, 668; O. T. points of contact with Gilgamesh epic, 495; with deluge story, 506 ff.; parallels betw. Adam and Eabani, Eve and Ukhat, 511; betw. Samson and Gilgamesh stories, 515-6; 3d chapter Genesis compared with Adapa legend, 551; Hebr. Sheôl ∥ Bab. Shuâlu, 560; Hebr. Shôel ∥ Bab. Shâ'ilu, 560; Hebr.-Bab. custom of inquiring of the dead, 560; parallelism betw. Sargon I. and Moses, 562; conceptions of nether-world in O. T. and in Bab., 606; parallels betw. temple of Solomon and Bab. temple, 623, 632, 652-3, 655; libation of oil in O. T. and in Ass.-Bab., 665; sacrifices in O. T. compared with Ass.-Bab., 667-8; teraphim and Ass.-Bab. amulets, 674; Hebr. and Bab. New Years, 681; Purim compared with Bab. 15th Adar festival, 686; Ashera and tree worship in Babylonia, 689.

Omens, division of religious literature, 247; purposes of, 248, 331; comparative age of, 253-4; an indirect means of forecasting the future, 329; directions for the priest in recognizing o., 330; relationship betw. o. and prayers, 331; part of magic element in the ritual, 331; occasions for seeking an o., 331 ff.; derived from offered animals, 332; of a public character, 332 ff., 362, 364, 374, 401; questions of an omen seeker, 333 ff., 369; list of, 337, 362; their relation to reports, 368, 372; o. ritual, 338; connecting link betw. incantations and o., 352; variety of o. literature, 355, 362; o. from stars, 356; the more variety, the more significance — a principle of general application in interpretation of o., 358; other guiding principles, 358 ff., 388, 401; private o., 362, 403, 405; o. series and mode of their composition, 363; omens deduced from observations of eclipses, 357, 364; restricted application of o. no hindrance to their practical use, 366, 372; vagueness of o. intentional, 367; interrelation betw. reports and o., 368, 372-3; importance of o. deduced from eclipses and more ordinary phenomena, 368-9; omens deduced from observations of planets, esp. Ishtar, and of other heavenly bodies, 371-3; omen calendars, 375, 382; omens from terrestrial phenomena, 383 ff.; logical principle controlling the interpretation, 384; offshoot of sympathetic magic, 384; birth omens, 384; partly public, partly private character, 386; the rarer the phenomena, the greater the significance, 385; ideas of sympathetic magic in the interpretation of o., 388; omens from offsprings of animals, 391 ff.; omens from the actions of animals, 397–402; omens from dreams, 402-4; o. of a private character, 403; popular phase of augury, 403; omens from individual experiences, 404; dividing line betw. omens of individual and of public character, 405; the practical working of the omen belief, 406.

Ophites, a gnostic sect, 699.

Oppert, Jules, expedition to Babylonia, 8.

Oracles, see also Omens and Witchcraft, direct means of forecasting the future, 329; occasions for asking o., 338 ff.; blank forms for o., 341; form of, 341 ff.; Marduk, god of, 342; asked of the sun-god, 334 ff.; of Ishtar of Arbela, 342; ceremonies accompanying o., 345; relationship to penitential psalms, 347; practical purpose of, 349; by means of dreams, 349 ff.; generally vague language, 344; occasionally definite language, 360; objects with which o. are concerned, 360; given by priestesses, 485, or priests, 329, 560, 657-8; asked of the dead, 559-60, 657; asked on the New Year's festival, 628-9.

Pantheon, divisions and development, 48-50; sources, 51; comparison betw. p. in historical and in incantation texts, 297; comparison betw. B. and A. pantheon, 189, 201.

Papakhu, chamber of the god, 627; cosmological significance, 629.

Pap-sukal, i.e., divine messenger, epithet of Nin-shakh, Nebo, and Nusku, 93 (cf. 463, 571); in incantations, 273; 10th month sacred to P., Ishtar, and Anu, 463.

Pap-u, god, in the Cassite pantheon, 162, 172; offspring of E-sharra, 174; function, 174.

Paradise, belief in, among Babylonians, 578.

Parakku, chamber of the god, 627.

Parnapishtim, immortal, 488, 577; P. and Gilgamesh, 492 ff.; son of Kidin-Marduk, 488, 496; born in Shurippak, 496; his epithet Adra-Khasis, 505; bears more resemblance to Lot than to Noah, 507.

Pa-sag, god, 51; "the leader of the land," 101; identity with Ishum, 101; lieutenant of Shamash, 107; in Gudea's pantheon, 106.

Patesi, 198.

Patron gods, of persons, 216, 235; Nabu, patron of Ramman-nirari III., 228; of places, 49, 69–70, 106, 111.

Penitential psalms, points in common with and differences from incantations, 312; national origin of, 312; marks relationship betw. god and man, 313; purpose to appease the anger of the gods, 315, 688; advanced religious conceptions, 314-5, 326; dialogue form, 315; language, 316-7; age, 317; anonymity of the deity addressed, 318; p. for specific purposes, 324, 688; relationship to oracles, 347.

Persepolis, wedge writings, 16.

Persian Gulf, sacred to Ea, 497; not the source of the deluge, 497; confluence of the streams, 577.

Persian wedge writing, 19.

Personifications of human arts, 178.

Peters, John P., explorer, 11.

Pilgrimage, 684.

Place, Victor, excavations, 8.

Place of Fates, name of temple, 641.

Planets, observations of, 370; identifications of p. with deities, 370, 459 (*cf.* 619); prominence of Ishtar-Venus, in astrological texts, 371; regarded as auguries for the chiefs and the general welfare, 373; planets and zikkurats, 619.

Politics, affecting religion and literature, 108, 110-1, 134-5, 201, 239, 690-1.

Popular Belief, see *Theology and Popular Belief.*

Prayers, see also *Hymns,* occasions, 663; in connection with incantations, 293, 299; without accompaniment of incantations, 294; curses regarded as p., 296; no line of demarcation betw. incantations and p., 297, 299, 307; ethics in, 298; power of words, 328; no p. in its highest form, 329; relationship betw. prayers and omen, 330; efficacy dependent on their being uttered in the right manner and by the right person, 353.

Priestly codes, 362.

Priests and priestesses, divisions of, 269, 241-2, 657-8; p. as exorciser and his function, 271-2, 330, 657-8; mediator betw. man and god, 315, 331, 353, 374, 560, 627, 692; prognostication of future, 329, 560, 657; importance of, 353; "Priests of Ashur," association of priestly functions with early kingship, 374; priests and priestesses in their functions, 485, 655 ff., 692; priests purifying the dead, 578, 602; general name for priest, 657-8, 676; priestesses as dirge singers, 604, 658; as judges, 625, 658; intellectual leaders, 693; as sacrificers, 657-8; eligibility to priesthood, 658-9; women priests, 485, 659-60.

Proper names, see also *Names,* composition of, 165; source of study of divinities, 166; evidence of age of cult of gods (Ishme-Dagan), 208; Samsi-Ramman, 209.

Psalms, see *Penitential Psalms;* also *Hymns, Prayers.*

Ptolemy, see *Claudius Ptolemaeus.*

Pudilu, builds temple of Shamash at Ashur, 209.

Purat = Euphrates, 27.

Purification, see *Rituals.*

Purim, compared with the Bab. solar festival, 15th of Adar, 686; not to be compared with Puru, 688.

Puru, a festival ceremony, 688.

Puzur-Shadu-Rabū, captain of the ship of Parnapishtim, 500.

Ra, Egyptian sun-god, 210.

Rabbinical literature, bearing upon B.-A. religion, 3, 697.

Races, of Mesopotamia, 24, 33.

Ramman, god, Shala his consort, 102, 161, 212; associated with Anu, 154, 207, 212; associated with Shamash, 145, 157-8, 160, 211; associated with Sin and Shamash, 158, 163; associated with Nergal and Nanâ, 159, 164; rivals of Marduk, 158; ideographic and other readings of the name, 156-7; meaning of name, 156-7; extent of his cult, 159; cult by Aramaeans, 159; indigenous to Assyria, 159; rival of Ashur, 161; his two aspects as storm-god, 160; epithets, 156, 158, 160, 212, 498; in Hammurabi's pantheon, 162; in Nebuchadnezzar's I. pantheon, 162; = Martu, 166, 212; popular in Assyria, 211; his instruments of destruction, 212; "the mightiest of the gods," 212; name of one of the eastern gates of Sargon's II. palace, 237; brings abundance, 237; temple at Borsippa, 242; temple at Kumari, 242; 11th month sacred to R., 463; R. in the deluge, 500; declines to fight Zu, 541.

Ramman-nirari I., king of Assyria, 155; cult of Ramman, 159; of Anunnaki and Igigi as spirits of earth and heaven resp., 185; repels the Cassites, 199; his pantheon, 237, 593.

Ramman-nirari III., king of Assyria, gives prominence to Nabu cult in Assyria, 128, 228; erects temple to Nabu at Calah, 228; Nabu his patron god, 228.

Rassam, Hormuzd researches, 9.
Rawlinson, Henry, explorations, 9.
Regulus, observations, 372.
Religion, unity of church and state, 690; influence upon Hebrews, see

Old Testament; upon Christianity, 698; upon Egypt, Persia, and Greece, 699-701.

Religious texts, 12-3, 467; sources for religion, 51, 661; in Bab. theological schools, 134; reshaping of r. t. during Hammurabi's time, 140-2; divisions, 247-51; age, 691; comparison betw. Ass. and Bab. r. t., 251-2; their value as source for knowledge of sacrifices, 661; votive inscriptions on statues, 669; on other objects, 671-2; worn as amulets, 672; plague tablets, 536, 674.

Rim-Sin, of 2d dynasty of Ur, "called" by Bel and Ea, 62; cult of moon and sun-god in Ur, 70; of Nanâ in Ur, 81; builds temple of Nin-shakh at Uruk, 93; his wife builds temple to Nin-gal at Ur, 97.

Rituals, establishment of, 115; and incantations, 247-8, 253-4, 283; manner of growth, 255; purification, 284, 688; incantations the oldest fixed r., 294; penitential psalms, 312 ff., 688; bodily castigation, 320, 688; offerings, 328; prayers, 293 ff.; never without ulterior motive, 328; oracles and omens, 328 ff.; composition and growth, 329-30; strictness in observation of, 347.

Rustem, son of Sal in Armen. and Mandaean legend, parallel to Etana, 520.

Saba, district in southern Arabia, 491.
Sabitum, maiden in Gilgamesh epic, 490-1; the goddess of Siduri, 491.

Sacred objects, 651.
Sacred period, 686.
Sacred quarter, 622 ff.
Sacredness of animals, meaning of, 397–8, 662; of trees, 662–3.
Sacrifices, when not to be offered, 378; when offered, 663, 667–8; offered by priests, 657–8; Semitic view of, 660; comparison with Hebrew, 667–8; as determined from religious and historical literature, 661; development of, 661; two kinds of, 661; connected with prayers, 663; use of oil and wine, 664, 666; daily, 667; monthly, 668.
Sâdu, the hunter in the service of Gilgamesh, 475; associated with Ukhat, 511.
Safa, hill in Mecca, 687.
Sag-ila = Marduk, in proper names of the 2d Bab. period, 169.
Sal, father of Rustem, 520.
Samsi-Ramman, king of Assyria, builds temple to Ramman, 154, 159; builds temple to Ashur in Ashur, 198; his name as evidence of age of Shamash cult, 209.
Samson, parallelism with Gilgamesh, 515 ff.
Samsuiluna, king of Babylon, 56; builds sanctuary of Belit, 56; builds Dur-padda, sacred to Ramman, 158; his pantheon, 162; builds wall of Zakar in Nippur, 172; builds wall of Lugal-mittu in Nippur, 172.
Samuel, prophet, his spirit called up, 559.
Saracus, last king of Assyria, 229.
Sargon I., "builds" temple E-ulmash of Nanâ in Agade, 82; myth of Sargon I. to an incident in Moses' life, 562; his exploits incorporated in a religious text, 562; "builder" of temple of En-lil in Nippur, 642, 645.
Sargon II., of Assyria, restores "laws and customs of Harran," 77; builds sanctuary to Shamash, 211; names Kar-Nergal in honor of Nergal, 219; builds sanctuary to Sin at Khorsabad and Magganubba, 219; patron of learning, 229; prominence of Nabu cult, 229; erects sanctuary to Nin-gal at Khorsabad, 231; restores Magganubba, 232; revives the triad, 236; his pantheon, 237; his palace at Khorsabad, 225, 237; his zikkurat at Khorsabad, 617; sacrifices in Babylonia, 664; institutes special festival, 687.
Sarpanitum, consort of Marduk, 121, 224, 228, 636; interpretation of name, 121, 449; shrine in E-Sagila, 121, 241, 636, 641; her statue recovered by Agum, 122, 152, 670, 687; her subordinate position, 121–2; goddess of matrimonial fertility, 122, 684; of secret knowledge, 122; amalgamation with Erua, 122; epithets of Sarpanitum-Erua, 123; called Belit, 224, 684; shrine in E-Zida, 241; rarely in incantations, 276; 25th day of Siwan her festival, 684; festival instituted by Agum, 687.
Saturn = Ninib, planet, 371, 459.
Saul, king of Israel, and the witch, 559.

Semites and non-Semites in Babylonia, 21-2, 32-4.

Sendschirli, excavations in, 579.

Senkereh = Larsa.

Sennacherib, king of Assyria, 200; takes statues of Ramman and Shala back from Babylon, 212; erects temple to Nergal at Tarbisu, 219; his pantheon, 238, 644, note 2.

Seven spirits, cause eclipse of moon, 264, 276; 12th month sacred to them, 463; Sibi, collective personification of the s. p. associated in war with Ishum, 533.

Sex, inferiority of female to male in the B.-A. pantheon, 75, 79, 104; confusion of female cults, 80; variety of "ladies" in pantheon, 98, 104; position of female deities as consorts of male deities, 104, 586, 594; male deities becoming female and consorts of male deities, 177, 280; association of sexes in cosmology, 411; association of sexes in the creation of the gods, 413; female deities and the months, 463; sex in witchcraft, 267, 342, 660; sex in priesthood, 485, 659-60; sex in furnishing oracles, 485, 660; sex among musicians and dirge singers, 660 (see *Dirge*); position of woman, 694.

Shabat, 11th month, sacred to Ramman, 463; sacred to Ninib, 215, 684.

Shabra, god, temple at Lagash, 635.

Shâilu, a designation for priest, 560; ¶ Hebr. Shôel, 560.

Shala, consort of Ramman, 161, 212; in proper names of 2d Bab. period, 169; in Ass. pantheon, 189; meaning of name, 213; other applications of the name, 213; epithets, 213.

Shalman, god, in Ass. pantheon, 188.

Shalmaneser II., king of Assyria, gives prominence to Shamash cult, 205, 215; his pantheon, 237.

Shamash, or Utu, 51, 277; signification of name, 68; relations to the moon-god, 68-70, 98, 305; centers of worship, Sippar and Larsa, 69, 117, 143, 176, 241, 628, 640, 646; relative age of the centers, 70; temple Ebabbara, 70, 628, 640, 645; attributes and functions, 71, 120, 210; in incantations, 71, 211; probable age of these conceptions, 72; his other names and their meaning, 72-4, 176; local uses thereof, 73; Malkatu his consort, 74-5, 176, 241-685; offspring of Nin-gal, 98; in Lugalzaggisi's and Gudea's pantheon, 110; in Hammurabi's pantheon, 162; warrior of heaven and earth, 144, 211; mighty hero, 152; position in Bab. pantheon during and after Hammurabi, 144; position in Ass. pantheon, 144, 209-11; associated with Ramman, 145, 157-8, 160, 211; associated with Sin and Ramman, 158, 163; associated with Ishtar, 163, 511; associated with Malik and Bunene, 176; often called Malik, 176; symbol of Shamash, 176-7; temple at Ashur, 209; protecting deity, 209; ethical level in Ass. pantheon, 209-10; judge of heaven and earth, 210, 274, 279, 297, 527 (*cf.* 640); prominence of sun cult during reign of Ashurnasirbal and Shalmaneser II., 210, 646; under Esarhaddon, 646; sanctuary by Sargon II., 211; cult influenced by that of Egyptian Ra, 210 (*cf.* 699); name of one of the eastern gates of Sargon's II. palace, 237; grants victory, 237; Nebuchadnezzar II. and Shamash cult, 646; Nabonnedos gives prominence to Sh. cult, 240-1, 647; temple in Babylon, 242, 640: Sh. in incantations, 280; in hymns, 300 ff.; in omens and oracles, 334, 344; Shamash and Sin, 305, 647; 7th month sacred to Sh., 463, 685; patron of Gilgamesh, 471, 479; identical with Lugal-Marada, 486; patron of Etana, 520; controls Zu, 538; on seal cylinders, 540; Si-gar, a festival of, 684; festival days, 685.

Shamshi-Ramman, king of Assyria, gives prominence to Ninib cult, 214.

Shamuktu, a class of priestesses of Ishtar, 660.

Sha-nit(?)-ka, goddess, in Ass. pantheon, 188; associated with Damku and Sharru-ilu, 232; mistress of Nineveh, 233; = Ishtar, 233.

Sharru, title of Marduk, in the deluge story, 500.

Sharru ilu, god, associated with Damku and Sha-nit(?)-ka, 232; meaning of name, 232; evidently a title, 232; perhaps a foreign god, 232; worshipped at Magganubba, 232.

Shar-sarbi = Belsarbi, 242.

Sherua, minor god in Ass. pantheon, 234; foreign deity, 644.

Sheôl, 560; O. T. conceptions of Sheôl ‖ to Babylonian conceptions, 606 ff.; see also *Shuâlu, Dead*.

Shinar = Babylonia, 613.

Ship, construction of, 498-9; Puzur-shadu-rabu, captain of ark, 500; a sacred object, 653-4; its uses and significance, 654; compared with the Mahmal and the ark, 655.

"*Ship of Light*," name of Sin's ship, 655.

"*Ship of Malku*," name of the ship of Nâru, 655.

"*Ship of the Brilliant Offspring*," name of Bau's ship, 655.

Shir, god, in Nebuchadnezzar's I. pantheon, 162; local god, 163; patron of Bit-Khabban, 176.

Shirpurla, see *Lagash*.

Shuâlu, designation of the district of the dead, 560 ff.; meaning, 559; ‖ to Hebr. Sheôl, 560.

Shubu, in Nebuchadnezzar's I. pantheon, 162; local character, 163; patron god of Bit-Khabban, 176.

Shu-bu-la, god, in proper names of the 2d Bab. period, 169; patron of Shumdula, 169.

Shu-gid-la, see *Shu-bu-la*, 169.

Shukamuna, Cassite god, identical with Nergal, 152, 163, 172; head of Agum's pantheon, 152, 172; consort of Shumalia, 173.

Shul-gur = Nin-gir-su, 51.

Shul-pa-uddu, god, 51; meaning of

name, 99; age and extension of cult, 99; decline of cult in favor of Shamash and Ninib, 100; position in Babylonian astronomy, 100; solar deity, 99, 531.

Shumalia, in the Cassite pantheon, 162-3, 172; in Nebuchadnezzar's I. pantheon, 162; consort of Shukamuna, 173; epithet, 173.

Shumdula, city in Babylonia, cult of Shubula, 169.

Shum-gar, see *Si-gar*.

Shurippak, city on Euphrates, destroyed by rainstorm, 495; comparison with Sodom, 496, 507.

Shurpu series, 290.

Shu-sil-la, see *Shubula*, 169.

Sibi, collective personification of the seven evil spirits associated with Ishum, 533.

Sibittum, minor deity in the Etana legend, 521.

Siduri, Sabitum, the goddess of Siduri, 491.

Si-gar, festival of Gula, 683; festival of Sin, 684; festival of Shamash, 684; meaning, 684; date of installation of Ashurbanabal, 684.

Silili, mother of one of Ishtar's associates, 482.

Sin, god, see also *Nannar*; worshipped in Harran, 76, 241, 641, 647; temple at Ur, 76, 241, 295, 640, 644, 687; occurrence of the name elsewhere, 77; amalgamation with Nannar, 78; chief trait, 78; lunar cycle and sun calendar, 78; epithets and functions, 76, 78-9, 219, 462; gradual decrease of Sin cult, 78-9; in Lugalzaggisi's and Gudea's pantheon, 110; associated with Shamash and Ramman, 158, 163; in Hammurabi's pantheon, 162; patron of Bit-Khabban, 163; head of 2d triad, 163; associated with Ishtar, 163, 571; father of Ishtar, 565; temple at Calah, 219; sanctuary at Khorsabad, 219; sanctuary at Magganubba, 219; god of wisdom, 78, 219; god of war in Ass. pantheon, 219; first-born son of Bel, 76, 219; subordinate position in Ass. pantheon, 219-20; Sin and astronomy, resp. astrology, 219-20; temple at Babylon, 242; in incantations, 280; in hymn, 303-4; Sin and Shamash, 305, 647; first-born of Bel, 219, 462; Siwan, 3d month, sacred to Sin, 462; chapel in E-Zida, 639; Sin cult under Nabonnedos, 77, 648; Sin's ship, 655; zagmuk of, 678; Si-gar, festival of, 684.

Sinai, a peninsula (metals and stone), 627, 652.

Sin-gamil, of Uruk, builds sanctuaries to Nergal at Cuthah, 66.

Sin-gashid, of Uruk, servitor of Lugal-banda and Nin-gul, 95-6.

Sin-iddina, of Larsa, builds sanctuary to Shamash in Larsa, 69; builds temple of Sin in Ur, 76.

Sippar, temple and archives, 16; ancient center, 35, 245; center of worship of Shamash, 69, 117, 143-4, 241, 628, 640, 646; temple of Nun-gal, 168; worship of Shamash, Malik, and Bunene, 176; temple of Nin-karrak, 294; temple of Malkatu or Â, 640; zikkurat, "Threshold of Long Life," 641.

Sir, serpent god, in proper names of the 2d Bab. period, 170.

Sirius, observations of, 372.

Siwan, 3d month, sacred to Sin, 462, 687; sacred to the god of brick structures, 463; 25th day of Siwan sacred to Belit of Babylon, 684.

Slaves, standing of slaves a measure of social ethics, 695.

Smith, George, explorations, 9.

Sodom, destruction of, point of contact with Gilgamesh epic, 495-6, 507.

Sokkaros, grandfather of Gilgamesh (Aelian), 524.

Solomonic temple and the sacred quarter in Nippur, 623-4; horns of altar compared with Bab. custom, 652; "sea" compared with Apsu, 653; ark compared with the Bab. ship, 655.

Sorcer, Sorceress, see also *Witchcraft*; relationship betw. s. and oracle-giver, 342.

Spirits, in proper names, 166, 180; Nun-gal-e-ne, a class of, 168 (*cf.* 184); their symbols, 174, 182; functions, 174; lists of, 180; classification of, 181 ff.; of disease, 181, 186, 246; of the field, 182; of the nether-world, 183; dividing line betw. gods and spirits, 181, 183, 231, 266, 274; of evil, 260, 264; activity of, 260-1; representations of, 263; habitations of, 260, 263; the seven spirits, 264; strength attribute of, 266; relationship betw. demons and witchcraft, 267; differentiation of demons, 262.

Spiritualization of mythology, 304, 306; characteristic of later times, 297; in penitential psalms, 313, 319.

Splendor of Heaven and Earth, name of temple, 641.

Stars, writing of heaven, 454; division of, 455.

Storm, symbols of storm (birds and bulls), 537 ff.

Subartu, name of country, 532.

Sugi, name of country, 675.

Sukhal-ziku, name of mythical fountain, 572.

Sumer and Akkad, ethnological-geographical, 32-3; S.-A. language in incantations, 259.

Sumerian question, 21-4, 32-4.

Sun, see *Shamash*; gates of s., 435, 443; representation of sun in creation story, 461; sun and moon in astronomy and religion, 461.

Susian wedge writing, 19.

Syllabaries, 135.

Syncellus, source for B.-A. religion, 1, 5.

Systematized religion, see *Theology*.

Taboo, meaning of, 397.

Talisman, see *Amulet, Teraphim*.

Tammuz, agricultural deity, 58, 588; relations to Ishtar, 84, 482, 484, 547, 564, 574; T. and Gish-zida doorkeepers of heaven, 546; solar deity, 547; 4th month named for T., 547, 682; intercedes for Adapa with Anu, 548-9; brother of Belili, 575; T.'s day = All-Souls' Day, 599, 605, 682; identified with Nin-girsu, 58; associated with Nin-gish-zida, 546, 588.

Tammuz, 4th month, sacred to Ninib, 462; named for god Tammuz, 547, 682; sacred to the servant of Gibil, 463.

Tarbisu, city north of Nineveh; temple of Nergal, 219.

Tar-gul-le, names of some demons let loose by Dibbarra in the deluge story, 500.

Tashmitum, goddess in pantheon of Hammurabi, 130; a new creation, 131–2; consort of Nabu, 130–1, 228–9; meaning of name, 131; her quasi-artificial character, 131–2; called Nanâ, 132; shrine in E-Sagila, 220, 241; in the subscript to Ashurbanabal's tablets, 229–30; shrine in E-Zida, 241.

Tashritu, see *Tishri*.

Taylor, J. E., excavations, 8.

Tebet, 10th month, sacred to Papsukal, Ishtar, and Anu, 463; festival of En-meshara, 588.

Tel-Id, mound near Warka, site of ancient capital of Mar, 100.

Tell-el-amarna, see *El-amarna*.

Tell-Ibrahim = Cuthah.

Telloh, excavations, 11; temple records and legal documents, 165.

Tell-Sifr, temple records and legal documents, 165.

Temple records, see also *Literature*; source of study of the deities, 167.

Temples, 612 ff.; names of t., 638 ff.; history of t., 642 ff.; as financial establishments, 650; minor part played by the temples in Assyria, 659.

Terah, *Terahites*, appearance in Palestine, 2; migrations, 2; home of, 9.

Teraphim, talismans parallel to Ass.-Bab. statuettes of gods, 674.

Teumman, king of Elam, 296.

Thamud, Arabic tribe destroyed, 496.

The Brilliant House, name of temple, 641.

"*The Lesser Light*," name of Ningal's ship, 655.

Theology and popular belief, 89, 114, 131, 180, 235, 249, 411, 414, 416, 458, 494, 527, 584, 614, 619, 629–30, 689; Gudea's system, 108; interaction betw. political fortunes and positions of divinities, 108, 110–11, 134–5, 201, 234, 235; genealogical arrangement according to Amiaud, 108; family theory according to Davis, 109; its value, 109; tendency towards recognition of certain great gods, 111, 147, 171, 190, 234–5, 696; organization of cult and ritual, establishment of dogmas, 115, 133, 247, 690; pedagogical activity, 135; formation of the great triad, 147; re-systematization of gods by Hammurabi, 171, 276; systematization of spirits, 184; attempts to systematize series of gods, 213, 216, 233; theology in cosmology, 412 ff., 418, 443; in the 12th tablet of the Gilgamesh epic, 512–3; in the Etana legend, 527; theology in the Zu epic, 542.

Thomas, Felix, excavations, 8.

Thousand and One Nights, 494.

Threshold of Long Life, name of zikkurat in Sippar, 641.

Tiâmat, mythical monster, conquered by Marduk, 140, 197, 408;

fought by Anu, Ea, 197; synonymous with Apsu, 411; female principle, 411; personified chaos, 411, 414; dominion of T. and Apsu precedes that of the gods, 412; gods product of the union of T. and Apsu, 413; mythical monsters product of the union of T. and Apsu, 414; associates of T., 419; Ummu-Khubur, epithet of T., 419; Kingu her consort, 420; Tiâmat epic compared with Zu myth, 543; comparison with Nergal-Allat fight, 585.

Tiglathpileser I., king of Assyria, nomenclature of Bel, 146; dedicates temple to Anu and Ramman, 154, 159; as a hunter, 216; rebuilds temple of Bel at Ashur, 225; pantheon, 236; dedicates captured gods, 675.

Tiglathpileser II., sacrifices in Babylonia, 664.

Tigris, course of, 28-9; comparison with Euphrates, 30; in garden of Eden, 2 (*cf.* 506); one of the four streams forming the confluence of streams, 506 (*cf.* 2).

Tishri, 7th month, sacred to Shamash, 462 (*cf.* 681, 685); 7th day sacred to Shamash, Malkatu, and Bunene, 685.

Tombs, see *Dead*.

Triad, the great, Anu, Bel, Ea, 107; relationship of the members, 147; product of theology, 147, 149; development of, 148; extraneous position, 149; representative of the three kingdoms, 155; punish the violator of monuments, 207; fix the name of the months, 208, 236; general position in Ass. pantheon, 236; give victory, 236; grant rule, 236; associated with Ashur, Ishtar, and Igigi, and Anunnaki, 236; in incantations, 273; associated with fire-god, 279; in Gudea, 418; in the cosmology, 418; ancestors of the triad, 418; symbolizes the eternal laws of the universe, 432.

Triad, second, Sin, Shamash, Ramman, 163; in incantations, 273.

Tubal-cain, biblical father of metal workers, 178.

Tur-lil-en, in Nebuchadnezzar's II. pantheon, 242.

Tychsen, Gerhard, decipherment of wedge writing, 15.

Ubshu-kenna, council chamber of the gods, 423, 629, 687.

Uddushu-Namir, a divine servant, created by Ea, 571.

Ud-zal = Ninib, 166.

Ukhat, in the Gilgamesh epic, 475, 476 ff.; parallelism betw. U. and Eve, 511.

Ukháti, sacred harlots of Uruk, 475, 531, 660.

Ul-mash-shi-tum, in proper names of the 2d Bab. period, 170.

Ululu, 6th month, sacred to Ishtar, 462, 684; sacred to Ashur, 463, 685; sacred to Ninib, 215, 684; 3d day of U. sacred to Shamash, Malkatu, and Bunene, 685.

Ululu 2d (intercalated), sacred to Anu and Bel, 463.

Umu, goddess, 51; priestess of Uruk, 102; in Lugalzaggisi's pantheon, 110.

Umun-pa-uddu = Shul-pa-uddu, 99.
Ur, city, home of Terahites, 9; dynasties, 36-7; sacred to Sin or Nannar, 69-70, 75, 242, 640, 647; sanctuary of Shamash, 70; starting point of Hebrew migrations, 77; association with Harran, 77; temple of Nanâ, 81; temple of Nin-gal, 97; temple of Sin, 70, 242, 295, 640; literary center, 245; zikkurat at Ur, 617; temple E-kharsag, 638; temple E-gal-makh, 639.
Ur-Bau, patesi of Lagash, builds sanctuary of Belit, 56; builds sanctuary to Ea in Girsu, 61-3; builds temple of Ninni in Gish-galla, 80; builds temple to Nin-Mar in Mar, 100; builds temple to Ku(?)-anna in Girsu, 102; erects a zikkurat in Nippur, 645.
Ur-Gur, 2d dynasty of Ur, builds sanctuary to Shamash in Larsa, 69; preserves local cults in Larsa, Nippur, Uruk, 69; builds temple to Sin in Ur, 76; builds temple to Nanâ in Uruk, 81.
Ur-Kasdim = Ur.
Ur-Nin-Girsu, of Lagash, priest of Anu, 90.
Ur-Shul-pa-uddu, ruler of Kish, 99.
Uru-azagga, quarter of Lagash, 57; temple of Bau, 59, 103.
Uru-gal, "great city," designation of nether-world, 592; Nin-azu, god of U., 592.
Uruk, ancient center, 9, 35, 245, 445, 472; excavated, 9; rulers, 37; temple of Nin-shakh, 93; temple of Lugal-banda, 95; temple of Nin-gul, 96; origin of cult of Nisaba, 102; Nanâ, or Ishtar, the great goddess of Uruk, 81, 84, 103, 242, 311, 445, 473, 475, 645, 648; importance of Uruk in Nippur inscriptions, 103; worship of Nisaba, 111; temple of Nanâ or Ishtar, 81, 242, 311, 531, 639; Uruk supûri, 472; city of the Kizrêti, Ukhâti, and Kharimâti, 475, 531; conquered by Gilgamesh, 473, 513; attacked by Khumbaba, 430; Uruk under Cassites (?), 480; attacked by Dibbarra, 531; dwelling of Anu and Ishtar, 531; zikkurat at U., 619, 639.
Uru-kagina, patesi of Lagash, 53; king of Girsu, 56; erects temple of Bau at Uru-azagga, 103.
Utu, surname of Shamash, 72; etymology, 73.
Utukku, a class of spirits, 260 (*cf.* 511).

Vases, sacred objects, 652, 674-5; comparison with vases in the Solomonic temple, 653.
Venus = Ishtar, name of planet, 370.
Votive inscriptions, see *Religious Texts*.
Votive offerings, 51, 57, 660 ff.; lists of, 165; popular character, 668-9; statues of kings votive offerings, 669; occasions for, 670; offered by kings and laymen, 671, 675; various objects, 671, 675; captured gods as offerings, 675.
Warka, see *Uruk*.
Water, see *Fire* and *Ea*; means of purification, 276, 279, 282, 289.

Wedge writing, styles and varieties, 19, 20; origin, 21 ff., 454, 455.

Witchcraft, origin of belief in, 267; relationship betw. w. and demons, 267; the sex in w., 267, 342, 485; means of w., 268; protection against, 269; release from, 285, 657; causes of punishment by, 291.

Worship, tree worship compared with Hebrew-Phoenician Ashera cult, 689; symbolical in Bab., 689.

Xenophon, contemporary of Ctesias, 1.

Xisuthras, 505; see *Adra-Khasis.*

Yakhin, name of column in Solomon's temple, 624.

Zab, lower, tributary of Tigris, 192.

Zabu, king of Babylon, restores Shamash temple at Sippar, 117; restores Anunit temple at Agade, 117.

Zag-muk, festival of Bau, 59, 677; festival of Marduk, 127, 631, 678-9; festival of En-lil, 678; festival of Sin, 678; festival of Nanâ, 678; propitious time for asking oracles, 628-9; spring and fall the time of the z., 678; compared with Jewish New Year, 687.

Zakar, god, meaning of name, 172; place of worship, 172; "wall of Zakar," 172; relationship to Bel and Belit, 172.

Zamama, god of the 2d Bab. period, 168; sanctuary to Z. in Kish, 169; god of battle (identified with Ninib, 640), 169; Ninni his consort, 169; in incantations, 273; temple of Zamama-Ninib, 640.

Zarniu, son of Bau, 103.

Za-za-uru, son of Bau, 103.

Zikkurat, staged tower, 615; imitation of mountain, 615; house of oracle, 622; names of zikkurats, 638 ff.

Zodiac, z. system outcome of religious thought, 247, 434; zodiacal interpretation of the gods, 82, 310-1, 434, 462-3. 676; almost the entire zodiac known to the Babylonians, 456.

Zoroastrianism, 45.

Zu, personification of storm, 525, 537; myth of Zu, 537 ff.; compared with Tiâmat epic, 543; explanation of name, 537; the chief worker of evil, 538; under the control of Shamash, 538; robs the tablets of fate, 540; conquered by Marduk, 542.

Zurghul, city in Babylonia, 578.

ANNOUNCEMENTS

HANDBOOKS ON THE HISTORY OF RELIGIONS

Edited by MORRIS JASTROW, JR., Professor of Semitic Languages
in the University of Pennsylvania

THE distinguishing features of this series will be: first, each volume will deal with the history of a special religion, which is to be intrusted to the hands of a competent specialist; second, the treatment of the subject in the various volumes will follow so far as possible a uniform order; a third division will embody a full exposition of the beliefs and rites, the religious art and literature; a fourth division will give the history of the religion and set forth its relation to others. Three volumes are now ready.

NOW READY

I. THE RELIGIONS OF INDIA

By EDWARD WASHBURN HOPKINS, Professor of Sanskrit and Comparative Philology in Yale University. 8vo. Cloth. xviii + 612 pages. List price, $2.00; mailing price, $2.20.

II. THE RELIGION OF BABYLONIA AND ASSYRIA

By MORRIS JASTROW, JR., Professor of Semitic Languages in the University of Pennsylvania. 8vo. Cloth. xiv + 780 pages. List price, $3.00; mailing price, $3.25.

III. THE RELIGION OF THE TEUTONS

By P. D. CHANTEPIE DE LA SAUSSAYE, Professor in the University of Leiden. Translated by B. J. VOS, Associate Professor of German in the Johns Hopkins University. 8vo. Cloth. viii + 504 pages. List price, $2.50; mailing price, $2.70.

IN PREPARATION

IV. THE RELIGION OF ISRAEL
By the Rev. Professor JOHN P. PETERS, New York.

V. THE RELIGION OF PERSIA
By Professor A. V. WILLIAMS JACKSON of Columbia University.

VI. INTRODUCTION TO THE HISTORY OF RELIGIONS
By Professor C. H. TOY of Harvard University.

VII. THE RELIGION OF ISLAM
By Professor MORRIS JASTROW, JR., of the University of Pennsylvania.

VIII. THE RELIGION OF THE ROMANS
By Professor JESSE BENEDICT CARTER of Princeton University.

GINN & COMPANY Publishers

www.ingramcontent.com/pod-product-compliance
Lightning Source LLC
Chambersburg PA
CBHW061733300426
44115CB00009B/1196